Ninth Edition

A Child Goes Forth
A Curriculum Guide
for Preschool Children

BARBARA J. TAYLOR

Professor Emerita
Brigham Young University

MERRILL,
an imprint of Prentice Hall
Upper Saddle River, New Jersey   *Columbus, Ohio*

Library of Congress Cataloging-in-Publication Data

Taylor, Barbara J.
    A child goes forth: a curriculum guide for preschool children
  Barabara J. Taylor.—9th ed.
     p. cm.
    Includes bibliographical references and index.
    ISBN 0-13-916354-9
    1. Education, Preschool—Curricula. I. Title.
  LB1140.4.T388 1999
  372.19—dc21   98-17013
                                             CIP

Cover photo: © Doug Martin Photography
Editor: Ann Castel Davis
Production Editor: Sheryl Glicker Langner
Production Coordination: Linda Zuk, WordCrafters Editorial Services, Inc.
Photo Coordinator: Patty Carro
Design Coordinator: Karrie M. Converse
Cover Designer: Ceri Fitzgerald
Production Manager: Laura Messerly
Electronic Text Management: Karen L. Bretz
Director of Marketing: Kevin Flanagan
Marketing Manager: Suzanne Stanton
Marketing Coordinator: Krista Groshong

This book was set in Zapf Book Light by Clarinda Co. and was printed and bound by
The Banta Company. The cover was printed by Phoenix Color Corp.

 ©1999, 1995 by Prentice-Hall, Inc.
Simon & Schuster/A Viacom Company
Upper Saddle River, New Jersey 07458

Earlier editions, © 1991, 1985 by Macmillan College Publishing Company; © 1980 by Burgess
Publishing Company; © 1975, 1972, 1966, 1964 by Brigham Young University Press.

Photo Credits
pp. ix, xi by Doug Martin; facing p. 1, pp. 3, 6, 12, 17, 19, 20, 26, 29, 33, 34, 43, 47, 50, 58, 62,
67, 69, 79, 85, 89, 100, 104, 107, 122, 130, 136, 140, 142, 147, 151, 156, 162, 165, 172, 178, 182,
196, 201, 209, 211, 216, 220, 228, 234, 237, 241, 248, 252, 253, 256, 266, 271, 275, 277, 280, 282,
286, 289, 296, 302, 312, 315, 317, 322, 327, 331, 334, 339, 344, 347, 351, 359, 365, 372, 376, 384,
389, 392, 395, 400, 403, 410, 412, 416, 422, 425, 426, 429, 434, 440, 444, 448 by Glenn Anderson;
pp. 10, 93, 437 by Dan Floss/Merrill; pp. 38, 95, 113, 190, 223, 244, 259, 354 by Anne
Vega/Merrill; p. 117 by Barbara Schwartz/Merrill; pp. 325, 363 by Julie Peters/Merrill; p. 408
by Scott Cunningham/Merrill

Printed in the United States of America

10 9 8 7 6 5 4 3 2 1

ISBN: 0-13-916354-9

Prentice-Hall International (UK) Limited, *London*
Prentice-Hall of Australia Pty. Limited, *Sydney*
Prentice-Hall of Canada, Inc., *Toronto*
Prentice-Hall Hispanoamericana, S. A., *Mexico*
Prentice-Hall of India Private Limited, *New Delhi*
Prentice-Hall of Japan, Inc., *Tokyo*
Simon & Schuster Asia Pte. Ltd., *Singapore*
Editora Prentice-Hall do Brasil, Ltda., *Rio de Janeiro*

To young children everywhere

There was a child went forth every day,
And the first object he look'd upon, that object he became,
And that object became part of him for the
*   day or a certain part of the day,*
Or for many years or stretching cycles of years.

Walt Whitman
From "Autumn Rivulets"
in *Leaves of Grass*

Preface

As I sat down to write this new edition, I pondered several questions, such as: What is the current status of the young children in our country—and the world? How can new, fresh information make a difference in the lives of young children and the adults who interact with them? Do early experiences really make a difference in attitudes, perspectives, and outcomes? The Preface to the eighth edition of *A Child Goes Forth* began with these words:

> Over time, children have been looked upon in different ways: as miniature adults, as chattel, as hurdles, as punishment, or various personal interpretations. Those who saw children as the future of civilization instituted educational paths, parental education, and health and safety measures, and recognized individual differences within and among children. We have come a long way—but as long as children in any part of the world are undervalued, underfed, exploited, or inappropriately cared for, we have a long way to go. (p. v)

What kinds of changes have we seen since the eighth edition was published in 1995? In many parts of the world—including our own country—children are still undervalued, underfed, exploited, or inappropriately cared for. Will the new welfare laws make the road easier or more difficult for those who come under its provisions? We still have a long way to go. But are we even headed in the right direction, and are children and families any better off? I like to think we are making progress, even if it is slow, rocky, and sometimes unsure. How can early childhood educators make the road a little safer, a little easier, and more rewarding for children, parents, and educators? This is one of those difficult, often unanswerable, questions. This edition of *A Child Goes Forth* is an attempt to provide some guidance and reassurance along the way.

Aimed at enriching the lives of children between ages 2 and 5 and those who teach them, this text is written with a sincere desire to offer logical information, based on knowledge and experience, and encouragement to adults who love, learn with, and live with young children. One begins at the beginning—the environments that produce happier, healthier, and more productive citizens. But can one say that the same environment will bring the same results for everyone? And how do we equalize the environment for all—or is that even possible or desirable?

Chapter 1 describes developmentally appropriate practices (DAP) and names some important educators who promoted this concept many years ago; but the term *DAP* has been popularized by the National Association for the Education of Young Children (NAEYC) in recent years. Throughout the book (including Appendix A), the theories of these early educators are mentioned, reinforced by current theories and practices. Knowing the names and philosophies of influential educators is important in the field of early childhood education.

Boxed "nuggets" appear in each chapter; they are intended to help the reader focus on words and ideas that can make a difference in daily lives. The Reflections encourage the reader to ponder a possible situation and then reflect on how and why he or she would respond.

Curriculum chapters have been updated in an effort to show how each topic not only stands alone, but has tremendous influence upon the total growth and development of each young child. The teacher may have preferences in subjects—as do children—but the total experience helps both teachers and children have a better understanding of the world in which they live.

Guidance principles, the subject of Chapter 2, are necessary in all walks of life and provide ways for children and teachers to act and interact in more positive, productive, and acceptable ways.

In researching the Chapter 3, The Value of Play, I became convinced that we need to provide, accept, and understand the ways of children if we are to be advocates for them, and if we are to be instruments in promoting better kinds of behavior.

I was pleased and excited to see how the math and science scores of American children have improved since the previous edition was published. I sincerely feel that teachers and parents of young children can encourage more interest in and understanding of these subjects by the way we talk and act—embracing spontaneous or planned activities and displaying sincere interest and inquisitive minds.

I have made a deliberate attempt to focus upon how the individual child feels about himself and others. Personal and multicultural experiences and attitudes are important aspects in learning.

As an example of how the text fits together, think about Chapter 12, Transition Activities. Note that it suggests ways to incorporate a good environment, guidance principles, play, and curriculum (language, creative expression, music and movement, science, mathematics, social studies, and nutrition and health) into a happy, inclusive experience for children and teachers.

The final paragraph of the Preface to the eighth edition still represents my thinking about teaching and loving young children.

> Whether children are grouped by one age or mixed ages (family grouping), teachers need to understand and plan for differences in skills, interests, and needs. Rigid programs and expectations do not meet the needs of individual children. When things are not going well, teachers need to *modify the curricula and expectations*—not the children. This book is full of practical and meaningful tasks, activities, and opportunities for young children. (p. vi)

OVERVIEW OF NINTH EDITION CHAPTERS

Chapters of the ninth edition:

1 Good environments: happy and healthy home and neighborhoods; love of and respect for other people; simple, inexpensive, wholesome experiences

2 Guidance: good techniques for building good relationships; rules and requests that show respect and promote growth

3 Play: types of activities; individual and group play; safety; satisfaction; constructive versus destructive play

4   Curriculum development: children's responsibilities; sequencing events

5   Language development: reading, talking, listening, explaining, questioning, interacting, imitating, sequencing, planning. Early experiences with books are invaluable.

6   Creativity: individuality, thinking, use of materials, activities, discussing, appreciation

7   Music and movement: listening, similarities, meanings, body usage, self-confidence and skill building (motor, social), memory enhancement

8   Science: bubbles, bulbs, magnets, water, weather, time, repetition, labels

9   Math: counting, using fingers, one-to-one correspondence, units, daily activities, sequencing, sharing

10   Social relationships: people—cultures, ages, differences, techniques

11   Nutrition and health: food selection, purchasing, preparing; immunizations, personal hygiene and exercise; appropriate clothing; general nutrition

In Walt Whitman's poem "Autumn Rivulets," a child becomes part of all he sees and does. Children of all ages are curious, imitative, and growing, and the title *A Child Goes Forth* reflects this involvement of children with the world around them. Part of what has made *A Child Goes Forth* a successful text for early childhood education courses is the book's emphasis on the individuality of each child, and in each successive edition there is greater emphasis and clarity on providing programs and activities that are *developmentally appropriate* for children. In order to provide such programs, parents and teachers should understand and insist upon the components necessary for good environments for young children—inside and outside the home. Adults should not be intimidated by commercial materials, academic pressures, or outspoken but uninformed adults. All facets of a child's personality—social, intellectual, spiritual, physical, and emotional—are interrelated; a relaxed, unstructured yet carefully planned atmosphere is most conducive to effective learning.

I would like to thank photographer Glenn Anderson, Instructional Media, Brigham Young University, for his contribution to this edition. Thanks also to centers where photographs were taken, including "R" Kids Child Care Center, Utah Valley Regional Medical Center, Provo, Utah, Anita Spainhower, director; Kids On the Move, Orem, Utah, Karen Hahne, director; Adventure Time, Provo, Utah, Ginger Wooly, owner. Finally, thanks to my husband and family for their love, patience, and endurance.

Introduction

A NOTE ABOUT THE CHILD ON THE COVER

Lea is fourteen months old. She was born in Western Samoa and now resides in the United States with her parents and an older brother. She has had many experiences in her young life which encourage her to be curious, outgoing, friendly, secure, and teachable.

While the primary focus of this text is on children between the ages of 2 and 6, the experiences and preparation that occur before and after these ages are vital in the total learning and development of children of all ages. A brief overview of the chapters in this text can also relate to younger children or children who do not attend preschools or child care centers before entering public school. Children of all ages need to have experiences in each of the following 11 areas, which correspond to the chapters of this book.

1. Participate in *environments* that include happy and healthy homes and neighborhoods; love and respect for themselves and others; and conditions where simple, inexpensive, and wholesome experiences are prevalent.

Example: Lea has freedom of movement, but unsafe conditions are noted and enforced; she feels loved and valued; and many of her daily activities revolve around simple activities available in the home.

2. Know that parents and others will provide appropriate *guidance* to the young children who are inexperienced and in developing stages of growth.

Example: Lea is redirected from areas and activities that may cause her harm: open staircases, unsafe places to climb, toys that are inappropriate, and so forth. As a result, she has learned to go up and down stairs safely and to play in secure places.

3. Explore and play.

Example: Lea likes to explore new areas, play with familiar and new things, and repeat prior activities. It is the role of the adult to help her learn how to play alone or in a group, to provide activities that are safe and satisfying, and to help her learn how to play constructively.

4. Utilize available materials and learn personal responsibility.

Example: Lea learns how to care for her toys, where they belong when they are not in use (blocks are stacked, books are shelved, pieces are grouped), how to use toys creatively, and how her toys can represent daily activities. Her use of toys increases as she develops new skills.

5. Hear and use language.

Example: Lea has been talked to and sung to, and has engaged in other activities involving language. Since four months of age, parents and others have read to her, shown her pictures and objects, played with her, and made her a very active part of the family. She now sits quietly and looks at books for long periods of time. When asked to choose a book for an adult to read to her, she knows where to find a book, chooses the one she wants to hear, and climbs up on a lap. (Too many adults think books and reading are for older children!) Lea identifies various animals and makes their sounds. She listens carefully to distinguish between sounds, a skill that will aid in the development of later reading ability. Early experiences with books are invaluable.

6. Be creative and self-expressive.

Example: Lea is learning to do things in a variety of ways and to express her needs and desires in different ways. When she wants someone to sit by her, she pats a cushion; when she wants an object, she points and says "Dat." There are many inexpensive and available toys and materials for her creative expression. She needs someone to talk with her about her activities and to value her ideas and abilities. Her attempts should be acknowledged and appreciated.

7. Hear and enjoy music and movement activities.

Example: Lea enjoys hearing music and imitating movement. A scarf or different rhythms encourage locomotion, and the activity itself encourages her body usage, self-confidence, motor skills, and enjoyment. Musical games ("Ring around the Rosy," "Head and Shoulders, Knees and Toes") help her identify body parts, stimulate participation, develop social and mental skills, and improve memory.

8. Experience science concepts.

Example: Lea is fascinated by motion: air, water, weather, toys, and her own body. Things like bubbles, magnets, changes in weather (falling snow or rain,

gentle breezes, color changes), food combinations, sensory objects, and sound are very interesting to her. On a fall walk, Lea is very interested in the crunching of the dry leaves. When taken from her stroller and placed in the leaves, she crumbles them, kicks them, sits in them, tosses them in the air, expressing great delight in the many things she can do with them. Opportunities for exploration are always available and inexpensive (concepts of time, sequencing of events, labels for objects or activities, food, experimenting with colors, etc.).

9. Learn math skills.

   Example: Lea loves finger games. When asked how old she is, her first finger is quickly raised. She attempts to raise different fingers for number games. She likes to hear counting while pointing to objects (one-to-one correspondence), multiples (two socks, two shoes), and sequencing activities (after you finish your cookie, we will go for a walk).

10. Build social relationships.

    Example: Lea is a very social person who likes to be included in whatever is going on. She vocalizes enough to let you know that she is part of the conversation, and frequently repeats words or labels. She knows she is valued as a family member. She uses some of the social graces (please, thank you) in her immature way and knows that they are important to those around her. She is learning to share objects and to play cooperatively. She blows kisses, waves bye-bye, and gives hugs.

11. Develop and maintain a strong and healthy body.

    Example: Lea's health needs are important. Her immunizations are on schedule, her illnesses are promptly cared for, and she loves to eat what others are eating and to be part of a family setting.

In preparing this text, it has been a joy to have Lea as a guide and model for me. She has emphasized the importance of very young children—who are not just waiting to grow up and "be" something, they are *already something very special!*

In summary, activities for all ages (sometimes divided by category and sometimes combined with other topics) should be *enjoyable* rather than restrictive, *growth promoting* rather than growth stunting (stereotyping), *positive* rather than negative, and often *child initiated* rather than adult imposed. Adults need to be aware at all times that:

1. Very young children are active learners and will respond positively or negatively depending on how the environment is planned and utilized.

2. It is very easy to stimulate and encourage young children to value themselves and their environment.

3. "A child goes forth" from a very young age, and individuals in their environment can be positive, negative, or noninfluential.

4. *Every* child deserves the right to a happy, productive, and enriched life.

Contents

Chapter 8   SCIENCE AND TECHNOLO0GY   267

Chapter 9   MATHEMATICS   313

Chapter 10   SOCIAL STUDIES, ANTI-BIAS CURRICULUM,
                       AND FIELD TRIPS   345

Chapter 11   NUTRITION AND HEALTH   385

Chapter 12   TRANSITION ACTIVITIES   423

A Child Goes Forth

Good Environments for Young Children, Teachers, and Families

1

MAIN PRINCIPLES

Creating a good environment for children involves the following:

1. Acknowledging and promoting developmentally appropriate programs—that is, knowing the optimum methods, sequences, and timing for each child's best learning.
2. Knowing some names and theories of advocates of developmentally appropriate practices and how these theories can help one better promote optimal interactions with young children.
3. Being aware of misconceptions about behavior and learning styles, about how children learn, and about developmentally appropriate practices, to help one plan for and interact better with young children.
4. Distinguishing between practices that are developmentally appropriate and ones that are *in*appropriate for young children.
5. Being aware of the many influences in a young child's environment.
6. Promoting healthy peer interaction.
7. Acknowledging differences in a child's environment and providing a healthy, happy experience for children.

A good environment for teachers includes the following:

1. Opportunities to participate with young children in a comfortable setting. To do so, one must have knowledge and experience concerning how children grow and learn.
2. Training and practice with capable teachers and/or supervisors.
3. Opportunities to learn and use good observation skills.
4. Feelings of worthwhileness, value, and acceptance.
5. Opportunities to learn and grow as a person and as a professional.
6. Ability to give and receive information (with supervisors, peers, parents, and others).
7. Knowledge of, belief in, and commitment to using good ethical behavior with colleagues, children, and families.
8. Commitment to building positive relationships with all children.
9. Active participation in professional organizations, reading current information, and discussion and implementation of concepts that will make a better environment for children, teachers, and families.

A good environment for families of children in out-of-home situations includes the following:

1. Being valued as parents/families and the roles assigned to them; recognizing parents as children's primary educators; having a place where they can learn more about children, families, and interaction outside the home.
2. Feeling that their children are cared for and taught by loving teachers in wholesome and safe settings.

3. Learning and using observation skills.

4. The ability to give and receive information from teachers and others.

5. Federal and organizational support for children beginning school by the year 2000—high-quality programs (including nutritional and health programs) for *all* children.

6. Awareness of the kinds of child-care education available in their neighborhoods and within their financial range.

7. Willingness to understand, cooperate with, and participate in good settings for their children.

FOR YOUNG CHILDREN

How often have you heard the statement, "Children are our best resources," and then wondered just what was meant? If this statement refers to a child in a family, a community, or anywhere in the world, it could mean that the hopes of the family, the community, or the world reside in the abilities and performance of that child. Take, for example, the role of the *expecter,* who assumes that great rewards, returns, and benefits will occur (internally and externally) for individuals or groups. Then take, for another example, the role of the *expectee.* Will the child receive assistance, guidance, and encouragement along the way, or must the child stumble and progress as best as possible? Sometimes the messages that are sent and those that are received are quite different—depending on the frame of reference, confidence, and desired outcome of the sender and receiver. Expecting too much too soon, and without thinking through the myriad implications and complications, may invite premature failure or total disaster.

Adults who work with young children are really involved with the "pot of gold at the end of the rainbow." Young children are tender, malleable, trusting, lovable, curious, and teachable. It is as if the teacher or parent were seated at the potter's wheel, about to take the lump of clay and mold it into a thing of beauty and value. At the same time, the adult does not have the privilege of molding a child into a preconceived idea of "perfection"; rather, the adult must help the child to capitalize on his individual talents and abilities so he can live happily and healthily in his world and feel good about himself and his contribution.

This chapter identifies some of the important considerations in providing good learning and living environments for young children.

Most of the classroom examples in this book involve female teachers. Unfortunately, men have had a certain reluctance to enter an occupation that has been traditionally "female"; men in the field of education are often teaching older children or in administrative positions. Nevertheless, young children need and want male teachers, and one hopes there will be an increasing trend toward more men teaching young children.

How Young Children Learn Best

In early European history, children were treated like adults, were dressed like adults, worked like adults, and were considered adult in all ways except size. They were expected to carry their full share of responsibility in providing for the family. In some cases, children performed tasks that adults could not: they crawled into

Caring adults help children develop confidence and initiative.

small openings while working in mines, spent long hours in the fields, and survived on less food and sleep.

During the past century, observation and research revealed that children are not miniature adults. They have feelings similar to those of adults, such as fear, joy, and pain, but their learning patterns are different.

Many approaches, theories, and practices have been introduced regarding the growth, behavior, and learning of young children. This text is based upon the premise that experiences for young children should be based on abilities, interests, and experiences that are developmentally appropriate for each individual child. Theorists who advocate this idea include Piaget, Erikson, Dewey, Vygotsky, and Malaguzzi (the founder of the Reggio Emilia approach). Each will be briefly discussed here. The reader is highly encouraged to seek further information from Appendix A, from the original writings of each theorist, and from educators who are well versed in the trends of early-childhood education.

Jean Piaget (1896–1980)

Jean Piaget, the Swiss epistemologist, formulated a model for the stages of intellectual development in children as follows (1974):

Stage 1: Sensorimotor (0 to 24 months of age)

Stage 2: Preoperational (2 to 7 years of age)

Stage 3: Concrete operational (7 to 11 years of age)

Stage 4: Formal operational (11 years of age on)

The first, or *sensorimotor,* stage involves learning through the five senses, the emerging ability to control one's body movements, and a combination of learning through the senses and ability to control one's body movements. Children under 2 mouth and touch everything, listen intently, have a keen sense of smell, and notice even the smallest thing on the floor. They are into everything in or out of reach. They crawl into small or dangerous spaces without fear; nothing is safe from them.

The second, or *preoperational*, stage is the focal point in early-childhood education, representing expansion of the first stage. During the ages of 2 to 7, children are somewhat self-centered and still oriented toward learning through the senses and body skills. They broaden their scope of activity from the home base to other individuals and experiences. Their best learning is done through hands-on experiences. They live in a here-and-now world and need concrete experiences; they need opportunities to explore through the five senses and opportunities to interact with things that are real and present. They imitate, question, and practice. From birth, children are thinkers; during the second stage they begin to handle abstract concepts, although the ideas of past and future are difficult for them.

In addition to concrete experience and sensory involvement, children in this stage learn best when language is used to increase vocabulary and ideas, when opportunities to practice problem solving are provided, when activities are appropriate for their level of development (not too easy or too difficult, but challenging), and when they have interactions with other children and adults. Other aspects to consider are individual readiness, opportunities, materials, support, freedom to explore, degree of involvement, variety of experiences, and repetition. Practice, guidance, and motivation are important to children as they learn about themselves and their environment. It is hoped that most of their experiences will be positive so that children can develop self-confidence.

The third and fourth stages (*concrete operational* and *formal operational*) are beyond the scope of this book; however, the reader may find value in investigating these later stages. Many child-development texts or articles in professional journals are good sources of information.

Erik Erikson (1902–1994)

Erikson's theory of *psychosocial development* (1950)—that is, each person's relationship to the social environment—is age-related, and has been helpful to teachers as they plan for young children.

Approximate Age	Characteristic	Development of:
Birth to 1 year	Trust vs. mistrust	Hope
1 to 3 years	Autonomy vs. shame and doubt	Willpower
3 to 6 years	Initiative vs. guilt	Purpose
7 to 11 years	Industry vs. inferiority	Competence
Adolescence	Identity vs. role confusion	Fidelity
Adulthood	Intimacy vs. isolation	Love
	Generativity vs. stagnation	Care
	Integrity vs. despair	Wisdom

At the appropriate time, certain conditions need to be met for the child's healthy progress. For example, during the first year the child either learns to trust those who care for her basic needs or lacks confidence when in the care of others. During ages 1 through 3, she learns to be self-sufficient in many activities (walking, feeding, toileting, and so on) or to doubt her own abilities. From ages 3 through 6, she wants to do many adult-type activities, sometimes beyond her abilities, or she develops guilt feelings because of inadequacy. Ages 7 through adult likewise identify positive and negative outcomes for individuals and are beyond the scope of this book. Again, the reader is encouraged to investigate these steps for personal reasons and for understanding the ongoing growth patterns of individuals outside the limits of this text.

Erikson's theory is mentioned here because of its lasting popularity and because of its implications and applicability to healthful environments for young children.

The development of good early work habits is also important in learning and is based on the child, the task, and the adult. The child should be allowed to take the initiative, and may need some guidance in the tasks he undertakes, but the most important aspect is the intrinsic reward he personally feels for his efforts. Knowing what to expect and how to meet the needs of the young child, the adult plans for the child's success while conveying confidence in him. It has been concluded that children who learn the most persist at tasks, sometimes difficult ones; pay attention to and select tasks that are challenging; and work on tasks alone without unnecessary requests for adult assistance. Praise that comes from the adult should be related more to attempts and progress than to final outcomes. A teacher or parent who rewards less-than-optimal performance prevents children from developing an understanding of a relationship between effort and performance.

John Dewey (1859–1952)

Dewey saw education as being active, constructive, and a continuing reconstruction process of experiences. He valued uncertainty, saying that "knowledge is created through active inquiry," not in sequences of organized subject matter. Teachers and children alike were to be learners.

Dewey's philosophy implied radical changes in curriculum, permitting physical activity, free play, and a training ground for democracy, cooperation, productive work, and community experiences, such as field trips and classroom visitors. He introduced the term *subprimary* to distinguish his classes from the strict Froebelian approach of "gifts" (specially designed materials Froebel believed would help children develop knowledge of forms of life, beauty, and mathematics) and "occupations" (constructive play activities such as weaving, clay molding, paper folding, and embroidery that focused the child's attention and exercised fine motor skills).

Lev Vygotsky (1896–1934)

Vygotsky's work was unpublished until after his death, but he was a contemporary of Piaget. Both viewed the child as a biological organism; both credit the other for help in developing their theories.

Vygotsky's work had two major goals: (1) to create a Marxist psychology that would solve problems in psychology and guide the Russian people in their newly designed country, and (2) to help children solve physical and psychological problems. His main tenets included (1) the importance of language; (2) the idea that education leads development; and (3) the *zone of proximal development* (ZPD), or the distance between the child's ability to solve problems independently compared to his ability to solve them with the assistance of someone more competent than he. Vygotsky also taught that people are products of their social and cultural worlds, and in order to understand others, we must understand their environment.

The Vygotskian approach to education is one of assisted discovery. His classrooms include a heavy emphasis upon teacher-child and child-child relationships, a whole-language approach, the interests and competencies of children, mixed-age grouping, and activity centers where children can accomplish individual and group academic goals. Time, space, language, resources, type of learning, and associations are unlimited.

Reggio Emilia—Founded by Loris Malaguzzi (1920–1994)

Reggio Emilia, unlike other approaches, is named after a town in Italy. It was founded by Loris Malaguzzi and is supported by national funding of public preschools for *all* 3- to 6-year-old Italian children.

The central function of this approach is on social construction of knowledge—an emphasis of Vygotsky. Malaguzzi took many different theories (such as those of Dewey, Piaget, Erikson, and others) and wove them into a well-run and well-integrated early-childhood program.

Malaguzzi invited educators to reflect on a bill of rights for children, parents, and teachers. He stated that there are hundreds of different images and each one relates differently to a child. Our environment grows out of our relationship with the child in a unique and fluid way. Children are sensitive and curious and like attention, yet are immature in their physical, social, emotional, and intellectual development. Each child is considered to have positive attributes, such as competence, resourcefulness, creativity, knowledge, and so on. Adults need to be open and flexible and "to wait for the child" as they recognize and promote the rights and strengths of children.

Reggio Emilia utilizes the *project approach;* based on the interests of children, it may be short or last days or weeks. The learning goals of this procedure include knowledge, skills, dispositions (enduring habits), and feelings (emotional and affective).

Reggio Emilia's approach to early education reflects ideas from other theorists, including a constructivist view. Children negotiate in the peer group. Their needs, interests, and abilities, as well as the current thinking of parents, teachers,

Children learn from each other if they have time, materials, and opportunities that encourage cooperation.

and children, contribute in meaningful ways to determine school experiences. Teachers trust themselves to respond appropriately to children's ideas and interests; they trust children to be interested in things worth knowing about; and they trust parents to be informed, productive members of an educational team. The result is an atmosphere of community and collaboration that is developmentally appropriate for adults and children alike (New, 1990).

For similarities and differences between Reggio Emilia and American approaches to early-childhood cognitive education, see Appendix A.

Before we proceed further, a symbol that will appear throughout the text needs to be introduced. To demonstrate a point, to give the reader an opportunity to visualize a situation, to bring in practical experience, and to bring past and future learning into focus, *Reflections* will be used. The symbol denoting such examples is

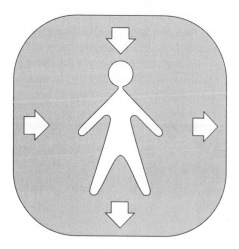

In studying the image, one notes that a child stands amid four arrows, used to signify learning and interaction between the child and her environment. The arrow on the left refers to the child's past experiences that have influenced and will influence present and future learning. The arrow on the right indicates that with experience and maturity, the child's horizontal learning increases—that is, she learns about different topics.

The arrow on the top refers to vertical (or depth) learning: at first the child learns few things about a topic, then—indicated by the arrow beneath the child—she learns more things about the same topic. As she grows and experiences, the child will learn *some* about more topics (breadth) and *more* about the same topics (depth).

Read the "planting" Reflection on page 8. See if you can determine how Shaun's past experiences and the hands-on activity increased his knowledge and feelings about planting. Then ponder how a planting experience could be integrated with other topics to give meaning to both (water, tools, weather, different ways to plant, satisfaction, and so on). Stretch your imagination, if necessary, to reflect on your similar past experiences and what would have helped you develop a more positive attitude toward tasks for children, planting and harvesting crops, independence, commitment, and so on.

As you probably discovered in this exercise, some situations are not black or white. For example, if a child cries when left in a strange situation, does it necessarily mean that the child was raised in a distrusting environment? Respond to each item in the exercise in two ways: (1) what would be the most common or expected reaction, and (2) what modifications would ensure growth for each girl?

Reflection

A group of preschool children were involved in a planting experience. They had a bucket of dirt, individual containers, spoons, bulbs, seeds, and a small watering can. Unnoticed by the children, the teacher became distracted. The children busied themselves with the task at hand. Shaun filled his container. Then, realizing it might not be a good idea just to lay the bulbs and seeds on top of the dirt, he emptied his container. This time he put the seeds and bulbs in the bottom and filled the jar with soil. Thoughtfully, he looked at the jar. Evidently deciding that this also was not the best idea, he spooned the dirt out until he reached the bulbs and seeds. The bulbs were easily retrieved, but the seeds became a problem. Carefully, he spooned the dirt onto the table. At first he tenderly stirred the dirt with his spoon but finally resorted to using his fingers to pick out the seeds one by one. Then he remembered how they had used cotton balls when they sprouted seeds previously. He got some small, white cotton balls from the shelf, lightly dampened them at the sink, and returned to the activity. He picked up each seed and placed it on a cotton ball. This time, as he filled his jar, he was very precise in placing the dirt, bulbs, and seeds. When the jar was full, he patted the dirt gently and slowly poured water from the can. His masterpiece was finished! By now the teacher had returned and was quietly observing the different skills and methods of the children. Shaun showed her his jar and told her of his different attempts at planting the bulbs and seeds and how he had finally succeeded. One could tell from the look of satisfaction on his face that Shaun was pleased with his planting experience. The teacher's smile and interest confirmed his ability to solve his problem.

Reflection

Relate this scenario to Erikson's theory, discussed previously:

During her first 4 years of life, Lea has experienced loving care—fed when hungry, comforted when distressed, warmed when cold, changed when messy or dirty, and included when lonesome. She has been encouraged to feed herself and to walk when ready, and safe objects have been available for her exploration. When imitating or modeling the behavior of others, she has been encouraged in a timely way. She has not been spoiled, but her needs have been met on a consistent basis.

During Becky's first 4 years of life, she has experienced care at the convenience of others, has been discouraged from feeding herself (too messy), from walking (to prevent her from getting into possessions of others), and from handling objects (she would lose or destroy them). When she imitated or modeled the behavior of others, she was discouraged and/or props were removed (her attempts were embarrassing to someone). Her interaction with others has been inconsistent and frustrating.

Lea and Becky meet as 4-year-olds in a group play situation. Identify and explain which of the following behaviors you would expect each child to exhibit.

- ○ Self-confidence
- ○ Cooperation and sharing
- ○ Self-direction and entertainment
- ○ Trust of children and situations
- ○ Security when parent leaves
- ○ Fear of failure
- ○ Verbal, inquisitive, and happy behavior
- ○ Handling own personal needs

Using the Reflection symbol (child with arrows) and its definition, described previously, what possible changes occurred for both girls through vertical and horizontal learning (for example, past experiences, learning or progress, and so on)? As a teacher, how can you provide experiences so all children in your classroom will show self-confidence, security, and positive ways of expressing themselves?

Misconceptions about Behavior and Learning Styles

In general, when 2-year-olds are mentioned, one's first thoughts are of behavior:

$$\text{age} + \text{negativism} = \text{"terrible twos"}$$

Although negative behavior might be expressed more vigorously at 2 years than at most other ages, this is not the only age when a person is negative. Some individuals never get beyond this stage. But because negativism is so often associated with the young child, this concept is briefly explored here. (See also Chapter 2.)

At 2 years of age, children are striving for independence but lack the knowledge and skill to get it. They may constantly use the word *NO!*, even when they want the opposite; they may become rigid or limp all over; they may use aggressive behavior, such as biting, kicking, and scratching; they may run away or, worst of all, throw a tantrum. They cannot verbalize feelings or desires, so they revert to behavior—with vigor. To them, negativism is felt but may often be short-lived. It does get results. Instead of ignoring or playing down the behavior, adults often force more negativism before attending to the behavior. The 2-year-olds then see that negative behavior has to be increased in intensity or duration in order to get results.

Hurlock (1964) has an early but still applicable and interesting discussion on negativism. She states that this tendency can result from aggressive discipline, intolerance toward normal childish behavior, refusal by the child to carry out requests when and how the adult requires, adult interference, inconsistent training, early toilet training, or reaction of people to different tempos. Negativism begins at about 18 months of age, reaches a peak between 3 and 6 years of age, and then recedes rapidly. The decline results partly from social influences, partly because children learn that compliance is to their advantage, and partly because parents learn to show more respect for the children. Negativism is usually more frequent and more severe in poorly adjusted children, but also appears in well-adjusted children. Between the ages of 4 and 6, children change resistance from physical to verbal forms. They also pretend not to hear or understand, refuse to see the point, insist on reopening issues, and complain or act irresponsibly.

Negativism is a part of the young child's life, but duration, intensity, and frequency depend in large measure on the response of the adult. Through behavior, adults can increase or decrease negativism by planning for and interacting with young children. Adults must see that issues are resolved without causing children to suffer loss of face, without trying to win a power struggle, and through a loving relationship. When thoughtfully handled, not only will the "terrible twos" be changed to the "terrific twos," but other ages and stages will be less stressful for both children and adults. In a broad generality, many adults try to do too much for a child at each age when the child is trying to become more and more independent, that is, a person in his own right with his own needs, abilities, and desires.

Like negativism, other aspects of behavior, such as independence, confidence, security, conformity, and conflict, recur throughout the child's life cycle, becoming notable again during adolescence and young adulthood.

Adult Misconceptions about How Children Learn

Over two decades ago, Elkind (1972), an early-childhood educator, thoughtfully brought to focus five important adult misunderstandings of children and learning:

1. Children are most like adults in their thinking and least like them in their feelings.
2. Children learn best while sitting still and listening.
3. Children can learn and operate according to rules.
4. Acceleration is preferable to elaboration.
5. Parents and teachers can raise the IQ of children.

Adults who have been around young children will recognize these five points as myths and react accordingly. Adults whose experience with young children is limited, however, will have to be observant to avoid these pitfalls. Young children do share the same emotional feelings with adults, but their cognitive structure is very different from that of adults. Children are doers—their thinking pattern does not allow them to sit and listen or to absorb and follow rules at this young age. They need *time* and *opportunities* to learn about their environment. Additional misconceptions could be added—for example, "All children of the same chronological age have the same interests, attention span, and abilities," "Extrinsic rewards are better than intrinsic rewards," or "Children learn best through vicarious experiences."

Since the publication of Elkind's list, support for his ideas has grown, research has been conducted, programs have been initiated, and there has been a

Good environments for children include indoor and outdoor play with peers.

movement to describe and provide developmentally appropriate practices for the education and care of young children. On the forefront of this movement has been the National Association for the Education of Young Children (NAEYC), which is an organization with officers and members contributing to and supporting the philosophy (see Bredekamp, 1987; Bredekamp & Copple, 1997).

Developmentally Appropriate Practices

Developmentally appropriate practices (DAP)* have been contrasted to developmentally inappropriate practices (DIP)* by Bredekamp, 1987, and Bredekamp & Copple, 1997. Traditional approaches to educating young children have been referred to by NAEYC as developmentally inappropriate practices.

The developmentally appropriate practices have been used in many classrooms and currently represent a philosophy of many organizations and individuals. The information has influenced the preparation of this book.

The terms *DAP* and *DIP* were coined and popularized by NAEYC and are descriptive. They have been well received in the field of early-childhood education. The components of these practices are clearly defined and documented, are easy to implement, and are applicable to administrators, teachers, parents, policymakers, and others who make decisions about the care and education of young children. A position statement of NAEYC reads: "a high quality early childhood program provides a safe and nurturing environment that promotes the physical, social, emotional, and cognitive development of young children while responding to the needs of families" (Bredekamp, 1987, p. 1). And further: "Some characteristics of early childhood programs have also changed in recent years. . . . Because culture and language are critical components of children's development, practices cannot be developmentally appropriate unless they are responsive in cultural and linguistic diversity" (Bredekamp & Copple, 1997, p. 4).

Several decades of research clearly demonstrate "that high-quality, developmentally appropriate early childhood programs produce short- and long-term positive effects on children's cognitive and social development" (Barnett, 1995; Howes, 1988).

Specifically, the revised NAEYC pamphlet addresses age appropriateness and individual appropriateness in the areas of physical, motor, language, cognitive, social, and emotional development at the different age levels. It also provides guidelines for (1) creating a caring community of learners (p. 16), (2) teaching to enhance development and learning (p. 17), (3) constructing appropriate curriculum (p. 20), (4) assessing children's learning and development (p. 21), and (5) establishing reciprocal relationships with families (p. 22). The sections on "moving from either/or to both/and thinking in early childhood practice" (p. 23) and "policies essential for achieving developmentally appropriate early childhood programs" (p. 24) are especially informative (Bredekamp & Copple, 1997).

Consideration must be made for children who fit the "norms" and those who deviate from them. Information should *not* be regarded as *final* and *specific* for all children of all ages. Circumstances that may cause deviations include nutrition, genetics, socioeconomic status, culture, illness, opportunities, and others.

---

*in chart form.

Misconceptions about Developmentally Appropriate Practices

Note some of the myths that have been associated with developmentally appropriate programs:

1. There are two dichotomous positions: one always right, the other always wrong.
2. Teachers are required to abandon all their prior knowledge and experience; former learning is unacceptable.
3. Classrooms are unstructured and chaotic.
4. Teachers offer no instructions; a traditional, "watered-down" curriculum results in less learning.
5. The DAP program meets the needs of only certain kinds of children.
6. DAP is a fad—soon to be replaced by another, perhaps opposite, trend. (Kostelnik, 1992, pp. 17–23)

As a matter of fact, teachers are most successful in developmentally appropriate practices when they capitalize on their prior knowledge, long-range objectives, fluid decision making, and input from the children (in the form of their asking questions, suggesting alternatives, expressing interest, developing plans, and looking for new directions in learning).

Curriculum

Curriculum opportunities for children should include and integrate all areas of development. Children should have an opportunity to explore materials and activities as well as to interact with adults and other children. Learning activities should be real and relevant to the child's world. "Workbooks, worksheets, coloring books, and

Well organized, but flexible, classrooms invite exploration and play.

adult-made models of art products for children to copy are *not* appropriate for young children, especially those younger than 6" (Bredekamp, 1987, p. 4). Wise teachers plan periods of active play interspersed with more quiet or restful periods so children do not become overly stimulated or bored. They should always encourage children to participate both indoors and outdoors as weather, conditions, and interest dictate.

Adult-Child Interaction

Children show their differing styles, needs, and desires, and adults must adapt and direct their responses quickly through focused attention, physical proximity, and verbal encouragement—such as defining situations, giving the child a future model, and helping the child express feelings verbally rather than physically—before things get out of hand. Teachers can initiate situations whereby the children feel confident, respected, and comforted—even when their behavior exceeds "normal" or expected boundaries.

Developmental Evaluation of Children

Testing results can be misused; therefore, they should be "used with caution to prevent discrimination against individuals and to ensure accuracy" (Bredekamp, 1987, p. 12). Likewise, decisions should not be made on the basis of single sources of information. The NAEYC pamphlet states, and I agree: "assessment of children should be used to evaluate the effectiveness of the curriculum, but the performance of children on standardized tests should not determine curriculum decisions." In other words, if children are not doing well on the provided curriculum, *it is the curriculum that needs revision to meet the needs of the children—not the children to fit the curriculum!*

Schweinhart (1987b) reminds readers that good early-childhood programs can be found *"in any setting that has adequate resources and qualified staff—in a private nursery school, public school, Head Start program, day care center, or day care home"* (p. 9). In another publication (1987a), he asks, "How important is child-initiated activity in early childhood education?" "Very important," he answers, and adds:

> [T]his is the consensus of early childhood leaders and parents, and it is supported by longitudinal research on program effects. The idea has its roots in the efforts of such historic early childhood experts as Friedrich Froebel, Susan Blow, Maria Montessori, John Dewey, and Jean Piaget. Yet, some early childhood curricula still may not be taking full advantage of the opportunities for child development inherent in child-initiated activity. . . . (p. 1)

Early-childhood education is not merely the transmission to young minds of the concepts of numbers, letters, shapes, and colors. It is our first public statement of the values we wish to pass on to our children. We say that we value personal initiative, collaborative problem-solving, and tolerance and respect for others. These, then, are the values that should be evident in every setting where young children spend their time and have the opportunity to create their futures (Schweinhart, 1987a, p. 10).

Not only must all who work in early-childhood education in any capacity (administration, teaching, support personnel) recognize what is important in the learning and developing child, but they must also be prepared to interpret and defend the basic principles to educators, legislators, parents, and lay people. They need to campaign actively for equipment, for resources that will better meet the needs of young children, and for the best-qualified and most nurturing teachers. They must call for preservice and inservice training that will keep teachers current, enthusiastic, productive, and feeling worthwhile.

Why do we allow inappropriate educational practices with our young children when research and leaders in early-childhood education are telling us more important and appropriate methods? Elkind (1986) says it is happening because in the 1960s "education became a ground on which to fight social battles that had little or nothing to do with what was good pedagogy for children" (p. 634). Some of the affecting situations included government funding of some early-childhood programs; the fact that schools were under attack for not keeping abreast with other countries' educational achievements; and the civil rights movement, which addressed unequal schooling of minorities. There were also shifting views about the growth and development of infants and young children, urbanization, the women's movement, and the growing number of middle-class women in the workforce. All of these changes were accompanied by increasing pressures to place children in educational programs and by a rapidly changing technological environment (computers, TV, and so on). So, if these changes were taking place, Elkind asks: "What harm is there in [more formalized education for young children]?" He says it is a matter of both short- and long-term "miseducation"

> whenever we put them [children] at risk for no purpose. . . . The short-term risks derive from the stress, with all its attendant symptoms, that formal instruction places on children; the long-term risks are of at least three kinds: motivational, intellectual, and social. In each case, the potential psychological risks of early intervention far outweigh any potential educational gain. (p. 635)

Other Influences

To this point, we have mainly considered the child in the family. But as the child grows, there are more and more influences on her life. There are parent(s), possibly siblings or extended family members, and interaction outside the home. Perhaps the child will attend a preschool or child-care center. So the opportunities expand from what is shown in Figure 1.1 to that in Figure 1.2.

This is just the beginning of what the child will experience. Parents want the best opportunities for each of their children, but suppose that parents want to give their children "all the things we never had." Then the situation moves from a dyad (two components), to a triad (three components), to multi-involvement; for example, parents may enroll their children in athletic programs, in music programs, in learning a second language, in academic acceleration, and so on. Then the child's world looks like what is shown in Figure 1.3.

Parents and children consider many decisions about the care or education of the children outside the home. Some they can make; others are imposed. For example, some states advocate school attendance for all 4-year-olds, some want longer school days for kindergartners, and some want reading and math to be taught to infants and young children; still others want formal education to be de-

Figure 1.1
The Child is Part of the Family Unit.

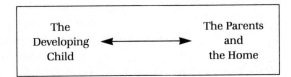

Figure 1.2
The Child Is the Connecting Link Between Home and Center.

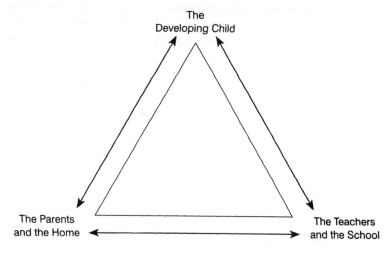

layed until age 8. It has been argued that preschool education should be part of public education, but with its own curriculum, methods of evaluation, classroom techniques, and programs of teacher education (Elkind, 1988). Curriculum and teaching strategies for early-childhood education need to best serve children's long-term development, both normative and dynamic (Katz, 1987).

Another characteristic of a good environment for young children has to do with *time:* time to explore, time to think, time to act, time to be with others and time to be alone, time to be active and time to be quiet, time to talk and time to listen, time to feel valued, and time to just be oneself. Adults have a tendency to hurry—to want something to show for their efforts.

Figure 1.3
Influences Outside the Home Increase the Complexity of the Child's Environment.

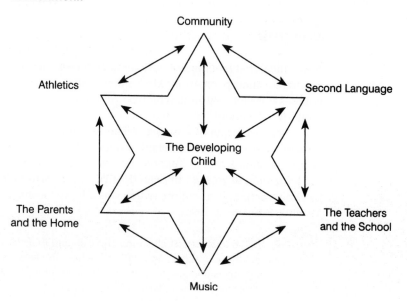

Elkind (1984) discusses two sources of energy that cause stress in young children: clock energy and calendar energy. *Clock energy* is used in pursuing the tasks of daily living, and it is replenished by food and rest. Symptoms of stress may appear as fatigue, loss of appetite, and decreased efficiency. *Calendar energy* is the energy involved in growth and development, and that determines our total life span:

> When the excessive demands continue without adequate time for replenishment, an individual must draw on his or her calendar energy. When this happens, such psychosomatic stress symptoms as headaches and stomachaches that can injure the organism and shorten the life span begin to appear. In young children exposed to formal instruction, both types of stress symptoms are frequently seen. (pp. 336–337)

The physical facilities and room arrangement are important considerations, as are the health and safety of the children in all situations. Guidelines need to be carefully explained and maintained. Compatible areas of curriculum should be placed near each other. Thoughtful consideration should be given to how easily the children can be supervised and to how toys, materials, equipment, and activities will be accessible so children can make and carry out independent decisions.

Diversity

There should be diversity in programs to create awareness of different cultures, abilities, and needs of individual children. Children come from varied backgrounds, genetic makeups, cultures, and so on. What fits one may not fit another, and vice versa. Sighted and hearing children have different modes of learning than children who have sight or hearing deficiencies, for example. Programs must be carefully thought through and administered so that they will be of value to the children who participate in them now—today! Children and parents have goals for "regular" learning—reading, writing, and arithmetic—but how and when children can use experiences and information may be vastly different for each child.

Other types of diversity (such as sex, culture, race, physical abilities, and so on) are further addressed in Chapter 10.

FOR TEACHERS

Training

It is critical that teachers of early-childhood education be properly and completely trained for their profession. Most states, and some districts, have carefully outlined courses for such training, which should differ from the training for elementary or secondary teachers.

As an example of how organizations and individuals can coordinate their efforts in an immensely important endeavor, two powerful and prestigious organizations, the Association of Teacher Educators (ATE) and the National Association for the Education of Young Children (NAEYC), have formulated a position statement regarding teacher certification, which was adopted in July/August 1991 (Association of Teacher Educators, 1991).

> *Purpose:* To ensure that all young children and their families have access to qualified early childhood teachers by guiding teacher educators and policy makers to (1) make informed decisions about early childhood teacher certification, (2) evaluate existing teacher certification standards, and (3) advocate for more appropriate early childhood teacher certification standards. (p. 16)

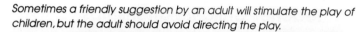

Sometimes a friendly suggestion by an adult will stimulate the play of children, but the adult should avoid directing the play.

Because teacher requirements vary for the age of the children taught, between states, in longevity, and in transferability between states, the reader is encouraged to seek current local, state, and national requirements from appropriate departments of education. (In recent years, Gwen Morgan at Wheelock College and Richard Fiene at the Bureau of Child Day Care Services in Harrisburg, Pennsylvania, have been active in identifying and promoting educational standards for training early-childhood education personnel.)

Ethical Behavior

As with other occupations and because of the great impact teachers have on the lives of children and families, it is understandable and important to have standards of ethical conduct. In this regard, Katz and Ward (1991) have prepared an expanded edition of ethical behavior for the National Association for the Education of Young Children, which includes the NAEYC code of ethical conduct and statement of commitment adopted in July 1989.

They summarize a code of ethics as statements about right or good conduct in the course of implementing one's goals and about courage to act in accordance with professional judgment of what is best for individuals served, even when they may not agree. (See page 28.)

Teacher-Child Relationships

We read in textbooks that honest, respectful, and nurturing teacher-child relationships are essential to children's security, self-confidence, and learning in early-childhood environments (see, for example, Elicker & Fortner-Wood, 1995).

As guidelines are developed and refined for early-childhood programs (NAEYC's position statements, for example), the warm, positive relationships between children and adults is strongly emphasized for children from birth to 3 years and clearly implied in guidelines for children older than 3 years (Bredekamp, 1987; Elicker & Fortner-Wood, 1995; Ainslie & Anderson, 1984; Hinde, 1979). In addition to providing emotional security, adults function as children's playmates, guides for learning, behavior managers, and providers of routine care.

Evidence from long-term studies supports the hypothesis that positive teacher-child relationships can improve the course of development for high-risk young children, including those who experience serious biological or environmental adversities early in life. A close, supportive relationship with a teacher or a caregiver can be a "resilience factor" for high-risk children (Elicker & Fortner-Wood, 1995, p. 73).

Teachers can find many opportune moments to build positive adult-child relationships: during conversations and play on the playground, while eating, at arrival and departure times, while caring for a pet or setting up activities, at private moments, during curriculum activities, and at special times when the child needs some quiet time. There is always much to do, but finding time to spend with each child to foster a positive relationship can have important benefits for his well-being and development. Attention to relationships with children can also make the job of teaching and caring for children more meaningful, rewarding, and enjoyable. To develop good relationships with children:

1. Make the relationship a priority.
2. Increase involvement with individual children.
3. Strive to make each relationship positive.
4. Build positive relationships with parents and co-teachers.
5. Plan routines and activities that focus on relationships. (Elicker & Fortner-Wood, 1995)

Child-Child Relationships

Howes, Hamilton, and Matheson (1994) found the following behaviors in peer relationships in child-care settings:

1. Children who had secure attachment relationships with their teachers were more gregarious, engaged in more complex play, and displayed more behavioral flexibility than did those with less secure teacher attachments.
2. Children who had higher emotional security with their teachers displayed fewer withdrawn behaviors and less hostile aggression toward peers.
3. When teachers mediated positively during peer interactions (for example, offered verbal or physical assistance), children were more likely to be accepted by their peers, whereas negative teacher mediation (interruption, punishment, or separation) was related to children's withdrawn behaviors and hostile aggression toward others.

A teacher can interest children in activities by using objects and language, then can encourage them to explore.

4. Children's relationships with teachers may have even stronger effects on their peer relations than do their relationships with parents because the teacher is available and ready to guide children in peer situations (Howes, Hamilton, & Matheson, 1994).

And further:

Finally, we have evidence that having secure attachment relationships with parents *and* teachers provides the greatest positive influence on young children's competence with peers. Howes and Clements (1994) found that children who were more sociable with both parents and teachers also tended to be more sociable with their peers. Howes found that children who had formed secure attachments with their teachers but not with their parents were more socially competent than those who had not formed secure attachments to *either* parents *or* teachers. These researchers suggest that having a secure attachment with a teacher or caregiver may at least partially compensate for insecure attachment with a parent. (p. 273)

Disadvantaged Children

Much needs to be said about disadvantaged, disabled, neglected, and mistreated children. It is acknowledged that caregivers, parents, and teachers should be aware of the conditions in their area and should be willing and able advocates for these children.

As both an opportunity and a challenge to early-childhood professionals, the demand for early child care continues to increase among economically disadvantaged families as welfare reform requires mothers receiving aid to return to school or work. Quality programs need to be designed to help children from low-income families, disabled children, and families with special needs reach their highest potential.

In the interest of focus, only one article will be referenced here (Campbell & Taylor, 1996):

> To provide a definitive investigation of the effects of preschool interventions for children from low-income families, a Consortium for Longitudinal Studies was formed in which eleven investigators followed up their participants to learn how long early benefits persisted. The consortium found important, lasting benefits in terms of: (a) fewer retentions in grade and fewer placements into special education for treated children; (b) positive changes in parental educational and employment levels; (c) modest but long-lasting IQ gains; (d) higher academic test scores and better progress through school; (e) "No one model emerges as clearly superior to another: positive benefits were found for limited interventions as well as for the most massive"; (f) greater cognitive gains when intervention begins in very early childhood; (g) care must be of the highest quality with particular attention being paid to socioemotional factors, (h) more research is needed on how best to foster healthy emotional growth in young children, (i) early childhood programs ultimately save taxpayer dollars in terms of reductions in the costs of education, welfare, and crime. (p. 79)

FOR FAMILIES (THE RELATIONSHIP BETWEEN HOME AND SCHOOL ENVIRONMENTS)

Parents play a vital role in the education of their children, for even when they think they are not teaching, they are visual, verbal, and physical models for their children. Parents shouldn't feel that "teaching" is the sole responsi-

Children frequently enact scenes from home and situations about which they feel safe.

bility of "teachers." Regardless of age, setting, or title, we are all teachers and learners.

At an earlier period there was a separation between the role of the parent and the role of the school—it could even have been called a chasm over which neither ventured. The child was shuttled between two different settings. Now both teachers and parents are more accepting of each other's roles in an effort to better educate children. However, teachers and parents are still learning how to deliver and receive messages that are accurate, clear, and helpful.

Reflection

Prior to the summer vacation, the teacher is planning a social with the children who have been in her preschool classroom for the past school year. She sends a vague invitation home with each child—it's unclear who is invited, whether it is a come-and-go or a stay affair, what the purpose is, how long it lasts, and so on.

Intentions of the teacher: The festivities will be simple, fairly short, outdoors, with light refreshments, a chance for the teacher to say good-bye to the child and for parents to pick up any items the child has left at school.

Interpretation of the parents: This will be a graduation for the child (even if he will return after summer), "I won't have to fix dinner," "We'll all need to dress up," "It will be difficult getting all of us ready and there on time," "It will be an opportunity for my child to perform for the other parents and children," "This will give my younger children a chance to play on the playground," "We had better invite all our relatives for this 'educational' achievement," and other parental hopes and anticipations.

The party does not meet the expectations of the teacher, the children, or the parents.

Exercise: With a partner, role play assuming you are the teacher. What message did you want to give to the parents? Why were your intentions misunderstood? Why were the parents so angry and resentful? Did any good things happen?

In a few minutes, switch roles and assume that you are the parent. Did you understand the teacher's intentions or did you feel you had to make them up? Did that disappoint you and/or your children? Do you have basis for being angry or do you just accept things as they unravel? Will this incident interfere with relationships between the home and school? How could future misunderstandings be avoided between the teacher and the parent?

Good environments for children are also good environments for parents. Parents trust the teachers, the staff, and the setting to be wholesome and growth-promoting for their family. Although the young child may be the only one in the family who attends the center, the experience will be felt by the entire family, large or small. Parents look for convenience, cost, expectations, and responsibilities. But the most important consideration of parents should be the philosophy of the center. Is it based on developmentally appropriate practices supported by research? Is it the best setting for *this* particular child and family? Will expectations cause undue stress on either the family or the center? When there is conflict, it is the child who is usually in the middle—uncomfortable at school and at home.

An environment where the child feels secure and happy is where she does best, where this child fits developmentally. Pushing ahead or holding back may please parents, but may not be best for the individual child. The child's behavior age, not her birthday age, should determine the time of school entrance and of subsequent promotion.

In addition to proposing teacher certification requirements, ATE and NAEYC (1991) promote a congenial relationship between the home and the school. Parents should be valued as educational partners, as educational objectives cannot be fully achieved without collaboration with families. This ability to collaborate with families and be a support to their child-rearing efforts demands an understanding of and respect for cultural and familial diversity.

Teachers can assist parents in cultivating realistic expectations regarding the development of young children, and parents can assist teachers in understanding the uniqueness of the child and family.

A national education strategy proposes goals for young children and families (as well as other points) (U.S. Department of Education, 1991, p. 61; Hostetler, 1991, p. 2). Goal 1 reads:

> Readiness for School by the year 2000, all children in America will start school ready to learn.

Specifics include the following:

    a. All disadvantaged and disabled children will have access to high-quality and developmentally appropriate preschool programs that help prepare children for school.

    b. Every parent in America will be the child's first teacher and devote time each day helping his or her preschool children learn; parents will have access to the training and support they need.

    c. Children will receive the nutrition and health care needed to arrive at school with healthy minds and bodies, and the number of low birthweight babies will be significantly reduced through enhanced prenatal health systems.

Head Start, NAEYC, ATE, educators, researchers, and others advocate a strong and reciprocal relationship between the school and the home, and give their full support to the preceding goals. The goals encourage schools to get ready to serve all children, urging that any definition of readiness must address both characteristics of the child and characteristics of the school (U.S. Department of Education, 1991). The information continues:

> Despite these cautions about possible misinterpretations of the goal due to the specific wording, we must recognize that establishing Goal 1 is perhaps the most significant statement ever made by our nation's leaders acknowledging the critical importance of early childhood experiences to later success in school and life. (p. 38)

NAEYC summarizes its commitment to universal school readiness by doing the following:

1. Addressing the inequities in early life experience so that all children have access to the opportunities that promote school success

2. Recognizing and supporting individual differences among children

3. Establishing reasonable and appropriate expectations of children's capabilities on school entry

Head Start funds have continually increased as a means of preventing young children from experiencing those things that diminish their self-image, health, learning abilities, and optimism for the future. Organizations and individuals have devised and implemented ways to help parents within the home, but the goal of reaching all children in need has not been rapidly or completely accomplished. Out-of-home experiences have not always been available or desirable for many diverse reasons.

This section is but an introduction to the importance of good environments for children, teachers, and home-school relations. More information and discussion on these topics are presented in subsequent chapters.

CHILD-CARE CENTER LICENSING

Much research has been done on current and long-term licensing; however, only the current study of Snow, Teleki, and Reguero-de-Atiles (1996) will be mentioned here:

> **Summary and Conclusions:**
> a. Child care licensing regulations continue to vary widely from state to state on three important indicators of child care quality between 1981 and 1995; child-staff ratio, group size, and staff education/training.
>
> b. *Positive* findings indicate that child-staff ratios and group-size limits have improved for infants as more states have established standards for infant care, and more states are now meeting recommended standards for child-staff ratio and group size; however, several states are still not in compliance with recommended child staff ratios, whereas an even larger number do not meet recommended group-size standards.
>
> c. *Negative* findings are that the child-staff ratio and group-size regulations for four-year-olds eroded in many places because of the demand for more service and the limited available federal and state dollars for purchase of care. The pressures to reduce regulations are likely to continue as welfare reform accelerates the demand for child care, especially for infants and toddlers. (p. 40)

APPLICATION OF PRINCIPLES

1. Name some characteristics of a good environment for:
   a. young children
   b. teachers of young children
   c. a good relationship between the home and the school.
   What advice would you give to parents considering enrolling a child in a child-care/education center?

2. Recall one of the theorists outlined in the chapter.
   a. Give some examples of his beliefs.
   b. Specifically, how would you use this information in preparing for or teaching young children?

3. Select a "misconception" listed in the chapter and indicate how you could correct or diffuse it.

4. Give three examples of developmentally appropriate and developmentally *in*appropriate activities; give examples of differences between age-appropriate and individually appropriate activities.

5. Think of a child between ages 3 and 5. What are some of the influences in that child's life? How could you help the child simplify some of the negative influences?

6. Consider two children who were fighting over a toy. How could you help the children become more friendly?

7. As a future teacher of young children, what personal and professional characteristics would *you* most likely develop? Suggest ways you could build good relationships with children, colleagues, and parents.

8. What are the differences between child-centered and adult-centered activities?

9. In what ways do adults hurry or put stress on young children?

10. Contact a department of education and get the requirements for becoming a certified teacher of child care and/or teacher of preschool children in your area.

REFERENCES

Ainslie, R. C., & C. W. Anderson (1984). Day care children's relationships to their mothers and caregivers: An inquiry into the conditions for the development of attachment. In Ainslie, R. C. (ed.), *The child and the day care setting: Qualitative variations and development,* 98–132. New York: Praeger.

Association of Teacher Educators (ATE) (1991). Early childhood teacher certification: A position statement of the Association of Teacher Educators and the National Association for the Education of Young Children (NAEYC). *Young Children,* 47(1), 16–21.

Barnett, W. S. (1995). Long-term effects of early childhood programs on cognitive and school outcomes. *The Future of Children* 5(3), 25–50.

Bredekamp, S. (ed.) (1987). *Developmentally appropriate practice in early childhood programs serving children from birth through age 8,* expanded edition. Washington, DC: NAEYC.

Bredekamp, S., & C. Copple (eds.) (1997). *Developmentally appropriate practice in early childhood programs,* revised edition. Washington, DC: NAEYC.

Campbell, F. A., & K. Taylor (1996, May). Early childhood programs that work for children from economically disadvantaged families. *Young Children,* 51(4), 74–80.

Elicker, J., & C. Fortner-Wood (1995, November). Research in review: Adult-child relationships in early childhood programs. *Young Children,* 51(1), 69–78.

Elkind, D. (1972). Misunderstandings about how children learn. *Today's Education,* 125–126.

Elkind, D. (1981). *The hurried child.* Reading, MA: Addison-Wesley.

Elkind, D. (1984). *All grown up and no place to go: Teenagers in crisis.* Reading, MA: Addison-Wesley.

Elkind, D. (1986). Formal education and early childhood education: An essential difference. *Phi Delta Kappan,* (67), 631–636.

Elkind, D. (1988). Educating the very young: A call for clear thinking. *NEA Today,* 6(6), 22–26.

Erikson, E. (1950). *A healthy personality for your child.* Washington, DC: U.S. Government Printing Office.

Ethics code revision: Recommended changes in the NAEYC Code of Ethical Conduct (1992, March). *Young Children,* 47(3), 12.

Fiene, R. (1993). *National early childhood program accreditation.* Annual report. Harrisburg, PA: Bureau of Child Day Care, 1401 Bertolino Building, 17105-2675.

Hinde, R. A. (1979). *Towards understanding relationships.* New York: Academic.

Hostetler, L. (1991, November). Healthy minds, healthy bodies, and health minds: Our goal one for young children. *Young Children,* 47(1), 2, 57–58.

Howes, C. (1988). Relations between early child care and schooling. *Developmental Psychology,* 24(1), 53–57.

Howes, C., & D. Clements (1994). Adult socialization of children's play in child care. In Goelman, H. (ed.), *Play and Child Care.* Albany, NY: State University of New York Press.

Howes, C., C. C. Matheson, & C. E. Hamilton (1994). Maternal, teacher, and child care history correlates of children's relationships with peers. *Child Development,* 65, 264–273.

Hurlock, E. (1964). *Child Development.* New York: McGraw-Hill.

Katz, L. (1987). Early education: What should young children be learning? *ERIC Digest.* Urbana, IL: ERIC Clearing House on Elementary and Early Childhood Education. ED290554.

Katz, L. G., & Ward, E. H. (1991) *Ethical behavior in early childhood education,* expanded edition. Washington, DC: NAEYC.

Kostelnik, M. J. (1992, May). Myths associated with developmentally appropriate programs. *Young Children,* 47(4), 17–23.

National Association for the Education of Young Children (NAEYC) (1996). *Ethical behavior in early childhood education,* expanded edition. Washington, DC: NAEYC.

National Association for the Education of Young Children (NAEYC) & National Association of Early Childhood Specialists in State Departments of Education (NAECS/SDE) (1991). Guidelines for appropriate curriculum content and assessment in programs serving children ages 3 through 8. *Young Children,* 46(3), 21–38. (Also in Bredekamp, S., & T. Rosegrant [eds.] [1992]. *Reaching potentials: Appropriate curriculum and assessment for young children,* Vol. 1, 9–27. Washington, DC: NAEYC.)

New, R. (1990, September) Excellent early education: a city in Italy has it. *Young Children,* 45(6), 4–6.

Piaget, J. (1974). *The child and reality: Problems of genetic psychology.* Trans. A. Rosin. New York: Viking.

Schweinhart, L. J. (1987a). "Child-initiated activity: How important is it in Early Childhood Education?" *High/Scope ReSource Magazine* (Spring/Summer). Ypsilanti, MI: High/Scope Press.

Schweinhart, L. J. (1987b). When the buck stops here: What it takes to run good early childhood programs. *High/Scope ReSource Magazine* (Fall). Ypsilanti, MI: High/Scope Press.

Snow, C. W., J. K. Teleki, & J. T. Reguero-de-Atiles (1996, September). Child care center licensing standards in the United States: 1981 to 1995. *Young Children,* 51(6), 36–41.

U.S. Department of Education (1991). *America 2000: An education strategy.* Washington, DC: Author.

Guidance Techniques and School/Home Interaction

CHAPTER 2

MAIN PRINCIPLES

1. A code of ethics for early-childhood education includes responsibilities for the practitioner, exemplary professional behavior, and practices that are required, prohibited, and permitted.

2. Adults play an important role in the lives of children and can help them develop prosocial attitudes and behaviors. Children need and want guidelines.

3. Preschool classroom management is based on eight positive steps: (a) commitment of the teacher; (b) respect for one another; (c) a positive atmosphere; (d) routines and guidelines; (e) consistency; (f) choice; (g) clarity; and (h) flexibility. Classrooms can be prepared to enhance learning and reduce behavior problems.

4. The three major approaches to guidance, each resulting in development of quite different kinds of character, are *authoritarian, permissive,* and *democratic.*

5. Good guidance techniques at school and home promote better behavior in both settings. Destructive or harmful behavior must be stopped immediately.

6. Both teachers and parents share in the care and education of young children. A good relationship between the school and home benefits both settings.

7. Good observation skills help parents and teachers better understand young children.

In Chapter 1, good environments for young children, teachers, and parents were discussed. In this chapter, attention is given to some workable interactive guidance techniques. Adults respond in various ways to children, and vice versa. Teachers, for example, are less emotionally involved and often act more objectively than parents do, making it easier to work with the children of others than with one's own. Moreover, parents feel they have more at stake than a teacher does because their children are extensions of them. Some adults are easier for children to understand—especially when the children feel secure and the adult is consistent in what is expected.

A CODE OF ETHICS: GUIDELINES FOR CAREGIVERS OUTSIDE THE HOME

Many daily decisions, moral and ethical, are required of those who work with young children, their families, and individuals who administer and license programs. In behalf of these children and adults, NAEYC (1996) has set forth a code of ethical conduct, describing paramount responsibilities to provide for:

- *children:* "safe, healthy, nurturing, and responsive settings . . . helping them learn to live and work cooperatively, and promoting self-esteem." (p. 58)
- *families:* "collaboration between the home and school in ways that enhance the child's development." (p. 58)
- *colleagues* (co-workers, employers, employees): "settings and relationships that support productive work and meet professional needs." (p. 59)
- *communities and society:* "to provide programs that meet its needs and to co-operate with agencies and professions that share responsibility for the welfare and protection of children . . . to serve as a voice for children everywhere." (p. 60)

The main features of the NAEYC code of ethics are the group's beliefs about:

- what is right rather than expedient,
- what is good rather than simply practical, and
- what acts members must never engage in or condone even if those acts would work or if members *could get away with* such acts, acts to which they must never be accomplices, bystanders, or contributors. (Katz & Ward, 1996, p. 4)

Why Is a Code of Ethics Important?

Katz and Ward (1996) identify and summarize a four-part answer:

1. *High power and low status of practitioners:* greater necessity for internalized restraints against abusing power. (p. 4)
2. *Multiplicity of clients:* parents are the primary group, children secondary, the employing agency and the larger community next. "Each group of clients in the hierarchy may be perceived as exerting pressures for practitioners to act in ways that may be against the best interest of another client group." (p. 7)
3. *Ambiguity of the data base:* "to remind practitioners to eschew orthodoxies, strive to be well-informed and open-minded, and keep abreast of new ideas and developments." (p. 7)

4. *Role ambiguity:* the importance of the developmental and stimulus functions of early-childhood practitioners; parental involvement; nutrition and health screening; and relevant social services. (p. 7)

"In summary, . . . it seems reasonable to suggest that the actual problems encountered by practitioners in the course of daily practice typically reflect combinations of several of these aspects" (p. 8).

RELATIONSHIPS BETWEEN CHILDREN AND ADULTS

Studying children in kindergarten through third grade, Carlsson-Paige and Levin (1992) assessed how conflicts developed over time and what methods the children used to resolve them. They found that how the children defined the conflict had a great deal to do with its solution. Kindergartners see conflict in the present moment, in physical terms, and egocentrically. Time helps them to see it from another's point of view and in a more broad and abstract manner—such as underlying motives, feelings, and intentions (1992). Learning to negotiate is difficult for young children; however, when their thinking becomes more flexible and interconnected, they can see options for solutions. By helping young children to develop problem-solving skills, adults help them gain skills of empowerment and techniques of getting along with others: "I (we) can solve problems and make others happy!" Children in the early grades can learn through class meetings, group discussions, and even role playing. These techniques help young children feel that they are *problem solvers*. People of all ages must find ways to solve conflict in ways that are satisfying to all parties and promote better relationships.

"Not surprisingly, if caregivers and teachers take time to encourage, facilitate, and teach prosocial behaviors, children's prosocial interactions increase and

Teachers calm children when the need arises.

aggression decreases" (Carlsson-Paige & Levin, 1995). In one early study, children (ages 3 months to kindergarten) who attended an experimental child-care program that focused on intellectual growth were rated by their kindergarten teachers as more aggressive than a control group of children who attended community child-care programs during their preschool years for a shorter amount of time.

Developmental theory predicts that with age, as children's thinking becomes more logical and flexible, they will become better able to think of win/win solutions.

In part two of a two-part article on prosocial behavior in classrooms, families, schools, and communities, Honig and Wittmer (1996) encourage child-sensitive, high-quality care in classrooms because those attributes promote prosocial behaviors. For example, they emphasize cooperation rather than competition; teach cooperative and conflict-resolution games and sports; set up play spaces and materials to facilitate cooperative play; use children's literature that includes empathy and caring; have discussions about feelings; encourage social interaction with special-needs children; train older children as peer mediators; work closely with families; and use other age-appropriate techniques. They conclude:

> [T]he more cherished a child is, the less likely he or she is to bully others *or* to be rejected by other children. The more nurturing parents and caregivers are—the more positive affection and responsive, empathetic care they provide—the more positively children will relate in social interactions with teachers, caring adults, and peers and in cooperating with classroom learning goals, as well." (p. 70)

McCloskey (1996) suggests preschool classroom management based on "loosening up" with eight positive steps: (1) be a committed preschool teacher; (2) show respect to each other; (3) deal in a positive atmosphere; (4) be guided by consistency, structure, and routine; (5) "mean what you say and say what you mean," (6) encourage choice but still maintain control; (7) be willing to clarify; and (8) if it doesn't work, scrap it!

To Praise or Not to Praise—That Is the Question!

Some teachers use lavish praise, some use moderate praise, and some use *no* praise. Where is the appropriate point on the scale?

"Publicly praising positive behavior has been advocated by teachers and teacher educators for generations . . . avoiding the use of negative comments," writes Marshall (1995, p. 26), but does that make it a good classroom practice?

When a teacher says, "I like the way . . . ," it can create problems in the classroom:

1. It can be used in an unequal and biased way.
2. Dependency on praise can regulate children's behavior in unnatural ways.
3. Focus is on approval rather than on learning.
4. Other children are expected to model the target child's actions.
5. It puts emphasis on teacher approval.
6. It can create unhealthy feelings between conforming and nonconforming children.
7. It can become a monotonous and meaningless statement.

To be most effective, praise needs to be personal, specific, valued, behavior-reinforcing, and honest. We can acknowledge and support what children have done and at the same time help them evaluate themselves. Rather than hearing the teacher say "I like the way . . ." as a general classroom statement, children prefer to have their personal efforts seen and acknowledged. When children with poor self-concepts hear a "general announcement," they feel excluded: "She couldn't possibly be talking about me!"

Alternate techniques to "I like the way . . ." that are less likely to have undesirable side effects are (1) stating what action is expected (what the child *is* to do); (2) helping children figure out *what* they need to do to be ready to learn (find a comfortable place, think about the experience, put toys away); (3) giving *expectations and reasons;* and (4) acknowledging *all* children. These techniques foster self-regulation, long-term effects, and self-motivated reasons (Marshall, 1995, p. 28).

Types of Guidance

Three major, very different approaches to child rearing and child care, which usually result in the development of quite different kinds of character, are outlined in Table 2.1. However, in cases of harm, danger, or destruction, the teacher steps in and stops the behavior without a second thought about which type of guidance he or she prefers.

Proactive guidance, in which teachers and children anticipate possible problems and consider acceptable solutions, is far superior to *reactive* guidance, in which interaction is generally negative or one-sided.

Example:
A group of 3-year-olds is going on a spring walk. In *proactive guidance,* the children and teachers discuss the route, expected behavior at various points, the purpose of the trip, items they will be taking, when they will return, and so on. The excursion is pleasant and satisfying to all involved. In *reactive guidance,* the children frolic freely, disregard any cautions, refuse to follow rules, and are unruly. Teachers become upset, children are ridiculed, and the excursion turns out to be unpleasant for all involved.

Guidance in the Classroom

There are many approaches a teacher can take to a variety of situations within the classroom to reduce discipline problems. This method, called *indirect guidance,* shows in the organization of curriculum areas, materials, traffic patterns, sequencing of events, use of space and time, and other items that consider the needs of the children individually or as a group. The following are some examples:

- Democracy and curiosity are encouraged.
- Children select the area and amount of time spent in play.
- Children have individual spaces for their personal items.
- Health and safety limits are identified and enforced.
- Incompatible areas and/or materials are separated within the classroom (for example, water is away from books, quiet away from noisy activities).
- Art projects are open-ended.
- Tools are appropriate in size, weight, and intended use.
- Blocks are used out of traffic areas and on a surface that muffles the sound.

Table 2.1
Approaches to Child Rearing and Child Care

TYPES OF CHILD-REARING PATTERNS	PARENT BEHAVIOR	TYPE OF PRESCHOOL EDUCATION PREFERRED
Authoritarian (autocratic, external control)	Values obedience over independence, conformity and convention over creativity. Punitive; as a result, children most likely react with anger, resentment, or submission.	Academic; authoritarian teachers. Rigid schedules and behavior. Seat work, where children work individually at their own pace. Little child-child interaction. Conformity.
Permissive (laissez-faire)	Extremely indulgent. Lacks limits in setting standards, behavioral and/or intellectual challenges, and development of social skills.	Pleasant setting but little intellectual content or challenge to children's thinking or social development. Laissez-faire teachers spend limited time (a) planning and/or preparing curriculum, (b) enriching play or providing meaningful activities, (c) helping children develop democratic interactional skills, and (d) providing guidance or suitable responses to individual children's needs. The need to play and other physical needs are seriously neglected.
Democratic (an approach advocated by Dewey, who defined it as a cluster of characteristics, interests, and motivations in an individual that are at once self-fulfilling and of benefit to the group. [Greenberg, 1992, March, p. 61] Dewey disagreed that all children of the same age have the same skill development, knowledge, and understanding, a common thought of teachers and parents who dominated children. An easily implemented approach that benefits and addresses rights, abilities, responsibilities, and actions of each person.)	Aware of and concerned with social interaction, thinking, and learning. Expects and recognizes behavior that is developmentally appropriate. Parents discuss necessary rules with children and build a democratic setting. Adults use proactive rather than reactive guidance.	Developmentally appropriate settings and learning experiences. Caring teachers, flexible activities, and a democratic atmosphere blend into a coherent setting of fulfillment for oneself and others.

Source: Greenberg, P. (1992, March). Why not academic preschool? Part 2. Autocracy or democracy in the classroom? *Young Children* (47)3, 54–64.

 ○ Materials are easily accessed and replaced, are self-help, and encourage repeated play.
 ○ Duplicate materials are available to encourage cooperative play.
 ○ Activities and materials are flexible depending on the skills and interests of the children.

Children can offer guidance and comfort to each other.

- ○ Bathroom fixtures and classroom furniture are child-sized.
- ○ Needs of children with disabilities are met.
- ○ Teachers are accessible when needed.
- ○ Group activities are kept to a minimum.
- ○ Tension-reducing activities and methods are appropriate.
- ○ Alternative plans and activities are available.
- ○ The classroom is "culturally friendly."

GUIDANCE TECHNIQUES FOR SCHOOL AND HOME

Good observational skills and accurate interpretation are great assets when guiding others. Figure 2.1 lists some techniques that adults in the school and/or home will find fruitful and easy to use. They are not presented in any particular order; they just work. Read through them and pick out one or two that you would like to try. Be persistent. Give each one a fair trial. After you have mastered a few, select others. Undoubtedly there will be a change in behavior for both you and the children you teach—at home or at school. The bibliography at the end of the chapter can lead you to further examination of the issues.

Young, immature, and inexperienced children need additional guidance and patience from adults.

Figure 2.1
Guidance Techniques for School and Home

1. There are two ultimate goals: to help the child develop self-esteem and self-discipline.
2. Listen *to* children and talk *with* them.
3. Plan experiences that will be challenging but successful.
4. Send and receive clear messages.
5. Reinforce the actions you want repeated.
6. Use a positive approach, but do not hesitate to stop inappropriate behaviors.
7. Provide guidelines for behavior.
8. Show respect for children.
9. Guide through love instead of fear or guilt.
10. Be a good role model.
11. Be on guard for warning signals.
12. Avoid power struggles.
13. Offer legitimate choices and accept decisions.
14. Encourage independence.
15. Provide acceptable avenues for release of feelings.
16. Help children learn through participation.
17. When needed, use discipline appropriately.

Reflection

I have had student teachers master a technique and feel comfortable with its outcome, only to find the children using the same technique (for example, positive statements, eye contact, and so on). The student teachers rush back and say, "The children are using those techniques on me! What do I do next?" My reply is: "If it is a *good* technique and it works, why can't children also use it?" Why do some adults think they always have to be one step ahead of children?

Discussion of Techniques

1. There Are Two Ultimate Goals: To Help the Child Develop Self-Esteem and Self-Discipline.   Adults are large and powerful enough to make children do what the adult wishes—and some adults like knowing they can control someone or something. Children feel undervalued or unimportant when they are expected to conform with little or no consideration.

One way adults express their power to children is by saying "I like the way . . ." (for example, that Charles is sitting, or Debbie waited for her turn to talk, and so on). This puts the emphasis on the teacher and what pleases her rather than stating the acceptable thing the child does. The situation could be turned more to the child's behavior by saying, "Thanks, Charles, for sitting up at story time," "Debbie, it was thoughtful of you to wait until Susan was through talking before giving us your ideas," "What a good idea you had, Stephen, about wiping your brush on the side of the jar to keep the paint from dripping on the floor," and so on.

Self-esteem is an important aspect of one's self-image. It is how we value ourselves, and reflects how others view us as well. "Changed self-esteem can result from changing the referent group as well as from changing self-perception. If individuals become more competent, the feedback they receive, both from the accomplishment of tasks and from others' view of the accomplishment, becomes enhanced," states Spodek (1991). He continues,

> It may be that the best way to help children improve their self-esteem is to help them gain competence and use that competence in activities that have serious purposes and real consequences. Such an approach may be more effective and more real in its outcomes than the programs available that "teach" self-esteem. (p. 164)

With reference to the school's role in enhancing self-esteem, Beane (1991) states that it must first help children cope with ambiguities and discontinuities in their lives, and second, help them deal with the persistent correlation between self-esteem and a number of "school-related variables, including participation, completion, behavior, self-direction, and achievement . . ." (p. 153). In this setting, one might expect children to be active in participation and classroom governance, where there is heterogeneous grouping and cooperative learning with emphasis on personal and social meanings. One would not expect "to see an autocratic, adult-dominated environment, either explicitly displayed or thinly veiled behind gimmicks, gadgets, and coupons that are meant to insidiously seduce children into prizing someone else's agenda over their own" (p. 159).

Lest any gains in self-esteem resulting from classroom activity be washed away by conditions outside the classroom, Beane suggests that "educators themselves become more active as advocates for children . . . both in rhetoric and action. Children cannot grow with dignity and self-esteem if they must live in a world that mitigates against these qualities, particularly for those who are not white, male, and middle-class."

And further:

> Many will recognize this as the language and politics of social reconstruction and they will be correct in doing so. But if "developmental" interests are sincere about the quality of life for children, then this is the direction they must take. Anything short of this will continue the superficial, culturally detached, utilitarian, and self-protective definition of self-esteem, a version that clearly does not serve the self-esteem of children. (pp. 159–160)

For children to survive in this complex world, they must be able to take responsibility for their own actions. If adults are willing to help children practice self-control when they are ready and able, children can develop trust and confidence in their ability to make and carry out decisions. These children will begin to make consistent choices and will be able to adjust to and accept the consequences. Do not expect too much of young children. They cannot take on situations inappropriate for their age or abilities. Do be patient as they become more able to assume responsibility for their own behavior, and do give them opportunities to practice responsibility in an accepting environment by helping them feel worthy of trust through sincere remarks.

2. Listen *to* Children and Talk *with* Them.   Have you ever heard a child who was questioned about a certain act reply, "But you said I could!" His response is a result of someone not listening! We often give our undivided attention to another adult but fail to hear the words of children—who sometimes have to tug and pull at us before we give them even divided attention. Children do have important things to say and ask. We should listen and explain in an affectionate and interested manner.

Young children often have difficulty expressing themselves because their thoughts move faster than their mouths. They will be more likely to try to express their thoughts if a patient and caring person will listen. When children are rushed or listeners are only partially interested, children do not often return for information or conversation. Listening adults find out information about the child, his interests, and his needs, and thereby are able to help the child gain confidence in himself and with others.

One way to give children your undivided attention is to stoop or kneel so that you have eye-to-eye contact. Then concentrate on their words. With a limited vocabulary, they may have difficulty conveying complete and desired messages. Interest helps communication. (If you have ever studied a foreign language, you will be more sympathetic to the child's difficulty in communicating.)

Besides being poor listeners to children, adults may speak differently to them than to others—talking down in tone or ideas. Listen attentively and speak normally. They want and need information but dislike long, unnecessary lectures. Talk with them about things of their interest and stimulate their thinking. Appreciate and enjoy your conversations with children. They are refreshing and enlightening.

At times it will be important to reflect the children's feelings to them—not by putting ideas or words into their mouths, but by helping them put feelings into words. Griffin (1982) states: "Efforts to comfort, argue a child out of his feelings, point a moral, criticize his attitude, or make up with him if he is angry have no place in this situation and end confidences. The best response communicates both understanding of the feelings and acceptance of them."

3. Plan Experiences That Will Be Challenging but Successful. Young children need to have successful experiences at least 80 percent of the time if they are going to develop confidence in themselves. Everyone likes success, but it is especially important to young children. They are just beginning to unravel their world; knowledge and skills are limited. They need encouragement to try new activities and to repeat old ones.

Knowing that young children are in the sensorimotor stage of development, adults can plan appropriate experiences with brief explanations, which will assist the children in their actions. Children sense the adult's confidence, which is important in attempting something new or difficult. Mastery brings about competence; competence brings about mastery.

Observe each child carefully; then give individual responsibilities and privileges accordingly. Express your honest appreciation and encouragement frequently. Let the child determine when her activity is finished and satisfying.

Reflection

Provide toys and materials for activities than can be concluded at any time or that can be extended if desired (block building, art materials, outdoor play, and so on). Suppose a child began making a collage out of the many types of materials to cut and paste. He can conclude the activity with few or many objects pasted on his masterpiece—and who is to say that it isn't finished or that the child hasn't had satisfaction in the process?

If children experience only situations they can manage easily, they will tend to repeat those and ignore challenging opportunities. If experiences are always too difficult, children turn away from them. Failure is an unpleasant feeling. Watch the children. See what interests them and how they attack various problems. Help them develop problem-solving abilities by providing toys and materials with endless experimental possibilities to stimulate curiosity. Plan time for their exploration. Introduce them to some new experiences to widen their horizons, but make sure these experiences are based on needs, levels of development, and interests. Avoid pushing when children are not ready, but keep curiosity alive when they are ready.

4. Send and Receive Clear Messages. When you make a request of children, be sure they understand what you mean. If they act unsure, then repeat, define, or clarify, but not in a belittling way.

For example, at the center, Rojas would stand near the gate until no one was looking, then run into the parking lot. The teacher showed him how busy the lot was, how fast cars went past the gate, and how difficult it was to see him because of his height. Her words went unheeded, so she warned him that the next time he went out of the gate, she would call his mother to come and take him home. His chance came, and he slipped out of the gate and was gone again. Because of her warning and the presence of real danger, the teacher called his mother, who came and took Rojas home. The next day when he arrived at school, he went to each child and said, "Do you know what happens if you run out of the gate?" and then explained, "Your mother comes and takes you home." He had omitted the reasons, but he was clear on the result.

Requests made of children should be reasonable, clear, and simple. Too many commands or something that seems unreasonable or complicated causes children to hesitate rather than respond. Think carefully what you are requesting, then be prepared to follow through, as in the case of Rojas. Your hesitancy or inability to follow through adds to the confusion of children.

Speak with confidence, and children respond in the same way. When you end a request with "Okay?", it means you are seeking their agreement to conform, and the children are frequently confused by this action. Another familiar phrase is, "You need to . . ." Griffin (1982) defines this as meaning that the teacher will not change his mind and that he has a good reason for anything he requires. Just use your voice as a teaching tool and expect the children to carry the request through matter-of-factly.

While sending good messages to children, be alert in receiving their messages. Are their words saying what they mean? Are there nonverbal messages? Gestural language often conveys more clues than verbal language. Let children know you understand their feelings by defining them. "I know you are mad because you can't swing. It's Lisa's turn, but when she is through, it will be your turn. Let's find something else to do while you wait." "It really hurts when you fall on the cement. A cool cloth will help your knee feel better."

Be honest in your praise of children and their accomplishments. They will appreciate your sincerity as well as your time to talk and to listen.

5. Reinforce the Actions You Want Repeated. It seems much easier (or perhaps more common) to comment on negative than positive behavior. Communication with a particular child may be only to describe her "bad" behavior. To get any recognition at all, she repeats the negative behavior. Is it better to have negative attention than none at all? Adults who look for and reward acceptable behavior indicate to children the types of actions that are accepted and expected. When children

Teachers who set and maintain limits encourage children to develop safe patterns to follow.

exhibit negative or undesirable behavior, they need to know it is the *behavior* and *not them* that is unacceptable.

Suppose a child picks up his toys and you say, "Thanks for picking up your toys. Your room looks so nice when your toys are on the shelf." By commenting, you are increasing the possibility of his repeating the behavior. But if you say nothing, he may think, "Why should I pick up my toys? Mother (or teacher) doesn't care. She'll just pick them up later." But how do you show approval for something that has never occurred (the child has never picked up his toys)? You have to watch for the behavior, or even catch the child doing the task. Even if he picked up only one toy, say, "That truck looks good on the shelf. Now it won't get stepped on," or "You'll be able to find your truck the next time you want it because it is on the shelf." The next time he may pick up two toys. Again, give honest praise. He will probably continue until all the toys are picked up if he gets more recognition for picking them up than for leaving them around. Notice when he is doing good things and acknowledge them.

If you look for good behavior to reinforce, you are likely to find it. If you look for the bad, you are also likely to find it. The more closely a reinforcement (a reward, an approval, a privilege) follows an action, the more likely that action is to be repeated. In fact, if you reinforce a child's action every time she exhibits good behavior, and then begin to taper off to reinforcing less frequently, she will continue to repeat that pattern, looking for the approval. Reinforce her occasionally and she'll continue the behavior, wanting the approval but not knowing when it will come.

In reinforcing actions, identify what was appropriate. Rather than saying, "You did a good job," or "I like what you did," say, "You did a good job in sweeping the floor and putting the broom in the closet," or "Thanks for putting the puzzle together. Now the pieces won't get lost." Kind words *(thank you, please, excuse me)* are important to children *and* adults.

Two schools of thought deal with inappropriate behavior. One is to ignore the behavior, which will increase its intensity and frequency as the child tries to regain attention. Finding this behavior unrewarded, the child will discontinue it. The second thought comes from Hendrick (1992):

> While on the subject of reinforcement, I want to comment that I agree with Bettye Caldwell (1977) that it is not effective to "extinguish" aggressive behavior in young children by simply ignoring it. In my experience such behavior does not subside when ignored—apparently because children interpret this laissez-faire attitude as permission (Bandura and Walters 1963). Not only that, one cannot overlook the fact that there are inherent gratifications (pay-offs) in attacking other children; these range from simply seizing what is desired to enjoying hitting someone—if you're angry, hitting somebody feels pretty good. For these reasons, it is important to take more assertive action and stop undesirable behavior rather than let it slip past on the ground that it will go away if no attention is paid to it.

6. Use a Positive Approach, but Do Not Hesitate to Stop Inappropriate Behaviors. When I tell my college students to be positive rather than negative, some of them rebel. A familiar comment is, "We've had nothing but negative comments all our lives. Now we are expected to adopt a different approach—just like that!" It is difficult to see value in and to use an opposing technique at first. But through diligent effort, students see children responding more favorably when positive rather than negative statements are used. The effort pays off.

Occasionally, an adult should analyze how his verbalizations appear to others: If the teacher thoughtfully considers the words that he uses in speaking to children, he may realize that many of them communicate disapproval, disappointment, criticism, impatience, and other negative attitudes, even though his general attitude toward children is a positive one.

Always telling children what *cannot* be done creates defiance. Turn that around: when children are told what *can* be done, all sorts of possibilities arise, creating a different attitude and encouraging rather than discouraging participation.

Think how you would respond to the following sets of statements:

"Hammer your nail in that wood," or "Don't hammer the table."

"Hang your jacket in your locker," or "Don't throw your jacket on the floor."

"Pour just what you want to drink," or "Don't waste juice!"

If the first of each pair of statements seems too commanding, read them again. Realize that the child is being redirected, that is, given a possible response, an appropriate action. The second statement in each pair leaves him hanging: "Well, what *do* you expect me to do?" He may continue the behavior because no alternative is available.

Positive statements work well with anyone. When a person knows how she is expected to act, the chance of her acting that way is increased. Most people respond better when addressed in a positive way. They feel respected and appreciated. The world of preschoolers is so full of *"don'ts," "quits,"* and *"stops"* that the children are left with the feeling, "Whatever I do is wrong." Using the positive approach opens new avenues for children and their behavior, as do humor and modeling.

In her book *Guiding Young Children,* Hildebrand (1994) gives some excellent advice. Pay particular attention to ways to appreciate positive behavior, ways to cope with troublesome behavior, qualities of significant adults in the lives of children, and ways to involve parents in their children's schooling.

Now a couple of *DON'T*s along with the *DO*s. First, do not be misled about *never* using negative statements. When danger is imminent, do or say whatever it takes to stop the action before an injury occurs. Then survey the situation and proceed with positive words and actions. Second, don't overuse praise! It can become so common that the children see no value in it and can almost mock the teacher's words before she says them: "Oh, that is so *wonderfully wonderful!*" Make sure your praise is appropriate, honest, and fits the situation.

Reflection

As a little homework, keep track of your interaction with a child (or adult) for a few days. Mark down every time you respond to that person and see whether your positive responses outweigh your negative ones *and* whether you use a variety of appropriate responses.

7. Provide Guidelines for Behavior.   Good discipline includes creating an atmosphere of firmness, clarity, conscientiousness, and reasoning. In other words, it must be clear what is expected and why it is important. Bad discipline involves unduly harsh and inappropriate punishment and is often associated with verbal ridicule and attacks on the child's integrity.

As an undergraduate student, I remember learning early about the three red flags in discipline: The child is not allowed to hurt himself, hurt someone else, or destroy property. This advice has served me well and has been passed on to my students.

Limits should be considered very carefully and important ones upheld. Unimportant limits should be discarded. Nothing is magical about a set number of limits—have only those that are important for the health and safety of the children and teachers. Help children understand what the limits are and why they are necessary, and give as much freedom as possible. As children grow and develop, alter the guidelines. Children's increasing reasoning power, skills, and experiences cause them to act more independently. Be consistent, but not inflexible, in enforcing the guidelines. Certain conditions call for altering guidelines, not breaking them or removing them.

If possible, let the children help establish rules. "What do you think we ought to do about . . ." "Can you think of something that would make that situation safer?" "Where should you ride the trike?" Allow for discussions. Establish reasons why a certain thing does or does not occur. Keep stating the reasons (from time to time) until the children understand the rationale. Reasons are important in their learning.

The best time to handle a situation is before it occurs. Watch for trouble spots. Talk about and set up limits before there is an accident. ("When we cross the street on our walk today, we will wait at the corner and all cross together.") With prior admonition, children will know what is to occur and as a consequence will behave acceptably.

Hymes (1981) reports that there are classrooms with "sixteen million rules and regulations" and those with only the most general rules: "Be kind to other people," or "Take good care of property." He suggests a three-step method:

> Step One, to build understandings: Establish some classroom rules and regulations. Step Two: Don't set up so many that the children gag on them. Step Three calls for great sensitivity. Your classroom rules and regulations must fit your boys and girls. You want reasonable requirements. If you ask more than youngsters can live up to, only evil results.

Make sure the established guidelines are within the developmental abilities of the children.

Griffin (1982) captures the feeling of most teachers:

> Setting limits is probably the most difficult part of her job for many a teacher. Children need to be prevented from doing some things, and they need to be required to do some things. But in either case, more important than just what limits are set or what is required is recognition of a child's feelings about limits and requirements.

Children need to feel that limits are for their health and safety.

Sometimes inappropriate behavior must be rebuked. In such a circumstance, make sure the children are aware of the seriousness of the offense. Then let them know you reprimand only their action, that you still love and care for them by the tone of your voice, the gentleness of your touch, and by being close to them.

When children need to be disciplined for inappropriate behavior, make sure the punishment fits the crime. Do not be like the old woman in the shoe, who didn't know what to do with all her children, so first she fed them (a common reinforcer) and then she punished them all in the same manner. Were they bad for being children or for being too numerous? Did they misbehave? Will their punishment prevent misbehavior (whatever it was) from happening again? What did they learn from the episode?

In his wisdom and experience, White (1975) recommends child-rearing practices. In his book *The First Three Years of Life*, he also gives four child-rearing practices he does not recommend: (1) overemphasis on intellectual growth, (2) expensive educational toys, (3) unsupervised play groups, and (4) overindulgence. Consider these items seriously.

Whenever a child has been removed from a situation or activity, some legitimate way of returning is extremely important; she must decide when she is ready, and she must have another chance to participate where she misbehaved. Without these two conditions, how can she build self-control?

8. Show Respect for Children.   When an adult shows respect for children, the children increase in feelings of competence and value while also improving relationships with peers. Hymes (1981) says it is important for children to "develop good feelings about themselves, about their peers and the other humans around them, about the world of reality in which they live."

Children who are totally immersed in activities that need to be prematurely terminated appreciate a friendly notice. For example, Lee was used to a few minutes' warning before lunch, but he finished his activity early one day. He called, "Mother, aren't you going to tell me it's a few minutes before lunch?" She replied, "Not quite yet." Lee stood silently for several minutes until Mother's warning. Happily, he washed his hands and went to the table.

Another way to show respect for children involves their personal belongings. Encourage them to share as good social etiquette, but never force them. If a child has a personal possession that he doesn't want to share, say to the other child (or children), "This is very special to him. He wants to keep it now, so we'll look for something for you." The child is not made to feel guilty because he does not share; rather, he feels that his rights are respected. Remember that sharing *follows* possessing! At school the problem of sharing may arise infrequently because all the toys belong to everyone; however, one child may be using a particular toy when another wants it. Be fair when handling disagreements between two children. When possible, allow them to settle their own differences. Allow each child to maintain her dignity; avoid forcing guilt feelings on her. Be proactive!

Children should also be respected for the individuals they are, for what they can do, and for just being themselves. Help them build a good self-image by pointing out assets: "You are able to ride the bike so well." "You have the prettiest blue eyes." "My, but you are strong to help move the table." Show in words and actions that you value them. Avoid comparing abilities, characteristics, activities, and behavior with those of other children. Such comparisons breed dislike and unhappiness.

9. Guide through Love Instead of Fear or Guilt.   When an offense occurs, place emphasis on the action and not on the child. In a loving and kind way, help the child to see the infraction and how to resolve it in ways other than blind obedience. Then let him know you reprimand only his action and that you still love and care for him.

When appropriate, ask the children to define the situation. "Do you know why you can't do this?" If they are inaccurate or unclear, explain: "Because it is very dangerous, and you might get hurt (or whatever is the case). I love you, and I would feel very sad if something happened to you." Or, "I care enough about you to stop you when you are doing something that could hurt you or someone else."

Trying to rule through fear or guilt is a growth-stunting procedure; children never learn to make valid decisions or see true issues. Instead, build a loving and trusting relationship so that you both are able to survive the inevitable rough times.

10. Be a Good Role Model.   When we ask or expect children to act in a certain manner, and then we do the opposite, they receive mixed messages. Consider the teacher who tells the children that it is time for *everybody* to go inside, and then turns back into the playground to put away some equipment. Or the parent who strikes a child, at the same time saying, "How many times have I told you not to hit your little brother?"

The mere fact that we are moving, speaking beings means that we are providing a model for someone. Imitations of good qualities are flattering, but imitations of bad qualities are embarrassing. As parents or teachers we see behavior reflected in the words and actions of children (a comment, a gesture). Sometimes we recognize these behaviors as our own; sometimes, oblivious, we wonder where the children could have seen or heard such a thing!

If we have a happy attitude, the children around us are likely to have the same attitude. If we are harsh and critical, so will the children be. Be sure your words and actions say the same thing. If you tell your child to get ready for supper, you get ready, too. If you continue to sit and read the paper while you are telling her to hurry, she becomes confused. If she sits (as you are doing), do not get angry with her for imitating you. She usually follows your actions more readily than your words. When your actions and words do not support each other, you are sending a double message.

Some children have difficulty participating in active play.

Keep calm. Be nurturing. Give valid reasons for what you request from the children. An adult who is authoritarian, permissive, or inconsistent does not help the children to form productive behavior patterns. If you are unappreciative of the way the children are acting at home or in the classroom, try to analyze what the problem may be. The best way to change someone else's behavior is to change your own. Maybe you are expecting too much or not enough; maybe you aren't sure what to expect! Maybe you act defensively, and so do those around you. Try to be more understanding and patient; look for the other person's point of view. Pleasant understanding reduces tension. Evaluate carefully and then make specific plans for improvement.

11. Be on Guard for Warning Signals.   When you anticipate that a dangerous situation is about to occur and immediate action is called for, step in unhesitatingly and stop the behavior. If verbal means deter the action, fine ("Put that shovel down," or "Don't hit him with the shovel!"). If that doesn't stop the action, physical means may be necessary ("I'll have to hold onto your arm so you won't hit him with the shovel."). Then discuss the situation with those involved. "When he stepped on your road, it made you want to hit him; but when you hit him, he doesn't know what you want. Tell him with words." Let the child know that you understand his behavior but that there are other, more positive ways of expressing his feelings. Children will not learn the value of property if they are allowed to destroy it. They will not build good interpersonal relationships if they are allowed to harm another individual. Being inquisitive is one thing, but deliberate destruction or injury must not be tolerated.

Being observant can reduce or prevent misbehavior. Children usually give some signals. You can see the tension building in the block area or other places. Children who cannot see at group time will begin subtle physical or verbal actions. Children who need to use the toilet begin to wiggle. The signs are there—learn how to read and respond to them before a problem arises.

A number of authors list causes of misbehavior. For example, Hymes (1981) says there are four causes of misbehavior: (1) the stage of growth the child is presently in, (2) unmet needs, (3) the present environment, and (4) not knowing it is inappropriate. Other authors identify the following reasons for misbehavior: to gain attention, to display power, to gain revenge, and to express inadequacy and passivity—that is, to give up. To be sure, children misbehave for different reasons.

Reflection

Tommy, a 3-year-old, was brought to a center by his mother. He was new and uncomfortable. As they approached the door, he began to draw back, cry, and hit his mother. She could not understand why he acted this way, but because she was in a hurry, she pushed him in the door. His feet stood firm, and he leaned back against her with all his strength. She tried reasoning, threatening, and then bribing. Still he refused. Even the teacher's invitation was not accepted. Finally the mother bribed him with gum (and who knows what else), and he reluctantly and stubbornly entered the room. He went from toy to toy, kicking or throwing each one. He pushed the other children and took their toys. The teacher's first inclination was to tell him that if he was unable to act friendly, he would not be able to come to the center. That was just what he wanted! Instead, she tried to involve him in interesting activities, one after another. He momentarily became involved—and then remembered to throw the toys and hit the children. It took the entire morning, under the teacher's watchful eye, to help him settle in. His best involvement was in large-muscle, vigorous activity where he could legitimately "let it out."

Osborn and Osborn (1977) discuss three modes of child discipline. The first describes children surrounded by a continuous wall of *NOs*; they cannot break down the wall. Adults make decisions for them, and the children feel that they are bad and unsuccessful. In the second mode, they are allowed to move freely in any direction with no walls or *NOs*. The children become frustrated, insecure, and sometimes hostile. The first mode gives no freedom; the second gives too much freedom. The third mode has low walls with doors that can be opened to go in or out. Children are aware of limitations but are free to make choices within the avenues open to them; this is freedom with control. Through this last mode, children gain the self-control so important in getting along in society.

Recently there has been much discussion and research about the stress in the lives of young children—both in and out of the home. Teachers who are aware of problems or difficult situations the children face can deal with them in more direct and kindly ways.

Angry feelings, associated with feelings of dependency, sadness, or depression, should be distinguished from aggression. Anger is a temporary emotional state caused by frustration, and aggression is often an attempt to hurt a person or to destroy property (the red flags). When either of these feelings arise, they call for action that teaches and protects, not punishes.

In an article on stress that proposes a more accepting attitude toward *all* crying in young children, Solter identifies the following ideas (1992):

1. Crying (less acceptable in boys than in girls) is an important and beneficial physiological process in helping children cope with stress.

2. There appears to be a relationship between crying and learning ability. Children become more enthusiastic and successful learners when the need for emotional release is recognized and accepted.

3. There are many sources of stress in young children's lives that create a need for crying: abuse (physical, sexual, verbal); neglect; illnesses, injuries, and hospitalization; confusion and anxiety; parental substance abuse; quarreling, separation, or divorce; violence, death, and war; a recent move; a new sibling; fatigue or hunger; and so on.

4. "Children need an environment that permits them to cry without being distracted, ridiculed, or punished. In this manner they can help free themselves from the effects of frustrating, frightening, or confusing experiences." (p. 67)

As teachers and parents, we need to practice our guidance techniques not at the expense of the children, but in an effort to enhance their self-image and internal control. When misbehavior persists and we have exhausted all avenues, Hendrick (1992) summarizes five steps for helping children learn self-control: (1) warn them, (2) remove them from the activity while keeping them with the teacher, (3) discuss feelings and rules, (4) wait for them to make the decision to return to the activity, and (5) help them return and be more successful. Help them practice these steps until they can control themselves—they'll be happier when they are socially successful, and so will you.

12. Avoid Power Struggles.   Adults may make a demand or a request of children. When the children do not comply, the adults become angry. They ask or tell the children again. If this still is unsuccessful, adults become defensive, especially if they are questioned or ignored. Do children have the right to question adults? When they are told to do something, they should obey! Or should they? Are the requests reasonable? Do the children understand the nature of the requests? What do adult actions mean to children? Are children being deliberately disobedient? If both adults and children analyze the situation, if adults give rationales for requests, if children verbalize noncompliance, the situation is resolvable. If, on the other hand, each decides stubbornly to win, a power struggle results, and neither wins.

Gordon (1970) suggests a no-lose method of resolving conflicts through the following steps of negotiation: (1) identifying and defining the conflict, (2) generating possible alternative solutions, (3) evaluating the alternatives, (4) deciding on the best acceptable solution, and (5) following up to evaluate its success. The adult becomes an active listener and the children practice problem solving. This method is superior to having an adult winner who uses authority, power, superior knowledge, and experience, or a child who wins because the adult does not want to lose her love, misunderstands about permissiveness, or is too tired or uninterested in negotiating. One winner means one loser, and this brings about resentment, lowered self-image, and breakdown in communication.

13. Offer Legitimate Choices and Accept Decisions.   Choice making should be a practice developed from early childhood. Choices should be within the child's ability, legitimate, and character-building.

Some interesting research from the Gesell Institute of Child Development suggests that ease or difficulty of choice making is related to age. The average child of 3, 5, 7, or 10 has an easier time deciding between two alternatives because at these ages he is under less inner stress and strain than at other ages. He is therefore able to accept choices without too much emotional conflict. Children do not make good decisions at any age when they are ill, fatigued, bombarded, or pressured. Are adults any different?

If a child has a legitimate choice, let her practice decision making. Bearing in mind that you must be prepared to accept her decision, be careful to form appropriate choices: "You can wear your blue shirt or your green one." "You can play inside or outside." "You can either hear one more story or play a short game before bedtime." If she has no choice, you make a simple outright statement about what is to occur: "Put on your blue shirt." "You will have to stay inside." "It is time for bed now." To offer a child a choice ("Do you want to drink your milk?") and then refuse to accept his answer ("Well, that's too bad; you have to, anyway") increases the negative aspect of his world. Also remember that when a question is worded in such a way that either yes or no can be the answer, the child is most likely to answer in the negative, even if she really wants it to be positive.

Sometimes adults think they are democratic in offering choices to children, when in reality they are weighting the questions in their favor. "Do you want to watch TV, or do you want to help me so we can go and get a treat?" "Do you want to pick up your toys or go to your room?" If children are going to be able to make good decisions, they need to develop a sound basis on which to make choices. They need legitimate choices for practice. They also need to be willing and able to handle the consequences of their choices.

14. Encourage Independence.   Preschool children like to do things themselves. Often, in the interest of time or energy, the parent or teacher assists the children or actually does the task rather than letting children try their skills or problem-solving abilities. Admittedly, some tasks are too difficult for preschoolers to attempt. In such instances, the adult can offer assistance and encouragement. If the task is one the children can handle, let them. It might take longer, but the results are worth the patience.

Encouragement is essential in building independence. "Try, and if you need help, I'll help you" is often enough incentive to get the children started. Then remain nearby. If assistance is needed, help—through either verbal or physical means. On completion, give some honest praise: "You did that so well," or "I'm glad you tried. I think you will be able to do it by yourself next time."

Children can be responsible for tools and behavior.

Seek long-range goals for children—development of good work habits, initiative, self-direction, and the ability to tackle a job.

15. Provide Acceptable Avenues for Release of Feelings. Frustration and anger come easily to preschoolers. They need to express these feelings in such a way that they feel better—not worse. If they are hitting, tell them to hit the clay, the stuffed animal, the punching bag, the pillow, or other suitable objects; but they cannot hit the baby, the television set, or people. Large-muscle activities—such as painting with big strokes, moving to music, riding a stick horse, throwing a ball, or finger painting—are often suitable outlets. At any rate, look for activities that help each child to release his feelings.

The younger the child, the more likely she is to use physical rather than verbal releases. With encouragement, experience, and practice, she will learn acceptable verbal ways of releasing and defining feelings.

16. Help Children Learn through Participation. Children can learn through observation or lecture, but the most efficient way is through participation. Instead of always telling them, provide opportunities for them to experience the results firsthand. Allow plenty of time and materials for exploration.

When asked to perform a task, children should be allowed to do it their way, unless it is dangerous or harmful. Offer suggestions only if the children need them. With freedom to try ideas, children may find better ways to do tasks.

17. When Needed, Use Appropriate Discipline. As you will recall from Chapter 1, various teaching methods and their effects on children have been investigated. Repeatedly, research shows that the single most important factor in children's learning is the effectiveness of the teacher. Similarly, in counseling, regardless of the method employed, the counselor makes the difference in the therapy. As an adult involved with young children, you are both a teacher and a counselor. You have the responsibility of seeing that your attitudes and personal attributes are such that they will be more instrumental in helping children reach their potential than if your life had not crossed theirs.

Greenberg (1990) makes this point:

Lest anyone misunderstand, we hasten to state that all leading early childhood educators believe in discipline, because it's in a context of discipline that each child develops *self*-discipline. On this, as on many things, teachers in academic and developmentally appropriate programs for young children agree. Children need routines, rules, boundaries, behavioral expectations and standards, procedures, policies, limits . . . children need control. They need reasonable, age-appropriate control, and of course understanding. They need fair, firm discipline at home (both homes if the parents are divorced). They need it in child care settings. They need it everywhere else they spend significant amounts of time . . . children left largely undisciplined, lacking guidance in slowly but steadily growing up, indulge their most primitive impulses greedily, devour the time and attention of beloved adults, whiningly demand the first turn, the longest turn, and the most turns, struggle for the best possessions, bite, sulk, howl, and throw half-hour raging tantrums. Many child development specialists are opposed to pressing and stressing children beyond their capacity to cope, but these specialists still strongly believe in child-guidance-style discipline. (p. 79)

RELATIONSHIPS AMONG SCHOOL, HOME, AND GUIDANCE

Teachers and parents share in the care and education of young children. The bond should be constructive and for the good of the child. Good communication between the school and home is important if problems are to be avoided and misunderstanding prevented. Messages sent and received from both school and home should be friendly and open. Teachers who use educational jargon need to make sure the parents interpret the messages accurately—sometimes communication requires use of different terms or explanations.

Some schools or teachers offer individual conferences to parents. When conferences are not a part of the program, a parent may request a meeting. In all circumstances, teachers of preschool children should be careful in the types of information they give lest it be inaccurate or that parents misinterpret or misuse it.

Home visits, another valuable tool for preschool teachers, may cause anxiety in parents if they think the teacher is coming to inspect the living quarters or if teachers do not understand differing family values. Seeing the child in his daily habitat often gives the teacher new insight into the child, the family, and ways to prepare the school environment for the most effective teaching.

Together, adults in the school and home settings can carefully observe the child, share their findings, and better meet the child's total needs. Teachers can help parents sharpen their observation skills by suggesting things to look for, and parents can identify and clarify the child's home behavior.

Children may become acquainted with children of other cultural, economic, and health backgrounds. Emphasis should be on a healthy blend of different factors in the home as well as at school.

School

In order to understand and promote good environments for children, adults need to have the same opportunities as children—to learn through experimenting, solving problems, trying and re-trying, hypothesizing and testing, asking questions, talking with others, planning and adjusting, using a variety of materials, and having time to explore and reflect. For the new teacher in the classroom, it is important to develop observation skills and an opportunity to discuss with others, experienced and inexperienced, what they have seen and interpreted.

Observation Skills

If teachers do not already have some good observation skills, they should carefully consider what skills they need to develop in order to better understand the needs of the children in their classrooms. They could consider the following type of observations:

Special Curriculum.   Are there some activities or items that could be implemented that would better help their students understand and utilize the activities provided (special needs of children, more understanding of principles and procedures, better use of toys and/or materials, and so on)?

Fine/Gross Motor Skills.   Do some children need more experiences in order to develop better fine, gross, or fine/gross motor skills?

Relationships.   Are children inclusive or exclusive of some, all, or none of the other children?

Indoor/Outdoor Preferences.   Do some children always want to play in a certain setting? Why do some children avoid indoor activities and other children avoid outdoor activities? How could both environments be more inviting and growth-promoting to these children?

Verbalization.   Which of the children verbally participate with other children and in most activities and settings? How could less verbal children be encouraged to verbalize more freely?

Socialization.   Which children socialize most of the time? What causes children to be more or less social?

Interpretation.   How do teachers evaluate the behavior, development, and progress of their students?

> *Objective evaluations:* These include making written notes of exactly what is occurring, without bias, prejudice, or interpretation.

> Example:
> Tim and Sarah are digging in the sand. Tim quickly fills his bucket by using a large shovel with quick movements, compacting the sand after each shovelful. Then he turns the bucket upside down and taps the bottom of it with his shovel. Carefully, he lifts the bucket up and observes a mound in the shape of his bucket. He says to Sarah, "Look, I've got an empty bucket and a full pile." Sarah looks at him, smiles, and continues putting sand in her bucket.

> *Subjective evaluations:* These include not only recording what is observed, but interpretive feelings, ideas, or impressions of the person making the observation.

> Example:
> Tim and Sarah are digging in the sand. Tim likes playing in the sand, but Sarah is afraid of getting dirty. Tim is pretending he is a giant steam shovel as he piles sand in the bucket. When he is satisfied with the amount of sand in the bucket, he turns it upside down. In the meantime, Sarah acts uninterested, thinks about a story they heard yesterday, and wishes she were painting a picture or wearing a hat to keep the sun out of her eyes.

Think carefully about the differences in the examples. Which evaluation would be more meaningful in a child's file? What are the dangers of subjective evaluations? What conclusions could parents make from each of the examples?

Supervisors or directors can assist novice teachers to develop and sharpen their observation skills by giving simple observation assignments and providing verbal or written feedback. Another option is to have trainees observe as a trainer points out activities or relationships that are occurring within the classroom. These two steps may be inverted (observation and discussion with a more experienced person and then individual observation). Observers must be taught how to record what transpires within the classroom without imposing their own feelings, motives, or prejudices.

Through training and experience, novice teachers can understand the needs and development of the young child. In many settings, academic skills are reinforced and children participate as a group, in circles, and within a time limitation. In DAP programs, play skills are emphasized (see Chapter 3, The Value of Play). As Piaget stated, "To understand is to invent," and children learn most important things by interaction with the physical world with other children and by constructing their own knowledge. Adults at school and home should have these same opportunities to construct their knowledge. In this way adults have a better opportunity to connect theory and practice for themselves and the young children they teach.

And what about the teachers who have not developed a feeling of self-esteem—which some children also lack? By helping these adults experience their world firsthand (and through observing the actions of children), they can enhance their feelings about themselves, their willingness to try new things, and their interaction with others.

Parents should be encouraged to visit the classroom to do some inconspicuous observations of *all* children so as to get a clear picture of what children are like and what they do at certain ages. It often makes parents feel more comfortable and confident in how their children behave. If possible, a supervisor or teacher could observe with the parents and point out some important happenings (curriculum areas, child interaction, language development, child reaction to materials/activities, and so on).

Children can resolve conflicts with peers, but do so in a different manner than adults.

Parents can also be invited to participate in observing their child (and other children) at home or in various settings, looking at the same behaviors just outlined, and to share their observations with teachers during conferences or casual conversations. Some parents will be objective, some will be defensive, and some will use the information to learn more about their child and children in general.

Reflection

A prospective parent is visiting your classroom. Together you glance around the classroom and notice that some of the children are in the domestic area, some are building with table blocks and others with large unit blocks, some are painting at the easel, some are quietly looking at books and using visual aids on the flannel board, and still others are outside digging and planting a garden, riding trikes, and climbing.

The parent remarks: "I think it is a rather expensive program for children to just play all the time. And how do you keep track of all the children at once?"

What a golden moment and what a captive audience for the teacher to show the parent the philosophy of the classroom as the following items are pointed out:

1. Children manage most of their own activities because of the types of things provided.
2. Children are free to remain or leave according to their interests.
3. Children assist each other.
4. Teachers are aware of all the children, position themselves strategically, and assist if needed.
5. Children gain self-esteem and self-discipline because of the attitude of teachers and security in the environment.
6. Planned and spontaneous learning occurs in all areas of curriculum and through personal interaction.

There is more about observation in Chapter 3, The Value of Play (see the section titled "Adults' Perception of Play").

School/Home Contacts

From the beginning inquiry about the classroom, teachers should make parents feel important, wanted, accepted, and like team members. When children are happy, parents are happy; when parents are happy, teachers are happy; when teachers are happy, children are happy. It's an endless circle.

There are a number of things the school can do to inform and encourage parents. The initial contact will undoubtedly be for information. Further contacts deal with more specifics: daily routines and commitments, responsibilities and privileges of home and school, and so on.

Primary Contacts (Initial, Preparatory, Information-Gathering, and Casual)

1. Parents are encouraged to make on-site visits.
2. The philosophy of the program is articulated.
3. Individual orientation is conducted.

Secondary Contacts (Sequential, Information-blending)

1. Parents and children are encouraged to make additional on-site visits.
2. Individual and/or group orientations broaden the scope of the home/school relationship, and may be more focused, blend data, and encourage team membership.

Ongoing Contacts

See Table 2.2 for a list of ways to keep contacts ongoing.

Learning Cards

As a classroom teacher, I frequently had comments and requests from parents about what we did at school. The children wanted to sing songs, do art projects, read books, or have other activities as an extension of the classroom. Learning cards resulted—actually, they began as 3″ × 5″ cards, and that resulted in their name. They include the date and theme, a quick review of the day's activities, and a suggested follow-up for parents. See Figure 2.2 for an example.

Today, as I think about the behavioristic and rigid way the learning was perceived by children and parents, I shake my head! I found that the children really loved the cards—wouldn't go home without one—and the parents used them as an examination tool. Parents were often heard to say: "Okay. Name the three primary colors! Tell me what colors you are wearing! How do you make (orange)?" and other comments to see if their child had really learned! That was not the intent of the cards at all! It was merely to inform the parents so they could build on the learning whenever it was convenient or spontaneous, but they were using the cards as a requirement for leaving the daily classroom!

Table 2.2
Ongoing Contacts

ABOUT THE SCHOOL	ABOUT THE CHILD(REN)	WITH THE HOME
Philosophy and procedures	Enrollment procedures/forms	Explain and show "Learning Cards"
Parent handbook	Home visits	Explain and show "Learning Packets"
Daily contact with parents	Daily contact with parents	Ways home can supplement school
Newsletters	Telephone messages	Feedback on ideas or material used
Bulletin boards	Conferences	Ideas initiated at home
Parent education	Individual needs	Home visits
Parent meetings	Written communications	Telephone messages
Announcements about school and community events	School participation (artifacts, job)	Written messages
Suggestion box	Materials available for check-out	School visits
Teaching calendar of events and home follow-up	Small study or discussion groups	Receiving child's materials, when appropriate

Figure 2.2
Learning Card

> Date: 10/3/97   Theme: Color
>
> Today we talked about the primary colors—red, yellow, and blue. We sang a song about the colors in the children's clothing and noticed different colors in our classroom and playground. At creative art time we mixed the primary colors and then let the children use the colors separately and combined. At snack we talked about the color of the food. We heard a story and imitated a record that had a game about colors.
>
> As a result of today's theme, your child should be able to name the primary colors; to pick out red, yellow, and blue in his or her environment; to tell or demonstrate how to make secondary colors, and to play a color game.

The cards were tedious to prepare each day, so a weekly sheet was prepared for the parents—but in a much more informative and flexible manner. Rewritten in the vein of developmentally appropriate philosophy, the learning card now includes the date and theme (for future reference for parents and teachers), a brief overview of the related activities, and then casual suggestions that could easily be carried out at any time. Compare the learning card in Figure 2.2 to the one in Figure 2.3 and note the changes in the last paragraph.

Learning Packets

A learning packet may consist of a single item in a manila envelope (such as an article on a prescribed topic) or it may consist of many items (articles, community resources, art activities to do at home, children's story books, songs sung at school, or a variety of means to inform parents on current issues, things happening in the community, and so on).

When the center has sufficient learning packets, it can distribute a list of topics for individual parental selection, or it might suggest reading on a specific topic. Often parents do not know where to get accurate and current information, so they turn to individuals who may not be knowledgeable. A center can be a valuable source for parents.

Materials that go into the home should stress the individuality of children and the approximate age at which children can handle the suggestions so that parents

Figure 2.3
Example of a Day on Color

> Date: 10/6/97   Theme: Color
>
> Today we talked about the primary colors—red, yellow, and blue. We sang a song about the colors in the children's clothing and noticed different colors in our classroom and playground. At creative art time we mixed the primary colors and then let the children use the colors separately and combined. At snack we talked about the color of the food; we heard a story and used a record game about colors.
>
> When appropriate, talk with your child about the colors he is wearing or those around him. Be patient in helping him learn the names of colors. Play color games with your child now (for example, What things can you see that are blue?) and at a later date (for example, What things can you think of that are blue?). Make color learning fun and not a dreaded activity.

will refrain from forcing their children into inappropriate activities. Elkind (1987) states: "The wrong things at the wrong time" can only create stress, frustration, and a sense of failure in young children (p. 25). Parents need to know what to expect of children of different ages and individual characteristics. Material of this nature could be invaluable to parents.

To initially prepare a variety of learning packets may require more time, effort, and cost than a center can afford; however, packets can be prepared occasionally until there is a comprehensive source of different topics and developmental domains that have been tried and proved helpful to parents. Until there is material available for each family to have their own copy of materials, a check-in and check-out service is helpful.

Through information that goes into the home (for example, learning cards or packets), parents can become involved in the education of their children. The following information about the value of learning packets is adapted from Spewock (1991). Learning packets:

Establish lines of communication between school and home.

Provide parents with access to information appropriate for their child's stage of development.

Are convenient and helpful resources for working parents who want to spend quality time with their children.

Are concise and easy to read.

Provide current information written by reliable writers and researchers.

Make parents aware of inexpensive materials (and activities) readily available within the home that are pleasurable for themselves and their children (for example, how to read to young children, reading times, topics children enjoy, values of activities, art and music experiences, simple science, physical activities, and so on).

Newsletters

Written correspondence from school is often refreshing and informative. It makes parents feel a part of their child's schooling and makes contact with parents who are hard to reach. A good newsletter can make parents as eager to receive it as children are to receive learning cards.

Suggestions for Newsletters about the School.   Share events of interest to young children and/or families. Use the newsletter to provide information and follow-up for topics being taught at school and for sharing the school calendar. The newsletter can encourage children to develop healthy attitudes toward learning (for example, math, numbers, science). It can recognize or highlight a teacher or staff member.

Suggestions for Newsletters about Children.   The newsletter can provide current child-rearing topics and information and ideas to promote growth in each domain (physical, intellectual, social/emotional). It can suggest ways and props to encourage play, such as thinking games (specifically rules, counting, turn-taking), and finger dexterity skills (toys, tools, puzzles, fasteners).

Suggestions for Newsletters about the Home.   The newsletter can help children develop a good self-image and self-discipline. It can promote the importance of good health, such as nutrition, cleanliness, and being immunized. It can instruct how to safety-proof the home, including what the child should do, whom to call, where to go, and so on if there is trouble. Other issues that can be discussed through a newsletter include ways to promote understanding and appreciation of ethnic groups, ways to promote good communication skills between parent and child (listening and speaking), how to promote cooperation and healthy attitudes, and how to select toys and books for children. The newsletter can share interesting and inexpensive ways to have fun at home and suggest ways children can help with food preparation, household chores, and so on. It can request information about parental needs and interests.

Suggestions for Newsletters about the Community.   Events of interest to young children and/or families can be shared, along with good places to visit. The newsletter can suggest resources for resolving child/family problems, meeting and/or learning about culturally diverse people, and learning about different occupations within the community. Rules of safety when riding or walking through the community can be discussed. Community pride can be encouraged through suggesting how to prevent various types of pollution and encouraging family support of service projects. Holiday and seasonal celebrations can be announced.

A newsletter can provide many other services—depending on the school, on the community, on the home, on current happenings, and on the individual.

APPLICATION OF PRINCIPLES

1. Why is a code of ethics important in early-childhood education? Everybody loves children! How could you support the code?

2. Identify ways that adults (teachers and parents) can help reduce conflicts between children.

3. Suggest methods of promoting good child behavior *instead* of saying, "I like the way . . ."

4. Name and contrast the three major types of guidance. Give an example of proactive and reactive guidance. How can you prepare yourself to use proactive guidance?

5. Select one of the guidance techniques you would like to work on. Write goals and how you can achieve them. Put the technique into practice. After a period of time, evaluate your progress. Select another technique (preferably one you feel weak in) and repeat the process until you feel more secure in using it with young children.

6. Make it a practice to listen carefully when you are around young children. Are their words conveying their true message? Are yours?

7. Make a chart listing each child in your group. Observe the behavior of each child and record it on the chart. Note which children need help in social situations. List how you can help each child to control her own behavior.

8. Ask for a set of guidelines or rules for your center or classroom. Discuss them with other staff members. Make sure you know and understand what is expected of staff, children, and parents. If you have suggestions or questions, discuss them with your supervisor, teacher, or employer.

9. Carry a piece of paper and a pencil. Note the situation and tally the number of times you or another staff member uses a negative approach (*no, don't, can't, stop*) inappropriately. Make an effort to use positive approaches in dealing with children and adults.

10. Practice offering choices. Is there really a choice? How do you follow through when you have offered an inappropriate choice?

11. If there is a child or parent who needs professional help, to where would you refer him in your community? Make a list of agencies in your community that counsel on mental, social, emotional, and physical problems.

12. If you feel someone is inappropriately controlling you, how can you change or eliminate her behavior?

13. Practice your observation skills. Record children in different types of activities. Ask a colleague or teacher to evaluate how often you record objective information and subjective information.

14. Select a method of contact with the home (learning packet, newsletter, meeting, phone call, "Notes to Home," "Notes from Home," or another method) and propose a way to use it.

REFERENCES

Beane, J. A. (1991, April). Enhancing children's self-esteem: Illusion and possibility. *Early Education and Development,* 2(2), 153–160.

Carlsson-Paige, N., & D. E. Levin (1992, November). Making peace in violent times: A constructivist approach to conflict resolution. *Young Children,* 48(1), 4–13.

Carlsson-Paige, N., & D. E. Levin (1995, July). Can teachers resolve the war-play dilemma? *Young Children,* 50(5), 62–63.

Elkind, E. (1987). *Miseducation: Preschoolers at risk.* New York: Knopf.

Gordon, I. (1970). *Parent effectiveness training.* New York: Wyden.

Greenberg, P. (1990). Why not academic preschool? Part 1. *Young Children,* 45(2), 70–80.

Greenberg, P. (1992, March). Why not academic preschool? Autocracy or democracy in the classroom? Part 2. *Young Children,* 47(3), 54–64.

Greenberg, P. (1992, July). How to institute some simple democratic practices pertaining to respect, rights, roots, and responsibilities in any classroom (without losing your leadership position). *Young Children,* 47(5), 10–17.

Griffin, E. F. (1982). *Island of childhood: Education in the special world of nursery school.* New York: Teachers College Press.

Hendrick, J. (1992). *The whole child,* 5th edition. New York: Merrill/Macmillan.

Hildebrand, V. (1994). *Guiding young children,* 5th edition. New York: Macmillan.

Honig, A. S., & D. S. Wittmer (1996, Jan). Helping children become more prosocial: Ideas for classrooms, families, schools, and communities. *Young Children,* 51(2), 62–70.

Hymes, J. L. (1981). *Teaching the child under six.* Upper Saddle River, NJ: Prentice Hall/Merrill.

Katz, L. G. & Ward, E. H. (1996). Ethical behavior in early childhood education (Expanded edition). Washington, DC: NAEYC.

Marshall, H. H. (1995, January). Beyond "I like the way . . .". *Young Children,* 50(2), 26–28.

McCloskey, C. M. (1996, March). Taking positive steps toward classroom management in preschool: Loosening up without letting it all fall apart. *Young Children,* 51(3), 14–16.

NAEYC code of ethical conduct: Guidelines for responsible behavior in early childhood education (1996, March). *Young Children,* 51(3), 57–60.

Osborn, D. K. (1980). *Early childhood education in historical perspective.* Athens, GA: Education Associates.

Osborn, D. K., & J. D. Osborn (1977). *Discipline and classroom management.* Athens, GA: University of Georgia, Early Childhood Learning Center.

Solter, A. (1992, May). Understanding tears and tantrums. *Young Children,* 47(4), 64–68.

Spewock, T. S. (1991, November). Teaching parents of young children through learning packets. *Young Children,* 47(1), 28–30.

Spodek, B. (1991, April). Reconceptualizing early childhood education: A commentary. *Early Education and Development,* 2(2), 161–167.

White, B. L. (1975). *The first three years of life.* Upper Saddle River, NJ: Prentice Hall.

The Value of Play

CHAPTER 3

MAIN PRINCIPLES

While play is important for the entire life span, and differs according to interests and development, this chapter focuses on the child from 2 to 5 years of age.

1. Play is a child's world, his prime educator.
2. Play enhances the physical, social, emotional, and intellectual development of the young child.
3. A child needs opportunities for play that are active and quiet, spontaneous and planned, indoors and outdoors, done alone and with peers, of her choosing and duration, and enriching rather than competitive.
4. Young children go through progressive stages of play.
5. Adults can enrich or hinder the play of children.
6. Valuable learning comes from dramatic play and from appropriate selection of play materials by adults.
7. Dramatic play and block play are valuable in learning about oneself and one's environment.
8. Although there are gender-play preferences in young children, activities, materials, occupations, and so on are gender-, culture-, and race-free.
9. Children with special needs (children with disabilities, gifted children, late developers, language-impaired or non-English-speaking children, and so on) often engage in the same activities as other children; however, modification is made to accommodate the individual needs of each child. Diversity among the children should be acknowledged, accepted, and respected. Activities that promote multicultural awareness should be positive and frequent.
10. The assumption that learning occurs indoors and physical release occurs outdoors is false. Learning and release should be provided in both settings.
11. Health and safety should be of prime importance when planning environments for young children.
12. Planning of and participation in outdoor play is important in the development of the young child. Toys and experiences should be well planned and carefully supervised.
13. Disruptive play may be caused by numerous influences.
14. Violent play can be avoided or controlled through the actions and planning of parents and teachers.
15. Young children learn different behaviors through aggressive and nonaggressive play.

Notable Quotes

"Many animals play, but primates play more, and humans play the most" (Eibl-Eibesfeldt, 1970; Bruner, 1976).

"The child's play interests reveal many of the interests of humankind" (Piaget, 1963; Vygotsky, 1976).

"We are curious about the social and physical world and reach out to explore it . . . to see what will happen and how things and people function. . . . [P]lay reveals children's interests and nourishes the growing edges of their competence . . . [they] try to play with everything in their environments and with each of their own motor and mental capacities" (Bronson, 1995).

"Human play is characteristically imaginative and symbolic" (Piaget, 1962; Werner & Kaplan, 1963).

Refer to Chapter 1 for some basic information regarding theories of early-childhood education, and to Appendix A for information on theorists who support play in the lives of young children.

Why do some people question the value of play for young children? Are they so product- and time-conscious that they want the children to get past playing and get on to "learning"? Do they realize the importance of firsthand experiences? A child may seem to be wasting time at play, but to the child, play is his work, his way of learning about his environment. Consider how development is furthered through play experiences (see Table 3.1).

DEVELOPMENT DURING YEARS 2 THROUGH 5

Freud and Erikson, psychoanalysts, maintain that play contributes to the development of a healthy personality. Piaget determined that play affects cognitive development as children note cause-and-effect relationships in the process of constructing their own knowledge about their environment. But play is a topic of many disciplines—not just child development and psychology (for example, anthropology, sociology, physical education, education). Frost (1992) concludes the following:

> After having reviewed major theories of play spanning the last 3,000 years, from Plato to Piaget, it is still not possible to arrive at a simple, clear, scientific definition of play. Erikson advises that play has a very personal meaning for each individual. Perhaps the best thing that we as adults can do to discover this meaning is to go out and play; to reflect upon our own childhood play; to once again look at play through the eyes of the child. (p. 21)

Motor Development

Physical changes in the young child are more obvious than changes in other areas of development. Through physical increase, the child gains independence, develops body skills and coordination, masters his environment, and learns to cooperate. Her body is used as a vehicle of expression. Through body movements, she learns spatial relationships and bilateral movements. She learns about motion, speed, and force. Many of these activities are symbolic and are satisfying at the time and also in later learning. Numerous studies have shown the important relationship between a child's physical skills and her self-concept. When she feels competent, she is willing to attempt new and different experiences.

Table 3.1
Values of Play for Young Children

VALUES OF PLAY FOR YOUNG CHILDREN	
Domain	*Enhancement*
Motor	Health, perceptual-motor abilities, physical fitness; rejuvenation; new or advanced skills; coordination; fine and gross muscle development.
Social-emotional	Freedom to explore rich environments; builds knowledge of self and others; self-esteem and personal power; builds the foundation for success and personal competence; teaches us to value differences; cooperation through curriculum areas; healthy competition; sharing; lengthening interest span.
Cognitive-language	Increased verbal fluency; thinking; problem solving; planning; cooperation; imagination; developing powers of concentration, curiosity, and self-determination.
Combination of domains/body parts	Using arms, legs, and eyes together; using hands, fingers, and eyes together; remembering what is seen; remembering what is heard; communicating with others through expressive language; listening to others; showing interest in words and books; classifying; comparing, and sequencing; understanding numbers; comprehending stories; controlling and expressing emotions.
	Skills required in sociodramatic play are related to the cognitive skills required for academic success and the social skills required for successful school adjustment (Smilansky and Shefatya, 1990).
Overall	Play is more than running off excess energy; relaxing and relieving tension; reliving earlier periods and preparing for later ones; it is somewhat archaic with insufficient explanations (Frost, 1992).
Other factors	A well-organized classroom environment; ability and opportunity to play; brainstorming; spontaneity; ability to solve problems; choice; responsibility and follow-through; a feeling of belonging; culture; novelty; complexity and realism; adult and peer models; role play ideas from life, media, books, and so on.

For the most part, and mainly because of inadequate space indoors, most large-muscle activities are performed outside. However, some provision should be made for indoor large-muscle play, giving consideration to space needs, type of equipment, appropriate activities, and noise level. Children should play outdoors each day, even during inclement weather, but sustained large-muscle development is difficult when it is wet or cold. On such days children profit from indoor large-muscle activities. A portable jungle gym, ladders, and boxes can be brought in, or sheets thrown over furniture can suffice for props. Set up the limits—the stick horses can be ridden in one room, but not throughout the building—and watch the enjoyment!

Social Development

Social-skill learning, a complex task, can be fostered through play. Some skills are self-related and some are interpersonally related. Every child wants to participate with other children, and the first few years are the most important for practicing social living.

Studies over several decades show the relationship between the absence of pleasure and the failure to develop normally. Some years ago, Spitz observed that infants in a foundling home developed severe psychological disturbances, even though physical care was adequate.

Some play is not without conflict. In her concluding paragraph of a study on kindergarten children, Ditchburn (1988) states:

> Conflict management is a requisite social skill at every stage of life and in all social situations. Further, conflict is endemic in our stressful, modern society. That young children demonstrate sophistication in conflict management gives some pause for reflection. Play is readily available, cost efficient, and a safe occasion for the exercise of socially acceptable conflict management. . . . Learning through play is not merely a trite phrase supporting academically impoverished practice—rather play is a lesson in life. One cautionary note, however, is in order. We need to examine which strategies achieve desired ends and which children typically achieve their conversational goals in situations of conflict. There are important moral and gender-related questions which have not been addressed in the literature on children's conflict. (p. 69)

Play helps young children learn and practice roles of leading and following, essential aspects of effective social participation. Trawick-Smith (1988) found the following:

> Never to lead is never to be heard, never to have ideas carefully considered by others, and never to have an impact on the behaviors or thinking of peers. Never to follow, on the other hand, is never to benefit from the ideas of others or be swayed to another's viewpoint. Total absence of the skill or the confidence to lead or follow, when these are genuinely desired or needed, can be a barrier to human interaction that teachers can help young children overcome. Helping young children develop leadership abilities, whether a child chooses to exercise these frequently or only occasionally, is a worthwhile objective of early childhood programs. (p. 58)

Play incorporates all areas of development.

In their study of play behaviors, Quay, Weaver, and Neel (1986) find that children engage in more social than nonsocial and more positive than negative behavior (also stated by Marcus [1987] and Read, Gardner, & Mahler [1987]). More negative social behavior occurred in woodworking and doll/dollhouse environments. By gender, boys played more in woodworking, manipulative, and language centers; girls played more in paints, housekeeping, games, art, and book centers.

Maturation is a factor to consider in assessing a child's readiness for specific types of play activities. It sets limitations on his skills, experience, and techniques.

Emotional Development

Some adults have little patience with and understanding of a child's emotional development. That is one reason why play opportunities are so important for young children. Through play, children learn trust and confidence in themselves, in others, and in their environment. They recognize their self-worth and develop inner satisfaction. Instead of feeling helpless in many situations and showing fear or rage, they reduce these feelings or gain mastery over them and formulate acceptable age-related emotional releases. In play they can exercise rule making and direction following; both are important for interaction with others and for later learning.

Play is a medium through which children can express their positive or negative feelings. For a time they do not have to conform to adult ways and can have relief from high expectations in childlike ways. Whenever a child has a successful experience, her feelings of self-worth and ability increase. Success also releases her from a sense of powerlessness. She actually can control and manipulate her environment.

During the ages from 2 to 4, the child is less inhibited than she will ever be. His self-image during this period depends on his play. He is very egocentric and he desires power. According to Caplan and Caplan (1973), "Healthy personality development is tied to each child's own biological time clock, to her endowment, and his very early life experiences."

Within a group of peers, the child can learn about sharing, taking turns, and property rights. She learns that at school there are toys, activities, and people to be shared. At times she uses these things; at times someone else uses them—but sharing is *not* giving up one's rights. A child who has had opportunities to possess (at home or elsewhere) finds that rather than relinquishing all rights, she will again be able to use the item(s). And while she is sharing, she should be redirected to another activity or toy, rather than just wait! Then, at the appropriate time, the child is offered another opportunity to use the shared item.

At times some children become so upset that they cannot control themselves. On these occasions, so that the child does not lose face or upset the other children, it may be wise to remove the child. Help her to gain control and return to the setting without his feeling the isolation as a form of punishment or rejection.

According to Read, Gardner, and Mahler (1987),

> There are times in the lives of all children when they are not free to play because they are overwhelmed by the new, the strange, or the feared. A child may become overwhelmed at times of illness, accidents, death, or family problems. Demands to perform beyond his ability or teasing can overwhelm him. It is important that all children who cannot play or whose play is disorganized and aggressive find a trustworthy, reliable adult in their center. They need a teacher who will not push them to be busy, but rather one who will take time to build a trusting relationship and will help them find ways to cope with their particular stresses. (pp. 217–18)

According to Soderman (1984),

> Children at 4 and 5 . . . have a genuine need to play, and the quality and quantity of the time they spend playing are later seen (or observed to be lacking) in their creative thought, ability to make decisions, and potential for coping with stressful situations. . . . The American Academy of Pediatricians has expressed concern about the dramatic increase of "stress-related" symptoms being seen in young children.

Cognitive and Language Development

Many people think intellectual development must be taught through structured academic experience. They think that children must be taught early to perform the three Rs. Some teachers are so anxious to look good and to prepare children for the next grade that they are introducing topics earlier and earlier. Hymes calls this the "dribble down disease" (1981, p. 25). Why are adults not just as concerned about training children in the basics of life? Have they ever stopped to think that children who are helped to live fully as 3-, 4-, 5-, 6-, or whatever-year-olds will be happier and more productive throughout their entire schooling and lives? Young children may read, write, or do arithmetic, but do they know how to play?

The preschool period is not a valueless waiting time. Much is to be gained from play experiences: sustained attention and deep concentration, so necessary for reading; imagination; curiosity to explore, examine, and discover; initiative to try one's own ideas; opportunity to use memory in relating, recalling, and thinking; a chance to play and organize; leadership and group participation; a larger repertoire of responses; language development; creativity; acquisition of knowledge; self-enhancement; flexibility; understanding of one's personal problems; and the ability to exercise divergent thinking.

How can children or adults be expected to make good decisions based on logic, cause and effect, value, or consequences if opportunities are not provided throughout their lives to exercise judgment, originality, and independence? Development and use of the ability to think divergently are essential.

Levy (1984) conducted an extensive review of research on the role of play in language and cognitive development and drew several major conclusions:

1. Play stimulates innovation in language.
2. Play introduces and clarifies new words and concepts.
3. Play motivates language use and practice.
4. Play develops metalinguistic awareness.
5. Play encourages verbal thinking.

Lawrence K. Frank (1968), author and lecturer on human growth and development, has this to say about play and learning:

> With his sensory capacities, the child learns not only to look but to see, not only to hear but to listen, not only to touch but to feel and grasp what he handles. He tastes whatever he can get into his mouth. He begins to smell what he encounters. He can and will, if not handicapped, impaired or blocked, master these many experiences through continual play . . . the most intensive and fruitful learning activity in his whole life cycle. (p. 433)

The teacher or parent should accept the challenge of designing and providing appropriate play activities that enhance the child's intellectual development. Most kinds of opportunities, such as dramatic, sensory, or scientific exploration, are meaningful, but especially so are creative or artistic endeavors. Deciding *what* to do and *how* to do it sharpens the child's intellect. These activities also provide for exercise of the brain, eye, hand, and other parts of the body.

Intellectual development (academic learning) can be developed through play experiences. For example, Henniger (1987) reports that attitudes about curiosity, divergent thinking, motivation, and so on—so essential to learning math and science—are formed during play activities.

Play themes are acquired in many ways—from books and stories children hear, daily episodes they see, their own imaginations, vicarious experiences, media, curiosity, spontaneous or planned activities, ignorance, or a desire to test and learn about the world. All these ways, and many more, cause the child to develop and stretch his mental capacities.

See Table 3.2 for a list of instructional items to provide for the various ages and areas of development.

Table 3.2
Areas of Development

AGE	MOTOR	SOCIAL AND EMOTIONAL	COGNITIVE AND LANGUAGE
2–3	blocks: unit, hollow, plastic, and cardboard wooden figures rocking boat simple climbing equipment large wooden nesting boxes big cars and trucks wheel toys easels, paints, and brushes manipulative toys	doll house dolls stuffed toys simple doll clothes and blankets telephones child-sized furniture domestic play items dress-up clothes riding toys music	books with action, rhyming records record player puzzles crayons markers paste brushes clay soft balls
4	**add:** walking boards planks, boxes wheelbarrows tricycles swings slide woodworking bench and tools sand toys triangle set coaster wagon jungle gyms stick horses balls hoops	**add:** chest of drawers sand and water table clothesline and pins puppets puppet theater career clothing costumes wheel toys multicultural books and toys	**add:** chalk, peg, and bulletin board blunt scissors large colored beads and patterns for stringing manipulative toys card games aquarium pets cooking opportunities
5	**add:** giant dominoes construction sets balls roller skates scooter construction sets ladders, ropes jump ropes obstacle courses	**add:** small tent traffic signs	**add:** flannel board and counting set counting games magnets magnifying glasses games with rules action books

General Discussion

How one reflects on one's own childhood is a personal matter. Some adults recall playing neighborhood games such as tag, hide and seek, kick-the-can, marbles, hopscotch, follow-the-leader, jump rope, cops and robbers—depending on where and when they grew up. Some adults recall games and activities where play space was limited in size, opportunity, and safety. Others made up their own activities—role playing occupations, pretending to be famous people in sports, movies, science, or other timely topics—with and without props.

At times games were short-lived; at others the play continued for hours, days, or even months. Our games taught us language skills, how to take turns, learning and following rules, different roles, positive human relations, imagination, skills and competence, and change. Perhaps if adults returned to thoughts of their growing-up years, they would have a better appreciation for the play needs of children.

Educators in many settings (classroom, spontaneous conversations, departments of education, coffee shops, and so on) are discussing and accepting the importance of developmentally appropriate practice (Bredekamp, 1987; Bredekamp & Copple, 1997) but when it comes to actually putting it into practice, there are as many differences in definition and practice as there are individuals discussing it. Kagan (1990) notes that "[o]ne of the central issues that emerge as teachers attempt to define the best practice for young children is the role of play in the curriculum" (p. 174). The most common answer is that play is the child's work or her way of learning. Play is complex and multifaceted. "One of the major issues teachers and researchers struggle with is the precise nature of the relationship of play to the concepts and skills valued by our educational system," write Nourot and Van Hoorn (1991, p. 40).

"To understand is to invent" is a reminder from Piaget. Young children learn most important things through personal involvement—through play—not by being told but by constructing knowledge for themselves in interaction with the physical world and with other children. Teachers can carefully observe the play of children and try to interpret it as the children do—not through the mind and experience of the teacher. He can relate the play to theories and application through study and discussions with others in an attempt to better understand it. See Figure 3.1 for a list of different types of play.

Torbert (1980) has proposed replacing musical chairs and other exclusive games with those that foster inclusion rather than elimination, that encourage collaboration rather than competition, and that allow play time for all rather than the varsity-bound few. She advocates activities that teach skills such as trust, initiative, and autonomy. All of this, she says, builds self-esteem and fosters peace (in the world and the neighborhood) through social interaction as it generates alternatives, working together, and imbuing respect for both body and soul.

Figure 3.1
Suggested Types of Play in Young Children

Simple	One child plays alone (solitary)—looking at books, manipulating toys, entertaining self.
Complex	Usually two to four children (parallel or cooperatively)—with art materials, at water/sand table, in block area.
Super	Usually up to eight children (cooperatively)—in dramatic play, construction, table, or floor games.

Children like to repeat familiar themes.

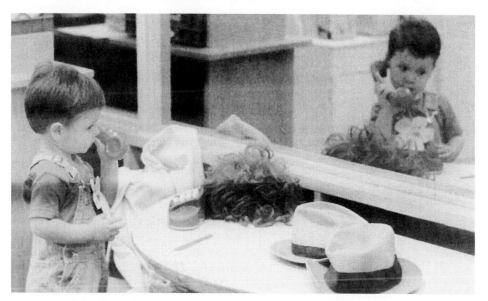

In an article titled "The Physical Education Hall of Shame," Williams (1992) likewise discourages the use of elimination and competitive games with young children, such as dodge ball; "Duck, Duck, Goose"; kickball; relay races; and of course musical chairs. Like Torbert, he has been criticized for his ideas, and adds, "We're seeking to maximize participation in physical activity"; he advocates games that give every child lots of turns, that permit success at various skill levels, and that allow social acceptance (not ridicule) of differences in ability. Elimination games may cause children to have feelings of sadness, worthlessness, laziness, being squashed, and being a dumbbell.

In contrast, Brian Sutton-Smith, a professor emeritus of educational psychology and folklore at the University of Pennsylvania and respected for his research on play, finds Torbert's games unrealistic. According to Sutton-Smith, play reflects society's value system. "If you live in a competitive society, then you have competitive play." And "the games as they now exist . . . [impart] discipline," he says. "If you don't conform to the rules of the game, you don't get to play." Neither Torbert nor Sutton-Smith has won the other over.

I feel that competitive and large-group games do not meet the needs of the young child. Rules are hard to interpret and follow, skills are limited, waiting for a turn is difficult, and playing for an extended time (as many games require) is exhausting. It appears that small-group games can be beneficial if they do not occur too frequently, everybody gets lots of chances, the emphasis is placed on the fun and excitement, and children feel they have been successful. This is also my interpretation of what would be developmentally appropriate for young children.

Our job is to help teachers and parents understand the complexities of play and what the child is learning. We can also offer suggestions on ways that parents can extend their child's play experiences at home. Instead of asking a young child, "What did you do at school (or another playing situation) today?"—to which the child most often answers, "I played"—ask more open-ended questions while moving the conversation in a specific direction, such as what kinds of toys or roles were played. Teachers and parents are facilitators of play experiences as they offer new materials, comment on what they observe, and offer suggestions of new things to try.

STAGES OF PLAY IN YOUNG CHILDREN

Parten's traditional stages of play (1932–33; Table 3.3) have been useful in identifying when young children develop certain skills in playing with each other during the early years.

Parten's descriptions of play are now referred to as the *traditional view* and were formulated when most research involved young children whose interactions with peers were limited to occasional play groups of short duration. Current research is not entirely consistent with the traditional view mainly because today children spend more time in the company of peers in child-care centers, family child-care homes, and other programs, which necessitates reassessing the age ranges and kinds of play in which they participate. A second reason is that more research is being conducted on the topic.

Recent research shows that, given the opportunity to be with peers, even infants participate in parallel play, which had previously been considered to be absent from children's repertoires until the age of 2. As early as 12 months of age, infants have been observed spending more time watching the activity of their peers than that of their mothers, and were more likely to touch, get close to, look at, and imitate a friend than a stranger (Oden, 1982). Important opportunities to practice social skills in the early years and to learn new ones through frequent and sustained peer contacts encourages 2- and 3-year-olds to engage in associative and cooperative play (Anselmo & Franz, 1995).

Ross and Lollis (1989), observing 20- and 30-month-old children over time in small peer-group play sessions, found that (1) even at that young age, children formed relationships with individual friends that were qualitatively different from their interactions with other people; and (2) these special relationships continued across a number of play sessions with surprising stability. They suggest that it is possible that positive interactions draw children into social relationships and, once these relationships are established, conflict naturally merges as a normal part of social development.

In yet another study, Caplan et al. (1991) studied conflict in the peer relationships of 12- and 24-month-old toddlers, examining the theory that conflict is due to frustration over play equipment and toys. They found that rather than the scarcity of toys being related to conflict, the greatest amount of conflict occurred among 24-month-olds when there were scarce resources and no duplicate toys available. The conflict among the 12-month-olds occurred when the toddlers found a toy attractive when another child had it—even if there was another duplicate toy available in the room and sometimes even when the child was holding the duplicate toy. The ability to cooperate increases over the ages of 12 to 30 months, due to the child's

Table 3.3
Parten's Traditional Stages of Play

AGE	NAME OF PLAY	BRIEF DESCRIPTION
0–24 months	Solitary	Children interact only with an object or familiar person
2–3 years	Parallel	Children play near each other but independently
3–4 years	Associative	Children participate in small groups but have a very limited sharing or interaction with each other
4 years on	Cooperative	Children share ideas and roles and interact in increasingly more complex play

ability to separate himself from others cognitively, known as *self-other differentiation* (Brownell & Carriger, 1990).

"Conclusion: The vast literature on children's play reveals that its contributions to child development can be looked at from diverse vantage points. Psychoanalytic theorists have highlighted the emotionally integrative function of pretense, pointing out that anxiety-provoking events, such as a visit to the doctor's office or discipline by a parent, are likely to be revised in the young child's play, but with roles reversed so that the child is in command and compensates for unpleasant experiences in real life" (Erikson, 1950). Piaget underscored the opportunities that make-believe affords for exercising symbolic schemes. And both Piaget and Vygotsky recognized that pretense allows children to become familiar with social-role possibilities. In cultures around the world, young children act out family scenes and highly visible occupations—police officer, doctor, and nurse in Western nations; rabbit hunter and potter among the Hopi; and hut builder and spear maker among the Baka of West Africa (Garvey, 1990). In this way, play provides children with important insights into the link between self and wider society (Berk & Winsler, 1995, p. 79).

How to Plan for Sustained Play

The presence of an interested adult is important in helping children to sustain and extend their play. As teachers improve their observation skills and knowledge about individual children, they will become more objective and see new

Children playing side by side may be involved in solitary or cooperative play.

and additional benefits of play as they watch individual children and the group as a whole. They will share pleasure in the growth and development of the children. "When I do something good (or hard) and it works, I feel wonderful. I can imagine how Helena feels because she was finally able to dress the doll by herself." Good and satisfying behavior is likely to be repeated by children and adults!

Teachers who can step back and observe the play of children experience a higher level of understanding in the importance of providing proper activities and materials for the children's use. This stepping back *does not mean* that the teacher does not play at all with children. It lies in the teacher's ability to know when stepping in elevates the play and when it destroys the play.

Reflection

At the Valley View Center, the teachers wondered how to stimulate interest in the neglected dramatic-play area. To get into the refrigerator, the children had to lean over the table. Guests had to stand. The dolls were stacked in the cradle as if it were a storage bin. The cooking and eating utensils were mismatched, cracked, and dented. At a serious glance, the teachers decided the activity lacked space and interest. Much needed were some attractive dress-up articles for both gender roles, reduction in the number of dolls, new dishes and utensils, and more space! When these changes were made and a colorful tablecloth was added, this became the most popular area.

The time frame for play in early-childhood programs should depend on the *interest of the children*. Some general guidelines, partially consolidated from the study by Christie and Wardle (1992), are presented in Figure 3.2.

DRAMATIC PLAY

Dramatic play, sometimes referred to as *sociodramatic play,* is defined as "a form of voluntary social play activity in which young children participate" (Smilansky & Shefatya, 1990, p. 21). Its importance in the preschool curriculum cannot be underestimated because it gives children a chance to touch and live different ways of life (see Table 3.4).

Some centers have a policy of restricting items from home (toys, food, pets, or other unnamed items). In this way toys and opportunities are not lost, broken, misplaced, or unjustly claimed. Some centers find that play is more spontaneous and inclusive when certain items are not available—clothing fads (Superman cape, hero toys), media themes, food advertising, and so on. War play can be disruptive, negative, and exclusive; so can hero play. (See the section titled "Violent Play" later in this chapter.)

Values for Children

Children often reenact what they see or hear at home. To them, this reenactment is realistic living, not dramatic play, and helps them understand the adult world. Anything is possible; a child can be the mother, father, baby, street sweeper, engineer, doctor, or whatever she likes. Roles may even change rapidly. Such play should be encouraged. Studies indicate that playful children are more advanced in their ability to think divergently than are their nonplayful counterparts. Note the learning young children can gain from dramatic play in Figure 3.3.

Figure 3.2
Hints for Sustaining Children's Play

<table>
<tr><td align="center">Do</td><td align="center">Don't</td></tr>
<tr><td>

- Plan daily free-play periods of a *minimum* of 30 minutes—with longer periods at least several times during the week.
- Plan sustained times rather than brief periods scattered through the day.
- Have sustained play periods when most (or all) the children are present.
- Reduce the amount and kinds of interruptions.
- Reinforce the importance of play with the children (in the physical environment, interest areas, stimulating materials and activities, and so on), in staff training (personal and curriculum development), and interaction with parents (interest areas, workshops, newsletters, meetings, informal conversations, community events, check-out materials, and so on).
- Help the children to be successful in play activities.
- Plan frequent opportunities to play outdoors.
- Vary the kinds of play and vary the manner of play (repetitive or prolonged).
- Watch for the interest levels of children and provide items that will increase their participation and development.
- Frequently add new materials or activities to stimulate their thinking.
- Observe the children carefully in order to meet their individual and group needs.

</td><td>

- Use elimination of play or exclusion from the group as a means of punishment. (Disruptive children need experiences with other children and activities—but recall the three red flags.)
- Use outdoor time just to get rid of wiggles, release tension, or reduce energy levels.
- Overload play periods with academic performance (counting, sorting, and so on).
- Set unnecessary restrictions on children or uses of materials.
- Let adults dominate the play of the children.
- Be unnecessarily restrictive on the noise or activity level in the classroom and playground.
- Provide props (books, clothing, occupation, and so on) that encourage gender, cultural, economic, or other biases.
- Provide materials that could cause harm or danger to the children.
- Use materials that are especially fragile.
- Promote games that exclude children because of skills.
- Expect children to be excited over a long period of time with the same toys.
- Expect the children to have the same interests, skills, and attention span.

</td></tr>
</table>

Figure 3.3
What Do Young Children Learn from Dramatic Play?

- To interact with other children (with age, ability, and interest differences); to develop personal relationships
- To cooperate: sharing and turn-taking, being a productive member of society
- To experience different types of curricula: art, music, language, and so on
- To take and experiment with different roles
- To communicate: social skills, negotiation, expressing ideas
- To attain personal goals and act within appropriate limits
- To explore and experiment with their environment
- To exercise their imaginations and ideas
- To take responsibility (roles, preparation, cleanup)
- To understand others: gender roles, cultures, privileges, responsibilities, empathy, and so on
- To enjoy themselves, others, the environment, and so on
- To develop initiative, accountability, social competence, and so on
- To identify pleasurable activities; to find positive ways to release energy and ideas
- To play with other children, regardless of developmental delays or behavior advancement

Table 3.4
Ideas to Encourage Dramatic Play

TYPE OF ACTIVITY	SUGGESTED PROPS
Family/home	Dress-up clothes—masculine and feminine, occupational, multicultural. Full-length or hand-held mirrors. Different rooms, different activities, different family members. A visit by child's family. Pictures of children in various kinds of activities posted at eye level. A mother bathing a baby. Books, stories, and pictures.
Clothing	Ethnic, gender, specialty articles of clothing (sports, occupational, etc.). Nonsexist ideas and discussion. Books, stories, and pictures.
Government offices—post office, bank, school, museum, police or fire station, etc.	Appropriate clothing and tools (badges, kits, bags, money, vehicles, etc.). Practicing courtesy and safety. Books, stories, and pictures.
Animals	Different habitats—pet shop, kennel, zoo, natural settings. Items for pet care. Replicas of different kinds of animals: zoo, farm, circus, and dinosaurs. Healthy and friendly animals within the classroom or on a field trip. A bug hunt on the playground. A bird's nest, a beehive, a cocoon. Books, stories, and pictures.
Food	Furniture and equipment for a restaurant, tools for planting, equipment and opportunity for food preparation, plastic replicas, good pictures. A field trip to a bakery, grocery store, pizza shop, produce farm, etc. Books, stories, and pictures.
Local industry	Depends on individual community: farm, dairy, water sport or fishing, etc. A safe and interesting place recognized by the children. An involved parent, clothing worn, and good pictures. Books, stories, and pictures.
Health center—doctor's office, clinic, hospital, etc.	Medical clothing and equipment. A unit on health. A visitor to the classroom. Books, stories, and pictures.

Reflection

It is not unusual for a child to dramatize a familiar theme. Simon and Ann were playing in the domestic area. Ann handed a block (representing his lunch bucket) to Simon and told him to go to work. He did so. Shortly she called to him and told him it was time to come home. Dutifully he returned, only to have her throw her arms around him and say, "Oh darling, I'm so glad you're home." Startled, Simon dropped the block and said, "Let me out of here!" With that, he ran to another area. This may have been a familiar scene to Ann, but it was foreign to Simon.

Table 3.4
continued

TYPE OF ACTIVITY	SUGGESTED PROPS
Water	Cooking and eating utensils. Boats, funnels, tubes, measuring equipment, water wheel, and water. Mixing paints for use. Investigating porous and nonporous materials. Doll clothes, a washtub, and soap. Books, stories, and pictures.
Environment	Rearrange, rotate, and add something special. Observe and discuss pollution—noise, litter, water, air. Child-sized and easily moved equipment and furniture. Combination of equipment and activities within the classroom. Enough (or duplicate) items for cooperative and sustained play. Manipulative toys for construction and building. Items to encourage singing, dancing, moving (records and recorders, tapes and cassettes, musical instruments, streamers, soft balls, scarves, etc.) A flannel board and objects of different colors, sizes, shapes, animals, people, etc. Books, stories, and pictures.
Sports	Family members to demonstrate their sport activities. Different sports items (hats, shoes, equipment). Books, stories, and pictures.
Nature	A walk during different seasons of the year, noting the surroundings. Items for making a collage. Places animals live and what they eat. Weather conditions at your center and those in other climates. Local and seasonal items of nature—leaves, snow, flowers, etc. Books, stories, and pictures.
Transportation	Uses of different vehicles. Sounds of different vehicles. Vehicles added to blocks, table toys, sand, etc. Books, stories, and pictures.
Interests of individual children	To be filled in by individual teacher.
Things to introduce to the children	To be filled in by individual teacher.

Most young children enjoy this area of expression. When interest begins to dwindle, a few props (like those mentioned at the beginning of this section) may be added.

Water has a magical attraction, but limits must be set as to where the water can be obtained and used.

Role of the Teacher

Dramatic play occurs in any area: domestic, block, sand, art, snack, language arts, or anywhere children are. Either teachers or children can be the initiators, but the actual activity should be child-centered. A story may trigger an activity, or the teacher can initiate dramatization of a story the children have just heard. A field trip is reinforced by dramatizing it on return.

How the teacher feels and prepares for dramatic play is very important in encouraging or discouraging participation. Children are usually eager for such experiences. Still they want and like the approval of the teacher.

Appropriate pictures placed in the domestic area add the stimulation some children need, but positioning a mirror so the child actually sees his participation, not just thinks it, is magnetic. Listening to what transpires is refreshing and revealing. In a wholesome atmosphere, the children fully enjoy dramatic play.

On occasion, something can be made to encourage later dramatic play. For example, airplanes could be fashioned at the woodworking table for use after a trip to the airport, and musical instruments can be made and used at music time. A discarded box from a new appliance can be sawed, painted, and decorated to become a house, store, bus, airplane, or whatever the children imaging.

Dramatic play adds new life to the children and to the program. With appropriate props, the children can dramatize home life, camping, vacations, and visits. They also should try occupational settings such as a bakery, airport, barber shop, beauty salon, medical office or hospital, construction site, school, library, pet store, restaurant, or gas station. They can be vehicle drivers, garbage collectors, bankers, firefighters, dancers, members of an orchestra, or anything they can imagine.

It is very important that play materials and opportunities are made available to help the child investigate personal interests, motivation, and skills. Early-childhood education practitioners and theorists, such as Froebel (1975), Montessori (1964), and others, designed and provided classroom materials to support their theories. Caroline Pratt, for example, designed the classic unit blocks to provide more open-ended materials for young children. Debates continue about

Figure 3.4
Criteria for Selecting Play Materials for Young Children

Items should:
1. be interesting and appealing to the particular child
2. support the exercise and refinement of the child's skills (remembering that children's interests expand)
3. have lasting play value
4. provide a foundation for future development
5. invite desirable types of play
6. stimulate interest, imagination, and learning
7. provide for parallel, solitary, and/or group play and various themes
8. be sturdy, durable, and safe (compare them to adult tools so they will stand up to wear and tear)
9. match the developmental age and individual needs of each child (and should have special adaptations for motor, visual, or auditory disabilities when appropriate)
10. include stimulation for social and fantasy play; exploration and mastery play; music, art, and movement; gross and fine motor play; intellectual development; solitary and group activity; seasonal play; and areas of personal interest.

There are government regulations, toy industry voluntary standards, and Consumer Product Safety Commission standards. For further information about these issues, write to the U.S. Consumer Product Safety Commission, Washington, DC 20207, or call the toll-free hotline: (800) 638-CPSC.

There is a "Guide to Play Materials by Type" in Bronson, 1995, pp. 129–153, for young toddler through primary-preschool ages.

the appropriate mix of structured (or closed-ended) and open-ended materials that should be available in the early-childhood classroom (Bredekamp & Rosegrant, 1992). Educational theorists, teachers, and others continue to create play materials to fit the goals and needs of individual children. Recent emphasis has been on materials that fit a wider age range of children and also are appropriate for children who are more mature or less mature than their chronological age. In other words, materials and play should be appropriate to the developmental abilities rather than the chronological age of the child.

Figure 3.4 helps adults focus on important criteria for selecting play materials for young children.

In many classrooms, teachers permit play as a reward for behavior or accomplishment, use it as a time filler for faster students, or devote little time planning for it. One is less likely to see classrooms that have no guidelines, in which the children "play" all the time. Either extreme can be hazardous. Since play is the work of children, they learn many personal and group attributes by participating in it.

Play fosters all aspects of the child's development. Through play, children integrate what they are learning and stretch toward further possibilities. In a developmentally appropriate early-childhood program, play is the center of the curriculum.

BLOCKS

Blocks are important in the education of young children both at home and at school.

Types and Use

Blocks are of many different kinds: large and hollow with handle openings, solid, unit, dimensionally proportioned, plastic, cardboard, vinyl, or fabric. Some are intended for use on the floor, others for use on tables. They are made in different sizes, shapes, and colors. Children enjoy putting blocks together to make new shapes or color combinations. Dramatic play is often enhanced with the addition of props to blocks. Two areas in the center may be joined together with the use of blocks (blocks and trucks, blocks used to enclose a reading area, and so on).

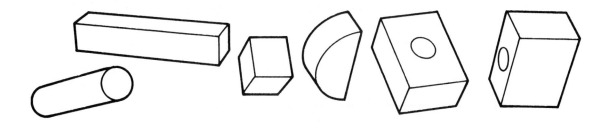

Good planning should go into the purchase of blocks. All blocks should be designed to fit together mathematically, each size twice as long or wide as the preceding size. Not only will they serve better purposes in building, but they will stack compactly when not in use. All types of blocks should be either shellacked or waxed. This finish will be more practical than paint.

A teacher wanted to promote block play with a group of 4-year-old children. The space in the room was limited, so she moved out part of the furniture and the domestic equipment. The first day after the equipment was gone, the children all asked, "Who took our stove?" "Where did the refrigerator go?" They wandered around aimlessly. The second day, they noticed a stack of large blocks in the corner and began using the blocks in their play. By the end of the week, they had experienced many joys from using these blocks. They worked cooperatively and came up with some rather ingenious ideas—including making furniture. The use of blocks was no longer a problem.

Role of the Teacher

Physical Arrangements

Plenty of space and uninterrupted time are necessary for good block play. As in the preceding example, equipment can be moved to another area or room if necessary to provide sufficient floor space. Because of the noise they create, blocks are used on a rug or carpet if at all possible. This protects the blocks from damage when they tumble down, keeps the children's knees from a cold or hard surface, and softens sounds.

Blocks should be out of the traffic pattern. For several days, two children had tried to build a block fence to house some new farm animals. Every time they got ready to play with their creation, someone either knocked it down or they had to pick it up. This day they were determined to have success. Quickly they gathered up the needed blocks and animals. They selected a different spot and started building. Soon one child after another rushed past and down went the blocks. In total disgust, they complained to the next child, who replied, "I didn't mean to—but I just had to get in to the toilet." The children had selected the most vulnerable spot in the room—right in front of the bathroom door!

A unit of time should be allotted to use a completed structure. At one center, day after day the children played that they were going to Africa to catch zoo animals. One child had recently been to a nearby zoo and had shared his ideas. Seeing how sustained the play was, the teacher began the basic structure so the children could finish it and get on with their trip to Africa. Otherwise, they never would have been able to play—they would always be building!

The teacher should be conscious of the time and warn the children in advance to end the activity at the appropriate time. Sometimes good constructive play can be continued and some other activity shortened or eliminated. Simply saying "It's almost time to pick up the blocks" or "It will soon be time for snack" gives the children an opportunity to prepare to end the activity. If possible, the structure is left up for later play.

Supervision

The teacher should indicate to the children what the guidelines are for the block area. She should be nearby, but needs not actively participate. Her verbal support is often enough to sustain activity in this area.

When structures get too tall or wobbly, a positive suggestion redirects the activity. Statements such as "Build as high as your nose," or "It's time to start another stack," are usually readily accepted by the children. Safety is important. The teacher should show appreciation for a structure but avoid overemphasis, never giving the children the idea that they must make certain structures in order to gain approval.

To interest children in the block area, a teacher may have to provide a pacesetter, that is, an eye-catcher or attention-getter. It should not be elaborate—just attract the children. One day it may be a tall structure, another day a farm or single block road leading to transportation vehicles.

As noted previously, children should be involved in cleanup. If shelves are low, near the building area, and have predrawn shapes, the children generally are willing to help put the blocks away. A teacher might say, "You pick up that size and I'll pick up this size," which gets the cleanup under way. The block area is watched carefully, and as interest begins to decrease or the children start being destructive, the teacher immediately steps in and helps the children decide whether they want to continue to play constructively, or if it is time to put the blocks away. To bring a child back from another area to help pick up blocks is not the most effective idea. When children take many blocks off the shelf at one time, the task of replacing them looks insurmountable. Here the teacher uses his initiative and wisdom in directing the children.

GENDER DIFFERENCES

In general, research over the last fifty years indicates that typical gender themes and topics for play have not changed much: boys more likely engage in rough-and-tumble play, aggressive themes, and play with vehicles and building materials; girls are more likely to engage in domestic roles and themes, sedentary indoor play, and goal-oriented construction or craft projects (Nourot & Van Hoorn, 1991; also see Figure 3.5.)

But Wardle (1991) says we may be shortchanging boys because they are usually the ones who are disruptive, generally appear in case examples, and are diagnosed as hyperactive almost twice as often as girls. Minority males have the most difficult adjustment in the traditional classroom. He continues,

> Informal observations in my program show teachers (female) less often in the block area, doing woodwork, on the floor with children, or involved in active play (inside and outside). Research suggests women teachers do not respond to cues of male youngsters; and male involvement in the classroom positively affects the behavior of boys, without negatively affecting the behavior of girls. (p. 49)

When female teachers become involved with boys who are engaged in typical male behavior, the amount and quality of play increases, and disruptive behavior decreases (Wardle, 1991).

Teachers should not expect children to be quiet and stationary in their play. Children do engage in large motor activities every day—bringing noise and action to the classroom. They like to collect materials and toys from one area and take them to another for different or more involved play. Barriers between distinct

Figure 3.5
Some Differences between Young Girls' and Boys' Style of Play

Girls	Boys
• More advanced socially	• More rough-and-tumble play
• More advanced in cognitive and language development	• More aggression and fighting
• Prefer table play and sitting activities	• Prefer floor play, push-pull toys, blocks, wheel toys, and sand
• Prefer arts, crafts, puzzles, coloring, dolls	• Prefer outdoors
• Use materials in a more educational way	• Choose superhero play
• Prefer domestic activities	• Boisterous
• Less active and noisy	• More gender-role oriented

learning areas should be eliminated or removed when possible, helping to destroy the notion of boys in blocks, girls in dramatic play.

ADULTS' PERCEPTION OF PLAY

Rothlein and Brett (1987) reported on interviews of children 2 through 6 years of age and questionnaires completed by parents and teachers regarding their perceptions of play. Children's favorite play activities according to children, parents, and teachers were outdoor play, dramatic play, blocks, and art activities. Parents thought of play as fun or amusement and did not support having their children spend a large amount of time in play during preschool. Teachers saw play both as fun and as development of cognitive and social areas, but did not view it as an integral part of the curriculum—instead, they saw a learn-play dichotomy.

In 1924, when children were still being reminded that they must speak only when spoken to, a group of mothers from Muncie, Indiana, chose three traits they wanted their children to develop: strict obedience, loyalty to church, and good manners. During the 1920s parents emphasized obedience, conformity, and respect for home and church (Remley, 1988). In a replication of a 1924 study, Caplow, Bahr, and Chadwick (1989) found that 54 years later mothers emphasized independence, tolerance, and social mindedness. "Parents no longer want their children to follow them out of blind obedience," explains Dr. Bruce Chadwick. "Now they want their children to be able to think things out and to be dependable and responsible because the kids decide that's what they want to be."

Summary

The principal source of development in the early years is play, according to Vygotsky (1976). Play is a basic ingredient in learning in kindergarten (Simmons, 1983) and the "way a child learns most efficiently" (Simmons & Brewer, 1985, p. 178). Davis (1965) states, "Play is the mirror of an individual's developmental pattern" (p. 222). When reviewed as a learning process, play becomes a vehicle for intellectual growth and continues to be the most vital avenue of learning for kindergartners. Play involves not only materials and equipment, but also words and ideas that promote literacy and develop thinking skills. In addition to the three Rs, play promotes problem solving, critical thinking, concept formation, and creativity. Social and emotional development are enhanced through play as well. Play fosters holistic learning (Moyer, Egertson, & Isenberg, 1987, p. 238).

Reflection

Recall the Reflection in Chapter 2 in which the parent of a prospective student, after watching the children in many indoor and outdoor activities, stated: "I think it is a rather expensive program for children to just play all the time." From additional information you have gained since reading this chapter on play, would you respond differently to the parent than you would have after reading the example the first time in Chapter 2? How convinced are you that play is very important in the life and learning of a young child? Give specific examples. Do you still need to convince yourself?

SPECIAL NEEDS OF CHILDREN

Throughout this book the theme of meeting the needs of children individually and in groups will be stressed. Children with special needs—whether it be developmental, cultural, racial, or whatever—are recognized and identified for the kind of help they require without putting undue attention or pressure on the children, the school, or the home. Some children will need experiences scaled down and others will need them scaled up; some need to interact in small groups, and others benefit from action with large groups; some must remain inside the classroom (for health and safety reasons), and others react better in open spaces and fresh air. Teachers should make every effort to see that opportunities are open-ended—they can be terminated or expanded at any point. If a child has a disability, it is related to the ability of the specific child and not compared to other children who have similar or different disability.

SAFETY IN PLAY

Whether play materials are used indoors or outdoors, *safety* must be of utmost concern. Unbroken, nontoxic, well-fitting toys should always be used. Activities that include possible danger should be either closely supervised or not used at all. Woodworking is an example. It has so many developmental values for children that to exclude it would be unfortunate; however, when woodworking is used, *the teacher must remain with the tools, must define the guidelines for participation, must provide tools that are appropriate and in good working condition, and must feel comfortable about working with the children.*

Some areas or activities (indoors and outdoors) require more supervision than others. The teacher should make sure children have opportunities to get, use, and replace materials independent of teacher direction. Occasional teacher contact or interaction may sustain children in an activity or may encourage them to try different methods.

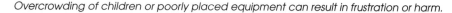

Overcrowding of children or poorly placed equipment can result in frustration or harm.

When a teacher has thought through the entire activity (preparation, availability, use, and cleanup), there is less chance of misuse of materials, inappropriate behavior, or danger.

When children are climbing, running, or particularly active, accidents may happen. Teacher awareness of these activities, or of particular children, can reduce possible problems. When accidents do happen, teachers must be quick, accurate, and calm in handling them.

Indoor Precautions

A number of safety factors inside the facility need the close attention of teachers and parents. They include, but are not limited to, the following:

> Art materials (See Table 6.1 in Chapter 6, Creative, Artistic, and Sensory Expression)
>
> Houseplants (may be poisonous) (see Alber et al., 1990; Taylor, 1997)
>
> Traffic patterns
>
> Floor space and activities
>
> Types and number of doors
>
> Temperature of water
>
> Lighting and heating (including cords for cooking)
>
> Toys (some have small parts that could be swallowed)
>
> Pets (some may be unfriendly, mistreated, or carry diseases)
>
> Water activities (slipping)—if a wading pool is used, extra precautions need to be taken
>
> Carpets, floor coverings, furniture
>
> Alarms (smoke, open doors, unsafe areas)
>
> Emergencies and an exit plan
>
> Seat belts
>
> Supervision
>
> Behavior limits
>
> One's rights and beliefs
>
> Construction materials (asbestos, lead, others) (see *Lead and Your Child's Safety*, National Paint and Coatings Association, 1500 Rhode Island Ave. N.W., Washington, DC 20005; "Lead Toxicity—Is Your Program at Risk?" [1992, September]. *Young Children*, 47(6), 35.)

Outdoor Precautions

Some important changes have been made in outdoor playgrounds for young children.

1. The U.S. Consumer Products Safety Commission (CPSC) (Washington DC 20207) has updated its guidelines for public playgrounds, and has made two changes that are significant for the child-care industry. It has specifically in-

cluded child-care facilities in its definition of "public" playgrounds, and, even more important, it has included specific playground guidelines for preschool children ages 2 to 5, in addition to the guidelines for school-age children from 5 to 12 years that were previously recommended.

The *Handbook on Public Playground Safety* states:

> Preschool and school-age children differ dramatically not only in physical size and ability, but also in their cognitive and social skills. Therefore, *age-appropriate* playground designs should accommodate these differences with regard to the type, scale and the layout of equipment.

This is the first mention of "age-appropriateness" by this federal agency responsible for informing the public of potential product hazards (Landscape Structures, 1992, Fall, p. 1).

2. Title III requirements of the Americans with Disabilities Act (ADA) pertain to places of public accommodation, including more than five million private establishments—among them, private schools and day-care centers, according to highlights from the law published by the Department of Justice.

The highlights continue:

> Existing facilities: Removal of barriers: Physical barriers must be removed when this can be accomplished (1) easily, and (2) without much difficulty and expense. What is "readily achievable" will be decided on a case-by-case basis in light of the resources available.

> New construction: New facilities must be accessible to individuals with disabilities to the extent that it is not "structurally impracticable."

The rules apply to any facility occupied after January 26, 1993, "for which the last application for a building permit or permit extension is certified as complete after January 26, 1992" (Landscape Structures, 1992, Summer, p. 1). (For a free packet of information on the ADA, write: Office of the Americans with Disabilities Act, Civil Rights Division, U.S. Dept. of Justice, P.O. Box 66118, Washington, DC 20035-6118.)

The Consumer Federation of America has compiled a checklist of problems to look for in a playground, and recommends that any concerns be addressed to the individual playground supervisor or owner.

Child Injuries

The American Academy of Orthopedic Surgeons (AAOS) says that nearly 270,000 children under age 15 were treated in hospital emergency rooms in 1992 for injuries related to playground equipment. More than 67,000 children ages 5 to 14 received injuries related to swings and about the same number to climbing equipment.

The AAOS has begun a national public education campaign, "Play It Safe," based on the playground guidelines of the U.S. Consumer Product Safety Commission.

In 1988, the Centers for Disease Control (CDC) conducted a study of playground hazards at fifty-eight child-care centers in Atlanta, Georgia; identified the hazards at these playgrounds; pointed them out to the director at each center; and gave playground safety instruction to the directors. Licensing inspectors returned to the sites two years later and found that "the sites where directors had been shown the hazards and given information about them actually had higher hazard scores. . . . They found that the playgrounds of sites that had changed directors had fewer hazards than those where the director was the same."

As a result of this study, the CDC researchers found that pointing out hazards and providing information to directors was not enough to correct hazardous situations; therefore, the researchers suggest several interventions: more explicit regulations, better training of regulators, support for enforcement of regulations, more extensive training of child-care center directors, increasing parental awareness, and posting the inspection report in a conspicuous place at the center (Aronson, 1992).

Remember that some children are accident-prone. Some are more susceptible to accidents when they are hungry, fatigued, or inexperienced, or when equipment is new and challenging. Staff should be especially alert on the playground around climbing equipment, with tools (woodworking, cooking), with overstimulated children, and in crowded facilities. Young children *can* be taught how to use toys and equipment safely.

Through an awareness program, children and parents can learn and practice safety measures at school and home. Items to include are activities for children to hear, see, and practice, and articles sent to the home for parental awareness and implementation (pedestrian safety, poison safety, water safety, gun safety, pollution).

CHILDREN AND THE OUTDOORS

Often overlooked or underestimated, outdoor play is essential for the health and well-being of young children. The traditional school model contends that outside activities are to rejuvenate children (and teachers) and inside activities are for learning. How far from the truth! Anything that can be done inside a classroom can also be done on the playground—art, music, science, socialization, physical development, and on and on.

When weather permits, move easels and paint, dramatic play, music and movement, obstacle courses, wheel toys, and typically indoor activities onto the playground. In inclement weather, some climbing pieces, selected wheel toys, and open classroom space provide some of the opportunities often limited to the outdoor areas.

Typical *indoor* resources include furniture, art, music, dramatic play, block play, manipulative materials, movement experiences, food preparation, mathematics, science, language, resting areas, and sometimes water play.

Outdoor resource centers usually allow for greater action, more noise, sometimes an incline or hill, sand, water, swings, a climbing apparatus, playhouses, blocks, woodworking and carpentry, loose materials, a gardening area, animals, a group-activity area, a wheel-toy area, a quiet place, and a natural area. Creative teachers plan to integrate activities and areas to give greater flexibility and more interest to the children whether in indoor or outdoor areas. Materials for sensorimotor, construction, and dramatic play outdoors include those shown in Table 3.5.

Often teachers use outdoor equipment and space with less planning than for indoor activities. Stationary equipment is always available and may become the only activity on the playground unless some other focal point is provided daily, such as climbing apparatus arranged in a new or stimulating way, sturdy tools for gardening, games, musical activities, stick horses, and wheel toys.

Table 3.5
Props for Construction and Dramatic Play Outdoors

TYPE OF PLAY	PROPS
Sandbox	Water, bottle caps for decoration, rocks and sticks, bowls, cups, wooden spoons; small trucks and cars; small people and animals
Art	Easel with paints, paper, and brushes; collage materials; dough
Music and movement	Record or cassette player, records or tapes, streamers, musical instruments, balls, hula hoops, scarves
Construction (exercise caution)	Large materials: wooden or cardboard crates, large blocks, large pieces of wood, vehicle tires, blanket or tarp, ladders, gardening tools
Dramatic play	Dress-up clothes, food cans, dolls, furniture, towels, drying rack, mirror, miscellaneous items
Water	Buckets, tubs, funnels, bowls, siphon, tubes, plastic containers, soap, washable items, brushes, towels
Wheel toys	Tricycles, wagons, carts, wheelbarrows, tires

Role of the Teacher

The teacher's role outdoors is similar to that in other areas:

- To provide for the individual child and her needs
- To "pace" the area to be inviting and stimulating
- To set up and maintain necessary limits
- To be flexible in her teaching
- To provide a variety of experiences in the fresh air
- To stimulate and encourage children to explore
- To appreciate the interests and enthusiasm of the children
- To enjoy being with them
- To exhibit a positive attitude toward outdoor play
- To meet the needs of both girls and boys while removing superficial or real barriers related to gender, race, culture, or other destructive measures
- To see play as a fun but growth-stimulating opportunity for young children in all the developmental domains
- To enlarge children's vision of and participation in areas where they feel less secure (woodworking, climbing)
- To take some risks in activity planning and supervision, to respond to individual learning styles, and to initiate ways to combine interests and activities of the children
- "To act as a catalyst to help children experience and enjoy sociodramatic play and to improve each child's ability to extend and elaborate play themes" (Smilansky & Shefatya, 1990)
- To prepare "the environment and schedule blocks of time for play, intervening as matchmaker, peacekeeper, or coach" (Nourot & Van Hoorn, 1991)

Good planning is necessary for maximum use of the playground and its equipment. The area can be beautiful yet functional, with space for freedom of movement. Needs of the children can be provided for without a great deal of cost.

The children should play outside independently, but not unsupervised. Equipment and activities should provide opportunities to make decisions, try ideas, work, and play with others without fear of harm or destruction. The focal point should be obvious to the children and should attract them to it, either to use as provided or to stimulate their creativity.

Of course, the attractiveness of the playground is important for children to enjoy the area; however, the design and appearance will not ensure that the area will meet the needs of the young child. Adults who plan outdoor play areas must consider the goals and objectives for children's development. And in line with other learning areas, toys and activities should be age-appropriate for the development of the children, especially their large-muscle involvement. Lovell and Harms (1985) stress that some areas should be refined for social skills; that there should be opportunities to solve problems using both physical and social skills; that there should be enhancement of relationships (such as in/out, up/down, over/under, high/medium/low, heavy/light, hard/soft, and fast/slow); that creativity should be expressed through art, carpentry, music, movement, and block building; that opportunities should exist for physical knowledge about weather, growing seeds, animals, balance, distance and speed, and volume and shape; and that the outdoor environment should be a comfortable place to eat, paint, read, and engage in other activities.

According to Frost (1992), teachers would be wise to remember that "insensitive, unskilled, excessive intervention in children's play by adults can interrupt the flow of play themes, block leadership roles of children, encourage dependency on adults, stifle self-confidence, and lead to the breakdown of play itself" (p. 341).

Values for Children

Large-Muscle Development

The young child needs the proper equipment to help him exercise his large muscles. One of the most versatile is a good assortment of sturdy boxes and boards that can be moved easily and arranged in a manner stimulating to the interests and abilities of the children. Equipment constructed to take the abuse of energetic bodies should be brightly colored to attract attention. A board can be used directly on the ground for beginners, then raised to various levels as imaginations and skills dictate. One minute the board may be a road; the next, a bridge to crawl under. Boxes should be large enough for children to climb into, onto, or over. Boards and boxes can be combined into interesting obstacle courses. If funds are limited, large cardboard boxes can be obtained from floral, appliance, furniture, or grocery stores.

Outdoor play allows the children to connect with the community, to socialize, and to expand their horizons. On large, fixed equipment, children develop their bodies while experiencing basic physics (gravity, inertia, and optics [being upside down]) (Rivkin, 1995).

A jungle gym or climbing apparatus of some kind (ladders, nets, trees, hills) that presents a variety of possibilities for activity is best. Such equipment stimulates imagination and exercises muscles as well.

A paved area should be provided for wheel toys. Tricycles and wagons can be used separately or jointly. Most pedal cars are difficult for preschoolers because the pedals and steering are not coordinated as they are on a tricycle. Some 5-year-olds are ready to ride a two-wheel bike but must constantly be reminded about safety (stopping, running into people and obstacles, going into traffic, and so on).

Fresh air, friends, and fun as children learn and practice social skills indoors and outdoors.

Swings have little to offer children between ages 2 and 5 (although the adult gets pushing practice). The 2-year-old is not coordinated enough to pump the swing; therefore, she gets no exercise and must depend on someone to push her. Accidents occur, also, because children walk into the path of the swing, or the swinging child decides to let go. Moreover, swinging takes a child away from group or active play. She has opportunities elsewhere (at home or in a park) for this type of experience. The 5-year-old, however, uses the swing in more advanced ways: pumping while sitting or standing, resting on her stomach, and twisting and turning in more cooperative and creative ways than the younger child.

Although large-muscle and cooperative activities are encouraged in young children, competitive games are best avoided, because the young child lacks the physical skills and emotional stability to make such competition a growth-promoting experience. Young children enjoy some appropriate outdoor games, but children should not be required to stay and play for a long period of time. Other activity suggestions include the following:

- A broom handle (or even a string) can be placed between two chairs or posts and the child encouraged to go under or over it at various heights.
- Tires or tubes help children release excess energy. Large truck or airplane tubes are exciting to roll in, climb through, jump on, and bounce on.
- Stick horses provide good exercise at a low price. They can be stored in tall garbage cans when not in use.

○ Either blocks built for outdoor use or large barrels add interest to the play-ground.

○ Large wooden or plastic carriers used by milk carriers make good stacking and storage units.

○ Parachutes (or large sheets) provide fun and muscle practice.

○ The play yard can be explored for such treasures as nests, insects, and rocks.

○ Digging equipment of all kinds (sand, garden, and so on) encourages explo-ration and interest.

○ Scientific equipment (pulleys, magnets, microscopes, and so on) takes on new challenges when used outdoors.

○ The bottom and side beneath the handle of a gallon plastic container can be cut out to make a scoop for scoop ball. Partners throw and catch a ball or beanbag.

○ A rope can be tied in a high place, such as a tree or the frame of a swing. Knots are made at 2- or 3-foot intervals so the child can sit on one knot while reaching for the next higher one and pulling himself up. Careful supervision is required.

○ A steering wheel attached to a large wooden frame initiates interaction.

○ Equipment can be put in different combinations or locations. In warm weather, materials and activities generally used inside can be taken outside.

More woodworking examples are discussed in Chapter 6.

Social Interaction or Dramatic Play

The theme and complexity of play depend on the age of the child. The 2-year-old child plays silently and alone. Variations continue up to the 5-year-old, who chatters incessantly, needs other children, and may initiate and continue elaborate play over a period of time lasting from minutes to days.

Much equipment discussed in this chapter stimulates socialization and group and dramatic play. Children often initiate an unusual use for a piece of equipment. For example, two children were building with large blocks when one discovered that his arrangement looked like a horse! (See Tables 3.4 and 3.5.)

Role playing takes on a new and vigorous light outdoors. The entire play-ground is the stage. A rowboat, for instance, provides hours of imaginative and co-operative play. It can be brightly painted and strategically placed, with some holes drilled in the bottom to facilitate drainage. Other similar possibilities are an old car frame, a tractor, or a cockpit from army surplus.

Strategically placed props can suggest and sustain dramatic play. For example, moving housekeeping items outside near a water outlet can encourage washing dishes or clothes, bathing dolls, pouring and measuring, and other activities that may be too messy to include indoors on a frequent basis. Or props such as a play-house, a trunk, suitcases, occupational hats, and wheel toys bring new life, action, and practice for young children. Areas of partial seclusion (not unsupervised areas) bring excitement into the play of children (a small tent, large cardboard boxes, sheets or a parachute, low area dividers).

Sensory Experiences

Experiences with water are more fully undertaken outside than is possible inside. When weather permits, water makes an occasion special. Many parents object to their children's playing with water at home; opportunities should be provided at the center. Precautions are taken, of course, to see that children are properly dressed for this activity in bathing suits, boots, or cover-ups. Painting with water, sailing boats, or even watering plants can be fun. (See Chapter 6, Creative, Artistic, and Sensory Expression, and Chapter 8, Science and Technology, for further suggestions about water experiences.) On a hot day, it is refreshing to let the hose run on the slide, cooling it and adding an extra zip as the children slide down. A wading pool filled with water at the end of the slide adds zest to the experience but must be closely supervised.

Sand is another item that is better used outdoors. It holds many possibilities, especially with the addition of props such as strainers, spoons, molds, buckets, shovels, cars, and various toys.

Creative art materials used outdoors can allow more freedom of movement and expression than materials used indoors. There need not be the degree of concern outside that there is inside—but if there is fear of spillage (of soap, which kills plants; paint that stains concrete; and so on) a cover of newspaper, plastic, or cardboard could be placed under especially messy activities. Placement of creative art materials outside should include consideration of glare from the sun, disturbance or distraction by other activities, access to materials and cleanup items, sunburn of children, and the need for adult supervision.

Learning about Nature

The beauty and tranquility of the area will increase the children's enjoyment. A variety of flowers, a garden plot, an area for rest and relaxation, and a place to watch and listen assist children's learning.

The landscaping around the playground area can be planned to stimulate children's interest in nature. Shrubs of differing sizes, colors, and characteristics can be planted either in the ground or in large tubs. A large tree for climbing is desirable, if available. Check with a gardener or landscape architect to ensure that leaves, berries, shrubs, and other plantings are not poisonous or harmful to children if chewed, eaten, or touched. Planned experiences, such as feeders and animals, and unplanned ones, such as the weather and bugs, add to environmental learning.

Planning the Area

The playground should provide large areas of space away from equipment. A garden or digging area provides many opportunities for children to use proper tools, to plant, and to harvest. Free-flowing paths are inviting to fast-paced youngsters, too. They resemble curves found on modern highways.

As a result of playing and building outdoors, a child adds to her experiences. Crates and large wooden cartons are fun to build with, as are old tires, wooden and metal frames, and boards. The weight of the object should challenge but not tax the ability of a child. She will also learn about cooperation, interdependence, independence, balance, size, and gravity. Through use of her body, she will develop skills and dexterity.

Following are suggestions for types of areas and items for an outdoor play area:

aesthetic design (color arrangement, variety)	barrels
	bedspread over box
animals	blocks (hollow)
areas: domestic, open, private, planning, running	boards for crawling, jumping, bouncing
art materials	boxes (large packing)

cars (doors removed)
climbers (wood, metal), rings,
    ropes, poles, platform
clocks
cockpit
easels
fishing net
gardening equipment and plot
gas pump
housekeeping items (dolls, dishes,
    dress-up clothes)
inner tubes
ladders (horizontal or perpendicular;
    made of rope, wood, or metal)
levers
nets over frames
parachute
plants, flowers
playhouse
pulley
pumps (water, tire)
punching bag

radios
ramps
ropes (use with caution)
sand tools and toys
sawhorses
shovels
signs (road)
slides
sounds: pleasant, varied
stick horses
storage
storm drainpipe
surfaces: grass, dirt, asphalt
swing (tire)
tent
terrarium
trees
trucks, cars
trunk, suitcases
water and toys
wheel toys (wagons, tricycles)
woodworking equipment

TOYS AND MATERIALS

Often parents buy toys too advanced for children, hoping the children will be ready for them early—almost like buying a pair of shoes that are too large now but hoping the child will get more use out of them as his feet grow! Perhaps parents lack buying knowledge of what is characteristic for different ages. Frequently parents buy toys that interest them (the parents) in hopes that their children will also be interested. The best advice to offer parents and to sustain a child's play is to buy toys that match the child's abilities and interests.

For the young child the best types of toys are those that offer a variety of uses. Wind-up toys may be interesting for the moment, but then what do you do with them? Building materials, art materials, and other versatile toys stimulate the imagination and provide many hours of pleasure and exploration. Toys have to be fun, evocative, and creative; interactive toys stretch the child's imagination.

Complex toys often hinder play; the simpler the toy, the more complex the play. As Albert Einstein once said, "Imagination is more important than knowledge."

Although computers can be educational, they don't teach children how to get along with people—the kinds of lessons you learn from a good old-fashioned board game or a box of building materials. (See the discussion in Chapter 8 about computers.)

Parents at home and teachers at school should be aware of the pressure they place on children to always be doing something, have something to show for their time, show positive changes in behavior, mature too rapidly in all areas of development, and be popular.

Teachers can obtain a current catalog from any manufacturer of toys for young children.

VIOLENT PLAY

By now the reader is probably wondering whether the topic of violent play will be ignored or addressed. It is a very timely topic and needs much careful thought and consideration.

One cannot discuss other types of play (dramatic, skill, outdoor, solitary, and so on) without some focus on unacceptable, mainly violent, play that occurs when children get together. Parents as well as teachers need to know how to direct play so that it is constructive, growth-promoting, and valuable to young children. There is additional discussion on this topic in Chapter 2, Guidance Techniques and School/Home Interaction.

Since the deregulation of children's media in 1984, there has been a steadily increasing amount of entertainment violence marketed to children with the supporting linkup of toys to those TV shows. Manufacturers who are driven more by profits than by what serves the best interests of children have become a powerful influence over children, competing with teachers and parents in shaping children's values, behavior, and play. "A blanket disapproval of these toys and images and movements that are so important to our kids (yes, because of successful media coercion) just alienates the child from adults and from school and our ability to provide guidance. A TV show that glorifies aggression and antagonism is not appropriate for our children," states Greenberg (1995).

Outdoor play can release tensions and reduce aggressive actions.

The United States is the most violent country in the industrialized world, with homicide, rape, assault, and battery rates many times those of other countries . . . [The] reasons are many and go to the very root of social and economic injustice; the mass media play a significant role in socializing young children into violence (Garbarino et al. 1992; American Psychological Association, 1993). Crime rates are increasing most rapidly among youth who were in their formative early years when children's TV was deregulated and violent programs and toys successfully deluged childhood culture. (Levin & Carlsson-Paige, 1995, p. 67)

Parents, teachers, and others have noted the increase of violence in the behavior of young children. Some parents have even supported the behavior by purchasing certain items (toys, clothing, and so on) and providing opportunities for children to act out the behaviors. Some teachers have banned such items from the classroom, only to find that while the banning gives children the strong message that violence is bad and that even pretending to hurt others is unacceptable, violent behavior continues to plague both parents and teachers. Banning such play also carries with it serious problems; it can encourage children to hide from their teachers the things that really interest or concern them (Greenberg, 1995). "And more important, it prevents teachers from having any direct influence on all that children are learning about violence and social behavior as they engage in war play outside the teachers' view. . . . So if teachers ban war-related play, they are faced with a new set of challenges" (Carlsson-Paige & Levin, 1995).

Reflection

One center was having trouble with games involving Batman, Ninja Turtles, and all the violent media heroes because the children were hurt and frightened while playing these games. The teachers had a discussion with the children; parents received a letter from the center about the negative impact of the play along with suggested ways to downplay these heroes in selection of clothes, toys, books, and accessories, and in TV and movie watching (for example, de-emphasizing children's exposure to them, providing alternative toys and media viewing, suggesting more appropriate ways to play with the toys, selecting other designs for children's clothing, leaving "questionable" toys at home, and so on). (Duffy, 1991)

Aggression occurs under normal circumstances, even without the presence of heroes. During the preschool years children are just learning to distinguish reality from fantasy (real victims and fictional ones) and how to act acceptably with peers and adults. Even normal play indoors and outdoors can degenerate into a hitting, negative, hurting situation. We should strive to help children keep their negative feelings to a minimum and their positive ones to a maximum.

An alternative to banning classroom violence is to work directly with children's war play to counteract the messages children learn from media and toys (see Figure 3.6). It can also help them make meaning of the violence they have experienced in order to get some resolution or mastery over it (Groves & Mazur, 1995). As teachers facilitate children's dramatic play, children develop better skills for working out the powerful issues in their lives, including violence, through play (Gowen, 1995). But this choice, too, creates special challenges for teachers over how to maintain a sense of safety for all children in the classroom while beginning to work with these difficult themes in children's play (Carlsson-Paige & Levin, 1987; Levin & Carlsson-Paige, 1995).

Figure 3.6
Possible Causes of Violent Play in Young Children

TV programming
Toys supporting violent TV programs, games, and so on
Video games
Books displaying violent themes or characters
Movies—including cartoons
Music (lyrics and gestures)
Games—group
Sports—participation or observation
Inappropriate expectations of adults
Peer reinforcement
Developmentally delayed behavior—immaturity
Adult models and encouragement (macho, powerful, dominant, possessive)
Lack of good models, lack of better ways of solving situations, or lack of cooperation skills
Status symbols—clothing, colors, insignias, hair styles, belonging
Allergies to food, fabrics, animals, toxins, and so on
Other things that may be "child-specific"

To sum up: "Whatever teachers choose to do in their classrooms, it will not be easy, and it will not be enough . . . the power of one person's actions in creating change, there are many things we all can do to reduce violence in children's lives, both in our communities and in the wider society. We feel that early childhood educators need to work together, using the full power of our professions, to unite with parents and to advocate for changes in society that eliminate the marketing of violence to children and that create a safe, healthy work in which *all* children can fully exercise their right to play (Piaget, 1973)" (Carlsson-Paige & Levin, 1995, p. 63).

Bergen (1994, p. 301) has noted: "[V]iolent play themes are drawn from real life and fantasy . . . but the basic structure consistently revolves around dominance and submission . . . someone who is more powerful 'winning' and someone who is weaker being 'defeated'." This gives a message that guns and other violent objects or actions can be effective in solving problems. And, further, "boys (i.e., men) are more likely to accept violence as a method of solving problems than girls (i.e., women)." Girls are more likely to be reprimanded by adults for their aggressive play.

As early-childhood educators, we need to recall that there is a sequence to growth and development. Such is the case of progress that children proceed through in learning to define a problem. They [kindergartners] tend to see problems in the immediate moment, in physical terms, and from their own point of view. "Only with age and experience do children slowly learn to see problems in a larger context; in more abstract terms that involve underlying motives, feelings, and intentions; and from more than their own point of view. Until they are able to do this on their own, therefore, the teacher needs to help" (Carlsson-Paige & Levin, 1992, p. 7). To use Piaget's terms, children proceed from concrete to abstract thinking, from one to more than one point of view, and from segments to the whole problem: causes and effects. They learn to think of potential solutions and then to think through negative and positive consequences of each. Developmental theory predicts that with age, as children's thinking becomes more logical and flexible, they will become better able to think of win/win solutions (Selman & Demorest, 1984). Carlsson-Paige and Levin (1992) did not find an increase in win/win solutions as children's age increased, even when they saw general advances in their cognitive levels. They continue their findings:

> The static thinking of younger children makes learning to negotiate difficult. They have a hard time moving from one state in a conflict to another or seeing how that might be done. They often seem totally immersed in the conflict, unable to see a way out. Only when children's thinking becomes more flexible and interconnected do they begin to see how to get from a state of conflict to a solution.
>
> When we help children develop skills they can use in resolving their own conflicts, we help them feel . . . that *I am a problem solver*. . . . Time and again they insisted that there was nothing they could do to improve difficult conflicts they described from their own lives. (p. 10)

Aggressive play has been a topic over many years, and is certainly not just the result of more violent television programming or supporting toys (see Figure 3.7). Bandura (1973), noted for using an inflatable child-sized doll in experiments, proposed a social learning theory, which stressed that children who see aggressive acts performed by powerful models (adults) or similar models (peers) will be likely to also act aggressively. To control this type of behavior, teachers need to (1) convey to children and parents in their classrooms that violent play is not acceptable, and (2) remember that models who are rewarded for their violence in-

Figure 3.7
Effects of Violence on Children

Children need to feel safe. Experts describe the impact of violence on many children as *post-traumatic stress disorder* (Garbarino et al., 1992).

The younger the child, the greater the threat of exposure to violence to healthy development. Chronic exposure to violence can have serious developmental consequences for children, including psychological disorders, grief and loss reactions, impaired intellectual development and school programs, truncated moral development, pathological adaptation to violence, and identification with the aggressor (Craig, 1992; Garbarino et al., 1992).

Children exposed to violence have difficulty focusing on schoolwork or engaging in any of the other playful activities that should be reassured experiences of childhood (National Television Violence Study, 1996).

It is estimated that up to 80 percent of all children exposed to powerful stressors do not sustain developmental damage (Rutter, 1979; Werner, 1990).

Most children are able to cope with dangerous environments and maintain resilience as long as their parents are not stressed beyond their capacity to cope (Garbarino et al., 1992).

Schools and child-care programs can be vitally important support systems by strengthening children's resilience and providing resources for parents so that they can serve as psychological buffers to protect their children (National Television Violence Study, 1996).

The National Association for the Education of Young Children (NAEYC), the nation's largest professional organization for early-childhood educators, is committed to actions (1) to decrease the extent of violence in all forms in children's lives by advocating for public policies and actions at the national level, and (2) to enhance the ability of educators to help children cope with violence, promote children's resilience, and assist families by improving professional practice in early-childhood programs (National Television Violence Study, 1996, p. 23).

Creative art materials encourage constructive thoughts and actions.

crease their violent tendencies, and also those tendencies of others. Erikson (1977) supported a psychosocial viewpoint, which interprets aggressive actions in play as a way children can constructively deal with their emotions and gain a feeling of power and control over their environment. Thus, violent play is a natural and relatively harmless outlet for aggressive feelings within activities that the children control through their play, and can be expressed, mastered, and ultimately dissipated. This type of play allows children to feel more powerful and thereby express and master their natural anger in a "low-risk" manner; however, there must be limits.

Bergen (1994) summarizes:

> Playing with violence should be only a small part of a fully balanced player's life. Both boys and girls should be encouraged to play with caring and teachers should facilitate such play development. . . . Many teachers and many parents must be committed to finding strategies that will make our societal goals congruent with such play. Because play is such a powerful medium for learning, the behaviors and attitudes children practice in their play have the potential to affect the future. The stance teachers take toward appropriate expressions of violence, both within and outside the classroom, will affect that future as well. (p. 301)

The National Television Violence Study (1996), a three-year effort to assess violence on television, reports key findings and recommendations. The *findings* include the following: violence on television poses risks to viewers; perpetrators go unpunished in most violent scenes; negative consequences of violence are omitted from the programming; handguns are frequently used; programs contain a very limited amount of antiviolence; explicit or graphic violence is limited; different television channels show different amounts of violence; children's programs are least

Figure 3.8
Lessons Learned from Play

Aggressive Play	Nonaggressive Play
Rewards aggressiveness. May or may not satisfy the child, but annoys teachers and children.	Encourages children to find better ways of interacting, working out feelings.
Gives the child a false sense of security or acceptance, negative self-perception.	Values each child: protects the rights of the shy child and shows the aggressive child better ways to control anger, desires, and so on.
Shows the teacher and others that the child needs attention.	Requires good teacher planning, classroom cooperation.
Involves much teacher time, sensitivity, and firmness.	Makes materials and props more flexible.
Makes other children feel insecure.	Helps teachers and children learn and work cooperatively; promotes productivity.
Focuses teaching/learning time on less important matters.	Attention can be shared with all class members.
Can consume much time and energy.	
Attention may be focused on a few students.	

likely to show long-term negative consequences, and violence is frequently portrayed in a humorous context (see Figure 3.8).

The study gives the following recommendations:

For the Television Community:

1. Less violence
2. Increased portrayals of powerful nonviolent heroes and attractive characters
3. Scheduling high-violence shows in late-evening hours
4. Codes for types of programs
5. Advisory information in programming guides (which are revised periodically)
6. Limiting the time devoted to sponsor, station, or network during public service announcements

For Parents:

1. Watch TV with the child
2. Encourage discussion and evaluation of the program content
3. Consider the child's developmental level when selecting programs
4. Be aware of potential violence
5. Recognize that different kinds of violent programs pose different risks for each person

In addition to the TV guidelines just mentioned, parents should establish and follow rules for firearms within the home. Specific information and enforcement can prevent many accidental gunshot deaths involving young children. See Goble and Bomba (1995) for information and a handout for safety rules for parents.

Teachers can choose from a range of options (Carlsson-Paige & Levin, 1987), but none of them is perfect. What seems most important is to be aware of the options and implications of each approach so that you can adapt and change your approach as you try to meet the needs of everyone in your classroom.

With the Children:

1. Keep safety in your classroom as your prime guiding principle.

2. Plan a total curriculum that presents children with alternatives that resonate with their deep developmental needs and inspire dramatic and artistic recreations.

3. Help them be able to see problems from more than a single point of view and use skills for negotiation that go beyond stating ultimatums and bottom lines. Find solutions that can work in the end for everyone—not solutions in which there will be winners and losers. Introduce children to conflict-resolution skills in ways that they can understand and enjoy, thereby helping them grapple creatively with conflict and to make the kind of peace that can benefit everyone (Carlsson-Paige & Levin, 1992).

4. Talk with children on a regular basis about whatever approach you are taking in the classroom—sharing your reasons, as a teacher, and listening to children's thoughts and feelings and reasons for them.

5. Reach out to parents to involve them in discussions on the issue—through newsletters, meetings, workshops, and so on.

6. Regulate children's television programming to limit media exposure to violence and restrict practices that market violence through the linkup of media, toys, and licensed products (National Television Violence Study, 1996).

Manipulative toys can challenge creativity in children, encourage use of their small muscles, and promote comradeship.

7. NAEYC (1993) encourages commitment of members of the early-childhood profession to helping children cope with violence in their lives and promoting their resilience through partnerships with parents; early-childhood programs and curriculum; and professional preparation, development, and support (National Television Violence Study, 1996).

With Parents, Adults, and Community:

1. Speak out against violence and violent play for all ages by creating public awareness of the problems.

2. Write to producers and sponsors of TV shows, newspapers, magazines, toys, and others, stating your objections.

3. Join local and national organizations to fight violence.

4. Promote play, games, books, and other activities that show better ways of resolving problems.

5. Every sector of our society must assume some responsibility for the problem. Insist on policies that reduce the number of risk factors for all children, but especially for children from low-income families. Policies should target the greatest number of resources toward children in the preschool and elementary years, when children are most vulnerable to developmental damage as a result of exposure to violence (National Television Violence Study, 1996).

6. Allocate resources to prevention of violence.

7. Revitalize neighborhoods through ensuring peacekeeping and targeting the delivery of human services, such as job training, health care, early-childhood education programs, and parent education (National Television Violence Study, 1996).

8. Look for, read, and share antiviolence literature. One concentrated source of information appears in *Young Children*, July 1995, (50)5 where four viewpoints about violent play are discussed (Klemm, Carlsson-Paige & Levin, Kuykendall, and Greenberg).

Note to reader: If you are wondering why the play chapter is so long, it is because: (1) play is important in the life and development of the young child, (2) there are so many different aspects of the topic, (3) it is frequently misunderstood and underrated, and (4) *FOREMOST, it is the basis for the entire book.*

APPLICATION OF PRINCIPLES

1. Observe two or more children between the ages of 2 and 5. Note the type of play most frequently exhibited (solitary/with a companion, verbal/nonverbal, sharing/competitive, awareness/unawareness of others, and so on.

2. Discuss the motor, social-emotional, cognitive-language, and combined areas of development most common in children between the ages of 2 and 5. In which of the areas of development do you find it most difficult to see changes in the young child?

3. Through your observations of young children, describe how learning is manifested in play activities.

4. Discuss the role of competition for young children. Do you think it is a help or a hindrance in the child's development?

5. Name and implement ways to sustain children in their play without directing their activities.

6. Describe the stages and timing of play in young children.

7. Why is dramatic play important for young children?

8. What modifications need to be made for successful play of children with special needs?

9. How can children enhance their development through outdoor play?

10. How is violent play enacted by young children and how can a teacher or parent change it into productive, healthy play?

11. Carefully describe your personal feelings about play during the life cycle of an individual.

REFERENCES

Alber, J. L., D. M. Alber, D. R. Santoliquido, & D. Allen (1990). *Baby-safe houseplants and cut flowers.* Highland, IL: Genus Books, Box 351, 62249.

American Psychological Association (1993). Violence and youth: Psychology's response. *Summary report of the APA Commission on Violence and Youth,* Vol. 1. Washington, DC: Author.

Anselmo, S., & W. Franz (1995). *Early childhood development.* Englewood Cliffs, NJ: Merrill.

Aronson, S. (1992, May). Is playground safety being taken seriously? *Exchange,* (85), 47–48.

Bandura, A. (1973). *Aggression: Social learning analysis.* Englewood Cliffs, NJ: Prentice-Hall.

Bergen, D. (1994, Annual Theme). Should teachers permit or discourage violent play themes? *Childhood Education,* 300–302.

Berk, L. E., & A. Winsler (1995). *Scaffolding children's learning: Vygotsky and early childhood education. Research in Practice,* Vol. 7. Washington, DC: NAEYC.

Bredekamp, S. (ed.) (1987). *Developmentally appropriate practice in early childhood programs serving children from birth through age 8,* expanded edition. Washington, DC: NAEYC.

Bredekamp, S., & C. Copple (eds.) (1997). *Developmentally appropriate practice in early childhood programs,* revised edition. Washington, DC: NAEYC.

Bredekamp, S., & T. Rosegrand (eds.) (1992). *Reaching potentials: Appropriate curriculum and assessment for young children.* Vol. 1. Washington, DC: NAEYC.

Bronson, M. B. (1995). *The right stuff for children birth to 8: Selecting play materials to support development.* Washington, DC: NAEYC.

Brownell, C. A., & M. S. Carriger (1990). Changes in cooperation and self-other differentiation during the second year. *Child Development,* 61, 1164–1174.

Bruner, J. S. (1976). The nature and uses of immaturity. In Bruner, J. S., A. Jolly, & K. Sylva (eds.), *Play: Its role in development and evolution.* New York: Basic.

Caplan, F., & T. Caplan (1973). *The power of play.* Garden City, NY: Anchor.

Caplan, M., J. Vespo, J. Pedersen, and D. F. Hay (1991). Conflict and its resolution in small groups of one- and two-year-olds. *Child Development,* 62, 1513–1524.

Caplow, T., H. Bahr, & B. Chadwick (1989, May 26). Brigham Young University, *Y News,* 14(36).

Carlsson-Paige, N., & D. E. Levin (1987). *The war play dilemma: Balancing needs and values in the early childhood classroom.* New York: Teachers College Press.

Carlsson-Paige, N., & D. E. Levin (1992, November). Making peace in violent times: A constructivist approach to conflict resolution. *Young Children,* 48(1), 4–13.

Carlsson-Paige, N., & D. E. Levin (1995, July). Can teachers resolve the war-play dilemma? *Young Children,* 50(5), 62–63.

Christie, J. F., & F. Wardle (1992, March). How much time is needed for play? *Young Children,* 47(3), 28–32.

Craig, S. (1992). The educational needs of children living with violence. *Phi Delta Kappan,* 74(1), 67–71.

Davis, D. (1965). Play: A state of childhood. *Childhood Education,* 4(4), 222–244.

Ditchburn, S. J. (1988, December). Conflict management in young children's play. *International Journal of Early Childhood* (OMEP), 20(2), 62–70.

Duffy, V. M. (1991, January/February). Who are our heroes? *Exchange* (77), 45.

Eibl-Eibesfeldt, I. (1970). *Ethology: The biology of behavior.* New York: Holt, Rinehart & Winston.

Erikson, E. H. (1950). *A healthy personality for your child.* Midcentury White House Conference on Children and Youth, December 1950. Washington, DC: U.S. Government Printing Office.

Erikson, E. H. (1977). *Toys and reasons.* New York: Norton.

Frank, L. K. (1968, March). Play is valid. *Childhood Education,* 44, 433–440.

Froebel, F. (1975). *The education of man.* New York: Appleton.

Frost, J. L. (1992). *Play and playscapes.* Albany, NY: Delmar.

Garbarino, J., N. Dubrow, K. Kostelny, & C. Pardo (1992). *Children in danger: Dealing with the effects of community violence.* San Francisco: Jossey-Bass.

Garvey, C. (1990). *Play.* Cambridge, MA: Harvard University Press.

Goble, C. B., & A. K. Bomba (1995, January). A parent meeting: Young children and firearm safety. *Young Children,* 50(2), 81.

Gowan, J. W. (1995, March). The early development of symbolic play. *Young Children,* 50(3), 75–83.

Greenberg, J. (1995, July). Making friends with the Power Rangers. *Young Children,* 50(5), 60–61.

Groves, B. M., & S. Mazur. (1995). Shelter from the storm: Using the classroom to help children cope with violence. *Child Care Information Exchange,* 102(3), 47–49.

Henniger, M. (1987, February). Learning mathematics and science through play. *Childhood Education,* 63(3), 167–171.

Hymes, J. L. Jr. (1981). *Teaching the child under six.* Columbus, OH: Merrill.

Kagan, S. L. (1990). Children's play: The journey from theory to practice. In Klugman, E., & S. Smilansky (eds.), *Children's play and learning: Perspectives and policy implications*, 173–185. New York: Teachers College Press.

Kuykendall, J. (1995, July). Is gun play OK here? *Young Children*, 50(5), 56–59.

Landscape Structures, Inc. (1992, Summer). *Child's play: A newsletter about outdoor play for the child care industry.* Issue 2, p. 1. 601 7th Street, South, Delano, MN 55328.

Landscape Structures, Inc. (1992, Fall). *Now CPSC has guidelines for child care centers.* Issue 3, p. 1. 601 7th Street, South, Delano, MN 55328.

Lead toxicity: Is your program at risk? (1992, September). *Young Children* 47(6), 35.

Levin, D. E., & N. Carlsson-Paige (1995, September). The Mighty Morphin Power Rangers: Teachers voice concern. *Young Children*, 50(6), 67–71.

Levy, A. K. (1984). The language of play: The role of play in language development. *Early Child Development and Care*, 17, 49–62.

Lovell, P. & T. Harms. (1985, March). Can playgrounds be improved? A rating scale. *Young Children*, 40(3), 3–8.

Marcus, R. F. (1987). The role of affect in children's cooperation. *Child Study Journal*, 17(2), 153–168.

Montessori, M. (1964). *The Montessori method.* New York: Schocken.

Moyer, J., H. Egertson, & J. Isenberg (1987, April). The child centered kindergarten. *Childhood Education*, 235–242.

NAEYC position statement on violence in the lives of children (1993, September). *Young Children*, 48(6), 80–84.

National Paint and Coatings Association. *Lead and Your Child's Safety.* (N.D.). Washington, D.C.

National Television Violence Study: Key findings and recommendations (1996, March). *Young Children*, 51(3), 54–55.

Nourot, P. M., & J. L. Van Hoorn (1991, September). Research in review: Symbolic play in preschool and primary settings. *Young Children*, 46(6), 40–50.

Oden, S. (1982). Peer relationship development in childhood. In Katz, L. G. (ed.), *Current topics in early childhood education*, Vol. 4. Norwood, NJ: Ablex.

Parten, M. (1932–33). Social participation among preschool children. *Journal of Abnormal and Social Psychology*, 27, 243–269.

Piaget, J. (1962). *Play, dreams, and imitation in childhood.* New York: Norton.

Piaget, J. (1963). *The origin of intelligence in children.* New York: Norton.

Piaget, J. (1973). *To understand is to invent: The future of education.* New York: Grossman.

Quay, L. C., J. H. Weaver, & J. H. Neel (1986). The effects of play materials on positive and negative social behaviors in preschool boys and girls. *Child Study Journal*, 16(1), 67–76.

Read, K., P. Gardner, & B. C. Mahler (1987). *Early childhood programs: Human relationships and learning*, 8th edition. New York: Holt, Rinehart & Winston.

Remley, A. (1988, October). From obedience to independence. *Psychology Today*, 5–59.

Rivkin, M. S. (1995). *The great outdoors: Restoring children's right to play outside.* Washington, DC: NAEYC.

Ross, H. S., & S. P. Lollis (1989). A social relations analysis of toddler peer relationships. *Child Development*, 60, 1082–1091.

Rothlein, L., & A. Brett (1987, March). Children's, teachers', and parents' perceptions of play. *Early Childhood Research Quarterly*, 2(1), 45–53.

Rutter, M. (1979). Protective factors in children's responses to stress and disadvantage. In Kent, M. W., & J. E. Rolf (eds.), *Primary prevention of psychopathology: Social competence in children*, Vol. 3, 49–74. Hanover, NH: University Press of New England.

Selman, R. L., & A. Demorest (1984). Observing troubled children's interpersonal negotiation strategies: Implications of and for a developmental model. *Child Development*, 55(1), 288–304.

Simmons, B. (1983). Children's play: A basic ingredient of learning. In Vernon, L., et al. (eds.), *Early learning: A life-long legacy.* Texas Elementary/Kindergarten/Nursery Education Association.

Simmons, B., & J. Brewer (1985). When parents of kindergartners ask why? *Childhood Education*, 61(3), 177–184.

Smilansky, S., & L. Shefatya (1990). *Facilitating play: A medium for promoting cognitive, socio-emotional and academic development in young children.* Gaithersburg, MD: Psychosocial and Educational Publications.

Soderman, K. K. (1984, March). Schooling all 4-year-olds: An idea full of promise, fraught with pitfalls. *Education Week*, 14, 19.

Taylor, B. J. (1997). *Early childhood program management: People and procedures*, 3rd edition, 459–460. New York: Macmillan.

Torbert, M. (1980). *Follow me, too: Handbook of movement activities for 3–5 year olds.* Reading, MA: Addison-Wesley.

Trawick-Smith, J. (1988). "Let's say you're the baby, OK?" Play leadership and following behavior of young children. *Young Children*, 43(5), 51–59.

U.S. Consumer Products Safety Commission. Washington, DC 20207. 1-800-638-2772.

Van Hoorn, J., P. Nourot, B. Scales, & K. Alward (1993). *Play at the center of the curriculum.* Upper Saddle River, NJ: Prentice-Hall.

Vygotsky, L. S. (1976). Play and its role in the mental development of the child. In Bruner, J., A. Jolly, & K. Sylva (eds.), *Play: Its role in development and evolution.* New York: Basic.

Vygotsky, L. S. (1978). *Mind in society: The development of higher psychological processes.* Cambridge, MA: Harvard University Press.

Wardle, F. (1991, May/June). Are we shortchanging boys? *Exchange*, 79, 48–51.

Werner, E. E. (1990). Protective factors and individual resilience. In Meisels, S. J., & J. P. Shonkoff (eds.), *Handbook of early childhood education*, 97–116. Cambridge, England: Cambridge University Press.

Werner, H., & B. Kaplan (1963). *Symbol formation*. New York: Wiley.

Williams, N. (1992, August). The physical education hall of shame. *Journal of Physical Education, Recreation & Dance*.

Curriculum Development

CHAPTER 4

MAIN PRINCIPLES

To plan properly for young children, a teacher needs to do the following:

1. Understand how and what young children should learn.
2. Support good curriculum planning principles.
3. Be able to define *webbing* and show how to effectively use it with young children.
4. Know the developmental and individual characteristics of children at each age level.
5. Establish educational goals for the children and teachers.
6. Respect and value each child.
7. Understand the role of the teacher.
8. Perfect, execute, and evaluate good planning skills.
9. Take teaching and planning as an important privilege and a serious responsibility.
10. Value parents and keep them informed about their child and school activities.

In her teaching, "the teacher must attend to what she knows about the prior learning of the children in the group so that she can teach in their *zone of proximal development* (Vygotsky 1978), that is, the range of tasks that the child cannot yet handle alone but can accomplish with the help of adults or more skilled peers" (Berk, 1994).

"The process of learning is complex and has been described in many ways. One helpful way of thinking about learning is to visualize the process as 'a recurring cycle that begins in awareness and moves to exploration, to inquiry, and finally, to utilization'" (NAEYC & NAECS/SDE, 1991, pp. 32–36). "This cycle is not developmental in the pure sense of the word because it is similar for children and adults when they acquire new knowledge or skill" (Bredekamp & Rosegrant, 1995, p. 19). "Curriculum decisions not only involve questions of *how* children learn, but also *what* learning is appropriate and *when* it is best learned" (Katz & Chard, 1989).

The NAEYC and NAECS/SDE (1991) have identified some theoretical perspectives on development learning that acknowledge many theories of learning and development with various explanations of phenomena. Specifically, early-childhood professionals have found some theories to be more comprehensive, explanatory, and useful than others, such as Piaget (1952), Vygotsky (1978), and Erikson (1963), and have used these theories to inform their document (NAEYC & NAECS/SDE, 1991, p. 24). (For more information on these theorists, see Chapters 1 and 3 and Appendix A.)

The NAEYC and NAECS/SDE document identifies specifically:

1. *How* children best learn:
   a. when their physical needs are met and they feel psychologically safe and secure (p. 25)
   b. when they construct knowledge
   c. through social interaction with adults and other children
   d. when learning reflects a recurring cycle that begins in awareness and moves to exploration, to inquiry, and finally, to utilization (p. 26)
   e. through play
   f. when their interests and "need to know" motivate learning
   g. by individual variation (p. 27)

2. *What* children should learn (most important or worthy): The foundation for developmentally appropriate practice advocated here and elsewhere relates to at least two of Eisner's conceptions of curriculum (1990); (a) it promotes the development of cognitive processes and (b) it also emphasizes the role of personal relevance in curriculum decisions.

3. *How* definitions clarify (summarized in NAEYC and NAESC/SDE, 1991):

   Curriculum is an organized framework that delineates the content children are to learn, the processes through which children achieve the identified curricular goals, what teachers do to help children achieve these goals, and the context in which teaching and learning occur. The early childhood profession defines curriculum in its broadest sense, encompassing prevailing theories, approaches, and models.

   Assessment is the process of observing, recording and otherwise documenting the work children do and why they do it, as a basis for a variety of educational decisions that affect the child, including planning for groups and individual children, and communicating with parents. Assessment encompasses the many forms of evaluation available to educational decision makers. Assessment in the service of curriculum and learning requires teachers to observe and analyze regularly what the children are doing in light of the content goals and the learning processes. (pp. 21–22)

However, the dominant rationale for the kind of child-centered, experiential learning advocated here is its consistency with democratic values. NAEYC clearly acknowledges that the principles of practice it espouses have their roots in Dewey's vision of school and society (Bredekamp, 1987, p. 66).

CURRICULUM DEVELOPMENT

It is somewhat unrealistic to think that there is a specific course of study in early childhood. Of course, there are some theories and programs that have specific lock-step study programs. But when one believes in developmentally appropriate curriculum for children of specific ages and interests, that is the curriculum. We look at children individually and collectively and discover that there are some common interests and some unique interests. So one begins thinking about curriculum by watching the children as they play and by listening to their comments and conversations. Curriculum is happening all around the home, the school, the playground, and wherever young children gather. Perceptive teachers can help enrich and enhance what is happening.

"In early childhood education, curriculum isn't the focus, children are. It's easy for teachers to get hooked on *curriculum* because it's so much more manageable than children. But curriculum is *what happens* in an educational environment—not what is rationally planned to happen, but what actually takes place" (Jones & Nimmo, 1994, p. 12). Teachers can set the classroom stage for different types of play and activities, but the children are the ones who make the production. Most preschool teachers do not write or expect typical school-type lesson plans to be effective with young children. They may follow a format (perhaps a theme, learning activities, classroom arrangement, sequencing, and so on) but these items should be skeletal and flexible. Writing the plan after the day's activities would be more productive than writing it before the action begins. An *emergent curriculum* is in continuous revision. What works one day, or with one group of children, may be entirely inappropriate another day or with another group of children. Flexibility on the part of teachers, availability of resources for quick revisions, and active children make for exciting and active classrooms.

Van Hoorn et al. identify three types of curriculum: (1) *play-generated curriculum,* which emerges directly from teacher observations of the interests and themes of the children; (2) *curriculum-generated curriculum,* which leads the teacher to include materials or techniques that he suspects will match the spontaneous interest of the children; and (3) *recasting the curriculum* through play, in which the teacher provides opportunities and asks questions that encourage children to use newly constructed knowledge derived from the curriculum in their play. This aspect of play is very important (1993, pp. 60–61).

Bruner (1963) coined the term *spiral curriculum* to represent the idea that at many stages of their development, children may grasp basic concepts, each time returning to the same ideas at a more sophisticated level of understanding. This aspect of play is important in children's development.

Emergent Curriculum

The term *emergent curriculum* was introduced by Betty Jones in her introduction to the NAEYC publication *Curriculum Is What Happens,* edited by Laura Dittmann in 1970. Emphasis was given to each word in the term: *emergent* emphasizes that planning comes from children's own interests and spontaneity; *curriculum* conveys that planning occurs. Both aspects of emergent curriculum—spontaneity and planning—were brought forth in her text. And simply put, "emergent curriculum asks that we be responsible to particular people, in a particular place, at a particular time."

It would be difficult to identify the original source of most of our planning—it grows from every possible source as we try to invent functional systems for needed resources. Emergent curriculum is sensible but not predictable. It would be wrong to assume that everything simply emerges from the children—their ideas are extremely important but just one of many possible sources. Emergent curriculum is a continuous revision process of what is actually happening, but a responsible adult organizes, sets the stage, and keeps the production on track (Jones & Nimmo, 1994, p. 12).

The children are always the focus of attention in early-childhood education programs, and curriculum is what takes place in that environment. Teachers who prepare the physical environment to respond to children have the basis for interaction with materials, individuals, and ideas. To get your children acquainted with the outdoor playground or the indoor play areas, try a scavenger hunt, as described in Figure 4.1.

In your planning, include rules for behavior and rules for using materials and toys. Children need genuine rules for safety as well as opportunities for responding to the democratic rights of a group. "Taking into account individual and cultural differences may, at times, override the need to be universally consistent in the application of preset rules in group care and education" (Jones & Nimmo, 1994, p. 24). Unless we can look into a crystal ball and see how children and situations evolve, we need to anticipate revising rules as children mature, experience, and learn. This involves negotiation, risk taking, and willingness to deal with complexity. When safety is threatened, children need the security of clear limits, as well as when fairness and a sense of community call for a rule evenly applied (p. 24).

Children may improvise their own uses of materials.

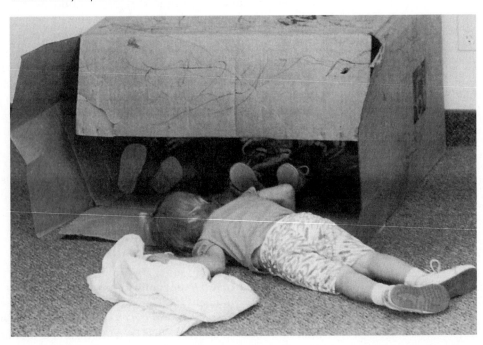

Figure 4.1
Scavenger Hunt on Your Playground

Look for things that:
- need repair (toys, equipment, swings, fences, and so on)
- are dangerous (open gates, nails, unattended swings, and so on)
- people can move (shovel, ball, boxes, toys, and so on)
- can move people (wagon, swing, wheels, and so on)
- are made of a certain material (wood, fabric, plastic)
- are favorite toys of children
- children can climb (slide, climber, hill)
- water can be used with (buckets, washing equipment, water fountain)
- are shady (under tree, in shed, under bushes)
- have a certain texture (rough, smooth, soft, and so on)

Suggest some curriculum activities based on the hunt.
Try a spin-off for your indoor play spaces.

(The scavenger hunt idea is suggested by Jones & Nimmo, 1994, p. 21. This example is original.)

Try one of the following to acquaint children with the physical environment, safety rules, participation, or interaction:

- Introduce a new toy, game, procedure, field trip, and so on.

- Encourage the children to help set rules or limits. Consider appropriate praise or restrictions. What should we do when children follow the rules? What should we do when children do not follow the rules? Do we need to re-think our plan: too many things to consider, too many new things, or inflexible expectations of children's responses?

- Prepare some sensory stimulation experiences for the children. Include items that are hard/soft, wet/dry, cold/warm, pleasurable/annoying, odorous/non-odorous, loud/soft, sweet/sour, smooth/rough, movable/stable, and so on. Omit anything *harmful*. Stimulate various senses.

Sensory stimulation can help a child to learn about her environment. There are some qualities or textures that we want in a child-care setting. For example, softness can be in furnishings (furniture, wall hangings, floor coverings, toys, or other items). In the outdoors, there may be grass, sand, dirt, and so on. Manipulative materials may be messy, rough, soft, fluid, hard, or other textures. Quiet places are likely to have soft, cuddly materials; loud places may include blocks, riding toys, digging, or other activities. Objects and materials that respond to the senses are very important for young children.

Flexibility in Planning

A truly appropriate curriculum will not look the same from one classroom of children to the next, from one school district to another, from one year to the next, or for teachers who have used the topic or information before—to be a duplicate would violate the philosophy of being developmentally appropriate for the children within the present classroom. However, early-childhood teachers can benefit from the experiences of other teachers, classrooms, printed material, or strategies if proper adjustment has been made for current children and classrooms. A curriculum is "grass roots" in the sense that it is responsible to the "common people" (the children, the teachers, the parents, and others) (Cassidy & Lancaster, 1993, p. 47).

At the beginning of the school year, or at any time during the year, teachers may put emphasis on the classroom atmosphere (attendance, playmates, rules, weather, playground, or other elements). Later, she may try to "web" earlier curriculum into additional meaningful experiences, such as rearranging the playground, creating new combinations of friends, or providing additional cooking or other experiences. Or the teacher may prepare (or substitute) new items for an "interest" table to encourage exploration by the children. Some materials and toys may remain in the classroom on a semipermanent basis. Units and themes emerge from use of items rather than from a pre-planned length of time. Popularity of ideas may change as children use or ignore them.

Spodek (1973) made some interesting observations and concluded the following about rigid or stereotyped planning:

1. Themes, as traditionally implemented, proved to be limiting and counterproductive to the task at hand.

2. The cookbook approach to curriculum planning was ineffective in planning developmentally appropriate curriculum.

3. Activities that were age appropriate existed within the teachers' repertoire of ideas . . . but the teachers didn't have specific information about what the individuals in the classroom needed or were interested in until they had an opportunity to observe and interact with the children on a daily basis.

4. Although child observation formed the foundation of the curriculum, the curriculum was neither prescriptive nor reactive in nature but rather *interactive*—a dialogue between teachers and children.

5. Observations were affected by teacher bias. (p. 84)

Appendix B, Suggested Curriculum Topics, and Appendix C, Suggested Miniplans for Curriculum Chapters, are intended as "stimulators" or beginning points for classroom focus or webbing purposes.

To include flexibility in the curriculum, the teacher need look no further than observations of the children. They have some interests in common; yet at times they have totally diverse interests. At any rate, their use of materials, their conversation, their response to others, their sustained or divided interests, and their mortality add humor, seriousness, interest, and diversity. Children make a major contribution to the curriculum, but not the sole contribution. Teachers clearly are decision makers in this process.

Documenting comments of children, uses of materials, input from parents, spin-offs to other topics, better notes, or other information (a valued practice in Reggio Emilia classrooms) helps teachers have a more solid basis upon which to introduce or expand a particular topic at other times.

Appropriate Group and Individual Curriculum

As teachers consider topics for classroom use, they should carefully consider the values of the school, community, family, and culture. The children themselves initiate play or suggest ideas that may be timely and urgent, or temporary and fleeting. Their ideas should be considered and valued; however, teachers should carefully justify topics for group exploration. For example, some children may be frightened while others express defiance through mass media or toys that expose unwholesome themes (see the section titled "Violent Play" in Chapter 3). Teachers need to assess the potential of any interest for in-depth learning by both the individual child and other members of the adult-child classroom community. Teachers of young children also need to contemplate topics that support hands-on experiences (local geography, current events, family values) and leave more abstract teaching (outer space or unfamiliar land/water phenomena, for example) until the children are better able to handle them. In other words, focus on the child, the family, the school, the community, and the immediate environment before introducing topics that even adults shy away from. If something is of present interest, such as the discovery of the world's largest spider in the fall of 1996, address it and the children's questions and interest, and then move on.

Watch for the children who are not interested in available topics or materials. What hands-on activities could interest them? How could the topic be woven into something in which the child has interest? What could this child add that would be of value to the other children? Watch also for the interests of children as individuals

Equipment placed in a different locale can encourage new playmates and themes.

and as group members. Plan activities in which they can take active part—find a book, bring in items for dramatic play, combine activities and materials, encourage group activities, or provide props where the child can independently explore without disturbing others.

Curriculum Negotiations

Teachers do decide some aspects of curriculum; however, its use, frequency, and popularity will be determined by the children. Teachers who maintain structured classrooms may offer only one choice—and where this happens, some children may elect the "not-to-do" option (Herndon, 1968). Others will try to do, and fail; others—the majority, if the teacher has planned appropriately—will succeed.

When teachers make a conscious effort to negotiate the curriculum (Jones & Nimmo, 1994, p. 48; Katz & Chard, 1989), "there are likely to be planned discussions between teacher and children: What do you already know about this? What do you want to learn? With younger children, however, negotiation often appropriately takes the form of action rather than discussion. The teacher provides ideas and materials, but the children ignore them to pursue their own ideas. Deciding when to insist, when to try it another way, and when to let go of one's plans altogether is a never-ending challenge for the teacher of young children" (Jones & Nimmo, 1994, p. 48).

Some teachers plan together, perhaps for the same classroom or different ones. While they may not necessarily agree on what to provide, how much, when, what limitations, or other items, dialogue among teachers can be a significant source of mutual learning. This practice is strongly emphasized in the child-care centers of Reggio Emilia. It characterizes in-depth emergent curriculum.

Curriculum "Requirements"

A less-than-ideal teaching situation is one in which curriculum "requirements" are imposed. "Cookbooks" seldom fit the needs of the individual children. The terms suggested by Jones & Nimmo (1994, p. 77) for this type of teaching are amusing and appropriate:

> Canned: curriculum from the district, the state, the textbooks, workbooks, and tests; intended to be "teacher-proof."
>
> Embalmed: total of teacher's materials and years of experience—unmodified.
>
> Accidental/unidentified: curriculum just happens, and no one names it or follows up on it.
>
> Emergent: curriculum is more work, more fun, and a value choice.

In a speech given to and published by NAEYC, Margaret Mead (1973) described a pre-planned, rational curriculum as "the transcendent boredom—to be shut up in a room, away from anything that moves or breathes or grows, in a controlled temperature, hour after hour after hour—means that we are taking away from them any kind of chance of responsiveness." "When this occurs, it is a problem shared by teachers and children alike. Teachers shouldn't model giving in; they should model intelligent problem solving" (reported in Jones & Nimmo, 1994, p. 77).

Good Ideas Flow Freely

Most adults who think "open-endedly" find more ideas than they can ever use in their daily teaching. Rather than overload the children with too many ideas, not enough time to use them, and cursory examination, some adults have to consciously let go of some ideas—there will be other times and other children who can benefit from new ideas (including those from the children).

In the Reggio Emilia approach, in the planning stages, adults discuss various possibilities, hypotheses, and potential directions that the project might take (Rankin, 1993, p. 192). "Isolating a teacher in a classroom and giving her or him a prescribed curriculum that presents only one hypothesis at a time is the opposite approach to ensuring quality in education. It assumes the possibility of 'teacher-proof' canned curriculum rather than reliance on teachers' continuing growth as the source of quality" (Jones & Nimmo, 1994, p. 51).

Some Topics Cause Negative Emotions

At Reggio Emilia, teachers actually plan activities and experiences knowing that they may worry or frighten some children. When asked why they would purposefully provide such an experience, the explanation, simply enough, was that children need opportunities, within the safety of the group setting, to understand and learn how to cope with their own and others' feelings. "The American preoccupation with protecting young children from experiencing negative emotions is a marked contrast to this practice," describes New (1993, p. 226).

Instead of intensifying a fear (of darkness, animals, water, people, or whatever), adults can help children to understand other aspects of the fear: What is interesting, different, useful, beautiful, and so on? How could one harmoniously deal with the fear? If one pays close attention, what will one find out?

Teaching "Touchy" Topics

No matter what the subject, the educational setting, or the political or religious orientation of the locality, some topics will raise "red flags" for some parents, students, and others. Refer to Chapter 10, Social Studies, Anti-Bias Curriculum, and Field Trips.

Teachers are always cautious about teaching subjects that may need discretion, sensitivity, poise, accuracy, and other considerations. Some particular topics may be special occasions (holidays), religion, race, violence, food habits, and customs. When or if these topics are taught, they should be done with respect and accuracy and geared to the level of the children in the immediate setting. Some topics can be taught separately; some must include a combination of ideas to give a complete picture. Most of the teaching decisions will be determined by school or government policies, personal feelings of teachers and parents, allotted classroom time, community pressure, or other limitations.

Curriculum Interests

Teachers, inexperienced and experienced, are sometimes perplexed about what to provide for young children: something new, something based on a former topic (emergent curriculum), something children suggest, something they have always wanted to try, something "way out." If you are "stumped," try using your imagination and props at hand to set up an *exploration space*. You might use table, floor, or wall space to display a number of replicas or real objects—for example, a plastic alligator, a large feather, real vegetables or fruits, hats, some straw, a piece of foam, seeds, a hula hoop, a peanut in a shell, a stuffed animal, a totally unfamiliar object, a holiday symbol (mask, basket, flag), a photograph of a person or location in the community; you can add more. Select ideas that are *open-ended* and are *starting points*, characteristics of emergent curriculum. Stand back and watch, or better still, have someone tape the responses of the children so you have a permanent, accurate record, whether there is much or little reaction. Always be alert to unexpected events. Documentation can be the driving force behind your curriculum development.

For additional value of the exploration space, plan on webbing ideas so that the children will see ideas as connecting and supporting entities rather than just separate bits, pieces, or time consumers. (See the section titled "Curriculum Webbing" later in this chapter.)

A developmentally appropriate (emergent) curriculum is a result of interaction between teachers and children, who both contribute ideas and react to them. Curriculum reflects both children's interests and adults' interests and values. "Units" in a developmentally appropriate classroom are not pre-planned activity segments with a standard time length. Themes that emerge from brainstorming, an event, or introduction of materials are interconnected and flow from one to the other as children ask questions and develop new interests (Cassidy & Lancaster, 1993).

Some values of children may be at odds with the values of the adults in their lives (violent play or war play, for example). When this happens, Carlsson-Paige and Levin (1987) offer four options: (1) ban the play, (2) permit or ignore the play, (3) permit the play with specific limits, or (4) actively facilitate the play. They further suggest that the teacher might try to "bring in new content for the play, such as new props, roles, and physical settings, which grow out of current content and will help children vary and elaborate the play. This is especially important for those children who seem to be following a television script or acting out the same theme over and over in the same way." For further discussion on violence and war play, see the section titled "Violent Play" in Chapter 3.

Some teachers fill their walls with commercial or teacher-made patterns thinking they will stimulate interest in learning. Rather, children's creative work, documentation of prior activities, and items of interest (another important feature of Reggio Emilia classrooms) should adorn the classroom because of child pleasure, parent awareness and support, and further stimulation for teaching.

Curriculum Selection

Those who work in programs with other adults find collaboration very helpful; however, those who work in isolated family child care, one-classroom sites, or centers have no interaction and often find planning difficult and challenging.

Sources of emergent curriculum include the interests of children and teachers; developmental tasks; things and people in the physical environment; curriculum resource materials; unexpected events; relationships with others; and values held in the school, community, family, and culture (Jones & Nimmo, 1994, p. 127). Other sources of stimulation, encouragement, and support come from the children and parents. A resource book is available (Jones, 1993). For stimulating discussions of values and curriculum, see Kessler (1991) and Bredekamp (1991).

When selecting curriculum for the classroom, teachers should ask themselves questions about the worth of the content (Is it meaningful and relevant?), whether it will be firsthand or vicarious, whether it is accurate and credible according to the recognized standards of relevant disciplines, whether there are realistic and attainable expectations, and whether the timing is better now or after other skills have been acquired (Bredekamp & Rosegrant, 1995, p. 15).

"Narrowing the curriculum to those basic skills that can be easily measured on multiple-choice tests diminishes the intellectual challenge for many children. Such intellectually impoverished curriculum underestimates the true competence of children, which has been demonstrated to be much higher than is often assumed (Gelman & Baillargeon 1983; Gelman & Meck 1983; Edwards, Gandini, & Forman 1993; Resnick 1996)" (Bredekamp & Copple, 1997, p. 20).Bredekamp and Copple (1997) provide the following guidelines for decisions about developmentally appropriate practices:

1. Teachers must integrate the many dimensions of their knowledge base: (a) child development, (b) how to teach, (c) what to teach, (d) how to assess what children have learned, and (e) knowing the particular children they teach and their families.

2. The curriculum guidelines, each carefully defined, address five interrelated dimensions of early-childhood professional practice: (a) creating a caring community of learners, (b) teaching to enhance development and learning, (c) constructing appropriate curriculum, (d) assessing children's development and learning, and (e) establishing reciprocal relationships with families (pp. 16-21).

Criticisms of Developmentally Appropriate Practices

When new programs, guidelines, or policy statements are presented, questions, objections, misinterpretations, and/or modifications often arise. The broad assumptions and definitions of "developmentally appropriate practices" given in Chapter 1 were such an example.

A discussion by Kostelnik (and others) (1992) put inaccuracies to rest, concluding:

While teachers carefully consider long-range objectives, their moment-to-moment decision-making remains fluid in order to capitalize on input from the children. Children ask questions, suggest alternatives, express interests and develop plans that may lead the instruction in new directions. (p. 22)

Curriculum Content and Assessment by NAEYC and NAECS/SDE

NAEYC and NAECS/SDE (1991) have defined curriculum content and assessment and have developed guidelines that reflect key points in deciding appropriate curriculum content and assessment for young children. Thinking about their framework and using it as a tool for analyzing and conceptualizing appropriate curriculum expectations for individuals and groups of children, early-childhood educators and curriculum developers can better prepare for their daily work with children (NAEYC & NAECS/SDE, 1991).

Standardized Testing

Standardized tests, especially for young children, have been under fire currently, periodically, and continually. Some teachers devise their own methods of evaluating children and have difficulty in administering mandatory tests. What do they mean anyway? The condition of the room, the health and attitude of the child, external pressures (parents, peers, school, geographical location), and many other variables determine the child's performance. Tests for young children cannot be watered-down versions of tests for older children. NAEYC and NAECS/SDE have identified assessment measures for use with young children.

Testing can be a very powerful tool; it has "the power to change teachers' and children's perceptions of themselves and their view of the entire educational process. Teachers and researchers have studied this phenomenon extensively (see Bredekamp & Rosegrant, 1992), but our daily experience provides the most convincing evidence about how powerful tests have become" (Meisels, 1993, p. 35). And further, "group-administered tests focus on the acquisition of simple facts, low-level skills, superficial memorization, and isolated evidence of achievement. Of greatest concern, they rob teachers of their sense of judgment—of how to help children develop to their optimal potential (see Jervis, 1991)."

Assessing Young Children

One contemporary assessment approach for preschool through third grade asks teachers to use checklists to enhance the process of observation and make it more reliable (Meisels, 1993, p. 35). It covers the domains of personal and social development, language and literature, mathematical and scientific thinking, social studies, art and music, and physical development. Each child has a summary report completed during fall, winter, and spring that includes brief summaries of the child's classroom performance, based on teacher observations and records, and is transformed from the checklists into easily understood and interpreted documents for parents, teachers, and administrators.

In order to make any assessment meaningful, teachers must learn to become astute observers—knowing what to look for, what it means, and how to interpret it to others. Parents also become a part of the assessment process. They can be guided to see that standardized tests and typical report cards are poor substitutes for observations and participation of teachers and parents. Parents can also become more involved in their children's school behaviors, activities, and accomplishments.

CURRICULUM WEBBING

Semantic webbing, especially the integration and connections among webs, may become the central feature of any curricular approach. Developmentally appropriate activities and outcomes for children result from teachers responding to the children's interests. The preschooler thinks about the world primarily in terms of actions that can be performed, so the choice of concepts must provide for action-oriented, child-initiated plans and activities; "by working with several webs simultaneously, children are encouraged to see connections among concepts," write Workman & Anziano (1993, p. 5).

Creating a curriculum web is based on a well-used concept in early-childhood education circles: building on interests of children and their existing

Teachers are always seeking new ways to interact with and involve children.

knowledge. Basic concepts should include topics that are manageable, related to one another, part of a cycle, and universal (Workman & Anziano, 1993). The natural interrelations among these webs support the developmental interaction approach of Biber (1977), who, along with others, has advocated for preschool curricula in which cognitive, affective, and social processes are all interdependent.

For example, suppose a child brings a cocoon to school. Beginning with the cocoon, diagram the many events and ideas that could lead up to the cocoon in its present form. Then sketch what will happen to the cocoon as it matures. How many ideas can be created that would be developmentally appropriate for 2-, 3-, 4-, or 5-year-old children, or children of mixed ages?

How many different curriculum areas could be involved (language, creativity, music/movement, science, social studies [visitors or field trips], mathematics, food, and so on)? After brainstorming by yourself, ask an adult to contribute, and then ask preschool children to "think" with you. How do the ideas expand or change as other individuals share their ideas? What ideas could be tried in your classroom?

Now think of an item that has been brought to school by a child or contributed by an adult. How did you go about incorporating it into your classroom curriculum? How did you expand upon it—or did you use it just once—possibly without prior planning or follow-up? What happened when you ignored an item or event completely?

Reflection

"From the very beginning their educational experiences must enable children to:
- be knowledgeable, be able to learn, and continue to learn even more about themselves and the world in which they live;

  think, learn to make decisions, and experience the consequences of these decisions; and

  learn to become a member of a group and to feel a oneness with others."
  (Seefeldt, 1993, p. 4)

A curriculum that does not originate from the children, their interests, their needs, or their "own environment, whatever or wherever it may be" (Mitchell, 1934, p. 16) has little chance of being meaningful for children.

Without meaning, children are ill able to construct the type of knowledge that promotes freedom of mind. "Knowledge needs to be made meaningful in order to be made critical and transformative" (Giroux, 1992, p. 9).

Curriculum that enables children to construct knowledge that will free them to learn today and tomorrow stems from knowledge of each child and the environment in which he lives, as well as knowledge of subject matter. Teachers "study relations in the environment into which children are born and watch children's behavior in their environment to note when they first discover relations and what they are" (Mitchell, 1934, p. 12).

Teachers must study the goals of the classroom to determine the best ways to introduce experiences to the young children. They will find ways to introduce the key concepts of a given discipline (Bruner, 1966) through their experiences with the environment.

"Each teacher and each school will make its own curriculum for small children," records Mitchell (1934, p. 12).

When curriculum addresses the culture and heritage of the children, their interests and needs, it also addresses their environment. Thus they make sense of their world and their personal lives. Meaningful knowledge satisfies children's need for mastery today and may be the only knowledge that will enable them, in the future, to "reach beyond themselves, to wonder, to imagine, to pose their own questions" (Greene, 1988) and to continue to want to learn (Workman & Anziano, 1993, p. 6).

Young Children, Peers, and Adults

If a child is to keep alive his inborn sense of wonder without any such gift from the fairies, he needs the companionship of at least one adult who can share it, rediscovering with him the *joy*, excitement, and mystery of the world we live in. . . . [I]t is not half so important to *know* as to *feel*. . . . (Carson, 1956, pp. 42–45)

There are times when children need to depend on adults to guide their thinking, decisions, and actions; however, under the right circumstances, children need to make decisions for themselves. In quality education programs, young children are given at least partial responsibility for making personal decisions and the opportunity to experience the consequences of their decisions. This enables them to develop the ability to think and decide for themselves throughout the day. Yet Dewey

(1944) believed that another type of decision-making experience was necessary if children were to develop minds that would enable them to be free. In an attempt to push children into true decision making and thinking, Dewey called for classroom use of raw materials (those without any predetermined end or goal, such as blocks, clay, paper and paints, sand, water, boxes, and so on—which he labeled "stuff"). The children were to decide what to do with the materials and when their goals with the materials had been achieved. Achievement of their goals, determined only by themselves, brought joy and satisfaction; failure meant personal adjustment to their plans and actions. "Workbook sheets, workbooks, computer-assisted instruction, even units of group projects that are determined and directed by a teacher do not permit thinking because often much of the doing has been completed by someone else. There is little left for the child to decide or think about. . . . [W]ithout a solid foundation of decision making built during early childhood, children will be ill prepared to set goals for themselves and achieve these but may be ready and prepared to achieve goals established for them by others" (Workman & Anziano, 1993, p. 7).

Classrooms should be arranged to sustain greater individualization on one hand and a broad sense of community on the other (Dewey, 1944; Greenberg, 1992). Opportunities for formal give-and-take with others are arranged "because one cannot share in intercourse with others without learning—without getting a broader point of view and perceiving things of which one would otherwise be ignorant" (Dewey, 1944, p. 123). Through naturally occurring interchanges, children are challenged to adjust their egocentric thoughts, assimilating and accommodating different points of view. "If they are to get along at all, children must consider the ideas, thinking, and wishes of others" (Dyson, 1988).

Group experiences, planned and informal, bring children together where they learn to value the perspectives of others. Spontaneous play, field trips, group interactions (lunch, outdoors, or wherever) provide opportunities for children to listen to, talk to, and interact with each other. They begin to share their thinking with others. And even though the children share the same experience, it has a different perspective for each child. Reflection, considering others' views, and sharing one's own views all further the thinking process and modify each life.

Through raw materials, play, stories and books, music and dance, and science and social studies, young children can have many opportunities to make decisions, interact with others, and develop values. The entire curriculum is important to their later attitudes about education, relationships, and themselves. Teachers can set a healthy learning stage for the children and offer them the type of education that "brings together the need for wide-awakeness with the hunger for community, the desire to know with the wisdom to understand, and the desire to feel with the passion to see" (Greene, 1988, p. 23).

BLENDING FLEXIBILITY AND CONTENT

Now that the groundwork has been laid for meeting the needs of young children, one must find a way to bring relevant, appropriate experiences into the classroom. Before implementing the curriculum for young children, several important questions must be considered:

What are the children like?

What is developmentally appropriate for the age levels and interests of individual children? (See Chapter 1 for review.)

What kinds of experiences should be included?

What is the role or responsibility of the teacher?

What does a good plan look like?

What Young Children Are Like

What a child is and does as a 2-year-old certainly is reflected in what she is and does as an older child. Likewise, how a child reacts as she moves into schoolwork will also depend on how she has spent her earlier years.

At the outset, the reader must be cautioned about individual differences of children in age, skills, interest, family backgrounds, and opportunity. The following paragraphs note some expected behavior of children ages 2 through 5. Just knowing whether behavior is typical of an age can help the adult in planning for and understanding children, but it does not take into account deviations from the "norms."

2-Year-Olds

Adam and Beth have recently passed their second birthday. Adam, seated on the floor near Beth, plays quietly with a few assorted toys. Beth is handling a book, which is upside down. As she attempts to turn the pages, she accidentally drops the book, which starts a wheel toy in motion. Both Beth and Adam reach for the toy and begin to scuffle over it. They begin jabbering at each other and pulling on the toy. A teacher steps in and offers a similar toy to each child. The children hear music and hurry to join in songs, stories, conversation, and other activities. They are semi-involved in a movement experience, but their jumping, running, and imitating are immature, uncoordinated, and slower than that of the other children; however, they are great imitators, curious, and full of energy. They soon tire and then individually drift off to another activity.

Characteristics: Play is usually solitary; children have a short attention span and are easily distracted. They use limited and often unclear language, often need adult assistance, and exhibit uncoordinated physical development.

3-Year-Olds

Cristi is attempting a puzzle and Devin, playing nearby, is using blocks to make a garage for his car. Cristi becomes distracted as Devin's blocks fall on his car. Cristi moves near Devin and asks, "What's happening?" Devin shrugs his shoulders and starts restacking the blocks. Cristi watches, gets an idea, sits down by Devin, and hands him a block. He takes it and makes a roof for his garage; the "roof" slides off and lands on his car. Cristi shows him how to move the blocks closer so the roof is supported by two blocks. Devin looks at her, accepts the solution, hands her another car, and asks her to help with building a barn. They play side by side with limited conversation until Cristi returns to her puzzle, picks up a piece and talks to it as if it were "real." The teacher announces lunch; Devin and Cristi hurry to wash their hands and find chairs next to each other at the table.

Characteristics: Children play near others (parallel) and begin cooperative play—a move from watching to "doing"; an increased attention span leads to more independence, more interaction, more cooperation, and increasing skills; verbalization consists of longer sentences, more ideas, and more use of language, but children may still participate in collective monologue. Large muscles are increasing in strength and coordination; however, agility is lacking. Use of small muscles is still limited, even though it is increasing all the time. Lack of eye-hand coordination

Younger children need more assistance and more opportunities to interact with a caring adult.

and of precision in small muscles makes it tiring for a 3-year-old to stay with small-muscle activities (puzzles, pegboards, or scissors).

The child's ability to distinguish reality from fantasy is limited—everything is possible, and the 3-year-old attempts to demonstrate rather than verbalize ideas.

Growth tapers off, causing dawdling over food and poor appetite.

4-Year-Olds

Ethan and Frankie are heading for the playground. They find the shed latched, but not locked. Ethan gets a box to stand on while Frankie steadies the box. Grace approaches and offers suggestions, which are ignored by the boys. Finally getting a stick to knock the latch out of the clasp, the boys race inside, get matching trikes, and speed off, apparently continuing play of a prior time. Their conversation, ranging from moderate to loud, directs and reflects accurate portrayal of their play, and sometimes addresses the activities of other children.

Characteristics: Children make definite strides for independence and, for the most part, are assertive and boastful. They express caring behavior toward others and usually prefer a friend of the same sex. Their interests are much broader and continued play is common. They want realistic props and roles for each participant. Attention is gained by showing off, expressing displeasure, and being aggressive or loud. Gross and fine muscles are becoming better coordinated, but large-muscle activities are still preferred over small-muscle tasks.

Language is used increasingly in accurate reflection of the child's play, in interaction with others, to gain desired things, to gain information, and in self-expression. Serious answers are wanted with verbiage.

Four-year-olds make some distinction between reality and fantasy, but there is still some confusion. When such actions as displays of superhuman strength or impossible feats are viewed on television or in movies, 4-year-olds insist they can be performed.

5-Year-Olds

Hettie, Ivan, Jacquie, Kenna, and Lamont are busily engaged in reenacting their roles of the previous day. Sequences have been briefly reviewed and minor adjustments have been made. Periodically they stop to make additional minor adjustments in order to modify the direction of their play. As their interest begins to dwindle, they leave their dramatic play to participate in other attractive activities. Hettie and Kenna move to where a teacher and a few children are making applesauce for lunch, Ivan and Lamont head for the woodworking table, and Jacquie joins a group of children who are dancing with scarves and lively music.

Characteristics: Children at 5 years of age are more independent, dependable, self-assured, and conforming than younger children, but they like approval from others. They are protective toward younger siblings. They prefer to play with children of the same sex and age, and their play is cooperative, sustained, and more complex than formerly. Eye-hand coordination, gross and fine muscle movements, and ideas work cooperatively. Body control is good; they can throw and catch a ball, jump rope, skip, and use their skills to interact with other people. They use scissors with more precision than younger children and enjoy making things. They love stories and school and can remember sequences of numbers or letters. Although 5-year-olds tend to be obedient, cooperative, and empathetic, they also brag about accomplishments, exaggerate, and enter into short quarrels. They understand and use language freely in expressing their feelings and in complying with requests. They differentiate better between truth and make-believe and can verbally explain some differences. They still enjoy dramatic play but are interested in the "real" world.

Summary

From the preceding descriptions, specific differences can be noted among children between ages 2 and 5; however, the match between a child and his age characteristics is another thing. Some fit so well that the movement from one age to the next is evident; others pass casually through the stages. Along with individual differences are periods when development is more continuous and smooth than others. When children are in a period of rapid development, behavior is less stable than when development is slower. For instance, the behavior of 2- and 4-year-olds, who are in periods of rapid development, reflects more negativism or egocentrism than that of 3- and 5-year-olds.

Young children from financially, educationally, nutritionally, or experientially restricted backgrounds would probably not fit into the preceding age characteristics as easily as other children. They may have the same tendencies toward these characteristics, but may not have the opportunity to explore or experience, or be motivated or encouraged.

Let us make a quick note about *attention* and *interest,* mentioned earlier. *Webster's New World Dictionary* makes the following distinctions: "Attention: the ability to give heed or observe carefully." "Interest: a share or participation in something." It may be said that young children have short attention spans. That is very logical if they are expected to observe carefully. Participating or sharing in an experience is very different. Young children are not observers—they are participants. If their attention or longer involvement is desired, active involvement rather than "showing" is required. Here is an example of how the interest span of a group of 2-year-olds was lengthened.

Reflection

Balls of play dough were placed in front of each child. Without delay, it was tasted, pinched, and smelled. This wasn't too exciting or interesting. As two children started to leave the table, the teacher brought out some flour sifters and flour. The children turned back to the activity. Sifting flour was fun for a few minutes; rolling the flour into the dough also took some concentration. Again a couple of the children were ready to leave. The teacher placed a small rolling pin in front of each child. Nothing was said, but eager hands reached for the pins. Now the children were tasting, pinching, flouring, and rolling. This continued for several minutes. Then, as lack of interest began to set in, the teacher placed cookie cutters and a pan on the table. Again, the eager fingers and minds were diverted back to the activity. All in all, the children stayed at the activity for a length of time that was notable, especially considering their age and short interest span.

What was it that kept the children interested? New and varied materials, attention from the teacher, peers, or success? Each of these components must have added to the experience.

COMPONENTS FOR A WELL-ROUNDED VIEW OF THE WORLD

Creative planning for young children is essential. Opposing the belief that children waste time until they are old enough to enter formal school, research in the field continues to indicate the importance of formative years. Early educators and researchers such as Montessori and Gesell felt that (1) development was a process of "unfolding" related to maturation, and (2) the rate of unfolding was determined genetically. More recently, educators and researchers have come to believe that a stimulating and planned environment can influence the learning capabilities of young children, especially those from deprived environments.

Although some children are prepared for group experience earlier than others, there is some general agreement that children are ready for peer contacts around the age of 3; however, more and more children are being placed in group care at age 2 or younger. Factors other than chronological age must be considered in evaluating the total social, emotional, spiritual, physical, and intellectual needs of each child. How secure does the child feel in the home? How well does his physical development fall within the expected range for his age? What opportunities does he have to be with children his own age? How does he respond to strangers (peers, adults)? What is the relationship between the child and his parents? What significant happenings in the home (new baby, recent move) may disturb his security or insecurity? What could the child gain from a group experience that he could not get at home? How would costs or arrangements change the family budget or routines? As these questions suggest, a group experience must be entered into with caution; the child must be given time to adjust, whether he does it slowly or rapidly.

Either daily or frequently, the young child should participate in various curricula on a developmental level that is appropriately challenging and interesting. Other provisions include individual concentration and play as well as group involvement; periods of activity and periods of quiet; indoor and outdoor play; and opportunities for physical, social, emotional, intellectual, and moral development. The focus should ever be on helping each child to acquire a healthy self-concept and to reach her potential more fully.

Goals for teachers and children should be short- and long-range. Whatever the duration, careful planning and foresight are necessary. Good teaching does not just happen.

To determine realistic and appropriate goals, the individual child's characteristics are considered first, then the philosophy or model used at the school. Setting goals without considering the children first is ineffective and is the same as saying, "We'll mold the children to fit the program." We must say, "Children *are* the program, and we'll plan to meet their needs." Also, goals for one group or year very possibly would not be effective for another group or year.

ROLE OF THE TEACHER

Even though the teacher has training in curriculum, there are often hidden curriculum clues for children, such as the kinds of toys available; the room arrangement; the sequence and schedule of activities; the number and variety of opportunities; whether the child plays alone or with others; whether there is sufficient time for sustained or repetitive play; weather and/or temperature; indoor/outdoor flow; how and when the teacher interacts with the children and parents; the child's ability to gain trust in adults, peers, and the school environment; and other items.

Teaching is a great responsibility. Being a teacher of young children is even more important. Teachers should take their stewardship seriously by building good relationships with and among staff, parents, and children, being professional at all times, and keeping confidences. Snap judgments should not be made without facts. Frequent and friendly contacts with parents are essential.

The number of teachers required to operate a center efficiently depends on the number and ages of the children, physical facilities, experience of the teachers, and local regulations, when applicable; however, at least *two* trained teachers are needed per group. More are required when a group is composed of only 2-year-olds or more than sixteen children. (State and local requirements vary, but the recommended maximum is twenty-four children per group, with the ideal number being between sixteen and twenty for children ages 3 through 5.)

Why is one trained teacher insufficient to handle a group of young children? How can a center afford two trained teachers per group? *Trained* does not necessarily refer to a four-year college degree in early-childhood education. Training can be obtained through a trade/technical school, working for an associate degree or child development associate (CDA) credential, or on-the-job training.

The program works best with two distinct teacher roles—the *lead* teacher and the *support* teacher. (A third teacher could also be assigned the role of support teacher.) As the name suggests, the lead teacher leads an activity, taking the major responsibility for planning, organization, and actual teaching. Support teachers assist the lead teacher. Although the roles differ in specific assignments, they are of equal importance. All teachers must have the training necessary to function competently in either role and to rotate roles easily and successfully.

For a brief clarification of the two roles, consider Teacher A (TA) and Teacher B (TB) in the same classroom. Both teachers have planned together for the day; however, TA takes the lead for the opening time, snack, and art, while TB takes the lead for the group theme time, outside activity, and language time. (See Appendix C.) A brief outline defining the two roles is shown in Table 4.1.

TA takes the initiative to set up free-play activities. Both teachers participate with the children as needed. At cleanup time, TA follows through; TB assists at the beginning and then moves to group time so he will be ready as the first children arrive. He begins some interesting activities. The children put away their toys and join TB. When TA is through with cleanup, she joins the children in the group and assists with incidentals while TB presents. At the conclusion of this period, both teachers help the children get ready to go outside. TB accompanies

Table 4.1
Assignment Chart for Teacher A and Teacher B

TIME	ACTIVITY PERIOD	DESCRIPTION	MATERIALS NEEDED	TEACHER
_____	Opening	Free choice	(Complete this column according to activities planned)	A
_____	Gathering	Theme setting		B
_____	Activity	Outdoor		B
_____	Gathering	Snack		A
_____	Gathering	Language		B
_____	Activity	Creative art		A

them while TA sets up the snack, with the help of two children, after which all three also go outside. To be ready when the children arrive at snack, TA precedes them into the classroom and assists them as needed. TB brings in the stragglers and joins the other children at the snack table. As this activity concludes, TB moves with the first children to another group time for stories and songs. TA clears away the snack, prepares the tables for art activities, then joins the group in progress. During art, both teachers move freely among the children, giving verbal support, physical help, or manipulating the materials when appropriate. At the end of the day, both teachers help the children make the transition from school to home.

Clearly, two teachers are needed to work individually or cooperatively according to the needs of the children or the experiences planned. On another day, the teachers could change roles, with TA planning and presenting the curriculum areas that TB had done the previous day, or one teacher might keep the same role for a longer period of time. The best teaching occurs when plans are made well in advance of the teaching day; a week ahead gives plenty of time to gather materials, make contacts, and solidify ideas. This new two-teacher model eliminates the teacher-aide model, in which one person had the teaching responsibility and the other had a less important role. Each teacher now takes primary responsibility for some activities.

The basic inner qualities of the teacher are more influential on the learning of the young child than any other single factor (Elkind, 1970); therefore, the teacher must accept the following responsibilities:

To Herself:

To grow professionally; to be progressive and creative

To remain in good physical and emotional health

To be enthusiastic, loving, and patient

To know, understand, and value herself

To gain good observational and reporting skills

To the Children:

To build good relationships with them; to value their uniqueness

To determine and meet their needs through appropriate experiences

To enjoy being with them

To respect them as individuals and encourage independence and self-control

To help them build a good self-image

To assist them toward reaching their potential

To the Parents:

To listen to their needs and encourage feedback from them

To build a good relationship with them; to value their uniqueness and ideas

To use their cultural and personal uniqueness as a valuable curriculum re-source

To provide good counseling and/or appropriate referrals

To provide information and materials at the developmental level of the child and to assist in planning for the well-being of the child

To keep them informed about school practices and activities, thereby bridging the gap between home and school

To Team Members:

To build a good relationship with and among them

To support and value them and their ideas

To share ideas and knowledge; to work as a team

To encourage and assist in their professional growth

To gain the attention of children, the teacher may invite them to participate, or just begin a new activity.

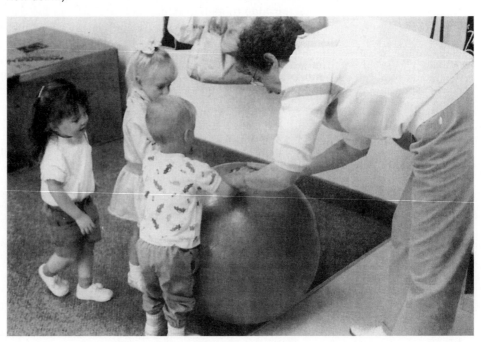

To the Community:

To be active in solving its problems

To participate in local professional early-childhood organizations and functions

To disseminate information about the importance of growth, development, and education for the young child

The preparation of teachers of young children is extremely important. Some states have specific requirements for caregivers; some states have specific requirements for teachers or directors of preschool programs; and most (if not all) states require an additional certification for teachers of young children in public and private schools. (See the section titled "For Teachers" in Chapter 1.)

Regardless of the setting (child care, nursery school, preschool) or sponsorship of a program for young children (government, private, corporation), only the most stable and well-trained individuals should be with the children.

The following are suggestions for teachers in their relationships with children:

Treat each child as being unique; understand and value differences.

Make sure the setting is child-centered. Give support when needed, but allow each child the time and opportunity to explore and solve problems. Put his needs before your own.

Know how many children are in the group daily, where they are, what they are doing, and where the other teachers are.

See that behavior limits, when necessary, are set, understood, and maintained. Be consistent (in your expectations and with other adults) without being inflexible.

Use your voice as a teaching tool. A soft, pleasant voice receives better response than a loud, gruff one or a high-pitched, overly excited one.

Make sure your words and actions indicate the same thing. When it is time to go inside, for instance, tell the children and then go inside yourself.

Use verbalization as a technique to gain cooperation from the children. Help them to understand what is expected of them. Speak with confidence.

Get on a child's physical level when speaking to him by either kneeling, stooping, or sitting on a low chair or the floor.

The following are suggestions for teachers personally in their approach to children:

Check your curriculum frequently to avoid any biased or inappropriate activities, materials, aids, and so on.

Rotate curriculum activities and materials to stimulate new and/or sustained play as indicated by the children.

Get adequate rest and proper nutrition.

Leave your problems outside the center.

Dress properly for the job, the weather, and activities.

Be prompt. Have things organized and ready when the children arrive. Control is difficult to regain if children get ahead of you.

Keep current by reading professional periodicals, books, and pamphlets and by attending professional workshops and conferences to aid you in becoming a more effective teacher.

Plan ahead. Make sure the next activity is ready before warning children to finish their current involvement.

When another teacher is handling a situation, do not interfere unless your help is requested.

Be a good housekeeper both indoors and outdoors. Keep the center clean and attractive; however, avoid being so involved in cleanup that children are unsupervised.

Be totally aware of what is going on. Just furnishing a warm body is insufficient.

Strike a balance between giving needed one-to-one attention and keeping peripheral awareness of other activities.

Share your experiences and ideas with other staff members.

In all ways be a good support and lead teacher.

Be honestly enthusiastic about being with the children.

Relax and smile!

WHAT TO PLAN

First—the Children.   Consider each child individually and all children collectively—interests, knowledge, security, skills, and other known information.

Second—Experiences.   Consider interpersonal relationships, sensory experiences, exploration of natural and physical surroundings, intellectual stimulation, muscle development, language opportunities, and other available information.

Third—the Curriculum.   What do the children already know—and are the concepts true and on their developmental level? What are the most effective ways of teaching new information? How can curriculum areas be integrated, strengthened, and made more useful? How can teachers be most effective?

Fourth—Evaluation.   How can teachers determine how effective the learning has been? What would be effective follow-up? Discussing events immediately after the departure of the children, an important responsibility, enhances planning skills, the ability to evaluate objectively, and relations with other staff members. Serious evaluation leads to better understanding of children and better planning (see Figure 4.2).

When teachers are aware of the individual characteristics of each child, they know which children are ready for new experiences, what will appeal to many children, what activities will support the experiences, and how to follow up on them. Rather than plan for a *specific,* nonflexible day, they consider attitudes and desire for participation as they are expressed by the children.

Figure 4.2
Daily Curriculum Checklist

1. Development	Have all domains of development been provided for?	
2. Observation	Will teachers have an opportunity to observe and record (at least some of) the activities of (some of) the children?	
3. Interaction	Has the environment been prepared so children learn through active exploration, through interaction with other children and adults, and across developmental domains and curriculum areas?	
4. Interests/abilities	Are activities and materials interesting, slightly challenging, concrete, real, and relevant to the lives of young children?	
5. Flexibility	Does the plan provide for activities with increasing difficulty, complexity, and challenge so children with either less or more developed skills will be interested and challenged?	
6. Choice	Can children choose from among a variety of activities, materials, equipment, playmates, and time spent to become immersed, stimulated, and satisfied?	
7. Balance	Is there provision for active and quiet, indoor and outdoor, individual and group play? (Equal time is not always the best plan.)	
8. Diversity	Has there been concerted effort to avoid anticultural, biased, exclusive, and competitive play?	

Teachers expect to clarify, increase, and stimulate the interests of children. They do so by being observant of children's actions and conversations. The written plan is merely a guide to assist teachers in providing breadth and depth experiences for the children, who are at varying levels of cognitive and physical development.

MULTICULTURAL EDUCATION

There are several advantages for children of a multiculturally sensitive classroom:

- They develop pride in and appreciation for their own culture.
- They increase their awareness of other cultural groups.
- They learn to promote diversity.
- Their activities are integrated into the curriculum.
- They begin a lifelong search about people who make up our world.
- They develop their own self-concept.
- They make new friends.
- They enlarge their view of families and the community.
- They develop sensitivity to others.
- They notice new and different ways to do things.
- They become curious about other aspects of family life.
- Their own lives are enriched and expanded to include issues beyond their immediate experiences.

For the teacher, incorporating a multiculturally sensitive classroom entails the following tasks and suggestions:

- Be curious about the children within your classroom regardless of their color, sex, or culture.
- Discover their interests and present knowledge.
- Seek out and bring materials into the classroom that will create interest in new and different ideas and things.
- Be patient and observant.
- Gradually, with authenticity and respectfulness, introduce cultures of children within your classroom.
- Ask parents for suggestions, resources, and assistance.
- Encourage curiosity and acceptance.

(Ideas that promote cultural sensitivity have been included at the end of each curriculum chapter.)

Reflection

Using a multicultural theme of your choice, design an activity or daily theme. To make it successful, you will want to consider the following:

- Applicability (or interest) to the children
- Planning (before, during, and after)
- Preparation of the classroom and the children
- Ways to keep the activity child-centered
- Outside or special props or people
- Integration into known curriculum and familiar routines
- Any special instructions or restrictions
- Responses of the children: how to lengthen or shorten the activity
- Possible questions or concerns of the children
- Information for parents
- Follow-up
- Other

A GOOD LESSON PLAN

It may seem inconsistent to say that lesson plans should be flexible and then suggest a formal plan. In presenting the following information and format, it is assumed that the planner is always aware of the children he teaches, their interests, and their abilities, and is constantly aware of blending concepts together to aid children's learning. (See the section titled "Curriculum Webbing" earlier in this chapter.)

A good lesson plan is used as a guide and not as an end in itself. Planning is an ongoing procedure designed to meet the needs of young children. The process includes three general stages: preassessing, teaching, and evaluating. A complete lesson plan has seven components: theme, preassessment and findings, ideas to be emphasized, schedule of the day, items for special attention, evaluation, and follow-through for parents.

Prior to the day the lesson material is to be used, the teachers sit down together, before the children arrive, and review the activities and responsibilities so that everything is fresh in their minds. (See Figures 4.3 and 4.4.)

Figure 4.3
Thumbnail Sketch of the Day

Daily Planning Outline

Teacher/Planner   Date

THEME

PREASSESSMENT AND FINDINGS

IDEAS TO BE EMPHASIZED

SCHEDULE OF THE DAY

| Time | Activity period | Description | Materials needed | Teacher |

ITEMS FOR SPECIAL ATTENTION

EVALUATION

FOLLOW-THROUGH FOR PARENTS

Figure 4.4
Lesson Plan Checklist

1. Theme	Consider ideas suggested by both children and adults, but make sure the topics are within the understanding of young children.
	Include ideas that have local, seasonal, or current interest, but also introduce new ideas when feasible.
2. Preassessment and findings	When questioning is used, be sure questions are thoughtful and open-ended.
	When using props or activities, make sure they are realistic and familiar.
	In reporting findings, use clear responses.
3. Ideas to be emphasized	Include the most important information related to the topic. Prepare simple, moderate, and advanced information to meet the needs of all the children. Assume that this information will be the basis for building on this topic.
4. Learning activities and tentative schedule of the day	Use ideas and activities that are realistic, are concrete, and teach the desired concepts. Include specific and detailed information about transitions, stories, outside activities, and so on, and when they occur.
	Have activities for all areas of the curriculum and provide for all domains of development.
	Provide large blocks of time—be prepared to lengthen or shorten periods depending on the interest of the children.
5. Evaluation	Reflect on how plan areas overlap and support each other (preassessment with activities, ideas and evaluation, and so on).
	Give specific examples of conversation and/or activities that show learning of individual children and the group as a whole.
	Consider how misconceptions can be corrected and how concepts can be used as a basis for future learning.
	Plan on using this topic at a later time, making appropriate modifications or additions.
6. Aids: books, records, other	List books on the theme and how they will be used. List books for diversion (include author, title, and publisher for future use).
	List records/tapes that will be used (include recording company and number).
	List other aids to be used (songs, visual aids, musical instruments, props, and so on).
7. Parental information	Give a brief overview of the day/week with brief and logical suggestions for parental follow-through. Include date and group.
	Make information neat, showing value for the teacher, child, and parent.

Theme

A theme may not always be selected; however, it does give some direction and continuity to activities provided. Teachers may get theme ideas from comments or play of the children—and may be surprised at play preferences or disinterests of children.

Some children might ask, "What are we talking about today?" and some may not pick up on a theme, but with a variety of open-ended opportunities the child is likely to gather subjective knowledge whether or not it is theme-related. The theme itself suggests the best ways to present the concepts.

Using the idea of webbing, consider (1) what led up to the selection of this topic and (2) how it can be expanded at a later date.

A theme is not used to impart knowledge that can be memorized or regurgitated. Nor is it taught once and forgotten. On their own, children will revive, elaborate on, or continue a theme while adding variety and dimension. Rather than being a one-shot overdose, the topic is used again later on, or frequently as the interest of children suggests.

Reflection

In order to get to the classroom, the children had to detour through a toy and supply area. Every day Alan spotted a package containing plastic dinosaurs, and every day he asked to use them. Thinking the dinosaurs would be of little or no interest to the 4-year-olds and forgetting to remove them before the next day, the teacher finally gave in. Alan spent most of the morning with the dinosaurs—and so did many of the other children. They would take a replica to the teacher and ask, "What's he called?" Unprepared, the teacher made a few excuses and then remembered a book about dinosaurs that was also tucked away in the storage room. Alan (and others—including the teacher) began matching the pictures to the replicas. In no time they could describe the animals, give their proper names, and tell something special about them (body, eating habits, and so on). Much learning, interacting, and excitement went on that day—and others. Thanks to Alan!

For some suggested curriculum topics, see Appendix B.

Preassessment and Findings

Once teachers know the interest of the children, the next step is to find out what the children already know about it, collectively and individually. Do have in mind some introductory, intermediate, and advanced ideas for children in different stages of learning. In this way the beginner will not be overwhelmed or the advanced learner demeaned. Some basic information can be used for review and some can be used for initial introduction of materials and activities. Children with prior knowledge are used to help inform the others, and each child is taken just beyond his present knowledge. Raw materials and unlimited time can help children find their knowledge and interest levels.

Preassessment is made before developing a plan and is done casually or formally. The casual approach yields general information; the formal, specific. The following are two examples of preassessment on shapes:

1. *Casual.* Approach individual children or a small group and ask them if they know any shapes. If so, which ones? On a table, place items in the different shapes you plan to teach. See what the children say about them or do with them. With this method you are trying to see if the children can name shapes without the shapes being present; then you are supplying the actual shapes and seeing if this gives the children clues. Observe, listen, and take notes.

2. *Formal.* Prepare some of the desired shapes. Then individually ask each child to hand you a specific shape. Also ask her to look around the room and tell you if she can see things in the room that are of the same shape. Can she give the right name for each shape and point out an example?

In the preassessment section of the planning checklist (Figure 4.4) are some guides. Preassessment is employed to acquire significant information. Teachers should pay close attention to the responses of the children, rather than deciding before the preassessment what they'll provide in the classroom and what they'll teach regardless of the present knowledge or interest of the children.

Several ideas or themes may be presented during an activity period. Materials planned with a certain child in mind may not be of interest to him at the time—but other children will probably join in.

*Fun activities, good tools, a place to work, and a friend nearby
provide a soothing atmosphere.*

Ideas to be Emphasized

The central ideas, which are a direct result of the preassessment, bind the theme and the activities together. Known ideas are used as a foundation on which to add new ideas. The latter should be in the form of simple, true statements based on the developmental level of the children. The number of new ideas depends on the amount and depth of information to be taught without overwhelming the children.

Again, expect children to use materials in a variety of ways—some will be even better than the ones the teacher had planned. Be observant as the children interact with the materials and with peers. They don't have to respond as the teacher planned in order for the experience to be a success!

Schedule of the Day

This part of the plan can be in written or graphic form and reflects the teacher's creativity, thoroughness, and versatility (see Table 4.2).

The following are some suggestions for opening/activity play time:

- Creative art
- Books/flannel board and objects
- Manipulative toys
- Science table
- Dramatic play
- Music and movement
- Blocks

Table 4.2
Suggested Daily Time Frames

SUGGESTED DAILY TIME FRAMES		
Period	*Setup*	*Particulars*
Opening	Classroom is set up with a variety of centers. Children choose play situations and companions.	Transition from home to classroom. Flexible depending on the arrival of children. Teachers greet children. Parents depart. Child engages in activities.
Activity play time	Learning centers. In some cases materials are set out; in others, children get and replace toys of their choosing.	Can combine opening and activity play. Longest part of day. Flexible; avoid interruptions. Child-centered. Options in different areas and with peers. May recur throughout the day. Indoors, outdoors, or both. Teachers are available but do not direct play. Chance to encourage and broaden child's interests.
Gathering	Usually for stories, snack, music, language opportunities, a guest, special information, events important for the group.	Short and infrequent. Teacher/group-oriented. Indoors or outdoors. Social interaction: sharing, spacing self to see, turn taking, listening/speaking, instruction, information, peer relationships, participation, and so on. Drawbacks: child must leave what he was doing, may not be too interested, resent being directed, want more activity, and so on.
Closing time	Children replace toys, do wind-down activities, and gather personal items to take home.	Flexible—depending on arrival of parents. Teacher helps child prepare for departure as other teacher remains with other children.
Evaluation		

- Floor toys
- Water/sand table
- Outdoor climbing
- Outdoor wheel toys
- Food preparation and eating

Items for Special Attention

Items may or may not be listed here daily, but the reminder is invaluable when needed. The staff may need to carefully watch a certain activity (a transition, for example) or a certain child (perhaps one has been especially listless lately). A reminder to recontact someone for a future activity, such as a field trip or a visitor, can be written here. A note can be made to rearrange the indoor or outdoor areas, to order more supplies for an activity (wood for the woodworking table for Thursday), or to check the drain on the water table before filling it with water and boats.

This space is not used for personal reminders (personal phone calls, errands, appointments, etc.).

Evaluation

This is how to determine how well the day was planned, how well the children responded, how well the staff performed, and what changes can be made before the plan is used again (webbed). Notes can be written right on the plan as reminders to make any additions, deletions, or modifications.

To be most effective, the evaluation is held as soon as possible after the children leave the center. All the staff who worked with the children that day are included, if possible. At times just the lead and support teachers participate.

On the lesson plan, in the form of questions, statements, or mere reminders, valuable ideas evident during planning should be written. They give a starting point to the discussion and, it is hoped, help make the evaluation meaningful. Productivity of the evaluation and not the clock decides the length.

To get the staff in a constructive mood, discussion should begin with things that went well. Open-ended questions, ones requiring thinking, recalling, observing, and interpreting, help make for effective evaluations. For example, compare these two questions: "Did the children like the activities today?" "Which activities did the children seem to enjoy the most today?" The first question calls for a yes or no answer; the second, for careful thought and response.

Things that did not go well are also discussed, continuing until ideas come up on how they can be done differently, avoided, or turned into learning experiences instead of failures.

The progress of each child should be assessed frequently. Looking at one or two children per week may be sufficient, or there may be a child who needs more consideration. The children should be the focal point of the center.

Follow-Through for Parents

This section gives space to consider, during planning, the parents and the home. Some teachers prefer to send home a note daily telling what has transpired during that day, and some prefer a weekly or monthly newsletter; still others post a lesson plan daily and remind parents to read it. Whatever the method, the closeness between home and center is vital, and the child is the connecting link.

A little time and effort are needed to prepare a message for the parent, but they are worthwhile. As the parent brings or picks up the child, a spontaneous or common topic can be shared. The teacher's message should never be a tool of interrogation. Rather, it should keep parents informed and encourage valuable feedback so that misconceptions, comments, or interests of the children can be used in future planning. (See the discussion in Chapter 2.)

The teacher may find a skeleton plan helpful. Samples of miniplans will be found in Appendix C on selected curriculum areas.

CONCLUSIONS

The following paragraph receives my full support:

> NAEYC has devoted more than 60 years of activity to ensuring the best for children. We would never advocate subjecting children to inappropriate environments. At the same time, we cannot support policies such as readiness testing, transition classes, holding

younger children out of school, or raising the entrance age, which we know at best are short-term solutions and at worst harm individual children and contribute to inappropriate expectations. (Bredekamp & Shepard, 1989, p. 23)

Not all teachers have been trained in the developmentally appropriate program (DAP) method. Some, hearing about it recently after university training and years of teaching in the field, have misgivings and frustrations. Consider the following report of Carter (1992):

Not everyone is a believer in the discovery approach in early childhood education; some teachers still use the direct-instruction method. Interns can help bridge the gap that exists between the two philosophies. This will not be easy because everyone would rather resist change, especially if they have "*always* done it this way." Tenured teachers would benefit from seminars that would help them bridge the gap between the direct-instruction way they may teach now and developmentally appropriate practices. Teachers need to see the reward they would get for changing the way they teach now, and that reward is *children who can think.* (p. 72)

APPLICATION OF PRINCIPLES

1. Define *curriculum* and how it applies to young children. How can one blend flexibility and content into the planning?

2. Describe some of the "myths" of developmentally appropriate practices as they apply to young children.

3. Describe *webbing*. Using the topic of air, brainstorm some themes that could be presented to young children. Remember that webbing leads up to and provides follow-up for ideas.

4. Compare and contrast the general characteristics of children between the ages of 2 and 5 years to assure that you plan accurately for children of different ages.

5. Outline the role of the teacher in planning curriculum for young children. What are the differences between lead and support teachers?

6. When planning for young children, what are the four aspects to consider?

7. Using Figure 4.2, evaluate a day in preschool.

8. Write a lesson plan (using the seven elements listed in the chapter) and compare it with the outline in the chapter. Identify the areas which are *easiest* and *most difficult* for you to plan. Ask a teacher or classmate for assistance.

9. Explain how relations between home and school can be strengthened.

10. Make a floor plan of your present classroom and suggest some possible options in space and activities. Discuss your ideas with a teacher or classmate. (If possible, try some of them.)

REFERENCES

Berk, L. E. (1994). Vygotsky's theory: The importance of make-believe play. *Young Children, 50*(1), 30–39.

Biber, B. (1977). A developmental interaction approach: Bank Street College of Education. In Day, M. D., & R. K. Parker (eds.), *The preschool in action,* 2nd edition, 423–460. Boston: Allyn & Bacon.

Bredekamp, S. (ed.) (1987). *Developmentally appropriate practice in early childhood programs serving children from birth through age 8,* expanded edition. Washington, DC: NAEYC.

Bredekamp, S. (1991). Redeveloping early childhood education: A response to Kessler. *Early Childhood Research Quarterly, 6*(2), 199–209.

Bredekamp, S., & C. Copple (eds.) (1997). *Developmentally appropriate practices in early childhood programs,* revised edition. Washington, DC: NAEYC.

Bredekamp, S., & T. Rosegrant (eds.) (1992). *Reaching potentials: Appropriate curriculum and assessment for young children,* Vol. 1, 9–27. Washington, DC: NAEYC.

Bredekamp, S., & T. Rosegrant (eds.) (1995). *Reaching potentials: Transforming early childhood curriculum and assessment*, Vol. 2. Washington, DC: NAEYC.

Bredekamp, S., & L. Shepard (1989, March). How best to protect children from inappropriate school expectations, practices, and policies. *Young Children*, 44(3), 14–24.

Bruner, J. (1963). *The process of education*. Cambridge, MA: Harvard University Press.

Bruner, J. (1966). *Toward a theory of instruction*. Cambridge, MA: The Belknap Press of Harvard University Press.

Carlsson-Paige, N., & D. E. Levin (1987). *The war play dilemma: Balancing needs and values in the early childhood classroom*. New York: Teachers College Press.

Carson, R. (1956). *The sense of wonder*. New York: Harper & Row.

Carter, G. J. (1992, September). How can the teaching intern deal with the disparity between how she is taught to teach and how she is expected to teach in "real world" primary grades? *Young Children*, 47(6), 68–72.

Cassidy, D. J., & C. Lancaster (1993). The grassroots curriculum: a dialogue between children and teachers. *Young Children*, 48(6), 47–51.

Dewey, J. (1944). *Democracy and education*. New York: Free Press.

Dittman, L., (ed.) (1970). *Curriculum is what happens*. Washington, D.C.: NAEYC.

Dyson, A. H. (1988). The value of time off task: Young children's spontaneous talk and deliberate text. *Harvard Educational Review*, 57, 396–420.

Edwards, C., L. Gandini, & G. Forman (eds.) (1993). *The hundred languages of children: The Reggio Emilia approach to early childhood education*. Norwood, NJ: Ablex.

Eisner, E. (1990). Who decides what schools teach? *Phi Delta Kappan*, 71(7), 523–26.

Eisner, W. E., & E. Vallance (eds.) (1974). *Conflicting conceptions of curriculum*. Berkeley, CA: McCutchan.

Elkind, D. (1970, January). The case of the academic preschool: Fact or fiction? *Young Children*, 25, 132–140.

Erikson, E. (1963). *Childhood and society*. New York: Norton.

Gelman, R., & R. Baillargeon (1983). A review of some Piagetian concepts. In Mussen, P. (ed.), *Handbook of child psychology*, Vol. 3, 167–230. New York: Wiley.

Gelman, R., & E. Meck (1983). Preschoolers' counting: Principles before skill. *Cognition*, 13, 343–350.

Giroux, H. A. (1992). Educational leadership and the crisis of democratic government. *Educational Researcher*, 21(4), 4–12.

Greenberg, P. (1992). How to institute some simple democratic practices pertaining to respect, rights, roots and responsibilities in any classroom (without losing your leadership position). *Young Children*, 47(5), 10–17.

Greene, M. (1988). *The dialectic of freedom*. New York: Teachers College Press.

Herndon, J. (1968). *The way it spozed to be*. New York: Simon-Schuster.

Jervis, K. (1991). Closed gates in a New York City school. In Perrone, V. (ed.), *Expanding student assessment*, 1–21. Alexandria, VA: Association for Supervision and Curriculum Development.

Jones, B. (1970). In Dittman, L., (ed.), *Curriculum is what happens*. Washington, DC: NAEYC.

Jones, E. (1993). *Growing teachers: Partnership in staff development*. Washington, DC: NAEYC.

Jones, E., & J. Nimmo (1994). *Emergent curriculum*. Washington, DC: NAEYC.

Katz, L., & S. Chard (1989). *Engaging children's minds: The project approach*. Norwood, NJ: Ablex.

Kessler, S. A. (1991). Alternative perspectives on early childhood education. *Early Childhood Research Quarterly*, 6(2), 183–187.

Kostelnik, M. J. (1992, May). Myths associated with developmentally appropriate programs. *Young Children*, 47(4), 17–23.

Mead, M. (1973). Can the socialization of children lead to greater acceptance of diversity? *Young Children*, 28(6), 329.

Meisels, S. J. (1993). Remaking classroom assessment with the work sampling system. *Young Children*, 48(5), 34–40.

Mitchell, L. S. (1934). *Young geographers*. New York: Bank Street College.

National Association for the Education of Young Children (NAEYC) & National Association of Early Childhood Specialists in State Departments of Education (NAECS/SDE) (1991). Guidelines for appropriate curriculum content and assessment in programs serving children ages 3 through 8. *Young Children*, 46(3), 21–38.

New, R. (1993). Cultural variations on developmentally appropriate practice: Challenges to theory and practice. In Edwards, C., L. Gandini, & G. Forman, (eds.), *The hundred languages of children*, 215–231. Norwood, NJ: Ablex.

Piaget, J. (1952). *The origins of intelligence in children*. New York: International Universities Press.

Rankin, B. (1993). Curriculum development in Reggio Emilia: A long-term curriculum project about dinosaurs. In Edwards, C., L. Gandini, & G. Forman (eds.), *The hundred languages of children*, 189–211. Norwood, NJ: Ablex.

Resnick, L. (1996). Schooling and the workplace: What relationship? In *Preparing youth for the 21st century*, 21–37. Washington, DC: Aspen Institute.

Seefeldt, C. (1993, March). Social studies: Learning for freedom. *Young Children*, 48(3), 4–9.

Spodek, B. (1973). *Early childhood education*. Englewood Cliffs, NJ: Prentice-Hall.

Swanson, L. (1994, May). Changes—how our nursery school replaced adult-directed art projects with child-directed experiences and changed to an accredited, child-sensitive, developmentally appropriate school. *Young Children, 49*(4), 69–73.

Van Hoorn, J., P. Nourot, B. Scales, & K. Alward (1993). *Play at the center of the curriculum.* Upper Saddle River, NJ: Prentice-Hall.

Vygotsky, L. (1978). *Mind in society: The development of higher mental processes.* Cambridge, MA: Harvard University Press.

Workman, S., & M. C. Anziano (1993, January). Curriculum webs: Weaving connections from children to teachers. *Young Children, 48*(2), 4–9.

Language Arts

CHAPTER 5

MAIN PRINCIPLES

1. Opportunities for language development are important in the life of the young child.

2. The four areas of language development discussed in this chapter are listening, speaking, reading, and writing.

3. For the optimal development and learning of all children, educators must accept the legitimacy of children's home languages.

4. Language can be responsive or restrictive.

5. Language and literacy learning are continuous processes.

6. Proponents of the whole-language approach (Vygotsky and others) stress that it is not a single instructional strategy, or even a group of strategies, but a comprehensive theory of language learning and instruction.

7. Print serves the many needs of children.

8. There are several criteria for selecting books and stories for young children.

9. Young children should be given frequent opportunities to verbally express their ideas.

10. In the case of preschool children, "reading" more frequently consists of being read to than children actually reading.

11. Developmental characteristics of "writing" for the young child include scribbling, left-to-right and top-to-bottom, and recognition of letters.

12. Parents, teachers, and other adults can stimulate and encourage children in the areas of listening, speaking, reading, and writing.

By design and because of its importance, this chapter on language arts follows the chapters on good environments, relationships and guidance techniques, play, and curriculum. Without language, none of the preceding or following chapters would have much meaning. But there need to be decisions and rationale. Young children are encountering language experiences from the day of birth; other curriculum areas fall into place with the opportunities and development of the child.

The goal in language arts is to help children develop and improve their ability to communicate. Language is oral, auditory, and visual and may be used to express personal or social ideas. One depends on it to clarify norms, to inform, and to transmit needs, feelings, and desires. Inability to communicate with another, whether due to a language barrier or sensory impairment, impresses one with how much language is taken for granted and how much we depend on it in our daily lives. See Figure 5.1 for the symbols associated with the four areas of language, which are the thrust of this chapter.

This chapter is designed to emphasize the importance of the four areas of language (listening, speaking, reading, writing) and their interdependence especially for children up to the age of 6. Not within the scope of this book are details about language acquisitions, problems related to each of the areas of development, possible referrals for diagnosis and treatment, specific approaches to teaching and reading, and ways of dealing with bilingual children. However, it is intended that the information and activities herein will aid teachers in communicating with children from all backgrounds and language experiences.

Young children should be encouraged to actively participate in activities that allow for experimentation with listening, speaking, reading, and writing. When they participate with adults and peers in oral and written opportunities, they increase

Figure 5.1
Symbols of the Four Areas of Language: Listening,
Speaking, Reading, and Writing

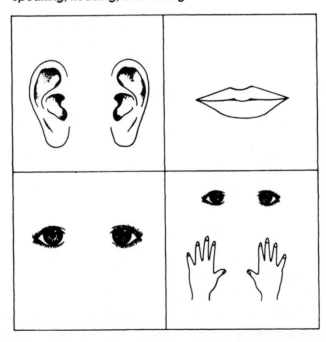

their awareness and understanding of their world. These early experiences lay a foundation and create interest for the child's later learning.

Poetry, an important part of a young child's life, can introduce language, rhythm, sounds, and concepts in a delightful way. Any topic can be highlighted, any time is appropriate, and humor is spontaneous with young children; however, some books or ideas that are humorous to adults fail to be so with children due to a mismatch with their learning ability and interest. Using humor can facilitate children's social, cognitive, and language growth. (See Jalongo, 1985.)

When language acquisition in young children is delayed, it may be caused by "physical or structural deficits (such as hearing loss), physiological or neurological impairments (such as cerebral palsy), mental retardation, or emotional problems" (Dumtschin, 1988, p. 16). Generally, early-childhood teachers are not trained to diagnose language problems or to prescribe therapy; however, they should be alert to hearing and speaking deficiencies and refer parents to appropriate agencies. Because of the complexity of hearing disorders, this topic is not within the scope of this text.

As discussed in Chapter 3, play is an important component in the healthy development of young children. Literature (language arts) helps provide familiar and vicarious experiences.

Language arts is a very broad category, for it includes verbal, written, pictorial, and performing media in all their forms for children and adults—it is much more than just children's literature or storytime. Language should be integrated into all areas of curriculum, with all individuals, and at all times. As you will discover while reading this chapter, language is one of the most important ways we communicate with each other—and sometimes our communication doesn't come out the way it was intended! So we use language for clarification, elaboration, justification, and personalization.

NAEYC has issued a position statement (1996) responding to linguistic and cultural diversity regarding young children. It states:

> For the optimal development and learning of all children, educators must *accept* the legitimacy of children's home language, *respect* (hold in high regard) and *value* (esteem, appreciate) the home culture, and *promote* and *encourage* the active involvement and support of all families, including extended and nontraditional family units. (p. 5)

The report summarizes: Early-childhood educators can best help linguistically and culturally diverse children and their families by acknowledging and responding to the importance of (a) the child's home language and culture, (b) administrative support for bilingualism within the educational setting; (c) modifying the classroom to meet the individual needs of children, (d) learning and practicing ways to support children and families from linguistically or culturally different backgrounds, and (e) providing high-quality care and education for *all* children. (p. 12)

According to the Bureau of Labor Statistics (Silvestri, 1993), the number of child-care workers in the United States is expected to grow by 49 percent by the year 2005. These caregivers play an integral role in children's development, including their literacy development. This is especially critical in light of the fact that as many as 35 percent of kindergarten children come to school unprepared for formal education, according to teachers surveyed for the Carnegie Foundation report *Ready to Learn* (Boyer, 1991).

Communicating, influencing, and cooperating with others help build one's self-esteem.

To encourage literacy in young children, teachers can share books, poems, songs, and rhymes whenever and wherever they can throughout the day. These activities can be child- or adult-initiated, group or one-on-one. Teachers will want to initiate new selections periodically and invite *all* children to listen—not just the persistent, verbal ones. Barclay, Benelli, and Curtis (1995) suggest the use of Big Books as children explore how print works. These books on nursery rhymes and song charts make pictures easily distinguishable from the well-spaced print. Benelli and colleagues also encourage signs and labels on children's cubbies, lockers, toy shelves, and other convenient places to help children understand the function of the printed word, and to convey information (p. 28). They conclude: "Books and other print-related materials are valued and necessary ingredients for each day for the children in our center. Through their intense involvement with literacy materials, they are developing important concepts about print, an increasing ability to retell stories from illustrations, and a love of books" (p. 28). (See also Cornell, 1993.)

The International Reading Association (IRA), with representatives from five national professional organizations (including NAEYC), has set forth recommendations for literacy before the first grade that call for the use of "reading materials that are familiar or predictable, such as well-known stories, as they provide children with a sense of control and confidence in their ability to learn" (IRA, 1985). NAEYC and NAECS/SDE (1992) suggest that children use language to communicate effectively and to facilitate thinking and learning. The children become literate individuals who gain satisfaction as well as information from reading and writing (p. 18).

LANGUAGE INTERACTION

Responsive and Restrictive Language

Stone (1993) identifies two ways to interact with others, using either responsive or restrictive language:

Responsive Language	*Restrictive Language*
Shows regard and respect	Shows disregard and disrespect
Is democratic	Is authoritarian, intimidating, and disrespectful
Encourages give-and-take	
Uses alternates and choices, reasons and explanations;	Uses threats, punishment, and criticism
Includes elaboration for understanding	Discourages independence
	Is condensed and impersonal
Shows sensitivity and caring	(Condensed from Stone, 1993)

Responsive language gives the individual options of what to do or how to do things better. Restrictive language is limiting and makes the individual feel inferior. In interacting with children, helping them to see a positive outlet (and to feel worthwhile) is far superior to being left hanging on a limb—when one often does not have the strength to hold on! Behavior problems can erupt. Research has shown that there is a correlation between caregiver use of responsive language and the use of other recommended practices (Stone, 1993).

Literacy

Teachers should load their classrooms with award-winning books from many available sources. Not only should books *be* in the classroom, but they should also be used, reused, and overused. Verbal encouragement, time, and comfortable places will help young children become involved with print. Literacy begins with print awareness in children as young as 3 years old as a response to their experiences in a print-rich environment.

Enriching classroom play settings with message-bearing signs and labels and providing time for interaction among the children helps them develop the ability to read words, particularly when the print is embedded in its supporting context in a play setting and has important implications for classroom practice.

Providing print experiences means "awakening interest by providing continuous encouragement through positive discourse and by creating a warm and supportive atmosphere in which children can take risks without fear of failure" (Williams & Davis, 1994, p. 41).

Social Convention

Some researchers place more value on the social component of language development; for instance, Vygotsky states that "children solve practical tasks with the help of their speech, as well as their eyes and hands" (1978, p. 26) and that "language arises initially as a means of communication between the child and the people in his environment. Only subsequently, upon conversion to internal speech, does it come to organize the child's thought, that is, become an internal mental function" (p. 89).

Language and Literacy Learning— A Developmental Continuum

Language and literacy learning is a continuous process. All children develop at their own rates and in their own directions in their sociocultural environments. Maturation and environmental experiences vary from child to child. *It is therefore virtually impossible, nor is it desirable, to provide a definitive sequence or an age-regulated timeline for language and literacy development.* "Children acquire a common fund of concepts but the point of entry and the path of progress may be different for any two children" (Clay, 1975, p. 7).

Whole-Language Learning and Assessment

An approach to reading and writing instruction has evolved that has caused much interest and controversy among educators. Known as *whole language*, this approach is based on the premise that young children best learn to read and write in the same way they learned to speak—from whole to part (Harste, Woodward, & Burke, 1984, p. 193). That is, they learn language as a whole process using many reading, writing, and speaking skills and then, gradually, they refine the

Due to immature speech, toddlers may use props and actions instead of words to get attention.

different skills that make up the language process. The instructional focus is primarily on language meaning, rather than on specific skills (Educational Research Service, 1991, p. 1; Edelsky, Altwerger, & Flores, 1991, p. 8; Weaver, 1990, p. 6; Reutzel & Hollingsworth, 1988, p. 412; Watson, 1989; Goodman, 1986; Heald-Taylor, 1989).

"Finally, implicit in the whole language approach is the belief that children have already learned a great deal before they begin school. The variety of backgrounds, cultures, and interests children bring into the classroom is considered a valuable part of whole language learning by teachers, who often seek ways to incorporate these attributes into the curriculum in an effort to make learning more relevant to each child" (Goodman, 1986, p. 10). And further: "In whole language, students are guided to learn language 'incidentally' by their voluntary exposure to various forms of language" (p. 6).

Researchers who have documented the influence of the classroom environment on children's development (Loughlin & Martin, 1987; Loughlin & Suina, 1982) recommend an environment that supports language and literacy and reflects a child's point of view. Immersing children in functional print and making the literacy environment as constant and pervasive as the oral-language environment is encouraged. In addition, adults should ensure that print is used for *real* purposes, as opposed to practice or ornamental purposes (Ortiz & Englebrecht, 1986).

In whole-language classrooms, children use the four classifications of language (speaking, listening, reading, and writing) in integrated ways to receive and express information, feelings, sensory perceptions, and ideas, and to play. Collaborative experiences are very important, yet children need time to develop their own interests and abilities through personal effort, to support the tension between personal invention and social convention, and to integrate all subject areas through both social and individual experiences (Strickland, 1988).

Based on their knowledge of their individual classroom students, teachers who develop rich, holistic, authentic learning experiences meet Elkind's recommendation (1991) that "curriculum should never be final but always open, flexible, and innovative. That sort of curriculum is exciting for the teacher as well as for the pupils and makes the learning and curriculum innovative and a cooperative venture" (p. 11).

Classrooms often become flooded with abundant but frequently nonfunctional print that has no meaning for children but is provided by well-meaning teachers. Print should be used as a real resource for children and adults so that children are "exposed to all these functions of literacy within the everyday interactions of . . . school life rather than within contexts constructed for instructional purposes. Hence . . . preschoolers [are] not so much surrounded by print as they [are] surrounded by adults who routinely choose to use print because it [is] effective in many contexts and for many purposes in their everyday lives" (Schieffelin & Cochran-Smith, 1984, p. 8).

Print needs to serve as a real resource for children and adults, as suggested in Figure 5.2.

Vygotsky (1978) emphasizes the importance of play and its relationship to literacy, "determining that early writing evolves through play and gesture. . . . Play is important for all children, even beyond age 8, because it gives children opportunities to experiment with uses of writing, to invent freely, and to practice more approximate literacy behaviors in nonevaluative settings."

Observation, anecdotal records, and informal means of assessment help teachers evaluate and assess the progress of children. Portfolios, work accumulation, observation, parent conferences, and other means provide an opportunity for children and teachers to collect meaningful assessment records.

Figure 5.2
Sources of Print for Classroom Use (From the Child's-Eye View)

Information:	*Useful* information, such as a schedule (for those who use one), special events, alphabet, lunch menu, date, weather, and so on
Integration:	Language and activities across areas of curriculum and throughout the day (math with play, literature with social studies, art with science, play with physical development, and so on)
Pleasure:	Printed literature (books, poems, songs), new books or activities
Recording:	Observations, weather logs, attendance, lunch count
Dramatic play:	Special props for various kinds of play
Home-school:	Information to share between home and school
Special events:	Field trips, celebrations, announcements, guests, new toys and activities
Follow-up:	Thank-you notes, recording of special events (visitors, field trips)
Curriculum:	Introduce new information, highlight a special activity for the day
Notices:	Information of interest—especially on topics suggested by the children

Home-School Relationships

Early childhood educators are responsible for building on each child's knowledge from home. . . . [R]edefining the traditional relationship between schools and homes . . . based on partnership and communication, with the mutual goal of providing children with supportive and successful educational experiences, must replace the common relationship marked by fear, intimidation, anger, and resentment between teachers, principals, and parents (Bredekamp, 1987; Shannon, 1995).

Appropriate and Integrated Curriculum

If young children are to reach their potentials, the curriculum *must* be developmentally appropriate and begin with the individual characteristics of the children involved. They need firsthand experiences in exploration, practice, and learning.

Bredekamp (1987) has outlined specific guidelines for appropriate K–3 classrooms. For example, a carefully planned and prepared curriculum includes:

1. Materials and activities that are relevant, meaningful, appropriate for the ages and stages of the individual children, integrated with other topics, and placed throughout the day

2. Opportunities for personal and social growth

3. Sufficient and flexible play materials and work places

4. Opportunities in specific and integrated curriculum areas

5. Individual and group experiences with language

6. Carefully selected toys and activities (multicultural, nonsexist) to enhance self-esteem, and appreciation of differences and similarities between the children (pp. 67–72).

Webbing

Consider Bromley's definition of *webbing* (1991):

> In nature, a web is a network of fine threads that a spider weaves. This network forms a complicated structure that is the means by which the spider snares its prey. A web can also be a complicated work of the mind that represents objects or concepts and the relationships a person perceives among them. In a classroom, the term *web* borrows something from both definitions. A semantic web, used as an instructional tool in a classroom, is a graphic representation or visual display of categories of information and their relationships. (p. 2)

Webbing was discussed in Chapter 4, Curriculum Development. In this chapter it will help to emphasize the importance of written and spoken language in relating concepts, in personal relationships, in everyday life, and in making sense of the world to the young children we teach.

Literacy development is a continuous process that begins in infancy. It is learned through oral and written language. Its roots are found everywhere in the environment, beginning in the home and spreading as the child's literacy learning grows out of a variety of experiences.

LISTENING

Early-childhood teachers have long realized the importance of role playing and dramatic play for the children in their classrooms. These teachers reinforce and give firsthand meaning to stories, books, and everyday experiences by providing props and materials, replicas, pictures, flannel board and flip-card stories, space, time, and a host of other necessities. Through these activities, children learn facts, concepts, and principles in addition to the literal and implicit content of the story.

Developmental Characteristics

Age 2

Understands most simple words and sentences. Likes to hear commercial jingles and catchy tunes. Listens to simple stories. Likes nursery rhymes.

Age 3

Likes to hear familiar sounds (animals, transportation, household). Likes one-on-one reading experiences. Has rather short but attentive listening span.

Age 4

Listens longer to stories. Still likes one-on-one experiences. May bring favorite stories to be read. Follows simple directions.

Age 5

Seems content to listen for period of time. Enjoys stories, songs, finger plays, and rhymes. Can follow more directions. Carries on conversations.

Children within earshot of conversations, even if they appear not to be listening, learn about language. As reported by Garrard (1987): "Excellence in language does not come from a kit. It comes from children conversing with caring adults while busy playing and living in general, especially with adults who speak well and who encourage children to converse freely" (p. 17).

Too often, adults do not listen to young children, even though they can learn much about them and their concerns merely by doing so. Adults who expect children to listen need to model good listening. A child can be complimented by saying: "What a good idea!" "You thought of a different way to do it!" "You are a good thinker." Such approval tells the child that the adult can listen, too.

Because research reveals that auditory discrimination correlates positively with reading achievement, good listening experiences must be planned and executed often. A child learns to be selective by giving attention to others or to the task at hand (when important) rather than attending to the fly on the wall, other children outside, or thoughts within her head. Listening experiences help the child to increase her vocabulary, learn the structure of spoken language, add concepts and ideas, increase her speech accuracy, and interact with others. They also stimulate her imagination.

Some periods are natural for language development. One is during group time when stories, poetry, finger plays, and songs are used; another is during free play with friends and props.

We could all be better listeners: teacher-child, parent-child, husband-wife, sibling-sibling, employer-employee, and so on. A person may send a message in a particular way, and the receiver (based on former experience—or inexperience) receives the message in a logical (or illogical) way and acts upon it. Both sender and receiver may show confusion. It is particularly important for adults to carefully consider their information or request as a child may receive it, for a child responds from a limited background; the response could result in action that is inappropriate, unexpected, or unappreciated by the adult but perfectly natural or logical for the child.

Reflection

The following story provides *a thought-provoking but poor example of teaching a concept—hopefully this will never occur in your preschool classroom!*

A preschool teacher wanted to teach the children about rain. She carefully prepared her visual aids and gave a lengthy demonstration about evaporation. A few of the children got a glimmer of the concepts, but in order to move on to an activity of individual selection, the teacher required each child to give her a verbal explanation, using some of her terms, of what she had just demonstrated. Some older children parroted back the teacher's words and moved on to other play. But, the younger, less verbal, less interested, limited-speaking children had a very difficult time. The children and teacher found the experience to be very frustrating.

Hopefully, the teacher will pledge to herself that she will be more careful in her future planning and requirements. As an observer of this experience, offer some constructive, but specific, suggestions to this teacher.

Of all the language skills that human beings acquire, listening is the one they use the most throughout life, particularly during early childhood. The sense of hearing functions even before birth, and the typical child amasses extensive experience with listening long before he speaks, reads, or writes. But good listening is

Hearing impairments should not exclude children from experiences with peers. Both gain valuable experiences and understanding.

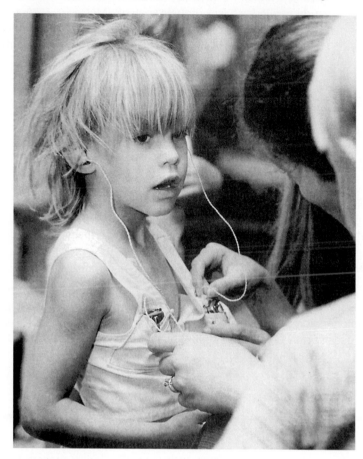

more than hearing. Listening is the process used to convert spoken language and sound into meaning in the mind (Lundsteen, 1979; Jalongo, 1996). At this point I would like to remind the reader that diagnosis, treatment, and special handling of children with hearing impairments will not be discussed in this text; however, these children can and should be included in regular classrooms.

Building children's listening skills is dependent upon creating a positive classroom communication environment. Jalongo (1996) suggests that teachers listen to themselves and use the following guidelines for self-assessment:

> Do I model good listening habits? Is there evidence that my classroom is a listening environment? Do I set a purpose for children's listening? Do I communicate clearly? Do I assess children's background knowledge and keep them actively involved in the lesson, project, or activity? Do I listen attentively to each child? (We can't expect children to listen to us if we don't listen to them.) Do I have projects and activities that are interesting to almost all children? Why should they listen if nothing worthwhile is going on? Do I work with parents to build listening skills at home? Are listening goals part of the curriculum?

Each question is followed by examples and dialogue.

To encourage listening, teachers must use clear, concise messages, use jargon-free language, consider what nonverbal communication says to children, *and,* above all, show respect for the children's home languages and cultures. "Listening is one of the primary methods by which children acquire the beliefs, norms, and knowledge bases of their society" (McDevitt, 1990, p. 571). When teachers build children's listening skills, they are making an important contribution that will serve the child well, not only during early childhood but also throughout life.

Reflection

Teachers' Attitudes Regarding Language and Its Usage

Personal

Showing respect for (1) home languages and cultures; (2) culturally and linguistically diverse families and individual differences in second-language learning; (3) those who have language differences (are nonverbal, have speech/hearing problems, and so on); and (4) children who need extra time to express themselves or understand concepts.

Classroom Attitudes

Using: (1) literature and activities that reflect the children in the classroom; (2) diversity in curriculum activities (music, art, and so on); (3) interpersonal relationships; (4) new languages and/or customs; (5) repetition; (6) information about language/hearing deficits; (7) specific guided information related to differences within the classroom; and (8) sensory deprivation as a positive teaching tool about others who are different from us.

Some ideas suggested by Soto, 1995, p. 47.

Language is frequently viewed as being spoken, but listening is a very important part of language development. If a person does not hear, she cannot respond. If she does not respond, she may be inappropriately classified. And language can be used privately (reading, self-communication) or publicly.

Aimed at children who are slightly below the ages considered in this text but who will very shortly be in our focus, the National Institute for Child Health and Human Development child care study, the most comprehensive to date on child care in the United States to compare the progress of children in child care and those under their mother's care only, has identified linguistic interaction as a key to intellectual growth in infants (reported in 1997 in a local newspaper article. [This information is given here to alert the reader to research in progress on this topic.]). What researchers have found so far is simple, logical, and subtle: Quality and meaningful interaction between caregivers and children is a powerful influence on the children's intellectual progress—not the educational toys, the family's status, or even the security of home care—but caregivers who speak often and directly to children with respect, sincerity, and sensitivity. The right environment, in which children and caregivers can listen to each other, is critical—and that can be compromised in large groups in some child-care centers. "Quality interaction, apparently, can happen anywhere there's a motivated adult," says Huston, a professor of child development at the University of Texas at Austin and a researcher on the NICHHD study. "It doesn't matter what the topic of conversation, the trick is to speak to children at their level, and then open the door to two-way conversation by listening for their responses," adds Huston.

The sensitive and caring caregivers in the study who were adept at this used simple words, talked softly and answered even babies' vocalizations—creating a language recognized by researchers as "Motherese."

Stories and Storytime

The response of children to stories varies greatly. Some sit quietly during storytime; some make frequent comments; some do neither. If one child is disturbing the others, the teacher can say, "After we finish the story, I'd like to hear more about that. Could you tell me later?" She must then follow through and let him tell what he was thinking. The time lapse may or may not dampen his desire to talk. Although the teacher does not want to stifle one child's interest or imagination, she must also consider the rest of the children.

Books attractively displayed on a rack or table beckon children. Children like to sit quietly, undisturbed, while they look at books or have a story read to them individually or in a small, intimate group. A variety of books should be provided—some favorites, some new.

The teacher can be aware of the interests of the children and encourage them to spend time with books. One child may be fascinated with spiders, another with boats, another with weather. The teacher should point out to the individual child that she can learn more about her interests through looking at the books. The teacher might select one or more of these special books to use during group storytime.

The attitude and feelings of the teacher will greatly influence the children's interest in the story. One teacher felt sure the children would not enjoy the story she had prepared. She was right; they picked up her attitude about it. On another day the same teacher was very excited about the story she had prepared. She was surprised when the children responded to her enthusiasm.

Storytime should be relaxed and leisurely, with the length depending on the children—not the clock! They should be comfortably seated on the floor. If they get restless but need to stay in the group, some activities can be started to involve them more, such as finger play, an exercise, or a song.

Thorough preparation of the story (whether it includes use of visual aids or just reading) will add interest for the children and flexibility for the teacher. When necessary, the teacher should be able to lengthen or shorten the story.

Storytime is when the two-teacher model works well. The lead teacher can begin and conduct the storytime while the support teacher assists with slow children, those who need quieting, or other interruptions. A child's attention may be regained by mentioning his name. When it is necessary to separate two children, the support teacher can move in casually but confidently and say, "I would like to sit by Denise and Michael today." He can then sit down and attend to the story. A support teacher can often reinterest a child merely by putting her hand on his shoulder or hand. If a particular child has an extremely difficult time enjoying storytime, it may be better for her to sit quietly in another area, not as punishment, but as preparation. She is always given the option of entering the group when she is ready.

Books are helpful to children who need time to assimilate the many facts thrown at them. Casually looking through a book may help children develop some concrete ideas or new concepts pertaining to their world. Occasionally they should be encouraged to act out a story.

Teachers should take advantage of teachable moments. One day, after a heavy snowstorm, the teacher told the children about the many things she had observed on the way to school. It sounded like a story! One child said: "Tell it again, teacher."

Individual and group language experiences are helpful. For a group of preschool children who are less attentive and rather disruptive during group story-time, one teacher found that the following suggestions recapture the children:

1. Spend a few introductory minutes discussing the story and making predictions.
2. Pause during the reading so children can join in with a familiar word or phrase.
3. Point to the pictures to emphasize the story.
4. Interject *brief* comments to help explain the text.
5. React positively to children's comments with a nod of your head or a short oral response.
6. Wonder aloud and invite the children to voice questions about pictures or text that might be difficult to decipher or understand, and ask open-ended questions.
7. Encourage the children to discuss and dramatize the story and to create art projects to enhance their enjoyment and comprehension of the story (Conlon, 1992, pp. 16–17).

Criteria for Selecting Books and Stories

Realistic, Accurate Material

The materials should be realistic and reported accurately. Factuality helps children develop validity of concepts and form mental pictures for future use. Young children have difficulty distinguishing between what is real and what is fantasy. The younger the child, the more he needs realistic stories. Most children can more appropriately deal with abstract concepts after their fifth birthday. Human characteristics (talking, dressing, feeling) given to animals, objects, or things confuse young children. Some children handle abstract or inconsistent ideas at a younger age than do other children. Fantasy stories should be used in small proportion to such realistic stories as here-and-now experiences until the children can better distinguish real from unreal.

The question of telling fairy tales to young children always arises. During the preoperational stage of development, young children are unable to understand fairy tales. Many fairy tales produce fear, deal with advanced concepts, or contain morals. They are better left until the school years (Kohlberg, 1966; Spock, 1976; Taylor & Howell, 1973).

DeVries (referred to by Bee, 1981) did an interesting experiment with 3- to 6-year-old children and a tame cat named Maynard. The children petted the cat and made friends with it. Then DeVries hid the front end of the cat behind a box and instructed the children to watch the tail end. Behind the box, DeVries put a very lifelike dog mask on the cat's head, showed him to the children, and asked if he could now bark, whether he would eat dog or cat food, whether the new animal would play like a cat or a dog, and so on. Young children thought the mask had essentially changed the animal into a dog and that he could bark and do other dog things. The 4- and 5-year-olds understood that the mask did not change the animal into a dog. This experience shows the level of belief in young children.

In *Island of Childhood* (1982), Griffin discusses animal disguises, animals smaller than children who need protection and security, animation of machines, competitive themes, extravagantly unreal happenings, bizarre creatures, imagination, hidden emotional problems, morals, and folk and fairy tales. This book is recommended to teachers of young children.

Another avenue of inquiry concerns the use of Mother Goose rhymes. These are often accepted because of the rhyme and rhythm, the humor, the suspense, and the repetition, but they should be used discriminately. Mother Goose rhymes, originally written as adult political satire, are usually enjoyed by young children. Avoid those that express or encourage aggression.

Support of Firsthand Experiences

Books promote learning by supporting firsthand experiences. A book may be used to introduce a new idea, especially when followed by a direct experience, such as a field trip, a visitor, replicas, or other personal involvement.

Books help children clarify concepts about their environment. Books may also be used to stimulate dramatic play, give role models, define behavior, or encourage curiosity. Books often put into words and pictures things the children want to know about but lack skills to ask.

Using flannel board characters can stimulate a child's imagination and vocabulary.

Young children like to hear stories about familiar things that they can also do, such as participating with the family, caring for a pet, visiting the community, developing new skills, or learning new information.

Literary Value

Literature should have value for the reader or listener of any age. For young children, the following are important:

- A definite plot (ability to discern author's purpose and fulfillment)
- Interesting sounds or plays on words (catch phrases, repetition of incidents or ideas)
- A light element of surprise or suspense
- Language that is clear, descriptive, and understandable
- Direct conversation that adds interest and helps children develop respect for language
- An uplifting effect (A book that contains familiar elements and helps to promote sound concepts is generally appropriate. Elements that produce fear, nightmares, poor social relationships, or emotional upsets should be used with caution. Some excellent books depict children conquering fears of potentially upsetting situations. These help children learn to deal with normal experiences.)
- Accurate portrayal of gender, ethnic, and social models
- Interest for the age level of the children, reflecting their point of view in timeliness, problem solving, creativity, and so on
- A positive influence on language arts experiences in listening, speaking, writing, and reading
- The ability to stimulate the imagination

Each year the John Newbery Medal is given for the best literary contribution to children's literature; however, it is not limited to books for preschool children. Librarians know the Newbery Medal winners and should be able to help determine their appropriateness for a specific group. Also check with local libraries, bookstores, and the Internet for lists of past and present Newbery Medal winners.

Some interesting questions are asked in the article "What Are We Really Saying to Children?" (*Child Care Information Exchange,* March, 1987). It encourages adults to look for the messages in children's books, and specifically asks for evaluation of the characters, the situation, the illustrations, the messages, the author/illustrator's credibility, and the selection as a whole. Too often these aspects are overlooked before books are purchased or read to young children.

Good Illustrations

Young children like visuals that are clear and fairly large and that clarify the text. Books should have an appropriate art style and be aesthetically appealing. Abstract illustrations are generally confusing and annoying to young children.

Most adults prefer color in picture books, and so do most children; however, some favorite picture books are in black and white, sepia and white, or only two colors. Children consider clarity more important than color. The pictures should be uncluttered, yet contain some supportive detail. Children enjoy discovering a ladybug or butterfly in the grass, but when the text calls for a brown-and-white cow and the picture is of a black one, the children are confused by the inconsistency.

Action in the picture gives further clarification, especially when the visual adds an element of information not generally known (instead of a goat just standing in the field, he might be eating a tin can or pulling a small cart, for example).

Photographs are interesting for children because they often give space relationships that may not be obvious in an artist's drawing. Photographs also give a mental picture to correlate with firsthand experiences.

Another annual award, given for the outstanding picture book, is the Caldecott Medal. Libraries often have a display of these books. The teacher can look through them for ones appropriate for his group of children. Not all the winners are of interest to preschool children. Also check with local libraries, bookstores, and the Internet for lists of past and present Caldecott Medal winners.

Group Storytime

When planning a group storytime, consider the following factors:

○ *Appropriateness of the story.* The teacher should know the children well enough to plan according to their needs, interests, abilities, interest span, and maturity level.

○ *Variety.* Children are more willing to attend the group experience if it is interesting and challenging. They like some repetition but also some variety.

○ *Length of time the children are expected to sit.* This depends on the children. Usually a 3-year-old sits quietly for a shorter period than a 4-year-old, but there can be differences among children, from day to day, or as weather changes. If the children grow restless, they can be allowed to participate more in the story; the teacher can also eliminate parts of the story or add interesting elements to it.

○ *Visual aids.* Often these add interest, but should be used wisely.

○ *Preparation of the teacher.* The teacher should be well prepared and have all of her materials before the story begins. Often, if a teacher leaves to get something, the children want to leave, too. The teacher should evaluate her personal actions, such as how often she reads instead of tells a story, her voice, her eye contact, and other techniques that add to the appeal of this experience for the children.

To create extra interest in storytime, whether the group is large or small, methods of presentation should vary. Some examples are as follows:

1. Use the book.
2. Tell the story, with or without aids.
3. Use flannel board aids.
4. Use only one picture and display it at an appropriate time.
5. Use flip cards.
6. Use real objects or replicas.
7. Have the children dramatize the story after it is read or discussed.
8. Act it out as you tell it.
9. Use your own creative methods.

Teachers should be alert to children who have difficulty listening to books or stories; some children may need special placement in order to see or hear, and others may have physical difficulties in sitting on the floor or in a crowded area. For children to enjoy stories and social times, they need to be comfortable and interested in the proceedings.

Some benefits of reading aloud suggested by Conlon (1992) include closeness to an adult, attention to visuals and ideas expressed, opportunities to learn about the act of reading, a chance to practice making sense of stories with a deeper understanding through repetition, support of their own development (emotional, social, and cognitive), a love of books and reading, hearing language and ideas, and an individual or group social experience. See Figure 5.3 for a list of evaluation questions when considering picture books.

Sources of Books for Young Children

In past editions of this book, an appendix has contained numerous books suggested for the various curriculum topics. In preparing this edition, I found that many of my favorite books are out of print, publishers have changed their names and/or ad-

Figure 5.3
Evaluation Questions for Picture Books for Young Children

Content Evaluation
1. How does the book compare with other picture books of its type (favorable, average, unfavorable)?
2. Do your colleagues, local educators, or librarians recommend or endorse the book? (Be very careful here. Some colleagues, educators, and librarians disagree on what is good literature or even what is popular. Not all good books can win awards or accolades of professionals.)
3. Is the story free from ethnic, racial, or gender-role stereotypes?
4. How could the story apply to or enhance the lives of the children in your group?
5. Are the pictures and text complementary?
6. From a literary standpoint, are elements of plot, theme, character, style, and setting used effectively?
7. Is the theme developmentally appropriate for the children?
8. How do preschool children respond to the story and pictures?
9. Does the book appeal to the parent or teacher?

Illustrations
1. Are the illustrations and text synchronized?
2. Does the mood conveyed by the artwork (humorous/serious, rollicking/quiet) complement that of the story?
3. Are the illustrative details consistent with the text?
4. Could a child get a sense of the basic concepts or story sequence by looking at the pictures?
5. Are the illustrations or photographs aesthetically pleasing?
6. Is the printing (clarity, form, line, color) of good quality?
7. Can children view and re-view the illustrations, each time getting more from them?
8. Are the illustrative style and complexity suited to the age level of the intended audience?

Note: Based on Huck (1979). No complete reference given.

---

dresses or gone out of business, a current list of publishers of children's books was not available, and many new books have been written for young children. To offer some direction, I now suggest:

1. checking with a children's librarian at the local library
2. getting acquainted with a buyer of children's books at a local bookstore
3. contacting a teacher of children's literature courses at a local junior/community college or university
4. contacting known reputable publishers of children's books for catalogs containing descriptions and age levels
5. searching the Internet for publishers of children's books, especially looking for Caldecott Award– and Newbery Award–winning books of current and past years (only some of them are for preschool children).

If at all possible, purchasers of books for young children should *read the books before buying them or checking them out of a library.* Some publishers mail an annotated catalog with an age guide, but some books listed as appropriate for preschoolers may be too advanced or too simple or may cover too broad an age range for a particular group of children.

In addition to using stories and books as good listening experiences for young children, the value of poetry, finger plays, and Mother Goose should be taken into consideration (see Chapter 12).

Items in the following list are used to increase listening ability:

- Poetry
- Finger plays
- Mother Goose rhymes
- Sound boxes, tubes, and cans
- Tape recordings (commercial or classroom). Listen to a taped story. Play it again. Stop it at various places and ask what will happen next. Make a tape of children's voices and familiar sounds and have them guess who or what it is.
- Record player and records
- Listening walk
- Rhyming words and nonrhyming words
- Repetition in stories
- Rhythm. The teacher beats the rhythm and the children repeat it.
- Simple directions
- Sounds in the classroom. Have children imitate them.
- Sounds in the environment, such as those from a household, a playground, or transportation. Use sounds with and without pictures.
- Puppets. Have children listen and then repeat words or actions.
- Games such as "Simon Says"; the teacher says, "I am thinking about an animal and its name sounds like *how*" (children guess); "Mother and Baby" (One child pretends to be a mother animal, makes the appropriate sound, then closes eyes. Another child, pretending to be the baby animal, hides, and also makes the appropriate sound. The mother finds the baby); "Head, Shoulders, Knees, and Toes."
- Telephones (answering, dialing, etiquette)

- ○ Stories. Have children listen and then dramatize.
- ○ Field trips. Tell children what to expect; dramatize later.
- ○ Whispering times
- ○ Objects. Provide children with a box or bag of objects. Describe an object and have each child find it in her bag.
- ○ Prepositions. Give directions ("Sit on the chair," "Roll under the table," "Stand beside the box") and have children respond using their bodies. When children are thoroughly familiar with the prepositions, continue the game at a future time by using a toy ("Put the car under the rug," "Put it between the blocks," "Put it beside the truck," and so on).

SPEAKING

Young children should not be pressured to produce responses. Sometimes they lack understanding of what is required, sometimes they feel silence is safer than being incorrect, and sometimes their words just don't come out! The problem could arise if a teacher has expectations of, and demands, responses that are at a level beyond the child's development.

Adults may insist upon spoken language. Children who are reluctant to speak may feel uncomfortable, frightened, inexperienced, unaccepted, or coerced. French (1996) writes: "There is much documentation of cultural differences in the extent to which children are encouraged to express themselves verbally at home. Also, considerable differences sometimes exist between children's language abilities at the comprehension level and at the production level; that is, children might be able to comprehend incoming language but still have difficulty in producing language expressing their understanding" (p. 20).

While story interests vary, most young children enjoy realistic ("I can do . . .") themes.

Young children should be given frequent opportunities to express their affective and cognitive ideas. Mentioned previously in this chapter was the stimulating and beneficial use of poetry and nursery rhymes, either spontaneous or planned. Maclean, Bryant, and Bradley (1987) concluded: "The direct practical implication of our research is that an increase in the amount of experience that 3-year-old children have with nursery rhymes should lead to a corresponding improvement in their awareness of sounds, and hence to greater success in learning to read" (p. 280).

Developmental Characteristics

Age 2

Has favorite word: "No!" Tries to say simple words; may use short sentences and carry on simple conversations. Names simple objects (body parts, pictures). Likes short responses.

Age 3

Can carry on a conversation. Uses simple words and short sentences (three to four words). May carry on a monologue. Asks "Why?" to gain adult attention.

Age 4

Is quick to pick up new words. Learns words for ideas, actions, and feelings. Combines more words. Is integrating rules of grammar; may have difficulty with irregular past tense or plurals. Is boastful and quarrelsome. May carry on a monologue. Talks about imaginary companion. Experiments with language. Asks "Why?" for knowledge.

Age 5

Has highly socialized speech. Is a continual talker. Uses "because" sentences. Has wide vocabulary, uses six- to eight-word sentences. Can verbally compare two or more objects.

In recent years, wordless books for young children have been appearing on the market. Do they have any value for these children? Hough, Nurss, and Wood (1987) record that stories told by young children about wordless books were more elaborate than stories they originated about a single picture, but less complex than original stories told by the children. They also encourage "busy pictures and wordless books" as idea givers to children because they encourage children to invent their own original stories.

"Literacy develops best in relational contexts that are meaningful to children as opposed to activities that are separate from their day-to-day pursuits" (Wishon, Brazee, & Eller, 1986, p. 91). Young children need stimulating learning experiences based on contextual cues, encouragement, and opportunities to practice new words and ideas if they are to express themselves, build concepts, and enlarge their knowledge base. Familiarity with books and experiences (such as field trips, filmstrips or videos, books, discussions), adjusting content level, and using descriptive language—all based on the developmental level of the children involved—provide the child with a sense of control and confidence.

Oral language is used to share, exchange, or test ideas; to express feelings; to gain new knowledge; to develop auditory acuity; to build relationships; to practice words and grammar; and to provide enjoyment. The younger the children, the less they verbalize; rather, they use physical methods for egocentric purposes. They take things, walk over others, bite, cry, kick, and scream. As children mature, they progressively use more verbalization.

Helping young children increase their speaking skills is desirable, but adults may do the opposite. When children receive too much attention, they do not need to speak; they can point, grunt, or cry. Children may use behavior below their developmental level just because it pays off. Adults may carry on their own two-way conversation by commenting and responding to themselves rather than giving the children a chance to respond. An adult may offer a choice to a child and when the child hesitates (or when the adult knows what he expects), the adult may respond as if making a democratic choice for the child.

Young children need attractive environments that are conducive to play, promote cooperation and enjoyment, and encourage verbal interaction. When they have thoughts, they want and need to express them. In some classrooms, however, teachers are known to talk 75 to 90 percent of the time to give instructions, keep order, and teach the children. When teachers use language in these ways, children speak infrequently. Frequent use of positive support comments decreases the need for disciplinary or negative statements and commands. In one study done by Serbin and O'Leary (1975), nursery-school teachers were found to reward boys for aggression and girls for passivity. In other words, they were "teaching girls to shut up"!

The teacher must learn how to establish rapport and a spontaneous flow of communication that provides comfort and security for each child. When teachers talk with children about interesting things, they get a rewarding response. The teacher can also help the shy child to verbalize by providing a variety of experiences, such as stories, songs, finger plays, new encounters, and friendly companions. Teachers, acting as resources for children's language, should be as precise as possible in their conversations, using many concept words, descriptions, and abstractions that help the child relate to the experience.

The teacher who shows sincere interest by getting down on the level of the children, by listening attentively, and by making appropriate comments, can expect other "talking times" with them. The teacher further encourages language by expanding conversations ("Yes, I see your new shoes," when a child says, "New shoes") and by elaborating on what children say without controlling the whole conversation ("Your new shoes have two straps and two buckles"). The teacher may also need to assist very young children who are trying to use words and verbs that are irregular in forming plurals or past tenses.

Several authors discuss two popular myths about learning language: (1) that children learn by imitation, and (2) that children learn by being corrected. Imitation by itself is insufficient, and correction does not occur with enough frequency to change verbal patterns. Many theories of language development agree that experience, conceptualization, and communication continuously influence the way children develop language.

Following are some suggestions teachers could use to increase the speaking ability of children:

- Poetry
- Finger plays
- Mother Goose rhymes
- Puppets (stick, sack, felt, cone, sock, glove, finger). A puppet stage is also useful. Remind the children that the puppets are kind and gentle, thus avoiding aggressive and loud behavior.

- Telephone (for courtesy and conversation)
- Just talking about things that are of interest to the children
- Props. Put on various articles of clothing and ask the children to guess your occupation (firefighter, sports figure, doctor, skier, mail carrier, construction worker, nurse, baker, soldier). Stress that occupations can be for either males or females.
- Recordings (video or audio). Record original poems or songs and what the children say about their activities. Play back the recordings and try to identify voices.
- Stories. Discuss a story; let the children retell a story using visual aids; use a wordless book and let the children supply the story; tell a group story (each child tells part of it); have the children tell stories to each other.
- Television. Make a large cardboard TV set. Slip different pictures into its window and ask the children to tell about them. Provide a large box and let the children pretend they are actors.
- Naming (especially for younger children). The teacher points to a body part, and the children name it; the teacher shows an object or picture, and the children name it.
- Field trip. Discuss preparations and behavior with children, such as what they should ask, what they think they will see, and how they should act. Provide dramatic play as a follow-up.
- Songs
- Questions. Ask open-ended questions that require thought and verbalization rather than yes, no, or one-word answers; propose questions (why, what, where, when, how) and help the children find out the answers.
- Food experiences. Let children help shop for, prepare, and eat different foods. Encourage conversation at snack time.
- Dramatic play. Provide an area in the classroom where the children can reenact a variety of themes.
- Show and tell. This may be less effective with younger children. Also, some children feel compelled to have something every time, so you may need a schedule. This is a time for children—not teachers—to talk.
- Spotlight. Have a place in your room where you display interesting science things. Rotate the display, but give the children enough time to enjoy and investigate. Use this area to stimulate curiosity and conversation.
- Microphone. Encourage the children to pretend they are talking through a microphone (use a small can, tube, or fist).

Drama

Young children can learn from dramatic play and also from informal drama—reenacting stories, making up situations, and using props that suggest activities. Through this type of play, children practice physical skills, social and emotional situations, cognitive and language development, and multisensory experiences as ideas unfold or are enhanced in the presence of others—actors and audience.

A supportive adult may need to be nearby to see that the dramatizations do not become negative, exclusive, or competitive. Teachers may also need special training, understanding, and confidence to make drama a delightful part of language development.

Show and Tell

Show and tell has become a part of some early-childhood programs and has become extinct in others. On the one hand, it sounds like a good opportunity for children to verbalize with a group of their peers, but what often happens is that a child, as excited and desirous as he may be, becomes nervous, embarrassed, and nonverbal. The teacher does most of the talking—asking questions that can be answered with a nod, or repeating facts that the child (or parent) has previously given.

If show and tell is a part of the program, guidelines need to be precise or the following problems may occur:

> *Inconsistency:* A school policy of no toys coming from home, and then expecting show-and-tell participation.

> *Taking turns:* Some children want to participate *every* time.

> *Embarrassment:* Not able to speak in front of a group.

> *Parental/family fatigue:* Always having to come up with something to take—and it usually turns out to be of more value or interest to a family member than to the particular child. Unusual show-and-tell items include a 4-year-old sneaking her little sister onto the bus while the mother was in the shower, the mother's diamond ring, a brother's sports equipment, Dad's fishing gear, the neighbor's pet, worn-out shoes, and food stuffed into the child's pocket.

> *Lack of interest of other children:* Giving up valuable time for something that bores them.

> *Concern for the item:* A child may be so afraid of losing or having to share the item that she becomes very protective of it and loses interest in the activities and the other children.

Burrell (1992) reports:

> For some programs, the advantages of having a "S & T" time outweigh the disadvantages. When children are encouraged to bring in things from home, they begin to understand that each one of them is a "teacher," with something to help others learn about. As they share something of themselves with one another, they gain confidence in becoming the focus of the group's attention, they gain speaking skills, they find out that others are interested in them, they discover that there are things they know about, and they feel good about themselves doing it! (p. 30)

Burrell suggests that the name be changed to *sharing time* or *children's teaching time* and encourages

> clear guidelines for parents and children to follow, such as something found in nature; exotic or little known food; safe *hand* tool; photo from newspaper, magazine, or book or snapshot taken with a home camera; items the children have made themselves; items that represent someone's job, hobby, or favorite sport; children's books on any of the above topics, any current classroom themes, or any other topic that children and parents feel might be valuable to the class. Arrange the scheduling of the sharing experience so that it maximizes its advantages and minimizes any impact on your regular teaching time—like once per week. (p. 30)

READING

(In the case of preschool children, reading more often consists of *being read to* than children actually reading.)

Many young children are pressured to read by being subjected to drills or rigid, formal prereading programs. Both of these expectations are inappropriate for the experiences and skills of the children—but some adults (parents and educators) feel that early reading is possible and a sign of intelligence. In the home and in a preschool or kindergarten setting, many experiences prepare a child for learning to read. Children who are read to at an early age develop better reading habits and demonstrate significantly greater gains in vocabulary and reading comprehension than children who have not had this advantage.

Developmental Characteristics

Age 2

Many recognize objects, turn pages in books, and point to or name objects.

Ages 3, 4, and 5

May learn to read simple words (some memorize or remember). May identify words that look alike or different. Recognize a few words (own name, logos, signs, television words, food containers).

Children who see adults reading observe eye movements (or finger movements) to follow the print, page turning, picture support, and enjoyment. Books become important to the children, too. Besides using books, adults can point out words and signs in the child's environment, assist the child in writing his name (using capital and lowercase letters, of course), and provide opportunities for eye-hand coordination and discrimination tasks.

Sensory experiences are vital in helping young children learn to read:

Visual discrimination: matching (buttons, colors, shapes, letters and/or pictures [cards, books, and so on]) and sorting (cans, groceries, clothes, pans, and so on)

Auditory discrimination: sounds, telephone experiences, hearing stories, singing songs, and conversations involving descriptive ideas or recalling information (loud/soft, same/different)

Tactile discrimination: feeling many objects (fabrics, plastics, wood, and so on)

Oral discrimination: tasting, smelling, chewing

Some adults become anxious about teaching alphabet recognition, naming, and writing. Read, Gardner, and Mahler (1987) issue this reminder: "Learning to recognize and write the letters of the alphabet is not an appropriate activity for most three-year-olds, but it is often included in these programs" (p. 290). Smith (1985) states:

Of course, it does not hurt a child to have some acquaintance with the alphabet. . . . But learning the alphabet is not a prerequisite for learning to distinguish words, and

Children enjoy the closeness of others while hearing stories.

the alphabet can be a handicap if adults use it to try and train children to sound out words before they are able to make sense of what the adults are talking about. (p. 122)

And Kontos (1986) reports:

Letter name knowledge is frequently shown to be an important indicator of reading readiness. The research on letter name knowledge . . . is concerned with letter identification but not alphabetic sequence. Recitation of the alphabet does not necessarily indicate letter name knowledge. . . . Across studies, children as young as 3 are shown to be capable of recognizing some letters and 5-year-olds are shown to have nearly mastered letter name knowledge. (p. 62)

Many children learn to read before they come to school. Formal instruction is obviously not essential. Learning to read early is not determined by social or economic class, or by size of family, age, maturity, intelligence, an intact home, specialized programs and materials, or any specific geographical location or neighborhood (Smith, 1985). In order to read, children need to have reading experiences. Anbar's study (1986) shows that early reading can be achieved at home in a natural, nonpressured manner, with child and both parents enjoying the process by making a distinction between "pushing" and "encouraging" the child. (See Figure 5.4.)

Reading demands visual and auditory acuity, language ability, and the ability to learn (Smith, 1985). With regard to inventories of prerequisites for reading readiness, Smith calls them "shopping lists" of everything the compiler thinks might be relevant to reading, ranging from "knowledge of letters and sounds" to physical and emotional maturity and even "correct body-book posture" (p. 146). Smith continues:

The basic requirements are easily stated: on the part of the learner an interest in learning to read (or more precisely, in making sense of print) and for the teacher, the ability

Figure 5.4
Ways to Stimulate Reading in Young Children

1. Let children see an adult reading (modeling).
2. Arrange a comfortable reading area with magazines, newspapers, picture books, and so on.
3. Take children to the library: get a library card, choose books, and get acquainted with other media there.
4. Read road signs, store signs, package labels; find license plates for different states.
5. Reward children for reading achievement with *honest* praise, a trip to the library, or the purchase of a new book.
6. Make book projects: maps, special words, bookmarks, or other book-related activities.
7. Write down a story as a child tells it, then reread it.
8. Give children or help children make their own bookcases.
9. Limit television watching, or watch together.
10. Give books as presents.
11. As children draw and talk about their pictures, record descriptions and other information.
12. Show pictures and ask questions; prediction is an important reading skill.
13. Establish a daily pattern to read to your children (same time, same place). Talk about books you have read; anticipate what will happen next; recall a favorite thing or character. Talk about why the child liked the story. Ask the reader questions about the story; has something similar happened to the adult or the child?

to find interesting print that the child can make sense of. In the latter respect, teachers can be just as "unready" as learners. (p. 147)

Some parents search for magazines specifically published for preschool children. Scofield (1986) tested the appropriateness of seven magazines published for children between 2 and 6 years of age. She found that only one of the seven periodicals "solely and completely provided young children with entertainment and interesting information which offered many opportunities for extended discussion." Sometimes those who decide an age level for books, magazines, toys, and other materials for children are swayed by information other than the developmental characteristics of the children.

$$READING = written\ symbols + experience + meaning$$

If children do not have the repertoire of ideas to make sense out of something, the reading makes no sense, either.

Present-Day Concerns

There is concern that preschool programs have become too academic and are creating stress for children. This concern can easily apply to language arts—where stress may be on speaking frequently and fluently (in making one's needs and wants known, in getting along with others, in expressing one's feelings, and so on) or emphasis on learning to read and write.

Warnings about the dangers of including academics in preschool programs have appeared recently in both the popular and professional literature (Elkind, 1987; Kantrowitz & Wingert, 1989; Schickedanz et al., 1990; and others). It seems that teaching methods and what is being taught have not been differentiated in

Reflection

Ivan, a happy 5-year-old, sat looking at *The Wall Street Journal.* His mother had called him several times to prepare for dinner. Still he sat and looked. Finally, his mother became exasperated. "Ivan, if you don't come to dinner right this minute, I'll give your food to the dog!" Reluctantly, Ivan laid down the paper and strolled to the table. Still in deep thought, he finally said, "Mom, I just can't figure out why Dad likes that paper so much. It doesn't have any pictures, and it is all the same color!" Ivan was trying to equate his own reading experiences with those of his father. Ivan liked pictures, action, and color.

When young children are read to frequently and when parents are good models of reading, children begin their reading careers early. As Ivan and a parent sat down to read together, Ivan talked about the pictures, asked questions, and added new dialogue. He turned the pages when he was ready. Sometimes he or his parent made additions to the text and sometimes deletions. He memorized his favorite books and could tell when a word was misused or omitted. He figured out that the marks on the pages had something to do with the pictures, an important discovery in developing reading skill and comprehension. He also noticed that when he asked questions that his parents or teachers could not answer, they went to books, so, when he had questions, he looked at books. He did not always find what he wanted, but he knew the procedure followed by adults.

these discussions. For example: "Early instruction miseducates, not because it attempts to teach, but because it attempts to teach the wrong things at the wrong time" (Elkind, 1987, p. 25). The truth is that many 5-year-olds aren't ready for reading—or most of the other academic tasks that come easily to older children (Kantrowitz & Wingert, 1989, p. 52). Katz and Chard (1989) say that throughout the early years, teachers tend to overestimate children academically but underestimate them intellectually.

There is some agreement that presently many preschool and kindergarten children are being subjected to inappropriate teaching methods in many settings. Schickedanz et al. (1990) state: "We shouldn't keep academic learning out of preschool. We should have it there with home-like teaching methods" (p. 9). In other words, they are suggesting happy, nonpressured experience and appropriate, interesting ways for children to explore both tools and writing skills. Home and school environments should keep adult/child ratios as low as possible so adults can ask and answer questions, make observations and comments, reflect what children say and do, and be aware of materials children need and enjoy during their literacy experiences. High ratios of children to adults, pushy adults, inappropriate methods, strict time frames, at-risk children, and insufficient materials cause problems for young children.

The following elements help increase reading ability in children:

- Games where sound and listening are important
- A cozy place to read (loft or tent with pillows)
- A variety of good books appropriate for the child
- A discussion about the care of books
- Enrichment of the child's vocabulary
- Seriation (size, variation in color, or stacking of shoes, socks, sticks, cups, jars, ribbons, and so on)

Telling stories to a doll reflects the pleasure a child receives when an adult reads to the child.

- ○ Classification. Have the children put objects into appropriate groups and then look for other ways of grouping.
- ○ Card games (bingo and picture variations; old maid; go fish; matching pictures of shapes, sizes, and colors; combining two properties such as size and shape; large cards with numbers and letters the children can arrange)
- ○ Poster or chart. Use a helper chart on which each child's name is placed by a picture with a word for an activity or an assignment. Make a word dictionary as children learn new words (include pictures).
- ○ Visual discrimination opportunities (similarities and differences, missing items, comparison, shapes, sizes, and so on)
- ○ Uninterrupted time
- ○ Models who read and enjoy it
- ○ Experiences and conversations that stimulate conversation
- ○ Food. Make a list, go to the grocery store, buy food for lunch or snack (observe labels). Make something using a recipe.
- ○ Typewriter or computer
- ○ Curriculum areas. (1) Have a pattern for toys that go in certain places. (2) Provide puzzles and rubber stamps of objects, letters, and numbers. (3) Supply sewing cards. (4) Have children reproduce designs with pegs, beads, or blocks.

- Symbols. (1) Place a sticker or design on each child's locker. (2) Wear name tags daily. (3) Write each child's name on the back of her artwork. (4) Use one picture of only boys, one of only girls, and one of both boys and girls; hold up one picture and have pictured children respond to actions or questions (no verbalization is used).

- Artwork. Ask children to tell about their artwork. On the back side or a separate page, write down what they say and read it back to them.

- Community. (1) Take a trip to the local library. (2) Observe safety and speed signs. (3) Go to some interesting places and observe signs. Write a thank-you note.

- Decentering. Help children focus on more than one aspect at a time. They will need to recognize parts and whole if they are to learn to read.

- Practice. Give the children opportunities to practice concepts of conversation, reversibility, seriation, whole-part relationships, and multiple and simultaneous classification. (Some examples are listed here and in Chapter 9.)

Symbol-Reading Exercises Just for Adults

Throughout this book, activities are suggested to increase skills and abilities in children. Figure 5.5 shows shorthand and Japanese symbol-reading exercises and Figure 5.6 shows music symbol-reading exercises just for adults.

Figure 5.5
Shorthand and Japanese Symbol-Reading Exercises for Adults Only

A

B

KAGOME KAGOME	〈 かごめ　かごめ 〉
KAGOME KAGOME	かごめ　かごめ
KAGONO NAKANO TORIWA	かごの 中の 鳥は
ITSU ITSU DEAU	いついつ であう
YOAKENO BANNI	夜明けの 晩に
TSURUTO KAMEGA SUBETTA	鶴と 亀が すべった
USHIRONO SYOMEN DARE	後の 正面 だーれ？

Identify the individual words and meaning of the shorthand (A) and the Japanese (B).

Figure 5.6
Music Identification Symbol-Reading Exercises for Adults Only

Hum the music and identify the two songs (do not use a piano or other musical instrument).

As you approached each of these exercises, you probably looked for familiar signs. If you felt comfortable with one option more than the other two, you probably concentrated there. If none of the three exercises gave you any clues, you probably became frustrated and moved on to the next paragraph. Young children learning to read look for familiar symbols in their environment (names, road signs, designs) and then try to match them to symbols in written material. You just went through a similar experience.

WRITING

Rich (1985) describes a method of

> promoting an interest in reading in young children by giving them access to important materials (e.g., books, paper, crayons). . . . These items would help stimulate a child's interest, take advantage of the important relationship between drawing and writing, and provide an outlet for children's natural curiosity about print as they see it being used.

To think that children under 6 years of age can maneuver writing implements with accuracy and precision or that they have mental organizational skills sophisticated enough to compose a short story indicates total ignorance as to how young children develop and learn. More realistic is the image of a young child crudely holding writing tools, making indistinguishable strokes at scattered locations on the page, giving first one description of his marks and then another, and combining unrelated ideas. Children do pretend to make up, write, and read stories of their own. They see adults do it, so why can't they?

Developmentally appropriate early writing stages include *scribbling* (written symbols that carry meaning and a message); the *linear mock writing stage* (left-to-right, single-line, top-to-bottom, sometimes reading written work to someone else); and *mock letter writing* (recognition of letters, imitation of the conventional alphabet) (Kuball, 1995).

Developmental Characteristics

Age 2

Scribbles; repeats radial or circular pattern. Uses whole-hand grasp, whole-arm movement. Fills whole page. Is fascinated by markings.

Age 3

Prints large, single, capital letters anywhere on page. Likes to draw and paint (images are large, simple, and incomplete).

Age 4

May recognize a few letters, including own name. May write name or a few capital letters (large and irregular). Likes to draw and paint. Human figures are stick, drawings crude. Draws circles and squares.

Age 5

Prints first name (large, irregular letters increasing in size). Frequently reverses letters and numbers or writes from right to left. Prints numbers (uneven and medium-sized). Can write some capital and lowercase letters. Has better grasp on writing utensils. Likes to draw and paint. Pictures are more complex and complete. Combines squares and circles. Likes to copy a model. May ask about spelling.

"Learning to write can sometimes become a meaningless activity for children. The physical problems of trying to copy or trace the written word are tremendous. This is particularly true of the young child who is beginning to write his name," writes Lowenfeld (1987, pp. 51–52).

"Children who are encouraged to draw and scribble 'stories' at an early age will later learn to compose more effectively, and with greater confidence than children who do not have this encouragement" (U.S. Department of Education, 1986, p. 14).

Parents can stimulate and encourage children in writing experiences through (1) providing writing equipment (paper, pencils, crayons, envelopes, cellophane tape, staples, a comfortable place to work, and so on, so that the children can explore writing at any time; (2) providing blank forms, order forms, menu pads, and so on for play that stretches children's imaginations and broadens their experiences; (3) helping them write letters, cards, and so on to others; (4) putting notes in lunchboxes; (5) making books for children to write and draw (some folded sheets); (6) modeling writing—notes, lists, and so on; (7) praising their attempts and showing the relationship between print and speech; and (8) eliminating criticisms of neatness, spelling, or grammar.

Handwriting has several aspects: physical ability, organizational skills and idea presentation, and language skills (vocabulary, syntax, grammar).

Physical ability includes good use of hands and fingers. Writing requires more than a whole-hand grasp and uncontrolled large gross movements. The fingers need to have a good grasp of the utensil, and the arm needs to rest comfortably on a tabletop. The physical prerequisites are often lacking in 4- and 5-year-olds. Their control generally is still imprecise and awkward. Practice and some instruction are needed.

Schickedanz et al. (1977) note the following:

> As in most areas of learning, learning to form letters takes time. It is a lengthy process for several reasons. First, the movements are not easy to make. Second, there are many letters. Third, some letters are very similar to other letters, making it easy to confuse one with another. Fourth, the child must learn that with these special two-dimensional symbols, orientation is a significant attribute. It is not just the configuration of the lines that makes one letter different from the other, but the left-right or up-down orientation as well. . . . If allowed to proceed at their own pace and in their own way, without pressure and fanfare, children will often approach learning to write letters with mastery behavior similar to that used when working puzzles or building with blocks.

The second aspect of writing, *organizational skills* and *idea presentation*, is difficult for young children, who are still in the egocentric stage and have difficulty expressing ideas or seeing things from another's viewpoint. They think others can see into their minds and know their thoughts and that others have the same view as they do. Expressing simple, often unrelated, ideas is the extent of their ability.

The third aspect of writing, *language skills,* is also difficult for young children. They know nothing about the use of capital letters, punctuation, placement of elements in the sentence, spelling, or the use of descriptive words. It will be some years before these attributes are developed.

Beginning writing experiences include the use of jumbo crayons and pencils, large sheets of paper, something interesting to draw, and motivation. When utensils and materials are readily available, the children are encouraged to use them.

Young children should learn manuscript letters (printing) before cursive ones for two reasons. First, when children have had extensive experience with drawing and painting, they may have already mastered the basic strokes required in handwriting. Second, as children begin their initial reading, manuscript letters more nearly resemble the print.

When a child expresses interest in writing, parents generally teach the capital letters only. When this occurs, the child must learn two different ways of writing. As a beginner, it is easier for the child to learn capital and lowercase letters in simple words such as his name and familiar objects and terms. Again, this type of writing looks like the type in books. When teachers in the classroom write names on possessions, they should start in the upper left-hand corner and use capital and lowercase letters. The adult should sit down by the children and make the letters neatly as a good model for the children to follow. Writing from across the table or in an awkward position distorts the letters.

Writing is not generally one of the regular curriculum areas for young children, but most preschools give help with writing as each child indicates interest. Individually, the experience can be one of joy and success. In some kindergartens, writing practice is one of the regular curriculum areas. Generally, teachers have a specific way of presenting the different letters that is not necessarily consecutive. Many preschool children memorize the alphabet before it has actual meaning to them.

The following activities are recommended to increase writing ability:

○ Practice in using and strengthening small muscles (pegboards, cutting, puzzles, stringing, lacing, zipping, drawing, painting)

○ Body movement. This helps children to observe; gives them a sense of high, low, and other directions; and teaches them shape and line. (For example, they can be told to swing their arms in a circle or to hold their legs straight.) The teacher can also ask the children to make their bodies into shapes shown on cards (see Chapter 12).

Figure 5.7
Sticking golf tees into Styrofoam or pegboard helps
increase abilities needed for writing.

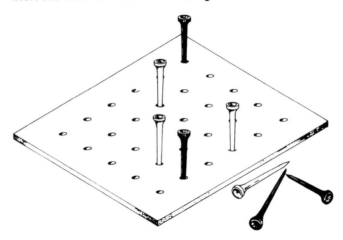

○ Practice in right-left concept ("Hokey Pokey"; body movement)

○ Use of manipulative toys (Tinkertoys, snap blocks, magnetic boards, blocks)

○ Games (Twister; "Do as I'm Doing"; circle games such as "Mulberry Bush" or "Ring-Around-a-Rosy"); spinner games

○ Practice with letters (letters of the child's name to put together like a puzzle; letters and numbers to use on the flannel board, or magnetic ones to use on magnetic boards; stencils to trace)

○ Drawing. This includes completing partially completed designs; reproducing designs; following patterns, making slanted, straight, and curved lines with crayons (teepees, boxes, a road); making designs and letters in the air; connecting dots or drawing lines to matching items (mother and baby animals, two shoes, go-togethers).

○ Labeling. Each child wears a label with her name that she can put into a chart to indicate an area she will play in, put into a helper chart, or use as a model when writing her name.

○ Art. The children can write in finger paint or sand; paste a variety of shapes to make letters and designs; weave paper, fabric, or yarn mats; stick golf tees into Styrofoam or pegboard (see Figure 5.7); and hammer small nails into fiberboard.

○ Sewing cards

Remember: Literature refers to listening, speaking, reading, and writing.

ROLE OF THE TEACHER

A teacher who wants to encourage language use and development in young children must be a good listener, a good model, and an interested and caring person. He must also provide for individual needs of the children. The teacher plans wisely so that language is an integral part of each day and each area of the curriculum. To say, "Now it's language time" would be foolish and inaccurate. Language time is all the time. Nonverbal or body language is often better understood than verbal language. One can easily tell from a facial expression, movement of the body, or breathing whether the sender is pleased or displeased.

Hendrick (1992) lists seven basic ways to foster language development: (1) listen to the children; (2) give them something real to talk about; (3) encourage conversation and dialogue; (4) use questions to generate and develop language; (5) provide auditory training; (6) seek professional assistance promptly, when necessary; and (7) become acquainted with and draw on research-based language development programs.

A review of additional references indicates that generally desired components for language development include favorable socioeconomic background, enriching experiences, sensory practice, respect for the child, interaction with other children, quality adult models, using the same language at home and school, attentive listeners for the child, a noncritical attitude toward the child's language skills, flexibility in the child's life, and time to enjoy speaking and listening experiences.

If language is so much a part of living, why is it important to provide specific opportunities for children to just talk or listen? Consider these values of language:

1. It enriches or supplements firsthand experiences.
2. It enhances self-image and builds self-control.
3. It promotes diversity.
4. It helps establishment of social relations through sharing.
5. It facilitates accurate conceptualization, clarifies ideas and stimulates new ones, and presents information.
6. It fosters aesthetic appreciation and stimulates creativity.
7. It provides literary experiences.
8. It acquaints children with another way of learning about their environment.
9. It provides auditory experiences and practice.
10. It provides opportunities for a change of pace and enjoyment of materials and people.

Thorough planning by the teacher is crucial if she is to utilize the many opportunities to foster language and identify and meet the needs of children individually and collectively. Following are some suggestions related to the four areas of language development: listening, speaking, reading, and writing.

Listening

- Be an attentive listener.
- Take time to talk with, not to, each child. Plan something interesting and exciting that encourages questions and increases knowledge.
- Provide some appropriate listening experiences (records, tapes). Be aware of loudness to prevent hearing problems.
- Read to a child or small group of children often. Use a variety of topics but don't get too concerned if someone asks for favorites. Find a cozy place and time without interruption. Closeness (on your lap or next to you) increases the pleasure.
- Tell (instead of read) stories often. Encourage the children to join in.

- Play the "position" game with the children (learn about prepositions) or give simple commands and see if the children can follow them.

Speaking

- Give your full attention to the child or children when conversation, questioning, information, or permission is directed to you.
- Give honest praise frequently.
- Speak clearly; be positive, joyful.
- Avoid baby talk or talking down.
- Help the children establish rules.
- Play a game, such as "What would happen if . . ." Ask the children to respond.
- At group or other appropriate times, let individual children introduce a poem, song, idea, or activity.
- Write down descriptions of the children's pictures, novel sayings, and poems.
- Talk about rhyming words.
- Increase each child's vocabulary by introducing and defining appropriate words and terms. Allow firsthand opportunities for the children to understand the new terms.
- While you are doing tasks, errands, or activities, briefly explain what is happening.
- Make your verbal and nonverbal language (gestures, actions) compatible. How would you expect a child to respond if you said, "Be friendly to our pet," while you shied away from it or refused to handle or feed it?
- Help the children resolve problems verbally rather than physically.

Following a teacher's presentation or at the children's selection, stories can be retold or originated with appropriate props.

Reading

- Provide quality listening experiences.
- Take the children to the center or public library, when possible. Let them help select and check out books.
- Purchase good books for the center.
- Help children find out things by using books.
- When children are interested and ready, have some alphabet or number cards for their exploration.
- Provide magazines to be looked through, cut up, or written in.
- Point out pictures and ideas in magazines.
- Talk about the care of books.
- Provide a quiet, comfortable, well-lighted place to read, away from distractions.
- When reading to and with the children, take time to look at the pictures; frequently let a child choose the books.
- Have books arranged but available for use.
- Provide a variety of books, but keep them in the classroom long enough for the children to become familiar and friendly with them.
- Choose books that are physically appropriate to the age level and stage of the children (for example, cardboard for 2-year-olds); also note the size and shape.
- Remember the role of parents in a child's interest in reading:

  Either consciously or unconsciously, parents do identify and define the reading process for their children and they do model behavior that either supports or negates the value of reading. Because of the importance of modeling and the impact of the home environment, there is a need for parents to serve as *informed* guides for their children (Simmons & Lawrence, 1981).

- Value reading by encouraging children to look at books each day. (Don't use books or reading simply as fillers of time or as punishment.)
- Use a variety of storytelling techniques (flannel board stories, flip-card stories, one-picture or object stories, puppets, and so on) to keep the interest of the children.
- Vary your tone of voice, speed, inflection, and loudness, without being overly dramatic.

Writing

- Do your note taking and recording with a positive attitude.
- Give each child some paper (or a booklet) and let him draw a story; you write down the comments.
- Help the children write a letter or thank-you note to someone.
- Provide good writing tools and time to write.
- Appreciate attempts at writing.
- Show each child how to write her name and other words as interest is indicated (use capital and lowercase letters).

○ Place names of individuals and objects around the room.

○ Encourage the use of small muscles (pegboards, puzzles, paintbrushes, stringing, and so on).

SELECTED NEEDS

Positive experiences with books are critical for young children's reading development. Making books an integral part of a young child's life is a goal that any early-childhood center or family can attain. Gottschall (1995) states: "The rewards of creating book-centered classrooms are readily apparent in children's seeking out books, 'reading' them, sharing the pictures and stories with others, and developing imaginative play from the stories. Less apparent, but equally important, is the knowledge about books and reading that young children accumulate as they participate in a book-friendly environment. Classrooms and homes that promote this love of books and reading prepare young children to enter primary school eager and ready to learn to read" (p. 35).

Reflection

Because it is difficult to select stories and books for whole-group reading, the following are some possible considerations (adapted from Wolter, 1992):

1. *Grouping:* The activity may be divided by age or interest, or provided for all children; advance preparation is important. Some preschool and kindergarten teachers group children by listening levels and/or background knowledge; others include the whole group. The story area should be comfortable for the children.

2. *Selection:* Consider child development practices; backgrounds of children (ethnicity, cultures, diversity, family groupings); language ability of the children (domestic, bilingual, limited); timing of events; books brought from home; variety in topics (humor, science, relationships, support of classroom play, expanded knowledge, exploration); repetition; good visuals; and flexibility.

3. *Presentation:* Include different types of visual aids (original book, flannel board, object, enactment, puppets, recording); use intonation, originality, and interest; have the children reenact the story; reread the book to individual children or at another group time.

4. *Children:* Consider individual and group interests and their ability to understand and sit still.

5. *Variation in literature:* Use children's books; poetry and other rhymes; nonfiction; letters, notes, and postcards; child participation; visitors; books made by the children; photographs with captions; items found while visiting the school or public library.

6. *Extension of storytime:* Use ideas that can be extended into other activities, such as art, dramatic play, and outdoor play. Books attractively displayed and accessible to children will increase their interest in and use of books.

APPLICATION OF PRINCIPLES

1. Briefly describe the four distinct but interrelated areas of language as they pertain to young children.

2. Using a storybook for visuals, tell the story to a group of children. What do you need to remember about your voice? Your eye contact? Interruptions from children?

3. Give some criteria for books for young children. How often should you use fairy tales? Why?

4. Write and illustrate an original story for young children. Use it with a small group of children. Discuss the experience with another teacher.

5. Detail some activities that could help young children develop language skills (poetry, sensory experiences, social opportunities, hearing stories, manipulative toys, and so on). Be specific.

6. Record the conversation of two or more children. Did their conversation contain more responsive or more restrictive language?

7. Briefly describe whole-language learning to a friend or colleague.

8. How does webbing apply in language development?

9. What precautions could you take to ensure that a group storytime would be interesting to the children?

10. What would you say to a parent who *insisted* that you teach her 3-year-old how to read?

11. Outline some activities that could help prepare "interested and ready children" to learn to write.

12. Engage three to five children in a spontaneous conversation. Talk about their interests.

13. During creative art time, note how children of different ages hold writing implements. Should you encourage a child who is using his left hand to change to his right hand? Why?

14. Display some meaningful words around the room, such as name tags for the children, labels on furniture, and words under pictures. Note which children comment, show interest, or attempt to write their own name or words.

15. Use games, toys, or other ways to help children discriminate and describe colors, shapes, and sizes.

16. Note the specific interests of several of the children, then plan experiences to enhance their interests through books, activities, discussions, and so on.

17. Recall some of your favorite childhood books. Why did you like them and not others?

18. Do you recall any picture books that stereotyped the characters? If so, were you ever in the minority? How do you feel about "questionable" children's books, such as *Little Black Sambo*, Indian folklore, or sexist or moralistic books? How do you think they make children feel?

19. Carefully observe the types of books children prefer. Are the pictures black-and-white or colored? Realistic or abstract? Is the plot one that children could reproduce and enjoy?

20. Go to the area where children's books are located at a local bookstore or library. Randomly select four to six books. Sit down and read them. Note whether the characters are correctly depicted—sex, age, ethnicity, culture. Note the publication date of the book to see whether ideas are current with regard to portraying characters, roles, occupations, and other interests of young children.

21. What would be your plan of action if you had a child in your classroom who had immature or delayed verbal skills?

REFERENCES

Allen, A. M., D. N. Allen, & G. Sigler (1993). Changes in sex-role stereotyping in Caldecott Medal Award Picture Books 1938–1988. *Journal of Research in Higher Education*, 7(2), 67–73.

Anbar, A. (1986). Reading acquisition of preschool children without systematic instruction. *Early Childhood Research Quarterly*, 1, 69–83.

Anderson, M. P. (1996, January). Frequently asked questions about NAEYC's linguistic and cultural diversity position paper. *Young Children*, 51(2), 13–16.

Barclay, K., C. Benelli, & A. Curtis (1995, May). Literacy begins at birth: What caregivers can learn from parents of children who read early. *Young Children*, 50(4), 24–28.

Bee, H. (1981). *The developing child*, 3rd edition. New York: Harper.

Boyer, E. (1991). *Ready to learn: A mandate for the nation.* Princeton, NJ: Carnegie Foundation for the Advancement of Teaching.

Bredekamp, S. (ed.) (1987). *Developmentally appropriate practice in early childhood programs serving children from birth through age 8,* expanded edition. Washington, DC: NAEYC.

Bromley, K. D. (1991). *Webbing with literature.* Boston: Allyn & Bacon.

Burrell, S. (1992, September/October). New ideas for "show and tell." *First Teacher,* 13(5), 30.

Clay, M. (1975). *What did I write?* Exeter, NH: Heinemann.

Conlon, A. (1992, March). Giving Mrs. Jones a hand: Making group storytime more pleasurable and meaningful for young children. *Young Children,* 47(3), 14–18.

Cornell, C. E. (1993, September). Language and culture monsters that lurk in our traditional rhymes and folktales. *Young Children,* 48(6), 40–46.

Dumtschin, J. U. (1988, March). Recognize language development and delay in early childhood. *Young Children,* 47(3), 16–24.

Edelsky, C., B. Altwerger, & B. Flores (1991). *Whole language: What's the difference?* Portsmouth, NH: Heinemann Educational Books.

Educational Research Service (1991). *The whole language approach to reading and writing instruction.* Arlington, VA: Author.

Elkind, D. (1987). *Miseducation: Preschoolers at risk.* New York: Knopf.

Elkind, D. (1991). Developmentally appropriate practice: A case study of educational inertia. In Kagan, S. L. (ed.), *The care and education of America's young children: Obstacles and opportunities.* Ninetieth yearbook of the National Society for the Study of Education, Part I, 1–16. Chicago: University of Chicago Press.

French, L. (1996, January). I told you all about it, so don't tell me you don't know: Two-year-olds and learning through language. *Young Children,* 51(2), 17–20.

Garrard, K. R. (1987, March). Helping young children develop mature speech patterns. *Young Children,* 42(3), 16–21.

Goodman, K. S. (1986). *What's whole in whole language?* Portsmouth, NH: Heinemann Educational Books.

Gottschall, S. M. (1995, May). Hug-a-book: A program to nurture a young child's love of books and reading. *Young Children,* 50(4), 29–35.

Greenberg, P. (1990). Why not academic preschool? *Young Children,* 45(2), 70–80.

Griffin, E. F. (1982). *Island of childhood: Education in the special world of nursery school.* New York: Teachers College Press.

Harste, J., V. Woodward, & C. Burke (1984). *Language stories and literacy lessons.* Portsmouth, NJ: Heinemann.

Heald-Taylor, G. (1989). *The administrator's guide to whole language.* New York: Richard C. Owen.

Hendrick, J. (1992). *The whole child,* 5th edition. New York: Merrill/Macmillan.

Hough, R. A., J. R. Nurss, & D. Wood (1987, November) Tell me a story: Making opportunities for elaborated language in early childhood classrooms. *Young Children,* 43(1), 6–12.

International Reading Association (IRA) (1985). *Literacy development and pre-first grade: A joint statement of concerns about present practices in pre-first grade reading instruction and recommendations for improvement,* revised edition. Newark, DE: International Reading Association. Also in *Young Children,* 41(4), 10–13.

Jalongo, M. R. (1985, November/December). Children's literature: there's some sense to its humor. *Childhood Education,* 62(2), 109–114.

Jalongo, M. R. (1988). *Picture books and young children: Literature from infancy to six.* Washington, DC: NAEYC.

Jalongo, M. R. (1996, January). Teaching young children to become better listeners. *Young Children,* 51(2), 21–26.

Kantrowitz, B., & P. Wingert (1989, April). How kids learn. *Newsweek,* 50–56.

Katz, L. G., & S. C. Chard (1989). *Engaging children's minds: The project approach.* Norwood, NJ: Ablex.

Kohlberg, L. (1966). Cognitive stages of preschool education. *Human Development,* 9 (Parts 1 and 2).

Kontos, S. (1986, November). What preschool children know about reading and how they learn it. *Young Children,* 42(1), 58–66.

Kuball, Y. E. (1995, January). Goodbye dittos: A journey from skill-based teaching to developmentally appropriate language education in a bilingual kindergarten. *Young Children,* 50(2), 6–14.

Loughlin, C. E., & M. D. Martin (1987). *Supporting literacy: Developing effective learning environments.* New York: Teachers College Press.

Loughlin, C. E., & J. H. Suina (1982). *The learning environment: An instructional strategy.* New York: Teachers College Press.

Lowenfeld, V. (1987). *Creative and mental growth,* 8th edition. New York: Macmillan.

Lundsteen, S. W. (1979). *Listening: Its impact at all levels on reading and the other language arts.* Urbana, IL: National Council of Teachers of English.

Maclean, M., P. Bryant, & L. Bradley (1987, July). Rhymes, nursery rhymes, and reading in early childhood. *Merrill Palmer Quarterly,* 33(3), 255–281.

McDevitt, T. M. (1990). Encouraging young children's listening. *Academic Therapy,* 25(5), 569–577.

NAEYC position statement: Responding to linguistic and cultural diversity—recommendations for effective early childhood education (1996, January). *Young Children,* 51(2), 4–12.

National Association for the Education of Young Children (NAEYC) & National Association of Early Childhood Specialists in State Departments of Education (NAECS/SDE) (1992). Guidelines for appropriate curriculum content and assessment in programs serving children ages 3 through 8. In Bredekamp, S., & T. Rosegrant (eds.), *Reaching potentials: Appropriate curriculum and assessment for young children,* Vol. 2, 9–27. Washington, DC: NAEYC.

Ortiz, L. I., & G. Engelbrecht (1986). Partners in biliteracy: The school and the community. *Language Arts,* 63(5), 458–465.

Parent's guide to choosing children's books (1996, January/February). *Early Childhood News,* 8(1), 38.

Read, K., P. Gardner, & B. C. Mahler (1987). *Early childhood programs: Human relationships and learning,* 8th edition. New York: Holt, Rinehart & Winston.

Reutzel, D. R., & P. M. Hollingsworth (1988, March) Whole language and the practitioner. *Academic Therapy,* 23, 405–417.

Rich, S. J. (1985, July). The writing suitcase. *Young Children,* 40(5), 42–44.

Schickedanz, J. (1986). *More than the ABC's: The early stages of reading and writing.* Washington, DC: NAEYC.

Schickedanz, J. A., S. Chay, P. Gopin, L. L. Sheng, S. Song, and N. Wild (1990, November). Preschoolers and academics: Some thoughts. *Young Children,* 46(1), 4–13.

Schickedanz, J., M. E. York, I. S. Stewart, & D. White (1977). *Strategies for teaching young children.* Englewood Cliffs, NJ: Prentice-Hall.

Schieffelin, B. B., & M. Cochran-Smith (1984). Learning to read culturally: Literacy before schooling. Goelman, H., A. Oberg, & F. Smith (eds.), In *Awakening to literacy,* 3–23. Exeter, NH: Heinemann.

Scofield, M. E. (1986). An evaluation of magazines for the very young. Master's thesis, Northern Michigan University.

Serbin, L. A., & K. D. O'Leary (1975, December). How nursery schools teach girls to shut up. *Psychology Today,* 113–116.

Shannon, K. (1995). *At home at school: A child's transition.* Bothell, WA: Wright Group.

Silvestri, G. (1993). Wanted: Child care workers. *Parents,* 68(5), 84.

Smith, F. (1985). *Reading without nonsense,* 2nd edition. New York: Teachers College Press.

Soto, L. D. (1995, November/December). Children and language. *Scholastic Early Childhood Today,* 10(3), 47.

Spock, B. (1976, June). Are fairy tales good for children? *Redbook,* 136–138.

Stone, J. (1993, May). Caregiver and teacher language—responsive or restrictive? *Young Children,* 48(4), 12–18.

Strickland, D. (1988). A model for change: Framework for an emergent literacy curriculum. In Strickland, D. S., & L. M. Morrow (eds.), *Emerging literacy: Young children learn to read and write,* 135–146. Newark, DE: International Reading Association.

Taylor, B. J., & R. J. Howell (1973). The ability of three-, four-, and five-year-old children to distinguish fantasy from reality. *Journal of Genetic Psychology,* 122, 315–318.

Vukelich, C. (1994). Effects of play interventions on young children's reading of environmental print. *Early Childhood Research Quarterly,* 9, 153–170.

Vygotsky, L. (1978). *Mind in society: The development of higher psychological processes.* Cambridge, MA: Harvard University Press.

Watson, D. J. (1989, November). Defining and describing whole language. *The Elementary School Journal,* 90, 133–141.

Weaver, C. (1990). *Understanding whole language: From principles to practice.* Portsmouth, NH: Heinemann Educational Books.

What are we really saying to children? (1987, March). *Child Care Information Exchange.*

Williams, R. P., & J. K. Davis (1994, May). Lead sprightly into literacy. *Young Children,* 49(4), 37–41.

Wishon, P. M., P. Brazee, & B. Eller (1986). Facilitating oral language competence: The natural ingredients. *Childhood Education,* 63(2), 91–94.

Wolter, D. L. (1992, November). Whole group story reading? *Young Children,* 48(1), 72–75.

Brochures on Early Literacy Development

(As Listed in Young Children, 1994, March, p. 21):

National Association for the Education of Young Children (NAEYC)
1509 16th Street, N.W.
Washington, DC 20036-1426

American Library Association
50 E. Huron Street
Chicago, IL 60611

Reading Is Fundamental, Inc.
P.O. Box 23444
Washington, DC 20026

International Reading Association (IRA)
600 Barksdale Road
Newark, DE 19714

Creative, Artistic, and Sensory Expression

CHAPTER 6

MAIN PRINCIPLES

1. Individuals are creative in different ways.
2. Raw materials, uninterrupted time, and freedom to choose activities and playmates are valuable to both the child's development and her artistic expression.
3. Over time, educational theorists have advocated the important role of creative expression in the development of humanity.
4. Children need many different ways to express themselves that are healthy and acceptable to society.
5. Adults who are supportive, noncritical, and good listeners encourage a child's future experiences in self-expression and the child's good feelings about himself and his abilities.
6. Safety factors are as important in self-expression opportunities as they are in all other curriculum areas.
7. Children who share multicultural experiences with others establish their own identity and respect the differences in others.

Creativity is defined differently by different people. Those who feel they have little creativity look at it as being negative and hard to come by, and are spectators rather than participants in things viewed for their beauty, originality, or value. Those who have spontaneous or new ideas look at creativity as a gift, something natural, or just needing expression—whether through visual or performing arts. Then those in the middle, just neutral, feel they are creative sometimes and not others, do what they have to do under the circumstances, or feel their work is to be neither praised nor criticized. Too often the "creativity" is related to compositions of art or music when it should be seen as something much more broad. A creative idea may be a new way to do something (set the table, prepare food, solve problems, sew on a button, file materials, play a game). It may be a private or a shared experience.

One dictionary defines *creativity* as "artistic or intellectual inventiveness," and then defines *artistic* as "done skillfully, aesthetically satisfying." This indicates that any and all of us can be creative—and we are creative in individual ways. Children are just beginning to explore art materials, movement to music, skill in manipulating their bodies, and interacting with others. They do it the best way they can—and for now it is through sensory, firsthand experiences. Perhaps adults should start there, too.

Nothing is quite so delightful as seeing a young child wholly absorbed in creative self-expression. She may be creative when she moves to music, engages in dramatic play, exercises large muscles, or prepares food. This chapter is devoted to creative, artistic, and sensory expression. Dramatic play and block building, forms of creative expression, were discussed in Chapter 3. Music and other forms of creativity are covered in later chapters.

Not all children enjoy things that are "messy," but the need for expression is still there. The teacher is responsible for seeing that children have many opportunities for self-expression, that these ways are acceptable in society and meet developmental needs, and that children feel good about them.

In order for a child to be creative, writes Schirrmacher (1988), he needs to choose (1) what he wants to make (content), (2) how he will go about making it (process), and (3) what it will end up looking like (product). Adults who are supportive, noncritical, and good listeners encourage the child's future experiences in this area and the child's feelings about himself and his abilities.

Davis and Gardner (1991) present an insightful illustration of the consequences of not understanding the knowledge embedded in early-childhood curriculum activities. They describe a classroom incident in which a young child has drawn figures representing her family during a classroom exercise. The teacher engages the child in conversation, asking her to tell about her drawing. The teacher then labels each figure in the drawing and writes the title, "Lucy's Family," at the top of the child's paper.

The teacher acted as most early-childhood teachers would. In doing so, Davis and Gardner argue, the teacher is telling the child that words are better symbol systems than are drawings. The teacher has also violated the child's compositional integrity by writing on the drawing. In addition, the teacher is sending a power message to the child: she can write on the child's work without fear of trespassing (Spodek, 1991). A separate page or the back of the picture could be used for comments made by the children while still preserving their masterpieces.

Too frequently one observes artifacts created during *art time* by children who have been taught to carefully follow directions. Each creation looks similar to all others and reflects themes and patterns from prior years (especially at holiday times and seasonal changes).

An example of the integration of art with content learning is an easy-to-envision *doing* example of the type of subject-integrated education going on in many classrooms across the country (Dever & Jared, 1996). It can be used with any topic. The primary goals of the unit are conventional and simple: to help the children enhance their understanding of the world and to meaningfully integrate art activities with other curricular areas.

"Inquiry learning is a generative process that encourages children to view life experiences as a continual process of building new understandings from their experiences" (Watson, Burke, & Harste, 1989). The teacher's role is (1) to provide many and varied experiences through primary resources: direct experiences to observe, interact, or manipulate, such as through dramatic play, art materials, field trips, oral discussions, and so on; (2) to provide many secondary sources, such as books, videos, visitors, storytellers, pictures, props, and so on; and (3) to provide ways for children to share what they have learned.

Whenever possible, teachers should ensure that children have real experiences before encouraging them to reproduce them through art or dramatization. Early on, teachers should make a distinction between arts (individual expression using a variety of materials) and crafts (product-oriented, pattern-directed activities) and their role in the lives of young children. "Crafts and expressive art are two different things," states Schiller (1995, p. 36). There will be more about this later in this chapter.

Art activities can serve as an expressive medium and a means of advancing the children's understanding of topic content, and there is an additional benefit as the children actively manipulate the art materials. They make discoveries about what they can make with the materials—perhaps unique shades or different images from the stroke of the brush. Colors created with paint, crayons, and markers are different and interact differently with different media, such as paste, dry ingredients, fabric, and others.

Teaching and learning must address the whole developing child. Art should be integrated into a curriculum for young children in ways that encourage them to express their ideas and feelings. Such activities provide children with the opportunity to experiment with various art materials as well as to express their ideas aesthetically. Creative expression should not isolate the child from other subjects; rather, it should be purposefully and meaningfully integrated into the curriculum, providing support for developing skills and for advancing knowledge about their world.

As I was sitting at my computer writing this chapter, we had one of the heaviest snowfalls in years. I wondered to myself, "How could I use this spontaneous event to stimulate young children to think about this wonderful event?" I noticed the birds flying to their nests, the animals running to their holes, and the humans scurrying for shelter. I imagined myself with a group of children, as had happened many times over the years, and what this snowfall would mean to them: romping in the snow, heavy clothing, cold feet and hands. Snow means moisture—leading us into the water cycle and water sports, planting cycles, warm weather, and on and on. And what about the animals now and later? They grow heavier coats and need protection and access to food. Oh, where are the children when I need them most?

Theoretical Background of Art for Young Children

Art is not an automatic consequence of growth or development. It is the result of active exploration and inquiry that cannot occur without some adult assistance to draw, paint, and sculpt with interest and determination (Vygotsky, 1978; Brittain, 1979).

Teachers need to provide materials, space, and encouragement and realize that art is vital for all young children—not just a talented few. Children who are encouraged to pursue a medium or topic seriously for an extended period of time are capable of creating surprisingly complex and sophisticated works of art (Katz & Chard, 1989). Teachers and parents sometimes resort to highly directive methods of "teaching" young children to draw, which limit children's choices and encourage replication of an adult-produced model.

Art educators have become more directly involved in the preparation of early-childhood teachers and have shown increasing concern in creative activities for young children. Art for young children is no longer considered an exclusively developmental phenomenon, but also a form of activity which deserves serious consideration as people experience art as part of their history and culture.

Art lessons for young children lead them to want finished products. A young child's progress is measured by the intensity of the child's involvement in art activities—her capacity to spend ever longer periods of time engaged in ever more ambitious projects and pursuits.

Dewey's Influence on Creative Art for Young Children

John Dewey, the American empirical philosopher and educator, was concerned with democratizing the arts—bringing them into everyday life and experience. In school, both fine arts and crafts (identified as woodworking and other hand skills) were to be available to all children as fundamental means of expression and communication. In his Laboratory School at the University of Chicago, art was valued equally with other subject matter (Engel, 1995).

Fortunately, a product is unimportant in many activities.

Artistic activity has been recognized as one of the primary ways that children can learn by doing and document what they learn (Dewey, 1934):

> [L]ack of an appropriate outlet for expressing strong feelings, no matter what their origin, results in frustration and unhappiness. . . . Psycho-analytically oriented educators became interested in mental health in schools and saw art as playing a crucial role in its maintenance—a way of providing access to, and allowing expression, of repressed feelings. (Engel, 1995, p. 9)

Other Supporters of Art in Early-Childhood Education

In 1914, Margaret Naumberg founded and co-directed the Children's School (later renamed the Walden School) in New York City. She was one of the first educators to change classroom practice in response to the new psychology and encouraged free exploration and expression in all areas of learning. Children chose their own media and subject matter in art. Art lessons were eliminated and adults were "reluctant to correct, judge, or react to children's work at all for fear of inhibiting spontaneous expression. Art as therapy came first and art as aesthetic experience second, although the two purposes were inseparable in practice" (Engel, 1995, p. 10). (Following their respective personal philosophies, Dewey emphasized art more as an aspect of community experience, while Naumberg used it as an outlet for the repressed feelings of the individual.)

Cyril Burt, a British psychologist, was one of the first to specify in detail a series of developmental stages, his aim being to establish norms of human intelligence for testing purposes. Some of his seven developmental stages are similar to contemporary formulations: scribble (ages 2–5), line (age 4), descriptive symbolism (ages 5–6), descriptive realism (ages 7–8), visual realism (ages 9–11), repression (ages 11–14), and artistic revival (early adolescence) (Engel, 1995, p. 15). (Burt, a highly respected professional, falsified data to support his own beliefs about inherited intelligence [Engel, 1995, p. 51]).

Near the same time as Burt, Viktor Lowenfeld published an important work on art and young children, which is still important today (Lowenfeld, 1947; Lowenfeld & Brittain, 1967). He emphasized divergent thinking (original solutions) while denouncing coloring books, adult standards for judging children's art, and competition between children. "Not all children move from one stage to another at exactly the same time; except for the abnormal or exceptional child, these stages follow one another, however, and a description of each is valuable in understanding the general characteristics of children and their art at any particular time" (Lowenfeld, 1987, p. 37).

Art and Development

Teachers who are concerned with manipulative skills put emphasis on products rather than on the process. For children, art is a way of learning and not something to be learned (Lowenfeld, 1987, p. 47). Their products often do not reflect the eye-hand coordination that one might expect.

Attempts have been made to teach certain concepts to children before they were able to cognitively grasp those particular concepts. For example, Brittain (1969) attempted to teach preschool children the simple task of copying a square by thoroughly saturating them with the square concept, but he was not able to improve their square-making ability. However, at the age of 4, children that he worked with did accomplish the task of copying a square. But those children who were not so lucky as to be taught square-making abilities also accomplished the task successfully at the age of 4.

Developmental Stages in Art

Scribbling: Ages 2–4

Children make random marks on paper; this is mainly a motor activity and can be considered a reflection of physical and emotional development. (Lowenfeld, 1967, pp. 196, 204). Materials suggested for this stage: large unwrapped crayons, white chalk on blackboard, fiber-tipped pen; old newspapers, wallpaper samples, wrapping paper; tempera or poster paint; clay; fingerpaint (p. 214).

Preschematic: Ages 4–7

Children make their first representational attempts, typical head-feet presentation; they begin to draw a number of other objects in their environment, randomly placed and varying in size.

"The ability to copy geometric forms is sometimes used as a measure of young children's developmental level. Although the circle can be copied by most children at the age of three, it is not until four that a square can be copied successfully" (p. 205).

Schematic: Ages 7–9

Children develop a definite form; their drawings symbolize parts of the environment; children usually repeat with some variation the schema that they have developed; they arrange the objects they are portraying in a straight line across the bottom of the page; their works of art look quite decorative.

Dawning Realism: Ages 9–12

Children are interested in detail and no longer make the large free drawings made at a younger age; they hide their drawings from adult observation; their drawings symbolize rather than represent objects.

Adapted from Lowenfeld, 1987, pp. 38–39.

The arts can play a tremendous role in learning and may be more basic to the thinking processes than the more traditional school subjects. Every drawing demands a great deal of intellectual involvement: what to do, how to do it, what to use, where to place ideas, how much to include (or exclude), and so on. The procedure is the same for a scribbling child or a high school student at the peak of learning efficiency.

In the 1940s, a number of books dealing with art for children were published. Then art began to be interesting in itself. Goals and purposes of including art in the curriculum for young children were established: (1) Children need to have the opportunity to be expressive; (2) they need to pass on some heritage in the area of arts; (3) they have an inborn drive to be creative; (4) technical skills can be taught if there is a better understanding of children's growth—emotional, intellectual, physical, perceptual, social, aesthetic, creative, and so on (Lowenfeld, 1987, pp. 57, 59–71). Art encourages divergent thinking (no single correct answer); intelligence tests stress convergent thinking (the *correct* response).

The following quotes further clarify Lowenfeld's stand on art:

Preschool children learn in an active way rather than in a passive way. . . . Pictures on the wall are not art in the usual sense to preschool youngsters. Art is what they make themselves. However, nursery school children usually do not remember their own drawings or paintings after a few hours, and it could not be expected that they can develop any aesthetic awareness as adults understand it. (1987, p. 120)

There is no place in the art program for those activities that have no meaning for the scribbling child. Occasionally a nursery school or kindergarten teacher may plan certain art activities such as pasting, lacing, tracing, folding, or cutting; these are designed for a particular end product. . . . Such activities are worthless and should never be included in a program planned for scribbling children because they only point out the inability of children to perform on a level foreign to their understanding and ability. . . . Any new material should be looked upon with a great deal of care to make sure that it can further the natural development of children. It must not obstruct their ability to gain control over the material; rather it should promote creative expression. (1987, pp. 215–16)

Comparing Piaget's stages with his own, Lowenfeld states: "Although Piaget's stages are for intellectual development, it is not surprising to find the same stages in art" (1987, p. 45).

At about the age of two every child begins to scribble . . . on paper . . . on fresh concrete. . . . To the adult, scribbling may seem senseless, but to the child it is as natural as eating a cookie; it is a natural thing to do with fingers and toes—and it is meaningful. (Kellogg with O'Dell, 1967, p. 13)

Reflection

"The little girl who went to the park for a drawing lesson and drew a tree with a red trunk and blue leaves is a good example of how too many children are nudged away from art. When her grade-school teacher asked the supervisor what could possibly be done with such a child, and though great artists have painted blue leaves and great writers have described them as such, the supervisor said, "Take her back to the park.""

Source: Kellogg with O'Dell, 1967, p. 87.

In the mid-1980s, American educators became aware of an early-education program, the Reggio Emilia approach in Italy, which was based on art. Attention was brought to this approach through a traveling exhibit, "The Hundred Languages of Children." The accompanying catalog (Commune of Reggio Emilia, 1987) explains that the pedagogy of the schools is "on the side of a genetic, constructivist and creative perspective" (p. 18) and sees art as a language for which children have an inborn capacity. "Observing children's artworks, both the process and product, allows teachers insight into how children are constructing the world" (Engel, 1995, p. 23).

Of current interest is the philosophy and operation of the Reggio Emilia (city-run) child-care centers in the northern Italian city of the same name. The approach is acclaimed as one of the best preschool education systems in the world (Edwards, Gandini, & Forman, 1993; *Newsweek*, Dec. 2, 1991, p. 52).

Lacking in North American early-childhood programs, but an essential part of the Reggio Emilia approach, is an art studio, or *atelier*. Katz (1993) describes one of the primary lessons she has learned from her visits to Reggio Emilia: that young children can use graphic languages—paint, drawing, collage, construction, and so on—

"to record their ideas, observations, memories and so forth . . . to explore understandings, to reconstruct previous ones, and to co-construct revisited understandings of the topics investigated" (p. 20). She is now convinced that "many of us in the United States seriously underestimate preprimary school children's graphical capabilities and the quality of intellectual effort and growth it can stimulate" (pp. 20–21).

An Emergent Curriculum

Much of the recent interest in curriculum and artwork from Reggio Emilia is focused on their style of emergent curriculum. Teachers at Reggio Emilia "express general goals" (Gandini, 1993, p. 7) but do not predetermine where children's study will take them. There is flexibility in planning, as the process of each activity is adjusted. As with other areas of the preschool curriculum, talking about art should spring from the interests of the children and be initiated, for the most part, by them through (1) frequent opportunities to use open-ended materials (paints, clay, markers) in original ways, (2) a variety of well-displayed, good-quality materials used every day with self-determined time frames and children seeing their work attractively displayed, and (3) crafts (product-oriented, pattern-directed activities) offered only occasionally. "Many high-quality programs for young children include art appreciation and aesthetic education in their curriculum, as well as an abundance of expressive art experiences" (Schiller, 1995, p. 36).

Teachers in Reggio Emilia are not alone in endorsing the cognitive theories of art. The 1992 National Art Education Association's standards for the visual arts include the goals of fostering children's ability to:

- effectively communicate ideas, attitudes, and feelings through the visual art form;
- innovatively express ideas with visual arts forms;
- interpret the meaning of works of art; and
- use art media, tools, techniques, and processes skillfully (Seefeldt, 1995, p. 40).

There is understanding and psychological motivation in the Reggio Emilia approach. The role of teachers is more direct in Italy, as they model processes and products for the children and offer frequent praise and conversations about what is transpiring. The displays of children's art appear to be more like a museum presentation and therefore differ from the informal display used in other schools (Seefeldt, 1995, pp. 42, 43).

Art is viewed as serious work in Reggio Emilia. It represents the thoughts, ideas, and emotions of the children. With goals in mind, teachers offer children sufficient experiential motivation so that they will have something to express and psychological safety in which to do so.

Teachers who are serious about children's art carefully consider their role. They understand that talking with children about their art can foster children's ability to express themselves through the visual arts. "Talking to children about their art enriches their immediate experience and expands their understanding of the nature of visual forms and their own activity as artist" (Thompson, 1995). (See Figure 6.1.)

Expanding the Area of Art Education for Young Children

The current movement in art education that questions a heavy emphasis on creative expression as the purpose for art-related activities with young children might appear to be in conflict with developmentally appropriate practices (DAP) (Bre-

Figure 6.1
Experiences That Motivate Creativity in Young Children

- A repertoire of experiences to think or feel about. Being able to think about something not present and then find a way to express it is a major cognitive accomplishment for young children (Raines and Canady, 1990; Golumb, 1992).
- Time, opportunity, and encouragement to explore media. For an experience to be meaningful, children must "act upon it, do something with it" (Dewey, 1944, p. 139).
- Stimulation of all the senses:
  Visual—real objects, replicas, pictures, photographs, etc.
  Auditory—hearing about the item or its uses.
  Tactile—actually handling the item.
  Olfactory—smelling and/or tasting *safe* items.
- Teachers who understand the cognitive theories of art and who select motivational and teaching strategies appropriate for the age/interests/abilities of individual children (a Reggio Emilia and U.S. concept).
- Stunning displays of art, including that done by the children.
- Feeling secure, safe, and comfortable with themselves, teachers, other children, and their surroundings (Brittain, 1979; Moyer, 1990).
- Teachers who avoid "asking children to complete patterned artwork or to copy adult models of art, as far too many children are asked to do in the United States . . . [It] undermines children's sense of psychological safety and demonstrates disrespect for children—their ideas, abilities, and creativity—more than anything else can" (Seefeldt, 1995, p. 42).

dekamp, 1987) as defined by the NAEYC. The Piaget-based model of curriculum outlined by NAEYC suggests that children have the opportunity "for aesthetic expression and appreciation through art and music . . . [and that] a variety of art media are available for creative expression, such as easel and finger paint and clay" (p. 56). Some individuals advocate that this is not a complete experience and that art education should also be introduced without compromising the standards of NAEYC.

Recently the National Art Education Association published a briefing paper addressing developmentally appropriate practices in art education for young children, focusing on three major themes in high-quality early art education, namely the need of children (1) to have many opportunities to create art, (2) to have many opportunities to look at and talk about art (which is most often neglected in preschool classrooms), and (3) to become aware of art in their everyday lives (Colbert & Taunton, 1992).

Schiller (1995) found classroom environments that either encourage or discourage an appreciation of art: "[I]f a teacher depends on cartoon-like images in the classroom or uses photographic images exclusively, it gives children little choice in what they view and what they have the opportunity to respond to. Providing books on art topics and opportunities to talk about art and artists supports and extends a rich art environment" (p. 34).

Although most preschool art activities are organized to have children interact and experiment with art materials in a non-teacher-directed format, early-childhood classroom teachers can take art to another level, one of discussion and understanding, by fostering art appreciation through nondirective means.

Product-Oriented Activities

It is not unusual for many teachers to spend hours preparing parts, patterns, and activities for young children to glue together according to a specific pattern. They call this art. One should know clearly the differences between art and crafts, as described earlier in this chapter.

Many adults who work with children enjoy cutting out patterns; it's hard to get them to stop. That's what their teachers did when these adults were children in school; now it's their turn to play teacher. Walls decorated with such things reassure other adults, including parents, that the preschool really does have a curriculum. Thoughtful communication is necessary to help adults understand children's need to make their own representations and see models of their own works (Jones & Reynolds, 1992).

In an interesting account of changing adult-directed art projects to child-directed experiences (and thus to an accredited, child-sensitive, developmentally appropriate school), Swanson (1994) reports the following: the children disliked coercion, threats, group "have-to" times, and directed periods. What they did like was being part of the planning, carrying through with their plans, and learning to be responsible for their actions. "By fall the art *projects* were out, and art *experiences* were coming in." The children were asking interesting, open-ended questions; participating in small groups; using materials and toys for extended periods of time; and being more creative. Circle times became lots of fun.

Classroom Decorations

Patterned borders or pictures in halls and classrooms teach children to be conformists rather than encouraging them to create for themselves, practice divergent thinking, and make unique representations of their ideas and experiences (Figure 6.2).

VALUES FOR CHILDREN

Sensory experiences are very important to the young child; through these experiences, he learns about his world.

Independence

Keeping materials and supplies where children can get and return them stimulates independence. When interest is high, it should be satisfied. If children feel inclined to make a picture, play a record, or enter into dramatic play, and if props are at

Figure 6.2
Advantages of Raw Materials and Ideas over Patterned or Precut Materials

- Children can freely express themselves in design, color, and media.
- Competition and conformity are removed.
- Children may or may not select an art activity at a determined time.
- Their interests, choices, and abilities can be pursued.
- Creativity offers opportunity to express oneself constructively.
- Most children enjoy using the media; they may not have these experiences in other settings.
- Most materials and equipment can be set up permanently, or made easily accessible, for child selection.
- Valuable traits can be learned: responsibility (for getting and returning items), cooperation (sharing of items), respect (for others' space, accomplishment), socialization (conversations, questions), choice of activity, and more.
- Children learn to be resourceful and responsible.
- Children determine the amount of time to spend in the area.

their disposal, they make the transition smoothly rather than having to wait for help or for another time.

Through the use of creative materials, children express their individuality and learn social techniques, such as sharing and cooperating.

Ronald, 3 years old, was given several different opportunities at school to finger paint. He thoroughly enjoyed each experience. The request came from home to "quit finger painting at school because Ronald finger paints in everything at home—especially his food at mealtime!" Here was a child who needed more, not fewer, sensory experiences.

Aesthetic Appreciation

By setting a good example, having a wholesome attitude and atmosphere, encouraging the children, and giving them honest praise, adults help them appreciate the beauty surrounding them. If children develop appreciation for aesthetics at a young age, their environment becomes more meaningful. By taking an interest in what children do, adults help them see the unusual in the usual and hear that which they have not heard before. This builds an awareness of the environment.

Teachers who live in a community where paintings can be borrowed from a local source, such as a library or university, should plan to change the paintings in the classroom often. Teachers can teach about famous artwork by pointing out the colors, the lines, and the meanings, but this must be done on a level children understand and appreciate.

"Adults frequently show young children pictures of fruit or farms or families. Why not also show them a lovely still life by Cezanne, a fine landscape by Corot, or a beautiful mother and child by Mary Cassatt?" writes Wolf (1990). She continues, "The early years, when children are so fascinated with picture books, are the natural sensitive years for them to become familiar with paintings." And rather than always showing large framed pictures, she encourages postcard-sized reproductions that fit easily in a child's hand and can be used for a variety of activities such as matching, pairing, sorting, and placing in chronological order.

Children can learn about and enjoy art of the past and present, but the teacher will be the facilitator working between the piece of art and the children. They can begin by looking at and describing the art using divergent questions, such as "What do you see in the picture?" "What do you suppose they are thinking?" "How are you feeling about what you are seeing?" These kinds of inquiries help children bring themselves into the piece rather than giving convergent answers ("How many people are in the work?" "What articles of clothing are they wearing?" and so on). When children are actively involved in the discovery of meaning in works of art, they exercise intellectual (logical and creative thinking), social (valuing opinions of others, purpose of piece, listening and speaking skills), and emotional (verbalizing personal feelings, pleasure in the piece) skills (Cole & Schaefer, 1990).

Satisfaction and Enjoyment

The conversation of young children during creative or dramatic play is enlightening. They should be encouraged to give verbal comments: "It's gushy!" "It holds onto my fingers." "It scratches!" "Look how funny I am in this floppy old hat!"

Two essentials for gaining the most value from the use of creative materials are time and space. Time is so important in the lives of young children—even though they seem to waste it at times. They need time to investigate and to live through each experience in their own way. They also need space in which to move; traffic lanes, cramped quarters, or competition with the clock or other experiences discourage children at the outset. It would cause less frustration in children and adults if an art period or activity were omitted rather than included when time is limited.

When children know that they can complete an activity without interruption, they are more likely to be interested in it. Analyze this episode: Several children were finger painting; some entered eagerly into the activity while others watched. Ann debated whether or not to get involved. Some of the children finished and left the table. Ann gingerly put one finger into the mixture. It seemed acceptable; she put her finger in again and quietly pondered. She was about to involve herself when the teacher came with a sponge and told her they were through for the day. She rushed Ann away from the table and finished cleaning it herself. Wouldn't it have been better for Ann if she had been allowed to stay longer, or if she had been encouraged to help in cleaning the table?

Emotional Release

Artistic expression can be a means of soothing feelings; sliding hands through slippery finger paint, boldly pounding clay from one form to another, or building in the block area can be relaxing to most young children. Beating a drum, playing a role in the domestic area, or moving to music are also creative ways for children to relieve pressures.

Collaboration results in a different type of experience than does a solitary activity.

Reflection

Betty carefully guarded her finger painting as she tenderly carried it to the car. A few moments later an angry young uncle stormed into the classroom with the painting and shouted, "If you think you're going to put that junk in my car and mess up the upholstery, you're sadly mistaken!" Betty ran after him with tears in her eyes but made no comment; she was heartbroken. One wonders how long it was before she tried finger painting again.

David sat quietly waiting for his father. As his father appeared, David proudly displayed his picture. The father studied the picture appreciatively, nodded his head, and smiled. After a short pause, the child looked at his father and asked, "Well, what is it, Dad?" as if the father saw much more in the painting than the child did. The father pointed out several appealing parts of the picture. Think how much more David was encouraged to pursue creative activities than was Betty.

Good Work Habits

Even work habits involve creative expression. Wiping up finger paint made from soap flakes adds a new and exciting dimension. Lisa felt that staying clean was important. She would stand near the creative tables and watch the children as they enjoyed using the materials. She automatically wiped her already clean hands on her clothes. Whenever cleanup was initiated, she was the first to get a sponge. To her, it was unacceptable to get dirty but it was very acceptable to clean up. This was her introduction to creative materials.

Children enjoy participating, and valuable learning experiences can be gained from doing so. They need to be involved in the whole cycle of an activity. They should be encouraged to mix, to use, to clean up, and to prepare materials for storage. This may take longer, but the satisfaction is priceless. Children develop good work habits if they get the right cues from adults.

An art experience should not be confused with an exercise in following directions. The art experience allows children the freedom of creating. If you want to know if children can follow directions, then tell them to color the ball red and the pumpkin orange. If you want them to be creative, let them decide what color to use or what they want to do.

Recall the importance of good work habits in helping young children learn. Also recall how the behavior of the teacher helps children establish good patterns.

Muscle Development

Through self-expression, children can develop gross and fine muscles. The large ones are exercised through such activities as woodworking, movement to music, and active play. Small-muscle activities include cutting and pasting, working with collage, coloring with large crayons or chalk, drawing, making puzzles, or manipulating other table toys such as pegboards or small blocks. For young children, activities that encourage use of large (gross) muscles should predominate over those that encourage use of small (fine) muscles. Some children enjoy using their small muscles; these activities are provided for dexterity and eye-hand coordination, but young children should not be required to stay with this type of activity for any length of time.

Exploration and Transformation

Through the use of raw materials, children often learn to think for themselves. Those who wait for other children or adults to tell them what to do or when to do it profit from experiences with such materials, which can be used in many creative ways. Use of the material is more important than the finished product. The creation of the very young child changes name and focus as the materials are used. A 5-year-old may decide in advance what her creation will be and then set out to accomplish it, but one should not be surprised or disappointed if it, too, changes from the original plan.

Children enjoy repetition of materials and activities—not to limit their experiences, but as opportunities to further explore, manipulate, and exercise their imaginations and initiative. When new ideas or materials are introduced to children, plans for repeated use should be included. One exposure is not enough.

Studies indicate that creativity increases in preschool children until the age of 5, when a sharp decrease begins. Contributing to this decrease are parental influence, need for conformity, patterning, adherence to unrealistic standards, peer pressure, and commercial materials. Television also plays a role in shaping the child's image of reality and interferes with his creativity.

Divergent thinking can be developed in young children when teachers encourage individual thinking, exploration, cooperation, and curiosity. They can discover different ways to use or assemble different objects and many ways to ask and answer questions that require discussions rather than a simple, limited answer. There will be many times when thinking is directed (convergent), so children need opportunities to exercise their brains in divergent ways.

When children feel free to explore, they find many creative uses for "junk" or other items found in the environment. Many are discarded items, such as cardboard, candy papers, containers, eggshells, labels, string, and tickets. You be the supplier; let the child be the designer and builder.

Over time, children's explorations become more organized and intentional. They begin to make events happen and reflect on the relationships among these events. Piaget (1976) refers to this kind of understanding of relationships among actions or events as *logicomathematical knowledge*. To build an understanding of how one event is related to another, a child must have countless opportunities to make events happen, to vary the related actions, and to reflect on the subsequent variations in outcomes (Kamii & DeVries, 1978; Forman & Kuschner, 1983; Forman & Hill, 1984; Chaille & Freeman, 1988).

> Three transformations or changes to which play dough lends itself particularly well involve its consistency, color, and identity. Children can easily participate in changing play dough's texture from dry to sticky, its color from primary to a secondary, its identity from a meatball to a pancake. (Goldhaber, 1992, p. 26).

Whether you call it fooling around with play dough or teaching physics, it's both.

Transformation also applies to the physical environment of the child's classroom. One criticism of American teachers is that they spend an inordinate amount of time and money making or buying "things" to apply to their classroom walls. Teachers in Reggio Emilia programs display the work of the children, more commonly called "documentation."

Art Activities and Separation Anxiety

Art activities at the center can help reduce or eliminate parent-child separation anxiety; increase trust of others at the center; promote healthy attachments to teachers and peers; provide a supportive, trusting atmosphere that allows children to communicate; help children share similar feelings; strengthen peer relationships by offering children alternatives to taking out their frustrations on other children; and remind them of comforting feelings within the classroom. Even a young child can recognize that other children have similar issues and feelings (Muri, 1996, p. 31).

Suggested activities where two or more children can cooperate on a project include puzzles, books, building, puppets, dramatic play, art, and others.

Expanding One's Horizons

Children can be encouraged to expand their participation in art activities by hearing stories about colors, shapes, activities, scenes, or other experiences. Many good stories are available about the child's environment—or the teacher can make an original story using the names of the children and situations in their particular setting. "Creativity *is* feeling free to be flexible and original, to express one's *own* ideas in one's *own* way . . . [and] fosters thinking and confidence" (Edwards & Nabors, 1993, p. 79).

Four characteristics of creativity have been identified by Torrance (1970), a pioneer in the study of the creative process. They include:

- *fluency* as ideas emerge and thoughts change while children manipulate the colors around the paper (body and material interaction);
- *flexibility* in a purposeful activity, which gives the children freedom to experiment in their own ways with different approaches to changing colors and designs;
- *originality* as children decide what designs to make and how to make them; and
- *elaboration* as children add new colors, more detail, or other elements to their activity.

The focus of early childhood art *must* be on the process; something that is *theirs.* To encourage creativity in young children, teachers and parents should allow the children to enjoy the freedom that each basic material provides, let the children use their own ideas for selecting materials and themes, provide plenty of time for exploration and manipulation (they'll let us know when they are finished), and show honest appreciation for their efforts (see Figure 6.3).

Figure 6.3
Ways to Encourage Children to Participate in a Variety of Wholesome Activities

- Relate the activities to the present knowledge and experiences of the children.
- Allow ample time, space, and permission to be fluent.
- Encourage new ways of experiencing the situation.
- Be flexible in your instructions and/or expectations.
- Value their originality.
- Repeat successful experiences by providing new, stimulating props.
- Help the children see how experiences build related experiences.
- Suggest and encourage new relationships.
- Listen to the children's ideas and responses. Give positive feedback.
- Offer positive suggestions if play turns destructive.
- Offer new opportunities based on positive aspects of previous play.

Example:

It will be difficult for a child to make a clay animal if she isn't familiar with the animal, the medium, the responses of teachers, or the time frame. Perhaps the experience would be more successful if the child (1) has a better introduction to the animal (sees one; uses books, pictures, or puzzles; talks about firsthand experiences); (2) can select from a variety of media and tools (clay, crayons, markers, and so on); (3) has special interest in making a specific item; (4) has been given prior encouragement for successful endeavors; and (5) knows that time is plentiful.

Caution: Provide opportunities for child growth by expecting results within the child's developmental abilities.

ROLE OF THE TEACHER

Observation

Through the teacher's constant and casual observations of children and activities, she will note the awareness, special interests, and developmental progress of each child in all areas of development. She will learn when to intervene, make a suggestion, ask a question, add new materials, or merely observe the process because of her increasing knowledge base on how children learn and develop. She will make mental or written notes about the types of play the children enjoy, when repetition of themes with or without new props would help the children clarify points in their environment, and activities and materials that discourage destructive or negative types of expression.

Attitude

Some teachers have positive feelings toward messy and open-ended activities and time frames; others do not. But in order for children to gain experience, confidence, and enjoyment from artistic expression, they need understanding and supportive teachers. Perhaps teachers need to ask themselves how they personally feel about participating in art activities. Are they enthusiastic or negative? Are they curious? Do they enjoy experimenting with materials? Do they think it is a waste or good use of time? Do they enjoy or just tolerate "messes"? Do they realize the effect their attitude has on the children related to gender, personal characteristics, different types of play and expression, such as block, dramatic, and roles? Do they stimulate children's expressions?

Proper Materials

Materials should be appropriate to the developmental level of the children. Large sheets of paper, large brushes, and jumbo crayons are easiest for children to use. Children enjoy making large, free-arm movements and they develop eye-hand coordination and show interest in the various uses of materials.

Covering the table with newspaper or plastic before an activity begins is a great aid at cleanup time. Simply roll up the paper containing the excess paint, clay, paste, or other spilled materials and place the roll in the waste container. A sponge quickly and easily cleans plastic; an old shower curtain or canvas under creative materials is also a time and energy saver.

Reflection

In one center, a substitute teacher went to assist. As creative materials were being prepared for the day, she asked: "Why not use this bucket of earth clay, which is already prepared?" Several teachers agreed with the one who replied, "Our children don't like clay." The substitute persisted, volunteering to supervise, and the teachers agreed. As the children entered the center, they drifted to the clay table. There the substitute teacher was rolling and pounding the clay and remarking that it was cool, soft, and so forth. Many of the children sat down at the clay table and remained for a long period of time. Others stayed a short time, but during the period all of the children had been to the clay table. The conversation was delightful. At the end of the day, the teachers remarked, "We don't understand why the children went to the clay table. They haven't liked it before." The magical thing that drew the children was the attitude of the substitute teacher. The children felt her enjoyment and enthusiasm and wanted to share these feelings with her. At evaluation, the other teachers confessed that none of them enjoyed the messiness or the feel of clay. No wonder the children "didn't like it." Even though they had not expressed their dislike verbally to the children, the teachers had convinced them that something was wrong with the experience.

Materials should help to release feelings, not create frustrations. At one center, several children were enjoying pegs and boards. Guido was not as adept as the others and soon became discouraged. Then he became frustrated and pushed the pegs and boards onto the floor. Painting at the easel or playing in the block area would have better met his needs.

The teacher provides a number of different things, which the children use as their imaginations dictate. The number of different materials supplied at one time depends on the ages and development of the children involved. Young children adequately handle three or four materials, and other children delight in a larger selection. The children also need access to specific materials related to the activity they are engaged in (scissors, paste, something to paste on, and plenty of time when making a collage).

Placement of Materials

The placement of equipment for self-expression is most important. Messy materials should be near a water supply, in a well-lighted area out of the traffic pattern. Interruption by others passing by is discouraging to a child.

Materials placed on low shelves or cupboards are readily accessible and help children to be independent. Seeing materials often encourages their use. Of course, dangerous materials or activities require close teacher supervision.

The children should be allowed to help prepare the materials as much as possible. Children can easily make earth clay, dough clay, paint, and other media, and they should be expected to help clean up. Swishing a sponge around on a tabletop, a plastic cover, or a tray is fun.

Because most children like to take their creations home, a place should be provided where artwork can dry. If space is limited, a portable rack can be used and then folded out of the way. Some artwork can remain at the center overnight to dry; however, children do like to take it home the day they make it, if possible.

Goals and Objectives

Creative experiences must be well planned and executed. Using an activity to consume a block of time is unacceptable. Goals and objectives should be clearly defined, flexible, and within the abilities of the children. Providing teacher-centered materials for children detracts from the experience and may even discourage further participation.

Besides other reasons, a creative art period can be provided just for fun. Activities do not always have to promote the objectives of the day.

Teachers should refrain from patterning for the children; they can manipulate the materials, encourage conversation, and give support, but their role should be minor. They should listen to enlightening and interesting conversation about the way the children think. They should not be like the teacher who thinks all pictures have to be done exactly the same or they won't be displayed.

Necessary limits must be clearly defined and consistently maintained. Each head teacher may designate different limits, so all teachers in a classroom must become aware of the limits of their individual group. One teacher may confine finger painting to paper; another may permit finger painting on tabletops or the glass in windows or sliding doors.

Limits should be explained to and understood by the children. If each child is to clean up his own space when he is finished, he should be told in advance: "Here's a sponge to wipe up where you have been working." Also let the children know if the product is to be saved or if all the materials will be placed back in containers for another time.

Concern for Process or Product?

In our complex society, it is possible to become too product- and time-conscious. Too often parents are heard outwardly encouraging their children to "make something" to account for at least part of their time.

The teacher plays many roles; least of all is that of directing children's art activities.

One child received daily urgings from her mother to make something while at the center. This weighed heavily on the child's mind. On entering school one morning, she walked directly to the easel, grabbed a brush, dipped it in red paint, and made two large lines across the paper. As she left the easel, she was heard to say, "There, I've made a picture for Mother and now I can do what I want!"

One center was having difficulty with some product-minded parents. The parents were pressuring the children—and the center—into making something to take home each day. The teacher recognized that the children were not enjoying the materials as much as previously. She therefore arranged for the children to finger paint directly on the plastic tabletops. On another day, a large piece of butcher paper was placed on the floor, and the children made a group mural. (What conversation and cooperation!) When it came time to go home, the children had no products. Explaining the rationale to the parents helped them understand about pressuring their children. Shortly thereafter, the children again enjoyed the materials without feeling they had to "make something."

Patterns, Stereotyped Cutouts, Coloring Books

Patterning of any kind should be eliminated from art experiences for young children. It stifles rather than encourages creativity. Children draw things as they see them. Lines made by others are meaningless, and young children have difficulty staying inside lines created by someone else.

Coloring books stifle creativity in young children, cause frustration again because of the need to stay in the lines, discourage drawing because the child cannot draw as well as the model, require muscle skills that most young children do not have, and are often limited in size. Adults should never use coloring books or predrawn figures with young children and call them "art" projects. Coloring books may provide teachers with good sources for visual aids, however.

One mother was called to a conference with a kindergarten teacher because her child "refused to color anything" given to him by the teacher. Everything provided was stereotyped and provided no interest for the child, who had always been encouraged at home to draw his own pictures.

Some adults entertain children by drawing for them. Then when the child draws, he becomes easily frustrated because his pictures do not have the realism of the adult "artist." He refuses to attempt drawing because he compares his work to that of the adult. See Figure 6.4 for a list of the values of activities that are best suited for preschoolers. Table 6.1 shows safety tips when using art materials.

Summary of the Teacher's Role

Teachers with good observational skills and those who use the information about individual children as well as the group are much more successful in providing creative experiences that are good and rewarding learning experiences for children.

Developing a positive attitude toward themselves, the children, and the activities is a beginning point for teachers. Teachers who display a positive attitude, are personally secure, and are confident in their interpersonal relationships help others develop the same characteristics. Knowing the individual children helps teachers plan expressive activities and prepare the classroom for the enjoyment of all present.

The teacher should clearly define the goals and objectives of creative activities, define and maintain necessary limits, be supportive of and available to the children, and know why certain activities are more enjoyed and more developmentally appropriate for the children in his classroom.

Table 6.1
Safety in Art Materials

MEDIA	AVOID	USE
Clay	Silica (in powdered clay) because of easy inhalation and harm to the lungs	Damp clay to avoid dust inhalation
Glazes	Those with lead content	Poster paints
Paints (requiring solvent cleaning)	Those requiring chemicals to clean brushes and other tools	Water-based paints
Paint	Powdered tempera because of additives	Liquid tempera or any nontoxic paint
Dyes	Chemical additives, cold-water or commercial dyes	Natural dyes from vegetables
Papier-mache	Instant papier-mache because of lead or asbestos	Newspaper (printed with black ink only) and library paste or liquid starch
Glue	Epoxy, instant or solvent-based glues because of chemical additives	Water-based white glue or library paste
Woodworking	Unwieldy or toy tools; tools that don't work; short nails or those with small heads; small or cluttered areas; unsupervised areas	Sturdy tools built for children; nails with large heads that are long enough to hold; workable tools; good supervision

For additional information, contact Art Hazards Information Center, 5 Beekman St., New York, NY 10038. Chart adapted from Kendrick, Kaufman, and Messenger (1988) and Aronson (1991). A list of arts and crafts materials that cannot be purchased for use in kindergarten through grade six is available from the California Department of Health Services, Health Hazard Assessment Division, 714 P Street, Room 460, Sacramento, CA 95814.

Creativity emerges from the process and the results of children's learning experiences. Their novel thoughts, solutions, and products are brought forth from the types of learning experiences that help them express themselves and represent the world around them as they explore, inquire, and engage their minds, hands, and bodies. Patterns, stereotyped cutouts, and coloring books do not provide opportunities for young children to achieve these objectives.

The object of creative and expressive opportunities for young children is to help them expand their horizons of understanding and manipulative skills that may lie dormant within their maturing bodies. Benefits from such experiences are endless and priceless.

SUGGESTED EXPERIENCES

(*Note:* In each of the following activities, teachers should take caution to provide paints, paper, and other materials in skin-tone shades of different ethnic groups.)

Clay

Clay can be used in many ways—for short or long periods of time, with or without utensils, alone or in the presence of others. It can represent a form or figure, can be changed, and can satisfy one's developmental needs—and through these characteristics, failure is eliminated.

Figure 6.4
Values of Specific Activities for Preschoolers

ACTIVITIES	Sensory experience	Exploration	Satisfaction and enjoyment	Self-expression	Manipulation	Emotional release	Exercise imagination and initiative	Good work habits	Learning experience	Skill and concentration	Eye-hand coordination	Harmony, rhythm, and balance	Insight into own feelings	Develops large muscles	Develops small muscles
Blocks Large	▲	●	●	□	□	●	▲	▲	▲	□	□	●	●	●	▲
Blocks Small	□	●	□	□	□	▲	▲	▲	□	□	●	□	□	▲	●
Chalk	▲	▲	▲	▲	▲	▲	▲	□	▲	▲	□	▲	▲	▲	□
Clay	●	●	□	●	●	●	●	●	□	□	□	▲	●	●	□
Collage	●	●	●	●	●	●	●	●	□	□	□	▲	□	▲	●
Crayons	▲	▲	▲	▲	▲	▲	▲	□	▲	▲	□	▲	▲	▲	□
Cutting and pasting	□	□	□	□	□	□	□	●	□	●	●	▲	▲	▲	●
Domestic area	□	●	●	●	□	●	●	●	●	□	□	▲	●	□	□
Painting Easel	□	●	□	□	●	□	□	●	□	□	□	▲	□	●	□
Finger	●	□	●	●	□	●	□	●	□	▲	□	▲	●	□	□
Sponge or block	□	●	□	□	●	□	□	●	□	□	□	▲	□	□	●
Miscellaneous	□	□	□	□	□	□	□	●	□	□	□	▲	□	□	□
Sand	●	□	□	●	●	□	●	●	●	□	□	▲	□	●	□
Stringing	▲	▲	□	▲	□	▲	□	□	▲	●	●	□	▲	▲	●
Water	●	●	●	●	●	●	●	●	●	□	●	□	●	●	●
Woodworking	●	●	●	●	●	●	●	●	●	●	●	□	●	●	□

Key: ● Best □ Average ▲ Least

Earth clay must be prepared in advance of its use, and the children delight in helping. Some teachers feel that a center cannot be successfully operated without a large bucket of earth clay readily available for experimentation and release of feelings.

Earth clay is most effective when the children use their hands freely. Cookie cutters, rollers, and other objects detract from the sensory experience with this type of clay.

With dough clay, however, the child may use her fingers, her hands, or cookie cutters and rollers. The medium closely resembles cookie dough, and the use of cutters and/or rollers makes the experiences more realistic because one often uses cutters and rollers with this type of food dough. Cookie dough provides sensory and manipulative experiences but does not stimulate the same kind of creativity as earth clay; therefore, it is not used as a substitute for earth clay.

Reflection

To stimulate the interests of the children in the clay area, one teacher discussed building a bird's nest and then helped the children gather leaves, twigs, string, and other materials. They took these materials to the clay table and there learned a great deal by making nests. (The clay will not be reusable because of the materials added.)

Clay is an inexpensive medium for exploration, representation, language and social development, and personal development. When it is prepared, stored, and used properly, it will last for a long period of time and children can get and return it easily. Clay experiences can help children release their frustrations through pounding, twisting, rolling, and discussing, yet some teachers limit the frequency of its use, if they allow its use at all, for various personal reasons. It can come in a variety of colors, depending on where the clay was originally acquired. Clay is a safe medium, but some rules may need to be established until the children are more familiar with the experience. In providing an activity using clay, one teacher talked about it (and played with it), mentioning such things as it comes from; that flowers, vegetables, and other plants grow in the ground; volcanic and earth changes over time; and how clay changes consistency when it is cooked (fired). During subsequent clay experiences, the teacher noted the appearance of universal themes (families, school and city life, transportation, food, natural phenomena, and other topics) as the children manipulated the clay (Neubert, 1991).

For recipes of different kinds of clay, see Appendix D.

Suggestions Related to Clay

Multicultural Awareness

Display pieces of pottery made in different cultures for children to see and duplicate.

Use natural-colored clay (reds, browns) and let the children paint designs on them.

Display pictures of other cultures making and using clay items (pottery for cooking, eating, and so on).

Explore and share how clay is used in your community. Perhaps displaying and talking about tiles, slates, and other related materials would be of interest.

Special-Needs Children

Make sure that materials are nontoxic.

Provide objects that children can easily manipulate (size, weight, use, and so on).

Provide experiences that are open-ended so a child can feel success at any termination point.

Support the child physically, verbally, and socially without isolating her from other children or materials.

Clay can be totally involving.

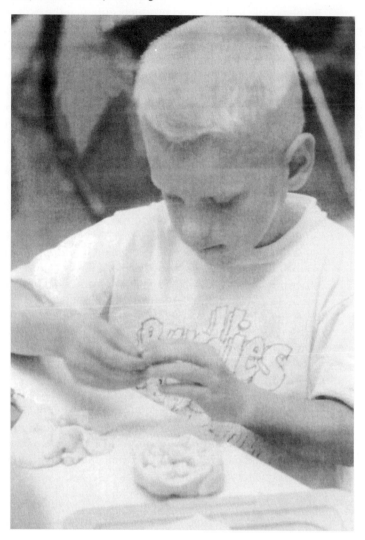

Collage

Webster's New Universal Unabridged Dictionary, deluxe second edition, 1979, printed by Dorset and Baber, defines *collage* as (1) "a kind of surrealist art in which bits of flat objects, as newspaper, cloth, pressed flowers, etc., are pasted together in incongruous relationship for their symbolic or suggested effect," and (2) "a picture so made."

Reflection

Here is a helpful hint when using glue: Place a blob of glue on a piece of paper towel glued to the tabletop on the right side of right-handed children and on the left side of left-handed children. The child can use a small brush or his finger to apply glue. When finished, the child can wrap up the paper and the excess glue and deposit it in the wastebasket. A damp sponge or paper towel helps in final cleanup (Clemens, 1991, p. 9).

Of serious concern is the question of using foodstuffs in creative art projects. Some people feel that food products enhance the experience (some children might not enter the experience if food were not a part of it); some say it broadens the child's acquaintance, reacquaintance, imagination, and exploratory ability with the products. Some feel it is unsanitary for children to "play with food." Others strongly feel that when people in our country (or worldwide) are hungry, foodstuffs should not be "wasted" as play materials (Jones & Nimmo, 1994). When edibles and non-edibles are used interchangeably, one can count on both items being placed in mouths—a rather hazardous situation. Keep in mind that objects small enough to be placed in eyes, noses, ears, or mouths should not be used around young children.

Objectional experiences include (but are not limited to) macaroni or breakfast cereals for necklaces; pasta and beans of different colors for collage; pudding for finger paint; flour and salt to make play dough; and rice, wheat, flour, or cornmeal in the sensory table. Some of the recipes in Appendix D call for some of the questionable ingredients.

Individual teachers need to decide if and how they will use food in teaching. Young children need rich and varied sensory experiences. Raw foodstuffs, among other things, offer such experiences. Commercial products for art activities are also available; however, the purchaser is cautioned against buying any product that contains harmful elements, for the safety of the children. Substitutes include using birdseed, raw grains, and other nonharmful items. (For a clear statement of the view that food, a precious resource, is only for eating, see Holt, 1989, pp. 156–57.) See Table 6.2 for suggestions of other materials to use in collages.

Junk can be made into beautiful pictures. Lots of boxes, tubes, and materials of all kinds and sizes should be on hand. Appropriate cutting tools are needed, as are good, strong ways to attach objects (glue, staples, and other materials). Let the children color and embellish the product. Through this kind of creative play, children learn skills, dexterity, scale, and balance. The intellect is stimulated to decide what items to use, where to place them, and how to attach them. The following are suggestions for cultivating creativity:

Place materials between two sheets of waxed paper and then press with a warm iron to seal the design (especially good for crayon shavings and leaves).

Paste materials on cloth or wallpaper instead of paper for a different experience.

Apply colored tissue paper (with liquid starch as the adhesive) on nonwaxed paper plates for an interesting experience involving color.

Using heavy paper and strong glue, let children make a collage with noodles, cornflakes, and similar materials.

Glue small boxes (match, food, or other) together for an interesting design.

Take small pieces of wood and let the children arrange and paste them onto another piece of wood or cardboard.

Cut pictures out of magazines and let the children paste them on a sheet of paper. Encourage the children to do their own cutting when possible. You might have pictures for the children to arrange in groups (foods, colors, things to wear).

Backgrounds can be of a number of surfaces: paper, cloth, cardboard, wood, plastic, wallpaper, or other surfaces.

Table 6.2
Suggested Teaching Aids for Collage Use

	SUGGESTED TEACHING AIDS FOR COLLAGE USE
Building materials	bark, Celotex, fiberboard, foam insulation, gravel, linoleum, Popsicle sticks, rocks, sand, sandpaper, sawdust and shavings, screens, tongue depressors, washers, wire, wood
Fabrics	burlap, carpet, chiffon, corduroy, cotton, cotton balls, denim, felt, fur, interfacing, knits, leather, muslin, net, satin, silk, taffeta, velvet, wool, yarn
Paper and paper substitutes	aluminum foil, blotters, boxes (small), cardboard (boxes, corrugated, food boxes, shirt forms), catalogs, cellophane, confetti, construction paper, crepe paper, cups (candy), doilies, egg cartons, gift cards, greeting cards, gummed labels, magazines, newspapers, plates, reinforcements, stamps, straws, tape, tissue, towels, tubes, wallpaper, waxed paper
Plastic	doilies, egg cartons, flowers, foam, food containers, hair rollers, straws, Styrofoam, toothpicks
Sewing	beads, buttons, elastic, lace, ribbon, rickrack, sequins, spools, string, tape, yarn
Miscellaneous	acorns, bottle caps, brads, cans, clothespins, corks, cotton balls, cotton swabs, excelsior, feathers, flowers (dried or fresh), glitter, hairpins, jars (lids and rings), jewelry, keys, leaves, net sacks, packing materials, paper clips, pipe cleaners, shells, shoelaces, sponges, twigs (and sticks), weeds, wrappers (gum, candy)

In preparation for a collage experience, tear, break, cut, or otherwise divide supplies into manipulative sizes.

If people are to be represented, have materials to represent different skin tones.

Reflection

Gigi, age 4, exercised her ingenuity with materials provided. She used straws for arms and legs, a sponge for a head, heavy twine for hair, different fabrics for a blouse and skirt, and small pieces of foam for shoes. Such imagination!

To help promote cultural awareness, select items familiar to different cultures:

Paper products (origami, rice, crepe paper, and so on)

Fabrics

Objects of different designs

Wood products

Pictures of people, objects, landscapes, and so on

Tools for cutting and pasting (brushes, tools, and so on)

Cutting and Pasting

Cutting is difficult for many young children; however, if they are provided with good scissors, they learn to use and enjoy them. Make sure the blades cut, are free from paste or other materials, and are the appropriate size for small hands and fingers. Every center should have some left-handed scissors, which are available from a number of sources. Manufacturers are also producing plastic scissors with inserted metal blades, handles with four holes for adult assistance, and scissors with a spring action. Try a number of kinds to see what features best meet the needs of your children: left- or right-handed, sharp or dull tips, metal or plastic blades, serrated or smooth blades.

Most 3-year-olds are unable to use scissors; some 4-year-olds can use them in rather immature ways; most 5-year-olds are able to follow lines and cut. Once Stephen, age 3, learned to cut, that was all he wanted to do. He was proud of the sack of scraps he had cut. Although it was still difficult for him to accurately follow lines, especially the curvy ones, he loved his own scissors and had some magazines that were just his own, but he could not cut up Mom's magazines, fabrics, books, or the evening paper.

The following activities are suggested to encourage cutting and pasting:

- Color dry salt with powdered tempera. Brush paste on paper, then sprinkle salt over the paste. A saltshaker makes a good container.
- Take a sheet of black construction paper and cut holes in various sizes, shapes, and places. Paste tissue over the holes to make stained-glass windows.
- Get fabric samples from a decorator or use remnants. Paste objects on them to make wall hangings.
- Cut designs from paper or fabric. Paste on cans or jars for gifts.
- Tear or cut strips from magazines. Have children paste them in interesting designs.
- Fold paper. Cut or tear designs in it.
- Make a mural of the community, having children make and cut shapes for their homes, churches, and other important landmarks.
- Provide scraps of paper and paper bags. Children can make paper-bag puppets or masks.
- Paste objects on paper plates.
- Use materials such as those listed for collage.
- Paste colored paper or magazine pictures on tubes, rollers, or boxes.
- Cut pictures from magazines and have the children make their family (determine how many children they need, what sizes, what color of hair, and so on).
- Have the children paste shapes, ribbons, or floral tape into a plastic meat tray. They can also paste textures in the bottom (straw for a cow, fabric for a cat, leaves for a bird) and then paste on a picture of an animal who would live there.
- Decorate large (gallon) plastic jugs with paper, fabric, or marking pens.
- Paste single-color objects on same-color paper (for snow pictures use white paper, wadded white tissue, felt, Styrofoam, popcorn, doilies, cotton balls, salt, and so on).

- ○ Drip glue on dark paper. Sprinkle on salt or glitter.
- ○ Draw a large body on a large brown bag and let the child use his imagination to decorate it (gingerbread boy; provide such items as rickrack and fabric scraps).

In order to stimulate multicultural awareness, provide pictures of people, clothing, situations, animals, and objects from different cultures.

Drawing

Young children spend a lot of time drawing. Whether this is the best experience for them is debatable. Art development has stages, and scribbling is an important beginning. Until children develop eye-hand coordination, muscle control, and the thought process, drawings will be scattered, unrecognizable, and primitive. By examining the drawings of selected children between the ages of 2 and 6 years, we can see progress in ability. One must remember that each child is unique and that experience also plays an important part.

Many drawing utensils are small, require pressure, or are messy. Adults give pencils, pens, and paper to children to keep them quiet and occupied. Most pencils are inappropriate for small, undeveloped fingers; if the child does use a pencil, a jumbo one with a soft lead is preferred.

Perhaps because of their attractiveness, availability, and inexpensiveness, most children have access to crayons. These come in regular and jumbo sizes, with the jumbo being easier for young children to hold. Pressure needs to be exerted if a dark color is desired. Often, the expenditure of energy tires the young hand before the child has had ample opportunity for self-expression. Some suppliers stock plastic crayons, which are less messy than wax crayons and are very colorful.

Crayons can be used in a number of different ways:

Crayon twist. Lay the crayon on its side and rotate it.

Shavings. Grate crayons. Place between two sheets of waxed paper and press with a warm iron.

Crayon melt. Heat a frying pan or griddle to warm. Place a piece of aluminum foil in the bottom. Have the child make a picture with crayon on the foil. Then apply a piece of newsprint or construction paper over the drawing and press gently. The paper will absorb the crayon design. Wipe off any remaining crayon from foil and the next child can make his design.

Crayon texture. Place a flat object, such as a leaf, screen, or Popsicle stick, under newsprint. Color over it with crayon. Using a crayon directly on sandpaper is another sensory experience.

Large sheets of paper encourage large arm movements. Paintbrushes offer a much better experience for young children than do pencils, pens, and crayons. Standing at an easel, children can fully use their bodies.

Chalk provides many of the same experiences as crayons. Because of its dryness, chalk has a tendency to be messy and to rub off. It can be made more permanent if it is dipped into buttermilk or if the paper is rubbed lightly with buttermilk or water before the chalk is applied. Buttermilk brings out the color of the chalk and acts as a fixative. Chalk does not require much pressure but does soil the hands, which some children dislike.

Many adults supply *felt-tip pens* as substitutes for crayons; however, the pens can become messy. They often go into the mouths of children, and they mark anything they touch, such as fabric or bodies. Because such marks may be permanent, pens with ink that washes off hands and out of fabrics would be better for children to use. The pens do have the advantages of requiring less pressure and of being quite brilliant in color.

Children can be given blank sheets of paper or paper formed into a booklet to create their own books. They can make the pictures and dictate the text to an adult. With the child's permission, the book can be used at storytime (see Figure 6.5).

The following materials are suggested to use for drawing:

blackboard and chalk	oilcloth (use back side)
cardboard (lightweight)	poster paper
construction paper	sandpaper
fabrics	screens
manila paper	wallpaper
newspaper (want-ad section)	window shades
newsprint	wood

Painting

Painting can be done in different ways. Therefore, this section is divided into separate areas: easel painting, finger painting, sponge or block painting, and miscellaneous painting.

Easel Painting

A good easel is of sturdy wood or metal construction, has a place for paint jars and a clip for paper, and is easily cleaned. It should be the correct height for the child and portable, so that it can be used outdoors as well as indoors. Indoors, the easel should be out of the traffic pattern, under good lighting, and close to a sink, washroom, and sponges. Side-by-side use encourages children to cooperate and verbalize.

Paint.   The children can help prepare the paint. Two to four colors are sufficient. Primary colors are most appealing and educational. Children learn to mix them to create secondary colors. White and black should be offered occasionally.

Dry powder paint and a small amount of water are shaken in a screw-top jar. Red and orange paint mix best in warm water. A small amount of wheat paste or extender is added to thicken the paint. A small amount of liquid detergent in the paint facilitates cleanup of hands, brushes, and clothing, and a pinch of salt keeps the paint from going sour in a warm room. The paint should be stirred well before using.

Paint keeps indefinitely if tightly covered and stored in a cool place. Improper storage greatly increases costs.

Jars.   The following types of containers can be used:

- Half-pint jars with lids for storage
- Baby-food jars with lids for storage
- Quart milk cartons washed out and cut down
- Frozen-juice cans (6- or 12-ounce size)
- Small food cans, such as those used for tuna and tomato paste
- Muffin tins

Figure 6.5
Drawings of similar objects done by children ages 3, 5, and 6 years.

Age 3   Age 5   Age 6

Age 3   Age 5   Age 6

Age 3   Age 5   Age 6

Clothing. A cover-up of some kind should always be used. A smock, a large T-shirt, a fabric or plastic apron, or an old shirt worn backward will do. Use of a cover-up is one of the limits for participating in this activity, not because children are messy or infantile, but because it is good policy to protect their clothes.

Techniques.   The following recommendations are helpful:

- Using one brush for each color keeps colors true but does not provide much opportunity for the child to explore. Occasionally time should be allowed for experimentation.
- Before applying the brush to paper, the end should be wiped on the top of the jar.
- If easels are unavailable, paper can be placed on a large table or on the floor out of the traffic pattern. Paint is put in muffin tins and flat containers.
- A place nearby should be provided for hanging pictures to dry.

Cleanup.   Children should be encouraged to cover unused paint and wash out brushes and empty jars. They should hang their pictures to dry. If space is limited, a large, portable, wooden clothes-drying frame can be used, or newspapers can be placed on the floor out of the traffic pattern. Spills on trays, easels, and the floor should be wiped up. A tarp, a plastic sheet, or newspapers placed on the floor before painting aids in cleanup.

The following are suggested materials for easel painting:

Brushes: bristles ½ to 1 inch wide

Paper: butcher, cardboard, cartons, construction, corrugated, finger-paint, magazines, newspaper, newsprint, sacks, towels, wallpaper

Fabrics: burlap, cotton, leather, nylon, oilcloth, plastic, vinyl

Other surfaces or materials: clay, metal, rocks, seashells, wood (boxes, branches, scraps)

When a child is making or painting a picture, one great disservice we can do is asking questions such as, "What is it?" or commenting on the quality of the work. Young children will be more encouraged to paint often if they feel they are free to create what is in their hand and head; if they are not interrupted by questions about the content, use of materials, or quality; and if they enjoy the use of a variety of materials.

The wise teacher or parent will carefully observe the child's progress and provide interesting and challenging opportunities as the child indicates readiness. Perhaps the child is ready to move beyond easels and tempera, to a different applicator (brush, eyedropper, sponge, spray bottle), a new surface (canvas, wallpaper, fabric), additional items (leaves, coins, keys, new materials, watercolors, finger paints, colored shaving cream, and so on), or even combining curriculum areas—science *and* art, for example (tinting water with food coloring, making secondary colors, changing consistency) (Demerest, 1996, p. 83). Stepping in when children are in exploratory mode, by telling them "how" to do this or that, will often sour their interest. They need to play, experiment, feel, and experience.

Finger Painting

Finger painting is a good emotional release. Children can express many moods, such as joy, concern, interest, curiosity, and sorrow. They can show fear, for example, and then quickly wipe it away.

Finger painting provides an excellent sensory experience. Adding different substances to the paint—sand, glitter, rice, or paper—can change the experience. To color the paint, powder paint is added to dry ingredients or food coloring to wet

Using water colors and having one's own materials can be a good beginning painting experience for young children.

ingredients. (*Note:* Food coloring stains some surfaces. It can usually be removed from plastic surfaces by putting full-strength liquid detergent on the spot, leaving it a few minutes, then wiping it off with a damp sponge or cloth.)

Materials. Recipes for finger paint are found in Appendix D. A number of surfaces can be used, including paper (butcher, shelf, hard-surfaced wrapping), oil-cloth, tabletops, wood, wallpaper, cardboard, glass, plastic, or vinyl. Sponges are provided to dampen the paper or tabletop and for cleanup, and racks are needed for drying the paintings. The children should wear cover-ups. (See the discussion about using edible products earlier in this chapter.)

Procedure. The following suggestions will ensure a pleasant finger-painting session:

- Define limits for children and teachers.
- Dampen the table or paper with a sponge so the paper is smooth and adheres to the surface.
- Put a heaping tablespoon of finger paint on the paper. (Colorless paint may be used; the teacher can sprinkle powdered tempera on paper. If children sprinkle tempera, cans become messy and hard to hold.)
- Play several types of music during the activity.
- Mention that the children can also make designs with their fists, knuckles, palms, and fingernails.
- Encourage children to clean up. Have sponges and water ready.

Finger painting can also be done directly on tabletops. When this is done, a design can be lifted onto paper.

Sponge or Block Painting

Sponge or block painting is done by dipping a sponge or other object into thick paint and then making a print on paper. The procedure is repeated in different positions and colors to make designs.

Sponges are cut into small pieces. A spring clothespin makes an excellent handle. Other objects include cork, pieces of wood, spools, string, potato mashers, sink stoppers, and plastic forks.

Paints should be quite thick. A small amount of wheat paste is used as a thickener. The paint is placed in staggered cups of a muffin tin or small aluminum pie pans.

The best paper for printing is butcher paper or cardboard. Absorbent paper can also be used.

Miscellaneous Painting

Brush painting. Different kinds of brushes can be used for paintings. Some unusual ones include tooth, bottle, hair, food, and straws from a broom.

Crayon painting. The child makes a design on paper with crayons and then "washes" paint over it. The wax resists the paint.

Ink-blot painting. Paper is folded in half and reopened. A few drops of paint are placed on one side of the paper. The paper is then refolded and pressed firmly. This creates a symmetrical design. Newsprint is best for this experience.

Mural painting. Children are provided with a long sheet of butcher paper, paint, brushes, and encouragement. They will do the rest.

Painting on different materials. A number of materials give experience in texture: cloth, paper towels, smooth paper, sponge, glass, plastic, leather, linoleum, egg cartons, aluminum foil, cone-shaped spools, corrugated paper, mailing tubes, paper bags, pleated muffin cups, waxed paper, tissue paper, metal, stone, rocks, and wallpaper.

Painting with water. Children can paint with water on boards, sidewalks, and other large surfaces that water will not damage. They should be given small pans of water and large brushes.

Snow painting. The child paints over a picture (greeting cards are good) with a mixture of 1 part Epsom salts and 1 part boiling water that has been cooled before painting. Evaporation leaves crystals.

Spool painting. The edges of a spool are nicked for design. A wire is inserted through the spool and twisted to make a handle. The spool is then dipped into thick paint and rolled on the paper.

String painting. A long piece of string is dipped into paint and rearranged on one half of a piece of paper. The other half is folded over the string and pressed. The string is pulled out, and the design appears on both halves of the sheet. Different strings and colors of paint can be used for colorful designs.

Tempera wash painting. Glue or paraffin wax is dripped on paper and allowed to dry overnight. A wash with tempera paint is done over the design.

Towel painting. A design is painted on a plastic tabletop or similar hard surface, and a paper towel is pressed on the painted surface. The towel is then removed and allowed to dry. This can also be done over a finger painting. A paper towel can also be painted directly with brush and easel paint.

Vinyl painting. Vinyl is applied to a wall or rolled out on the floor. Children paint on it and then wipe it off.

In order to promote multicultural awareness, ask children how colors are obtained for different uses (fabric, household goods, beauty, aesthetics, and other things) in different cultures and how patterns are made and if they have any special significance.

Puzzles

While puzzles do not technically belong with "creative/sensory" development because of their lack of flexibility or creativity, they do add to the development and satisfaction of young children in many ways that art materials do. Frequently both art

More structured than most art activities, puzzle-making can enhance cognitive, perceptual, motor, and personal development.

and activities may be provided in the same time frame but not at the same tables. Puzzles are seen as enhancing cognitive, perceptual, and motor development. Color, size, shape, and texture are experienced as the child learns the primary mathematical concepts (the sum of the whole is composed of many pieces). This requires attention and concentration on the task (Maldonado, 1996, p. 5).

Reflection

The values of puzzles for young children include active participation, problem solving, learning, satisfaction in putting things together where they belong, and contentment as the child actively observes and detects likenesses and differences; physical manipulation; trial-and-error strategies; self-correction; making something "whole"; self-gratification; individual or cooperative participation; development of interpersonal skills and friendships (socialization and speech, for example); autonomy, competency, and success; concentration; color and shape matching; and other individual specific values (Maldonado, 1996).

Role of the Teacher

The teacher's role in puzzle making is to reinforce cognitive, language, problem-solving, and socialization skills in young children, who are learning to observe, analyze, share, and devise problem-solving strategies.

Characteristics of good puzzle-making situations include:

1. Appropriateness to each child's developmental abilities and needs.
2. Attractive, interesting, or familiar designs.
3. Puzzles designed and constructed at a high level of quality.
4. Easy access and return.
5. Time to ponder and place pieces.

Summary

"Historically, one of the most commonly found materials in the early childhood classroom has been the table puzzle. Early childhood practitioners know that puzzles are an important tool in helping children engage in the problem-solving process. The use of table puzzles in early childhood programs has gone unchallenged and unchanged over the century due to continuing positive experiences of children and their teachers. This pleasurable activity is one of the best ways to work toward some of our educational goals!" (Maldonado, 1996, p. 10).

Sand

Most young children are delighted to play in sand. They run their hands through it, smooth out roads, construct tunnels and ditches, and make cakes. They socialize in sand: discussing, sharing ideas and materials, participating in collective monologue, and learning to cooperate.

Whether sand is used in a large area on the playground or in a sandbox matters little as long as space is sufficient for exploring. Props such as trucks, shovels, buckets, sifters, measuring spoons and cups, and containers stimulate the imagination of young children. Seashells make an interesting and lifelike addition.

Definite limits are set up so the children know how the sand is to be used. These are expressed as follows: "Keep the sand in the sand area." "Shovels, hoes, and rakes stay close to the ground." "Sand is for building."

During the winter, a sandbox can be used inside the school; however, some floors are easily scratched and require extra maintenance. For these reasons, some schools prohibit sand use in the classroom. Canvas, plastic, or newspapers can be spread to protect the floors.

Water changes the consistency of sand and makes it easier to manipulate. In summer, a hose stimulates creativity for children. Sand is dampened for pretend cooking and molding. A board nearby is convenient for dumping cakes and products or for children to sit on if the whole area is damp.

Sand toys are best stored near the sand area, separating them from other toys. Trucks, cars, measuring cups, sifters, gelatin molds, and so on are placed on low shelves; buckets and shovels are hung on low hooks or nails. A messy storage area discourages children from using the equipment and may cause accidents.

Stringing

Stringing objects encourages the use of small muscles and eye-hand coordination. Some children lack the control and concentration necessary to make the experience pleasurable; others enjoy it.

Helpful Hints

- Allow plenty of time for children to experiment.
- Make sure needles are large enough for the children to grasp, have blunt ends, and have an object tied on the end to keep objects from sliding off. Use a double thread so the needle will not become unthreaded. Yarn may be better to use.
- If needles are not used, make ends of string or yarn firm by covering with transparent or masking tape, or by dipping in paste or wax and allowing to dry. A shoelace makes an excellent string because of the hard tip.
- Color dry macaroni with water and food coloring. Wood alcohol colors well and dries rapidly but may cause gastrointestinal upset if macaroni is ingested. When using food coloring, place small amounts of water and coloring in a small bowl and let the macaroni stand in the solution until the desired shade. Remove with a fork and place on paper towels until the excess moisture is absorbed. Spread individual pieces of macaroni on sheets of waxed paper and let dry overnight. If not separated, the macaroni will dry in clusters. (See discussion earlier in this chapter about using edible products as creative materials.)

Suggested Materials

Threading small objects can be a rather tedious task for inexperienced fingers; teachers may want to use larger objects as an introduction to stringing, such as the following:

Paper: Aluminum foil, construction, tissue, holiday, and others

Beads: Clay (see recipe in Appendix D); large, wooden; plastic; and others

Spools: Thread wire products, string, bubble wrap, and others

Plastic: Spools, straws (½-inch pieces), and other objects

Miscellaneous: Foam packing material, shredded packing, bubble wrap, dividers, plastic containers, and others

Water

Children need to have water experiences. Water has a soothing effect. It gives way to the motion of one's hands. At school, basins and sinks are generally low and available to the children. Water can be used daily or just for special occasions.

Water encourages action, as do props. When children participate in this activity, wearing a cover-up is a prerequisite. Sponges, towels, mops, and buckets should be close at hand and used by the children for spills and cleanup. The number of children at this activity is limited by providing only a set number of cover-ups.

If water is not desired in certain areas of the classroom, these areas should be separated by as much distance as possible and the rationale explained to the children. "Water in the book area could ruin our books." They should be told where and when water can be used.

One preschool teacher had difficulty accepting water play. She felt water was for drinking and washing only. In her particular preschool group were several children who never passed the water to play in the other areas. As children measured, spilled, poured, wiped, and experimented with water, the teacher's dislike for it intensified. After a considerable length of time (and admitting she could not eliminate water from the room), she realized that the experience had a therapeutic effect on the children, and she began to recognize other values as well. Perhaps instead of fighting the presence of water, she should have joined the activity!

Teachers may consider the following suggestions for water use:

○ Give children a bucket of clear water and a large brush and let them paint anything outdoors that water will not damage.

○ Get a plastic container with a squeeze handle similar to that used with window cleaner. Let the children squirt at waterproof targets such as a fence or tree.

○ Let the children bathe dolls or wash doll clothes.

○ Have a box of water toys readily available for use in the water table.

○ Provide containers, water, and food coloring. Children can make and mix colors. Eyedroppers and plastic egg cartons are easy to use and clean.

○ Encourage water play in the domestic area.

○ During the summer, have a hose running in the sand area or use a wading pool.

○ If other sources of water play are not available, cut a tire in half and fill each half with water. Or use a jug, a large tub, or a 5-gallon plastic jug with a spout.

○ Demonstrate the use of steam for cooking and pressing.

○ Point out and make use of community resources, such as lakes, rivers, ponds, or fountains.

○ Observe activities relying on water, such as fishing, logging, or boating.

○ Tell how plumbing works and what repairs are needed.

- Go through a car wash or let the children help wash the car.
- Take a trip to the fire station and have the firefighters explain how water helps put out fires, how hoses are used, and so on.
- Explain or observe irrigation of crops.
- Visit a shipyard or dock and learn about it through use of books, pictures, and replicas.
- Watch the water wagon as it washes the streets.
- Encourage children to help water a garden, plants, or animals.
- Talk about the characteristics of water and evaporation.
- Talk about rain, snow, ice, and other weather conditions.
- Involve the children in cleanup using sponges and water.
- Provide containers and spouts for measuring and exploring water.
- Introduce new terms and characteristics of water (recycling, buoyancy, volume, weight, leveling).
- On a stormy day, watch the change in clouds, the darkness of the sky, the falling moisture (the bounce of raindrops, the floating of snowflakes, and so on), and the different types of clothing worn to accommodate the moisture and temperature.
- Talk about a rainbow. Use such books as Freeman's *A Rainbow of My Own* (1966).
- When using water in the classroom, encourage the children to help set and enforce limits for its use (type of clothing to be worn, cleanup procedures).
- Place some rocks or shells in a small fishbowl and let the children examine them through the glass, under magnifying glasses, or by removing them from the bowl.
- Mix water and dirt.
- Look for and use books about water and weather.

See also the section on water in Chapter 8.

Don't overlook the enjoyment of bubbles. Solutions can be purchased or made: Mix 1 gallon of water, 1 cup of dishwashing detergent (some are better than others), and 50 drops of glycerin. Anything with a hole is wonderful for making bubbles: plastic six-pack soda holders make six big bubbles!

Young children seldom have to be invited to join water or mud play. Water is adaptable, appealing, inexpensive, flexible, sometimes clean, mixable with other items (liquid and solid), abundant, and on and on. Frequently both mud and water play have a calming effect on children.

Woodworking

Very young children enjoy pounding and banging; preschool children obtain satisfaction from using tools and wood. Their first experiences are exploratory. They like to build simple structures and should be permitted to use their imaginations. The names they select for their objects should be accepted without comments indicating they look like something else, need some additions or changes, or are poorly done. To them, the objects are real. Patterning, as in other areas, has no place in woodworking.

Safety

An excellent experience for both girls and boys, woodworking requires close supervision. Precise limits must be set and maintained for obvious reasons—and the children will pay more attention to the limits if they help set them. Consider the following possibilities:

- Talk about and demonstrate the proper use and storage of the tools; for example, saws have a back-and-forth motion, hammers are used for pounding, sandpaper is a rubbing motion and helps smooth the wood, and so on.
- Besides careful supervision, the teacher has other roles (how much help to give, which children are more apt to need physical or verbal support, what if the teacher becomes distracted or needs additional help, and so on).
- What tools are appropriate for young hands?
- Are the tools sturdy and appropriate (weight, size, and so on)? Improper or poor tools (adult-sized tools are too heavy, toy tools are ineffective) are the cause of many accidents.
- How many children can participate at a time?
- How will a child know when it is her turn?
- What are the children to do with their finished products? Will they be painted, used for a later activity, or taken home?
- How can uninterested children be involved?
- Are there special considerations for your center?

Tree stumps (such as those normally cast off when cutting firewood), a hammer, and some nails (1¼-inch roofing nails have large heads that are not only easy to grasp, but also offer an easy target for a hammer) make a fun experience for children—provided they have good equipment and close supervision! After the

Girls, too, enjoy woodworking and tools.

stump is completely covered in nails, a slice can be cut off the stump with a chainsaw and the stump will be ready for another hammering experience. Expect the hammering to be random; however, some children may try to make recognizable designs as their skills develop (Leithead, 1996).

Reflection

The values of a woodworking (hammering) experience include:

Social: Turn taking, predicting, discussing designs

Motor: Eye-hand coordination; strength

Intellectual: How hard to hit the nail; size of hammer to use; noise made when hitting the nail or wood; making designs; skills and procedures needed; math: measurements, number of nails for an area, number of strokes to bury a nail; using new tools; and so on

Emotional: "Venting" experience, sharing, cooperation

Woodworking is not used each day. Despite its many values and interests, the activity also has drawbacks—a limited number of children can participate at a time; constant, careful supervision is necessary; some children take a long time to finish a project—if they are hurried they become frustrated and careless, and if they take an excessively long time they deprive other children of the opportunity or miss out on other activities; tools and materials are expensive; and children can be easily injured.

Inexpensive substitutes for wood are masonite, sheet rock, Celotex, acoustical tile, or a log of soft wood. (Avoid all materials containing asbestos!) The children can hammer small nails into them. Pounding boards and pressing golf tees into plastic foam are not substitutes for woodworking.

Suggested Woodworking Equipment

Workbench. A workbench can be purchased or made by cutting the legs off a wooden table. The correct height is a little shorter than half the child's height. Sawhorses with a sturdy plank may also be used.

Hammers. A claw hammer, the most practical for general use, should be well balanced, have a broad head, and weigh 7 to 13 ounces. It should be made with the same careful workmanship and durable materials as regular carpenter tools. A toy hammer is not acceptable.

Saws. Both ripsaws and crosscut saws should be provided, and the teacher should know the use of each. An 8- to 10-point crosscut saw, 12 to 20 inches in length, is desirable. A saw is held gently and used with long, even downward strokes. A groove that makes sawing easier is initiated by drawing the saw toward one on the first stroke.

Nails. A variety of nails creates interest. Roofing nails are useful because of the large heads; however, they may split the wood. Fourpenny, sixpenny, and eightpenny nails, 1¼ to 2½ inches in length, are good.

Wood. A local lumberyard or carpenter will usually provide pieces of scrap wood. Soft woods, such as yellow or white pine or poplar, are easier for children to use. Wood of various sizes and shapes stimulates imagination. Wheels or dowels may be used as smokestacks, handles, and so on.

Plane. Many types and sizes of planes are available. The block plane is best for young children. They should be taught always to plane in an uphill direction and with the grain.

Vise. A vise mounted on the workbench holds the wood securely and allows the child to use both hands in sawing or hammering. Several vises may be mounted on the workbench.

Brace and bit. Children may need help in using a brace and bit. A 6-inch sweep is desirable for young children. Several different bits may be purchased. Recommended sizes are nos. 3, 4, 8, 12, and 16.

Sandpaper. Sandpaper can be used in a variety of sizes: fine 2/0, medium 1/0, and coarse 2 and 3. Sandpaper mounted on a wood block is easier for children to use.

Other tools and materials. Brushes, cans, carpenter's pencil, clamps (4- or 6-inch), fabrics, glue, leather, paint, paper, pliers, rasp, rubber, ruler, safety visor, screwdriver (4- to 6-inch handle, ¼-inch blade), spools, square, string, tongue depressors, wire, yarn.

Miscellaneous Sensory Experiences

Feel or Texture

- In a table used for water or sand, use nonharmful substances of various textures.
- Place items of various textures on a table and let children feel them. Try wool, silk, cotton, corduroy, velvet, oilcloth, felt, screening, paper, sawdust, shavings, and fur.
- Dip colored yarn into a thick wheat-paste mixture. Shape it on waxed paper and let it dry to make interesting designs.
- Place various objects in a box or paper sack. Let the children feel them and try to identify them before seeing them.
- Ask the children to walk around the room and touch objects that are similar (for example, those made of wood or metal, those that are smooth or cold).
- Put cornstarch in a bowl and add enough water so that the cornstarch is semiliquid or runny. The mixture, sometimes called *ooblick*, feels both moist and dry. It runs through the fingers but becomes hard when the hand is clenched. The recipe is in Appendix D.
- Have a small picture and a replica of some object, such as a dog. Put a number of replicas in a "feel box." Have the child look at the pictures and try to locate replicas by feeling in the box.
- Show replicas or pictures of objects and ask children to describe how they would feel. Then provide real objects, if possible, and feel them.
- Make a mixture using equal parts of liquid glue and cornstarch (try 1 cup of each). The substance has an unusual feel and can be molded and rolled. It is called *glarch* or *glurch* (glue and starch). The recipe is in Appendix D.
- Let children help prepare creative media, using their hands to feel them in different stages of preparation (for example, dough clay as dry ingredients,

when liquid is added, final use). It could feel warm, scratchy, smooth, cool, lumpy, and so on. Add the use of a garlic press, plastic knife, and so on and listen to the comments ("It's stringy," "Mine is globby," and so on).

○ The skin is a sense receptor. Touch something with fingers, the cheek, elbows, or feet, and explore whether objects feel the same when touched by different body parts. Talk about the meaning of *receptor*.

○ Make two identical feel boxes. Have a child place one hand in one box and the other hand in the duplicate box. Encourage him to find the same object with both hands simultaneously.

Smell

○ In small containers, place small amounts of common liquids that have odors (for example, perfume, extracts, vinegar, household commodities). Let the children smell them and try to identify them. Be sure to avoid harmful odors!

○ Show children pictures of things and ask them to describe what they think the items would smell like.

○ Ask children to name their favorite smells and tell why they like them.

○ Talk about how smell helps us (for example, the smell of smoke means danger).

○ In a water or creative activity, add scented bubble bath or food flavorings such as peppermint, vanilla, lemon extract, or others that would be somewhat familiar to the child. Is there more or less interest when a fragrance is added?

○ Match two smells from fragrance containers. How easy is it for the children?

○ Help the children learn and use only *safe* odors—avoiding those that are harmful to the body (glue, sprays, paint, and so on).

○ Make and use sniff-and-scratch cards by putting small amounts of fragrances on sand paper. When the surface is scratched, the aroma becomes more evident.

Taste

○ In small bowls, place staple items that look alike but have different tastes (white sugar, salt, flour, powdered sugar, tapioca, coconut). Taste them and talk about the differences.

○ In small bowls, place staple items that have the same name but have different characteristics (white sugar, brown sugar, raw sugar, powdered sugar, sugar cane, sugar cubes, and others). Taste them and talk about the differences.

○ Have plates of vegetables or fruits. Ask the children to taste and compare them (juicy, crunchy, sweet, sour).

○ Have the same fruit or vegetable prepared in different ways (raw, cooked, peeled, unpeeled, as juice). Taste and compare.

○ Have new foods as a snack or at lunch.

○ Talk about vegetables that are generally eaten raw (lettuce) and those that can be eaten raw or cooked. Serve some of them at snack.

○ Talk about nutrition frequently. Introduce the children to the current government pyramid chart.

○ With and without food products present, ask the children to describe the tastes of their favorite foods and disliked foods.

○ Talk about and taste food for babies (puréed, liquid, unseasoned, and so on).

You taste it first and if it's really good, we'll taste it, too.

Sound

- Fill containers with different items. Have the children shake them and try to guess what is inside.
- Have a group of duplicate containers with invisible contents. See if the children can correctly match them by shaking them.
- Play a record or tape and see if the children can identify the sounds. Pictures or replicas can go with the sounds. See if the children can match them.
- Make telephones with two empty juice cans and a string 10 to 20 feet long. Poke a hole in the bottom of a can, put string through the bottom, and tie a knot inside the can. Hold the string taut. Let the children talk and listen to each other.
- Borrow telephones from the telephone company (if available) to teach telephone courtesy and proper use.
- Record children's voices on tape. Play the tape back and see if they can identify the child who is speaking.
- Encourage the children to make poems or rhyming words.
- Have one child imitate a sound, such as an animal or vehicle, and another guess what it is.
- Behind a screen make sounds of common household items. See if the children can identify them.

- Tell a story of a child's day and have the children make the appropriate sounds (brushing teeth, turning on water, car starting, horns on the way to school, pet sounds).
- Have the children tell how they feel when they hear certain sounds, such as a dog, siren, band, familiar voice, or bell.
- Make the sound of an animal and have the children pretend to be that animal.
- Hide something that has a sound—ticking clock, rustling paper, squeaking toy, bell, musical instrument—and also some items that are soundless—flag, soft toy, hat. Inside an enclosed sack or box, make the item sound or sound-less according to the item. Have the children guess the item.
- Why do some items make sound and others not? What can you do to silence items with sounds and make sound from items that are soundless?
- Use tapes or records of stories and/or music.
- Use a story/tape such as *The Listening Walk* by Showers (1991). Take a listening walk around the classroom or playground.
- Listen to different volumes of the same sound—perhaps use earmuffs or a mute on a stringed instrument to soften sounds.
- Explore sounds in different cultures that would be of interest to the children (music, chants, animal sounds, and so on.)
- Read and/or use the "Noisy" books in Margaret Wise Brown's series (Harper Children's Books).

Sight

- Have the children look at various objects. Ask them to describe how the objects would feel before they touch them (hard, smooth, cold, and so on).
- Have the children look at a picture. Ask them to act out the scene.
- Have the children act out their favorite game or activity. See if the other children can guess it.
- Have the children put crayon shavings, things of nature (for example, flower petals, seeds, leaves), or small objects between two pieces of waxed paper and then press with a warm iron.
- Talk about the differences between opaque and clear things.
- Ask the children how they tell if something is hot just by looking at it.
- Have the children watch you complete a task and then model it.
- Show four to six objects. Have the children close their eyes while you remove one object. Have them name the missing object.
- From a variety of objects, have the children group items that are alike in color, size, or composition. Can the objects be grouped in other ways, such as by shape or use?
- From a group of objects, have the children select the things that would be used by a certain family member (father, mother, baby).
- Show a suitcase full of clothes. Have the children decide what articles are needed for different occasions or seasons.
- Be sure to have large and hand-held mirrors for the children to see themselves and in different activities (movement, dramatic play, and so on). This increases a child's self-awareness, self-esteem, interaction, and participation.

- Occasionally focus on a particular color in an activity or area of the room.
- Explain and show how and why animals camouflage themselves.
- Help the children identify and locate different shapes within the classroom.

Miscellaneous Ideas for Small-Muscle Development

- Pegboards
- Small, colored cubes
- Snap blocks
- Small plastic blocks representing bricks
- Puzzles (commercial or handmade)
- Tinkertoys
- Assorted table toys (small vehicles, people, animals)
- Geoboards. Use a piece of wood of any size but preferably about 4 by 6 inches or 5 by 8 inches. Hammer small nails into it about ½ inch apart. Give the children some small colored rubber bands and let them create their own designs by stretching the bands over the nails.
- Picture lotto or card games
- Mobiles. Use a coat hanger, string or yarn, and a variety of either purchased or handmade objects.
- Spool knitting
- Sorting buttons by size, shape, color, composition, and so on.
- Sewing cards (purchased or handmade)
- Sewing on burlap or soft fabrics
- Plastic objects that fit together (Multi-fits, Knoppers, Bristle Blocks)
- Creative arts (cutting, pasting, stringing, painting)
- Pipe cleaners. Let children make interesting shapes.
- Manipulation (zippers, buttons, snaps)
- Puppets (hand, finger, sack)
- Nesting objects (cans, boxes, barrels, containers)
- Objects (felt, metal) and appropriate boards (flannel, magnetic)

Perception of Multisensory Activities

- Describe how indoor and outdoor activities fine-tune the senses of young children. Are there some precautions to take (pollution, safety, health)?
- Invite teachers to recall the activities of one day (or period) and note the numerous planned and spontaneous multisensory activities of the children. Why is it important to be aware of multisensory opportunities? Do teachers need to be more aware of combining sensory experiences for young children?
- Brainstorm how creative, expressive, sensory, and multicultural ideas and activities could enhance the learning and understanding of young children. For example, how do children express themselves in other cultures—art, music? Are tools used differently for cultural reasons?

Children can be creative in different ways.

Developmental Characteristics

Some activities discussed in this chapter require almost the same materials for children of any age (blocks, clay, domestic area, and sand, for example). Children participate with raw materials in a manner consistent with their interests and skills. The intensity and duration of any activity differ with age; younger children most often play alone and immaturely; older ones, cooperatively and in more complex ways.

Planning for some of the other activities (collage, cutting and pasting, drawing, painting, stringing, and woodworking) varies with age level, as shown in the following examples.

CUTTING AND PASTING

Age 2

Cutting is minimal. Use of scissors needs careful supervision. Lines to be cut must be simple. Children are more interested in squeezing the glue or brushing on the paste. The picture has few objects pasted on.

Age 3

Some children attempt to cut. Again, use of scissors needs careful supervision, and lines to be cut must be simple. Pasting is still fascinating, but most children still have few objects on their pictures. Color, form, and balance are informal.

Age 4

Many children pick up scissors first. Cutting is often crude, but the child attempts it. Lines can be varied; the child may prefer to cut pictures from magazines. Applying paste is a minimal part of the project. Pictures begin to have form and balance.

Age 5

Most children are adept at using scissors and can follow a pattern when cutting. Activity seems to balance between use of the scissors and applying paste to make an aesthetic picture. Children may begin with preconceived notions of what they want the picture to look like.

STRINGING

Age 2

The child is not too interested in the activity. She may attempt to poke the string through a hole while the object is lying on the table, but does not try to steady the object or string (the other hand may not even be involved in activity). If an adult offers help, the child may turn away from the activity entirely, or after accepting help, may pull the object off and turn away.

Age 3

The child may observe activity with caution or attempt to string one or two objects. Large holes and objects are preferred. If the string becomes limp, the child becomes discouraged. He may accept help from an adult and watch as he is shown how to hold the tip of the string close to the hole and how to hold the object, but usually loses interest quickly.

Age 4

The child usually knows the relationship between holding the object and string and can string wooden beads easily. She now prefers a little challenge, such as a smaller hole or object, and may stay with the activity long enough to make a necklace or bracelet.

Age 5

The child enjoys stringing things and may ask for the activity or stay longer when it is provided. He introduces originality into the pattern and use of the finished string.

WOODWORKING

Proper use of woodworking tools is much more difficult for young hands than scissors, paste, or string. The children need the coordination of eyes and hands and strength in fingers, hands, and arms. Saws, hammers, and other tools can cause immediate and serious injury to the yielder or receiver of the tool. The younger the carpenter, the more simple the experience. Young children need help to get the feel of a hammer or saw or the motion of using sandpaper attached to a block. With age, experience, and supervision, children can begin to take more responsibility for the use of tools. They'll want to make more complex projects and may even want to paint them.

MULTICULTURAL EXPERIENCES

Art materials: Designs, colors, and textures; natural materials and colors; fabrics; pictures; experiences; patterns; tools; preservation; and so on

Blocks: To construct dwellings, buildings, activities; of different compositions, uses, and so on

Dramatic play: Materials and toys of different cultures and races and of both genders; dolls; communication devices; cooking and eating utensils; print or language of different cultures; games; replicas of food; storytelling materials; professions/occupations; fabrics; hobbies; and so on

Manipulative materials: Puzzles representing different cultures, activities, places, homes, and so on; counting and sorting pieces; typical sensory experiences; and so on

Music: Musical instruments (including construction: wood, metal, skin, and so on); types and records of cultural music; dance accessories; participation in movement and rituals; books and pictures of musical activities; and so on

Pictorial media: Picture/story books reflecting family, individual, and cultural diversity; illustrations (posters, cards, books, and so on) and objects related to culture; replicas of toys and play; clothing and food examples, and so on

Science accessories: Foliage used in home construction, toys, dress, and so on; measuring and building tools; pets (land/water/air); plants; weather and protection against it; food preparation and preservation; and so on

Some ideas for this section were adapted from "Multicultural Materials" (1995).

APPLICATION OF PRINCIPLES

1. Briefly describe creativity for young children.
2. List six ways that creative experiences can enhance the growth and development of young children. Include some personal examples.
3. If possible, observe children in the four different development stages of art suggested by Lowenfeld, as described early in this chapter.
4. Give some specific examples of how creativity can be webbed with other curriculum areas.
5. Describe the differences between creative and product-oriented activities.
6. From the ideas suggested in the chapter, what values for children most appeal to you? Why?
7. What role does the teacher play in helping young children express themselves through creative activities?
8. Observe which activities are most popular with the children in your center. Discuss with other adults how you could interest the children in a variety of creative materials.
9. Explain how you would set up an activity differently for the following:
   a. 2-year-olds and painting
      4-year-olds and painting
   b. 2-year-olds and sand
      5-year-olds and sand
   c. 3-year-olds and cutting
      5-year-olds and cutting

   d. 4-year-olds and woodworking
      5-year-olds and woodworking
   e. 2-year-olds and water
      5-year-olds and water
10. Plan and use two different sensory experiences with children between the ages of 2 and 5.
11. Role play with a partner. One of you plays a teacher who firmly believes in using food products in art experiences in the classroom; the other plays one who firmly believes that food products have no place in creative art. After three minutes, switch roles. Discuss your feelings in both roles.
12. Explain how you can introduce safety factors in creative and sensory activities and why it is so important. Be specific.
13. Refer to the curriculum checklist in Figure 4.2 to see if *each item* can apply to an art experience as well as the whole day. (Are there provisions for different areas of development, indoor/outdoor use, a wide range of skills and interests, repetitive or new play, and so on?)
14. Plan and use resources in your classroom to help promote healthy multicultural information and attitudes through creative expression.
15. Of all the suggestions listed in this chapter (or others), what are your favorite creative activities/materials to use with young children? Do you enjoy getting messy and making your own decisions about projects? Which experiences do you avoid? Why?

REFERENCES

Aronson, S. (1991). *Health & Safety.* New York: Harper-Collins. The best schools in the world. (December 2, 1991). *Newsweek*, pp. 50–56.

Bredekamp, S. (ed.) (1987). *Developmentally appropriate practice in early childhood programs serving children from birth through age 8,* expanded edition. Washington, DC: NAEYC.

Brittain, W. L. (1969). Some exploratory studies of the art of preschool children. *Studies in Art Education,* 10(3), 14–24.

Brittain, W. L. (1979). *Creativity, art, and the young child.* New York: Macmillan.

Chaille, C., & Freeman, L. (1988). Children's interactions with transformable materials. *The Genetic Epistemologist,* 16(3), 23–29.

Clemens, S. G. (1991, January). Art in the classroom: Making every day special. *Young Children,* 46(2), 4–11.

Colbert, C., & M. Taunton (1992). *Developmentally appropriate practices for the visual arts education of young children.* NAEA Briefing Paper. Reston, VA: National Art Education Association.

Cole, E., & C. Schaefer (1990, January). Can young children be art critics? *Young Children,* 45(2), 33–38.

Commune of Reggio Emilia (1987). *The hundred languages of children.* Reggio Emilia, Italy: Author.

Davis, J., & H. Gardner (1991). The arts and childhood education: A cognitive development portrait of the young child as artist. In Spodek, B. (ed.), *Handbook of Research on the Education of Young Children.* New York: Macmillan.

Demerest, K. (1996, March). Playing with color. *Young Children,* 51(3), 83.

Dever, M. T., & Jared, E. J. (1996, March). Remember to include art and crafts in your integrated curriculum. *Young Children,* 51(3), 69–73.

Dewey, J. (1934). *Art as experience.* New York: Putnam.

Dewey, J. (1944). *Art and experience.* New York: Free Press.

Edwards, L. C. (1990). *Affective development and the creative arts: A process approach to early childhood education.* Columbus, OH: Merrill/Macmillan.

Edwards, C., L. Gandini, & G. Forman (eds.) (1993). *The hundred languages of children: The Reggio Emilia approach to early childhood education.* Norwood, NJ: Ablex.

Edwards, L. C., & M. L. Nabors (1993, March). The creative arts process: What it is and what it is not. *Young Children,* 48(3), 77–81.

Engel, B. S. (1995). *Considering children's art: Why and how to value their works.* Washington, DC: NAEYC.

Forman, G., & F. Hill (1984). *Constructive play: Applying Piaget in the preschool.* Menlo Park, CA: Addison-Wesley.

Forman, G., & D. Kuschner (1983). *The child's construction of knowledge: Piaget for teaching children.* Washington, DC: NAEYC.

Freeman, D. (1966). *A rainbow of my own.* New York: Viking.

Gandini, L. (1993). Fundamentals of the Reggio Emilia approach to early childhood education. *Young Children,* 49(1), 4–8.

Goldhaber, J. (1992, November). Sticky to dry, red to purple: Exploring transformation with play dough. *Young Children,* 48(1), 26–28.

Golumb, C. (1992). *The child's creation of a pictorial world.* Berkeley, CA: University of California Press.

Holt, B. G. (1989). *Science with young children,* revised edition, 156–157. Washington, DC: NAEYC.

Jones, E., & J. Nimmo (1994). *Emergent curriculum.* Washington, DC: NAEYC.

Jones, E., & G. Reynolds (1992). *The play's the thing: The teacher's roles in children's play.* New York: Teachers College Press.

Kamii, C., & R. DeVries (1978). *Physical knowledge in preschool education: Implications of Piaget's theory.* Englewood Cliffs, NJ: Prentice-Hall.

Katz, L. (1993). What can we learn from Reggio Emilia? In Edwards, C., & L. Gandini, G. Forman (eds.), *The hundred languages of children,* 19–37. Norwood, NJ: Ablex.

Katz, L., & S. Chard (1989). *Engaging children's minds: The project approach.* Norwood, NJ: Ablex.

Kellogg, R., with S. O'Dell (1967). *The psychology of children's art.* Published by CRM, Inc. Distributed by Random House, New York.

Kendrick, A. S., R. Kaufman, & K. P. Messenger, (eds.). (1988). *Healthy young children: A manual for programs.* Washington, D.C.: National Association for the Education of Young Children (NAEYC).

Leithead, M. (1996, March). Happy hammering: A hammering activity center with built-in success. *Young Children;* 51(3), 12.

Lowenfeld, V. (1947). *Creative and mental growth,* 3rd edition. New York: Macmillan.

Lowenfeld, V. (1987). *Creative and mental growth,* 8th edition. New York: Macmillan.

Lowenfeld, V., & W. L. Brittain (1967). *Creative and mental growth.* New York: Macmillan.

Maldonado, N. S. (1996, May). Puzzles: A pathetically neglected, commonly available resource. *Young Children,* 51(4), 4–10.

Moyer, J. (1990). Whose creation is it, anyway? *Childhood Education,* 66, 130–132.

Multicultural materials (1995, November/December). *Scholastic Early Childhood Today,* 10(3), 46.

Muri, S. A. (1996, January/February). "Mommy! Don't Go Bye-Bye!" How art activities can ease separation anxiety. *Early Childhood News,* 8(1), 31–32.

Neubert, K. (1991). *The care and feeling of clay,* 4–5. Pasadena, CA: Pacific Oaks College.

Piaget, J. (1976). *The grasp of consciousness: Action and concept in the young child.* Cambridge, MA: Harvard University Press.

Raines, S., & R. J. Canady (1990). *The whole language kindergarten.* New York: Teachers College Press.

Schiller, J. (1995, March). An emergent art curriculum that fosters understanding. *Young Children,* 50(3), 33–38.

Schirrmacher, R. (1988). *Art & creative development for children.* New York: Delmar.

Seefeldt, C. (1995, March). Art—a serious work. *Young Children,* 50(3), 39–45.

Showers, P. (1991). *The Listening Walk.* New York: The Trumpet Club, 666 5th Avenue (A cassette tape is also available here.)

Spodek, B. (1991, April). Reconceptualizing early childhood education: A commentary. *Early Childhood and Development,* 2(2), 16.

Swanson, L. (1994, May). Changes—how our nursery school replaced adult-directed art projects with child-directed experiences and changed to an accredited, child-sensitive, developmentally appropriate school. *Young Children,* 49(4), 69–73.

Thompson, C. M. (1995). Transforming curriculum in the visual arts. In Bredekamp, S., & T. Rosegrant (eds.), *Reaching potentials: transforming early childhood curriculum and assessment,* Vol 2, 81–96. Washington, DC: NAEYC.

Torrance, E. P. (1970). *Encouraging creativity in the classroom.* Dubuque, IA: William C. Brown.

Vygotsky, L. (1978). *Mind in society.* Cambridge, MA: Harvard University Press.

Watson, D., C. Burke, & J. Harste (1989). *Whole language: Inquiring voices.* New York: Scholastic.

Wolf, A. D. (1990, January). Art postcards—another aspect of your aesthetics program? *Young Children,* 45(2), 39–43.

Music and Movement Education

CHAPTER 7

MAIN PRINCIPLES

1. Music is an enjoyable art form that aids self-expression and personal development.
2. Movement education is a viable curriculum area because of its enjoyment and value for children.
3. Alert teachers and parents bring many spontaneous and planned music and movement opportunities into the lives of young children.
4. Young children need many and varied opportunities to develop their bodies and abilities.
5. Music is a good medium for teaching other curriculum areas.
6. Music and movement education are certainly a part of creative expression but are discussed in a separate chapter for emphasis and enjoyment.
7. Music and movement from different cultures enrich children's lives and help them to better understand different racial and ethnic backgrounds.

Recall the following familiar nursery rhyme:

Jack and Jill went up the hill to get a pail of water,
Jack fell down and broke his crown
and Jill came tumbling after.

Now try this new version of the same rhyme:

A whistling Jack and a singing Jill went skipping merrily up the hill.
They filled their pail clear to the top and started home without a stop.
They both were quick, they both were agile;
Their bodies had developed so they were no longer fragile.
They sang and played the whole day through; they liked themselves, and oth-
ers, too.

Reflection

Consider the following helpful hints about music and movement education with young children (source: "Music for the Young Child," 1995, March):

"Dr. Benjamin Bloom from the University of Chicago states that forty per cent of everything we know we learn by age seventeen and fifty per cent of that knowledge has been learned by age four. He suggests that the age from six months to four years may be the most important time in a person's life." (p. 2)

"Research suggests that the brain cells stop their dramatic growth after about age four. Brain cell growth is stimulated by *vibration* (singing is intensified vibration), *exploration*, and *experience with the senses.* In order to provide for the most possible growth of a child's brain cells, we must lay a rich foundation for learning before age four. That *does NOT mean teaching skills,* but, instead, offering rich environment and exposure." (p. 2)

"Young children need to learn through their bodies. Everything they do with their bodies to explore and make sense out of the world at this young age transfers directly to higher forms of thinking as they grow older. They can represent something internally if allowed to explore it with their bodies while very young. Young children need to *move* to learn." (p. 2)

The feeling one has about his body and his abilities is very important in the development of a good self-image. One likes to feel confident in trying things, in interacting with others, and in exploring the environment.

From the time a baby is old enough to be aware of sounds, she attends to those that are rhythmic and melodious. Some of her first games are pat-a-cake, bye-bye, and peek-a-boo. Toddlers and young preschoolers readily sing and perform catchy commercials on the radio or television, while 4- and 5-year-olds enjoy songs, finger plays, and activities that have rhythm, repetition, and interaction of body parts as they play alone or with others. Music has a definite effect on the way one feels and moves.

The research in review by Andress (1991a) is an important and informative article, as it describes developmentally appropriate music experience for children, from birth through age 8, building on the framework of national music education standards established by the Music Educators National Conference (1994a, 1994b). Examples of typical behavior are cited to demonstrate how children at each stage of development may be expected to perform, create, listen to, describe, and value music as they sing, move, play instruments, read music, and write music (Andress, 1995, p. 99).

A CHILD-CENTERED CURRICULUM

A child-centered curriculum is based on the assumption that the learner (the child, in this case) is more important than what is to be learned (music, in this case). However, music has the power to add importance to the child's life. The music curriculum must include an understanding of the child's cognitive, physical, and socio-emotional development and the planner must be familiar with good music-education resources.

Characteristics of a child-centered music and movement program for young children include:

- Each child has musical potential and personal and unique interests and abilities.
- Children come from diverse backgrounds.
- Work is their play.
- Each child needs caring, effective, and knowledgeable adult models.
- They need exemplary musical sounds, activities, and materials.
- The best learning environment has pleasant and social settings.
- Very young children can develop critical thinking skills through musical experiences.
- They should perform at their own developmental level.
- They need diverse learning environments for individual growth. (MENC, 1994b, p. 9)

The Music Learning Environment in Early Childhood

"Appropriate musical content can best be explored in an interactive environment that is rich in manipulative objects, instruments, quality musical examples, and adults effectively modeling music. Music learning experiences for young children should occur throughout the day and the curriculum, as well as in special-interest areas and guided group play" (Andress, 1991a). Music across the curriculum, in special-interest areas, when choices are available, and during guided group music times are appropriate and encouraged.

Young children demonstrate their music abilities when they perform, listen, create, and describe music, as well as when they respond to pictures of musical ideas.

Appropriate Music Curriculum for Children from Birth through Age 4

Children of all ages should experience music daily in spontaneous and planned ways. Adults can encourage music experiences by:

singing, humming, and chanting;

using songs and rhymes representing a variety of meters and tonalities;

imitating the sounds infants and others make;

exposing them to a wide variety of vocal, body, instrumental, and environmental sounds;

providing exposure to selected live and recorded music;

rocking, patting, touching, and moving with the children to the beat, rhythm patterns, and melodic direction of music they hear;

providing safe toys that make musical sounds the children can control; and

talking about music and its relationship to expression and feeling (MENC, 1994b, p. 10).

Music Experiences for 2-, 3-, and 4-Year-Old Children

Singing and playing instruments

Creating music (improvising songs, instrumental accompaniments)

Creating short pieces of music (voices, instruments, sounds)

Responding to music (sounds, tempos, modes, styles)

Using one's voice to imitate voices

Using vocabulary to describe voices and other sounds

Moving or verbalizing to elements of music and changes

Demonstrating an awareness of music as a part of daily life (MENC, 1994b, pp. 10–12)

Music experiences for children from birth through age 8 must be planned to meet the needs of each child's unique learning style, interests, and abilities. In most cases, the activities for 5- to 8-year-old children are an advancement of what younger children can do. It is recommended that a rich and diverse learning environment be provided for all children at various levels for a successful music experience in early-childhood education.

In their article, Yinger and Blaszka (1995) do not address music specifically, but give some basic ideas that could be used to stimulate music activities: be creative; engage children in relevant tasks that are real and familiar; help children to be safe and social in a real-world environment; and challenge children in problem-solving situations.

ADVANTAGES OF MUSIC AND MOVEMENT EDUCATION

Following are some examples of how music and movement educate children.

Intellectual Development

Learning basic concepts (music and other), memories (recall), descriptions, problem solving, foundation for later skills (reading).

Learning musical concepts such as rhythm (steady and melodic pattern), tempo (fast, slow), pitch (high, low), timbre (tone quality of different instruments), dynamics (loud, soft), melody and related words, phrasing, accent, and mood.

Gaining concrete understanding of concept words such as *under, over, through, behind,* and so on.

Some theories suggest that music intelligence is only one of several forms of intelligence. Without active musical involvement, there is a loss of children's musical aptitude between ages five and six. . . . Research shows that music aptitude becomes stabilized before age nine, and that more consideration must be given to the musical experiences of children between the ages of three and eight. (Ball, 1991)

Physical/Motor Development

Releases excess energy, reduces stress, increases strength and coordination, uses body in individual and group activities, learns new skills, improves self-esteem, encourages leadership/followership, balance, own's own space, management of one's own body, indoor and outdoor activity.

"Clapping, chanting, and playing simple instruments help children to develop basic motor coordination and control over simple body movements" (Kranyik, 1993, p. 25).

Perceptual Awareness

Senses, body space, directionality (prepositions, obstacle courses, size, shape), sharpen auditory discrimination skills (listening).

For young children, music is primarily the discovery of sound—"Focused listening means helping children zero in on specific sounds or words that give direction. . . . Listening is the basis of all musical learning" (Bayless & Ramsey, 1982). "Early childhood educators are very aware of the value of helping children sharpen auditory discrimination skills, but many have never considered it a part of music education" (Wolf, 1992, p. 57).

Language Development

Verbalizing (describing movements, tempo, rules, prepositions); learning and using symbols; imitating sounds (objects, animals, household, transportation, and so on); putting rhythm with familiar activities and objects (clapping rhythm of names, activities, and so on).

A sensory approach to song learning that includes visual, kinesthetic, and aural stimuli increases children's vocabulary.

Social Development

Self-concept/body awareness—success, self-esteem, secure enough to risk, no "wrong way"; stress release; interactive singing and games.

Creativity Development

Guides imagery or make-believe; combines curriculum areas (stories and dramatization, movement and environment, language and action, social studies and interaction, and so on); provides artistic and expressive avenues.

Some children need to sit, watch, and contemplate before entering an activity.

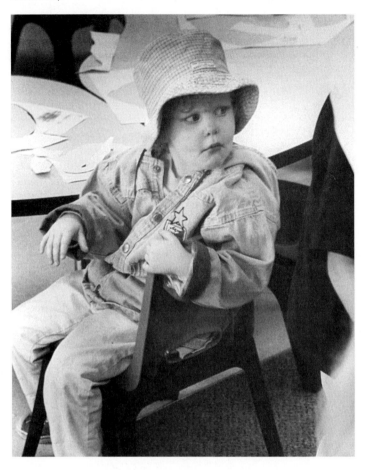

Cultural Development

Brings an awareness of music, instruments, folk songs, clothing, dances, games, and traditions of other cultures. "In our pluralistic society, music is a valuable way of linking different peoples together: I may not be familiar with your culture, but I like to hear and sing your songs" (Wolf, 1992, p. 58).

Environmental Awareness

Awareness of the community and peoples, of health and safety needs (pollution of water, land, and air; recycling); provides exploration of surroundings (walk in the community), different types of weather, landscapes, vegetation, and needs.

Music helps us understand the world. Friedrich Froebel, the father of the kindergarten movement, once wrote, "What the child imitates, he begins to understand. Let him represent the flying of birds and he enters partially into the life of the birds."

Development of a Combination of Skills

Kinesthetic activities and props (scarves, streamers—ideas familiar to the children); basic concepts; and so on. Music can be used as a companion to *all* curriculum areas.

Adults must make sure the concepts, activities, and materials presented to the children are well within the range of individual children and the group as a whole, and somewhat familiar to the children in order for the experiences to be meaningful.

In my personal experience with toddlers the past decade or so, I would be cautious about saying children of any age *can* or *cannot* do certain things. My professional training told me to include or avoid certain types of activities with young children, only to have these young children prove it right or wrong—it's the abilities and interests of the children you are working with at the time. Be willing to try different ideas—but be just as willing to discard them if they are too difficult or not well accepted at the time.

Developmental Characteristics

Age 2

Moves up and down to music, tries to imitate sounds, and is fascinated by simple songs.

Enjoys bouncing motion, swaying, swinging arms, nodding head, tapping feet, and clapping hands, but demonstrates little or no rhythmic accuracy for any length of time.

May walk with arms outstretched for balance.

Primarily a listener; jabbers.

Loves action songs and finger plays. Sings (or hums) parts of songs spontaneously with or without an adult but matches few tones correctly.

Experiments with rhythm. Walks on tiptoes. Pushes and pulls toys. Actively explores his environment.

Climbs stairs with both feet on each step; jumps immaturely (2-foot takeoff). Stands on low balance beam. Walks forward, sideways, and backward.

Rarely still—wiggles and toddles, bounces and waves, jumps and claps, springs and chases, hides and seeks.

Age 3

May or may not sing, but likes songs and rhythm.

Walks a 10-foot line, heel to toe. Hops two to three steps. Walks on balance beam for short distance. Climbs stairs with alternating feet. Throws ball about 10 feet.

Rides tricycle.

Is excited about walking backward without peeking.

No longer walks with arms outstretched. Gallops, jumps, runs, and walks in *fairly* good time to music.

Age 4

Creates own rhythm and keeps it somewhat. Enjoys singing, especially action songs. Is more observant of sound and rhythm around her.

Walks easily up and down stairs; runs well, jumps, and walks on a balance beam.

Likes to be independent; resists many instructions.

Feels quite confident about body skills; notes abilities of other children.

Has good balance; likes to carry liquids without spilling them.

Can throw objects at a target.

Enjoys climbing and obstacle courses.

Begins to kick large balls. Shows more controlled balance: swings back and forth, stands on one foot.

Fine movements are better differentiated.

Age 5

Enjoys singing; has large repertoire of songs.

Likes rhythm instruments; can keep time. Participates to records and tapes; is coordinated.

Has interest in musical instruments; enjoys guests.

Learns to skip. Has boundless energy; wiggles, runs, hops, jumps, and climbs with proficiency.

Attempts roller skating, rope jumping, stilt walking, and swing pumping. Is more coordinated at throwing and catching.

Broad jumps two to three feet.

Rides a two-wheel bike.

Plays games with simple rules; enjoys company.

LEARNING THROUGH MUSIC AND MOVEMENT EDUCATION—GENERAL

By now the reader may be questioning why music and movement education are not a part of Chapter 6, Creative, Artistic, and Sensory Expression. Consider the following:

1. Music and movement are certainly classed as creative and artistic expression; however, they deserve more attention than can be given in that chapter.

2. Teachers may need extra encouragement to include music and movement in their curriculum. Many feel inadequate to teach music or are self-conscious when singing or dancing with the children because of lack of formal training in either music or movement education. Although this training can add much to this area, many activities can be easily and inexpensively used, are growth-promoting, and have great benefit for children—and adults.

3. Music and movement are so much a part of the daily lives and activities of children. They enjoy music and rhythm.

4. Music and movement are great tools for integrating language, mathematics, science, social studies, art, nutrition, and health and safety subjects with children's natural and spontaneous interests.

5. Music and movement help children increase their self-esteem and their personal relationships with others.

Seeing an instrument up close and hearing it play familiar tunes make the experience more meaningful to young children.

Generally, music is thought of as a pleasant, enjoyable experience. Most young children are not exposed to practicing an instrument or performing in music competitions; to them music and movement are natural, spontaneous, and fun. Music is as respectable a curriculum area as any other, but doesn't appear to have the rigor or to inspire the fear often associated with math, reading, or science, for example. Still, there are many opportunities for music to interact with all other curriculum areas and to provide practice for personal skills and attributes.

Music can be easily used to help children think divergently—or creatively. For this to happen, they need adults (teachers and parents) who stimulate their thinking: "How else could a dog run?" "How would a tree bend in a slight breeze? In a strong windstorm?" "Could you show us another way to dance with the scarf?" But it is interesting to note that very few teachers ask children divergent-thinking questions automatically or consistently—and that training is necessary for teachers to use such questioning (Shaw & Cliatt, 1986). Goodlad (1984) found that less than 1 percent of time in school was devoted to open questioning that calls for skills other than simple memory, such as reasoning, problem solving, or forming opinions. Indeed, teachers do talk 70 percent of the time giving instruction, but part of this time could be used to gain—not always give—information.

Use familiar (or new) songs to help children solve problems. For example, "Eensy Weensy Spider" is loved and enjoyed by a particular group of toddlers. After singing the regular version using hand movements, they love to mouth the sound (no sound) and make the hand movements. Then they pretend to put their spiders in a quiet, safe place while other songs are sung. In another group of preschoolers, the teacher was singing "Do as I'm Doing" and then called up various children to lead a verse, but instead of letting them express their own ideas, the teacher would hold the child's hands and make the motions she thought were appropriate. The children quickly tired of this activity. How much more exciting it would have been for each child to present an action for the other children to model. Do things always have to be done a certain way, or don't some teachers trust children's ideas? An eternal favorite of young children is "The Wheels on the Bus." Sometimes the children will say, "Let's do it different this time. Let's make the daddy snore!"

It takes all the enjoyment out of an activity if it has to be done a certain way, with a certain amount of proficiency, and for a designated period of time. Take for example fundamental motor patterns: running, walking, jumping, throwing, catching, kicking, and combinations of these activities (skipping, running and jumping; catching and throwing a ball; and so on). Teachers can pre-assess the abilities of children just as well when they are performing these patterns in a group or when music is added as they can standing with a pad and pencil and testing each child individually. Music helps add beat, tempo, and meter to the activity. Balls, hoops and tires, ropes, beanbags, balance beams and boards, mat activities, and climbing apparatus are challenging and exciting while music is heard. Besides varying the movements in games, children can also solve problems such as how to involve more children, how to keep score, ways to use scarves or other props, or possibilities for accompanying singing with instruments.

As in other curriculum areas, children need "the security of having certain decisions made for them, of knowing the limits beyond which they may not go" (Riley, 1984, p. 8). Are the dancing drums to be used only by teachers? Will mishandling the instruments cause forfeiture of a turn to use them? Is jumping on and off the furniture permitted during music time but forbidden at other times? Are there certain drums to be played with mallets and some only tapped with hands? Not only are there rules, but if children can help establish those rules, they have greater understanding of the rules and greater respect for them.

When planning for young children, regardless of their ages or the curriculum area, adults should carefully study the research of developmental theorists and movement specialists in order to better understand the predictable movement characteristics of various age groups.

Since the 1980s, there has been increased emphasis and research on brain development and the functions of each half of the brain—the left for verbal and analytic thought, the right for intuition and for understanding patterns. The verbal-analytic half is extremely important in dealing with the object world and in learning spoken language as well as reading and writing. The right hemisphere is used to perceive and express novel and complex visual, spatial, and musical patterns. Both brain halves are specialized and complementary, but may be in conflict. The left hemisphere tends to be dominant (Galin, 1976). Therefore, specific experiences must be provided to exercise the right hemisphere. Creativity is one way, whether through music, art, science, or other means. "People with strong right-hemisphere processing skills seem to have their own sense of time and rhythm," write Cherry, Godwin, and Staples (1989, p. 243). (See also Taylor, 1997, pp. 34–36.)

Each person needs to find acceptable ways of expressing herself openly without fear of ridicule or embarrassment. Music or movement is more comfortable than verbalization for some individuals.

A child's acceptance or rejection of music depends on his age, his past musical experiences, cultural awareness, and attitude within his home. Children whose parents appreciate music and have musical talents are indeed fortunate, because parents share things they enjoy. A father who sings will sing with his children. A mother who plays the piano will play it with her children. Some families form their own musical groups—either singing or instrumental—and spend many delightful hours together. They also attend concerts and share their talents with others.

ROLE OF THE TEACHER

The role of the adult in structuring an environment that fosters and facilitates music and language growth in young children is identified by Bayless and Ramsey (1982) as the following:

1. Increasing their own awareness of the range of musical opportunities
2. Providing a wealth of music experiences
3. Making music an integral part of the day
4. Building a strong and varied repertoire of rhythms, finger plays, poetry, and movement exercises
5. Fostering a sharing, verbal atmosphere surrounding young children
6. Recognizing the individual differences reflected in each child's musical preferences
7. Delighting in music with young children
8. Interacting with children as they sing or speak
9. Helping young children put their own nonsense rhymes, riddles, and verses to music
10. Using music to expand memory
11. Playing a supportive role as young children experiment and discover music

A wise teacher discovers the developmental stage of each child and then plans beneficial experiences, avoiding activities that are too complex or frustrating. Andress (1984) states that when planning an age-appropriate music curriculum, adults need to observe the following: (1) how the child thinks ("often illogically, with single focus"), (2) how natural language acquisition influences the child's response ("from babbling, global properties of song, to more accurate pitch and rhythmic matching"), (3) how spontaneous the child's songs may be ("nurture these experiences as a means toward maintaining the child's creative tendencies"), (4) noting how play styles change as the child grows ("using settings that allow for playing alone, playing beside others, and with others"), (5) avoid exploiting the child ("provide experiences important and appropriate for the child, never for the ego-satisfaction of the adult"), and (6) acknowledge that children "are capable of interacting with and learning about basic musical concepts" (p. 61). When we use a child-centered approach in teaching young children in all areas of curriculum, the children have opportunities to solve problems, be creative, make decisions, interact with materials and people, and enjoy the lighter side of music.

The teacher should provide some type of music every day, and encourage spontaneous expression both indoors and outdoors, using a variety of methods and activities. She can pick up and encourage the rhythmic movements of the children. She must value individuality and plan accordingly for the children. If she is not musically inclined herself, she can arrange for another person to assist her, or use records, tapes, or a guest rather than eliminate music from the daily curriculum. She provides experiences that help the children release their feelings constructively, whether the feelings are of anger and hostility or of joy and excitement. She may even need to provide props that encourage creative expression, such as long, full skirts, crepe paper streamers, scarves, or yarn balls. Children develop a lifelong appreciation for music as a result of a pleasant introduction.

Reflection

Do the following two-part exercise:

1. From the previous discussions, select from the following list the music and movement opportunities that would be appropriate (DAP) and ones that would be inappropriate (DIP). Give rationales for your selections.

_____ Mixed ages of children riding stick horses

_____ 2- and 3-year-olds skipping outdoors

_____ 5-year-olds climbing on a jungle gym

_____ A teacher introducing a new song while using a tape recorder for the melody

_____ Toddlers singing a song, playing an instrument, and marching around the room—all children and all three activities at the same time

_____ 4-year-olds matching the beat of different rhythms

_____ Preschool children singing rounds

_____ Preschool children imitating the sounds and/or movements of animals, household items, transportation vehicles, and objects

_____ 4-year-olds throwing and catching a ball

_____ A teacher teaching math concepts (or other curriculum areas) to toddlers through singing and movement; to a mixed age group

_____ 5-year-olds using props (scarves, streamers, and so on) while moving to different types of music

_____ 3-year-olds learning a folk song and dance

2. Now, for all the activities you identified as being inappropriate, state a more appropriate age for the activity, or a more appropriate activity for the age given.

MUSIC IN GENERAL

Concerns have been raised about the music educator's approach to teaching prekindergarten children. Andress (1989) proposes a prekindergarten music curriculum model based on a synthesis of theories about the learning environment with the contributions of learning/play theorists and music educators. Music is primarily the discovery of sound. It should include purposive action or involvement, and should consider social, environmental, and procedural conditions (Wolf, 1992). Teachers will find that environmental conditions, such as space and attitude, are important components of successful music experiences.

Reassuring words and helpful ideas from Wolf (1992) give some comfort to music-shy teachers:

> A reasonable range (C to G or A) and uncomplicated rhythms add to the appropriateness. . . . Singing from the heart and setting aside any insecurities about singing will also boost the confidence of those early childhood teachers who shy away from singing with their classes. Children are not critics and actually learn best by hearing an unaccompanied voice. A child's ability to hear through harmony does not become sophisticated until after the age of five or six. . . . [M]usic can happen and often *does* spontaneously outside the group time we call *music time*. It is during these moments that the child appears to express the music from within himself. (p. 58)

Using a piano, the teacher can vary speed, sound, rhythms, and movements of children.

In early-childhood settings, teachers need to meet musically teachable moments with confidence by organizing music experiences to enhance the lives of young children and the total curriculum, while promoting good music education goals. Teachers with less musical education or background should not shy away from these important experiences, but should make a concerted effort to learn more about the basics of music and plan to include an abundance of focused listening, singing, and instrumental activities that encourage hearing and moving to the beat as well as music appreciation. Beat competency reflects the ability to keep time with or feel the pulse of the music (McDonald, 1979). As children grow they begin to go beyond their own personal sense of timing and develop the ability to relate to the timing of others (Bayless & Ramsey, 1982). Wolf (1992) states that keeping time with music is a skill that is gradually developed.

Singing is a complex skill. In order to sing, children must listen, remember what they hear, and then control their voices to imitate the sounds they hear (Wolf, 1992). In selecting music for young children, pay attention to the range of notes and tempo within the song—some songs are pitched too high, some are monotonous because of a limited range of notes, and others may be too complicated because of wide range or tempo.

For singing games, see Landeck (1950), Seeger (1948), and Glazier (1973, 1980). Other good sources are available at music stores or early-childhood education publishers.

Children love to sing their own improvised songs as well as structured songs of the culture. The developmental sequence as the young child grows in ability to sing alone or in a group involves (1) engaging in voice-inflection play, (2) singing her own rambling tunes, (3) listening to traditional songs of the culture, (4) singing global properties (most obvious words/melodic patterns) of traditional songs, and (5) displaying increased skill in performing lyrics with rhythmic and melodic accuracy (Andress, 1995, p. 102).

The Role of the Music Teacher

"The goal of the music educator . . . is to build through movement experiences toward musical understanding, rather than strive for the highly refined performance skills achieved by the movement educator. Movement experiences are a vital part of the music education program because they represent the sensing-doing stage of learning, which is a means to understanding more abstract musical ideas" (Andress, 1991b, p. 22). How the child responds to the experience depends on the child's disposition, developmental stage, and environmental factors.

The following suggestions were made by Andress (1991b) in encouraging movement and music experiences in young children:

1. A child-centered developmental approach: "As early childhood educators, it is important that we prepare young children to perform fundamental movement skills at an appropriate developmental level in order that they may feel and be physically competent" (Seefeldt, 1984, p. 35)

2. Modeling, imitated by 3- and 4-year-olds

3. Beat-keeping experiences for 4-year-olds—rather than clapping hands together to a given song, the teacher should beat the drum to the children's natural walking tempo (Andress, p. 25)

4. Arranging the environment for *enactive* (movement—such as swaying, bouncing, walking, and turning in response to the expressive whole of the music) and *iconic* (visual concrete representation using small props, including flowing scarves, streamers, and so on) levels of learning

5. Teacher interaction—combining modeling, describing, *and* suggesting so that the child's own creativity is allowed to flourish as awareness of music and movement is extended (p. 26)

6. Teachers who use types of interactional behaviors that reinforce music-related responses (p. 26)

Teaching Songs

A few general suggestions help teachers prepare for singing with the children. First, be enthusiastic! Learn the song well before presenting it to the children (and teach it to support teachers). Select songs that have appeal for you and the children (their interests, their abilities, their stage of development). Children especially like using their own names, nonsense, body parts, and familiar experiences. Sing slowly and clearly, repeating the song several times. Then invite the children: "Sing along with me when you are ready." Use appropriate visual aids (which can be optional).

Songs are to be sung, not to be talked about. Pitcher et al. (1974) remind us as follows:

The teacher should not expect a response on the first day or the second. It takes time for a young child to understand and remember the words and longer still to gain a clear conception of a melody. . . . Encourage him to sing, even if he isn't singing your tune. Vocal cords need exercise, and he needs vocal expression. Drill on either words or music is harmful for preschool children. Sing the song, straight through, and let him catch what he can, even if it is only the last note. Pitch will come on the wave of rhythm. (p. 47)

If teachers do not read music, play an instrument, or have access to a songbook or cassette, they can ask a suitable person (music teacher, friend) to make them a recording so they can learn the song by singing with the recording.

Teachers often mistakenly believe that a piano or guitar is necessary to accompany singing with young children. Only a skilled musician can sing, play a difficult instrument, and watch the children rather than their music. Your voice is your most important musical instrument. An ordinary voice is quite adequate. It is your enthusiasm that will make the difference.

Start your singing time with familiar songs so the children will get comfortable and join in. At times it may be interesting to record a music session, then later evaluate the responses, the attention span, and requests or comments of the children. Young children learn songs best through repetition. They do not read, their experience is limited, and they cannot remember new long sentences and phrases. The song should be short (no more than two phrases of words), easy to sing, and have familiar ideas, repetition, a distinct rhythm, and a limited range of notes.

Singing

"The wonderful result of including a lot of musical experiences in programs for young children—whether teachers view themselves as musical or not—is that children *learn* a lot about music, and also about language arts and much more, even if teachers can't itemize what it all is exactly" (Wolf, 1992, p. 56).

The Pillsbury Foundation Studies of 1937–1938 (Zimmerman, 1985), set up to discover the principles that govern children's relationship to music, resulted in four significant insights still meaningful today:

- For young children, music is primarily the discovery of sound.
- Music time with children should include their purpose, action, or involvement.
- In planning music time, it is necessary to consider social, environmental, and procedural conditions.
- Spontaneous music making should be carefully observed.

Some things to consider are developmental stages of the children; environmental considerations of the room; meeting musical and curricular objectives; focused listening, singing accuracy, beat competency, and music appreciation.

Helping children zero in on specific sounds or words that give direction is called *focused listening* and includes singing games, walking/running/skipping music, and songs that provide vocabulary for movement and silence for stopping. Careful listening is the basis for musical learning; it is the ability to focus the mind on sounds perceived. Activities that focus on auditory activity meet the same objective.

Auditory-discrimination skills are important in learning; however, some teachers have not considered music as one of the avenues for helping children develop these skills. Keeping in time to music, keeping in tune, or maintaining a steady beat heighten listening skills. Recordings that give directions or sound cues, songs that have movement cues, and games that require a response are examples of

Youthful enthusiasm makes singing a favorite activity of young children.

appropriate musical listening activities. Children (and adults) can learn to recognize patterns, cues, and interactions from musical listening activities—live or recorded. Thus, their focused attention is helping them develop accurate listening skills.

Expecting young children to sing with accuracy is premature. This accuracy is basically established by age 8 (McDonald, 1979); therefore, before we can assume the responsibility of teaching singing skills, we need to understand how young children learn to sing. Music educators have determined various stages of singing development. For instance, Smale (1985) organized these stages into a sequential list: (1) musical babbling; (2) tagging on; (3) talking/singing; (4) increased accuracy (ages 3–4); (5) accurate singing of simple songs, alone; and (6) accurate singing with a group. Wolf (1992) states:

> First the child listens to sounds. Babies are likely to first hear musical sound through the human voice, although TV, radio, records, and music boxes are also usually part of their environment early on. As a result, the child invents musical sound sometimes referred to as musical babbling. This invention precedes imitation, or copying what has been sung. . . . Imitation is observed as toddlers lag behind a bit or tag on to the end of a song. From the age of three or so, children progressively increase their ability to join in song. First they join in a little, and by school age they sing at group time with enthusiasm. Our job is to provide a repertoire of singable songs through recordings as well as teacher-sung songs. (p. 57)

Young children learn songs best by hearing an unaccompanied voice, when the range is reasonable (C to G or A), and when they listen attentively before trying to join in the singing. Their ability to keep time on their own often has no relationship to others (Wolf, 1992).

Singing with children is fun and should always be that way. Singing is a natural form of expression for young children. Teachers need to assume a posture of confidence, apply their newfound knowledge, use the tools and secrets, and enjoy. Many wonderful musical moments are ahead! (Wolf, 1994, p. 25)

Lyrics of Songs and Literacy

1. Language of song is natural for children.
2. Help children to more easily form a link from oral to printed language through rhyme, rhythm, repetition of vocabulary, and repetition of story structure (Lynch, 1986).
3. Lyrics overlap into curriculum areas, such as science, math, social studies, art, music, and others (see Figure 7.1).
4. Integrate skills. Karnowski (1986) encourages the integration of writing with music and art because "writing flourishes in a social environment where young children are free to use oral language, art, music, and drama to explore and enhance their writing" (p. 60).
5. Encourage language fluency or "meaning makers."
6. Use picture books to tie music and language together. Music and reading go together because singing is a celebration of language—consistent with the purposes of language—and puts readers in touch with satisfying meanings (Harp, 1988). Place the books in the book racks for children to explore and enjoy.

Chants in the Early-Childhood Classroom

Chants and other oral repetitions (poems, games, sayings, and so on) are beneficial for most young children—provided they are done in a voluntary, enjoyable manner. Research shows that children's success in reading and writing depends upon a solid background in the development of oral language skills (Hennings, 1990). With

Figure 7.1
Steps in Introducing Song Picture Books in the Classroom

- Teach the song: Use music, sing words, invite children to join in the repetitions of the song. Talk about the meaning, discuss special words, and encourage motions; then add all the elements together.
- Link the song to print: Use a song picture and ask the children to discuss the pictures; read the book; reread the book with children adding information and asking questions; show lyrics written on a chart; invite children to "read" along as you point to each word in the song; highlight repetitious phrases.
- Involve the children in extension of literature activities: Dramatize the song; tape and replay the song; help children identify the printed word with the spoken word; create big books; make the book available for children's exploration and enjoyment.
- Encourage children to find other appropriate songs: Help them to make a printed and pictorial chart using original ideas, other song books, story books, and experiences.

Selected song picture books are listed in the article on pp. 84–85.

Adapted from Barclay & Walwer, 1992, p. 78.

an increased awareness of whole-language philosophy, educators are realizing that meaningful, interactive experiences with language provide the most effective curriculum for developing speaking as well as reading, writing, and listening skills (Sampson, Sampson, & Van Allen, 1991). Teachers are trying to incorporate as many interesting language experiences into each day as they can (Buchoff, 1994, p. 26).

According to Anderson & Lapp (1988), a *chant* is any group of words that is recited with a lively beat. Through chanting, all children speak together in unison and need not fear intimidation. They learn the importance of clear and expressive pronunciation as their voices combine to make the message of the chant come alive.

The values of chants can include (a) perfection through repetitious or rhyming words; (b) success to even a shy child, a poor speaker, or a reluctant reader; (c) experience with and perfection of listening and writing skills; (d) introduction to poetry and rhyming; (e) cooperation and participation in a group; (f) rhythmic patterning; (g) supplementation to curriculum areas; (h) introduction to new cultures and situations; (i) humor; (j) practice in hearing and seeing words (on a chart); (k) body involvement (snapping fingers, tapping toes); (l) expanding curriculum (reading with speaking, body motions, and so on) and ways to learn a concept; (m) combining senses (seeing, hearing, playing instrument or clapping, dramatizing); and (n) thinking up new chants or dramatizing current ones.

Reflection

Should we wait for children to become verbal before we sing, chant, or verbalize with them? If we do, the child *may miss* these important benefits:

- Being soothed and feeling that someone cares
- Having a focal point
- Feeling a closeness with a caregiver
- Learning about daily routines and cooperativeness
- Building trust and self-esteem
- Comforting during times of separation
- Poetic experiences and visual imagery
- Opportunities to model or mimic sounds and phrases
- Stretching his mental abilities
- Experiences in humor and incongruities in verse
- Opportunities to practice large and small motor skills (rhythm, bouncing, whole-body movement, hand and finger manipulation)
- Eye-hand coordination and exercise
- Important language experiences
- Attentiveness to the human voice
- Listening experiences
- Many other benefits that affect children personally

Introducing Rhythm Instruments

Because of frustrating experiences with rhythm instruments, some teachers include this experience infrequently or never in their curriculum. Suppose someone placed in front of you a very exciting and new object—and told you not to touch it? Wouldn't that be frustrating? Now, also suppose that you knew what to do with the object and your body was saying, "Pick it up and see what you can do with it!" and somebody kept saying, "I'll show or tell you how to do it." The minute you got the go-ahead, wouldn't you do as much, as fast, and as loud as you could? Does it make sense to place something like a rhythm instrument in front of a child and then tell her not to touch it?

Teachers may want to introduce one kind of instrument at a time. They should try to have enough of the same kind so that each child can explore it on the same day. When first introducing the instrument, they may want to talk about its properties or use. Then they should identify a signal of when to start and when to stop playing and let the children try it. If the number of instruments is limited, the children take turns so that each child knows he will get a chance. On other days, different instruments are introduced. After the children are exposed to several kinds, the instruments are combined for a more advanced experience. Each child should have an opportunity to use all the instruments—even if for a short time.

On return use of the instruments, the children are allowed to select the instruments they want to play, with the understanding that there will be trading. The children can be responsible for passing out and gathering in the instruments.

Playing Musical Instruments

Instruments can be used in the learning environment to explore shape, size, and sound relationships; to organize, order, and classify sounds; to use sounds to express musical ideas (loud and soft composition created with a wood block) and nonmusical ideas (the wood-block sound of galloping ponies); or, when developmentally appropriate, to play simple accompaniments for songs and perform rhythmic and melodic ideas.

Weikart (1985), a pioneer in teaching rhythm to children, suggests that children pat the beat in a bilateral or parallel movement by simultaneously tapping their hands on their knees. This is conveniently done during chants, rhymes, or music that has a very evident pulse or beat. Until a child is ready to pat the beat, the teacher can pat the steady beat on the child's knees or shoulders as music is played or sung. The more experience the child has, the quicker the competency develops. Experiences with different types of music (marches, waltzes, polkas) encourage the child's ability to keep time with the music.

Using Recorded Music

Based upon her study, early-childhood music specialist Gharavi (1993) identified five basic problems with preschool teachers' current practices in using music with young children. Her major findings and some recommendations and ways that recorded music can help include the following:

1. Sing at a comfortable pitch for children's voices.
2. Expand your musical repertoire by borrowing a songbook from the library and/or by asking a friend who can sing and play to make a tape for you,
3. Become familiar with the best music available for young children.
4. Provide a wide range of musical styles, particularly ethnic music.
5. Provide opportunities for quiet listening. (p. 27)

Music is particularly important in the early-childhood program; leading theorist and Harvard professor Howard Gardner, who calls music one of the seven

It is frequently easier for children to familiarize themselves with rhythm instruments before they march with them.

forms of multiple intelligences, has concluded, "Of all the gifts with which individuals may be endowed, none emerges earlier than musical talent" (1993, p. 99).

Too often, teachers reserve music for just a few minutes each day during circle time because they lack confidence in their own musical abilities. Yet, as we know, children form enduring attitudes about music during the early-childhood years. Thus, teachers of young children—regardless of musical talent, training, and performance skills—have a special responsibility for developing young children's musical abilities (Jalongo, 1996, p. 11.) Some good references about books and journals, recorded music, sound recordings, sources for children's music, and big-book song/picture books are listed at the end of the Jalongo article.

When high-quality musical recordings are used effectively, they will make a powerful, positive influence on children during their lifetime (see Table 7.1).

Activities to Increase Music Abilities

Music is often limited to singing songs. Singing is fun and a good musical activity but is only one of many possibilities. Suggested activities in other chapters could be enhanced or varied with the addition of music. The following ideas are submitted as being useful; however, it is hoped that the reader will be creative when planning music experiences for young children.

- Use finger plays, chants, and poems.
- Provide experiences with a variety of musical instruments.
- Make and use rhythm instruments, or pretend to play some.

Table 7.1
Music and Young Children

CHARACTERISTICS OF YOUNG CHILDREN	HOW TO SUPPORT THEIR DEVELOPMENT THROUGH MUSIC, MOVEMENT, AND SOUND EXPERIENCES
They are active	Provide ways for them to touch, move, and manipulate their bodies (rhythm instruments, a song manipulative; a firm, steady beat; active participation).
They learn through play (specific developmental stages)	Encourage them to watch, play alone, play with others, play musical instruments, march, sing, and hear music.
They are inquisitive	Expose them to a rich environment of singing, playing instruments, listening to music, and creating music; be involved with them.
They have a limited voice range	Select and use songs that have a reasonable range
They like to mimic	Give them many listening experiences so they can reproduce a song, an experience, or an activity.
They like repetition	Even after you tire, give the child an opportunity to *re*-experience the music, the movement, and the experience.
They have a limited vocabulary	Introduce and verbalize music and language experiences and give them plenty of opportunities to repeat, repeat, and repeat.
They learn from models	Be a model (singing, movement, and so on) but encourage them to express *their own ideas*. A child copies what she sees. If models are excited, interested, and expressive, so will the child be.

- Play a variety of records, tapes, and music—classical, contemporary, instrumental, rhythmical, tempo, participation, listening, and so on.
- Teach the children how to use tape recorders. Tapes with songs, instrumentation, and stories can be checked out from many libraries. They make great individual or group listening opportunities. They last better than records; they don't scratch as easily, can be used in the car or outdoors, and are more available. (CDs are more expensive and may not have as appropriate a selection of music for young children at present.)
- Sing songs (with and without aids, with and without actions).
- Sing scale songs ("I Love Little Pussy," "Do, Re, Mi").
- Encourage children to sing while they play.
- Often, let the children choose songs to sing.
- For children who are reluctant to suggest songs, make a large cube with a picture for a song on each side. Roll the cube like a die and sing the song that comes up on top. Or make a singing tree. Pick a leaf off the tree. Turn it over for the song title. Or make a flower out of construction paper. Print the name of a song on it. Attach it to a straw and plant it in a clay pot of dirt. Let a child select a flower and then sing that song. Or place objects that represent certain songs in a basket. A child selects an object to sing about.
- Record and replay the children's voices (singing, talking, playing).
- Over a period of time, teach about three groups of instruments: woodwinds, percussion, and strings.
- Invite guests who sing, dance, or play musical instruments on the level of the children.
- Plan an activity around high/low, fast/slow, or loud/soft music.
- Identify natural rhythm in the classroom or play yard, such as clocks, squeaks, drips, bouncing balls, and swaying trees.

○ Go on a walking field trip to hear and identify rhythm.

○ Go places where music can be heard (band or orchestra practice, parade, sporting event, stores, television studio, dance studio).

○ During each season, go for a walk and listen to different sounds (for example, crunch of ice and snow, snap of a twig, rustle of leaves, pattern of rain, blowing of wind, stepping on stones or in puddles).

○ Combine experiences so the children can listen, create, sing, move, and experiment with sounds (based on the developmental level of the children).

○ Use music with other curriculum areas (art and science) and activities (free play and snack).

○ Be constantly aware of opportunities for spontaneous music.

○ Have some specific listening experiences. Make sounds and then have the children repeat and identify them.

○ Clap rhythm patterns to names, poems, and nursery rhymes and have the children repeat them or do them with you.

○ Use body actions to music ("Head, Shoulders, Knees, and Toes").

○ Exercise to music (aerobics are popular with children).

○ Provide props that encourage rhythm and music (blocks, sticks, coconut shells, shakers, bells).

○ Use a piano often, if available. You can vary the tempo and rhythm for exciting activities.

○ Obtain an Autoharp, an excellent instrument to use with children (available in different sizes and prices).

○ Fill matching film cans for identifying sounds.

○ Use visual aids to create interest in music (objects, posters, charts, pictures, movie boxes, transparencies, costumes, flip charts, drawing on a chalkboard).

○ Play circle games ("Mulberry Bush," "Ring-Around-a-Rosy," "Hokey Pokey," "This is the way we . . .").

○ Practice body sounds (hum, click teeth, snap fingers, blink eyes, clap, slap, rub, tap, shake).

○ Use music outdoors often.

○ Provide guidelines so children will know what is expected of them in various activities. Can they play the Autoharp, or is it just for teachers? How about the new dancing drum? Do the instruments stay in a certain area? Who can operate the record player and tape recorder?

○ Provide opportunities to support musical concepts such as rhythm, tempo, timbre, dynamics, and melody.

○ Sing and hum in the presence of children.

○ Put bells on different body parts—experiment.

○ Play music boxes that feature different tunes.

○ Use timers and clocks that produce unusual dings and ticks.

○ Use books with sounds: *Old MacDonald Had a Farm, This Old Man,* Margaret Wise Brown's series on sounds, and so on.

○ Play quiet background music.

○ Chant ideas (repetition).

○ Adapt familiar songs ("Mary Wore Her Red Dress").

  ○ Encourage parents to have music at home. Give simple ideas.
  ○ Play rhythm games.
  ○ Move or dance to music.

See the activities in the section titled "Listening" in Chapter 5.

MOVEMENT EDUCATION

"Movement, in addition to singing and playing instruments, continues to be one of the most important instructional tools available to the educator for setting an environment in which children learn to perform, describe, and create music," writes Andress (1991b, p. 22). To be developmentally appropriate, free choice and games without rules are more usable than structured music activities for this age group. Simple opportunities such as clapping or playing simple instruments help children to develop basic motor coordination and control over simple body movements. Children with more advanced gross motor coordination enjoy musical instruments and large-muscle movements as they move isolated body parts, practice and control their movements, and respond to rhythm using their entire bodies. But a child's response to music depends on disposition, developmental stage, and environmental factors.

Reflection

Observing a group of teachers in training, one notes that they are participating to "This Is a Song about Colors" (Hap Palmer record; check supply catalogs for ordering information). It has good rhythm, it makes one think and act simultaneously, it is fun to participate with others, it's exhilarating, and it's popular with adults. But then adults have learned to recognize colors in shades and hues beyond the abilities of children—and if one doesn't get to participate because he is wearing lavender, magenta, or chartreuse rather than the basic colors, one either enjoys the participation of others or pretends to have the right color. Now, look carefully at using the same experience with the following groups:

  ○ 3-year-olds (2-year-olds would be a disaster!)
  ○ 4-year-olds
  ○ 5-year-olds
  ○ special-needs or bilingual children
  ○ older children and adults

Consider the background of the individuals who would most benefit from the experience. Consider the feelings of children who have not learned their colors yet. Consider children who need more time to put together two ideas before acting (color and action). Now consider the preparation necessary for a color-song experience to be stimulating and successful for each of these groups.

Example: For 3-year-olds, you may use one or two colors only, and give each child a prop of that (or one other) color. You would surely want to slow down the tempo of the action—you could just say a color name and mention an action: "Red stand up." "Blue turn around." "Red smile." "Blue wiggle your toes."

Teachers need to modify ideas and activities so the children will enjoy the activities and find joy and success in them. You don't just use them because they are there or because others have enjoyed them. You modify and adapt!

Readers should not assume that children know how to move. That is, if the teacher wants the children to hop like a bunny, she should first talk about bunnies and how they move. Someone could demonstrate (before group hopping) how a bunny might hop. This way each child will have his definition of hopping (and all definitions are accepted) prior to the activity.

Movement exploration, a method of teaching that considers the development of the total child, encourages children to apply problem-solving techniques and to explore fantasies and relationships with others, while experiencing natural development of motor skills and knowledge of the operation of their own bodies. The self-concept of the children can grow in positive directions because the teacher establishes nonjudgmental techniques while demonstrating respect for each child's abilities (Sullivan, 1982, p. 1).

The Sullivan book (1982), available from NAEYC, provides countless movement activities mainly for working with 3- and 4-year-olds, but does extend through 8-year-olds. Activities allow for creativity with adult support and modeling. Different types, tempos, and instruments can add challenge or success to activities. The purposes of movement sessions include complementing free play, concepts to be taught, relaxation, interaction, change of pace, self-image development, and others.

Some of the equipment, materials, and activities that might be included in outdoor areas at various times during the year are included in Chapter 3, The Value of Play, in the section titled "Children and the Outdoors."

Props make a music experience more realistic.

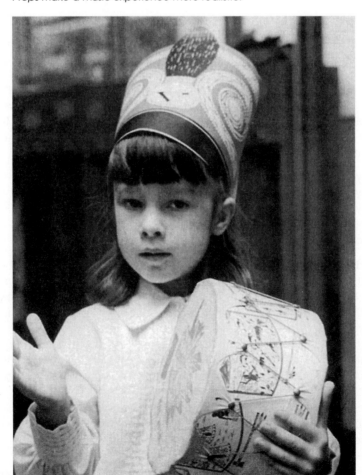

Movement and the Young Child

"The young child's movement is an important musical response because it is non-verbal and allows the observer to better understand what aspects of the music the child is sensing. Early movement activities center on the body (body touch, finger plays, song games) and responses to the wholeness of the music heard. The child begins to refine gestures to perform and describe introductory-level music information as heard in timbre, expressive controls, rhythm, melody, and form" (Andress, 1991a, p. 103).

For some reason, children's play is associated with noise and outdoor space. But much valuable play goes on within the classroom, provided there is time and space to do it. Both indoor and outdoor play are valuable. Movement and action are essential to children's development in general and to intellectual development in particular. Through it, children sense and act upon their environment.

Piaget (1974) called the first stage of children's intellectual development the *sensorimotor* stage, indicating the importance of experiencing the world primarily through their senses and motor abilities. He argued that the sensorimotor stage is the bedrock on which the subsequent hierarchy of all intelligence is built. Between birth and age 5 or 6, children's bodies, as much as their minds, are the organ of intelligence.

From Olds (1994) we read:

A facet of learning to read may illustrate the relationship between movement and learning. Until children have experiences orienting their bodies in space by going up, on, under, beside, inside, and in front of things, it is possible they will have difficulty dealing with letter identification and the orientation of symbols on a page. The only

As a new experience, toddlers concentrate on the flow of the scarves; locomotion comes later.

difference between a small "b" and a small "d," for example, both of which are composed of a line and a circle, depends upon orientation, i.e., which side of the circle is the line on? Zeller found that 98% of the 500 learning disabled children she tested were characterized as being physically *clumsy*. Similarly, Jean Ayres demonstrated that learning disabled children respond more readily to symbolic tutelage after being trained in the use of fundamental motor patterns that promote sensory integration—crawling, falling, rocking, and spinning. Thus, learning disabilities may be caused or exacerbated by immature or improper development of children's sensorimotor systems. (p. 33)

Movement is very important in the learning of a child, who must be personally and physically involved. It can only be done *by* the person, not *for* the person: her movements, her manipulation of materials. Overprotective caregivers must make the environment safe for the actions and interactions of *all* children. Movement is essential to the maintenance of the body's integrity. Adults should be aware of the rules, admonitions, and confinement they place upon children. True, adults need to take responsibility for the safety and protection of children, but they must plan for and accept the curiosity and exploration of children. Too many restrictions make children insecure rather than secure. Space is important and should be fully utilized. The requirement in many states is 35 square feet per child indoors to support gross motor play; others feel that is too cramped. Caregivers should carefully evaluate the amount of space they have available and the best use of it. At home some children must live in cramped spaces, but the center should find ways to make space for active indoor play. Limiting active play to the outdoors is not an option. "Failure to meet children's varied needs for movement prevents them from having experiences fundamental to their intellectual, social, and physical development," cautions Olds (1994, p. 33).

Reflection

Off-limits use of facilities includes:

- Climbing on tables
- Jumping off furniture (tables, beds, cupboards, and so on)
- Crawling under low furniture
- Sliding down banisters
- Balancing on ledges
- Hiding in closets
- Climbing in high or dangerous places
- Standing on moving objects (swings, wheel toys, and so on)
- Using ropes in an unsafe way
- Playing near hot equipment (heater, furnace, and so on)
- Using flame without adequate supervision
- Other hazards that may appear in *some* settings

Take a careful look around your indoor and outdoor spaces and add other specific "off-limits" activities. (For safety information, see Taylor, 1997, pp. 191–221.)

Activities should be based on available time and on equipment that is sturdy, safe, and well maintained. Activities should be supervised, developmentally appropriate, and stimulating. (See Figure 7.2.)

Figure 7.2
Activities That Encourage Movement

Balancing	*Balance beam:* vary width of board, adjust height, adjust slope *Rope:* vary width, vary length *Experiences:* vary body usage (one or two feet, on your back, on your stomach, seated, on knees, on hands, on head); balance on a stationary object.
Jumping	*Off* low (but stable) objects; from one object to another (such as colored paper shapes), on one or two feet, from a running or stationary position, *up* onto a safe object, onto something soft, *across* objects (small rope, a stuffed toy, ribbons, balls, puddles), *through* things (hoops, an inner tube, a large opening), *on* an old mattress, partially inflated inner tubes, or a small trampoline.
Swinging	Seated in a swing, on sturdy bars, using one or both hands, by knees (for children who are developed enough), holding onto ropes with knots to secure hands.
Throwing	Space, incentive, balls, beanbags, targets, companionship, challenge.
Body movement	Space, interesting props (streamers, ribbons, balloons—using caution with balloons—and so on), stories, music, companionship, dress-up clothing, encouragement, attention, experiences.
Climbing	Appropriate equipment, space, time, supervision.
Crawling	Interesting places, tunnels, suggested activities, reenacting stories, imitating (babies, animals).

Other activities to consider and plan for (according to the child's developmental abilities, safety, supervision, and other applicable conditions): hanging (to strengthen arms) and sliding (for coordination). Prepositions that encourage movement include *on (above), under (beneath), over, around, through, by, between,* and so on.

"Physical fitness refers to the level of health development and functional capacity of the body. A person needs to develop and maintain an adequate level of cardiovascular endurance, muscular strength, muscular endurance, flexibility, and body leanness to be deemed physically fit" (Seefeldt, 1984, p. 35).

Children move because it is essential to their development; they explore, discover, and interact with the world. They develop and strengthen muscles, refine motor skills, learn vocabulary and concepts, better understand their world, work out problems, and improve communication. Movement is in all areas of the curriculum and should not be limited to a certain time, place, or activity. The ability and flexibility to move freely in the classroom create an atmosphere that encourages interaction, divergent thinking, and individuality (Rodger, 1996).

Teachers need to think in terms of movement as they plan their physical facilities and prepare their curriculum activities. They must be flexible to the needs, responses, interests, and abilities of the children they teach. Movement interests of children may be spontaneous, planned, short-lived (seconds or minutes), or continued over a period of time (hours, days, weeks). Activities may be initiated by children (excited about a trip or experience) or teachers who are perceptive to spontaneous stimuli, interests of children, or the need for a change of pace.

All teachers and children move from location to location, activity to activity, or child to child. Transitions to facilitate these changes can be smooth, incidental, planned, or purposeful. (See the discussion of transition activities in Chapter 12).

Toddlers are cautions and curious about climbing and interacting with others.

Categories of Large-Muscle Development

Fundamental movement skills and combinations of movements that a child is neurologically ready to develop and refine during the preschool years include locomotor, manipulative, nonlocomotor, and perceptual-motor development skills (see Figure 7.3).

Recent research reveals that many young children have not developed their perceptual-motor skills, especially in the areas of visual awareness, auditory awareness and time awareness (Weikart, 1985).

> Many educators believe that children will automatically develop fundamental movement skills when they are ready. This is only partially true. Maturation provides a young child with the ability to perform a specific movement skill at a very low level of performance. It is only with continuous practice and instruction that a child's level of performance will increase. (Seefeldt, 1984, p. 35)

Figure 7.3
Fundamental Movement Skills

Locomotor	Walking, running, leaping, jumping, hopping, galloping, sliding, skipping, climbing, and propelling a wheel toy, such as a tricycle, scooter, or wagon
Manipulative	Throwing, kicking, punting, striking, volleying, bouncing, dribbling (hand), dribbling (foot), rolling, catching, and trapping
Nonlocomotor (balance)	Bending, stretching, twisting, turning, swinging, upright and inverted balances, body rolling, dodging, and beam walking (Gallahue, 1982)
Perceptual-motor	Involves monitoring and interpreting sensory data and responding in movement. It is generally accepted that this type of development includes awareness of each of the following: *Body skills:* Ability to name, locate, and identify the function of the body parts *Time skills:* Ability to move to a steady beat, perform a series of movements in a coordinated manner, speed up or slow down movements, and freeze movements without falling down *Spatial skills:* Ability to know internally how much space the body occupies and to control the body as it moves through space *Directional skills:* The internal ability to identify the dimensions of external space—up, down, in, over, under *Visual skills:* Ability to perceive and copy demonstrated movements *Auditory skills:* Ability to attend to verbal directions and discriminate between a variety of sounds

Adapted from Poest et al., 1990.

Helping Young Children Develop Their Bodies Properly

"Designing and implementing a developmentally appropriate movement curriculum will take time and effort. But it is worth it. If we are concerned with the whole child, we need to plan and implement appropriate activities that will facilitate the development of young children's motor skills" (Seefeldt, 1984, p. 35). We can do this through:

1. *Fundamental movement skills:* Teachers and parents cannot assume that young children will get enough of the age- and individual-appropriate motor activities to provide them with adequate motor skills.

2. *Physical fitness:* Daily fitness activities, good models, good stress-reducers, outdoor (walk, run, gallop, climb, jump) and indoor (music, imitate animals, variety of stationary movements) activities. Encourage children to try more challenging things and to do them longer, according to time, space, and interest.

Reflection

Little research has been done in the area of preschool fitness. We know, however, that:

> [T]he first signs of arteriosclerosis are now appearing at about age five. Children need to exercise aerobically at least three times a week and eat properly to reduce this disease process. (Institute of Aerobic Research, 1987)

> [C]hildren are not engaging in the moderate- to high-intensity physical activity necessary to increase cardiovascular fitness. (Gilliam et al., 1981; Ross and Pate, 1987)

> [C]ardiovascular fitness is not enhanced during most childhood sport and recreation activities, recess, or play time since the movement is not continuous. (Gilliam et al., 1982)

> [F]or every 100 children, at least 16 are obese (Mayer, 1968); the prevalence of obesity increased by approximately 40 percent from the 1960s to the 1970s in both children and youth. (Gortmaker et al., 1987)

> [Y]oung children are especially weak in the areas of muscular strength, cardiovascular endurance, and body leanness. The research seems to show that children are in worse physical condition now than 20 years ago. (Gallahue, 1987)

3. *Perceptual-motor skills:* Activities such as "Simon Says" for body awareness and visual clues; moving (tapping, marching, skipping, and so on); nursery rhymes, chants, songs; obstacle courses, directions in space: over, around, through.

Andress (1991b) states:

> We, as practitioners, tend to think from an activity base, constantly searching for "fun" ways to use movement and music in circle time sessions. We must abandon this practice now and use a child-centered approach wherein materials and activities reflect concerns for the various stages of development. (p. 27)

Young children are doers, talkers, and movers. Their bodies are not naturally still; however, movement should be encouraged in the right places and in the right ways, with time, space, ideas, and props.

When children discover the great potential in their body movements, they want to explore the possibilities. They test, try to understand and accept their bodies, and begin to feel confident and to lose self-consciousness. They feel joy and pleasure in free movement. Movement exploration can lead directly into a creative dance or a cultural experience. As such, it is the process, the solving of a problem, and the discovering of a new way, rather than an end product, that are important.

Movement may take place in a quiet and solitary setting or in an active group. Moha, a quiet 3-year-old, sat listening to a record. Then he commented: "It goes around and around!" His head began going around and around, then his arms, and finally his whole body. He was transferring the motion from the record to his body and finding it to be a delightful experience.

Movement is a viable and important part of the daily curriculum—not an add-on. It can easily be integrated as an expression medium. It is natural, essential, and valuable for physical and mental health and can also enhance academic learning; it aids in problem solving, exploration, and success. It helps to encourage inquisitive-

Although games of competition and exclusion are sometimes provided for young children, activities that promote cooperation and involvement help build children's self-esteem and personal relationships.

ness and creativity in children, who have an innate drive to master their environment through sensorimotor activities. Through space exploration, they can develop body control; ease and confidence in movement; and motor skills of coordination, strength, flexibility, balance, laterality, and directionality. Their bodies move in time (fast, medium, sudden, or sustained), in force (strong or light), in flow (bound, free, or a combination), in tension/relaxation, and in such relationships as near and far, front and back, over and under, lead and follow, or unison and contrast.

Factors that affect movement are (1) body awareness and actions (what is moved); (2) space (where one moves); (3) effort, or quality, of movement (how); and (4) relationship (with whom or what). Appropriate experiences can be provided so children can practice and become more proficient in the use of their bodies. Competition, such as pitting boys against girls or children against each other, is avoided. Rather, each child tries to improve his own physical skills and abilities.

Children who are restricted or forbidden to explore are at a definite disadvantage. One young child was given an ample number of playthings and good physical care and attention, but was restricted in space. She soon became listless, subject to illness, overweight, and insecure. Becoming concerned, her mother sought professional help, only to be encouraged to "open up the child's world." The child soon returned to her usual happy self when she was allowed more freedom to explore, find toys of her interest, interact with other children, and become more independent.

Activities to Increase Movement Skills

○ Place a series of footprints on the floor. Ask the children to walk or skip on them, jump from one to another, roll over them, and so on. Have footprints spaced at varying intervals that lead to another activity, a neglected area, and so on.

- Provide a balance beam. For beginners, have it close to the floor. Raise it as the children develop skill.
- Encourage the children to act out their feelings (stamp, pound, yell, glide, skip, dance).
- Tell them to act out movement in nature (sway, bend, tap).
- Encourage each child to move in her own way.
- Give mental images and have the children imitate them (rowing a boat, walking in wind, flying like a bird, walking with a broken leg, pulling a heavy load, carrying a vase on the head, and so on).
- Use records or tapes that encourage gross movement, listening, interpreting, and moving.
- Provide props that encourage movement, such as scarves, balls, clothes, and streamers.
- Make obstacle courses both indoors and outdoors. Verbally tell the children what is expected, or have indicators for *over this, around that, under this, between those,* and so on.
- Encourage the children to explore space by running, rolling, jumping, swinging arms, and so on. At times have them confined to a small area; at other times let them move as far as they desire.
- Provide a mat for tumbling, jumping, and rolling.
- Do activities using various body parts (touch your elbow; touch your elbow to your toe; put your hand on your knee; put your nose on your knee).
- Encourage the children to make their bodies tall, small, straight, or crooked.
- Provide many opportunities to practice locomotor skills (walking, crawling, hopping, jumping, running, leaping, skipping, galloping, rolling, climbing, sliding).
- Provide many opportunities to practice nonlocomotor skills (bending, swaying, rocking, stretching, turning, pulling, pushing, twisting, curling, standing, sitting, kneeling, reaching).
- Go on a walk; jump over cracks, straddle a rock, balance on a curb, skip around a fountain, and so on.
- Play the sponge game. Each child has a sponge (approximately 1 by 4 by 6 inches). The children follow the directions of a teacher or another child: Put your sponge on your head. Walk without letting it fall off. Put it on your shoulder, your arm, your shoe. Crawl with it on your back. Jump over it. Sit on it. Roll on it. Length of this activity is determined by the interest of the children.
- Dramatize stories or activities.
- Sing songs that encourage actions (for example, "Wiggle Song," "Head, Shoulders, Knees, and Toes," "Do as I'm Doing," "The Bus Song").
- Ask the children to go to various parts of the room without using their feet, like a ball, backward, and so on.
- Have the children pretend to be Raggedy Ann and Raggedy Andy (no bones).
- Use body cards and have the children model poses. (See Chapter 12.)
- Plan activities during which the children use their bodies to learn about location (especially good for learning about prepositions).
- Pantomime different activities.

○ Help children see movement in everyday things such as animals, people, or objects (clocks, faucets, cars, trains).

○ Suggest ideas to children and let them express their individuality (colors, moods, holidays). Be prepared for nonresponses. These ideas may be too advanced for young children.

○ Do simple aerobics with the children.

○ Make and use equipment (hula hoops out of plastic tubing, scoops out of plastic bleach bottles, and balls from yarn).

○ Use a hula hoop. Move inside of the hoop, roll it, jump into it, crawl through it, or share it with a friend.

○ Combine activities using a rope, hula hoop, beanbag, and ball.

○ Play games such as Twister, "Mother, May I?," "What Can You Do?," and tag.

○ Make body shadows.

○ Pretend to jump across a stream, narrow at first, then wider and wider.

○ Follow a rhythm chart. A picture of a hand indicates when to clap; a picture of a foot indicates when to stamp.

○ Practice ball handling as the children develop such skills as rolling, catching, throwing, bouncing, and kicking.

○ Use beanbags to throw at a target (bucket, box), kick them, or balance them on the head or back.

○ Provide rope experiences. Rope can be made into shapes, jumped over, crawled under, or used to circumscribe space.

○ Get a small parachute (a tablecloth or sheet may also work) and have children try the activities in the following list. Original activities are also encouraged.

Marshmallow: Hold parachute waist-high. On signal, throw arms and parachute as high as possible. Let parachute float down softly.

Waves: Gently wave parachute up and down and observe rippling motion.

Cover-up: Hold parachute waist high. On signal, extend arms upward and, while still holding on to parachute, turn around and squat on ground. Chute covers participants.

Bouncers: Place two yarn or other small balls in center of parachute. Try to keep them bouncing by shaking parachute up and down.

Catchers: Space teachers and children around the outside of parachute. Slowly move parachute up and down. On count of three, the teacher calls either "boys" or "girls." The called group runs under parachute, and others try to catch them.

○ Show pictures of animals and have children imitate their movements, such as sliding like a snake, jumping like a kangaroo, flying like a bird, and hopping like a bunny.

○ Have an animal walk. Imitate a bear, seal, crab, frog, duck, or monkey.

○ Take a field trip to a gymnasium, sports arena, or dance studio.

○ Have the children move as they would in different occupations (sanitation worker, engineer, baker, mountain climber, forest ranger, and so on). Note that occupations can be for both sexes.

○ Tell each child to form a circle with his body; then add a partner to form a circle; continue to add more children to form still larger circles. Do the same with other shapes such as a line, square, or triangle.

○ Show pictures of a circus. Have the children pretend to be dancing bears, prancing horses, stalking tigers, trunk-and-tail-holding elephants, and performing lions.

○ Let the children practice coordination skills by walking first on a piece of string or yarn placed on the floor, then on the wide side of a balance beam placed on the floor, then on the narrow side of the beam. Begin to raise the beam slightly from the floor as skills develop.

○ Make a number of pictures of animals and tape them to the floor. Bunnies mean *hop;* frogs *jump;* and ducks *sway.* Start with a series of the same animal; later, mix up the pictures so the actions will vary as the child moves around.

○ Demonstrate flexibility and stretching to children by using a large rubber band. Ask the children to use their bodies in the same way, stretching and flexing in various ways.

○ Take a make-believe ride in an elevator, stretching high, higher, highest as the elevator goes up and low, lower, lowest as it comes down.

○ Some music companies and distributors:

Children's Music Network
Pass It On! (newsletter)
267 Onota Street
Pittsfield, MA 01201

Kimbo Educational
P.O. Box 477
Long Branch, NJ 07740

Music in Motion
Box 645
Dallas, TX 76248

Educational Activities
P.O. Box 87
Baldwin, NY 11510

Miss Jackie Music
1001 El Monte
Overland Park, KS 66207

Piggyback Songbooks
by J. Warren
Totline Press
Everett, WA 98203P.O. Box 2255

Multicultural Music and Movement Activities

In addition to the previous activities, which provide multicultural music and movement activities, you might want to focus on the following:

○ Records and songs with international ties

○ Movement (games) and dances of different countries

○ Costumes (clothing) for dancing

○ Different instruments—for example, kalimbas, maracas, bells, gongs, castanets, guitars, and drums

APPLICATION OF PRINCIPLES

1. Make an effort to use more music with young children. Sing, hum, or move to music outdoors as well as indoors.

2. Encourage the children to use their large muscles by imitating animals, feelings, objects, or people, sometimes with and sometimes without musical accompaniment.

3. Over a period of a few weeks, learn and teach three new songs to young children. Use visual aids for one of the songs.

4. Use rhythm instruments, first without accompaniment and later with a record or piano, using a steady beat.

5. Invite a guest who has musical talents. What suggestions would you offer to that person?

6. Originate an outdoor game that involves the use of a ball, a parachute or small sheet, or an obstacle course.

7. Make a list of the five records and five songbooks you would like to own personally.

8. Sketch some possible obstacle courses. If possible, set them up and watch as the children participate.

9. Note the differing ages and physical abilities of the children. Are they within a "normal" range for their ages?

10. Consider how to modify suggestions for music and movement education for children of different ages or abilities.

11. Ask someone to help or coach you if you don't feel self-confident in music and movement experiences.

12. Refer to Figure 4.2. Which of the areas (1–8) have been planned for the day or period?

13. Does physical ability (or rhythm, sound, and so on) influence learning? Look over the information in the section titled "Advantages of Music and Movement Education" and the chapter discussion for important relationships between curriculum and development.

14. Using the information in the section on developmental characteristics, design some movement activities appropriate for each age group. (Play follow-the-leader as children march around the room, down the hall, outdoors, and so on).

15. Young children love to dance. Encourage them to create original dance steps to any musical selection.

16. Pick up the rhythm of children at play or tap out rhythm patterns (steady for walking, quick for running, uneven for skipping or galloping, slow for jumping). Change rhythm and see if the children can change their activities.

17. Take a familiar song (or one you are going to teach the children) and see how many curriculum areas are being taught through the words and actions of that song (science, social studies, creative art, language, math, music, reading, and so on).

REFERENCES

Anderson, P. S., & D. Lapp (1988). *Language skills in elementary education.* New York: Macmillan.

Andress, B. (1984). The practitioner involved young children in music. In Boswell, J. (ed.), *The young child and music.* Reston, VA: Music Educators National Conference.

Andress, B. (1989, October). Music for every stage: How much? What kind? How soon? *Music Educators Journal,* 76(2), 22–27.

Andress, B. (1991a). Developmentally appropriate music experiences for young children. In National Dance Association (ed.), *Early childhood creative arts,* 65–73. Reston, VA: American Alliance for Health, Physical Education, Recreation and Dance.

Andress, B. (1991b, November). From research to practice: Preschool children and their movement responses to music. Research in review. *Young Children,* 47(1), 22–27.

Andress, B. (1995). Transforming curriculum in music. In Bredekamp, S., & T. Rosegrant (eds.), *Reaching potentials: Transforming early childhood curriculum and assessment,* Vol. 2, 99–107. Washington, DC: NAEYC.

Ball, W. A. (1991). Music: An avenue for cultural literacy. Paper presented at the Annual Conference of the Southern Association on Children Under Six (SACUS) March 15, in Atlanta, GA. ED332799.

Barclay, K. D., & L. Walwer (1992, May). Linking lyrics and literacy through song picture books. *Young Children,* 47(4), 76–85.

Bayless, K., & M. Ramsey (1982). *Music: a way of life for the young child.* New York: Merrill/Macmillan.

Buchoff, R. (1994, May). Joyful voices: facilitating language growth through the rhythmic response to chants. *Young Children,* 49(4), 26.

Cherry, C., D. Godwin, & J. Staples (1989). *Is the left brain always right? A guide to whole child development.* Belmont, CA: Fearon Teaching Aids.

Galin, D. (1976, October). Educating both halves of the brain. *Childhood Education,* 53, 17–20.

Gallahue, D. (1982). *Developmental movement experiences for children.* New York: Wiley.

Gallahue, D. (1987). *Developmental movement activities for young children.* Paper presented at Annual Conference of the National Association for the Education of Young Children, November, in Chicago, IL.

Gardner, H. (1993). *Frames of mind: The theory of multiple intelligences,* 2nd edition. New York: Basic.

Gharavi, G. J. (1993). Music skills for preschool teachers: Needs and solutions. *Arts Education Policy Review,* 94(3), 27–30.

Gilliam, T., P. Freedson, D. Geenen, & B. Shahraray (1981). Physical activity patterns determined by heart rate monitoring in 6–7 year old children. *Medicine and Science in Sports and Exercise,* 13(1), 65–67.

Gilliam, T., S. MacConnie, D. Geenen, A. Pels, & P. Freedson (1982). Exercise programs for children: A way to prevent. *The Physical and Sports Medicine,* 10(9), 96–108.

Glazier, T. (1973). *Eye winker, Tom Tinker, chin chopper: Fifty musical fingerplays.* New York: Doubleday.

Glazier, T. (1980). *Do your ears hang low? Fifty more musical fingerplays.* New York: Doubleday.

Goodlad, J. I. (1984). *A place called school.* New York: McGraw-Hill.

Gortmaker, S. L., W. H. Dietz, A. M. Sobol, & C. A. Wehler (1987). Increasing pediatric obesity in the United States. *American Journal of Diseases in Children,* 141, 535–540.

Harp, B. (1988). Why are your kids singing during reading time? *The Reading Teacher,* 41, 454–456.

Hennings, D. G. (1990). *Communication in action.* Boston: Houghton Mifflin.

High/Scope Resource. They have a number of publications on movement, music, and folk songs for young children. Phone: (800) 40-PRESS. Fax: (800) 442-4FAX.

Institute of Aerobic Research (1987). *Get fit.* Dallas: Author.

Jalongo, M. R. (1996, July). Using recorded music with young children: A guide for nonmusicians. *Young Children,* 51(5), 6–14.

Karnowski, L. (1986). How young writers communicate. *Educational Leadership,* 46(3), 58–60.

Kranyik, M. A. (1993, January/February). Body music. *First Teacher,* 14(1), 25.

Landeck, B. (ed.) (1950). *Songs to grow on: A collection of American folk songs for children.* New York: Edward B. Marks Music and Wm. Sloane Associates.

Lynch, P. (1986). *Using big books and predictable books.* New York: Scholastic.

McDonald, D. T. (1979). *Music in our lives: The early years.* Washington, DC: NAEYC. Order #107.

Music Educators National Conference (MENC) (1994a). *Opportunities-to-learn standards for music instruction: Grades preK–12.* Reston, VA: Author.

Music Educators National Conference (MENC) (1994b). *The school music program: A new vision.* Reston, VA: Author.

Music for the young child. (1995, March and May). *Staff Notes for L. D. S. Church Musicians and Staff,* 7(2) and (3), 2. Salt Lake City, UT: Church of Jesus Christ of Latter-Day Saints.

National Dance Association (ed.) (1991). *Early childhood creative arts.* Washington, DC: NAEYC. Order #713.

Olds, A. R. (1994, May). From cartwheels to caterpillars: children's need to move indoors and out. *Child Care Information Exchange,* 32–36.

Piaget, J. (1951). *Play, dreams, and imitation in childhood.* New York: Norton.

Piaget, J. (1974). *The child and reality: Problems of genetic psychology.* Trans. A. Rosen. New York: Viking.

Pitcher, E. G., M. B. Lasher, S. G. Feinburg, & L. A. Braun (1974). *Helping young children learn,* 2nd edition. Columbus, OH: Merrill.

Poest, C. A., J. R. Williams, D. D. Witt, & M. E. Atwood (1990). Challenge me to move: Large muscle development in young children. *Young Children,* 45(5), 4–10.

Riley, S. (1984). *How to generate values in young children.* Washington, DC: NAEYC.

Rivkin, M. S. (1995). *The great outdoors: Restoring children's right to play outside.* Washington, DC: NAEYC.

Rodger, L. (1996, March). Adding movement throughout the day. *Young Children,* 51(3), 4–6.

Ross, J. G., & R. R. Pate (1987). The National Children and Youth Fitness Study II: A summary of findings. *Journal of Physical Education, Recreation and Dance,* 58(9), 51–56.

Sampson, M., M. B. Sampson, & R. Van Allen (1991). *Pathways to literacy.* Fort Worth, TX: Holt, Rinehart & Winston.

Seefeldt, V. (1984). Physical fitness in preschool and elementary school-aged children. *Journal of Physical Education, Recreation and Dance,* 55(9), 33–40.

Seeger, R. C. (ed.) (1948). *American folk songs for children.* Garden City, NY: Doubleday.

Shaw, J. M., & M. P. Cliatt (1986). A model for training teachers to encourage divergent thinking in young children. *Journal of Creative Behavior,* 20(2), 81–88.

Smale, S. (1985). *Music—basic for the young child.* Edina, MN: LEA/DECE Publications.

Sullivan, M. (1982). *Feeling strong, feeling free: Movement exploration for young children.* Washington, DC: NAEYC.

Taylor, B. J. (1997). *Early childhood program management: people and procedures,* 3rd edition. Upper Saddle River, NJ: Merrill.

Weikart, P. (1985). *Movement plus music.* Ypsilanti, MI: High/Scope Press.

Wolf, J. (1992, January). Let's sing it again: Creating music with young children. *Young Children,* 47(2), 56–61.

Wolf, J. (1994, May). Singing with children is a cinch! *Young Children,* 49(4), 20–25.

Yinger, J., & S. Blaszka (1995, November). A year of journaling—a year of building with young children. *Young Children,* 51(1), 15–20.

Zimmerman, M. (1985). State of the art in early childhood music and research. In Boswell, J. (ed.), *The young child and music: Contemporary principles in child development and music education,* 65–78. Reston, VA: Music Educators National Conference.

Science and
Technology

CHAPTER 8

MAIN PRINCIPLES

1. Young children want to learn about themselves and others. They have different interests and abilities to absorb knowledge at different ages.

2. All children, regardless of sex, race, age, or any other criteria, should have equal access to science and all areas of curriculum.

3. Children need multisensory opportunities to learn about their environment.

4. Children's natural curiosity can be enhanced and rewarded.

5. Teachers and parents can develop a positive attitude toward science.

6. Teachers and parents can encourage exploration and interests in young children.

7. Our world is a museum, a field trip, a laboratory, and a natural resource just waiting to be discovered, explored, and enjoyed.

8. There are ways to turn around negative attitudes, low interest, and limited science experiences for children and adults.

9. Formerly, the science and math scores for U.S. children through the eighth grade were lower than for same-grade students in foreign countries. The 1997 figures show that U.S. children are reversing these findings.

10. Young children are interested in computers and can use them effectively if certain criteria are met. Knowing and meeting the criteria is important in adult selection of computers, software, and classroom management.

Consider the following statistics from the Bureau of Labor. Did you know that by the year 2000:

> the United States will have a one-million-person shortage of trained scientists and technicians, according to estimates by the National Science Foundation;

> more than 80 percent of all jobs will require proficiency in math and science (right now, between 60 and 80 percent of career fields are closed to those with poor math and science preparation); and

> more than 40 percent of the college-age population will be African-American and Latino/Latina?

Reflection

It is curiosity, the drive to make sense out of something in our surroundings, that causes children to reach out, touch, and wonder and it is curiosity that moves scientists to do the very same thing. (Abruscato, 1992, p. 3) (See also Carson, (1956), under section entitled *Curriculum Webbing*, "young children, peers, & adults", p. 112.)

It is not true that the easier subjects should precede the harder. On the contrary, some of the hardest must come first, because nature so dictates, and because they are essential to life, states Alfred North Whitehead.

Students complain most, give more excuses, and feel more threatened in science than in any other curriculum area. Why is this so? On quizzing, one frequently gets answers like, "I hate science!" "I don't understand it myself, so how can I teach it to children?" "Please, *please,* let me do extra assignments in other areas instead." This is where toughness comes in—and usually pays great dividends. Offer assistance, but insist that teachers follow through.

Of all the curriculum areas, science is the most vital, for it encompasses all other topics. It is knowledge, and is found in relationships, in the environment, in art and the senses, in verbal and written communication, in music and movement, in living and physical things, and in daily living such as nutrition, health, and safety. It is discovered through play and one's interaction with the environment. But opportunities for science must be based on the developmental level of each child—based on her own foundation.

One reason I feel so strongly about science is that it is so exciting. Another reason is that it is so much a part of our daily lives. A third reason is that knowledge helps us live happier and more productive lives. And still another reason is a negative or fearful attitude in some circles toward anything scientific—and this worries me. I am speaking about learning scientific concepts in a realistic, meaningful, and growth-promoting way. I reject learning scientific facts merely to recite or write them to pass tests or because they are requirements. I encourage learning facts because they are interesting, useful, and satisfying.

One must not ignore the fact that American children were once not performing as highly in scientific or mathematical areas as were children of similar ages in selected countries throughout the world. A "crisis in education" was reported and discussed by Fisher in a two-part article (1992, August; 1992, September). He stated that "The National Science Board, the governing body of the National Science Foundation, echoed a 1983 dictum to plan to make U.S. elementary and secondary education in science and math 'premier in the world by 1995, as measured by achievement scores and participation levels' " (1992, August, p. 58). But instead, 300 reports attested to the fact that the scores of American children had gotten significantly worse. He continued, "In March of [1991], about 175,000 9- and 13-year-old students from 20 countries took standardized tests in science and math. . . . The Americans flunked the science test—taking thirteenth place. . . . In math, the 13-year-olds from the United States did even worse—landed in the next-to-the-bottom slot" (p. 59).

In the second part of Fisher's report (1992, September) he stated: "Poverty, discrimination against minorities and females, one-parent homes, poorly equipped schools, and inadequately trained teachers all contribute to the U.S. education crisis" (p. 50). The National Association of Eductional Progress (NAEP) 1990 Science Report (reported by Fisher, 1992, p. 51) concluded that students would perform better if they had access to more reading materials such as books, magazines, newspapers, and encyclopedias, read more than five pages for school each day, spent at least some time on daily homework, had both parents living in the home, and watched less television (p. 51).

The Third International Mathematics and Science Study (1997, January), or TIMSS report, showed that U.S. eighth-graders scored above average in science but below average in math compared to their counterparts in the United Kingdom, Canada, France, Germany, and Japan. The TIMSS report is the most thorough international study of math and science education ever conducted, comparing the performance of 500,000 students, of whom 40,000 were Americans.

To boost math and science achievement for U.S. students, the Department of Education will join the Academy of Sciences and the National Science Foundation to sponsor meetings across America to rally support for better teacher training and improvements in curriculum, textbooks, and testing (1997, January).

The Third International Mathematics and Science Study (TIMSS) report from July/August 1997 has a positive note:

> The recent results of the TIMSS show that our nation's fourth-graders are near the very top in science achievement in the world. America's fourth-graders are also doing better than ever in mastering the basics of arithmetic. This is the first time in any international comparison that American students in a given grade have exceeded the international average in both mathematics and science.

TIMSS is the most thorough international study of math and science education ever conducted, comparing the performance of a half million students, including 33,000 Americans, at levels corresponding to U.S. grades 4, 8, and 12. The fourth-grade findings were in contrast to the TIMSS results released last November showing that our nation's eighth-graders scored above average in science but below the international average in mathematics. . . .

> TIMSS data suggests that grades 4 through 8 are years that warrant special attention for U.S. students so that by the eighth-grade, all children can master challenging mathematics, including the foundations of algebra and geometry . . . so they will be ready for more advanced courses in high school . . . college, productive employment, and lifelong learning. (1997, July/August, p. 1)

Developmental Characteristics

The amount of intellectual development in children is often difficult to determine. Their lack of language and the adult's inability to determine precisely what and how to measure are both limiting factors. The age and size of the child can mislead adults into thinking children know more or less than they actually do.

Essentially, young children participate in many scientific activities. They may stay for long or short periods of time and feel joy or frustration. They are self-centered, seeing their own point of view, and center on only one aspect at a time. They are limited in their ability to handle abstract ideas.

Young children play alone or alongside another child. Eventually they join a small group; later they enjoy the companionship and ideas of others. They tend to judge others by their own acts. Not until later are they able to consider motives behind actions.

Intellectually, children begin by repeated experimentation with objects. They believe that natural phenomena are created by human beings and that inanimate objects have life and human characteristics.

To make science exciting and meaningful for young children, activities are based on familiar ideas. Children are encouraged to explore and discover; however, adults should be willing and able to assist when appropriate.

SCIENCE AND YOUNG CHILDREN

What Is Science?

Science is usually defined by delineating the content, procedures, and assumptions of the field. Science includes both knowledge about specific phenomena (characteristics, classifications, and principles that explain the universe) and the general strategies or processes used to collect and to evaluate such information (See: American Association for the Advancement of Science, 1989, 1993; National Center for Improving Science Education, 1990; National Research Council, 1994; Kilmer & Hofman, 1995, p. 43).

Home-School Partnership

"To achieve a good home-school connection, all involved need to know what types of experiences are appropriate for the child, what good science and math experiences are, and what strategies to use in engaging children" (Kokoski & Downing-Leffler, 1995, p. 35). (Note that many authors and educators use *experiences,* not *experiments.* The former connotes involvement; the latter, observation.)

"A good science and mathematics program fosters the development of lifelong skills and attitudes in children (Mechling & Oliver 1983). The most appropriate place to begin such learning is in early childhood programs. . . . Therefore, professionals in education must find ways to make connections between what is learned at school and what is learned at home. The home-school connection is the key to resolving this dilemma" (Kokoski & Downing-Leffler, p. 35).

Importance of Home/School Connection

1. The influence of parents and the home environment is recognized by professionals as a significant component of a child's education (McIntyre, 1984; Bybee et al., 1989).

Young children learn about science in a relaxed, non-threatening environment.

2. Academic learning activities that are completed at home promote children's achievement at school (Goldenberg, Reese, & Gallimore, 1992).

3. Parent and child attitudes about school become more positive through academic interactions at home, affecting the child's self-esteem. . . . Theoretically, acknowledgement of these benefits should lead to a more positive attitude toward and interest in science and mathematics (Kokoski & Downing-Leffler, 1995, p. 35).

Parents and educators need to know what types of experiences are appropriate for the child, what good science and mathematics experiences are, and what strategies to use in engaging with children at home.

Goals in providing appropriate science experiences for young children are defined by:

1. Kilmer and Hofman: "to lay a solid foundation for the continuing and development of an interest in and an understanding of science and technology with active participation for *every child*" (1995, p. 44).

2. National Center for Improving Science Education (NCISE): a general framework recommended for kindergarten through sixth grade, yet broad enough to serve as guidelines for planning experiences for preschool children as

well. Comprehensive in nature, the guidelines address attitudes, processes, and content. Specifically, they recommend: (a) developing each child's innate curiosity about the world; (b) broadening each child's procedural and thinking skills for investigating the world, solving problems, and making decisions; and (c) increasing each child's knowledge of the natural world (1990, p. 9). Objectives and ways to achieve these three goals are included in the article.

The general behaviors of science learning include the following: *observing, communicating, comparing, organizing, relating, inferring,* and *applying.*

For example: Four-year-olds in the sand area were observing the coarseness of the sand, talking about its roughness, comparing it to nearby soil, organizing a plan for road making, relating prior experiences with the medium, suggesting its best use, and applying their physical skills.

Or: Three-year-olds were observing some tadpoles, talking about their characteristics, and relating prior experiences with tadpoles. At this point they were using only some of the general behaviors needed to understand the full impact of the experience.

Reflection

Five-year-olds are organizing a "safari" outdoors.
Using your imagination and/or prior experience, fill in the blanks as to what the 5-year-olds might be:

Observing	
Saying	
Comparing	
Organizing	
Relating	
Inferring	
Applying	

THE SCIENCE CURRICULUM

How often we hear "Well, what did you learn today?" when children return to the presence of adults. What kind of a question is that? It's so broad, so vague, so overwhelming! (How would you, as an adult, answer it?) Isidor I. Rabi, a Nobel Prize winner in physics, suggests that one not ask "Did you learn anything today?" but "Did you ask a good question today?" The difference—asking good questions—"made me become a scientist."

Science is more than a collection of facts. Young children must live it. Older children and adults can learn about it in a more mature or abstract way through the scientific method (observation, predicting, testing predictions under controlled conditions, and interpretation), and younger children use these steps in a more primitive way. Young children may be easily discouraged in trying something new. The important thing is that they try, make modifications, and try again. Things that appeal most to young children are "things they can see, touch, manipulate, modify; situations that allow them to figure out what happens—in short, events and puzzles that they can investigate, which is the very stuff of science" (Paulu & Martin, 1992, p. 6). Science activities initiate language and problem-solving skills and involve touching, smelling, seeing, hearing, and exploring.

Science is a part of our daily lives. It is of vital importance to each and every one of us—through natural resources, through medicine, through production and consumption of goods and services, through life itself. If it is so much a part of us, why do some parents and teachers find the subject one that is intimidating, frustrating, and to be avoided? Young children are interested and excited about their environment. They need to keep that curiosity alive.

Science is the process of inquiry. Young children are natural scientists with spontaneous and ingenious ideas. They are, at this stage, egocentric. They see no reasons for things except for their benefit (parents make cookies because children are hungry, or the sun comes out so children can play). As they grow and have experiences, they become less egocentric; they look for physical, magical, or psychological reasons as causes for events. While in the preoperational stage, they live in the here and now. They believe all they see. "It's true! I saw it on television" is a common response. Then children try to duplicate some feats, only to end up injured or disappointed. They have limited ability to understand causality, reason logically, or predict consequences.

Young children often have misconceptions about their world; these need to be clarified and revised. By listening to or watching young children, adults receive clues as to when they need to offer a firsthand experience to get the child thinking in the right direction.

Reflection

A teacher demonstrated the principle of rain in the classroom. No questions were asked by the children, so the teacher assumed they had learned the concepts as she had planned them. The next day, a mother reported her daughter's comments: "Mother, God doesn't make the rain; I learned how to make it at school." Without this vital feedback, the teacher would have assumed the children had gained correct concepts. Instead, she was back to the drawing board for another attempt to teach about rain.

Adults have many opportunities to help young children understand the fascination of science. For example: Why is salt used in freezing ice cream? What makes popcorn pop? What is the principle of gravity? How can heavy airplanes stay up in the air, or heavy boats float? If you do not know answers, take the child to a book, or other resource, and find out together. Keep the information simple and on his level of understanding. Complicated lectures will discourage him from asking questions in the future.

While setting up some guidelines for science curriculum, see that all children are included—regardless of sex, race, age, or any other criteria. All children should have equal access to all areas of curriculum. All of them will be interested and ready for opportunities within their developmental and skill abilities. Because science encompasses their entire world, children will want to participate—maybe cautiously or hesitantly at first, but they will be interested. (Review, at least in your mind, the emphasis John Dewey [See Chapter 3 or Appendix A] placed on the importance of self-directed activity [active involvement]—he viewed children as scientists whose major occupation was problem solving.) Holt (1989) says: "I believe we are passing, to children, responsibility for a 21st Century Earth in shameful condition. Science and technology can only aid us if we all work at preserving, conserving, and sharing resources."

Life . . . and Death

It may be a touchy subject, but when one deals with life in science, one needs to also consider death—of plants and animals at first. The attitude, information, and method of presentation will all carry great importance.

Reflection

Ned's father had just returned from a trip to the desert and had brought Ned a horny toad. He excitedly put it into a shoebox and brought it to school one morning. Every time he showed it to someone, it jumped out of the box and ran. The children would run after it and try to catch it, a successful procedure at first. The teacher told him to keep the lid on the box until she could bring a small cage from the storage shed—but while she was gone, another child asked to see it. Proudly, Ned took off the lid and away went the horny toad again. The children ran after it and an unfortunate accident occurred: It ran in front of Del, and Del's inability to avert it caused him to step on it! The children ran to the returning teacher and said, "We don't need a cage. Del stepped on the horny toad and killed it—and we don't like Del anymore." The teacher tried to console the children and wondered just how much involvement she should exhibit. In an instant, and without the teacher's participation, one child said, "Well, I guess we had better bury it." Another one said, "We'll need some flowers." Still another said, "I'll get a shovel from the shed to dig a hole." Before the eyes of the speechless teacher, the children had organized and initiated ideas from their own experiences. A spot was selected, a hole was dug, the horny toad was buried, and flowers were placed on the grave.

On this topic Furman (1990) writes,

> [C]oping with death depends on first knowing what dead means. A basic concept of death is best grasped, not when a loved one dies, but in situations of minimal emotional significance, such as with dead insects or worms. Since all children encounter such deaths very often and since even toddlers notice and ask about them, we can help them by utilizing their experiences and interest instead of averting our or their eyes. Dead means the lasting end to signs of life. . . . (p. 16)

> Plants provide the most prevalent, accessible and emotionally neutral opportunities to learn about life and death . . . sweet potato in water, orange and grapefruit seeds, popcorn, top of carrot, beans in wet cotton. (p. 17)

With plants, children can learn about isolated experiences (planting seeds, watching plants grow, appreciation of product) and about the whole life cycle. With insects, young children can learn about their birth, care, habits, protection, and functions without needing to destroy them or be afraid of them. Of course, caution needs to be exercised when safety and health are involved. We also need to help young children value life—why pull every flower or stomp on every bug?

Adults must be very careful with the words and ideas they use when discussing death with young children, for, as just stated, children use their own experiences as references. Words like *old, sleeping, sick, tired,* and so on mean very different things to children. "Grandma is old." "If I go to sleep (or get sick or tired), will I not wake up (or will I die)?" How do young children relate to ideas such as *discard, replace, unwanted*? Do they apply to concepts about death?

Overview of Developmentally Appropriate Science

Developmentally appropriate science builds on children's curiosity and willingness to explore the things around them. It entails investigating phenomena facilitated by open-ended questions that encourage children to organize information and to reach their own conclusions. Following are some selected suggestions.

Science kits and curricula, with their attractive advertising and brilliant colors, should not give educators and parents a false sense of teaching "nature or the right way to teach young children" (Fenton, 1996, p. 10). Also, it is our job to be sure that each child's interactions with nature are safe and sensible.

Examining animal bones eliminates fear of confronting a live animal.

Ecology

Using good conservation policies in classrooms and centers can help children form environmentally sound lifestyles. Suggestions include durable dishes for food service rather than disposable ones; personal cloth towels instead of paper towels; saving paper scraps and other items for collages; turning off unneeded lights; prompt repairs of toys and equipment; and many other ways to protect our resources. Involving children in caring for living things (in gardening, composting, harvesting, and using food products) helps them practice responsibility and nurturing.

Along with some good ideas for seasonal nature, Galvin (1994) states, "To be a naturalist, all you need are curiosity, joy of exploration, and a desire to discover firsthand the wonders of nature. Young children are natural naturalists. Adults take a little longer" (p. 4).

Nature

People have a fundamental need to care for things outside themselves. This need can be met—and human life enriched—by caring for the natural world. A genuine concern for wild creatures and their habitats can promote great fulfillment in one's individual life and a sense of caring for other people (Wilson, 1995).

Books on the environment and ecology for children have greatly increased over the last decade. We should encourage children to be aware of environmental problems in conserving our resources, in loving nature, and in celebrating our earth (Dighe, 1993, p. 58). Walks in different types of weather, colors at different times of year, animals all around us, foliage in different stages, and other types of experiences are there for the taking. What are the assets and liabilities of nature around us? Are daily necessities such as farming, weather, water, and climate serious concerns? What are the most serious industry problems? Just look around the school and home environment to see how children could be encouraged to love and protect what is there.

Self-Expression

The arts are an extension of nature, culture, and education. "Encouraging children to express their interests and discoveries using art, music, dance, movement, and story-telling is one way to support and extend environmental learning" (Dighe, 1993, p. 61) and at the same time extend the child's learning environment and an encompassing education.

Water Play

Water play is basic raw material. It fosters curiosity, imagination, and experimentation (see Chapter 6 for other uses). The child has a natural affinity for water play indoors and outdoors.

Weather

When children study weather, informally and formally, they have many opportunities to use science process skills and to construct mathematical understandings in developmentally appropriate ways (Charlesworth & Lind, 1990). They learn to integrate science, math, and literacy in discovering and exploring weather (Bredekamp, 1987). Some activities they might participate in include gathering data and organizing study topics (rain and rainbows, clouds and precipitation, air and wind, the sun, and so on) (Huffman, 1996).

Water and air are simple elements but hold great fascination for young children.

Physical Science

See the section titled "Activities to Increase Awareness of Physical Science" later in this chapter.

As mentioned earlier in this text, the field of education is embracing a constructivist approach to early-childhood education. It moves children at all levels away from "one right answer" into the inquiry-based process, in which they construct learning through experience, research, and working cooperatively with others. Trained early-childhood educators provide children with a stimulating environment with opportunities and objects from which to "construct" learning. So it is with physical science. By handling, manipulating, reacting, combining, questioning, and other methods, children learn about their world. They experience, discover, and learn that while there may be one "right answer," this answer can lead them to further knowledge—memorization and rote answers are no longer conclusive.

Nor is physical knowledge limited to the science table. It happens in many ways, in many places, and in combination with other things. Every day, teachers can help children focus on exploration of the physical world by asking open-ended questions, extending children's thinking, and helping them build upon their experiences in developmentally appropriate ways.

The word *physics* itself brings fear into the hearts of many teachers and children. But it is fun and important, and it belongs in the early-childhood curriculum. It's true! "The pioneers in experiential learning through play—Lucy Sprague Mitchell, Caroline Pratt, Harriet Johnson, and John Dewey—were encouraging young children to explore objects in their physical world before the first half of the twentieth century (Pratt, 1924; Dewey, 1938; Johnson, 1972). Through the use of unit blocks, invented by Caroline Pratt, children gained experience with gravity, weight, balance, trial and error, the properties of matter, and the interaction of forces. Lucy Sprague Mitchell understood in the 1920s that children hone their spatial-relations skills by interacting with their environment. In *Young Geographers*, she writes about how children develop knowledge of their world through a process of discovery based on the relationships among facts of their physical environment (Mitchell, 1921/1971).

"In most classrooms," writes Sprung (1996), "science, particularly *physical* science, is not given equal importance with other areas of the curriculum. In too many classrooms the 'science area' is a table on which some shells or leaves are set out at the beginning of the year and remain, collecting dust, when summer vacation rolls around. For the most part, early childhood science curriculum revolves around plant and animal activities. While these activities are a very important part of science and are comfortable for most early childhood teachers to carry out, they are far too limited in scope to be considered a full-bodied curriculum" (p. 30).

Activities of physical science that are part of the curriculum include activities for children to discover the physical properties of objects using a process approach (Piaget, 1970). They are activities that encourage exploration through the manipulation of familiar everyday objects, such as water, sand, blocks, and rolling things. There is nothing esoteric about these activities. In fact, they are part of a long tradition in progressive early-childhood education (Sprung, 1996).

Reflection

The following quotes are from Bess-Gene Holt, a lifetime promoter of science with young children, and whose love for and dedication to science will influence teachers forever:

"I believe it is crucial to educate children in developmentally appropriate ways, and harmful to all of us and the world we live in to do otherwise. I believe science holds a special place in that process. I believe we are passing, to children, responsibility for a 21st Century Earth in shameful condition. Science and technology can only aid us if we all work at preserving, conserving, and sharing resources. . . . The clearer, more sensible, and happier science experiences and learnings are, the more likely children are to understand, cope with, and enjoy their lives in the world immediately and in the future" (pp. 12–13).

"Science is a way of doing things and solving problems. It is a style that leads a person to wonder, to seek, to discover, to know, and then to wonder anew. It is a style in which good feelings of joy, excitement, and beauty accompany these active mental and physical interactions with one's world. Not only children but adults can experience science. It is a way of life" (p. 18).

"Science experiences add momentum to our goal of helping children understand, enjoy, and cope with their lives and their environments in the present and in the future" (p. 5).

"Some attitudes in adults can certainly stop or slow down children's science inquiries. Very few young children have these obstacles in their heads. Far too many teachers do—and they can be contagious attitudes that ought to be classified as dangerous contaminants of effective science education" (p. 5).

"We should be very sensitive to establishing a nonsexist science approach for young children" (p. 5).

"[K]nowledge makes for more sensible behavior than ignorance" (p. 6).

"'[P]ersonal ecology' is the individual child interrelating, interweaving, and interacting with the phenomena that make up his own environment" (p. 118).

ROLE OF THE ADULT

Attitudes in adults can certainly stop, slow down, or give encouragement to children's science inquiries. Taking cues from adults, children can feel excited or frightened about happenings in their environment.

An atmosphere of wonder can be created, nourished, and sustained in young children when adults and teachers do the following:

- be sensitive, prompt, and responsible to voiced and unvoiced needs of children.
- lovingly hold and cuddle their child sufficiently that they both feel mutual comfort and joy.
- regularly show (model) their surprise, interest, and attraction to the natural world and its happenings.
- because they are close to the daily life of the child, interact with the child and her world with evident interest, spontaneous humor, and joy.
- encourage children to freely experiment, taste, feel, hear, see, explore, and get into things that are interesting and safe.
- show their pleasure and delight and create novelty in what otherwise would be life's daily mundane chores and routines.
- find something good about the mistakes children will make as they grow and learn.
- be flexible enough to postpone their planned activities from time to time to let a child's creative idea or direction lead the way.
- ask probing questions to encourage children to be successful observers (Klein, 1991).
- assist preschool children as they *communicate* and describe their observations with written and spoken language (Klein, 1991).
- provide social knowledge by reading books and sharing information in response to children's questions (Klein, 1991).
- construct an environment that supports scientific inquiry and experimentation (Klein, 1991).
- let children design curriculum through a collaborative effort in sharing ideas, planning activities, collecting materials, and exploring resources (Klein, 1991).

In order for the teacher to stimulate children to explore, investigate, and question, the teacher needs to have an inquiring mind, have a positive attitude toward curiosity and questioning, be knowledgeable and able to communicate on the level of the children, and feel informed.

In scientific discovery, teachers need to encourage the use of language in predicting, discussing, experimenting, and evaluating. In doing so, they must consider the child's level of maturity, his past experiences, his interests, his misconceptions, and his present and familiar concepts; they should be multisensory, firsthand, spontaneous, integrated, accurate, concrete, relevant, explained simply, and repeated.

Perry and Rivkin (1992) offer a two-part perspective on getting started on good science for children and teachers. In Part I they suggest ways of creating an inquiry program that contains three phases: teacher-planned tasks, child-initiated learning

With new and frequent discoveries, children are becoming more interested in dinosaurs.

("messing-about time"), and the "pull-together stage"—"sometimes teachers are the learners, and the children are our teachers" (p. 12). Part II allows for *teachers* to further read, think, and apply ideas as they appear.

Teachers and Science Curriculum

To help children have a broad understanding of science, teachers can easily use various areas of the curriculum to support firsthand experiences and increased knowledge.

Early-childhood educators should not feel intimidated by nature education. If they think they know too little about it, they can prepare in such simple ways as bringing in different items from nature (especially those that pertain to their area); growing plants from seeds, bulbs, or sprouts; posting interesting pictures; acquiring good books; taking walks around the center—stopping to examine trees, bark, insects, and foliage; picking up trash; visiting with a gardener or groundskeeper; watering and caring for plants and animals; and other things of interest in the area. The Science and Nature Library, available through Lakeshore Learning Materials (2695 E. Dominguez Street, Carson, CA 90749; (800) 421-5354) is an excellent source—included are six different books inviting children to meet a busy spider, watch tadpoles transform into frogs, learn about the rain forest, and explore the five senses.

Through observation, interaction, and study, the adult can determine appropriate kinds of activities for young children. Essentially the following should be considered:

1. The adult's personal attitude toward science
2. Activities that are neither too hard nor too easy

3. Activities that interest particular children

4. Activities that are best done individually (one's own way and pace) and some that are best done in small groups (cooperation without intimidation)

5. Giving choices between two activities

6. Timely interests (holidays, community, seasons)

7. Amount and kind of supervision needed, including safety factors—not to taste unless approved, use of safety equipment, preventing and/or handling accidents

8. The purpose, goals, and benefits of the activity

Check the Environment for Learning Possibilities

Consider teacher, child, home, and community involvement:

1. Is there a center for science and mathematics?

2. Are there libraries and other resources for science and mathematics?

3. Are there live plants and animals?

4. Are there hands-on/minds-on exploration opportunities (construction materials, supplies, running water, time allowances, peers, projects, books, and other equipment [calculators, microscopes, hand lenses, computers])?

5. Is there time to explore? Research indicates that young children require thirty to fifty minutes of free play/independent exploration time in order to fully engage in these types of environments (Johnson, Christie, & Yawkey, 1987). NAEYC (Bredekamp, 1987) and the National Council for Teachers of Mathematics (NCTM, 1989) support the strategy of providing large blocks of time for children to engage in meaningful learning, which includes play and exploration of materials as well as structured learning experiences. "Allowing children to move freely about the classroom, initiating learning experiences in a variety of ways, requires a movement away from rigid scheduling of discrete, subject-driven activities to an integrated, holistic view of curriculum, development, and learning" (Patton & Kokoski, 1996).

6. Is there encouragement for in-depth study rather than fleeting interests?

7. Are other subject areas combined with science and mathematics (literature, dramatic play, outdoor activities, and so on)?

8. How do you encourage some of the ideas for this "center" to come from the children? "A strategy for ensuring that every child has access to science, mathematics, and technology disciplines is for teachers to use an inclusive planning process" (Nelson & Frederick, 1994).

9. How do you encourage less-interested or shy children so that the area is utilized by *all* children?

10. Is this "center" available at all times for new or continued exploration?

11. How could you use webbing to include children and science in a variety of fun, meaningful experiences? (Construct a web and label only parts of it. Ask the children to help you fill in the blanks.)

12. Teachers: *Think and get excited!* Example: "What could you tell me about _____ ?" The teacher asks leading questions, and the children supply information. Then combine the information into a teacher-child web: language arts, music, art, dramatic play, social studies, sensory play, field trips or

Ladybugs are interesting and friendly.

speakers, math, parent involvement, science, food/nutrition leading up to a tasting party. (Specific information, related to each curriculum area, can provide interesting choices for the teacher to consider.)

13. How do you tie indoor activities with an outdoor or natural habitat (playground, field trip, and so on) to make it more meaningful? Is there a local "real" experience?

14. How do you keep parents informed as to classroom activities and how do you encourage them to further the experience? Is there provision for follow-up (classroom or community exhibits), home use, outside resources (books, pictures), and spin-offs?

15. How do you handle questions that you cannot answer immediately? (This requires careful, honest, and resourceful answers! Think about it very carefully!) Do you try to bluff your way? Do you say, "Let's find out together"—and then do so? Do you say, "I'm not sure but I will find out and let you know"—*and then do so*?

How to Change Attitudes toward Science

What are my suggestions for a turnaround?

1. Make science an everyday, exciting, hands-on experience.

2. Remove the stigma that science is hard and only for the bright students.

3. Encourage *all* children (regardless of sex, socioeconomic status, culture, age, or any other category) to be curious, to investigate, to explore, to revise and retry, to question, to seek solutions, and to understand their environment and the people around them.

4. Inform parents of ways to involve young children in activities and actions that help children protect and enhance their environment rather than destroy and distrust it.

5. Instill in children that science is a way of life and, therefore, understanding it will bring joy and satisfaction in daily life.

6. Help teachers and parents be aware of science opportunities in the daily environment—*not make learning (especially science) something that is separate, distasteful, boring, regimented, difficult, and competitive.*

7. Carefully plan curricula that include opportunities for children of all interests and abilities to become interested in spontaneous and/or planned scientific exploration—resulting in better understanding, more willingness to explore, and an increased feeling of self-worth.

8. Increase language opportunities for young children—exposure to print (books to look at and hear, magazines to peruse), listening experiences (others, tapes, stories), and casual and formal discussions with peers and adults. Adults can initiate conversations, but would probably be more useful if they provide a stimulating environment and respond to the children's needs vocally and physically.

VALUES FOR CHILDREN

Refer to Table 8.1.

In review: Through science experiences, children build confidence in themselves and in their environment; gain necessary firsthand experiences; develop basic concepts; increase observation skills; receive opportunities to use tools, equipment, and familiar materials; receive aid in problem solving; stimulate their curiosity for exploration and discovery while increasing basic knowledge; develop sensory, physical, emotional, intellectual, spiritual, and social attributes; develop language through increased vocabulary and an opportunity to ask and answer questions; and obtain many unnamed or child-specific values.

Schultz (1985) adds:

> We cannot expect children to grow up valuing trees, spiders, and snakes without positive experiences that touch them personally. Young children's direct contacts with nature awaken them to its beauty and the pleasure it offers. . . . And the children who had this (science) hands-on experience improved 80 percent in the area of science concepts, 167 percent in science vocabulary, and 15 percent in perceptual skills over their pre-instruction scores. Informally, I noticed that both teachers' and children's fear of animals decreased as their interest rose. (p. 49)

Still another value is perceived by Henniger (1987): "Young men and women with sound math and science understandings have many job opportunities and career choices unavailable to others" (p. 167).

Piaget (Elkind, 1981) effectively summarizes the challenge as follows:

> The principal goal of education is to create men who are capable of doing new things, not simply repeating what other generations have done . . . men who are creative, inventive and discoverers. The second goal of education is to form minds which can be

Table 8.1
Gains from Science Experiences in Early-Childhood Curriculum

WHO?	HOW?
Children can gain:	Experiences in problem solving, social skills, creative thinking, spatial relations, decision making, observation, sorting, categorizing, curriculum knowledge, estimating—all essential skills for later success in science
	Self-confidence when they can successfully manipulate objects in the physical world
	Skills in adaptive behavior to outdoor settings (balance, walking through different areas—snow, mud, fields)
	Survival skills
	Aesthetic development: sensitivity to beauty, seasonal changes, moisture, birds and animals; "beauty is not just in what can be seen but is present, also, in what can be touched, felt, and listened to" (Wilson, 1995)
	Cognitive development
	Skills in observing, listening, and responding to divergent information
	Communication skills: something to talk about
	Sensorimotor development: natural sights
	Understanding of space relationships (crawl under, jump over, slip through)
	Socioemotional development: caring for things outside themselves
	Improved personal and social behaviors
	(Sources: ideas from Wilson (1995), Sprung (1996), and present author.
Teachers can gain:	A sense of empowerment (overcoming a fear of science)
	Sharing of knowledge with children
	Security of not having to have all of the "right answers"
	Confidence ("it becomes apparent how interdisciplinary the activities are and what a boost they can give to the entire curriculum. New science activities can be a wonderful remedy for the midyear doldrums" (Sprung, 1996, p. 31)
Parents can gain:	An understanding of the importance of science for their children's futures and their role as teachers within the home
	Awareness that the science they know and use every day can become home-learning activities to do with their children
	Awareness of how their involvement plays an important role in children's success in school
	More involvement in their child's school education
	Satisfaction in everyday home activities, which are full of science learning: greasy pots become an experiment in how oil floats on top of water; storage (conservation); recycling; waste disposal; wheels, motors, and so on
	"Parents should know that their children's livelihoods may depend on how much math and science they know. Now, while the kids are in school, is the time for them to learn" (Sagan, 1989, p. 6)

Table 8.1
continued

WHO?	HOW?
Everybody wins because of:	Better trained individuals
	More confidence in "science" activities
	More knowledge and security in everyday lives
	More trust in each other to be better citizens (recycling, product uses, better use of their money and environment)
	Solutions to home/work problems
	"We live in a society exquisitely dependent on technology, in which hardly anybody knows anything about science and technology. This is a clear prescription for disaster" (Sagan, 1989, p. 6).
	Reread the statistics at the beginning of this chapter. Then apply them to the information in this table. How could we further improve our lives, our society, and our world?

critical, can verify, and not accept everything they are offered. The great danger today is of slogans, collective opinions, ready-made trends of thought. We have to be able to resist individually, to criticize, to distinguish between what is proven and what is not. So we need pupils who are active, who learn early to find out by themselves, partly by their own spontaneous activity and partly through materials we set up for them. We learn early to tell what is verifiable and what is simply the first idea to come to them. (p. 29)

Smith (1987) reports Piaget's findings concerning young children and science:

For Piaget, the foundation upon which all intellectual development takes place is physical knowledge, knowledge that comes from objects. This includes information about the properties of objects (their shape, size, textures, color, odor), as well as knowledge about how objects react to different actions on them (they roll, bounce, sink, slide, dry up). Children construct physical knowledge by acting on objects—feeling, tasting, smelling, seeing, and hearing them. They cause objects to move—throwing, banging, blowing, pushing, and pulling them, and they observe changes that take place in objects when they are heated, cooled, mixed together, or changed in some other way. As physical knowledge develops, children become better able to establish relationships (comparing, classifying, ordering) between and among the objects they act upon. Such relationships (logicomathematical knowledge according to Piaget) are essential for the emergence of logical, flexible thought processes. (p. 35)

Teaching science to young children can be easy, inexpensive, and rewarding. For example, a teacher could have a portable science kit ready to take out with the children on walks, on field trips, or just in the play yard. Contents of the kit depend on where the children are going, their ages, and what you are trying to investigate. Some suggestions are a magnifying glass, a tape measure, a flashlight, string, binoculars, plastic bags and ties, clear jars and other unbreakable containers, a small garden trowel or large sturdy spoons, plastic bags for treasures, and paper and pencils for note taking.

ACTIVITIES TO INCREASE AWARENESS OF BIOLOGICAL SCIENCE

Biological science is the study of plant and animal life. In this chapter, for ease in planning, the activities are divided into four areas: animals (broad definition), people, plants, and food. Examples of these four areas are also found in other chapters as they relate to different curriculum topics. Emphasis is placed on making experiences meaningful and appropriate for the children who participate.

Animals

- Have a small box with pictures of animals and also a duplicate of each cut into a silhouette from black paper. Children match the animal with its shadow.
- Make animal shadow pictures on a screen, using a strong light and imagination.
- Sing "Over in the Meadow."
- Make or purchase an ant farm or observe ants in their natural setting.
- Have animals in the classroom often. Teach about the care and characteristics of each. Some good classroom pets are ants, butterflies, caterpillars, earthworms, frogs, gerbils, goldfish, guinea pigs, hamsters, and hermit crabs. On special occasions, hatch eggs or bring in baby animals (a goat, lamb, rabbit, or other available animals).
- Build an insect collection in boxes or jars. Discuss local insects (bees, mosquitoes, fleas, and so on).
- Collect ants, ladybugs, caterpillars, earthworms, and butterflies from the play yard.

Sample Miniplan Involving Animals

Theme

Covering of animals

Ideas to Emphasize

1. Animals have specific body coverings.
2. Each type of covering feels different when touched.
3. These coverings help the animal.

Learning Activities

If possible, take the children to a nearby farm to observe animals. If this is not possible, bring tame caged animals to school. Talk about different coverings: hair on a horse or dog, fur on a rabbit, feathers on a chicken or other bird, wool on a lamb, a shell on a turtle, and scales on a fish. (If animals are not available, be sure to have some good samples of these coverings for the children to feel and examine.) Use the number of coverings you feel are appropriate for the children you are teaching—you can use this theme for several days. Discuss each type of covering, its color, how it helps the animal, how it feels, how it differs from other coverings, where the animal lives, uses of coverings to people, and other facts. Give the children time to ask and answer questions and make comments. At the end of the discussion, have pictures of animals with both similar and dissimilar coverings. Let the children group the pictures according to similar coverings.

- Take a walk and observe birds, insects, and animals common to the community.
- Make a bird bath or feeder (using a milk carton).
- Make self-correcting card games: (1) the same animals on two different cards for matching; (2) pictures of an animal and its habitat for matching; and (3) classifications of animals, such as those that fly or have four legs.
- Make a net out of a nylon stocking. Go bug-catching.
- Borrow a pet from a family, a farm, or a pet store. Make sure the animal is tame and free of disease. (A pet show of animals from home may be inadvisable because some animals do not get along!)
- When possible, bring in a guest who has an unusual pet or raises animals.
- Observe or discuss the characteristic movement of animals (some swim, some fly, some hop, and so on).
- Observe or discuss physical characteristics of various animals (for example, flippers, wings, webfeet, claws, or number of legs).
- Observe or discuss the diet of various animals (for example, hay, grain, milk, carrots, or nuts).
- Observe and discuss birth, nutrition, and habits of animals or insects.
- Observe frogs in various stages, from egg to tadpole to frog.
- Observe and discuss various housing for animals, such as a nest, hole, house, or cage.
- Observe animals with their young (care and feeding).
- Imitate animal sounds.
- Learn the names of adult male and female animals and babies.
- Discuss how animals protect themselves through camouflage, hibernation, claws, odor, horns, or stingers.
- If possible, feel the covering of various animals (for example, shell, fur, wool, skin, feathers).
- Observe animals at work (mule, bee, ant, spider, beaver, squirrel, or horse).
- Care for animals at the center or home by cleaning cages, feeding, and watering (this increases self-reliance). Discuss ways animals are cared for and limits in handling them.
- Using heavy paper, make a series of pictures about an animal, with each picture emphasizing a different part of the animal, such as the head, ears, or feet. Make identical pictures on cards for the children to match, to chart, or to form a puzzle.
- Observe wild animals at a park or zoo, if possible.
- Visit a ranch or farm to see poultry, sheep, cattle, or dairy animals.
- Rather than discussing general characteristics of animals, such as habitat, coverings, and diet, discuss many characteristics about one animal at a time (for example, where a cow lives, information about its calf, and sounds it makes).
- Make feeding places for birds in your play yard.
- Bring in a variety of bird nests.
- Catch a caterpillar, then watch it spin a cocoon and eventually emerge as a butterfly.

In a familiar and quiet setting, young children are more likely to interact with a live animal.

People

See also Chapter 10 for more information.

○ Focus on helping the children increase their self-image: draw an outline around each child's body and let him color or finish it; let the children make a "me" puppet; provide a place to make a mural of handprints and footprints; let the children participate in a group experience, such as holding visual aids for a story or song, introducing a toy, or choosing an activity.

○ Discuss things the children can do now that they could not do when younger or smaller.

○ Make a chart and show how the human body works.

○ Display photographs of the children at their eye level.

○ Weigh and measure each child. Post the chart.

○ Observe different characteristics of people (for example, hair, eye, and skin coloring; height, weight, sex). Talk about special characteristics of each child.

○ Give children some enjoyable, stimulating sensory experiences.

○ Help children recognize and appreciate different physical characteristics of children and adults. Discuss skills. Encourage development of a positive self-attitude.

○ Give children some quality experiences with older people (for example, grandparents, community workers, and so on).

○ Use a real skeleton or a replica to talk about bones.

○ Learn about such different parts of the body as the digestive tract, heart, tongue, hair, and eyes.

○ Stimulate the five senses (see Chapter 6).

- Visit a local health center, doctor's office, or hospital.
- Invite a resource person, such as a doctor or nurse.
- Visit community helpers or invite them to your classroom.
- Discuss the different places people live, such as apartments, houses, trailers, and dormitories, and then visit some of them.
- Discuss ways to stay healthy (for example, proper nutrition, clothing, rest).
- Observe someone with a cast on. Discuss the healing process.
- Observe a mother bathing, feeding, or dressing a baby.
- Discuss and enact roles of various family members.
- Make a family portrait by cutting pictures from magazines and pasting them on construction paper or paper plates.
- Throughout the day, help children solve problems through verbalization, cooperation, and sharing.
- Involve the children in establishing guidelines for behavior.
- Talk about common emotions. "How did it make you feel?" "How did it make someone else feel?" "What can we do to help someone feel happy?" "What should we do when someone is unhappy?"

Sample Miniplan Involving People

Theme

Sounds around us

Ideas to Emphasize

1. We hear through our ears.
2. Sounds are all around us.
3. Sounds help us identify people and things.

Learning Activities

1. Have the children place their hands over their eyes. Talk to them. Ask them if they can hear you. Ask them to put their hands over their mouths. Can they hear you? Have them put their hands over their ears. Can they still hear you? Discuss the use of ears.

2. Play a tape of familiar sounds while the children listen. Include sounds that are normal in the home, such as an alarm clock, brushing teeth, going downstairs, preparing breakfast, running water, beating or mixing, setting the table, a crying baby, pet noises, radio or television, a ringing telephone or doorbell, opening and closing a door, a running car, typing, and so on. Arrange the sounds in logical sequence so they can easily be used as part of a story. The second time the tape is played, stop it after each sound while the children discuss it. Be accepting of their ideas. Encourage them to make sounds they heard earlier in the day and let the other children guess what the sound represents. Also talk about how certain sounds protect us, such as those from smoke alarms, horns, sirens, or bells.

3. Play a game making and identifying the sounds of animals, transportation, occupations, and so on.

- Use a large hand mirror for the children to see their facial expressions for different emotions. Have at least one full-length mirror.
- Talk about the importance of good mental hygiene: thinking good thoughts, positive relationships, helpfulness instead of negativity.

Plants and Nature

- Talk about using plants for food, clothing, protection, beauty, and health.
- Talk about different ways to start plants from bulbs, seeds, sets, slips, or parts of the produce (potato).
- Observe and discuss trees and shrubs during different parts of the year.
- Prepare soil and plant a garden. Seeds for beans, melons, pumpkins, grass, and radishes germinate easily.
- If outdoor space is unavailable, plant a garden inside the classroom in a water table, pots, milk cartons, cans, jars, egg cartons, or paper cups.
- When possible, harvest, prepare, and use produce grown at school.
- Use *The Carrot Seed,* a story and record by Ruth Krauss.
- Soak bean seeds overnight, then open and examine them with a magnifying glass. Plant some beans against a glass container. Watch them grow, roots down, stem up.
- Observe how plants grow from seeds inside fruit (avocado, orange, apple). Note that they require light and water and grow toward the source of light. Also observe how some seeds grow faster than others. Sprout seeds for snacks, such as alfalfa, mung beans, soybeans, and wheat.
- Seal seeds and a picture of the produce in a small plastic bag. Have a second bag of the same seeds and picture separately. Have the children match them.

Caring for plants gives the child a sense of responsibility.

- Prepare a nature table using plants and produce. Change often, or use produce for snacks or lunch.
- Gather different kinds of seeds (fruit, vegetable, weed).
- Observe changes in nature during different seasons.
- Discuss the cycle of a tree and its uses for lumber and paper.
- Plant and observe growth of seeds in a terrarium.
- Have plants in the classroom. Let the children help care for them.
- Talk about and eat the different parts of the plant, such as seeds (peas, beans, corn, peanuts), roots (carrots, radishes, beets, onions, potatoes), stems (celery, asparagus, rhubarb), leaves (lettuce, cabbage, spinach), blossoms (broccoli, cauliflower), and fruit (apples, berries, grapes). Watch for allergies when using seeds and food.
- Observe the growth of plants in water (tops of carrots or turnips, bird seed on a damp sponge, sweet or white potato in a jar).
- With heavy paper or tag board make a series of pictures about a plant, each picture emphasizing a different part (blossom, root, leaf, or stem). Place pictures on a chart, and make individual cards identical to those on the chart. Children match the cards to the chart or form a puzzle.
- Go on nature walks often. Take a sack for gathering treasures to make a collage.
- Visit a plant nursery or greenhouse.
- Provide a variety of nuts. Let the children sort them by kinds and learn their names. Help them crack and taste the different kinds of nuts. Some may need to be roasted. Watch for allergies when serving nuts.
- Grow herbs and seasonings.

Sample Miniplan Involving Plants

Theme

Beans

Ideas to Emphasize

1. Bean seeds are usually larger than other seeds.
2. Beans grow on a vine or stem.
3. Beans are prepared for eating in different ways. Sprouts are eaten fresh while green beans are usually cooked. Dried beans need to be soaked and cooked before eating.

Learning Activities

Bean seeds, along with a variety of other seeds, such as beet, radish, carrot, and tomato, are placed on the science table. The teacher points out characteristics of the various seeds, and the children look at the seeds through a magnifying glass. During art, the seeds are used in a collage. An appropriate bean dish (for example, chili or string or lima beans) is served for lunch, and sprouts or bean salad for a snack. Bean seeds for sprouting and planting are soaked overnight. The children plant the beans in a terrarium or in paper cups to take home. Seeds for sprouting are placed in wire or plastic containers. The children care for the plants, noting daily changes.

- ○ Observe landscaping in your play yard.
- ○ Put a stalk of celery in a bottle containing water and food coloring. Observe how the water is carried to the leaves.
- ○ Purchase fresh cobs of popcorn. Let it dry; then pop it.
- ○ Purchase and observe Indian corn.
- ○ *Multicultural experience:* Provide a means of learning about different types of growth and climates—tropical (jungle), arid (desert), mountainous (forest), oceanic (rivers, seas, lakes), the local conditions, and others of interest.

Food

- ○ Discuss the different tastes of food, such as sour, sweet, bitter, and salty. Show a picture or replica of the tongue and point out where these different tastes are located.
- ○ Discuss different ways food grows—fish, shrimp, crab, oysters, and rice in water; apples and pears on trees; potatoes, carrots, and peanuts underground; and tomatoes and corn aboveground. (See the preceding section, "Plants and Nature.")
- ○ Let the children help prepare fruits and vegetables for lunch or a snack.
- ○ Observe differences in fruits and vegetables (color, taste, peeling, texture, and moisture).
- ○ Taste fruits and vegetables in various forms (raw, cooked, or as juice).
- ○ Experiment with coconut (husk, shell, liquid, chunks, shredded, toasted).
- ○ Prepare food using dairy products (ice cream, butter, pudding, cottage cheese, cheese).
- ○ Bake cookies, bread, and pies.
- ○ Use water to make soup and gelatin and to boil corn.
- ○ Observe a raw egg and see the difference when eggs are soft-boiled, hard-boiled, or fried.
- ○ Pop popcorn. Discuss how heat makes the kernel expand.
- ○ Make something for lunch or a snack (applesauce, spaghetti, sandwiches, fruit or vegetable plate).
- ○ Provide empty food containers to stimulate interest in the domestic area.
- ○ Use the food pyramid to discuss nutrition.
- ○ Provide a certain food commodity in various forms, such as sugar (raw, refined, brown, powdered) or wheat (grains, cracked, flour).
- ○ Examine food in various stages (for example, potato as seed, potato for eating, potato sprouting).
- ○ Purchase (or grow) squash or pumpkins. Eat the produce but save and dry the seeds. Roast and eat some of the seeds; plant others.
- ○ Purchase some raw peanuts. Shell and roast them. Make peanut butter. Watch for allergies when serving nuts.
- ○ Make a drying frame and dry some fruit. Make fruit leather.
- ○ Involve the five senses with food (smell different fruits and vegetables both raw and cooked; touch the various peelings; touch the food after it has been cooked; taste food as ingredients, and then cooked; sample foods that look alike but taste different, such as apple, pear, onion, turnip, radish, and white potato; compare peelings and meat of fruit and vegetables).

Sample Miniplan Involving Food

Theme

Apples

Ideas to Emphasize

1. Apples are prepared for eating in different ways.
2. Apples are green, yellow, or red.
3. Apples grow on trees.
4. An apple has different parts.

Learning Activities

Pictures of apples in different forms are placed on the bulletin board. A low table nearby, washed and covered with butcher paper, contains apples of different colors and sizes. With the children, the teacher discusses how apples are grown, their various colors, different ways they are eaten, and the kind of covering. Children wash their hands. Under careful supervision, the teacher and children peel, core, and cut the apples. The apples are placed in an electric saucepan, cooked, and served for a snack.

- Use household tools (grinder, peeler, beater, mixer).
- *Multicultural experience:* Provide a sensory table that features textures and smells from around the world (cinnamon, curry, pepper, extracts). Include coffee beans, grains, whole nuts, bark, dry leaves, kinds of flour, and raw cotton.

See Chapter 11 for further information on food.

ACTIVITIES TO INCREASE AWARENESS OF PHYSICAL SCIENCE

Physical science is the study of material things and their properties and reactions when they are changed or combined. It includes areas such as astronomy, chemistry, engineering, geology, physics, and other related fields. These subjects are difficult to teach to young children because they are more abstract than other sciences; nevertheless, children should be exposed to physical science. Children are natural explorers and are curious about many things. It is appropriate for the teacher to utilize the scientific method: observe the children, provide experiences to which they can relate, help them ask and answer questions, encourage their exploration, help them come up with alternate solutions, and introduce good terms and help the children practice them. Be excited yourself!

Here are some suggested activities. Use, modify, or discard them as you feel appropriate for your children.

Astronomy and Meteorology

Astronomy is especially difficult to teach at school because most observable activity occurs at night; however, you may want to discuss the warmth and light from the sun and encourage the children to notice sunsets and the stars and moon at night.

A visit to a planetarium is not the best for young children; they are often fearful when lights are turned off in an unfamiliar place. However, they may be interested in watching television reports about space exploration.

Cloud formations can be discussed and observed.

Chemistry

- Have the children mix things together and see the results. Even sand and water is of interest to them.
- Provide experiences to see how heat affects cooking, wearing apparel, and activities.
- Observe how light changes things (growth, warmth, appearance).
- Discuss the use of light (flashlight, lamp, sun, candle, sundial, shadows).
- Talk about the seasons and how people and animals prepare for them; note how the landscape changes.
- Observe the difference in temperature in the shade and in the sun, or during different seasons of the year.
- Investigate water. (See also Chapter 6.) It evaporates, cleans, changes things (rocks, sand), comes in different forms (liquid, gas, solid), is used for many purposes (mixing paint, drinking, play), and can be an excellent emotional release. Following are some suggested uses of water:

Siphon from one container to another.

Float objects (soap, toys, wood, metals); show effects of size and weight.

Pour water into different-shaped containers and note that the water takes the shape of the container.

Colored water could be poured into different clear containers and the children can note how the water changes color when they are poured together.

Pour warm water into four different small jars and provide bowls with sugar in one, salt in one, sand in one, and oil in one. Spoon one ingredient into each jar, shake the jar and let it set 30 seconds. Spoon another ingredient into another jar and repeat the procedure until all four items have been used. Note the differences in the four solutions (salt and sugar dissolve, sand sinks, oil forms droplets which then rise to top). Introduce appropriate terms about what is happening.

Water absorption: Give each child a sponge on a plate, an eyedropper, and a small container of water. The child drops water onto the sponge. When she is ready, she squeezes the water to measure how much water has been absorbed by the sponge, repeating the process as long as the child wishes. It appears that the sponge is drinking the water.

Blow bubbles:

Bubbles are bits of air or gas trapped inside a liquid ball. The surface of a bubble is very thin. Bubbles are particularly fragile when a dry object touches them. That's because soap film tends to stick to the object, which puts a strain on the bubble. So if you want your bubbles to last longer, keep everything wet, even the sides of the drinking straw. (Paulu & Martin, 1992, p. 17)

Observe reflections.

Wash and dry doll clothes (evaporation).

Build dams and canals.

Feel the force as water comes from the tap.

Observe evaporation by marking the water level in a pan and checking it daily.

Build a snowman; make snow angels.

Freeze ice, then watch it melt; use ice to set gelatin.

Stretch various materials (fabrics, plastic, paper, rubber) over a can and pour water over it. Show that water goes through some things easier than others.

Introduce the terms *porous* and *nonporous*. Allow experimentation.

Water plants.

Discuss wearing apparel for water (boots, umbrella, cover-ups).

Clean with water. Talk about absorption.

Observe the moisture on a glass of ice water on a hot day.

Boil water to produce steam.

Pour water through a funnel or from one container to another.

Prepare creative materials.

Drink water.

Prepare food and cook it.

Change the consistency of materials by changing the amount of water.

Play in water (sail boats, wash self or toys).

Talk about conservation, pollution, recycling.

Using different-sized cups or containers, have children pour water back and forth for experience in varying volume.

With different amounts of water in glasses or jars, have a child gently tap the glass with a spoon for different musical tones.

Have the children determine objects that would sink or float.

Make crystals (see "Sample Miniplan Involving Physical Science").

○ Make a discovery chart. As children are exposed to chemistry, they will discover different things about it. Help them make and post a chart of their new findings. Use their ideas in a group setting.

Geography

See Chapter 10 for more information.

Geology

- Discuss various kinds of rocks.
- Discuss various fuels and methods of heating (coal, oil, gas, electricity, steam, solar).
- Provide a museum or nature shelf with rocks, shells, and cones.
- On a science table, provide different kinds of soil, such as sand, clay, and volcanic ash. Place a magnifying glass nearby.
- Bring in a collection of rocks. Note how the rock changes color when it is wet.
- Examine pieces of coal with a magnifying glass.
- Point out and discuss the topography of your area (hills, mountains, valleys).
- Take field trips to local geological sites.
- Examine the properties of sand (varying volume, consistency with and without use of water).
- Notice the different surfaces of the play yard (sand, dirt, grass, asphalt, concrete). Discuss their uses.
- Take local field trips noting various geological formations.
- Make a discovery chart. As children are exposed to geology, they will discover different things about it. Help them make and post a chart of their new findings. Also use the chart in a group setting.

Physics

(See the section titled "Activities to Increase Awareness of Physical Science" later in this chapter.)

Many different types of science can be combined into one experience.

- Observe machines at work (dump truck, street sweeper, steamroller, garbage truck, derrick, steam shovel, farm, home).

- Familiarize children with gravity by placing a car on an inclined board or a wagon on a slope. Talk about roads.

- Talk about balance through use of blocks, a teeter-totter, and weights. Let children use their bodies in balancing.

- Discuss and have children participate in activities involving friction.

- Use a magnifying glass to examine various materials and objects.

- With the children, discover the use of a magnet and show things that are attracted and things that are not. Introduce, define, and experiment with new terms, such as *attract* and *repel*. Sprinkle pepper or lightweight visible material over water and watch it float. Dip small pieces of soap into the water, and watch the material go away from (be repelled by) the soap. Sprinkle sugar into the water, and watch the material float to (be attracted by) the sugar.

- Explore the uses of household tools and appliances (vacuum, eggbeater, mixer).

- Talk about various methods of communication (telephone, telegraph, radio, television, newspaper, magazine, letter).

- Use a magnifying glass to see what's hidden in soil or under leaves, what's on both sides of leaves, different patterns of snowflakes, and butterfly wings (Paulu & Martin, 1992).

- Make a game. Have the child focus on one dimension (color). When he knows this, add another dimension (shape). When he understands these, look for something that contains both the shape and color. Add another dimension, such as density (thick, thin). Have the child look for something that includes all three. Then add another (size), and look for all four. ("Look for something that is red, square, thin, and large.") Use only when the child is ready to combine dimensions.

- Observe shapes (round, square, oblong, triangular, hexagonal, octagonal, free-form); look for objects that are these shapes.

- Use a lever (for example, a claw hammer).

- Use wheels. Show how they aid in work, in play, and in the home (motors, pulleys, roller skates, toys, sewing machines, clocks).

- Provide substances and their opposites (wet and dry, long and short, hard and soft, hot and cold, sweet and sour, rough and smooth).

- Explore the weather (seasons, time of day, changes, temperature).

- Discuss how weather is influenced by sun, clouds, and wind.

- Observe and discuss fog (watch it move, lift); mist; rain (moisture it provides, appearance of sky, temperature); sun (warmth, light); frost; hail; snow. Talk about appropriate wearing apparel for different types of weather.

- Dress dolls or flannel board characters of children for different types of weather.

- Investigate the characteristics of snow (taste, feel, appearance).

- Make a simple chart that shows snow, rain, sun, and wind. An arrow can be turned to indicate the current weather.
- Discuss wind. Use kites, pinwheels, or balloons (with caution). Watch smoke. Observe dry leaves when the wind blows. Watch a weather vane or wind sock. Discuss the strength of wind.
- Explore air (movement made by a fan, how air occupies space but is unseen). Use a paper bag, balloon (with caution), pinwheel, whistle, parachute, weather vane, tire pump, and bubbles.

Sample Miniplan Involving Physical Science

Theme

Crystals

Ideas to Emphasize

1. Crystals are clear and angular in shape.
2. Crystals are found in the earth or can be made (jewelry, candy).

Learning Activities

1. The teacher shows the children different crystals and rocks. He explains what a crystal is and what things are crystals (sand, sugar, salt). Then he shows some crystals previously made. The children examine the crystals using a magnifying glass.
2. On another table are many objects. Some are crystals, some are not. The teacher helps the children identify the crystals.

- Use woodworking tools and materials.
- Discuss occupational tools and their uses.
- Bring in a camera (a box camera is good). Take pictures of the children. Talk about how the camera works.
- Bring in and explore lenses (a magnifying glass, an old box-type camera, binoculars, eyeglasses, a telescope, a jar with water in it).
- Investigate how water or air can cause pressure, as in a balloon, bottle, can, or parachute.
- Use a straw or medicine dropper to illustrate a vacuum being created as air is removed and another substance rushes in to fill space.
- Introduce vibration by using rubber bands, strings on a piano or other instrument, or a tuning fork.
- Go to a child's museum or aquarium.
- Build dams and canals.
- Provide scales, thermometers, prisms, and color paddles.
- Have an outdoor science area with boards and boxes, levers, wheels and axles, pendulums, and pulleys (clotheslines).

- Provide wind-up toys and objects (clocks) so that children can explore their workings.
- Help the children work with batteries, switches, bells, and lights.
- Provide gears and springs for exploration (alarm clock, gear-driven toys, music boxes).
- Acquire empty plastic gallon containers. Cut and use them as funnels, scoops, pots, vases or other containers, sieves, bug catchers, and so on (see Figure 8.1).
- Make a discovery chart. Through exposure, children will discover different things about physics. Help them make and post a chart of their new findings. Use the chart in a group setting.

TECHNOLOGY AND YOUNG CHILDREN

The use of computers with young children is a sensitive and controversial one. The basic question appears to be: Will the addition of computers to the classroom add to or detract from the desired development of the young child? The question involves performance, skills, language, socialization, creativity, self-image, and interest.

Some education specialists say that young children definitely should not be involved with computers; some advocate computer exposure in the classroom. Papert (1980), for example, says it is a means of developing intimate contact with an individual's thinking. Still others take the middle-of-the-road approach. Researchers list and discuss key issues regarding the cognitive stage of the child: socialization, isolation, real life experiences, and the "pushing" of children.

Figure 8.1
Empty plastic gallon bottles can be cut for funnels, scoops, pots, or sieves.

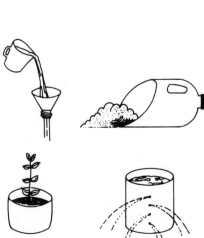

Many adults use computers on an individual or solitary basis. Would this also be true of children? Would they use fewer language and physical skills than in other activities? Would they expect to be entertained, or to seek the "one right answer"? Would adults and children see the computer as another means of pressure and preparation for future schooling? Would computer use emphasize a narrow or inappropriate view of the abilities of young children? Are there children who would prefer working with things (computers, for example) rather than people? Is there less or more of a threat to work with precise information or open-ended information? Is there a way to use computers as part of a program rather than *being* the program?

Many examples of developmentally appropriate programs have been given throughout this text. But how do they apply to computer use? First, a refresher about the DAP programs being age- and individual-appropriate. Sitting at a computer is a stationary, usually solitary, highly structured, and academic approach—somewhat uncommon for children under 6. Clements, Nastasi, and Swaminathan (1993) write, "Drill programs are not compatible with NAEYC curriculum guidelines" (p. 56), and "[W]hat we early childhood educators do the most with computers is what research and the NAEYC guidelines say we should do the *least*" (p. 57). One should recall information throughout the text dealing with too much too soon (Elkind, Katz, and others) and unnatural curriculum in the child's progression.

With reference to computers in the language arts areas of practice, talking, or writing, it has been found that placing computers in kindergartners' classrooms for several months significantly increases emerging reading skills; placing computers in the home as well yields greater gains.

An Overview of Recent Research

In reading the literature on computer advantages and disadvantages, one must pay close attention to the age of children in the study, the goal of the software, the teacher's preparedness with computers, availability of adults to assist the children, and the philosophy of the classroom.

One must answer questions for oneself about using computers with young children. Here are some questions to ponder:

1. Is the presence of computers in the classroom disruptive or enriching?
2. Do computers provide one or many values for young children?
3. How does computer use help enhance personal qualities in young children (self-esteem, autonomy, persistence, decision making, creativity, cooperation, socialization, and so on)?
4. When computers are available in the classroom, is there a decrease in the amount of time children spend in other activities?
5. Through familiarity with computers, are prereading and reading skills increased in young children? (Computer use is a part of language and cognitive development.)
6. If you were offered *one* choice, which would you select and why?
   a. A computer in the classroom for young children
   b. A computer for teacher use
   c. A classroom aide

NAEYC's guidelines for early-childhood curriculum accept the Piagetian notion that children construct knowledge through interaction with materials and people (NAEYC & NAECS/SDE, 1991). Are computers to be included among these materials? Some critics think computers are not concrete and that even shape drawing should not be included until children reach elementary-school age. Other critics and research indicate the opposite: that even preschool children can use *appropriate* computer programs, and that drawing experiences using the program Logo help the child create more elaborate pictures than the child could do manually. (Clements & Nastasi, 1992, provides a detailed review). Children modify their ideas and use these new ideas in all of their artwork (Vaidya & McKeeby, 1984).

"Drill programs are not compatible with NAEYC curriculum guidelines, but the most promising use of computers has nothing to do with programmed learning," say Clements, Nastasi, and Swaminathan (1993, p. 57). They continue: "In one study only children using drill-and-practice programs had significant *losses* in creativity. Children using open-ended software made significant gains in intelligence, nonverbal skills, structural knowledge, long-term memory, complex manual dexterity, and self-esteem" (Haugland, 1992).

These authors suggest that open-ended programs "such as Logo can have wide-ranging benefits, developing subject-matter knowledge and problem-solving and socioemotional competencies. This may be why entire school systems in Australia, Brazil, Costa Rica, Greece, the United Kingdom, and other countries—as well as some exemplary U.S. schools—are emphasizing Logo and related programs. These tools are used flexibly, across a broad range of content, to promote active, meaningful, deep learning—strikingly consistent with NAEYC guidelines" (p. 57).

Today's research offers directions at three crossroads where important decisions must be made:

Crossroad #1. Use simple computer games for "rewards" or occasional drill but do not integrate it into the wider educational program.

This path leads nowhere (Clements, Nastasi, & Swaminathan, 1993, p. 57).

Crossroad #2: Integrate drill and other structured software activities into the programs.

This path is educationally plausible, safe, and easy—for appropriate practice about ten minutes a day. (Clements, Nastasi, & Swaminathan, 1993, p. 63).

Crossroad #3: Use software and tools for problem-solving—word processors, Logo, and drawing programs—to extend and enrich the children's education.

This path is more challenging and offers the potential for substantive educational innovation consonant with NAEYC guidelines and those of other professional organizations (Clements, Nastasi, & Swaminathan, 1993, p. 62).

The easier, safer paths can be tempting, but perhaps this is, as Papert (1980) has claimed,

> inventing new gadgets to teach the same old stuff in a thinly disguised version of the same old way. Moreover, if the gadgets are computers, the same old teaching becomes incredibly more expensive and biased towards its dullest parts, namely the kind of rote learning in which measurable results can be obtained by treating the children like pigeons in a Skinner box. . . . I believe with Dewey, Montessori, and Piaget that children learn by doing and by thinking about what they do. And so the fundamental ingredients of educational innovation must be better things to do and better ways to think about oneself doing these things. I claim that computation is by far the richest known source of these ingredients. We can give children unprecedented power to invent and carry out exciting projects by providing them with access to computers. (p. 161)

Clements, Nastasi, and Swaminathan (1993) conclude their article:

> Research shows that decisions are not final. Many teachers take the second path, return one or more years later to the crossroads, and turn to the third path. Some see the

potential of computers and extend their vision. Others realize that different computer applications are more consistent with their child-centered, constructivist views. For many teachers, a variety of experiences leads them to reflect and reorganize their thinking about young children's learning. (p. 63)

Elkind, a contemporary and respected early-childhood education leader, provides his cautionary note and viewpoint regarding young children and technology:

growing prevalence of computers in our schools as well as in our homes and in our workplaces. . . . I have no doubt that computers will indeed change the way in which teachers teach, particularly at the elementary and secondary level. But when I read about the goals to be reached through having computers in the classroom, I was amused to discover that these were goals early childhood educators had attained long before computers. Here are some of these hoped-for, computer-mediated attainments:

> The role of the teacher changes dramatically in the well managed ILS (Integrated Learning System) classroom. Teachers are still responsible for students' learning, but rather than being dispensers of information they become guides to the learning process. They act as facilitators and organizers of learning activities; they are free to focus on small groups and individuals who need more specialized attention, helping them to make choices and validate their learning. (Van Dusen & Worthen 1995, 32)

If computers and educational software programs encourage primary and secondary school teachers to operate more like early childhood educators, these machines will

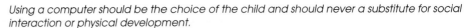

Using a computer should be the choice of the child and should never a substitute for social interaction or physical development.

most certainly bring about a miraculous transformation in teaching. Well before computers, many of us argued that teaching at all levels should follow the early childhood model. If the computer, with its high-tech image and authority, can bring about what all our efforts to disseminate developmentally appropriate practice has yet to achieve, I don't think any of us will complain or lament. (p. 22)

Multiple Intelligences

The theory of multiple intelligences, identified by Gardner as logical-mathematical, linguistic, musical, spatial, bodily-kinesthetic, interpersonal, and intrapersonal (1993), suggests that if we look directly at the functioning of all intelligences, we will have a multifaceted view of children, not just a focus on linguistic and logical-mathematical understanding (Wright & Shade, 1994, p. 7).

Wright and Shade describe children as artists, storytellers, designers, authors, mechanics, logical thinkers, and others, concluding that as "facilitators of an exciting learning environment, we must consider the computer's potential for exploration and growth and select programs that will offer opportunities for children to use their multiple intelligences freely" (p. 15).

Van Dyk (1994) observes that learning-style models provide exciting opportunities to:

1. recognize diversity of needs and celebrate a diversity of gifts;
2. sensitize teachers to the reality of individual differences; and
3. encourage teachers to enlarge their repertoires of classroom teaching strategies.

"By viewing interactions at the microcomputer from a multiple intelligences perspective, we have an opportunity to broaden our own perspectives on children's learning. Each child creates a unique set of images, and the observant teacher will look through this cognitive window and see the emergence of wonderful ideas" (Wright & Shade, 1994, p. 15).

What should we be teaching young children about technology? Bowman and Beyer (1994) suggest one agenda that includes the following concepts: people control technology, but there are rules that control how it works; it has languages, and provides different kinds of things in a variety of ways; and using computer programs requires different ways of organizing thinking (p. 24).

Criteria for judging the appropriateness of software as a learning tool include the following:

1. The child can use the program without asking for help, regardless of her reading skills, because the software uses graphical and spoken instructions rather than written ones.
2. The child controls the software.
3. The software provides several levels for exploration.
4. The feedback is instantaneous.
5. Multisensory learning is included.
6. The adult has evaluated the software (by reading the instructions, viewing it on a computer, and so on).
7. It hold's the child's interest and encourages spontaneous response.
8. The child feels empowered or successful (Narodick, 1992).

Three models for organizing learning experiences for children are proposed by Scardamalia and Bereiter (1991): First, the teacher focuses on the task, and learning is the byproduct. Classwork emphasizes activities rather than knowledge. Second, the teacher maintains control over the learning process and is responsible for setting cognitive goals, using children's prior knowledge, asking questions to stimulate discussion, and monitoring the comprehension process. Third, the teacher turns over the control to the child, encouraging the child to ask questions, monitor his comprehension, and take responsibility for his own learning. Scaradamalia and Bereiter have reached the conclusion that "the best computer tool for a learning child is one by which his intentions or concerns control the way in which he experiences new information or knowledge" (p. 28).

One group of researchers stated that if they had stopped their evaluation after a couple of months, they would have mistakenly concluded that computer learning yielded no effects. Only after one full year did the rich benefits emerge (Cochran-Smith, Kahn, & Paris, 1988).

Working with computers allows children to create, change, save, and retrieve ideas, and connect ideas from different areas (such as mathematics and art); provides situations with clear-cut feedback that children can interpret on their own; and allows children to interact, think, and play with ideas in significant ways, in some cases even with limited adult supervision (Clements, 1994, p. 42).

When young children work together at the computer, they seek help from each other and prefer help from peers over help from the teacher. Teachers of preschool children should be aware that young children need more structure and guidance than older children. At the computer they simultaneously show high levels of language and cooperative play.

In open-ended software such as Logo, young children are more likely to formulate and solve their own problems or collaborate with a partner.

Initially Bredekamp shared negative reactions with colleagues about computer use with young children: children had more important things to do, computer costs could better be used in improved staff salaries, and so on (Bredekamp & Rosegrant, 1992, p. 54). Further investigation brought this conclusion:

> Technology—including video and audiotapes and, especially, computers—should not be abandoned because it has at times been misused or because mismatches have occurred in the past. The potentials of technology are far-reaching and ever-changing. The risk is for adults to become complacent, assuming that their current knowledge or experience is adequate. Technology is an area of the curriculum, as well as a tool for learning, in which teachers must demonstrate their own capacity for learning. If teachers themselves become models of exploration and inquiry, children are likely to follow. Research demonstrates that computers can make a difference in a child becoming literate or not and can support self-esteem through the process. Sometimes a child who is not imaginative or verbal during other activities will demonstrate these capabilities when using computers. Computers can be an alternative way of making sure that children experience success. All of these potentials are achieved if, and only if, adults engage in the process of decision making. Computers cannot take the place of teachers any more than teachers can take the place of computers; but together the learning environment can be improved, and computers can be a powerful tool to help children reach their full potentials as learners and decision makers. (p. 61)

Social Interactions

An important environmental relationship must exist between the needs of the student and the total environment in the social context in which teaching and learning take place. Children generally prefer to work in dyads or triads rather than alone; in these small groups, they spontaneously teach, help, and encourage each other. "Interactions during computer activities are often more collaborative than those that occur during other activities. For example, preschoolers spent 63% of their time at the computer when working with a peer, compared to only 7% when working with puzzles. . . . In another study, the frequency of cooperative play at the computer was comparable to that exhibited during a fishing game (96% and 98%, respectively), but was much higher than that exhibited in other traditional preschool activities such as blocks (27%), Play-Doh (14%), and art (8%)," reports Clements (1993, p. 302), who continues:

> Thus computers engender social interaction among children in preschool and primary grades. Long-term developmental effects, however, depend on characteristics of the children as well as on ecological factors such as teacher support and computer programs. (p. 302)

Clements concludes:

> Most early warnings about computer use with young children and criticisms based on purported developmental limitations appear invalid. In appropriate environments, children use computers confidently, successfully, and enthusiastically, and they can benefit from such use. Nevertheless, warnings of *misuse* have validity, for example, purchasing technology without adequate attention to the selection of quality programs, the education of caregivers, and the integration of computers into the early childhood program consonant with that program's philosophy. (p. 311)

The reader is reminded that the Clements article was written mainly about kindergarten and primary grades.

Supporting Thematic Units with Computers

As with any area of curriculum, thematic units of study can include blocks, sand, outside play, movement experiences, mathematics, dramatic play, books, language arts, cooking, and other familiar or special activities to enhance learning. Teachers also can use computers to enhance units. For example, computers can support a unit on one or more levels:

1. Specific software using unit-related information
2. Tool software—for specific areas
3. Computer-related activities designed to build on specific computer skills or concepts
4. Building a "network" of related topics
5. Locating resource material (Davidson, 1994)

As reported in *Young Children,* NAEYC (1996) has issued a position statement on technology and young children:

> Early childhood educators must take responsibility to influence events that are transforming the daily lives of children and families. This statement addresses several issues related to technology's use with young children: (1) the essential role of the teacher in evaluating appropriate uses of technology; (2) the potential benefits of appropriate use of technology in early childhood programs; (3) the integration of technology into the typical learning environment; (4) equitable access to technology, including children with special needs; (5) stereotyping and violence in software; (6) the role of teachers

and parents as advocates; and (7) the implications of technology for professional development. (p. 11)

And further:

Although now there is considerable research that points to the positive effects of technology on children's learning and development (Clements 1994), the research indicates that, in practice, computers supplement and do not replace highly valued early childhood activities and materials, such as art, blocks, sand, water, books, exploration with writing materials, and dramatic play. Research indicates that computers can be used in developmentally appropriate ways beneficial to children and also can be misused, just as any tool can (Shade & Watson 1990). Developmentally appropriate software offers opportunities for collaborative play, learning, and creation. Educators must use professional judgment in evaluating and using this learning tool appropriately, applying the same criteria they would to any other learning tool or experience. They must also weight the costs of technology with the costs of other learning materials and program resources to arrive at an appropriate balance for their classrooms. (p. 11)

Shade (1996) comments on the NAEYC position statement regarding technology and young children, emphasizing the central role teachers must take to ensure that the potential benefits of technology are realized (see Wright & Shade, 1994, for further discussion). He identifies the most critical decision a teacher can make as that of software selection, adding that the computer is determined by the developmental appropriateness of the software selected. He cautions teachers to avoid drill-and-practice software, which requires children to respond to one right answer to closed-ended questions. Haugland and Shade (1994) estimated that approximately 25 to 30 percent of the software available for young children is developmentally appropriate.

Software companies are still trying to market large, integrated learning systems or solutions. Touted as all you need for your language arts or math curriculum, software applications like these have the least success in helping children read or do math, as research has clearly shown. (Clements & Nastasi, 1993, p. 18)

Schools continue to place computers in isolated labs where children are taught "computer literacy skills," which Papert (1993) states is the most useless thing we could teach children as the technology skills they learn today will not be the same skills needed in the future (p. 18).

Evaluating Software: What to Consider

Child features: Child-operated; concrete representations that the child can manipulate on the screen; accurate representations; expanding complexity for use by children of various developmental levels.

Teacher features: Cross-curriculum interchangeability; self-directed exploration by children; representative of diverse composition of classroom; empowers children to learn through self-directed exploration; ability of educators to have control over customizing software for the classroom or an individual child.

Technical features: Check the technical features of software to see if your computer will run it. See whether it is friendly or complex, and aesthetically pleasing. Research has shown that little correlation exists between winning an editors' or parents' award and being developmentally appropriate (Shade, 1996, p. 21).

In their chapter, Thouvenelle, Borunda, and McDowell (1994) explore three topics in the context of technology as an educational innovation: "(1) the increasing importance of technology in early childhood education; (2) the inequities in children's access to technology in education as a function of gender, cultural and linguistic background, and abilities; and (3) strategies that concerned early childhood professionals can adopt to promote equal access for all young children" (p. 151).

Educators today are being challenged to create educational activities and environments that are attentive to the needs of different communities. It has been found that software in one's native tongue enhances self-concept, personalizes learning experiences, and reaffirms culture.

Summary

There is a recent trend in some software publications that allows teacher editions to help integrate the computer into the curriculum with lesson plans, activities, and workbook pages. As with any classroom material, teachers must carefully assess the options provided. "Are they process- or product-oriented?"

> The fact that almost all drawing programs provide coloring book pages to be filled in should raise our awareness that we need to monitor the kinds of activities available on computers in light of guidelines for developmentally appropriate practice." (Davidson & Wright, 1994, p. 89)

Teachers and parents must advocate what is best for the children—not what is on the market.

Currently, there are limited resources for computers and teacher training for early-childhood education classrooms.

"It is critical for us all to use our intellectual energy and creativity to push the limits of the software and hardware industries, research and development efforts, and educational practice," write Char and Forman (1994, p. 177). For "only through our best collective thinking, hard work, and dedication will interactive technology offer valuable opportunities for young children's learning and development in the 21st century" (p. 177).

> We also argue for pushing hard on various fronts for greater integration, such as linking three-dimensional objects and computers; connecting different modalities and notation systems; merging video worlds and children's shared experiences in the immediate and familiar world; utilizing technology to support the social nature of the child; bringing technology-based learning centers into the real, physical center of learning in the classroom; and bridging the different and varied worlds of the child at home, at school, and in the community. (Char & Forman, 1994, p. 177)

Conclusion

The problems and solutions of computer inclusion can be common or unique to any classroom. Therefore, teachers and administrations need to carefully consider the benefits and liabilities.

After carefully reading and rereading all the current information you can find on the computer/young child issue, study these concerns and reach your own conclusions:

Children

What is the composition of the group (age, interests, abilities)?

Would a computer promote socialization and cooperation? What rules would be needed?

How could the computer support the varied developmental levels within the classroom?

Would its use be just for your classroom or would it be shared with staff or other classrooms?

Adults

How many adults would be available for assistance?

How knowledgeable are the adults about computers?

Are other adults pressuring for computers?

Does it lighten or increase the teacher's responsibilities?

Specifically, how would you use it with groups and individual children?

Computer

What could it offer these children that the teacher (adults) could not?

What guidelines would you establish with the children?

Would it displace or supplement firsthand experiences for the children?

Would its use be disrupting or enriching?

Is the software structured or flexible?

Is there software that would be appropriate for your group?

Classroom

Where could it be placed for best use?

Would it cause unreasonable financial adjustments?

Would there be upkeep problems—delays, costs, and so on?

Are opportunities abundant in the classroom for sensory experiences, construction, language, raw materials, firsthand experiences, choice of activity and playmates, and so on?

APPLICATION OF PRINCIPLES

1. Considering the Bureau of Labor statistics at the beginning of the chapter, give some curriculum suggestions for teachers *and* parents of young children.

2. Briefly outline your feelings about (a) science and (b) technology. Have your experiences been positive or negative? How can you reinforce positive feelings and eliminate negative feelings

about science and technology in yourself and others?

3. Considering science as a whole, what are your favorite areas? How could you teach these topics to young children?

4. Identify some negative attitudes toward taking science classes or planning some areas for young children. Make several plans whereby you can change those attitudes into positive, exciting experiences for yourself and children.

5. How do you think young children can learn to appreciate themselves and their immediate and extended environment?

6. Plan and take a nature walk with several children. What did you expect them to learn? What did you learn?

7. Identify and plan two simple, exciting activities to teach children about physical science. The first activity should include areas of your interest; the

second should include an area that you feel less sure about.

8. Brainstorm with a friend or colleague about the many ways an outdoor experience involves science. How about an indoor experience?

9. Quietly contemplate your personal experiences learning to use a computer (or why you have not learned to use a computer). Could you be a good example to others? Do you use a computer frequently or resist using one? Could you strengthen your positive attitude or diminish a negative one?

10. Briefly discuss multiple intelligences. In order of strength, identify different intelligences in yourself or someone else.

11. Describe a scene where young children could have an enriching experience using a computer.

12. If you were responsible to decide whether a computer would be part of a home or classroom experience for young children, *how* and *what* would you decide? Give reasons.

REFERENCES

Abruscato, J. (1992). *Teaching children science,* 3rd edition. Boston: Allyn & Bacon.

American Association for the Advancement of Science (1989). *Science for all Americans: Project 2061 report on literacy goals in science, mathematics and technology.* Washington, DC: Author.

American Association for the Advancement of Science (1993). *Benchmarks for science literacy.* Washington, DC: Author.

Bowman, B. T., & E. R. Beyer (1994). Thoughts on technology and early childhood education. In Wright, J. L., & D. D. Shade (eds.), *Young children: Active learners in a technological age.* Washington, DC: NAEYC.

Bredekamp, S. (ed.) (1987). *Developmentally appropriate practice in early childhood programs serving children from birth through age 8,* expanded edition. Washington, DC: NAEYC.

Bredekamp, S., & T. Rosegrant (1992). Reaching potentials through appropriate curriculum: Conceptual frameworks for applying the guidelines. In *Reaching potentials: Appropriate curriculum and assessment for young children,* Vol. 1. Bredekamp, S., and T. Rosegrant (eds.). Washington, DC: NAEYC.

Bybee, R., C. E. Buchwald, S. Crissman, D. Heil, P. J. Kuerbis, C. Matsumoto, & J. D. McInerey (1989). *Science and technology education for the elementary years: Frameworks for curriculum and instruction.* Andover, MA: National Center for Improving Science.

Carson, R. (1956). *The sense of wonder.* New York: Harper & Row.

Char, C., & G. E. Forman (1994). Interactive technology and the young child: A look to the future. In Wright, J. L., & D. D. Shade (eds.), *Young children: Active learners in a technological age,* 167–177. Washington, D.C.: NAEYC.

Charlesworth, R., & K. K. Lind (1990). *Math & science for young children.* Albany, NY: Delmar.

Clements, D. H. (1993). Computer technology and early childhood education. In Roopnarine, J. L., & J. E. Johnson, *Approaches to early childhood education,* Chapter 17, 295–316. New York: Macmillan.

Clements, D. H. (1994). The uniqueness of the computer as a learning tool: Insights from research and practice. In Wright, J. L., & D. D. Shade (eds.), *Young children: Active learners in a technological age,* 31–49. Washington, DC: NAEYC.

Clements, D. H., & B. K. Nastasi (1992). Computers and early childhood education. In Gettinger, M., S. M. Elliott, & T. R. Kratochwill (eds.), *Advances in school psychology: Preschool and early childhood treatment directions,* 187–246. Hillsdale, NJ: Lawrence Erlbaum.

Clements, D. H., & B. K. Nastasi (1993). Electronic media and early childhood education. In Spodek, B. (ed.), *Handbook of research on the education of young children,* 251–275. New York: Macmillan.

Clements, D. H., B. K. Nastasi, & S. Swaminathan (1993, January). Research in review: Young children and computers: Crossroads and directions from research. *Young Children,* 48(2), 56–64.

Cochran-Smith, M., J. Kahn, & C. L. Paris (1988). When word processors come into the classroom. In Hoot, J. L., & S. B. Silvern (eds.), *Writing with computers in the early grades,* 43–74. New York: Teachers College Press.

Davidson, J. (1994). Using computers to support thematic units. In Wright, J. L., & D. D. Shade (eds.), *Young children: Active learners in a technological age,* 178–180. Washington, DC: NAEYC.

Davidson, J., & J. L. Wright (1994). The potential of the microcomputer in the early childhood classroom. In Wright, J. L., & D. D. Shade (eds.), *Young children: Active learners in a technological age,* 77–91. Washington, DC: NAEYC.

Dewey, J. (1938). *Education and experience.* New York: Collier.

Dighe, J. (1993, March). Children and the earth. *Young Children,* 48(3), 58–63.

Elkind, D. (1981). *Children and adolescents,* 3rd edition. New York: Oxford University Press.

Elkind, D. (1996, September). Viewpoint: Young children and technology: a cautionary note. *Young Children,* 51(6), 22–23.

Fenton, G. M. (1996, March). Back to our roots in nature's classroom. *Young Children,* 51(3), 8–11.

Fisher, A. (1992, August). Crisis in education, Part 1: Science + math = F. *Popular Science,* 241(2), 58–63, 108.

Fisher, A. (1992, September). Crisis in education, Part 2: Why Johnny can't do science and math. *Popular Science,* 241(3), 50–55, 98.

Forman, G. E., & D. A. Kuschner (1983). *The child's construction of knowledge: Piaget for teaching children.* Washington, DC: NAEYC.

Furman, E. (1990, November). Plant a potato—learn about life (and death). *Young Children,* 46(1), 15–20.

Galvin, E. S. (1994, May). The joy of seasons: With the children, discover the joys of nature. *Young Children,* 49(4), 4–9.

Gardner, H. (1993). *Multiple intelligences: The theory into practice.* New York: Basic.

Goldenberg, C., L. Reese, & R. Gallimore (1992). Effects of literacy materials from school on Latino children's home experiences and early reading achievement. *American Journal of Education,* 100(4), 497–536.

Harlan, J. (1992). *Science experiences for the early childhood years,* 5th edition. New York: Merrill/Macmillan.

Haugland, S. W. (1992). The effect of computer software on preschool children's developmental gains. *Journal of Computing in Childhood Education,* 3(1), 15–30.

Haugland, S. W., & D. D. Shade (1994). Software evaluation for young children. In Wright, J. L., & D. D. Shade (eds.), *Young children: Active learners in a technological age,* 63–76. Washington, DC: NAEYC.

Henniger, M. L. (1987, February). Learning mathematics and science through play. *Childhood Education,* 63(3), 167–171.

Holt, B. (1989). *Science with young children,* revised edition. Washington, DC: NAEYC. Order #309.

Holt, B. F. (1990). *Science with young children.* Washington, DC: NAEYC.

Huffman, A. B. (1996, July). Beyond the weather chart: weathering new experiences. *Young Children,* 51(5), 34–37.

Javna, J. (1990). *Fifty simple things kids can do to save the earth.* Kansas City, MO: Andrews & McMeel.

Johnson, H. (1972). *Children in the nursery school.* New York: Agathon.

Johnson, J. E., J. F. Christie, & T. D. Yawkey (1987). *Play and early childhood development.* Glenview, IL: Scott, Foresman.

Kilmer, S. J., and H. Hofman (1995). Transforming science curriculum. In Bredekamp, S., & T. Rosegrant (eds.), *Reaching potentials: Transforming early childhood curriculum and assessment,* Vol. 2, 43–63. Washington, DC: NAEYC.

Klein, A. (1991, July). All about ants: Discovery learning in the primary grades. *Young Children,* 46(5), 23–27.

Kokoski, T. M., & N. Downing-Leffler (1995, July). Boosting your science and math programs in early childhood education: Making the home-school connection. *Young Children,* 50(5), 35–39.

Kokoski, T. M., & M. M. Patton (1994). Back-packing through science and mathematics. Paper presented at the National Science Teachers Association Annual Conference, March 30–April 2, in Anaheim, CA.

Krauss, R. (1989). *The carrot seed.* New York: Harper Children's Books.

McIntyre, M. (1984). Involving parents in science. In *Early Childhood and Science,* 134–135. Washington, DC: National Science Teachers Association.

Mechling, K. R., & D. Oliver (1983). *Science teaches basic skills.* Washington, DC: National Science Teachers Association.

Mitchell, L. S. (1921/1971). *Young geographers.* New York: Bank Street College of Education.

Narodick, S. (1992). Software as a learning tool. *Mac's Place:* 58.

National Association for the Education of Young Children (NAEYC) (1987). Outstanding science trade books for children. *Young Children,* 42(6), 52–56.

NAEYC position statement: Technology and young children—ages three through eight (1996, September). *Young Children,* 51(6), 11–16.

National Association for the Education of Young Children (NAEYC) & National Association of Early Childhood Specialists in State Departments of Education (NAECS/SDE) (1991). Guidelines for appropriate curriculum content and assessment in programs serving children ages 3 through 8. *Young Children,* 46(3), 21–38.

National Center for Improving Science Education (NCISE) (1990). *Getting started in science: A blueprint for elementary school science education.* A report from the National Center for Improving Science Education. Colorado Springs, CO: Author.

National Council for Teachers of Mathematics (NCTM) (1989). *Curriculum and evaluation standards for school mathematics.* Reston, VA: Author.

National Research Council (1994). *National science education standards* (draft). Washington, DC: National Academy Press.

National Science Teachers Association (1992). Outstanding science books for young children in 1991. *Young Children,* 47(4), 73–75.

Nelson, L., & L. Frederick (1994). Can children design curriculum? *Educational Leadership,* 51(5), 71–74.

Papert, S. (1980). Teaching children thinking; teaching children to be mathematicians vs. teaching about mathematics. In Taylor, R. (ed.), *The computer in the school: Tutor, tool, tutee,* 161–196. New York: Teachers College Press.

Papert, S. (1993). *The children's machine: Rethinking school in the age of the computer.* New York: Basic.

Patton, M. M., & T. M. Kokoski (1996, July). How good is your early childhood science, mathematics, and technology program? Strategies for extending your curriculum. *Young Children,* 51(5), 38–44.

Paulu, N., & M. Martin (1992). *Helping your child learn science.* Washington, DC: U.S. Government Printing Office. GPO Stock #065-000-00520-4.

Perry, G., & M. Rivkin (1992, May). Teachers and science. *Young Children,* 47(4), 9–16.

Piaget, J. (1927/1966). *The child's conception of physical causality.* Trans. M. Gabain. Totowa, NJ: Littlefield.

Piaget, J. (1970). *Science of education and the psychology of the child.* New York: Grossman.

Pratt, C. (1924). *Experimental practice in the city and country school.* New York: Dutton.

Rivkin, M. (n.d.). *The great outdoors: Restoring children's right to play outside.* Washington, DC: NAEYC. Order #108.

Rivkin, M. (ed.) (1992, May). Science is a way of life. *Young Children,* 47(4), 4–8.

Sagan, C. (1989). Why we need to understand science. *Parade,* 10 September, p. 6.

Scardamalia, M., & C. Bereiter (1991). Higher level of agency for children in knowledge building: A challenge for the design of new knowledge media. *Journal of the Learning Sciences,* 1(1), 37–68.

Schultz, C. (1985, May). Early childhood. *Science & Children,* 22(8), 49–51.

Seefeldt, C., & N. Barbour (1994). *Early childhood education: An introduction,* 3rd edition. New York: Merrill/Macmillan.

Shade, D. D. (1996, September). Software evaluation. *Young Children,* 51(6), 17–21.

Shade, D. D., & J. A. Watson (1990). Computers in early education: Issues put to rest, theoretical links to sound practice, and the potential contribution of microworlds. *Journal of Educational Computing Research,* 6(4), 375–392.

Smith, R. F. (1987). Theoretical framework for preschool science experiences. *Young Children,* 42(2), 34–40.

Sprung, B. (1996, July). Physics is fun, physics is important, and physics belongs in the early childhood curriculum. *Young Children,* 51(5), 29–33.

Taylor, B. J. (1993). *Science everywhere: Opportunities for very young children.* Fort Worth, TX: Harcourt Brace Jovanovich.

Taylor, B. J. (1995). *A child goes forth,* 8th edition. Englewood Cliffs, NJ: Merrill.

Third International Mathematics and Science Study (TIMSS) (1997, January). Stronger focus needed in improving math education, study shows. *Community Update,* #43, U.S. Department of Education.

Third International Mathematics and Science Study (TIMSS) (1997, July/August). Americans beat international averages in science and math. *Community Update,* #49, U.S. Department of Education.

Thouvenelle, S., M. Borunda, & C. McDowell. 1994. Replicating inequities: Are we doing it again? In Wright, J. L., & D. D. Shade (eds.), *Young children: Active learners in a technological age,* 151–166. Washington, DC: NAEYC.

Vaidya, S., & J. McKeeby (1984, September). Computer turtle graphics: Do they affect children's thought processes? *Educational Technology,* 46–47.

Van Dusen, L. M., & B. R. Worthen (1995). Can integrated instructional technology transform the classroom? *Educational Leadership,* 53(2), 28–33.

Van Dyk, J. (1994). Learning style models: Do we really need them? Paper presented at the Annual Meeting of the Association of Teacher Educators, February, in Atlanta, GA.

Wilson, R. A. (1993). *Fostering a sense of wonder during the early childhood years.* Columbus, OH: Greyden. See the annotated bibliography included in the appendix.

Wilson, R. A. (1995, September). Nature and young children: A natural connection. *Young Children,* 50(6), 4–11.

Wright, J. L., & D. D. Shade (eds.) 1994. *Young children: Active learners in a technological age.* Washington, DC: NAEYC.

Mathematics

CHAPTER 9

MAIN PRINCIPLES

1. Mathematics plays an important part in the daily lives of young children.
2. The ability to solve mathematical problems depends on the developmental stage of the child.
3. Mathematics provides an opportunity to think, discover, solve problems, and learn.
4. Teachers and parents can provide appropriate math learning experiences for young children.
5. In this chapter, mathematics is divided into four categories: sorting and classifying, counting, measuring, and exploring space and shapes.

According to Greenberg (1993),

> Let's face it, . . . *many* teachers don't like math. Many teachers don't like reading, ei-
> ther; they don't read in their spare time. Yet we would probably all agree that it's every
> early childhood educator's duty to try to instill love of stories and a variety of other
> "readiness to read" in the young children we work with. Isn't the same true of math?
> It's not a matter of whether *we* think reading or math is important, it's a matter of giv-
> ing each child a fair start in case *he* thinks so. (p. 76)

Unlike curriculum of older children and adults, mathematics for young children is
an integrated topic. In fact, interest in the topic is created when these young children
have a manipulative experience, when concepts are within their level of understanding, when learning is related to familiar things, and when there is an integration of
curriculum—such as number learning through music, art, food, science, language
arts, and other areas. Charlesworth (1988) also encourages blending of curriculum,
gives an example of combining math with science and social studies, and concludes:

> Early childhood teachers need to keep an imaginative eye out for opportunities to inte-
> grate mathematics into other curriculum areas in order to help students understand
> that mathematics is a useful tool and enjoyable and challenging to apply; not just an
> isolated, frequently boring, rote learning activity. (p. 31)

Math can be taught through many different curriculum areas. For example, it
can be easily taught through children's storybooks, songs, dramatic play, outdoor
activities, and other areas. All are readily available resources. Teachers must carefully review any sources to enhance math education, and should select books in
which illustrations portray correct mathematical ideas, are attractive, appeal to
young children, and are appropriate in size and detail for the child's developmental
characteristics. The text should be accurate, easily understood, and interesting to
young children. A number of resources are available; however, some counting
books are inappropriate for young children because of unclear illustrations, advanced concepts, or the misuse of cardinal or ordinal numbers. (For a refresher,
cardinal numbers indicate how many (1, 2, 3); ordinal numbers indicate the relationship with another item or event (first, second, third). "Research as well as experience, reveals that young children lack understanding of numbers' relationships
with one another" (Greenberg, 1993, p. 83).

Play is another avenue for children to learn about mathematics. They learn
about classification, comparison, ordering and ordinal numbers, one-to-one correspondence and rational counting, cardinal numbers, and number recognition.
Henniger (1987) notes:

> Childhood play provides numerous opportunities for creative responses to challeng-
> ing issues. It enables children to learn key concepts and develop essential attitudes to-
> ward learning. Its value and importance to mathematics and science learning should
> not be overlooked. (p. 171)

Many adults do not understand (and therefore dislike) mathematics. They
have difficulty in balancing their checkbooks, in having enough money, or in understanding physics and computers, so they want to shield children from math. On
the other hand, as soon as children are able, they are expected to tell their age and
also hold up the right number of fingers. Adults want children to learn sizes and
shapes and to get around easily in their environment. Further, they want children
to stack this, compare that, and even recite nursery rhymes or sing songs, many of
which deal with numbers. Does this sound as if adults are somewhat inconsistent?

In his review of research, Price (1989) gives this advice, with which other researchers in mathematics concur: Teachers should take pains "not to put math down," "not to make math seem difficult," and not to discourage "child-invented problem-solving techniques that work and that 'feel right'—for example, counting on one's fingers. Teacher discouragement of such techniques makes mathematics seem arbitrary, convention-bound, and counterintuitive. On the contrary, good mathematics is *intuitive*." Instead, "teachers who know how counting skill develops know when to notice, applaud, and appreciate the steps from 'novice' to 'expert' counter" (p. 57).

As mentioned in Chapter 8, Science and Technology, the Third International Mathematics and Science Study, or TIMSS report, showed that U.S. eighth-graders scored below average in math compared to their counterparts in the United Kingdom, Canada, France, Germany, and Japan. The TIMSS report compared the performance of 500,000 students, of whom 40,000 are Americans.

> Unlike many American students, Japanese students are trained to understand math concepts and apply knowledge to solve real problems along with the basics of arithmetic. The study also found that the topics taught in the U.S. math curriculum for eighth graders compare to the seventh grade level in leading countries. (TIMSS, 1997, January, p. 1)

The U.S. Department of Education *Community Update Report* #43 also states that stronger focus is needed in improving math education.

In the United States, there is no need to lag behind other countries in our thinking skills. We need to teach our children, from early life, to be thinkers and solvers—a concept whereby our youngest children can have experiences and opportunities to use their minds creatively, instead of being mere repeaters of facts. This chapter shows how activities and attitudes can influence the young child in beginning and continuing productive thinking—not just in math, but in all topics.

The child's mathematical concepts should be helped to move forward one step at a time.

Encouraging news of American student progress in math comes from a recent report (TIMSS, 1997, July/August) from the U.S. Department of Education:

> The recent results of the Third International Mathematics and Science Study (TIMSS) show that America's fourth-graders are also doing better than ever in mastering the basics of arithmetic. This is the first time in any international comparison that American students in a given grade have exceeded the international average in both mathematics and science.

President Clinton said in his announcement of the fourth-grade TIMSS findings: "We're doing a very good job in the early grades, but we've got a lot more work to do in the later ones." Early-childhood educators can interest and encourage young children to find satisfaction and accomplishment in math and science curriculum areas.

Math in Everyday Life

For Adults

Math concepts are used myriads of times in the daily lives of adults: How soon do we need to leave, how many will be here for dinner, how much money will it cost, what needs to be done first, how much gas is in the car, how much will we spend for Grandma's birthday present, and on, and on. Adults do much of their time and money planning as they do other tasks—they have had much experience with problems, planning, and solutions. They may entertain one or several concepts in their minds simultaneously, or think of only one thing at a time. They have learned that some things are within their control, and others are not. They can pass on to their children (or students) good ways of handling problems, or they may cause anxiety and hopelessness in children. The object of this chapter is to help both children and adults find easy, comfortable, and satisfying ways of dealing with number concepts—daily living, time, money, sequence (order), relationships of numbers (order, time and money), quantity, interaction with others, record keeping, pleasure (score or games), and so on.

For Children

From her extensive research and writing about number, Kamii (1995) organizes the teaching of numbers into three areas: (a) kinds of relationships (objects, events, and actions); (b) quantification of objects (thinking about numbers, logical comparison of sets—rather than counting—and movable objects; and (c) social interaction with peers and teachers.

She cautions: "Just as there are many ways of getting the wrong answer, there are many ways of getting the right answer." (p. 42)

> I would like to remind the reader once more that the child does not construct number outside the context of thinking in general throughout the day. The teacher must, therefore, encourage the child to put all kinds of things, ideas, and events into relationships all the time rather than focusing only on quantification (Principle #2a). (p. 42)

> Educators unfamiliar with Piaget's theory may believe in the importance of the child's manipulating objects. However, they are stumped when asked *how* children learn number concepts by manipulating objects. Most answer the question by referring vaguely to empirical abstraction. The most original and fundamental idea in Piaget's theory of number is that of reflective abstraction and the child's construction of the numerical structure through reflective abstraction. (p. 68)

Recall the statement in Chapter 6 in which Lowenfeld said that some things cannot be taught until a child is cognitively able to grasp the concepts, illustrated when Brittain (1969) unsuccessfully attempted to teach preschool children the concept of copying a square. Lowenfeld's follow-up was: "If we really expect to develop an inquiring mind in a child, one that is eager to tackle the problems of today, a mind that is flexible, inquisitive, and seeks for solutions in unusual ways, then the attention that we have paid to the so-called basic learning areas may be ill-placed" (1987, p. 53).

Constructivism in Math Experiences

"And so it began—this cycle of teacher learning from children who were learning from their experiences. Providing and/or taking advantage of appropriate mathematical experiences that would empower young children to make their own connections became a challenge. Understanding the *process* of connection-making became an even bigger challenge . . . the children were trying to tell me something and I needed to know more," expressed Anderson (1996, p. 34).

Mathematical problems and projects that lend themselves to investigations into a variety of curricular areas are seen as opportunities to make learning more relevant. Being aware of the "big ideas" within the math curriculum is important in organizing ideas (Schifter & Fosnot, 1993, p. 35).

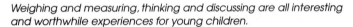

Weighing and measuring, thinking and discussing are all interesting and worthwhile experiences for young children.

In the constructivist classroom, manipulatives are available to assist the teacher and children in the process of constructing their own ways of arriving at answers (Anderson, 1996, p. 38). Autonomous children are able to take relevant factors into account and consider other points of view besides their own when deciding upon a viable solution, regardless of reward or sanction. Mutual trust and respect become the driving force in all aspects of classroom life (Kamii, 1985a, 1989, 1995; DeVries & Kohlberg, 1987; DeVries & Zan, 1994).

Obviously, autonomy (or the lack of it) changes the nature of classroom discourse dramatically. Wood, Cobb, and Yackel (1993) have carefully examined constructivist discourse. Their research has provided some important conclusions with regard to communication within these classrooms. They stress that one of the challenges of constructivist teachers is "to find ways to facilitate and build on their students' ideas to encourage the construction of increasingly powerful conceptual operations. This requires listening to children's explanations and developing an understanding of the underlying conceptual operations that underscore children's thinking" (p. 67). "Providing autonomy and questions to understand children's mathematical thinking is constructivist math education" (Anderson, 1996, p. 40).

STAGES OF DEVELOPMENT

The same question asked about reading could be asked about mathematics. Should it be taught to the young child? The answers range from an absolute *yes* to an emphatic *no*. The question is rather unfair without defining the term *mathematics*.

Mathematicians disagree as to what mathematics is. The higher the level, the more complex the definition. Some suitable definitions include: "an agreed-upon system for describing objects, time, and space in terms of quantity or magnitude"; "a study of relationships that exist between and among sets of quantity"; "assistance toward mathematical understanding by learning how to solve problems, becoming successful with activities of a mathematical nature, understanding the utility of mathematics, and having fun with it"; "to compute with facility as children learn to see how objects in their own environment are placed into a quantitative context"; and others—including ones you might originate. The experience should be of a *sensorimotor* nature, with the child using his senses and moving himself and objects about in space. As in other areas of curriculum, Piaget advocates teaching mathematics through the sensorimotor approach as preparation for logical operations; logic is based on coordination of action even before the development of language.

Piaget's second stage of mental development—*preoperational*—coincides with the ages from 2 through 6, just slightly older than the focus of this text. Broman (1982) says it is

> during this stage that children reason and explain through intuition rather than logic. They have difficulty expressing the order of events, explaining relationships, understanding numbers and their relations, understanding what others say accurately, and understanding and remembering rules.

Piaget (1965) states that mathematical learning takes place in three stages: (1) coordination within the field of perception, (2) operations that go beyond the field of perception, and (3) transition from perception to deduction, progressive coordination of operations, and gradual development of reversibility. Young children begin at stage one and move gradually into stage two. Not until they are in the *concrete operational* stage (ages 7 through 11) of Piaget's stages of mental development do they comprehend concepts of numbers, relationships, and processes.

Young children progress in mathematical knowledge if the activities and expectations match their abilities. In the preoperational stage, young children are very egocentric and generally incapable of seeing a situation from more than one perspective. However, they learn to discriminate color soon after shape and then become

> increasingly adept at working with progressively more difficult concepts of size, classification, seriation, and patterning. A child can work with numerals (chanting them, recognizing them, writing them) long before numeration can be comprehended appropriately. The abilities to use numerals in chanting or recognizing situations does not imply that a child can understand numberness. When the child can conserve, he or she moves from the preoperational to the concrete operational stage of the number concept. (Richardson et al., 1980)

When young children enter school, they have some mathematical skills. They can count some numbers and can classify and compare; most know the meaning of ordinal positions through *fifth;* they can recognize numerals from 1 to 10; they can answer simple addition and subtraction combinations; and most have some knowledge about coins, time, simple fractional concepts, and geometric shapes (Payne, 1975/1990). They also are developing concepts of one-to-one correspondence, number, shape, space, parts and wholes, sequence, measurement, and relating symbols and sets and applying basic knowledge through hypothesis testing and problem solving (Kamii, 1986; and others).

LEARNING OPPORTUNITIES

Teachers must have flexible expectations of young children and their mathematical concepts. Teachers should capitalize on spontaneous events to the degree that the experience is meaningful to the children. Many opportunities should be provided for children to see, manipulate, and test ideas in a friendly atmosphere. Children relate objects and activities as a means of putting their world into perspective. Children should be allowed to practice mathematical concepts; allowed to discover things for themselves through concrete, sensory, familiar, useful, and exploratory ways; and then helped to move forward one step at a time.

Some attainable goals, based on the developmental abilities of individual children in a relaxed atmosphere, are as follows:

1. To stimulate an interest in numbers and their uses
2. To show how number concepts can aid in problem solving
3. To increase worldly knowledge through mathematics
4. To introduce number symbols and terms as the children indicate readiness

Addition is the first form of mathematics learned by young children: "We need two more blocks to make this stack as high as that one." This is followed later by subtraction: "If I give you two of my cars, we will both have the same amount!" They can count the number of children and places for snack time and determine whether they need to add or remove some chairs. Mathematical terms can be introduced to children as long as these terms are defined and the children have opportunities to practice their meanings. When one wants (or needs) more of something, one adds (gets more). When one wants less (or not as many), one subtracts (or takes away). Some children understand what *equal* means. This is illustrated by placing the same number of children or objects on one side of a line as on the other.

Maria Montessori devised games, activities, and materials for teaching number concepts to young children. She thought the concept of *zero* (or nothing) was worth special teaching, and she taught numbers in a series of zero to nine just to give special emphasis to zero.

The importance of auditory skills in learning to read is stated in Chapter 5. The best preparation for successful math experiences, however, is visual development. Sight appears to be more important for success in math than in reading (Brophy, Good, & Nedler, 1975). If the child is unable to discriminate visually, learning mathematical concepts will be a problem.

Chapter 7 contains a short discussion on the two brain hemispheres: The left side controls verbal and analytic functioning and the right side controls intuition and understanding patterns. Piaget says that young children deal with intuition, yet the child must also be able to analyze if she is to perform mathematical tasks. Both hemispheres are utilized in learning mathematics.

Children need to be in an atmosphere where they can think, discover, solve problems, and learn. They need materials that are safe, malleable, and interesting, and they need to practice their kinesthetic senses through manipulation of objects and materials.

Math is not something that waits until a child enters a formal classroom at a prescribed age. From birth they have a desire to make sense of what is going on. Fisher (1992, September) supports and encourages the principles encouraged in this book and those described as developmentally appropriate—a hands-on approach, emphasizing experiment, discussion, cooperation, and participation—noting that student experiments and hands-on assignments have actually declined in recent years due to cost, limited teacher background and training, and outdated and inadequate math textbooks.

But there is hope on the horizon. First, teachers can encourage a good attitude about math through the experiences and success provided for preschool children. Second, and for later and continued success, the National Council of Teachers of Mathematics (1989) has set curriculum standards for grades K–4, 5–8, and 9–12. Each standard within the grade division is copiously illustrated with examples. The standards emphasize the development of children's thinking and reasoning abilities from kindergarten on, call for the appropriate use of calculators and computers, and specify what should be known at each stage for a broad range of content: measurement, computation, geometry, algebra, and—in what will be startling to many parents and teachers—statistics and probability, beginning in kindergarten. Shirley A. Hill, professor of mathematics and education at the University of Missouri and a key player in the development of the new standards, described them this way:

> There has been a long-time consensus about making mathematics-learning more about thinking and engaging the intellect and less about memorizing; more a task for the mind than a test of rote memory. That basic philosophy is now manifested in detailed and specific terms in a document that is the centerpiece of the profession's reform effort in mathematics. (Fisher, 1992, September, p. 55)

The new math standards of the National Council of Teachers of Mathematics have been accepted nationwide by a constellation of education constituencies: teachers, supervisors, unions, parents, school boards, professional societies, politicians, and university faculties (Fisher, 1992, September).

For decades, early-childhood educators have advocated the hands-on approach—and more recently they have emphasized the need for activities, materials, and relationships to be built on what is developmentally appropriate for each child, remembering that "[m]ath activities grounded in children's experience enhance interest in the solution, increase attention to the details of mathematical approaches, and lead to the generalization of concepts and procedures" (Northeast Foundation for Children, 1991, p. 42).

APPROPRIATE MATHEMATICAL EXPERIENCES

Role of the Teacher

As teachers of young children, we need to show enthusiasm for life and its challenges! In math, as in all other curriculum areas, teachers also need to do the following:

- know each child personally
- apply ourselves and our knowledge wisely
- provide stimulating (but not frustrating) experiences
- take advantage of spontaneous questions and situations
- plan open-ended activities so children at all developmental levels can experience success
- prepare an environment of math-rich and math-related experiences
- pose situations in which children can contemplate, try (modify when necessary), and enjoy their surroundings
- use math and thinking in other curriculum areas
- promote a healthy, positive attitude toward math
- help children learn different ways to solve problems (by actually manipulating objects but also brainstorming)
- find activities to interest particular children (dinosaurs, transportation, insects, books, curriculum areas, and so on) in math experiences
- provide large blocks of uninterrupted time for thinking
- place more quiet activities out of the traffic flow
- discover math opportunities in daily living and playing
- put emphasis on thinking and solving rather than table work or completion
- encourage children to solve problems individually or with others
- help a child move beyond present knowledge (and then what?)
- place themselves strategically so they can interact physically or verbally *when necessary*
- have a math-lush (but not overwhelming) environment—indoors and outdoors
- encourage children to select activities and time frames that help them enjoy and understand their environment (democracy)
- encourage use of all parts of the body in learning math concepts (large and small muscles, listening and speaking, seeing and touching, alone or with others, and so on)
- be receptive to different interests and moods of children
- assume with confidence that during meaningful, move-around activities, children will encounter problems and may need some assistance

○ continually review where children are in their mathematical thinking, the importance of concrete experiences, and how all curriculum areas support thinking and problem solving

Teachers should note how individual children respond to mathematical situations. This is far more important than whether they reach a "correct" answer. Constructivist teaching involves an understanding of each child's thinking in order to plan further learning opportunities that will take that child to higher, more inclusive levels of understanding; knowing how each child thinks in various cognitive domains is vital for the teacher in planning for each child. Teachers also need to consider how interesting each topic is and how the experience can be related to other experiences in each child's life.

When the teacher accepts and encourages a variety of answers and procedures, the children will respond in individual and creative ways. To reach a consensus (when important), the constructivist teacher helps children reach higher levels of understanding and learn more efficient procedures, as well as helping them clarify their thinking.

Seeking to understand students' points of view is essential to constructivist education. The more we study the learning process, the more we understand how fundamental this principle is. Students' points of view are windows into their reasoning. Awareness of students' points of view helps teachers challenge students, making school experiences both contextual and meaningful. Each student's point of view is an instructional entry point that sits at the gateway of personalized education. (Brooks & Brooks, 1993, p. 60)

Children learn fractions using familiar ideas, manipulatable aids, and support from others.

Within the last several years educators, cognitive researchers, and professional organizations have stressed the importance of children using their own procedures to arrive at a solution to promote true understanding (National Council of Teachers of Mathematics, 1989; Kamii, Lewis, & Livingston, 1993). The traditional method of teaching one procedure for getting an answer is increasingly seen as harmful for children. It encourages distrust in children's own thinking and discourages the development of number sense (Kamii & Lewis, 1993; Burns, 1994).

Reflection

Rather than having sequenced, planned math activities, note that young children can use math concepts in various ways, depending on the development and experience of the child:

- ◦ reasoning and problem solving (How can I get a turn with the toy?)
- ◦ one-to-one correspondence (How many cookies do we need so each child can have two?)
- ◦ recognizing and writing numerals 0 to 20 (How many is "3"?)
- ◦ communicating (How can I get a turn?)
- ◦ sets, classifying, comparing, and matching (Does the button go with the color, the number of holes, or the composition?)
- ◦ whole-number operations (How can we each have the same number of blocks?)
- ◦ spatial relations, shapes, and geometry (How can you fit things together when they are different shapes?)
- ◦ sequences (What happened first, next, last?)
- ◦ measurement (Which one is longer or weighs more?)

(Topics suggested by Greenberg, 1993; examples by the present author.)

In addition to expressing ideas about art and the young child, Lowenfeld (1987) has the following to say about math:

> The young child can recognize the number 5, but the parent or teacher does not know what meaning this has for the child. For example, a 5 can be an interesting shape, somewhat like a curled-up snake, and one must be careful not to confuse it with another curly one, the 2. On the other hand, the 5 may be part of a series falling between 4 and 6. There seems to be some order in numbers, and the 5 is sort of the middle one. Possibly the child sees 5 as a quantity. It is about as many marbles as can be held at one time or as many peas as will fit on a spoon. Possibly 5 is merely a symbol that indicates the location on the dial for a favorite TV program or the number over the classroom door.
>
> Meaningless drills often are part of the method of trying to teach these skills. Prepositions may be memorized, poems may be recited, or arithmetic tables may be learned by rote. Except for escaping the wrath of the schoolteacher, these seem to be of little value outside of school. Few of us can remember how to divide by fractions, and fewer of us ever use the skill in our daily activities. To think that reading, writing, and arithmetic have become so important in the learning process is to confuse the tools with the objectives. (p. 52)

It is worth repeating the concept that some things cannot be taught until a child is cognitively able to grasp them. If it is an inquiring mind that we seek, one that is flexible, inquisitive, and seeks for unusual solutions, then attention should be focused in this direction.

TEACHING MATH CONCEPTS

If counting is going to be meaningful to children, it must have a solid foundation upon which the children can build. They need to understand the following:

1. One-to-one correspondence—if you count another number, you have to touch another object; you can't skip over any objects, and you can't say the same number name twice—each number name means another object.
2. The further a number is from the beginning of the counting, the bigger it is (this is the number's quantitative significance).
3. Any number has a relationship to its neighbor numbers (the one just below it and the one just above it)—this is its ordinal relationship. (Greenberg, 1993, p. 78)

In yet another source, Greenberg states that children can understand addition and subtraction up to 10, a feat that is expected of children beyond kindergarten, but "*only* if they understand the relationship between numbers—that any number plus one $(n + 1)$ = the next higher number, any number minus one = the next lower number" (1994, p. 12).

A criticism of teaching numbers to young children is that adults hastily and repeatedly teach each number up to 10 but fail to relate each number with actual objects: they concentrate on the number name and sequence. Those who want to help children mathematically must spend a great deal of time giving children concrete opportunities and verbal prompts to help them relate the number name with an actual object (Greenberg, 1993, p. 78). It would be more productive to teach numbers through play (how many wheels on the cart), daily activities (one sock or two), curriculum components (music, stories), outdoor activities (buckets and shovels), and typical early-childhood education themes (pets, toys, family). Math is about thinking, figuring things out, and reasoning.

Some of the implications that flow from the research are that number understanding can be greatly enhanced if teachers:

are sensitive to children's thinking in relation to the stages of learning of key elements;

plan teaching and assessment programs that reflect these stages of learning of key elements; and

engage children in collaborative problem-solving situations as the basis for exploring, developing, and applying multidigit-number concepts and relationships. (Jones & Thornton, 1993, p. 17)

This approach is consistent with the set of recent reform recommendations for developing a sound understanding of numbers (for example, National Council of Teachers of Mathematics, 1989) and reflects a constructivist orientation to learning that has always been the strength of early school programs (Jones & Thornton, 1993, p. 17). Further, "[t]he teacher and the learning experiences provided by the teacher meet the learner halfway. This is *guided* discovery learning, not simply discovery learning" (p. 17).

Teaching One-to-One Correspondence

Most 3-year-old children understand *singular* and *plural* and groups of things (sets) better than they understand one-to-one correspondence and accurate counting. If we can, we should really further develop 3-year-olds' understanding of sets *before* introducing them to counting (assigning number words to things); it's children's interest in comparing sets (more crackers than, less crackers than, the same amount of crackers as) that stimulates interest in learning to count elements to ascertain the answer.

Math is about the relationships between things and numbers. The concept of a set is the basis of other mathematical concepts. "The best early childhood teachers teach largely through playing purposefully with children. Three-year-olds should be developing:

the idea of and ability to create sets (of blocks, sand toys, balls, fish in the tank, etc.),

the ability to compare whether sets have an equal or unequal number of elements; and

the ability to group sets according to different attributes (shape, color, etc.)" (Greenberg, 1993, pp. 79, 81).

For 4- and 5-year-olds, Greenberg states: "Number recognition, while prematurely and inappropriately stressed by many adults, *is* one of the many aspects of math we want fours and fives to learn, and being able to help themselves to these learning-through-play materials does facilitate learning" (1993, p. 83). Using Cuisenaire rods, counting individually or within a group, and looking at books or playing games are all helpful practices.

Math is about relationships among sizes, shapes, weight, and other dimensions.

Young children can learn one-to-one correspondence through various areas of the curriculum during dramatic and free play, music and movement, storybooks, transitions, theme-based units, math centers, and wherever they go.

Teaching about Sets

As children gather casually or deliberately and play begins, the children frequently select and distribute objects: "I want the red one, you can have the green one," or "You have more than me!" They are working with "sets" of objects and are in the beginning stages of addition and/or subtraction. Adding is joining things together, usually *sets* of things, and subtracting is taking things away. Most children younger than 6 or 7 don't add by counting on; they count *all* the objects.

Before they can count, add, or subtract, 18-month-old toddlers know something about numbers. They collect objects, remove and arrange them, and then rearrange them again.

> In mathematics a set is defined as a collection of objects considered as a whole. Much as they are enamored of sets, very young children can't see the single whole unless the set consists of an extremely small number of things in a predictable place (two eyes, two ears, five fingers, five toes) or unless two or three objects are close together in a line. If the objects in a group (set) *aren't* arranged in a line, a two- or three-year-old will have great difficulty determining how many there are even if she counts; she can't judge by assessing, and she becomes confused when she tries to count unaligned objects.
>
> If the objects in the "set" are not near each other, two- and three-year-olds don't recognize them as a set. . . . Three-, four-, five-, and six-year-olds need a lot of experience with small sets of people and things, too. *Keeping in mind the principle that a young child learns more if she constructs something than she does if she merely looks at something constructed by somebody else, we can see that a child will learn more about sets if we frequently ask her to* make *them, than if the* teacher *(or worksheet author) makes them and the child is only asked to compare them.* (Greenberg, 1994, p. 13)

Personal involvement with objects (touching them, moving them) is as essential a part of a child's learning about sets as it is an essential part of his learning about counting. "The less developed counting is in children, the greater the role movement plays" (Leushina, 1991, p. 85).

There is a firm conclusion that "instruction for small children should begin not with counting using number words but by having children actively create sets themselves and compare them by the techniques of superposition and association, so that the children gradually become familiar with equal and unequal aggregates. . . . Linear arrangements promote the most distinct visual perception of a set as a whole and of its elements" (Leushina, 1991, p. 87).

Number Opportunities throughout the Day

Greenberg's 1993 article is very logical and practical. She states:

> Teachers who feature democracy in their classrooms pay astute attention to how children treat each others' responses and mistakes. These teachers take time to reinforce respect as a requirement for all classroom interactions, and they themselves always speak respectfully to children. Many teachers already teach math more or less this way. If all this appeals to you, you can start moving in this direction. (References are listed at the end of the article.)

Teachers who have struggled to break free of the strings that have kept their initiative and creativity tethered to chalkboards and workbooks by years of training in teaching trivia, find that they can create great curriculum, be more effective educators, and have much more fun! (p. 84)

Reflection

Greenberg offers some helpful, specific hints about involving young children in successful math experiences: provide equity in gender, encourage participation, set a good example, help *each* child feel successful, play fair (equal turns and time), compliment each child's accomplishment (not effort), encourage child-child cooperation (including boy/girl), avoid letting one child dominate the group, encourage female and male participation in all sciences, and educate parents against sex stereotyping in the sciences (1994, p. 18).

Games in the Classroom

Games can enrich mathematical experiences in the classroom through the use of spinners, number cards, counting, or dice.

Games also provide an opportunity for children to become more autonomous or self-directed (Kamii & DeVries, 1980). Children can learn the rules of the games with the help of a teacher, who then can become a facilitator. Children think about the games and rules; ask pertinent questions; clarify thinking for themselves and others; and observe, assess, and evaluate the interaction. Also involved is rule negotiation, scorekeeping, counting, reaching agreement on how to approach a mathematical situation posed by a game, and successful resolution of problems.

Snack time can include a counting experience.

Group games include aiming games (marbles, targets, bowling); hiding games (some hide and some find), "how many . .."; and so on.

Only by moving objects and discovering . . . from playing with math games and friends . . . and through appropriate questioning by a curious adult . . . do young children come to realize that . . .

> *In addition to encouraging children to combine sets and to separate out subsets as we play with individuals and small clusters of children in the math center, natural math opportunities through which we can help children learn the rudiments of adding and subtracting abound in every classroom, waiting for us to think of them.* (Greenberg, 1994, p. 12)

Teaching Time Concepts

In helping preschool and primary children understand time concepts, Van Scoy & Fairchild (1993) report that "time is often taught to the children by having them recite social labels, such as the names of days of the week or months of the year. Children who recite labels in this way are being given an opportunity to construct *social knowledge* about time (Kamii, 1986). Social knowledge is knowledge of an arbitrary set of symbols and behaviors common to a society. Children who recite labels are not having experiences that will help them develop an understanding of the passage of time" (p. 21).

Piaget (1969) described the construction of two other types of knowledge—*physical* and *logicomathematical*. Kamii and DeVries (1978) state that

> physical knowledge is knowledge of objects which are "out there" and observable in external reality. . . . Logicomathematical knowledge, on the other hand, consists of relationships which the subject creates and introduces into or among objects. (pp. 16–17)

To help children understand the passage of time, we must relate time to physical objects and/or events that are meaningful to the children, by using innovative calendars, recording the passage of time, and discussing shared experiences or individual experiences.

Diagnosing children's levels of understanding of time and providing appropriate, personally meaningful learning experiences is challenging for teachers (Van Scoy & Fairchild, 1993, p. 24).

One useful way to help very young children determine the passage of time is to tell them a sequence of events ("We'll go outside, then have our snack and clean up before it is time to go home"). For older preschool children, a teacher may show a clock and talk about the numbers and placement of the hands and how they will change before "time to go home." At home we had a modernistic clock hanging on the wall. It was difficult for our children to learn to tell time because they didn't even have numbers for referents! Parents, beware—even digital clocks may confuse young children.

Adults live in a time-conscious world! But children understand the passage of time when it is related to their firsthand experiences or events that already have meaning to them.

And some adults teach children about placement of the hands on the face of the clock, so a child can relate, "The long one is at 6 and the little one is on 2," but the meaning is not there. And children who learn to tell time with a digital clock

Reflection

A 4-year-old was patiently waiting to go on errands with his mother. He kept saying, "What time is it?" and the mother would answer "10:30," "noon," and so on. But the child was persistent, and asked even more frequently. The mother became impatient and responded with "Quarter to one." The child, also becoming impatient, said, "No, I mean what time is it? Tell me what we have to do before we can go." To him sequencing was more important—not the actual time! Then the mother explained, "We need to get lunch, rinse the dishes, feed the dog . . . before we can go." "Oh," said the child, "now I know what time it is!"

and then are expected to transfer that learning to a "regular" clock often find it difficult and frustrating. Our actions help them better understand the urgency of the moment (If you say, "We have to go," and then just sit, they just sit! If you say, "We have to go," and then get going, so do they!).

Literature and Math

Many counting and number books are available. They can be helpful if they are used in combination with objects—not just counting on fingers, but live people and familiar objects.

Whiting has an interesting article in *Young Children* (1994) to help children learn from an enjoyable source:

> Many children view mathematics as a series of rules to follow or facts to memorize; they do not see the relevance of mathematics to their own lives. . . . One way that teachers might use these books is to connect literature to some of the daily events that naturally occur in their classrooms. This article suggests using children's books pertaining to five topics that teachers discuss with children on a regular basis: the calendar, celebrating birthdays, the daily schedule, taking attendance, and the lunch menu. (p. 4)

Before selecting books to teach about a certain concept, make sure the book meets good literature criteria and that it is developmentally appropriate for the children in the classroom. Modifications may need to be made to make the book more understandable for children of different ages and abilities.

Whiting (1994) suggests these resources:

1. About the passage of time:

   The Very Hungry Caterpillar by E. Carle (1969). New York: Putnam.

   Time to . . . by B. McMillan (1989). New York: Lothrop, Lee & Shepard.

   The Grouchy Ladybug by E. Carle. (1977). New York: Crowell.

   Five Minutes' Peace by J. Murphy (1990). New York: Scholastic.

   The Guy Who Was Five Minutes Late by B. Grossman (1990). New York: Crowell.

   The Stopwatch by D. Lloyd. New York: Lippincott.

2. From calendars to place value:

Anno's Counting book by Anno (1977). New York: Crowell.

Count and See by T. Hoban (1972). New York: Macmillan.

Counting Wildflowers by B. McMillan (1986). New York: Lothrop, Lee & Shepard.

Out for the Count: A Counting Adventure by K. Cave (1991). New York: Simon & Schuster.

3. Birthdays:

The Half-Birthday Party by C. Pomerantz (1984). New York: Clarion.

Happy Birthday, Sam by P. Hutchins (1978). New York: Greenwillow.

The Secret Birthday Message by E. Carle (1972). New York: Crowell.

Only Six More Days by M. Russo (1988). New York: Greenwillow.

Other publishers and authors have useful selections. Check also with local librarians, bookstores, experienced teachers, the Internet, and others.

Child Involvement

I used this example in an earlier publication (Taylor, 1993), but repeat it here because of its applicability:

A 3-year-old was asked to count to five. With his left index finger he counted the fingers on his right hand—"one, two, three, four, and five." He was then asked, "Can you count higher?" "Yes," he said, and climbed up on a chair, raised his hand, and began pointing to his fingers and counting, "One, two, three, four, and five." He was further asked, "Can you count backwards?" "Yes," was the reply. He climbed down off the chair, turned his back to the requestor, pointed to his fingers, and counted, "One, two, three, four, five."

Direct teaching cannot build concepts of conservation or of number. These concepts must be developed by the children themselves. Seefeldt (1980) notes:

> Many teachers have tried to teach conservation and other number concepts to children prior to the age of seven, but most have only failed in these efforts. Although you cannot teach such concepts directly, you can provide the atmosphere and materials that will facilitate the development of concepts of conservation as well as number.

Instead of planning specific number experiences and expecting the children to learn them, the teacher should plan a variety of opportunities whereby the child can manipulate objects and practice problem solving.

Kamii (1985b) reports, "[n]umber is something children construct by thinking, in their heads, and not by pushing pencils" (p. 5). She states that play is beneficial for their arithmetical learning and that worksheets are harmful, giving the following two reasons against worksheets:

1. They require children to write answers, and having to write interferes with the possibility of remembering combinations such as "3, 2, 5" and "4, 2, 6." Children can remember sums better when they are free to concentrate on these combinations, without having to write the answers.
2. They teach children to count mechanically when they don't know a sum.

Stone (1987) lists reasons why some teachers persist in using worksheets/workbooks with young children. Included are such ideas as "manipulative math materials are too costly; worksheets are more convenient; worksheets can be taken home and provide parents with evidence of useful work (accountability); worksheets provide an 'academic environment.'" She then counters each reason, and gives some simple, inexpensive, and fun ways to teach children about sizes, one-to-one correspondence, matching pairs, length, height, measuring tools, shapes, "twoness," number, and halves. If these ideas are unappealing, perhaps they will stimulate teachers to come up with alternatives for the children in their classrooms.

One early-childhood educator, Almy (1976), states:

> The child grows in understanding of the world by testing the way it responds to investigations and by observing the effects the child's own actions have. Such manipulation is essential in developing real comprehension. I am convinced that the reason most children are as intelligent as they are in the all too prevalent "look and say" curriculum found in most kindergartens and first grades and in too many preschools comes from the fact that they do actively explore their environment when they are outside the four walls of the classroom. (p. 95)

The involvement of mathematics provides excellent vocabulary experiences, with many new words to learn, meanings to explore, descriptions to use, solutions to discuss, and ideas to relate. There are times to contemplate silently and times to seek assistance.

One of the earliest math experiences children have is in counting. They may count as high as 3 (depending on their age); use randomly selected numbers up to

Children who have successful experiences are freer to explore their world.

20; or express an astronomically large number, such as 27! The introduction is through the number's cardinal name (how many). Children do not recognize symbols yet, but they have heard their names, so repetition follows, in or out of order. The next step will be in learning each ordinal name (or position, such as first, second, and so on). This often comes from hearing older children select positions or turns. Rote counting has value in repeatedly hearing the names and sequence of numbers; however, when the children are stopped in recitation, they return to the first number. The value of drilling young children in number sequence is questionable, because as yet numbers mean nothing to them.

Piaget has outlined the following concepts as appropriate when they correspond to the preschooler's development:

1. Classification (grouping by some common characteristic)
2. Seriation (ordering by a common characteristic)
3. Spatial relationships (distance, movement, and so on)
4. Temporal relationships (time)
5. Conservation (permanence of materials or objects)

Relationship is an important aspect of mathematics. A relationship is necessary to classify, order, and measure space or time, and also in the permanence of things. Relationship between sizes, such as small, smaller, smallest, is one of the more difficult concepts for young children to learn. For example, when given five items of mixed sizes, most young children cannot easily arrange them in appropriate sequence (Copeland, 1984). Margolin (1982) states about relationships:

> Children's realization of relationships begins to build a form of logic, thinking ahead, anticipating cause and effect. Mathematical concepts require anticipation of possible outcomes. The greater number of experiences of this kind that children have, accompanied by explanations of events by interested adults, the better will foundational skills be developed.

Relationships are comparisons, which give children words that symbolize mathematical concepts.

Source for Parents

The U.S. Department of Education (Office of Research, 1991) has prepared a helpful booklet to help parents become more involved with the mathematical teaching of their children. It states that children need instruction "that prepares them to use math not only to compute but also to deal with new technologies, to solve problems, to examine relationships, and to help make sense of the world around them" (p. 2). It encourages parents to do math experiences with their children (in terms of numbers and amounts and playing games that deal with things as logic, reason, estimation, direction, classification, and time). It further encourages parents to be supportive of their children, and to let schools know of parental concern. It recognizes that math comes "naturally" to some people and takes effort and interest on the part of the learner and support on the part of the parent. Some even need to make an attitude change about math and encourage their children in science and math courses.

Parents can help a child develop good study habits by providing a quiet place to study, making sure the child understands that solving problems is not always easy, encouraging persistence and discussing problem-solving ideas, and encouraging alternative strategies to find answers.

The booklet helps parents understand that "math is classifying objects, identifying shapes, reading and interpreting graphs, estimating all sorts of things such as distance, time, and amount, and becoming a detective to discover unknowns" (p. 4). With parental help, the child can understand the connections between math and the skills used every day on the job or in the home.

Here are some suggestions that could be used in the home or in the classroom:

Shopping: newspaper and magazine ads, comparing prices, weight, quantity, using a calculator, preparing a shopping list, working with a budget, managing one's allowance, collecting and sorting coupons

Traveling: directions, maps, street maps, speed limits and distances, time to get to a place, fuel cost and amount, counting cars or items, license plates, road signs

Gardening: what to plant and when, growing period, harvest, height and distances between plants, garden spot needed

Cooking and eating: measuring ingredients, cooking times, temperatures, amount needed, size and amount needed for each person, using measuring utensils, how to do things (chop, crush, roll)

Personal aspects: sorting clothing, family sizes (height, weight, clothing), time for activities, estimating measurements

Play: games that involve counting, finding patterns, and solving problems (tic-tac-toe, crossword and jigsaw puzzles, checkers, and chess). Buy your child a calculator and encourage playing with it to explore numbers and number facts. Relate sports to mathematics (player numbers, scoring, timing).

ACTIVITIES TO INCREASE MATHEMATICAL CONCEPTUALIZATION

As mentioned previously, mathematical experiences are divided into four areas: sorting and classifying, counting, measuring, and exploring space and shapes.

Miniplans

Teachers should think spontaneously, integrate ideas into the curriculum when it is most valuable *(spontaneous)*, and help the children see that the curriculum is expansive, exciting, and useful. When a teaching incident occurs and the teacher feels threatened or unprepared, it should be a warning and a challenge to commit oneself to reading, researching, or whatever it takes to fill this void. It may be a written plan that is implemented soon; it may be discussion with other adults; it may be more experience and practice.

Sample miniplans are included in each of the following mathematical areas and should be used as *idea givers, teacher builders,* and *mind expanders.* Learn to think ahead and respond to current needs.

Sorting and Classifying

When children are asked to put things that belong (or go together) in a certain place, they may group them differently than an adult would. Before responding to their appropriateness, or inappropriateness, seek further clarification from the children.

Art activities involve mathematical concepts, such as size, measuring, and sorting.

- Ask the children to sort a variety of objects by a common characteristic. Then ask for a different grouping. At first have two or three different possibilities. Use buttons as an example. Sort by color, size, number of holes; composition (wood, glass, plastic, fabric); use (men's, women's, children's); design; and so on. Also useful for this task are animals, cans, clothing, dishes, flowers, food, fruit, jars, leaves, marbles, rocks, seeds, and toys.
- Have objects in sets of four (three belong together, one is different, such as three animals and a pillow or three wheel toys and a shovel). Present the objects to the children and have them select the one that is different. This is an important experience.
- Let the child sort familiar objects (socks, shoes, boxes, and so on).
- Use commercial toys that have different-shaped objects to put in correspondingly shaped holes.
- Play or sort cards (old maid, go fish, and so on).
- Have the children place pictures or cards in the proper sequence and tell a story about them.
- Provide many opportunities to develop visual discrimination (for example, sizes, shapes, similarities, differences, symbols, and designs).
- Have a display of coins. Discuss characteristics and amounts of each.
- Use math vocabulary: add (more), subtract (less); wide, narrow; large, larger, largest; middle; and so on.
- Have duplicate cards showing a certain number of objects or dots on one and a corresponding written symbol on the other.
- Make sandpaper shapes and written symbols.

Sample Miniplan Involving Sorting and Classifying

Make a set of 40 number cards of light cardboard or heavy paper, 3″ × 4″ in size, individually numbered from 0 to 9, in four different colors. Along with the number, the card should show the number of dots represented by the card's number. Laminate the cards for longevity. (You may want more than one set to encourage interaction.)

Theme

Number, color, and symbol recognition.

Ideas to Emphasize

Give few instructions to the children. If necessary, suggest they look for something the cards have in common (color, numerals, design).

1. Each card has number symbols, colors, and a design. The cards can be put in stacks of things that are alike (color, symbol, design).
2. The cards can be put in order of quantity (low to high).
3. The cards could be used for playing games (taking turns, singing about colors or numbers, and so on).
4. The cards can be matched to other things in the room.

Learning Activities

1. Give few instructions to the children. If they can't figure out a way to use the cards, suggest they look for something the cards have in common (color, numerals, design).
2. Help them establish a name for each pile (color, number).
3. After familiarization with the cards, suggest that the children take a card and match it to something in the room (toy, numbered object, another activity, and so on). (Prior to the activity the teacher should be sure there are a number of easily accessible "matches" in sight.)

Counting

○ Provide many counting-out experiences (number of people for snack, cups for measuring, trikes to ride, and so on).

○ Do number finger plays and nursery rhymes.

○ Sing number songs.

○ Use books about numbers.

○ Recite poems containing numbers.

○ Focus on one number at a time (make a book about *four;* that is, talk about animals with four legs, involve four children in an activity, and so on).

○ Make and use a daily calendar.

○ Count items (number of buttons on a shirt; number of children wearing tie shoes; number of trees in the yard; spools, boxes, shovels, instruments).

○ Bring in and use a calculator or adding machine.

○ Talk about and show objects that have numbers: bottles, boxes, a calendar, cards, a cash register, a clock, flash cards, license plates, measuring spoons and cups, money, a phone, road signs, a ruler, scales, a speedometer, a sports player, tickets, a timer, a watch, a yardstick.

- Make a store. Provide cans, boxes, money, and a cash register. Write numbers (cost) on articles and amounts on money. Make it fun and simple.
- Earn and use tokens.
- Relate numbers to activities: how many times the ball bounced, the clock struck, the teacher clapped.
- Keep attendance records of the children.
- Make and post a class directory with addresses and phone numbers of the children and teachers.
- Use counters and containers (for example, an egg carton and poker chips; numbers written on a small juice can and Popsicle sticks to go in it).
- Talk with children about the difference between cardinal (1, 2, 3) and ordinal (first, second, third) numbers.
- Show how grouping helps in counting things.
- Go on a picnic. How much and what will you need to take?
- Play games with number symbol spinners.
- Use a die (dots represent numbers; numerals can be included on each face of the die).
- Count objects in a book or in the environment.
- Teach phone numbers to each child and how to use the telephone.
- Talk about numbers on athletic clothing.
- Point out numbers in the environment (speed limits, costs, quantity, and so on).
- Tell a story and have the children supply number parts (of legs on animals, distance, and so on).
- Count the number of children with a certain color of clothing, type of shoes, or physical characteristics. Count and name the parts of plants or objects.
- Set the table for snack or lunch. Decide how many things are needed.
- Have tickets for snack or lunch.
- Have a variety of clocks (number, digital, modernistic).
- Sell something for snack or lunch.
- Write numbers on spring clothespins. Hang a clothesline, yarn, or string at the child's level. Have the child take a clothespin from a box and hang it on the line in proper sequence (clothespins are easily moved around if errors occur).

Measuring

- Provide opportunities for various methods of measurement (length, width, time, size, amount).
- Provide opportunities for linear measurement (use string, stick, measuring tape, yardstick). Introduce the metric system for those who are ready for it.
- Weigh each child, measure her height, and post information about her on a chart or wall.

Sample Miniplan Involving Counting

Theme

Numbers

Ideas to Emphasize

1. Numbers are all around us.
2. Numbers can help us in work and play.
3. Numbers are represented in different ways.
4. Numbers are in a certain sequence.
5. Numbers can be fun.

Learning Activities

1. Prepare the environment so there are many opportunities to observe, count, and use numbers throughout the day.
2. Prepare number opportunities throughout the day—some to be spontaneous (suggested by the children) and some to be planned.
3. Take a planned or "pretend" field trip. We have _____ children, _____ teachers, and _____ cars. How can we take the trip without being overcrowded or understaffed?
4. Periodically throughout the day, involve children and numbers together (chairs for snack, toys to play with, instruments for music, and so on). Compare timers (clocks, watches, others) that use symbols and/or numbers.
5. Take children on a casual walk through your facilities. Gather up or make a list of all the things that have numbers on them (phone, clock, attendance list, toys, and so on). Talk about how numbers help us.
6. Show individual number cards and help the children arrange them in a numerical sequence.
7. Use your own imagination! Numbers are everywhere! Numbers are important to adults and children!

- Provide scales for weighing objects (this activity could also be used in a store).
- Introduce a thermometer and have ways for the children to use it (hot and cold).
- Introduce the concepts *zero, equal,* and *half* as the child is ready.
- Cut an apple. Ask how many pieces are needed to give each person a slice. Ask what the various pieces are called (half, quarter, eighth).
- Pack a sack. Talk about putting heavier things on the bottom.
- Use a compass, barometer, or speedometer.
- Relate measurement to an activity: how long you can stand on one foot, how far you can jump, and so on.
- Talk about center activities that are in the recent past or the near future (yesterday, today, tomorrow).
- Measure ingredients and make an art medium (such as clay).

○ Measure: heel-toe across room, for woodworking, or the amount of space in the block area.

○ Follow a recipe for food.

○ Compare size and number of objects.

○ Balance objects in a scale, on a board, or on your head.

○ Using measuring cups and spoons, see how many times you need to fill a smaller container to fill a larger one, or how many times a larger one will fill a smaller one.

Sample Miniplan Involving Measurement

Theme

Measurement

Ideas to Emphasize

1. There are different kinds of measurement: weight, size, time, amount, and so on.
2. Measurement can help us do things faster.
3. It is fun to measure things.

Learning Activities

1. Set up the classroom to stimulate children to participate in measurement activities: scales, tapes, art activities, measuring cups and spoons with a recipe, timing (cooking, endurance), new jargon, timing devices, new ideas suggested by children, and so on.
2. Help the children see how measurement is beneficial (saves time, better product, coordination, and so on).
3. Provide a container and objects of different sizes. How can you determine if the objects will fit?
4. Help the children determine a routine or schedule for the day (things they want to do before lunch or going home).
5. Talk about different sizes of things (clothes, houses).
6. If possible, have an artisan (carpenter, tailor, baker, and so on) come to class and construct something of his or her trade.

Exploring Space and Shapes

Suppose you were going to introduce different shapes to young children and help them begin to distinguish shapes. Which of the following would you do?

1. Trace the shapes on a piece of paper and give the children cut-outs to place over the traced shapes.
2. Give them three-dimensional shapes to place over traced shapes.
3. Talk with the children about different shapes, what their uses are (so they will roll—or not roll), and ask children to get examples from a set of blocks as the adult describes them or asks for them by name.

Making cookies is a favorite experience for young children. It provides good math opportunities—and a great snack!

Sample Miniplan Involving Space and Shape Exploration

Now it is your turn to plan and implement this topic. Make it spontaneous, important, and fun! You may want to walk into your classroom and see how many readily available things are already there.

Theme

Space and shapes

Ideas to Emphasize

Learning Activities

General Instructions

Use only a few, most familiar shapes. Explain the process to the child—how he is to use the objects in concert with the paper. Help the child verbalize the shapes and the procedure. Make sure the child does not identify the color of a cut-out with its shape (all "rounds" are red). Assist the child (verbally or physically, if necessary) in placing shapes into a composition. Is it easier for the child to use cut-outs or real objects? How were the child's senses and developmental ability shown in each case? What did you learn from this experience?

How would you change (or build on) each option to take the child further in shapes learning? Under what conditions would you display the child's work (if it was correct, if it was neat or complete, if the child at least initiated the task, if the child wanted to keep it, if the child showed creativity, if parents value "products")?

Analysis of Experience

1. Flat paper, sit-down job, all objects of same material (paper), no real distinction between shapes. Assist the child (verbally or physically if necessary) in placing shapes into a composition.

2. Three-dimensional objects that can be felt for shape, density, composition. Can better relate the shapes to similar objects in room. Has feel of shape (roundness, square corners, and so on).

3. Various means are used to determine the child's knowledge—language to describe objects or to ask questions; movement of hands to describe objects or body to get objects; sensory opportunities; thinking skills; creativity in learning how objects would fit or not fit, and so on.

Follow up the experience with two or more hands-on activities:

- Look for and label shapes within the classroom.
- Place similar shapes together (eating or cooking utensils, replicas of animals or food).
- Use tongs to group similar objects—nuts are fun and easy.
- Play a game like Twister.
- Stack objects (plastic barrels, socks, hats, and so on).
- Use body to form shapes; walk in shape patterns.
- Sequence similar objects but different sizes (dishes, shoes, brushes, toys, and so on).
- Use yarn or light rope to form shapes.
- Look at shapes of things (pizza) and see how the shape changes when it is cut.
- Ask children for suggestions about shapes.
- Have objects and articles of different sizes and shapes.
- Look around the room and yard for objects of the same shape.
- Take a shoebox and make openings of different shapes. Insert objects through a hole of the same shape.
- Have a discussion in the block area (shapes, sizes, number, relationship to each other).
- Make a poster board with various shapes and designs (keys, objects, people). Put corresponding objects or shapes and designs in a box. Have children select an object and hang it over the appropriate shape.
- Use nesting toys such as cups and dolls.
- Use puzzles.
- Using blocks of different sizes or shapes, ask the children to hand you specific ones or to make certain forms.
- Let the child experiment with geometric shapes.
- Supply dominoes for building or exploring.
- Use magnetic numbers and letters on a magnetic board.

- Toss beanbags into variously shaped holes.
- Match objects: bottle with lid, mittens, and so on.
- Have the children reproduce designs with beads, blocks, and so on.
- Play picture or number bingo.
- Using templates of paper, metal, wood, plastic, or cardboard, have the children trace geometric designs.
- Provide many opportunities for the child to develop visual discrimination (sizes, shapes, similarities and differences, symbols, designs, sequencing).

APPLICATION OF PRINCIPLES

1. Using available objects (too large to be put into mouths), design a way that young children can practice math skills (measuring, counting, comparing, and so on).

2. Using objects of similar properties (wood, for example), ask a child to help you use them in as many ways as possible. If the objects have more than one characteristic (size, shape, length, use), encourage the child to expand uses of the object.

3. Help a young child to learn how to "group" objects for easier counting (pairs, pattern, and so on).

4. Taking some or all of the following items, ask the children to construct as many games as they can: large buttons, familiar toy pieces, wood objects (blocks, dowels, checkers, and so on).

5. In daily living, at school or home, recount the ways numbers were used during one day (snack, attendance, classroom setup, board games, card games, transportation, and so on).

6. For experiences combining math and other curriculum areas, try the following:
   a. *Math and creative and artistic expression:* Help the children make one of the recipes in Appendix D or one of your favorites.
   b. *Math and cooking:* Help the children make one of the recipes in Appendix D or one of your favorites.
   c. *Math and music:* select one of the number songs or finger plays in Chapter 12, or one of your (or their) favorites.
   d. *Math and field trips:* Let the children help plan the trip (how many children and teachers, what to take for snack [napkins, cups, juice, crackers], time to go and return, and so on).
   e. *Math and literature:* Tell one of their favorite number stories, or read a book about numbers. Involve them in the counting.

   f. *Math through the day:* Carefully plan activities where numbers will be used: number of children in an area, chairs for snack, number of paintbrushes and scissors, games using spinners and counting, a broad schedule of activities, child/child and child/teacher ratios in certain activities, weigh and measure children and make an individual or group chart; involve all curriculum activities (songs, stories, outdoor play, creative activities, and so on). Make it fun—not an assignment filler!

7. Make a Reflection of your own. It may be a game, a story, physical involvement, a food experience, or an idea of your choice to illustrate math opportunities for young children. Think about the following ideas:

   a. *Daily living:* distribution of materials (even one-on-one); division of objects (equal snack items); collection of things (parental slips, number present or absent)

   b. *Keeping records:* attendance, books; cleanup (number of items that go in each box); voting (comparison of quantities)

   c. *A guessing game:* removal of a numbered card

   d. *Board games:* Candy Land, Chutes and Ladders, original games

   e. *Card games:* many excellent ones—choose for appropriate developmental level

8. Originate an enjoyable method of determining which children in your center can correctly identify number symbols.

9. Using materials in your center, or those suggested in the chapter, provide experiences for children in classification, seriation, and conservation. Observe closely the responses of each

child. Which experiences need to be modified or repeated? Why do some of the children have difficulty in understanding some of these concepts?

10. Use at least one mathematical experience each day in your center. Make it fun, stimulating, and desired. Never force a child to participate or to reach a certain level of performance.

11. Use nursery rhymes, songs, food experiences, and stories that mention numbers and number concepts.

12. When appropriate, encourage children to use numbers spontaneously.

13. Note the different activities in which children participate. Describe how the activities include math concepts (number, sequence, problem solving, and so on).

14. Suggest ways you could modify number concepts for special-needs or less advanced children.

15. Play noncompetitive number games, such as throwing beanbags through hoops, in which each child tries to improve her own previous score.

16. Introduce an activity in which children learn and use cardinal and ordinal numbers.

REFERENCES

Almy, M. (1976). Piaget in action. *Young Children*, 31(2), 93–96.

Anderson, T. L. (1996, May). "They're trying to tell me something": A teacher's reflection on primary children's construction of mathematical knowledge. *Young Children*, 51(4), 34–42.

Brittain, W. L. (1969). Some exploratory studies of the art of preschool children. *Studies in Art Education*, 10(3), 14–24.

Broman, B. L. (1982). *The early years in childhood education*, 285–311. Chicago: Rand McNally.

Brooks, J., & M. Brooks (1993). *In search of understanding: The case for constructivist classrooms*. Alexandria, VA: Teacher Association for Supervision and Curriculum Development.

Brophy, J. E., T. L. Good, & S. E. Nedler (1975). *Teaching in the preschool*. New York: Harper & Row.

Burns, M. (1994). Arithmetic: The last holdout. *Phi Delta Kappan*, 75(6), 471–476.

Charlesworth, R. (1988, Summer). Integrating math with science and social studies: A unit example. *Day Care & Education*, 15(4), 28–31.

Charlesworth, R., & K. K. Lind (1990). *Math and science for young children*. Albany, NY: Delmar.

Copeland, R. W. (1984). *How children learn mathematics: Teaching implications of Piaget's research*, 4th edition. New York: Macmillan.

DeVries, R., & L. Kohlberg (1987). *Constructivist early education: Overview and comparison with other programs*. Washington, DC: NAEYC.

DeVries, R., & B. Zan (1994). *Moral classrooms, moral children: Creating a constructivist atmosphere in early education*. New York: Teachers College Press.

Fisher, A. (1992, August). Crisis in education, Part 1: Science + math = F. *Popular Science*, 241(2), 58–63, 108.

Fisher, A. (1992, September). Crisis in education, Part 2: Why Johnny can't do science and math. *Popular Science*, 241(3), 50–55, 98.

Greenberg, P. (1993, May). How and why to teach all aspects of preschool and kindergarten math naturally, democratically, and effectively (for teachers who don't believe in academic programs, who do believe in educational excellence, and who find math boring to the max)—Part 1. *Young Children*, 48(4), 75–84.

Greenberg, P. (1994, January). How and why to teach all aspects of preschool and kindergarten math naturally, democratically, and effectively (for teachers who don't believe in academic programs, who do believe in educational excellence, and who find math boring to the max)—Part 2. *Young Children*, 49(2), 12–18, 88.

Harsh, A. (1987). Teach mathematics with children's literature. *Young Children*, 42(6), 24–29.

Henniger, M. (1987, February) Learning mathematics and science through play. *Childhood Education*, 63(3), 167–171.

Jones, G. A., & C. A. Thornton (1993, July). Children's understanding of place value: A framework for curriculum development and assessment. *Young Children*, 48(5), 12–18.

Kamii, C. (1985a). *Young children reinvent arithmetic, second grade: Implications of Piaget's theory*. New York: Teachers College Press.

Kamii, C. (1985b, September). Leading primary education toward excellence: Beyond worksheets and drill. *Young Children*, 40(6), 3–9.

Kamii, C. (1986). Cognitive learning and development. In Spodek, B. (ed.), *Today's Kindergarten*, 67–90. New York: Teachers College Press.

Kamii, C. (1989). *Young children reinvent arithmetic, second grade: Implications of Piaget's theory*. New York: Teachers College Press.

Kamii, C. (1995). *Number in preschool & kindergarten*. Washington, DC: NAEYC.

Kamii, C., & R. DeVries (1978). *Physical knowledge in preschool education: Implications of Piaget's theory*. Englewood Cliffs, NJ: Prentice-Hall.

Kamii, C., & R. DeVries (1980). *Group games in early education: Implications of Piaget's theory.* Washington, DC: NAEYC.

Kamii, C., & B. Lewis (1993). The harmful effects of algorithms in primary arithmetic. *Teaching K–8,* 23, 36–38.

Kamii, C., B. Lewis, & S. Livingston (1993). Primary arithmetic: Children inventing their own procedures. *Arithmetic Teacher,* 41(4), 200–203.

Kokoski, T. M., & N. Downing-Leffler (1995, July). Boosting your science and math programs in early childhood education: Making the home-school connection. *Young Children,* 50(5), 35–39.

Leushina, A. M. (English translation, 1991). *The development of elementary mathematical concepts in preschool children.* Vol. 4, *Soviet studies in mathematics education.* Reston, VA: National Council of Teachers of Mathematics.

Lowenfeld, V. (1987). *Creative and mental growth,* 8th edition. New York: Macmillan.

Margolin, E. (1982). *Teaching young children at school and home,* 249–273. New York: Macmillan.

NAEYC position statement: Technology and young children—ages three through eight (1996, September). *Young Children,* 51(6), 11–16.

National Council of Teachers of Mathematics (NCTM) (1989). *Curriculum and evaluation standards for school mathematics.* Reston, VA: Author.

Northeast Foundation for Children (1991). *Notebook for teachers: Making changes in the elementary curriculum.* Greenfield, MA: Author.

Office of Research, Office of Educational Research and Improvement, U.S. Department of Education (1991), *You can help your young child learn mathematics.* Washington, DC: U.S. Government Printing Office.

Payne, J. N. (ed.) (1975/1990). *Mathematics for the young child.* Reston, VA: National Council of Teachers of Mathematics.

Piaget, J. (1965). *The child's conception of number.* New York: Norton.

Piaget, J. (1969). *Science of education and the psychology of the child.* New York: Viking.

Piaget, J. (1970). *The child's conception of time.* New York: Basic.

Price, G. G. (1989, May). Mathematics in early childhood. *Young Children,* 44(4), 53–58.

Richardson, L., K. Goodman, N. Harman, & H. LePique (1980). *A mathematics activity curriculum for Early Childhood and Special Education.* New York: Macmillan.

Schifter, D., & C. Fosnot (1993). *Reconstructing mathematics education: Stories of teachers meeting the challenge of reform.* New York: Teachers College Press.

Seefeldt, C. (1980). *A curriculum for preschools,* 2nd edition, 253–266. Columbus, OH: Merrill.

Stone, J. I. (1987). Early childhood math: Make it manipulative! *Young Children,* 42(6), 16–23.

Taylor, B. J. (1993). *Science everywhere: Opportunities for very young children.* Fort Worth, TX: Harcourt Brace Jovanovich.

Third International Mathematics and Science Study (TIMSS) (1997, January). Stronger focus needed in improving math education, study shows. *Community Update,* #43, U.S. Department of Education.

Third International Mathematics and Science Study (TIMSS) (1997, July/August). Americans beat international averages in science and math. Community Update, #49, U.S. Department of Education.

Van Scoy, I. J., & S. H. Fairchild (1993). It's about time! Helping preschool and primary children understand time concepts. *Young Children,* 48(2), 21–24.

Whiting, D. J. (1994, January). Literature and mathematics in preschool and primary: The right connection. *Young Children,* 49(2), 4–11.

Williams, C. K., & C. Kamii (1986). How do children learn by handling objects? *Young Children,* 42(1), 23–26.

Wood, T., P. Cobb, & E. Yackel (1993). The nature of whole class discussion. *Journal for Research in Mathematics Education,* Monograph #6, 55–68.

Social Studies, Anti-Bias Curriculum, and Field Trips

CHAPTER 10

MAIN PRINCIPLES

1. Social studies, a part of science, are important for children to learn about themselves and their heritage and to help them understand and appreciate other people.
2. Through social studies, children can learn about their environment and its people through firsthand experiences.
3. Learning about others includes respect for diversity.
4. Anti-bias curriculum helps children better understand differences in gender, ethnic customs, age, race, family compositions, gifted and disabled children, and peaceful and violent living conditions.
5. Many interesting activities increase a child's awareness of social science.
6. Field trips can be valuable learning experiences for young children.

It should be noted early in this discussion that although we are recognizing and accepting many types of diversity, there are some types of diversity that we do not tolerate, such as abuse in any of its many physical, verbal, social, emotional, and intellectual forms. Nor do we tolerate adult or societal behaviors that may cause bodily harm to young children. In these cases we recognize (as in the cases of abuse, AIDS, and drugs), we teach (adults and children), we report to the proper authorities, and we do whatever is necessary for young children to grow up in a healthy, happy, growth-promoting environment.

As mentioned in Chapter 8, social studies are a part of science; however, because of the strong influence social studies have on the child and his view of himself and his world, information is extended to this chapter, which consists of three parts, each one equally important in the lives of young children and families: (1) learning about oneself, (2) learning about others using an anti-bias curriculum, and (3) awareness of social science.

Parents take their children to more places in the community than do teachers, so parents play an important role in familiarizing their children with activities, occupations, resources, and functions. They may take their children to the fire station, police station, post office, hospital, or an interesting landmark. They may also take their children to places of significance to the family, such as a church, a cemetery, the home of a relative, or a cultural event. As parents do daily errands, they should briefly tell the child how the people they see can help us (service-station attendant, cleaner, baker, banker, grocer). Children can learn firsthand about their extended families, or parents can invite guests into their homes or do something nice for a neighbor, relative, or friend.

Teachers can build on the experiences parents provide for their children. It may be easier for a child to understand and interact in dramatic play when she has seen or heard things related to that play (real animals on a farm, or a visit to a fire station). Teachers need to know the children and families well so they can reinforce family values, build understanding and acceptance, and support cultural heritage.

VALUES FOR CHILDREN

Studying social aspects for young children can help them do the following:

1. Learn about themselves, their family, and their environment.
2. Prevent feelings of inferiority or prejudice toward others.
3. Become more productive members of society.
4. Enlarge their horizon of knowledge and understanding.

LEARNING ABOUT ONESELF

Before children can learn about others, they must first learn about themselves. From birth they are learning to adjust to and accept themselves through their interaction with others and their environment.

Some children and families face problems not experienced by other children and families (for example, homelessness, poverty, illness, violence). The homeless child, for example, through no fault of his own, finds himself and his family living in a car, a tent, a box, or even an open park. There is little or no food, clothing, or shelter. Although the McKinney Act, which passed in 1987 with amendments passed in 1988, provides states with funds to assist the homeless, including assistance to

schools to assure that each child of a homeless family has access to free public education, these children and families face problems not conceived by other families
and need some special understanding and support if they are to maintain self-
respect and survival. Parents of homeless children want preschool staff to know
that their children are embarrassed about their homelessness; their families face
multiple problems (for example, spouse abuse, depression); they care deeply about
their children; some questions seem intrusive; the family is not necessarily a dys-
functional family; and some school requests cause embarrassment and frustration
to them (McCormick & Holden, 1992). Children from this situation or others equally
discouraging need extra love and attention if they are to feel they are worthwhile
and competent people.

The young child, even under the best of circumstances, has much to learn
about herself, her family, her environment, and her extended world. Children who
are raised in a loving home, have their developmental needs met, and feel good
about themselves have a head start in life. At first, young children depend on others
for their care and to fulfill their needs; later, they learn how to solve many of their
own needs; the success of this depends on how they feel individually and in the
presence of others. (Refer to Chapter 1 and Erikson's steps to a healthy personality.)

Further information seems appropriate here as the child learns about his
abilities and his relationship with other individuals. Self-esteem is a crucial aspect
of human dignity and requires home and school cooperation to help him build and
feel his worthiness. There is a widely publicized connection between self-esteem
and academic achievement. The school can help enhance self-esteem by helping
"children to cope with ambiguities and discontinuities in their lives and to avoid the

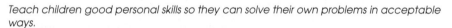

*Teach children good personal skills so they can solve their own problems in acceptable
ways.*

endemic self-destruction behaviors that are symptomatic of these conditions" (Beane, 1991, p. 153). For schools to play their contributing role, continues Beane,

> we might expect to observe a humanistic climate, participation of children in school and classroom governance, heterogeneous grouping, cooperative learning, thematic units that emphasize construction of personal and social meanings, self-evaluation, multi-cultural content, community service projects, and activities that involve making, creating, and doing things. We would not expect to see an autocratic, adult-dominated environment, either explicitly displayed or thinly veiled behind gimmicks, gadgets, and coupons that are meant to insidiously seduce children into prizing someone else's agenda over their own.

> . . . [N]o truly authentic project for self-esteem can proceed without a vision of a socially transformed world and a critique of the current status of our society (Ladewig, 1990). Many will recognize this as the language and politics of social reconstruction and they will be correct in doing so. But if "developmental" interests are sincere about the quality of life for children, then this is the direction they must take. Anything short of this will continue the superficial, culturally detached, utilitarian, and self-protective definition of self-esteem, a version that clearly does not serve the self-esteem of children. (pp. 159–160)

BEHAVIOR

Social

According to Cartwright (1993),

> We now know that it's not so much competition as cooperation that ensures survival in our fragile environment. . . . Cooperative learning in the classroom is not only relevant to life; it may be childhood learning at its best. (p. 12)

Teachers can stage classrooms so they promote or destroy cooperation. Consider Table 10.1 (see also Chapter 2).

Democracy

Greenberg (1992a) offered this account:

> My classroom is not child centered. It is not curriculum centered. It is not centered around researching the child's mind. It is developmental for each child, I hope—in other words, based on each child's physical, psychological, and social accomplishments, issues, needs, and readiness, as well as intellectual and academic accomplishments, issues, needs, and readiness. Isn't that what *development* means? (p. 10)

Let there be no doubt that parents and teachers are *always* responsible for the health, safety, and teaching of young children. It is the way they exercise these responsibilities that makes for a democratic or autocratic classroom. (See Chapter 2.) Democratic adults create and maintain necessary guidelines (with input from children), but the adults do not demand or command! They set the tone of the group and classroom through room arrangement, materials and equipment, enforcing the philosophy of the center, and personal interaction with children and adults. They also allow ample time and opportunities for spontaneous or child-initiated ideas. (See Figure 10.1.)

Table 10.1
Classroom Behaviors Depend on Teacher Preparation

COOPERATION	*CONTENTION*
Kinds of activities selected	Limited kinds of activities selected
Placement of materials for child use and replacement	Materials unaccessible for child use—no responsibility for replacement
Variety of opportunities	Few opportunities for personal selection
Adequate spaces	Cramped or traffic-pattern spaces
Uninterrupted time frames	Interruptions and time limitations
Types of toys and activities	One-of-a-kind toys or activities
Congenial and supportive attitudes of adults and children	Poor attitude of adults and children
Challenging, new, or repetitive activities	Broken, difficult, or one-turn toys
Sharing or trading toys and ideas	Limited use of toys and ideas (sharing means "losing")
Happy and secure children	Possessive or insecure children
Companionship—a sense of belonging	Isolation—a sense of rejection
Adults help children resolve conflicts in nonviolent ways (negotiation and conflict resolution)	Adults leave children to resolve disputes without giving them the skills or support to do so

Greenberg, 1992a, p. 14.

Seefeldt (1993) reminds us that quality programs for young children (1) "recognize that children are dependent on adults. At the same time, however, they realize that children must not learn the *habit* of being dependent on others but must learn to think and make decisions for themselves to develop independence"; (2) give children the responsibility of taking "at least partial responsibility for solving problems that arise from living, learning, and working with one another in a group"; and (3) also give children the opportunity "to experience the consequences of their decisions . . . determining which action they would change and how, or why the decision was or was not effective," helping them develop the ability to think and decide for themselves (p. 6).

Dewey (1944) believed another type of decision-making experience was necessary if children were to develop a mind that would enable them to be free. He called for more "stuff" in schools and encouraged teachers to use raw materials so children could develop the ability to think. He believed that raw materials, such as wood, clay, and paints—without any predetermined end or goal for their use—push children into true decision making and thinking. Seefeldt (1993) discusses Dewey's philosophy:

> Children are the ones who must figure out not only what to do with the materials but how they will do it and when they have achieved their own goals. . . . And when they reach their end goal, determined only by them—not by another—they are the ones who experience the joy of achievement and the satisfaction of developing a mind. (1993, p. 7)

In line with this thinking, Seefeldt adds:

> Worksheets, workbooks, computer-assisted instruction, even units of group projects that are determined and directed by a teacher do not permit thinking because often

Figure 10.1
Ways to Establish Good Social Relationships in the Classroom

Teacher-child	Provide a safe, trusting atmosphere where children will verbalize their feelings.
	Talk directly about issues and feelings.
	Role play if appropriate.
	Use terms and situations that are age-appropriate.
	Jointly establish goals and methods so children feel understood and accepted.
	Try to see problems and solutions from both points of view.
	Carefully listen to children's views and suggestions.
	Ask and answer questions in a responsive way.
	Talk at a special time that does not interfere with activities and child/child relationships (Armstrong, 1994, p. 22).
	Organize the environment to minimize stress and pressures put on children (noise, time, choices, interaction with others, special needs, curriculum).
	Be aware of each child's personal needs and interests.
	Invite children's input into the classroom.
Teacher-parent	Help parents to see the particular needs of their children (separation, unfinished activities, late arrival, and so on).
	Point out developmental progress in various areas of behavior.
	Be considerate of the stress and demands life makes on parents.
	Invite parent participation when appropriate.
	Respectfully seek information from parents and listen to parental concerns and input.

much of the doing has been completed by someone else. There is little left for the child to decide or think about. . . . Whenever the end goal of some activity has been predetermined by someone else, children only have to follow . . . but they will fail to develop a mind that could free them from the authority of others. Without a solid foundation of decision making built during early childhood, children will be ill prepared to set goals for themselves and achieve these but may be ready and prepared to achieve goals established for them by others. (p. 7).

Young children benefit from group experiences where they can try, test, share, and evaluate their ideas. They can listen to the ideas of others and compare them to their views. The child will find that some ideas may be better than his, support his, or be in total conflict with his. Until "individuals are able to identify with others, to empathize with others' thoughts and feelings and to develop the capacity for ethical respect, the world may never be free of tyranny and suffering" (Giroux, 1992, p. 7).

When teachers have these same opportunities as children (freedom to try, test, share, and evaluate their ideas), they provide settings for freedom, human dignity, individual rights, and responsibility toward others.

Moral Understanding

According to Buzzelli (1992),

As early as the second year of life, children begin to use standards in evaluating their own behavior and the behavior of others, an achievement that marks the beginning of moral understanding. . . . Most parents expect their children to have an awareness of

Young children generally respond carefully and quietly when a baby visits the classroom.

behavior standards by age three and to regulate their behavior according to the standards by age seven. (p. 48)

During the one- to three-year age period, conflicts involving opposing motives between parent and child first arise. It is no mere coincidence that as the toddler becomes more willful and able to say "No!" more often and more emphatically, parents become increasingly focused on teaching standards, enforcing rules, and using other types of discipline. Conflicts between children and caregivers take on special meaning not only because they represent constraints on the child but also because the conflicts are emotionally charged. Through such encounters, pride, shame, and guilt emerge. (p. 50)

In Buzzelli's research of moral development, the following implications are suggested for parents and teachers:

1. Adults must acknowledge and value young children's emerging morally relevant abilities, including increasingly sophisticated cognitive and language skills, which provide the foundation for moral understanding.
2. Adults need to set clear and appropriate standards and expectations for young children's behavior.
3. Parents and teachers support children's moral understanding when they respond to children's transgressions in ways that are consistent with the type of transgression.

4. Children in the constructivist classroom (DAP) were more cooperative with one another and used more negotiation strategies to solve conflicts than children in other types of classrooms.

5. Early-childhood educators know that from their earliest years, impressionable young children possess sophisticated abilities and understandings of their social world; therefore, they look to adults.

LEARNING ABOUT OTHERS

Diversity

A discussion regarding diversity was introduced in Chapter 1. Children with different backgrounds, genetics, cultures, physical characteristics, personalities, and expectations require teachers and parents to look for these differences and handle them in ways that meet the needs of individual children. Some parents have very definite and particular goals for their children—some parents have similar goals for their children. As educators of young children, we must see that the needs of all children are met in the very best way for each child. We can do this if we recognize that children utilize experiences and information in ways that may be vastly different for each child. See Figure 10.2 for different ways to respond to different situations.

A very useful list of children's books about diversity is found in the article "Enriching Classroom Diversity with Books for Children, In-Depth Discussions of Them, and Story-Extension Activities" (1993). It has a three-page list of books including children with special situations, cooperation, diverse abilities, diverse families, special relationships, diverse gender behaviors, environment, anti-animal stereotypes, low income and job loss, misuses of power, and general multicultural/anti-bias themes.

NAEYC has produced recommendations effective for early-childhood education that respond to linguistic and cultural diversity (NAEYC, 1996). These recommendations include specific guidelines for (1) working with children; (2) working with families; (3) professional preparation of early-childhood educators in the areas of culture, language, and diversity; and (4) recommendations for programs and practice. Their position reads:

> For the optimal development and learning of all children, educators must *accept* (hold in high regard) and *value* (esteem, appreciate) the home culture, and *promote* and *encourage* the active involvement and support of all families, including extended and nontraditional family units.

The article concludes that early-childhood professionals—by responding to the importance of the child's home language and culture—and families—by working toward the "school culture"—can provide a wholesome education for linguistically and culturally diverse children.

Multicultural Education

Multicultural education is a daily, ongoing process, and reaches beyond the typical food and dress in different cultures. It helps children to develop pride and appreciation for their own culture and to become sensitive to others. It is integrated into the curriculum and not merely added to it. It may be an initial cultural introduction for some children and should be done in a casual and accepting way.

Figure 10.2
Diversity in Response to Situations

Say . . .	*Instead of . . .*
The children are restless today (have lots of energy).	The children are wild as Indians today (downgrading a culture).
Tell her with your voice that you would like a turn.	You can't take that away from her (not promoting cooperation, peace).
If you ask in a friendly way, he'll let you have a turn in a minute.	You're just a bully and he doesn't have to share with you (downgrading a child).
This activity will be fun for all the children.	Just boys can play here (sexist).
Try to make it (or do it) yourself, and if you need help, I'll be here to help you (encouraging self-reliance).	Only strong (or smart) children can do this task.
Everyone has a different kind of family.	The best kind of family is white and has a mother, a father, two children, and a dog (insensitive to different family patterns).
Most children can do some things better than other things.	Children who can't hear stories and people talking (or can't run and jump) are not very smart (insensitive to abilities/handicaps).
It's nice to have Grandmas and Grandpas come to our classroom to see what we are doing and to help us out (valuing age).	Old people are grumpy, make trouble, and get in our way.
Let's think of ways men and women (boys and girls) could do the same job.	Let's think of all the jobs just men do and all the jobs just women do (sexist).
Which children in our group have blond hair? (Repeat for each hair color in the group, naming the children and counting them.)	Only children with black hair can swing today (segregating children, promoting competition, or indicating that one characteristic is better than another).
Find an activity you would like to do or a place to play until lunchtime (allowing choice of activity, time span, individual skills, and interest).	You may play wherever you like *after* you have completed *the* flower picture and written your name on it—but you have to hurry or you won't have time to do a good job.
In different families and places, people eat different kinds of food, wear different kinds of clothing, and do special activities (recognizing and learning about different cultures).	Children and families who eat different food than we do, dress differently than we do, or do different activities than we do are not as good as we are.
It is a good idea to take turns being the leader (democracy in choosing roles).	Paul is always the leader and Jennifer is always the caboose.
Sometimes parents get angry at children for the things they do or don't do (alternate discipline vs. abuse).	Parents have the right to hit or punish their children for bad deeds.
Tell her what it is you want or what she did to upset you (giving child a more appropriate response).	It is all right to hit children who get in your way or don't give you what you want.

Reflection

A 4-year-old boy from India asked his teacher one day, "Are we going to have any other children like me?" Not knowing the point of the question, the teacher asked for clarification. Pulling up his sleeve and pointing to his arm, the child replied, "You know, some children like me." The teacher knew he was asking about children of color, and quickly pointed out a Native American and several children with olive skin. The boy replied: "No, I mean *brown* like me!" What a golden and spontaneous moment to talk about the similarities and differences of the children in the group.

Children may engage in solitary or cooperative play as they learn about each other.

But don't wait for children to ask questions about cultural differences. Be aware of opportunities that are always there. Some young children have exposure to cultural differences and others do not. As children develop their self-concepts (during the preschool years), they do so as they make friends and interact with families and other individuals within their environment. When these interaction opportunities are not there, children become fearful of others—especially if others are different from themselves. They have a tendency to believe things they see and hear about others (collectively and individually). Even when there is cultural homogeneity, adults or children can talk about differences and encourage discussion without introducing competition, fear, dislike, or other negative aspects, such as comparing children against each other, family differences, physical characteristics, things people do, or kinds of clothing they wear, foods they eat, their housing, and so on.

Teachers in early childhood can implement multicultural education by being curious themselves, without being negative or judgmental, about the children in their classrooms. How do the children show affection or emotion? What are their attitudes toward school, themselves, and others? What materials can be brought into the classrooms that will introduce different ideas, expose the children to new things, and add an awareness and concern for others? Start where the children are now and focus on them. Change inappropriate things in the classroom and seek information and help from parents and others. Be sincere and respectful in your actions and dealings with children and adults. At the end of each curriculum chapter are some general suggestions to stimulate adult awareness of items and activities to incorporate in the classroom for a multicultural curriculum.

Caution: To begin with an extended exposure to many people at the same time, or to bombard the children with multicultural experiences, may just confuse or annoy them. Use wisdom in your planning—and make sure the children are the focus of your curriculum planning!

The suggestions can help creative positive relationships among different groups of people and help children gain interest in and concern with issues outside of their immediate experiences. Young children are usually more tolerant of changes if they meet them in a comfortable setting and if they have time to investigate and find out for themselves. Some teachers may feel that getting authentic information (dress, food, clothing, activities) on several different cultures is laborious and nonproductive. Begin with cultures or groups most likely to be in the lives of children within the classroom, then gradually broaden out to people who are in the community.

Reflection

At our university preschool, many of our student teachers have spent time in other cultures or have close friends who have done so. Many student teachers want to share their excitement and objects with the young children. Most experiences end up with adults talking to adults and uninterested children.

A head teacher and four graduate students found a need to plan a cultural demonstration in one classroom. They decided on Japan because of firsthand knowledge, authentic materials, and parental support. The morning consisted of child-sized kimonos and clogs in the housekeeping area (furnished by a parent of one of the children in the group), teachers wearing kimonos and clogs, cooking rice and eating it with chopsticks for snack, Japanese and English books in a quiet area (a simple picture book was read in Japanese and translated into English—noting the different way the book is printed and used), pictures of the teachers in Japanese settings and clothing, tasting Japanese food, hearing Japanese music, and learning to count to five in Japanese.

The children were fascinated with the clothing, toys, activities, and participation. One child mastered chopsticks—eating four bowls of rice! They talked about the different clothes, shoes, books, and food. Nobody wanted to go home and asked for assurance that we "could do this another time, too." It gave reassurance to our Japanese child and relationships blossomed.

Contrast the preceding experience with that of a group of 4-year-old boys who continually played together at the center following a series of World War II movies playing on television nightly. One boy was Japanese. After several days of reenactment of fighting, the Japanese boy said, quite fairly: "Why do I always have to be the Jap?" It appeared that the other boys recognized his features as being of the "enemy," but he could see no difference and wanted to know why he was singled out. How did he feel about himself? His heritage?

Children with Special Needs

Special laws regarding care and education have been adopted to protect the rights of young children with handicaps. Fink (1992) notes the following:

PL 94-142, the Education for All Handicapped Children Act of 1975, mandates that educators provide special education and related services within the least restrictive environment.

PL 99-457, the Education of the Handicapped Act Amendments of 1986 (amended by PL 101-476), requires all states to offer educational services to children between the ages of 3 and 5 who have handicaps.

The Americans with Disabilities Act (ADA), signed into law on July 26, 1990, by President Bush, prohibits discrimination on the basis of disability in a wide range of areas. Specific applications to early-childhood education programs (for children and their parents/guardians with disabilities) include:

1. *acceptance of children* with disabilities (each individual child considered on a case-by-case basis)
2. *accommodations* (perhaps some architectural changes that are reasonable and readily achievable, and/or subtle changes in the daily program)
3. modification of *behavior procedures* as needed
4. *staff training*
5. *termination of a child* (for reasons other than prejudice—failure to progress, incompatible program, health or safety risk for others—applied equally to all children)
6. *cost*—no additional cost to serve the child

Providers of public-school programs must educate *all* children to the maximum extent possible in the least restrictive environment, which may include changing the structure of the preschool program to an integrated model; one in which students are not grouped by age or severity of handicapping condition but are heterogeneously mixed through the school program provides an opportunity for homebound and kindergarten integration as well as increased integration of support services in the class. Incorporating the communication model provides the added option of within-class services for students with language impairments, and the motor program also expands the options available to students needing these services (Radonovich & Houck, 1990).

Parents of handicapped children feel favorable about having their children mainstreamed in a preschool setting (Miller et al., 1992).

Carran and Scott (1992) report a twofold shift in programs for preschool children with special needs: first, a shift away from longitudinal studies for predictive validity of screening instruments, and second, a shift toward the emphasis of risk analysis and interpretation—away from predictive validity. Further, Haring et al. (1992) state that the formula specifying significant discrepancy between potential and achievement of special-needs preschoolers is inappropriate for children under 6 primarily because "there are no standardized instruments with adequate predictive validity to establish any sense of potential achievement for children this age" (p. 169). They encourage identifying and providing services to children who need them and discourage any labeling of these children.

In a 1992 article, Mahoney and Robinson contrast the typical educational philosophy and procedures used in developmentally appropriate programs in early-childhood education (ECE) with programs currently used in early-childhood special education (ECSE). Their case is strong in suggesting that ECE programs are appropriate for special-needs children. Not being trained in special education, not wanting to take on the field, and not trying to be narrow-minded or directive, but having an interest in all children and having worked with young children with special needs over the years, these authors have proposed goals that are appealing and closely fit the ECE (or DAP) curriculum. See Table 10.2 for specific differences between the two programs as identified by Mahoney and Robinson.

In summary, Mahoney and Robinson encourage those in early-childhood special education to study, observe, evaluate, and cooperate as they develop much-needed alternatives to deficit-oriented special-education practices.

A program called "New Friends" was designed to teach preschoolers about similarities, differences, and disabilities using life-sized dolls with disabilities to in-

Table 10.2
Differences between ECSE and ECE Programs

EARLY-CHILDHOOD SPECIAL EDUCATION (DIP)	EARLY-CHILDHOOD EDUCATION (DAP)
This model more closely represents developmentally inappropriate programs (DIP) in that it does the following:	This model conceptualizes development as being driven by the child's introduction to and interaction with the environment, and does the following:
Emphasizes teacher-directed activities.	Is child-centered.
Views development as being driven by the acquisition of new skills.	
Tends to ignore or disregard children's interests.	Places high priority on supporting and encouraging children's interests and on accepting children's behavior as legitimate and worthwhile.
Acknowledges performances of the behaviors required of children.	
Is based on the notion that children need direction and guidance to perform desired developmental behaviors and activities.	Encourages the development of self-esteem, self-discipline, curiosity, and problem solving.
Encourages teachers to be directive and structured in their interactions with children.	Encourages teachers to be warm, available, and nonintrusive.

troduce four important concepts about specific disabling conditions (differences and similarities, and impairments of hearing, physical ability, and learning). Results indicated that exposure to the program led to positive changes in attitudes and to increased knowledge of disabilities. Thios and Foster (1991) note the following:

> However, no behavioral changes in social interaction patterns were observed. It is concluded that "New Friends" appears to provide a useful curriculum for use in conjunction with other procedures designed to enhance the acceptance of children with disabilities by their non-disabled peers.

ANTI-BIAS CURRICULUM

A filmstrip by the Council on Interracial Books for Children (1978) defines *stereotyping* as follows:

> A stereotype is an oversimplified, generalized image describing all individuals in a group as having the same characteristics, that is to say, in appearance, in behavior, in beliefs. While there may be a germ of truth in a stereotype, the image usually represents a gross distortion, or an exaggeration of that truth, and has offensive, dehumanizing implications.

Values for Children

Children benefit from learning about other people and cultures if activities and concepts are appropriately planned. The following criteria should be considered:

1. Developmental level of each child and of the total group, including interest, attention span, and skills

Reflection

It was summertime and a group of disabled children was housed next door to a group of nondisabled children—an arrangement heretofore not done. At first each head teacher scheduled a time for her group to be outside—therefore nondisabled children and disabled children were not on the playground at the same time. The disabled children had a joyous time indoors and outdoors, but the nondisabled children began to change. They pressed their noses to the glass when the disabled children were outside; they asked serious questions about the disabled children. They became quiet and fearful—of becoming the same way, of the unknown, of losing friends, and so on. The teacher of the nondisabled group began to notice these changes and the seriousness and lethargic response of the children. As they talked within the group, the children began to verbalize their concerns. The teachers began to bring things into the curriculum that the children were noticing—how would it be to be blind? Could a game with a blindfold ease or increase concerns? Would a wheelchair and crutches help the children to know how it felt to be injured or crippled? How would it be if you couldn't hear—or climb? Gradually, the children became less fearful and more curious. Disabled children were invited into their classroom. As tension eased, more and more children of each group were on the playground together. The nondisabled children wanted to ride in wheelchairs, try crutches, and assist the disabled children in many ways. By the end of the summer, the two groups were well integrated, had fun doing things for and with each other, and even had a parade and circus on the playground. What had started out as a fearful and negative situation turned into a cooperative and understanding experience for both groups of children.

2. Possibility of increasing existing knowledge or of clarifying concepts

3. Activities that are child-centered but may be adult-initiated

4. Possibility of increasing independence

5. Inclusion of many different aspects—for example, food, customs, music, and so on

6. Opportunity to increase understanding about and relationships with other cultures and people

Teachers of young children can do many things to avoid stereotyping. In their classrooms they can give wholesome examples of people of different races, ethnic groups, and family composition, and of people of both sexes doing the same and different things.

In using picture and story books in the classroom, the teacher should use caution; "young children are the most vulnerable to stereotypes and bias in books because books play a major role in shaping children's first images of the larger society" (Chambers, 1983, pp. 91–92).

Neugebauer (1987) suggests these guidelines for a visual/aesthetic environment: images of *all* children, families, and staff in your program, and in the U.S. society; images accurately reflecting people's current daily working and recreational activities; a numerical balance among different groups; a fair balance of images of women and men doing jobs in the home and jobs outside the home; images of elderly people of various backgrounds and activities; images of diversity in family styles; images of important individuals—past and present; and artwork—prints, sculpture, and textiles by artists of various backgrounds.

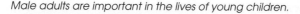

Male adults are important in the lives of young children.

The toys and activities planned for the classroom should include opportunities for children to learn about ethnic groups through books, dramatic play, written and spoken language, music, art materials, guests, manipulatives, blocks, food experiences, and other means. An excellent resource section on children's books (including publishing information; age recommendation; family, gender, people of color, and disabilities; work; prejudice; activism; comments; curriculum materials; and stereotyped worksheets) is found in Derman-Sparks & the A.B.C. Task Force (1989, pp. 119–145).

Gender

Teachers do not want to give the children the impression that *everything* has to be unisex—for it is important for the child to appreciate his or her own sex—but for them to also understand and appreciate the opposite sex. Some things can be done more casually than others. Instead of making name tags (when used) or locker symbols, for example, the teacher could let the child choose from a variety of pictures—not arbitrarily placing feminine symbols on girls' lockers and masculine symbols on boys' lockers. The classroom should include areas and activities that have typically been classed masculine (woodworking, trucks, and so on) and feminine (dramatic play, art, and so on), but *all* children should be encouraged to participate in all areas and feel that it is acceptable. One parent would almost threaten her son not to dress up, play with girls, or get messy. The more she pushed this idea, the more Abraham wanted to do these things—and the more guilt he felt when he did participate. The teacher and the mother discussed the problem, and the mother finally stopped making an issue. Abraham found more pleasure from these activities and then moved into other areas of play. Why shouldn't boys be nurturing, domestic, and creative? The mother's reasoning was she "didn't want him to be a sissy!"

Reflection

In one preschool, the mother of one child was a nurse and volunteered to show the children what she did at work. She also mentioned that many men where she worked were also nurses—and doctors were women or men. A teacher and a group of 4-year-olds were having a spontaneous discussion about the occupations of the parents. One boy said, "Well, my dad's a doctor!" and another one said, "Mine is, too." The teacher told the children that she was also a doctor. The response came back quickly and strong: "Oh, no, you can't be a doctor. You're a girl!" The teacher told them she was not a doctor who gave shots and took care of sick people, but she was a teacher-doctor. The first little boy responded: "Nope! You can be a teacher-nurse but you can't be a teacher-doctor!"

Conversations and ideas such as this inspired a mini-study with the children presently in our early-childhood lab. Each child (age 3½ to 5 years) was asked: "What do you want to be when you grow up?" Following a response, each one was asked, "If you were a boy (girl) rather than a girl (boy), what would you want to be when you grow up?" The answers were diverse. Many of the children of one sex just couldn't imagine being the other sex—or stated "I don't want to be a (person of the opposite sex)." Some answered quickly and surely about each sex. Most of the children (especially the younger ones) selected a familiar role (parent, community helper, or television character) for both roles, but there were a few different ones: pumpkin, snake, dinosaur, or pirate of one's own sex; and for the opposite sex: nothing, chicken, climb up rainbows, Superman, witch, and gremlin. Joshua said, "I hate to grow up—they never have any fun!" and no comment about being a girl. Michael just wanted to be "myself" for both answers.

An update of Weitzman's 1972 study of the appearance of male and female characters in text and illustrations in Caldecott Medal–winning children's books was made by Heintz (1987) for the years 1971 to 1984. Specifically, the picture books were examined as to (1) the difference in number of male and female characters, (2) the differences between the activities and occupations of males and females, and (3) whether a change has been made in the number and types of portrayals of male and female characters in picture books since the Weitzman study in 1972. Results indicated that males still greatly outnumber females in frequency of appearances (twice as often in the 1987 study as compared with eight times as often in 1972). The 1987 study also found that male characters are given three times as many career choices as female characters, and are pictured three times as often in those roles. The results continue to indicate a strong male bias; however, there has been a great improvement from the earlier study.

The Council on Interracial Books for Children (1980) has outlined ten quick ways to check for sexism in *Guidelines for Selecting Bias-Free Textbooks and Storybooks:*

1. Check the illustrations (stereotypes, tokenism, leadership/passive, males/females).

2. Check the story line (success, resolution of problems, role of women).
3. Look at lifestyles.
4. Weigh the relationships between people (whites/African-Americans, dominant/subservient).
5. Note the heroes (minorities).
6. Consider the effects on a child's self-image.
7. Note the background of the author or illustrator.
8. Check the perspective of the author.
9. Watch for loaded words (sexist).
10. Look at the copyright date.

The levels of understanding of children concerning gender are gender identity (the recognition of being either male or female) and when children begin to label the people around them according to their gender. It is still not clear to them what constitutes gender at this stage, and young children use external characteristics, such as hair length, clothing, names, and toy choices. A great deal of learning about gender is taking place between the ages of 3 and 8. Gender constancy develops around age 6 or 7, when children begin to understand that their sex is determined by their anatomy and it cannot be changed at will or by altering external appearance (Wellhousen, 1996). Once children have achieved gender constancy, they rigidly organize information from their world on the basis of gender, which results in gender-role stereotyping (Kohlberg, 1966).

"After reading books with characters in nontraditional gender roles, leading children's discussions is crucial to their understanding gender identity and gender constancy and to children's development of healthy, gender-fair attitudes. Teachers can encourage discussion by asking divergent or open-ended questions," states Wellhouse (1996, p. 83).

One of the most important responsibilities of teachers today is to make children feel capable and confident in their abilities. Teachers can promote children's understanding of gender and attitudes of gender fairness using children's books. By allowing children to express their feelings and ideas, teachers can plan responses to help children understand gender roles and to reinforce gender fairness (Wellhousen, 1996, p. 83).

Young children need to know that fathers (males) can be nurturing; mothers (females) can be breadwinners. Dramatic play with appropriate props, field trips, literature, music, and other curriculum segments can help reinforce these ideas.

Ethnic Customs

The celebration of special occasions or activities should be planned with discretion, depending on the children, their developmental level, the extent of their involvement, and the philosophy of parents and the center.

Holiday celebrations can be of national, cultural, or local interest. Throughout the country, one can find celebrations in common (patriotic holidays and some religious days). Asian children celebrate the Chinese New Year and Children's Day. Children in New Orleans probably know much about and look forward to Mardi Gras. Some families have specific celebrations and ways to conduct them. Teachers should learn about the families of the young children in their classrooms. They could also provide enriching experiences for other children by inviting families to share their beliefs and traditions.

The celebration should be held just before or on the actual day, if possible, and should reveal as much of the true meaning as the children can comprehend. Teachers and parents who start on the next holiday too soon after a current one often diminish the value of each holiday.

Special occasions are a means of informing children about the past and its importance. Because children have so much to learn about their world, celebrations are taken slowly. Often the children enjoy the activities but make no specific connection with a holiday or tradition. In time, there will be better integration. According to Seefeldt (1993),

> [h]oliday celebrations with young children can be pure fun and relaxation, and, at the same time, they can impart historical knowledge in an accurate and authentic manner. On the other hand, when poorly planned, they can become disasters and serve to perpetuate myths. Urging a realistic approach to the celebration of holidays, Parker and Temple suggest that it would be a mistake to attempt to explain the historical significance of the holiday, because young children could not understand it; rather, they believe that the social significance of the day can be realized by associating it with the activities and experiences of the children. (p. 6)

In other words, the holiday is integrated into the regular routine, the focus is kept simple and low-key, and a few appropriate concepts are selected. Parents can be involved when additional adult help is needed.

Special occasions need not always be grandiose. Attention can be centered on a special child, a visitor, or even on a fire drill. Children need to know how to handle a variety of situations. Experience in the center reduces fear and frustration in future happenings.

Teachers should have the following goals:

1. To teach true concepts about the occasion
2. To support or give firsthand experiences on the developmental level of the children
3. To increase understanding about one's own world
4. To build social relationships with others who have similar or different values
5. To inform about other customs and practices (family, religious, cultural, national, community)

In considering books, pictures, and other materials for young children, one should ask such questions as: Are people of different cultures and ethnic groups accurately portrayed? Are girls and women portrayed as active and successful? Is the language accurate and on the appropriate developmental level for the current children?

Holidays

The discussion of holiday curriculum is likely to arouse strong emotions in teachers and parents—some "for" and some "against." Some classrooms move out of one holiday and immediately into another—without a break in between. Such a practice can cause children to lose rather than gain interest in holiday celebrations. Some teachers see holiday celebrations as an arbitrary interruption of more developmentally appropriate activities.

Holidays can serve to connect children with patriotic, religious, and cultural traditions. On the other hand, many of these same holidays take one tradition for granted and ignore others—some that promote racist and sexist stereotypes.

Teachers and children can learn about other people through sharing good books.

Some questions about holiday celebrations outside the home are posed:

If some families have religious prohibitions against celebration of holidays with pagan roots (including traditional religious holidays), should we eliminate them from a school setting or should we promote them to give greater understanding to the children? Don't we need shared celebrations in order to create a better community understanding? What can we do about the formidable differences among us? Is it important to honor the rich cultural traditions of the families in an early-childhood program? How can this be done without trivializing symbolic meanings on the one hand, or offending people with different beliefs on the other? Would it be appropriate to downplay specific holiday-identified celebrations and look instead for the universally shared meanings underlying the holiday traditions of different cultures? Is there provision for dialogue between teachers and parents, or does the school have the final word?

Should there be no formal celebration of traditional holidays in the classroom? Perhaps a child-care program is an inappropriate place to celebrate holidays—end of discussion. While children love anticipation and planning and all the excitement that goes with festivity, consider the following:

1. It's extremely difficult to give holidays meaning that is developmentally appropriate for very young children. Most holidays are based on abstract concepts that are beyond their comprehension.

2. It's difficult to be inclusive. Are we going to celebrate holidays based in cultures represented in our program? What if there is little diversity? What if there is a great deal? What if some parents object to all holidays? Do we have the time and resources to do justice to them all? How much of our curriculum do we want to devote to holidays? What important activities are being displaced?

3. Many holidays are overdone anyway. Children see signs of the major commercialized holidays everywhere, so they'll be asking questions and their

families will be making choices. If families are celebrating, why do we need to celebrate too?

> When we make choices about what to celebrate, let us be very conscious of who we are doing it for. . . . If we are doing it for the families, we must choose carefully what to celebrate so that we are inclusive. If we are doing it for the children, let us be conscious of all the subtle messages inherent in what we do and choose things to celebrate that are meaningful, developmentally appropriate, and healthy for them. (Neugebauer, 1990, p. 42.)

Alternatives in a diverse classroom could be:

1. Integrate December holidays from several cultural groups; identifying common themes and observations.
2. Do December holidays other than Christmas.
3. Don't do December holidays at all in the classroom.
   (Derman-Sparks & the A.B.C. Task Force, 1989, pp. 91–93)

Age

Children not accustomed to being around elderly individuals (especially ones with disabilities) may be frightened, but once they understand that these individuals are nurturing and caring, the fears gradually dissipate. Talking with elderly people can help generate values in young children. They like to hear about "Tell about when you were little" and "Tell me about when I was a baby and the things I could do and say." This interaction can enhance the self-confidence and self-esteem of the children and enrich the lives of children and elderly individuals.

It has been noted in settings outside the classroom, such as being with senior citizens, that some children begin to express themselves verbally, begin to feel their own capacities, and smile more. The same may be true of the seniors.

Race

In a study using African-American 4- and 5-year-olds as one group and African-American 6- and 7-year-olds as another group, Branch and Newcombe (1986) report

> that the older children were significantly more pro-Black and anti-White than the younger children on the multiple-choice doll test. Parents' racial attitudes and attitudes about teaching their children about race varied with the age and sex of the child, and 1- vs. 2-parent family type. . . . Parents play a critical and complex role in shaping the racial attitudes of their children.

Not only must one be careful to include diversity in the curriculum and to plan for children of varied needs and background, one must also take precautions against ideas and attitudes that show bias toward some children and against others.

Throughout this book there is a focus on anti-bias curriculum. In some settings this will be easier to accomplish than where a strong bias feeling exists—but even in such settings, attempts should be made to reduce the negative or competitive feelings.

When children and older adults interact, there is often a special bond between them.

Cultures

[R]acial prejudice, societal stereotyping, and bias can begin during the preschool years, when children become aware of racial differences. It is also well documented that young children learn through the interaction of their own thinking with their experiences in the external world. (Kendall, 1983)

Children learn this bias through lack of contact with and information about people from diverse backgrounds. See Figure 10.3 for multicultural educational goals.

Figure 10.3
Goals for Multicultural Education

1. Teaching children to respect their own cultures and values as well as that of others
2. Helping all children learn to function successfully in a multicultural, multiracial society
3. Developing a positive self-concept in those children who are most affected by racism—children of color
4. Helping all children experience both their differences as culturally diverse people and their similarities as human beings in positive ways
5. Encouraging children to experience people of diverse cultures working together as unique parts of a whole community

Kendall, 1983, p. 3.

Parts of our country are more monocultural than others and children do not have daily contact with people of color or other cultural differences. Rather than thinking it is not their problem to teach multicultural ideas, adults (teachers and parents) can find ways to introduce diverse ideas. Perhaps they can team up with a companion school in another part of the country and exchange photographs, books, weather and natural conditions, songs, curriculum activities and other ideas, exercising caution that ideas are not too abstract for young children to grasp. Nevertheless, concepts of acceptance, uniqueness, self-identity and esteem, cooperation, democracy, and other principles can be taught within a classroom. The more realistic the experience (good props, visuals and stories, understanding and patient teachers), the more the children can gain from the experience.

Reflection

Using age-appropriate props, language, and time frames, try some of the following activities to inform young children about different cultures within the classroom or community (Boutte, LaPoint, & Davis, 1993):

- Read and talk about pictures, books, and artifacts of many cultures.
- Use music: sing songs, dance, imitate behaviors.
- Examine photographs and drawings.
- Provide replicas of clothing.
- Acquire appropriate props and encourage dramatic play.
- Provide cultural toys and games.
- Invite diverse visitors and resource people.
- Provide raw materials for exploration (wood, clay, paper, crayons, markers, paints, and so on—include opportunities to note various skin colors).
- Talk about interaction between people of similar and different cultures.
- Prevent such comments as preservice teachers label[ing] children of color "the quiet one" or "the maladjusted one," or [saying] "talking about race is not polite" when (actually, *not* discussing it is impolite). (p. 20)

There are two tremendous resources in *Young Children* (1993, March) about diversity (Seefeldt and "Enriching Classroom Diversity with Books for Children. . ."). Topics have been identified and references are clearly labeled and readily available. Some are resources for adults; others are books to be used with children. A description reads: "Think what a difference it would make in your classroom if you merely bought, often read and discussed, and sometimes did story-extension activities related to a number of these books! Buying and frequently using diversity books with your children can make the most homogeneous group more familiar with human diversity!" (p. 10).

A child's race is an intimate part of her self-esteem, a fact that teachers must realize. How one reacts to this aspect of a child has a tremendous effect upon her—racial issues in the classroom must be recognized and addressed! Teachers are the most powerful influences that young children encounter; these teachers can perpetuate or discourage racial problems within their classrooms.

"Unless educators provide encouragement and a nurturing environment in which all children and older students can learn and excel, negative misconceptions about their academic, communication, and social abilities will be perpetuated. In a diverse society, we as educators must learn to recognize subtle negative racial attitudes. Prejudice is no joke—it is ignorance!" (Boutte, LaPoint, & Davis, 1993, p. 23).

Native Americans

This group is selected here for emphasis because it has been underrecognized, misrepresented, and is easy to identify. They are scattered throughout the United States and belong to many different tribes, each having similarities and differences with other tribes.

The first thing should be to remove existing misconceptions and begin teaching true and accurate concepts. Unfortunately, written and visual media have portrayed Native Americans as warlike, uncivilized, and fearsome people. Teachers of young children can stop being culturally assaultive to these people by carefully selecting songs, books, activities, and references. Some teachers (and parents) teach concepts and promote ideas that are offensive and inaccurate without giving it a second thought because they learned and repeated these ideas from childhood. Now is the time to begin analyzing words to songs, examining text and pictures in media, thinking about activities prepared, and challenging erroneous, insulting, and discriminatory behavior—not only to Native Americans but to all cultures and races.

Although many Native American children adjust to the dominant society's school world, many of them experience a high degree of inner turmoil and lack necessary coping skills because of differences in child-rearing practices, indifference to material goods, acting out of need rather than by clock or plan, and inappropriate teaching methods currently used (Little Soldier, 1992).

To correct these problems, Little Soldier states:

> We have to encourage each child each day in various ways and in various areas of her development and learning—starting where she is. . . . It is imperative that these children—that *all* children—be taught how to think critically, solve problems, weigh alternatives, and make wise decisions. . . . Native American children need to understand who they are as Native Americans and why they feel and behave as they do. We must equip these children with values clarification and conflict resolution strategies so that inner harmony can be achieved. Teachers, paraprofessionals, counselors, administrations need to work together toward these ends. . . . (p. 21)

Little Soldier provides here another definition for **developmentally appropriate practices**—to work with each child in his culture, in his family, with his skills and interests, with appropriate values and opportunities to help him feel more comfortable and appreciate himself and his environment. True, children of all races in America need to know about the history and culture of this nation, but they should not be expected to give up *all* ideas, beliefs, and customs regarding their heritage. Figure 10.4 shows a letter written by a concerned parent, regarding the concepts being taught about Native Americans.

For those not directly involved in a particular point, or those who say, "Oh, it's only a fun little song," the parent's point of view is well taken. The little song may be unconsciously causing prejudice or stereotyping. How seriously does a teacher (or parent) need to take such things? And how can the teacher use curriculum ideas to promote positive attitudes toward different ethnic groups?

Follow-up activities for teachers include the following:

Subscribe to *Navajo Times*, P.O. Box 310, Window Rock, AZ 86515; $30 for 12 issues.

Figure 10.4
Parental Concern about Heritage

Dear Teacher:

I applaud the music experience the children have had in nursery school and the note of explanation you sent. I am very concerned, however, about the focus song on the handout:

> I'm a great big Indian chief
> With feathers in my cap
> I play my tom-tom all day long
> Now what do you think of that! Hmmmm

A study[1] by the League of Women Voters has shown that kindergartners have the following misconceptions:

1. All Indians are alike (no tribal or cultural distinctions).
2. Indians lived long ago.
3. Indians are threatening.
4. Indians live in teepees, wear headdresses, and are led by male "chiefs."

Sadly, by the sixth grade there is no significant change of perception.

You can see how this little song, with instructions to "chant" it, contributes to the described stereotypes. This concerns me for two reasons. First is my child's self-perception. [Name] knows his grandfather is Indian (Native American is a better term) but he has trouble connecting with all the scary or inane images projected by media—cartoons, picture books, songs, and Thanksgiving art projects. These incorrect and unpleasant ideas have been a source of inner conflict for [Name] that he certainly does not need.

Secondly, for children and parents who do not make the effort to distinguish between reality and stereotype, ignorance is perpetuated. This ignorance sows the seeds of racism. To fail to object to false images, to fail to properly educate is a racism more subtle, insidious and dangerous than open bigotry.

I realize that there is no malicious intent of the little song or the teachers. I know music is a wonderful medium for teaching. I am merely afraid of the underlying message of generalized falsehood in this song.

Sincerely,

[1] See Gretchen M. Betaille and Charles L. P. Silet, *The Pretend Indians*, Iowa State University Press, 1980.

Obtain a list of addresses of tribal headquarters from the Bureau of Indian Affairs by contacting the Office of Indian Education Programs, 1849C Street, N.W., Mail Stop 3530, Washington, DC 20240; (202)208-6123.

In learning about cultures, take the positive approach of making classrooms inclusive and assets to democracy; "stop being culturally assaultive" (Clark, DeWolf, & Clark, 1992); "stop tolerating erroneous, erasing, insulting, and discriminatory behavior on the part of others toward a child or children in our class or school" (Greenberg, 1992b, p. 30).

Different Families

The past image of the typical American family needs to be updated. Today there are many different family compositions: one parent (headed by either a male or a female), two parents (headed by a male and female, or two same-sex parents), interracial parents, stepparents, adoptive parents, extended families, no parent (raised by older sibling), and others. Children need to know that many family compositions exist. Some are harmonious and others experience difficulty of many kinds. "Educators must provide for children not living with their natural parents, children from abusive families, children who rarely see their parents, and children from single-parent homes," states Wardle (1987, p. 53).

> Early childhood educators are expected to create an environment of tolerance and justice for all people, including those unlike us in some way (religion, color, sexual orientation, family format, ability, socioeconomic status), and to promote tolerance and justice even for people with whom we disagree and of whose behavior we disapprove. This is the way of democracy, and democracy is the ideal of our country." (Wickens, 1993, p. 25)

The number of interracial marriages is on the increase. The 1983 census cites 632,000 interracial marriages in the United States; 125,000 are black-white unions. These figures reflect only current interracial marriages; they do not include divorced parents or interracial unions not resulting in marriage. Teachers, social workers, and psychologists often believe that the problems that interracial children experience stem from the fact of being interracial. (See Figure 10.5.)

> Because a child's identity is so dependent on setting, and it is in early childhood that the interracial child is exposed to the social pressure of being different, teachers must provide a supportive environment. Although almost nothing has been written about this issue, and there is still considerable debate as to the best approach to take, general indicators for professionals working with young interracial children can be suggested. (Wardle, 1987, p. 56)

Figure 10.5
Suggested Guidelines for Working with Interracial (and All) Children

Understand your own feelings and issues.
Treat parents as being concerned about their children.
Avoid stereotyping interracial children and families.
Seek help from parents in dealing with derogatory comments from others.
Feel love, support, and acceptance for each child.
With openness, discuss physical differences and similarities, feelings, and negative reactions.
Help the children protect themselves from verbal and physical abuse.
Encourage children to share and be proud of their heritage.
Help each child define his or her identity.
Provide materials, activities, and interactions among religions, heritages, races, and ethnic backgrounds.
Be sensitive about racial differences.
Help children to intermingle.

Adapted from Wardle, 1987.

There are eight to ten million children in three million gay and lesbian families in this country (American Bar Association, 1991). When parents disclose their same-sex parenting, usually when children are ages 3 to 7, teachers who have previously dealt with similar situations or who have had prior instruction usually handle the information better than teachers who are experiencing the situation for the first time or have strong feelings about the topic. Instruction on the topic helps teachers and parents handle the situation without trauma and shame on the part of either one.

> The inclusion of diverse family structures and family patterns in what we offer the children in our classrooms is important, whether the class has a child with lesbian or gay parents or not. In fact, teaching diversity of any kind is even more complex when diversity is *not* represented in the school. (Wickens, 1993, p. 26)

In addition,

> some teachers seem to be examining their curriculum, modifying stories and songs to present parents of both sexes in protective and nurturing roles, and creating a climate in which children can talk about their family structure, regardless of how conventional or unconventional it is. (p. 28)

One must not always conclude that because there are two male or two female parents that these parents are gay or lesbian. There are cases where two sisters, two brothers, or two unrelated same-sex adults are guardians of underage children.

Individuals working with young children should be caring and secure enough to discuss different types of families (single-parent, adoptive, extended, traditional, same-sex, homeless, abusive) without being judgmental. Corbett (1993) states:

> If we can learn to believe that gay people are meaningful, productive, equal members of our society, we will start thinking about the little ones we nurture who will one day join their ranks. (p. 30)

> How must the scores of children living with gay parents feel, never to see any representation of their lives in any book, any song, or any television program? The paucity of appropriate materials is admittedly great, but we owe these children and their families the same sensitivity we show everyone else we serve . . . some pictures of families with same-sex parents, a single parent, a grandparent as parent, two sets of parents/stepparents, and so on. Our attitude can be such that no child need feel ashamed to draw or discuss her family. (p. 31)

Gifted Children

Attention should also be placed on the gifted child so her talents are nurtured gently and naturally. To do so, Karges-Bone (1989) makes these suggestions to educators and parents: broader undergraduate training of teachers with experience and study of gifted children, using activities and materials that have many options, more opportunities to observe adults and gifted children in action, put more emphasis on the gifted, and study of gifted children in all domains of development.

Karnes and Johnson (1989), listing only four demonstration/research projects focusing on young gifted children, note that it is easier to spot gifted children from advantaged homes or those with no obvious disabilities than those from low-income homes or those with obvious disabilities. They note that giftedness comes in many forms (creative thinking, artistic, musical, mentally sharp, and others), and they underscore the importance of providing all children with stimulating and challenging activities.

Wolfle (1989) notes the following:

Although recent studies have found problems with all of the specific techniques used to identify gifted children, gifted preschoolers tend to have certain characteristics that teachers can look for. . . . Not only are gifted children often physically, socially, emotionally, and cognitively advanced, but they also exhibit unique characteristics that require *different* treatment rather than simply more of the activities usually associated with preschool. They also may demonstrate advanced ability and interest in a single area, such as reading or math, without demonstrating such ability in other areas. Before teachers can plan programs specifically for the individual children in their class they need to know each child's interest and abilities. (pp. 42–43)

In a developmentally appropriate program, *all* children, not just "average" children and children who are "behind," deserve consideration. A variety of open-ended activities to meet the differing abilities, skills, and interests of children becomes challenging and not frustrating or limiting.

In addition to having special talents, gifted children are still children and should be treated with flexible, responsive, and appropriate curriculum offerings according to their individual needs.

In a Teachers College Press publication, Roedell, Jackson, and Robinson (1988) offer twenty clues to use when looking for giftedness in young children. One has to do with building self-esteem, in that children who are capable and well-behaved do not get enough positive feedback from adults. Thinking there may be something wrong with them, ignored children "may simply stop doing the things that they think are wrong—questioning and experimenting." They add:

Allowing gifted preschoolers to enjoy and grow to their fullest as three-year-olds or four-year-olds is perhaps one of the best ways to prepare them for becoming enthusiastic kindergartners. As teachers of young gifted children, we must accept them for themselves and encourage them to do the same. This can, and must, be done by building on the abilities and interests of each preschooler in age-appropriate ways. (p. 48)

Disabilities

To make a classroom appropriate for children with disabilities, the teacher must adapt props and settings to help these children toward maximum independence— and be near and willing when things get too difficult. The teacher can help the speaking- or hearing-impaired child socially by helping other children listen carefully, speak slowly, and be patient without making the impaired child feel put down. Communicating with each other has a great deal to do with the quality of a relationship and is "useful in developing the children's verbal patterns; learning to give-and-take social exchanges; practice cooperative social behaviors, and build confidence in storytelling" (Brown, Althouse, & Anfin, 1993, p. 71).

It is strongly encouraged by Brown, Althouse, and Anfin (1993) that children who are different be included in regular classrooms for the benefit of all concerned:

The child with special needs receives the social interactions and stimulation necessary for full development of social skills and personality. The other children learn to accept and nurture others who are different and who may have special needs. This close contact and social interaction breaks down the barriers that lead to prejudice and discrimination. Parents gain confidence in their children as they watch them learn to function in a regular classroom and overcome their disabilities. Teachers find their professional skills challenged as they acquire new teaching strategies to help all

Young children can help set limits of behavior that encourage cooperation and peace.

children learn to interact. We strongly encourage including children who are different into regular classrooms because such integration provides all children with equal access to education and consequently gives them a start on the difficult path of attempting to gain equal access to society. (p. 71)

Peace/Violence

See also Chapter 3.

The promotion of peace and the reduction of violence have become of great importance. These ideas may be too abstract for young children; however, put into the context of here (in the school or home, for example) and now (conditions and situations), children can learn to deal with *peace* without using *violence*.

As noted previously, the younger the child, the more he uses physical and nonverbal methods of obtaining what he wants. Physical strength *may* get him what he wants but may include unpleasantries (injury, reprimand, loss of privileges, or other undesirable results). It is hoped that as he grows, matures, and experiences, he learns to use verbal means more (bargaining, substituting, reasoning) and physical means less.

In a peace education curriculum, four primary goals were used to provide developmentally appropriate experiences for young children (Freund, 1989). These goals have been adapted and expanded here (see Table 10.3). Each teacher is encouraged to construct, modify, and practice ways to help children in her classroom develop ways to promote peace.

It is very difficult to restrict gun play in preschools when so many children live with it every day—not just through the media but through actual experience. How

Table 10.3
Proposed Goals for Peace Curriculum

FOCUS	EXAMPLES
Learning to be a peacemaker	Introducing vocabulary and practicing concepts
	Practicing communication skills (courtesy, manners)
	Trying to see another's view
	Providing enough "things" to promote cooperation and diminish competition
	Promoting self-esteem in self and in others
	Learning that sharing is not giving up forever
	Using curriculum (songs, stories, and so on), activities, and role playing that promote peace (change words or concepts, if necessary)
	Talking about intrinsic rewards
Respecting nature and the environment	Cleaning up after oneself
	Cleaning up after others
	Enjoying nature
	Discouraging pollution of all kinds
	Being an advocate for life and living things
	Caring for plants and animals in the classroom
	Looking at the immediate environment and how one can enhance and protect it
	Learning about and practicing recycling
Compassion toward exceptional others	Respecting *all* individuals
	Being helpful but not overprotective or intimidating
	Appreciating oneself
	Learning about special equipment used by those with special needs (wheelchair, hearing aid, breathing aids)
Awareness of other cultures	Appreciating one's heritage
	Respecting rights and values of others
	Learning more about different cultures
	Visiting places and people
	Avoiding stereotyping or negative concepts

can you tell a child that guns are for protection when loved ones are being killed every day? Some adults find that restriction of guns and warfare makes them more desirable. We may control play in view, but what is the child still thinking and desiring—power! Can we give it to her in more constructive ways? The following are ways to reduce violence in young children:

1. Increase exposure to more peaceful ways and ideas.

2. Help children build their self-esteem and lessen their feelings of dependence, inferiority, and competition.

3. Teach them ways to act and react that are more acceptable.

4. Help them learn ways of self-discipline, thereby being more confident in their abilities and less influenced by others.

5. Provide curriculum and experiences more in line with their understanding and abilities. (TV or cartoon characters experience death—and return in the next episode.)

ACTIVITIES TO INCREASE AWARENESS OF SOCIAL SCIENCE

The study of social science includes anthropology, ecology, economics, current events, geography, history, political science, psychology, sociology, and other related fields. Some of these fields are more appropriate than others for teaching young children. A few ideas are given here; the teacher can develop activities of interest and value to the children he teaches.

- Experiences with *ecology:* Talk about such natural resources as water and energy. Talk about the care of the center and the community. Have a general cleanup.

- Experiences with *economics:* Provide activities that teach the children the principle of supply and demand (number and amount of creative materials, for example, and who will use them; care of unused materials). Give the children weekly or daily opportunities to help with center responsibilities. Teach care and respect for property and rules for behavior, such as sharing, replacing all toys and parts in proper places, and cooperating in play and ideas.

- Experiences with *current events:* Know what is going on locally, nationally, and personally within families. Help children verbalize happenings and the impact on them.

- Experiences with *geography:* Give the children experiences with various maps (for example, road, community, center, play yard). Have a fabric or plastic printed community with props, a farm with animals and equipment, a dollhouse and furniture, or a floor plan of a room or outdoor area, and ask for the children's help in rearrangement. Talk about concepts of direction, location, distance. Talk about the earth (land, sea, air; the solar system). Talk about geographic features in the community such as rocks, rivers, and mountains. Walk or ride on field trips around the school or community, noting routes, buildings, and landmarks. Make a mural showing important landmarks in the community such as homes of children, places of worship, stores, and parks.

- Experiences with *history:* Talk about the changes in the children. What are they able to do that they could not do earlier? (Use the book *The Growing Story* by Ruth Krauss [1947].) Talk about families and holidays.

- Experiences with *sociology:* Provide opportunities for children to participate in group living and learn cooperation, responsibility, courtesy, and sharing. Discuss ways people help each other. Help the children accept and appreciate peers who are of a different race, culture, size, or sex; those who have a disability; and those with diverse beliefs and ideas. Include nonsexist curriculum experiences. Provide props for dramatic play about families and careers. Ask the children what they want to be when they grow up; provide props (clothes, books, and games) for practice. Provide artistic materials for each child to make a picture about her family (she can draw, paint, or cut and paste pictures). Invite resource people to tell stories, share hobbies and interests, demonstrate skills, and bring objects from the past. Talk about behavioral guidelines. Let the children help establish and enforce necessary rules of safety, protection, and responsibility for the classroom, field trips, care of animals, and so on. Invite a safety guard or police officer to tell how she helps the children and the community. Make and post a helper chart for snack time, cleanup, and watering plants. Provide opportunities for children to select playmates, materials, and activities, and allow time to enjoy them. Invite community helpers and parents to share their occupations.

FIELD TRIPS (GEOGRAPHY)

Depending on one's location and school policies, some of the best and cheapest field trips are made on foot, followed up with a thank-you letter. For children who ride a school bus, teachers can design activities, present information, and role play situations that help the children feel secure and safe on their daily trip while becoming aware of environmental changes—the bus ride is not just a period before and after school.

Be sensitive to nature and the needs of living things as you complete your walk. Teach the children to be good observers and listeners. Patterns developed early can give a lifetime of enjoyment. Encourage children to make discoveries and to bring things back to the classroom when appropriate. Help them to combine development and curriculum areas—a good physical activity, science, art, music—depending on where you go and what you see.

Reflection

Be aware of the season and the reason for the walk. Perhaps in the spring you will look for new growth and color; in the fall look for seeds and color. Recently we took our 2- to 3-year-olds for a walk around the building. We looked for flowers and insects; to see if the wind was blowing our flag; birds; and seed pods. The thing that interested them most was large heads of milkweed seeds. Each child held and examined a seed. One said it looked like a parachute, another said it looked like an umbrella. After examination, they watched as the wind gently blew it away. Great follow-up activities could include examining seeds with a magnifying glass, covering the children's legs with stockings and letting them walk through weeds—then examine the different kinds of seeds, making a seed collage, sprouting then eating seeds, the cycle of seed growth, acting out the sequence from seed to plant, and other ideas suggested by the children.

Children can observe and study in the natural setting when trips outside of the familiar classroom meet their needs and interests. However, the frequency of the trips needs careful consideration; some children enjoy going often and others need the security of the classroom. Rather than continually going to new and different places, the teacher might well consider returning to a successful and well-liked location, particularly during a different season or when activities are different.

Values for Children

The following are considered worthwhile reasons for taking young children on field trips:

1. To gain firsthand experiences on their developmental level
2. To see career models (most occupations can be done successfully by males and females)
3. To increase and clarify concepts
4. To increase language skills by learning and associating new words with experiences
5. To increase their frame of reference and sense of observation

Field trips give children a chance to see things as they really are.

6. To develop initiative and creativeness in dramatic play
7. To help build good relationships with other children and adults through a group experience
8. To give parents an opportunity to participate
9. To have fun

Planning

One of the prerequisites of a successful field trip is a visit to the location in advance. Many a field trip has ended in failure because the person conducting them directed the information to the teachers rather than to the children. A successful field trip is one that involves the children and stimulates them to learn more about the particular subject.

At the advance visit, the teacher should insist on discussing the visit with the person who will conduct it when the children come. She should not accept the statement that "anybody who is here can take you through." It just does not work. The teacher needs to explain about the interests and abilities of the children—an informed person should meet the children.

During the advance visit, the teacher should inquire about bathrooms, drinking fountains, and any other things that may be important to or distract from the excursion (for example, change of shift, everybody out to lunch, special clothing to be worn, limits).

In the early stages, decisions are made regarding method of travel (bus, car, foot), cost, and how much supervision is required. Written permission is obtained from the school official. Unattended details can prevent a trip at the last minute.

The decision for a field trip must be carefully made. Perhaps the children have been some places many times; in other places, danger, loud noise, or unexpected activity may be encountered. There are also places to which parents want the privilege of taking their own children. See Figure 10.6 for a checklist to use for a field trip and Figure 10.7 for a suggested permission form.

Follow-Up

Bring to the children's attention some activities you used in preparation for the field trip. Now expand their geography into the real world.

Figure 10.6
Checklist for a Field Trip

CHECKLIST FOR FIELD TRIP

1. Destination _____

2. Proposed purpose _____

3. Pre-planning (check and record information) _____

    a. School policies _____

    b. Readiness of children _____

    c. Advance visit _____

        1. Person who conducts visit _____

        2. Safety _____

        3. Restrooms/fountains _____

    d. Mode of travel _____

    e. Supervision _____

    f. Permission of center official _____

4. Actual trip
    a. Time of departure and return _____

    b. Supervision (list people) _____

    c. Parental permission (check for each child) _____

    d. Transportation (list mode) _____

    e. Preparation of children (list ways) _____

    f. Assignment of children (give specifics) _____

5. Follow-up (informal discussion, art, food, dramatic play, pictures, classroom project, and so on)
    a. _____

    b. _____

    c. _____

6. Evaluation after trip
    a. What went well on the trip?
    b. How did the children respond to the experience and follow-up activities?
    c. How were problems solved?
    d. What changes are recommended for a future visit? (for example, preparation of children, follow-up, time)

Figure 10.7
Field Trip Permission Form

Dear Parent:

    We are conducting a field trip for the children. We will be visiting _____

_____*(place)*_____ on _____*(date)*_____.

We will go by _____*(foot, car, bus)*_____.

    If you give permission for your child to go, please sign below.

_____
(Child's name)

_____
(Date)

_____
(Signature of parent or guardian)

Many methods increase and stimulate knowledge of a field trip. A bulletin board, for example, with pictures and materials conveys information before the visit and reinforces it afterward.

Dramatic play clarifies and increases concepts. One teacher provided small cots and bandages and placed doctor and nurse kits strategically throughout the classroom. Many of the children wandered about aimlessly, paying no attention to them. That morning the class toured a nearby health center. When the children returned to school, there was much activity. They now had firsthand ideas about nurses, doctors, and a hospital. It was fascinating to see how their ideas had increased.

Because dramatic play after a field trip is important, the children should have sufficient time and props to work through their ideas. For example, large blocks can be used to make a bus after a bus ride, instruments can be played after a parade, or a cooking experience can be provided after a trip to the grocery store or bakery.

Stories, pictures, songs, and creative materials add to the learning experience of a trip. Children need more than one exposure if they are to develop correct concepts and a sound foundation. Relaxed talk about the trip elicits information from the children, but they should not be expected to spit back specific or detailed information.

The children are invited to help prepare a thank-you note and picture for the privilege of visiting a certain place. This will help the children express appreciation and also use some of their artistic and language skills.

Evaluation

As soon after the field trip as possible, the experience should be evaluated. What were the strong points? What were the weak ones? What concepts were learned by the children? Was the experience of interest to them? How could the trip have been improved or planned differently? What teaching aids could be employed to increase the children's knowledge and understanding? When could the topic be used again to the children's advantage?

Suggested Field Trips

You do not have to leave your classroom to have a field trip! Consider having self-contained experiences, such as (1) a sensory trip (look for things that stimulate each of the senses, preferably one at a time, or have some children look for "smell" things and others look for "feel" things), (2) a shape trip, (3) a color trip, (4) things made of similar materials (wood, for example), or (5) a "living" trip (plants, animals).

Keep in mind that a field trip should be on the *developmental level* of the children involved and should be *fairly close* to the school. Some places may be familiar to some children and unfamiliar to others. For example, Juan's parents operate a restaurant, and he spends a great deal of time there. He may have a special interest in visiting a restaurant or may be totally uninterested.

Know your community and special attractions. You might consider some of the following:

airport terminal	elevator/escalator	park
animal show	factory (food, clothing,	pet shop
apartment house	furniture, toy, other)	photo studio
aquarium	farm	planetarium
artist's studio	fire station	police station or car
athletic field	fish hatchery	post office
or building	fish market	pottery factory
aviary	flower garden or	poultry farm
bakery	show, florist, or	recreation areas (bowling
bank	greenhouse	alley, gym, hobby
beach or seashore	foundry	display, skating rink,
bird watching	garbage dump	swimming pool)
boat ride	grocery store	repair shop (bike,
body paint shop	hairstylist	car, shoes, watch)
bus depot	harbor	restaurant
bus ride	hobby shop	road construction
car dealer	hospital	building
car wash	house	road equipment
collector (rock,	junkyard	school
insect, coin)	laundry	seed store
community	library	service station
specialties (cave,	livestock show	sewage disposal plant
livestock show,	or auction	stable
cheese factory)	lumberyard	streetcar ride or station
construction site	lunchroom	subway
and equipment	manufacturer (car,	television, radio,
dairy	household)	or recording studio
dance studio	marching band	trailer park
dentist's office	museum	train depot
department store	music department or	truck terminal
dock	rehearsal	upholstery shop
doctor's office	newspaper	water (dam, lock,
(also eye doctor)	nursing home	lake, stream, river)
dog kennel	office	woods
dormitory	orchard	zoo

Summary

Field trips can support many areas of learning. The trips can be initiated by either parents or teachers and sometimes by both. Because of time, expense, liability, and availability, however, parents are more likely to take their children to certain places than are teachers.

Although a field trip is necessary to learn about certain locations or occupations, never underestimate the value of bringing a guest into the school. The principles for planning are similar for both.

According to Borden (1987),

> Our key concepts in all these activities are always: keep it simple; discuss, read, and plan in advance; encourage detailed observations while on community outings; ask questions and encourage thinking; give small amounts of information if children are interested; and provide time, materials, and enthusiasm for extensive follow-up play and projects. (p. 21)

APPLICATION OF PRINCIPLES

About oneself: Help the children learn about their bodies and build self-esteem by doing the following:

1. Acquire a skeleton—preferably a replica of the human body—from a library, university, museum, or other available source. Introduce it in an informal, nonfrightening way. Help the children feel their own bones and match those bones to the skeleton. Note that there are large and small bones. Place the skeleton where children can refer to it at their leisure or interest. Concepts you could introduce include the following: A skeleton is made up of many bones of different sizes; it provides shape to the body (human or animal); it gives strength to the body (ability to stand, play); it helps protect parts of the body (internal organs and brain); bones connect to each other through joints and enable movement; and the children will likely suggest others.

2. Following information on bones, help the children learn that muscles help humans (and animals) move in different ways—gallop, hop, crawl, reach, jump, run, carry, climb. Encourage children to think of all the ways they can move. Add rhythms of music that might suggest different ways to move.

3. Help the children discover and discuss a particular part of the body (head, arm, foot). How does this body part function individually and in concert with the other parts of the body or the body as a whole? (How are body parts similar to and different from those of someone else—shape of teeth or ears?)

4. Taking each one of the five senses individually (and later combining senses or all of them collectively), help the children discover how their bodies help them in different ways.

5. Combine curriculum ideas to help the children better understand about their bodies—cutting and pasting body parts, comparing the growth of their bodies to that of an animal or plant, singing songs, doing physical activities, cooperating with someone on a project, hearing activity stories, taking a walk through the playground, counting and naming body parts, nutrition, health and safety in activities, things they can do now that they could not do when younger, and so on.

About minorities:

1. Before planning and teaching concepts about Native Americans or any other minority group, learn true concepts and carefully plan activities. Correct any misconceptions or partial truths you currently have so you know and understand the particular culture.

2. Look through visual aids, materials, books, pictures, music, and other teaching materials to determine which ones teach true, accurate, and useful concepts about Native Americans and other minority groups. Discard inaccurate materials or modify them so they portray accurate concepts.

3. Purchase materials that are accurate and provide opportunities for children to learn and discover information about other peoples.

4. When teaching about minorities (cultures), involve ideas in addition to the food, clothing, and music of each group.

5. Are there some ethnic, religious, or cultural occasions that would be of value or interest to the children in your classroom? If so, select one and make plans to implement it. List some people and activities that could help the children gain a better understanding of the occasion.

6. Correct any misconceptions the children may have, such as "Indians are bad," "Indians scalp people," sitting "Indian style," "Cowboys kill Indians because Indians are the bad guys," "Indians live in teepees," and so on.

7. Teach through a variety of media: photographs, dress-up clothes, miniature people, puzzles, visitors and resource people, creative media (including all sorts of skin colors), field trips (when possible), and so on. Have props available so children can replay the themes over again as their interest indicates.

8. Talk about similarities and differences between the families of children within the group and those of other cultures. Point out things that are especially good about the culture (music, family relationships, art, housing, and so on).

9. Avoid teaching stereotyped ideas or using traditional projects (headbands, tomahawks, totem poles, Thanksgiving feast) that teach inaccurate concepts.

10. How do you personally feel about using nonsense songs or those that do not teach true concepts—especially those that might offend other races or cultures?

General:

1. Make a list of topics you think can appropriately be classed as "social studies" for young children.

2. Determine the social/ethnic problems in your area (gender, race, family composition, and so on). How can you help combat them? Focus on the young children.

3. Make a sociogram by casually asking children with whom they like to play (or by observing children over a period of time). Avoid making choices for children.

4. Explain how special occasions can be overemphasized. How would you handle a situation when parents objected to the celebration of a particular cultural or religious holiday?

5. List appropriate field trips near your center.

6. With another adult, select and plan a field trip. Fill out the checklist in Figure 10.6. If possible, take the trip, being sure to evaluate it properly on your return.

7. Why is it important to make a visit before taking a field trip with young children? What are the values of follow-up activities?

8. Devise a method of informing parents about field trips and of getting parental permission.

9. How appropriate are the center's present field trip policies for children, parents, and staff? Make constructive suggestions.

10. Evaluate the legal and moral responsibilities related to taking field trips. Are there state or federal laws related to transporting children (for example, liability, seat belts) that apply to your center?

11. Refer to the curriculum checklist in Figure 4.2 to make sure your planning covers the suggested points.

12. Write a lesson plan on some aspect of society—"Hats for My Head," "Shoes for My Feet," "Food for My Lunch"—and help the children learn about the people in their community.

REFERENCES

American Bar Association (1987). ABA Annual meeting provides forum for family law experts. 13 *Fam. L. Rep.* (BNA), 1542, 1543. Also 1991.

Armstrong, J. L. (1994, January). Mad, sad, or glad: Children speak out about child care. *Young Children,* 49(2), 22–23.

Beane, J. A. (1991, April). Enhancing children's self-esteem: Illusion and possibility. *Early Education and Development,* 2(2), 153–160.

Borden, E. (1987, May). The community connection—it works! *Young Children,* 42(4), 14–23.

Boutte, G. S., S. LaPoint, & B. Davis (1993, November). Racial issues in education: Real or imagined? *Young Children,* 49(1), 19–23.

Boutte, G. S., I. Van Scoy, & S. Hendley (1996, November). Multicultural and nonsexist prop boxes. *Young Children,* 52(1), 34–39.

Branch, C. W., & N. Newcombe (1986, June). Racial attitude development among young black children as a function of parental attitudes: A longitudinal and cross-sectional study. *Child Development,* 57(3), 712–721.

Brown, M. H., R. Althouse, & C. Anfin (1993, January). Guided dramatization: Fostering social development in children with disabilities. *Young Children,* 48(2), 68–71.

Buzzelli, C. A. (1992, September). Research in review. Young children's moral understanding: Learning about right and wrong. *Young Children,* 47(6), 47–53.

Carran, D. T., & K. G. Scott (1992). Risk assessment in preschool children: Research implications for the early detection of educational handicaps. *Topics in Early Childhood Special Education,* 12(2), 196–211.

Cartwright, S. (1993, January). Cooperative learning can occur in any kind of program. *Young Children,* 48(2), 12–14.

Chambers, B. (1983). Counteracting racism and sexism in children's books. In Saracho, O., & B. Spodek (eds.), *Understanding the multicultural experience in early childhood education,* 91–105. Washington, DC: NAEYC.

Clark, L., S. DeWolf, & C. Clark (1992, July). Teaching teachers to avoid having culturally assaultive classrooms. *Young Children,* 47(5), 4–9.

Corbett, S. (1993, March). A complicated bias. *Young Children,* 49(3), 29–31.

Council on Interracial Books for Children (1978). *Identifying racism and sexism in children's books.* New York: Racism and Sexism Resource Center for Educators (distributor). Filmstrip.

Council on Interracial Books for Children (1980). *Guidelines for selecting bias-free textbooks and storybooks.* New York: Council on Interracial Books for Children.

Derman-Sparks, L., & the A.B.C. Task Force (1989). *Antibias curriculum: Tools for empowering young children.* Washington, DC: NAEYC.

Dewey, J. (1944). *Democracy and education.* New York: Free Press.

Diamond, K. E., L. L. Hestenes, & C. E. O'Conner (1994, January). Integrating young children with disabilities in preschool: Problems and promise. *Young Children,* 49(2), 68–75.

Educating yourself about diverse cultural groups in our country by reading (1993, March). *Young Children,* 49(3), 13–16.

Enriching classroom diversity with books for children, indepth discussions of them, and story-extension activities (1993, March). *Young Children,* 48(3), 10–12.

Fink, D. B. (1992, May/June). The Americans with Disabilities Act. *Exchange,* 85, 43–46.

Freund, C. A. (1989). A peace education curriculum for preprimary children. Ed. D. practicum, Nova University. ED312089.

Giroux, H. A. (1992). Educational leadership and the crisis of democratic government. *Educational Researcher,* 21(4), 4–12.

Greenberg, P. (1992a). How to institute some simple democratic practices pertaining to respect, rights, roots, and responsibilities in any classroom (without losing your leadership position). *Young Children,* 47(5), 10–17.

Greenberg, P. (1992b, September). Teaching about Native Americans? Or teaching about people, including Native Americans? *Young Children* 47(6), 27–30, 79–81.

Haring, K. A., D. L. Lovett, K. F. Haney, B. Algozzine, D. D. Smith, & J. Clarke (1992). Labeling preschoolers as learning disabled: A cautionary position. *Topics in Early Childhood Special Education,* 12(2), 151–173.

Heintz, K. E. (1987). Examination of the sex-role and occupational-role presentations of female characters in award-winning children's picture books. Paper presented at the 37th Annual Meeting of the International Communication Association, May 21–25, in Montreal.

Karges-Bone, L. (1989, July/August). A new idea under the sun. *Gifted Child Today,* 12(4), 41–44.

Karnes, M. B., & L. J. Johnson (1989, March). Training for staff, parents, and volunteers working with gifted young children, especially those with disabilities and from low-income homes. *Young Children,* 44(3), 49–56.

Kendall, F. E. (1983). *Diversity in the classroom: Multicultural approach to the education of young children.* New York: Teachers College Press.

Kohlberg, L. (1966). A cognitive-developmental analysis of children's sex-role concepts and attitudes. In Maccoby, E. E. (ed.), *The development of sex differences,* 82–173. Stanford, CA: Stanford University Press.

Krauss, R. (1947). *The growing story.* New York: Harper.

Little Soldier, L. (1992, September). Working with Native American children. *Young Children,* 47(6), 15–21.

Mahoney, G., & C. Robinson (1992). Focusing on parent-child interaction: The bridge to developmentally appropriate practices. *Topics in Early Childhood Special Education,* 12(1), 105–120.

McCormick, L., & S. Feeney (1995, May). Modifying and expanding activities for children with disabilities. *Young Children,* 50(4), 10–17.

McCormick, L., & R. Holden (1992, September). Homeless children: A special challenge. *Young Children,* 47(6), 61–67.

Miller, L. J., P. S. Strain, K. Boyd, S. Hunsicker, J. McKinley, & A. Wu (1992). Parental attitudes toward integration. *Topics in Early Childhood Special Education,* 12(2), 230–246.

Mitchell, L. S. (1934). *Young geographers.* New York: Bank Street College of Education.

National Association for the Education of Young Children (NAEYC) (1996). *Responding to linguistic and cultural diversity—recommendations for effective early childhood education.* Washington, DC: NAEYC. Order #550.

Neugebauer, B. (ed.) (1987). Alike and different: Exploring our humanity with young children. Redmond, WA: Exchange Press.

Neugebauer, B. (1990). Going one step further—No traditional holidays. *Child Care Exchange,* 74 (Aug.), 42.

Radonovich, S., & C. Houck (1990, Summer). An integrated preschool: Developing a program for children with developmental handicaps. *Teaching Exceptional Children*, 22(4), 22–26.

Roedell, W. C., N. E. Jackson, & H. B. Robinson (1988). *Gifted Young Children*. New York: Teachers College Press.

Ross, H. W. (1992, March). Integrating infants with disabilities? Can "ordinary" caregivers do it? *Young Children*, 47(3), 65–71.

Seefeldt, C. (1993, March). Social studies: Learning for freedom. *Young Children*, 48(3), 4–9.

Thios, S. M., & S. B. Foster (1991). Changing preschoolers' attitudes toward children with disabilities. Paper presented at the Annual Meeting of the American Psycho-

logical Association, August 16–20, in San Francisco, CA. ED340516.

Wardle, F. (1987, January). Are you sensitive to interracial children's special identity needs? *Young Children*, 43(2), 53–59.

Wellhousen, K. (1996, July). Girls can be bull riders, too! Supporting children's understanding of gender roles through children's literature. *Young Children*, 51(5), 79–83.

Wickens, E. (1993, March). Penny's question: "I will have a child in my class with two moms—What do you know about this?" *Young Children*, 48(3), 25–28.

Wolfle, J. (1989, March). The gifted preschooler: Developmentally different, but still 3 or 4 years old. *Young Children*, 44(3), 41–48.

Nutrition
and Health

CHAPTER **11**

MAIN PRINCIPLES

1. Well-nourished children feel, act, and learn better than undernourished children.
2. Through food experiences young children learn about their world, their environment, and themselves.
3. Young children enjoy participating in food experiences.
4. The adult is responsible for teaching children about proper nutrition and food preparation.
5. Ethnic foods can be introduced to young children.
6. Nutritionists, medical people, educators, and others recommend a diet low in sugar, salt, and fats and warn about foods containing caffeine, chocolate, additives, and foods that may cause allergies or reactions in particular children.
7. Immunization is the most effective way to prevent many infectious diseases in children.
8. Health of young children includes nutrition, the educational setting, immunizations, and a pollutant-free environment.
9. Young children enjoy physical activities, which also help them develop body skills.

It is agreed and understood that nutrition and health are not curriculum areas and could easily be part of other chapters (science, social science, or others); however, because of their importance in the learning of young children, they are singled out and addressed here.

Some children do not have opportunities to participate in food preparation because some adults feel time pressure, do not understand the abilities of children, or are unwilling to involve them. Nevertheless, this area offers additional experiences in becoming independent, in learning about nutrition, in feeling accomplishment and satisfaction, and in contributing a service.

This chapter is intended to (1) give an overview of nutrition and its importance to young children, (2) discuss the involvement of children in food preparation, (3) give suggestions as to how to make eating more enjoyable for children, and (4) identify some important health factors for young children. Further reading is encouraged in the area of nutrition, especially as it applies to the growth and development of the young child. Local libraries, state departments, or welfare or social agencies can offer assistance. The National Dairy Council, with local offices in most states, has reference material, films, slides, and transparencies available at low or no cost to help in teaching about nutrition. Check for an office in your area or state.

Over 11 million children attend day care centers in the United States. These centers typically serve two meals a day plus snacks to children ranging in age from 6 weeks to 5 years old. The nutritional needs of these children should be a serious concern.

NUTRITION

When malnourished children are mentioned, one commonly pictures children from low-income homes or impoverished countries. Some of these children do come from such settings; some parents with limited food budgets lack good spending knowledge. But, some children of the affluent are also malnourished; some of these parents also lack knowledge as to effective use of their money—they spend freely on junk foods, do not consider nutritional value, or fail to plan well-balanced meals.

Basic nutrients to be included in the daily diet are carbohydrates, fats, protein, minerals, vitamins, and water. Amounts vary according to a person's age. Most nutrition books give proper amounts, as well as height and weight charts based on body structure.

A familiar way of identifying daily food requirements is the Pyramid Food Groups. Departments within the U.S. government have proposed a nutrition guidance and child nutrition program, which has been adapted in Table 11.1. The U.S. Department of Agriculture has recently revised the basic four food groups into a Food Guide Pyramid. Note the categories and suggested daily amounts in Figure 11.1.

Dietary guidelines provide for a variety of foods; a way to maintain ideal weight; avoidance of fat, sugar, and sodium; and food with adequate starch and fiber.

Humans need a variety of foods to obtain adequate nutrition. Their ability to adapt readily to eating substances that are available in their environment plays a central role in shaping food-acceptance patterns. Within each culture, people develop individual patterns of food likes and dislikes. Repeated exposure enhances children's acceptance of foods only when they actually taste the foods (Birch, Johnson, & Fisher, 1995).

Many child-care professionals understand the need for adequate nutrition and the role it plays in healthy child development; however, many have had little

Figure 11.1
Foods High in Nutritive Value (Basic Four Food Groups)

Eating Right Pyramid: A Guide to Daily Food Choices

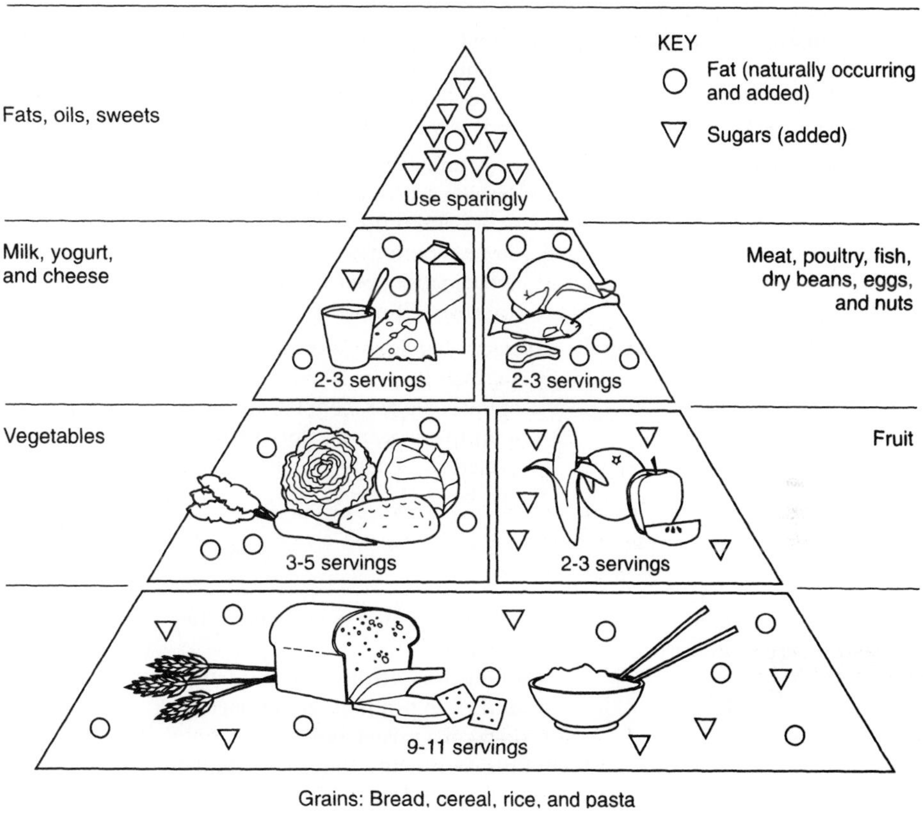

KEY

○ Fat (naturally occurring and added)

▽ Sugars (added)

Fats, oils, sweets
Use sparingly

Milk, yogurt, and cheese
2-3 servings

Meat, poultry, fish, dry beans, eggs, and nuts
2-3 servings

Vegetables
3-5 servings

Fruit
2-3 servings

9-11 servings

Grains: Bread, cereal, rice, and pasta

U. S. Department of Agriculture

nutrition training and few feel competent in planning menus (Bomba, Oakley, & Knight, 1996). Even some trained dietitians can plan well for the needs of adults but fall far short of the mark for good nutrition planning for young children. Still others can plan adequate basic menus for young children but have no concept of quantities consumed or the eating behaviors involved during meals (ability to manipulate utensils, size of food easiest to handle and eat, seasoning of food, fat content, restlessness, distraction, and so on).

Menus should meet one-third to one-half of the Recommended Dietary Allowances (RDAs) of key nutrients and energy (U.S. Department of Health and Human Services, 1994). Menus can be recycled as long as there is variety within each meal component: color, textures, temperatures, and flavors. Eliminate the use of added fats, salts, and sugars. Encourage children to drink adequate water and milk.

Breakfast and Young Children

It is hoped that most young children eat breakfast before going to school. Lately there has been more focus on breakfast and school performance and behavior. Children who are hungry are not as alert, often misbehave, and find attention and learning difficult. For many children, the choice is not between breakfast at home

Table 11.1
Nutrition Guidance for Child Nutrition Programs

GOALS	NOTES	EXAMPLES
Offer a variety of foods prepared in different ways	Nutrients important for good health: vitamins, minerals, water, carbohydrates, amino acids from protein, and certain fatty acids from fat	Milk for calcium; some bread, meat, and their alternatives for iron; fruits and vegetables for vitamins, minerals, and fiber
Serve meals that help maintain a healthy body and weight	For fun and relaxation; a healthy heart; develop positive attitudes; strengthen bones and muscles; healthy weight; develop motor skills, balance, and coordination; increase energy; and improve self-esteem	
Offer meals low in fat, saturated fat, and cholesterol	*Dietary Guidelines for Americans* suggests goals of 30 percent or less of total calories from fat, and less than 10 percent of calories from saturated fat to decrease obesity and certain types of cancer.	Butter, margarine, vegetable oils, salad dressings, cream, lard, egg yolks, and organ meats. In general, foods from animals (milk, meat, poultry, and fish) are naturally higher in fat than foods from plants. *Saturated fats* are found in animal products and some vegetable oils such as coconut, palm, and palm kernel.
Serve plenty of vegetables, fruits, and grain products	Foods differ in the kinds of fiber they contain. Carbohydrates from vegetables, fruits, and grain products are important parts of a varied diet. (A research team from Johns Hopkins University School of Medicine has identified a potentially potent cancer-fighting substance called sulforaphane, found in broccoli, kale, cauliflower, brussels sprouts and greens. *AICR Newsletter,* Fall 1992, Issue 37)	Include a variety of fiber-rich foods, such as whole-grain breads and cereals, fruits, vegetables, and cooked dry beans, peas, and lentils.
Offer and use sugars only in moderation	Main reasons for limiting sugar intake in children: excess calories, can lead to tooth decay	Sugar-coated cereals, candy, gum, cookies, ice cream, sweetened drinks.
Offer and use salt and sodium only in moderation	Table salt contains sodium and chloride essential to the diet; however, most Americans eat more than needed—much is added during processing and manufacturing. Reduce or omit salt during food preparation and help children avoid high blood pressure as adults.	Added salt includes cured and processed meats; cheeses; most snacks; ready-to-eat cereals, breads, and bakery products; prepared frozen entrées and dinners; packaged mixes; canned soups; and salad dressings.
Promote an alcohol- and drug-free lifestyle	Children and teens should not drink alcoholic beverages because of risks to health and other serious problems.	Some preschools and homes actively campaign to deter children and teens from using alcohol, especially among families and areas where alcohol abuse is a problem.
Build lifetime eating habits	Nutrition awareness is an essential part of education.	Education takes place during meals with the foods that are offered. It also happens throughout the day.

Developed jointly by U.S. Departments of Agriculture and Health and Human Services, 1992, April. Washington, DC 20250.

Meals for young children should be nutritious, carefully prepared, and served in a wholesome environment.

or at school; it is a choice between breakfast and no breakfast. (It is alarming to note that one of every eight children in America suffers from hunger.)

Breakfast studies continued throughout the 1960s, 1970s, and early 1980s, growing in sophistication and supporting researchers' beliefs that a nutritious breakfast also can have a positive impact on cholesterol levels, weight control, and learning. Nutrition has a strong physical, emotional, and intellectual impact on a child's ability to learn.

In 1987, Alan Meyers, M.D., of the Boston University School of Medicine, conducted a school breakfast and school performance study in which he examined the standardized test scores of 1,023 Lawrence, Massachusetts, schoolchildren in grades three through six. Results showed that increases in achievement test scores were significantly greater for school breakfast participants than for nonparticipants. Also, absenteeism and tardiness rates decreased for participants and increased for nonparticipants. The importance of school breakfast has also been substantiated by related studies such as the 1991 Community Childhood Hunger Identification Project (CCHIP) conducted by the Food Research and Action Center (FRAC), a nonprofit organization working in partnership with both national and local groups to end hunger in the United States. This study found that children who eat breakfast are less likely to suffer from fatigue, irritability, and inability to concentrate. (Sixty-eight percent of teachers report that undernourished students are a problem in class, according to The Carnegie Foundation for the Advancement of Teaching, 1987, National Survey of Public School Teachers.) A school district in rural West Baton Rouge, Louisiana, received a USDA grant targeting the district's 4,000 students and their families in topics such as nutrition units tied into science curricula and reinforced in the cafeteria; field trips to links in the food chain, such as a dairy or strawberry farm; billboard advertising; television and radio talk-show appearances; and even the publication of a breakfast recipe book.

Some schools and administrators decline to have breakfast programs for reasons such as the following: thinking it's the parents' responsibility—not the school's, lack of money, inadequate school facilities, mass confusion in scheduling, and thinking that breakfasts are geared just for disadvantaged children.

Children and Snacks

When we think about treats and snacks for children, we frequently focus on juice and cookies—maybe because of ease in preparation or availability. One should note that most of the cookies available in supermarkets today are high in fat and that many juices have additives and excessive sugar.

The *American Institute of Cancer Research Newsletter* (1992) states: "Let's face it, cookies will never go for a good-for-you snack. But you can avoid the monsters that are packed with fat and still satisfy your sweet tooth" (p. 4). Purchasers of snack foods (including cookies) are encouraged to *check labels and make wise choices.* Cookies vary greatly in their fat content, even though packages brag "no cholesterol" or "no tropical oils." "Generally speaking," continues the *Newsletter,*

> vanilla wafers, graham and animal crackers and fruit cookies have the least fat. Creme-filled sandwich, butter and oatmeal cookies fall in the middle. Fudge, nut and short-bread cookies usually have the most fat. . . . Remember, moderation is the key. It's fine to indulge every once in a while, but with cookies, fat and calories add up quickly. (p. 4)

Wise choices for children's snacks include foods that are nutritious and contain complex and unprocessed carbohydrates—fresh fruits and vegetables (including juices) and whole-grain products such as breads, cereals, and crackers.

One component of the Head Start program has been nutrition and health. This has been designed to help children develop positive food attitudes and eating habits, to provide nutrition education, and to increase parents' awareness and ability to meet the nutritional needs of their children and families. Phillips (1986) concludes that many disadvantaged preschoolers are hungry or poorly nourished, but that severe malnutrition is rare. Phillips points out that "[a] recent Harvard University study notes that 'silent undernutrition' is common in the United States, causing anemia, stunted growth, and failure to thrive ("The Physician Task Force on Hunger in America." *Hunger in America: The Growing Epidemic.* Boston: Harvard University, 1985)" (p. 45).

Seefeldt (1980) identifies some goals for nutrition education programs, including meeting total nutritional needs of the child while preserving and considering cultural and social needs of the child and family; encouraging healthful good habits promoted by a pleasant eating environment and increasing the variety of foods served; and continuing an educational program for children, parents, and staff regarding nutrition and health through making good choices and taking appropriate responsibility.

Some children have a group experience for four or fewer hours per day during which they likely have a snack. Children in all-day care should have two snacks and a meal, appropriately spaced. In the latter case, the center would undoubtedly come under local, state, or federal regulations. Caution must be exercised to see that the children receive at least part of their daily nutritional requirements.

By the time a child enters a group experience, she has had many prior experiences with food. In regard to nutrition, Powers and Presley (1978) state:

> The most important time of life for the child, nutritionally, is before birth . . . during his prenatal life. . . . The next most important time of the baby's life, nutritionally

speaking, is immediately following birth. The first "growth spurt" comes during early infancy, until around the child's first birthday.

During this period, adults (generally parents) have decided what, how much, and when the child will eat. They are disturbed when his appetite diminishes or he eats erratically. Powers and Presley (1978) note,

> Following this period of explosive growth in the first year of life, he reaches a "plateau" stage [from ages 1 to around 5] and growth is more gradual and almost unnoticed. What he eats is far more important than *how much* he eats. This especially applies to milk during preschool years.

Even though they seem to be burning up considerable energy in their daily routines, children do not require large quantities of food until they begin another growth spurt.

Influences on Children

Early experiences with food preparation may lay the foundation for a lifelong habit of eating nutritious foods. Good eating habits are promoted by nutritionists, social scientists, educators, Head Start planners, classroom teachers, and parents. Healthy meals, snacks, and cooking experiences have been part of many early-childhood programs for years. When children become involved in food preparation, they begin accepting responsibility for their own eating habits and feel a tremendous sense of personal satisfaction. Not only can they imitate adult tasks, but they can also enjoy the results!

Children enjoy the experience of preparing and serving food—something that may not occur at home. In serving themselves, they learn that taking a smaller amount of food and consuming it is more rewarding than overloading their plates and then not being able to eat it. (With our group of 2- to 3-year-olds, they often pour their own juice. They also know "two" cookies—one for each hand. Parents visiting a snack period are often amazed at the ability of the young child.)

When children participate in food activities, teachers should allow time for both planned and unforeseen occurrences, messes, questions, interruptions, and results, for this is an experience where adults and children can learn together. See Table 11.2 for a list of contrasting characteristics associated with nutrition.

Young children lack in literacy, worldliness, and experience. As a result, their eating habits and preferences are influenced by those around them (mainly through parental purchases and attitudes toward foods) and other stimulation (television). For years, debates have concerned the use of young children as agents in selling food products—children want what they see, and they believe what they hear.

Adults must be careful to purchase nourishing foods because children pick up food purchasing and eating habits from adults. To tell a child to eat or not eat a certain food while the adult does the opposite is poor and ineffectual teaching.

Many groups have tried to curtail the number and intensity of food commercials aimed at young children. Powers and Presley (1978) offer this account:

> Joan Gussow, a nutrition writer who testified before a Senate subcommittee, spelled out some of the objectional aspects of television promotion of food products to children. She and others monitored 388 network commercials during a week of viewing children's TV programs and learned that 82 percent of the commercials involved food, drink, and vitamin pill ads directed at children. . . . They urge children to eat the

Young children can pour their own juice and serve themselves.

worst type of food and swallow the worst type of drinks. Children are being lured into wanting the worst cereals that man has designed. Anything that is "fun, sweet, sparkly, gay, colorful, thick, and chocolately, magicky, or crunchily delicious" will eventually parade before the youngsters' eyes on the living room screen. Even vitamins become a vehicle for implanting the belief that if a child doesn't eat right it won't much matter— if he takes his vitamins. The major thrust, with the unstated thesis that only sweetened products are good, leaves a total impact. . . . This sweet pitch "sets up a conflict between the parent and child and in fact, between the child and any number of authority figures—doctors, dentists, and teachers as well as parents." . . . They conclude on a warning note that unless the trend is changed, "we can expect a continued growth of heart disease, hypertension, and poor dental health—the diseases that result from poor eating habits established in childhood which cripple and kill in adulthood."

It has been suggested that a critical period for the formation of food preferences is between ages 2 and 5. The factors that affect the development of food preferences have been identified as "familiarity (i.e., exposure to food); age; parents; peers; teachers and other significant adults; and programs that are designed to influence food habits" (Alles-White & Welch, 1985, pp. 265–266). Food presented as a reward enhanced the acceptance and preference for that food item (Birch, Zimmerman, & Hind, 1980).

Table 11.2
Contrast of General Characteristics Linked to Nutrition

WELL-NOURISHED	*POORLY NOURISHED*
Full of energy	Lethargic
Attentive	Attention lags
Good concentration	Concentration wanes
Happy	Irritable
Curious	Uninterested
Healthy	Frequent and prolonged illnesses
Verbal, cooperative	Nonverbal, uncooperative
Usually completes tasks	Frequently leaves tasks
Benefits from school	Dissatisfied with school
Plays with peers	Solitary play
Positive correlation of intelligence/ learning	Negative correlation of intelligence/learning
Good sleep habits	Poor sleep habits

In a study of children's food acceptance at nursery school and then later, Glasser (1964) found that earlier acceptance of foods does persist and that non-nursery-school attenders selected sweets more often than former nursery-school children. This study indicates the importance of creating an atmosphere in which children are encouraged to try a variety of new and nutritious foods— whether at school or home. Recommendations to increase the child's interest and acceptance of new foods (Figure 11.2) may include a discussion about the foods when they are introduced; preparing familiar foods in different ways; repetition of new foods; behavior at the table (adults eating with the children, encouraging the tasting of new foods, showing acceptance of the food, and acknowledging sampling); and serving familiar and new foods at the same meal (Alles-White & Welch, 1985).

Preference for a food has a great deal to do with how the food smells. The nose knows what the palate may expect. Some people are more sensitive to one taste than to another; taste varies among people and from time to time, with acuteness being the lowest just after meals and before breakfast.

Social Context

Most likes and dislikes of food occur in the absence of explicit teaching. Unfortunately, few children are involved in preparing and serving food for themselves and others, and sometimes they even need help in feeding themselves. One way to increase children's acceptance of disliked vegetables (not in a forced or shaming way) is to expose children to peers who like the disliked food (Birch, 1980). Rewarding children for eating disliked vegetables tends to reduce the child's liking for those vegetables (Birch, 1980). However, children do like a relaxed atmosphere where adults sit and eat with them.

Over the past several decades, the percentage of young American children being classified as obese has continued to increase; 1991 estimates indicate that 25 percent of young children are obese, and nearly one-third of young children are overweight (Dietz, 1991).

Figure 11.2
Hints for Developing Good Eating Habits in Young Children

- Give children many opportunities to participate in food experiences: preparing, tasting, shopping, growing, cleaning up. These experiences provide children with a greater opportunity to develop healthy lifetime eating behaviors.
- Encourage good health habits when preparing and eating food (wash hands, clean surfaces, use safe tools and sturdy utensils).
- Engage in interesting conversation—frequently initiated by the children.
- Eat with the children, eat what they are eating, and model the kind of behavior you expect from them. In a positive way—including pleasant facial expressions and positive conversation—provide frequent exposure to new foods and encourage (never force) them to taste the foods.
- Bake rather than fry meats and other items.
- Eliminate foods that are highly seasoned or have high fat or sugar content.
- Encourage variety in children's diets. Be aware of taste, color, and texture combinations.
- Make preparation and eating times pleasant.
- Serve a variety of foods.
- Allow children to serve themselves, encouraging a portion of each food.
- Talk about differences in the color, taste, and smell of the food as it is cooked.
- Provide finger foods.
- Check each child's personal records for allergies and prohibitions.

Baumrind's research on parenting style and child development outcomes (1973) reveals that "authoritarian or rigid control over children's behavior is associated with unfavorable developmental outcomes; for example, parents who use an overly restrictive style have children who are less self-reliant than are children of democratic parents. In contrast, democratic parenting fosters the development of a child's self-esteem and self-control"

Birch, Johnson, and Fisher (1995) suggest that parents and child-care providers "assume responsibility for providing children with a variety of healthful foods in a positive social environment and then [allow] children the freedom to eat what they wish" (p. 78).

Harmful Ingredients

Nutritionists, medical people, educators, and others in supporting fields urge adults to monitor children's diets. They recommend a diet low in sugar, salt, and fats, and warn about foods containing caffeine, chocolate, additives, and foods that may cause allergies or reactions in particular children. Alcohol should never be served to young children or teenagers!

Sugar

Sugar is especially harmful to children in two identified ways: development of dental caries and consumption of empty calories. Tooth decay results from the stickiness of sugar-containing food, the frequency of eating, oral cleanliness, and whether the sugar is consumed with other foods or is accompanied by a beverage.

Food containing empty calories dulls the appetite. Therefore, food served at snacks and meals should contribute to the child's balanced diet. Candy or gum la-

Snack should be a social as well as a nourishing experience.

beled sugar-free may still contain calories and in some cases may cause the preschooler gastric distress and diarrhea.

Other factors associated with reducing sugar consumption are the prevention of childhood obesity (often difficult to reverse) and psychological abuses of food—where it is used as rewards, is used for special celebrations, or has symbolic meanings.

The relationship between sugar and hyperactivity is a never-ending debate. The American Psychiatric Association (1981) has attempted to more clearly define hyperactivity as "a syndrome of attention and behavior disturbances that may improve when stimulant-drugs are administered" but there is a cry from parents and professionals about the overuse or misuse of some behavior-changing drugs.

Although many teachers and parents report excessive behavior of children following high sugar consumption (holidays, parties, and so on), it is difficult to find well-controlled studies to support these reports (Pipes, 1985; Worthington, 1981). However, some pediatricians maintain that lowering the sugar in children's diets has reduced their erratic or undesirable behavior. Each child requires an individualized approach. Often a combination of methods is used, some of which are considered to be controversial.

Some sugar substitutes have been introduced on the market; however, their effect on children has left questions unanswered. Inconclusive research indicates that saccharin may cause cancer; aspartame may cause irreversible brain damage to infants under 6 months old; overuse of sorbitol can cause diarrhea; honey is not recommended for children under 12 months and overuse can contribute to dental caries and consumption of empty calories—just like sugar! Much more research needs to be done on each of these substitutes.

Adults can limit children's sugar intake by obvious avoidance of high-sugar or "hidden" sugar foods, reducing amounts of sugar in recipes, and providing better food substitutes (fruits, vegetables, and natural foods) or nonedible items as treats (combs, soaps, jewelry, stickers, and so on).

Adults should read package labels. Ingredients are listed in order of total percentage of the food. If sugar is listed as the first ingredient, beware of its high content.

Caffeine

Caffeine is suspected of causing or increasing hyperactivity. Caffeinated drinks are readily available, well advertised, and addictive, but drinks have been introduced on the market with reduced or no caffeine. If adults realized the harmfulness of these drinks, they would restrict children and themselves from drinking them.

Powers and Presley (1978) describe the following effects of ingesting caffeine:

> Auditory perception and hand-eye coordination are significantly impaired. These conditions are accompanied by mental confusion and poor concentration and only add to those problems the hyperactive-learning disabled child is already struggling with. . . . Not only does caffeine tamper with the steady flow of blood sugar to the brain, but the side effects of that result may be expressed in a number of unexpected ways—nervousness, fatigue, and anxiety may increase.

Teachers who have children who habitually exhibit these symptoms should check with the parents to see how much sugar and caffeine the children are consuming.

Chocolate

Chocolate should be considered with foods in the caffeine category, but because of its popularity it is singled out for emphasis.

> Chocolate interferes with calcium metabolism and also places a great burden on the liver. . . . Cocoa and chocolate drinks are unacceptable, as the cacao bean, from which they are made, contains a chemical (an alkaloid) very similar to the one in coffee and just as stimulating. Most authorities on the subject claim that cocoa and chocolate can adversely affect the liver. (Thurston, 1979)

Pure chocolate contains 20 milligrams of caffeine per ounce. Carob, a substitute available in health food stores, is very similar to chocolate but is devoid of theobromine and other objectionable features of the cacao bean.

Additives

Salt has been linked with hypertension. Some researchers have successfully reduced blood pressure in hypertensive patients by using a low-sodium rice diet. Others feel that reduced sodium intakes may or may not be beneficial to children, but suggest the saltshaker not be placed on the table (Endres & Rockwell, 1994). Children generally do not like their food seasoned as much as adults do. However, when salt is used, iodized salt is highly recommended.

Lead pollution is also believed to cause hyperactivity, a symptom seen in persons with acute lead poisoning. Other environmental factors, such as noise (both audible and inaudible), fumes (including odorless), and light (natural and artificial), have been shown to cause hyperactivity in some children and adults.

In the 1970s Dr. Ben F. Feingold, chief emeritus of the department of allergy at Kaiser-Permanente Medical Center, San Francisco, introduced his Feingold Diet. Essentially, his findings showed that some hyperactive children were especially sensitive to artificial food flavorings and colorings, and that by removing these additives from their diet, their behavior could be better controlled. There were skeptics then and there are skeptics now.

Allergies

Many children have allergies—ranging from slight to violent reactions. Children can be sensitive to pollen, mold, dust, wind, animals, food, household products, and many other things. Frequently these allergies lead to various symptoms, such as runny nose, itchy eyes, sneezing, redness, swelling, or others, but they rarely result in serious medical problems. On the other hand, asthma can result in serious and even fatal reactions if not handled properly. Researchers from Johns Hopkins University described thirteen children, ages 2 to 17 years, who had serious allergic ("anaphylactic") reactions to candy, cookies, and pastry that contained peanuts, nuts, eggs, and milk. Six of the subjects had symptoms within 3 to 30 minutes of the ingestion of the allergen, and subsequently died. The other seven children survived, though their reactions were life-threatening (Sampson, Mendelson, & Rosen, 1992). The study concluded:

> Dangerous anaphylactic reactions to food occur in children and adolescents. The failure to recognize the severity of these reactions and to administer epinephrine promptly increases the risk of a fatal outcome. (p. 480)

It has been suggested that anaphylaxis to food may not be as rare as many people think. Teachers of young children should be especially conscious of common reactions in many children or specific reactions in specific children.

Some children, aware that certain foods cause itching or tingling in the mouth, constricted throat, cramps, vomiting, hives, or other unpleasant responses, may avoid these products, and some children will need constant reminders and supervision. (At a birthday celebration at preschool, a child brought cupcakes. One child, especially allergic to chocolate, asked what kind of cake it was. Assured that it was white, she accepted one, looked very carefully at the colored sprinkles on the icing, and proceeded to pick out any dark pieces. Unfortunately, there were a few minute chocolate pieces, and even though the child knew what her reaction would be—and carefully picked off the chocolate pieces—she became ill just from the chocolate *barely* melting on the icing.)

Children and adolescents with a food allergy should be evaluated and educated about food allergy by a knowledgeable physician, and the parents of such children should be taught ways of ensuring rapid response by schools and other public institutions in the event of the accidental ingestion of a food allergen. How fast the children receive medical attention has much to do with whether or not they survive their allergic attack ("Serious Allergic Reactions to Foods in Children," 1992).

Cleaning supplies, plants, toxins, paints, and other harmful substances should be kept in locked cupboards and under the strict supervision of responsible people.

Summary

Parents and teachers can get young children off to a good nutritional start: no commercial baby foods, sweets, or juices in infancy. Reward the preschooler with good food, not "goodies" and soft drinks; limit treats to "high holidays" only; never permit caffeine in any form (tea, coffee, colas, some root beers, or chocolate); and eliminate refined sugar as completely as possible (Powers & Presley, 1978).

If allergies are not listed on the intake form, the teacher should ask the parent if a child has allergies, and if so, what they are, how the child reacts, and how the situation should be handled if the child has an allergic reaction at the center.

FOOD PREPARATION

Through participation in the preparation of food, young children learn much about their world, their environment, and themselves. They have psychomotor experiences (coordinating eyes and hands and in spatial relationships), cognitive experiences (planning, sequencing, discriminating, deciding), and affective experiences (working and sharing with others, being persistent, feeling satisfaction). They develop and increase language skills through asking, answering, and listening. Academic opportunities lie in reading (interpreting the symbols of measurement and ingredients), in science (seeing how ingredients react to heat, moisture, and so on), in math (combining the right amounts of ingredients), in motor skills (stirring, beating, rolling, chopping), and in social skills (taking turns, verbalizing, eating, and sharing cultural experiences).

Food is not a separate or infrequently used topic and is included in all areas of the curriculum. Food of some type is prepared every day in the center and is a vital part of the children's activities. At snack time, food is used for nourishment as well as a socializer. The children have an opportunity to prepare and serve food and learn proper etiquette. Food is used as a science experience, in growing, harvesting, preparing, or eating. It is used in an art activity. It is used successfully and interestingly in math. It is used in a social-studies theme or a movement activity. It is frequently used as the topic of music, stories, or spontaneous conversation. Thinking and speaking are a part of each of the preceding activities, thereby stimulating verbal expression.

The greatest benefit from experience with food appears to be the change in the attitudes of children toward themselves. After preparing, cooking, and eating applesauce at nursery school one day, Pia asked her mother if she would buy a bushel of apples so that Pia could make more applesauce that afternoon. After another cooking experience, Joseph informed his mother, "I am going to make spaghetti for Dad for dinner tonight because I learned how to do it at school today." Still another child, Val, pleaded, "If you'd just let us make doughnuts at school, I'd show you how."

As with any activity, certain precautions are taken. When children use sharp knives, for example, the teacher must instruct and supervise. When they use cords, utensils, and other apparatus, the teacher indicates precautions or limits to encourage safety.

Some children have frequent opportunities at home to help with food preparation and cooking and find different ways of doing things. For example, some mothers mix bread with their hands, others with an electric mixer, and others with a hand-turned mixer. Some children aid in the process of bread baking from grinding the wheat through tasting the warm, fragrant product. But even these experiences take on new dimensions when done with a group of peers.

In food preparation, new terms and definitions are added to the vocabulary of the children, and opportunities provided for practicing them. Consider some of these terms—*measure, ingredients, recipe, beat, stir, fold*—or these processes—*dipping, scrubbing, shaking, spreading, rolling, peeling, cracking, juicing, cutting, grinding, blending, grating,* and *scraping.*

Different products have different characteristics: some are soft, others hard; some smooth, others textured; some crunchy, others "quiet." In bread, gluten is desired, so it is mixed a long time; in muffins, gluten is not desired, so the dry ingredients are stirred in quickly.

To aid children in independence and learning, a picture recipe (Figure 11.3) can be prepared and the children assisted in using it. If the cups, spoons, and so on

Figure 11.3
Picture Recipe for Children to Follow in Preparing Cookies

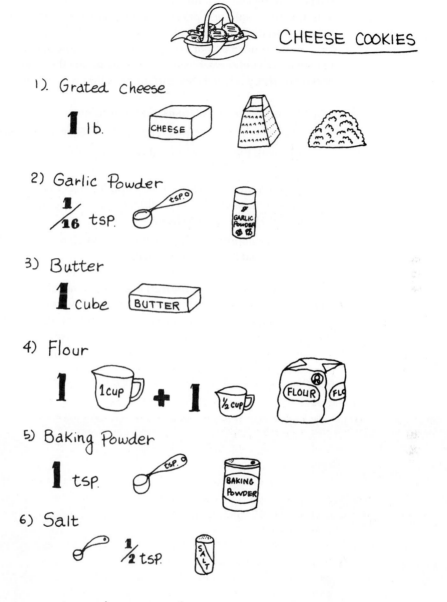

CHEESE COOKIES

1). Grated cheese

1 lb.   CHEESE

2) Garlic Powder

1/16 tsp.   GARLIC POWDER

3) Butter

1 cube   BUTTER

4) Flour

1 1 CUP **+** 1 ½ CUP   FLOUR

5) Baking Powder

1 tsp.   BAKING POWDER

6) Salt

½ tsp.   SALT

Mix cheese and garlic. Then add it to softened butter.
Sift baking powder, salt, and flour together. Add to
cheese mix.   Make balls and mash with fork.
Bake at 350° for 20 minutes.

are depicted actual size, the children hold them up to the recipe to "measure"
whether they have the right cup or spoon. Pictures from labels of the ingredients
(when available) also aid the children in getting the correct amount of the right ingredient. Making and eating the product takes on significance because of personal
involvement.

All children are allowed to participate, even though several may have to be involved at a time or the process repeated several times. The group is divided into two parts, with the lead teacher working with one half and the support teacher working with the other half, or a parent can be invited in to assist. Each child should have as many opportunities as possible.

At the time of actual preparation, health and safety are emphasized by (1) making sure each child washes and dries his hands thoroughly and puts on a cover-up, and (2) washing all surfaces and utensils that will be used. Then:

1. Show the recipe, utensils, and ingredients.
2. Explain why the recipe is read in its entirety before beginning to measure.
3. Talk with the children about what they can do and the sequence that will be used.
4. Be perceptive to the questions and feelings of each child. Be an observer and facilitator as much as possible. Be sure to mention when the food is to be eaten! They'll want to know!
5. On completion, involve the children in cleaning up the table and area as a normal part of the experience.

While assisting the children in food preparation, the teacher makes the experience calm and comfortable. She avoids hovering over the children and giving them too many strict instructions. A relaxed atmosphere, with the teacher entering into the action and verbalization when necessary, provides an enjoyable interac-

Creative activities and food experiences share common opportunities for children: measuring, mixing, satisfaction, and socialization.

tion. Encourage the children to use their senses, when appropriate: "Smell that aroma." "You can taste _____ ." "Did you see how he cracked the egg?"

Some special preparations are needed, depending on the type of food experience (washing fruit or vegetables, supervising dangerous tools such as knives and graters, getting proper equipment and ingredients). The recipe should have been tried beforehand, all tools should work properly, and all necessary equipment and ingredients should be available. The teacher can avoid a negative experience by being well prepared.

The teacher can be adventurous but secure in what is planned. When proper supervision is available, some different kinds of equipment and methods of preparation can be tried; children need and want some safe opportunities to try knives, for example. They should be helped to cut, spread, and slice. Grinders, choppers, peelers, graters, blenders, and other available appliances can be used, but with constant promotion of safety and proper use of tools.

Discussion of Checklist

See Figure 11.4 for a checklist for a food experience.

1. Decide on the specific experience.
2. Record the date. Avoid conflicts with holidays, other curriculum plans, or other teachers.
3. If necessary, discuss the experience with the appropriate person and get approval.
4. List all materials needed. Check to see that all supplies are fresh and available. Order necessary supplies, bring them from home, or have children bring them, if necessary.
5. List all equipment needed, including the equipment inside the classroom, such as tables, chairs, and cover-ups. Kitchen equipment might include bowls, appliances, pans, tools, hot pads, and cleaning supplies. Check all equipment for usability and safety.
6. Double-check both the list of materials and equipment needed. Failure of the experience could be attributed to poor planning.
7. Write down how you expect the adult to contribute to the experience (crack the eggs, encourage children to participate, get cover-ups, actually cook food). Discuss this with the adult.
8. List the specific participation of the child (cracking eggs, putting on a cover-up, measuring ingredients, cooking food).
9. Anticipate problems. Discuss possibilities with both adults and children so problems can be reduced or eliminated. Unexpected problems may still arise.
10. Check children's health records to be sure no one is allergic to the ingredients or end product.
11. Inform the children when the product will be eaten. Is it for snack time today or a picnic tomorrow? Can they take it home? Is it all right for them to taste during the experience? Eating the product is the highlight of the experience!
12. Be sure to evaluate the total experience and record your thoughts and feelings. Then you will have a foundation for planning similar experiences. Do

Figure 11.4
Checklist for a Food Experience

CHECKLIST FOR A FOOD EXPERIENCE

Food experience (name) _____

Date to be used _____

Approval (if necessary) _____

Materials needed (list each ingredient) _____

_____

_____

Equipment needed and preparation _____

_____

_____

Responsibility of adults _____

_____

Participation of children _____

_____

Any possible problems _____

_____

Disposition of food product _____

_____

Evaluation of experience _____

_____

_____

not be discouraged if the experience had some drawbacks or did not go the way you planned.

See Table 11.3 for snack suggestions based on the Food Guide Pyramid found in Figure 11.1. Recipes for some of these items can be found in Appendix D, or use some of your favorite nutritional ones. Be sure to include ethnic recipes as well as a discussion on cultural foods.

Try some food combinations that provide healthy choices: (1) Instead of serving bologna and cheese on white bread, serve turkey, lettuce, and tomato in a

Hygiene is always a part of a food experience.

whole-wheat pita. Why? Because the turkey combination contains less sodium and has fewer calories, and wheat bread has more fiber and vitamins. Of course, the dressing deserves consideration. Mayonnaise on either sandwich adds fat and calories. (2) As a side entrée, serve vegetable sticks or fruit chunks instead of something sweet or high in fat and calories (potato chips). (3) Instead of punch, serve milk because it is low in fat and supplies calcium and iron.

Enjoyment

It is possible that the only nutritionally balanced meals children eat are at school. Children may have specific food biases or habits. Listen to their concerns. Watch how they respond to the food that is presented to them. Place some attention on manners, but focus on helping the children develop healthy attitudes toward food and eating. Make gradual changes—and introduce new foods slowly and individually. Give them tasty and interesting food choices.

Food preparation is fun for boys and girls; therefore, it follows that good health and the making of tasty cuisine result in its enjoyment. Good health and safety habits begin early in the child's life; however, adults must provide information and supervision.

Food and eating habits may be heavily laden with emotion. If the child is to utilize the food she eats, she must do so in a loving atmosphere. Force, anger, hostility, and other unpleasantness should be absent from meals.

Here are some techniques to promote good attitudes toward food and eating.

Food

Understand the background of the children with regard to their culture and personal food preferences. Help the children enjoy a wide variety of foods—and the same food in a variety of forms to add interest to meals and snacks. Avoid the rut

Table 11.3
Snack Suggestions from the Food Guide Pyramid

GROUP	SUGGESTED FOODS
Milk, yogurt, and cheese group (2–3 servings daily)	Butter for crackers and bread Cheese chunks Cottage cheese Kabobs (cheese and lunchmeat) Milk (whole, powdered, canned) Puddings Sauces Yogurt
Meat, poultry, fish, dry beans, eggs, and nuts group (2–3 servings daily)	Creamed meat sauces (chicken, tuna) Dried beans Eggs Fish Lunchmeat (limited) Meatballs Meat loaf Meat sandwich fillings Nuts and nut butters Poultry Soy products (including tofu)
Vegetable group (3–5 servings daily)	Cooked, raw, juice, and a variety for finger foods, salads, dips, soups, dried (peas, corn, popcorn)
Fruit group (2–4 servings)	Cooked, dried (or leathers), fresh, juice (low in sugar), sauce, and a variety for finger foods, salads, dips, kabobs, frozen treats
Bread, cereals, rice, and pasta group (6–11 daily servings)	Bread (preferably whole-wheat or enriched; occasionally biscuits, bran muffins, bread sticks, melba toast, fruit and nut breads) Cereal (enriched, cooked or prepared, granola) Cookies (low in sugar and fat) Crackers (whole-wheat or -grain) Pasta (macaroni, noodles, spaghetti, other) Pizza (child-made)

of serving the same foods prepared in the same way just because you know that the children will eat them. Feature new foods or food combinations at least monthly.

Introduce new foods slowly, always in the presence of a known, and preferably liked, food. Even if the child only asks about it, fingers it, or ignores it, the food will be more familiar another time. Encourage her to taste it, but do not force her to eat it.

Use family style as appropriate. Children often eat more when they serve themselves; however, some take more than they can or want to eat.

Encourage small portions. Letting children ask for more gives them a sense of satisfaction rather than of failure for not being able to eat all their food.

Serve finger foods and expect children to be more adept with fingers than utensils.

Be sure a liquid is available to drink when dry foods are served, even if you can provide only water. Dry foods are hard for young children to swallow.

Serve food separately rather than in casseroles, stews, and mixtures.

Table 11.3
continued

GROUP	SUGGESTED FOODS
	Rice (unpolished)
	Sandwiches (enriched bread)
	Tacos
Combinations	Apple wedges with cream cheese, nut butter, or other spread
	Bacon and eggs
	Baked potato with cheese
	Cabbage, corned beef, and rice
	Carrot, raisin, apple, and pineapple salad
	Cheese melted on wheat crackers or enriched bread
	Chicken, dumplings or noodles, and vegetables
	Cottage cheese with fruit or vegetables
	Creamed meat sauce on toast
	Creamed peas and new potatoes
	Creamed tuna with rice or toast
	Custard with or without fruit
	Dairy dip with vegetables or fruit
	Macaroni and cheese
	Meat and vegetable soup
	Meatballs and spaghetti
	Milkshake (fruit)
	Nut butters on crackers
	Pocket sandwiches
	Puddings (rice, tapioca, and so on)
	Trail mix (nuts, seeds, fruit)
	Tuna casserole
	Yams baked with apple slices
	Yogurt pops (orange juice concentrate and yogurt, frozen on a stick)
Add a variety of ethnic foods in each category, as appropriate.	

Serve the food in bite-sized pieces.

Vary the consistency of food served at each meal (soft, crisp, and chewy).

When possible, let the children choose (for example, between two fruits or two vegetables).

Use peer influence in a positive way. Encourage children to bring their favorite fruit or vegetable. Let the group prepare them all, cut into bite-sized pieces, and have a tasting snack session. Be aware of the nutritional value of each food served.

Provide opportunities to taste food at times other than snack or lunch (tasting table, science).

Serve foods that are mild and natural in flavor; strong flavors are rejected by young children. Dilute strongly flavored juices (grapefruit, grape, pineapple) with water.

Encourage the children to drink water frequently.

Most young children prefer food served at room temperature; hot food may frighten them, and they often stir hard ice cream until it becomes liquid.

Never use food as a weapon, such as refusing to serve dessert until after all other food is eaten. A nourishing dessert should be as important as other foods.

Environment

Precede all eating situations with a calm, quiet activity. Excited or overstimulated children do not enjoy their food as much as tranquil children.

Require children to wash and dry their hands before eating or working with food. Let the children serve themselves when possible. Use child-sized pitchers, glasses, and utensils.

Make sure the children are comfortably seated, with feet touching the floor.

Let children assist in setting the tables.

Make the area attractive and peaceful.

See that the food is attractively presented in color, variety, and consistency. (Popular food colors for young children include green, orange, yellow, and pink.)

Meet children's social needs by providing time and association with peers.

Help the children use this experience in an educational way. Make it a time to learn about, identify, and talk about the food.

Assist the children in developing and using good table manners and etiquette.

Help build a bridge between home and the center in behavior during eating and in promoting and understanding about food habits in different ethnic groups.

Help the children become more conscious of nutrition and eating proper foods.

Make this nutrition program a part of the total school or child-care curriculum. Talk about food at noneating times—during stories, during a planting experience, while feeding animals, and at other spontaneous and planned times. Work closely with parents and others in the school program and within the community—visit a garden or farm, pick and prepare foods for meals, talk about the color of foods or different ways plants grow. Set small but successful goals.

Be patient and understanding about the different rates at which young children eat. Often eating takes less priority than socialization and exploration. Handle table accidents calmly and reassuringly (have sponges close at hand). Let the children resolve the situation as much as possible.

If a child refuses to eat, invite him to the table to enjoy the conversation rather than going to another activity.

For additional safety and sanitary concerns, see Figure 11.5.

Ways to Encourage Child Participation with Food

Have a tasting table with fruit or vegetable (carrots, broccoli, cauliflower, cucumber, cherry tomatoes, pepper strips) chunks. A dip could be made from sour cream, cottage cheese, or yogurt.

Have a sight and/or touch experience: use raw veggies and/or fruit. Encourage the children to describe the skin of the food before they touch it (peach is fuzzy, cucumber is prickly, cherry is slick, squash is firm, and so on). Talk about the covering of each. How does the touch differ when a food is peeled and unpeeled? Which ones are generally peeled before eating, and which ones are not? Talk about where the food is grown (bush, underground, tree, vine, and so on).

Have a smell table: See if the children can identify fruit and vegetables by their smell only. Which ones have strong odors and which have little or no odor? What is the difference between the smell of raw and cooked food (cabbage, for instance)?

After reading the story *Stone Soup*, by Marcia Brown (1986), ask the children how you could make soup at school. Through volunteers or assignment, the chil-

Figure 11.5
Monitoring Safety and Sanitary Concerns in Child Settings

1. Avoid foods that could cause choking: hot dogs, grapes, popcorn, peanuts, foods with small bones, and hard candies. *All staff must be trained in the Heimlich maneuver.*
2. Nutritionists recommend that meat, fish, and poultry products be cooked to an internal temperature of 160°F or until all the pink is gone.
3. Cool cooked foods to avoid burned mouths and tongues.
4. Avoid holding foods between 40 and 140°F for extended periods of time.
5. Plan carefully for supervision of classroom cooking experiences: sanitation, heat, utensils, cords, sharp tools, and so on. *NEVER* LEAVE A CLASSROOM COOKING EXPERIENCE UNATTENDED.

dren could each bring one ingredient for making soup at school. Assist the children in cleaning, cutting, and cooking the vegetables. Serve the soup for snack or lunch.

For information about using food for art activities, see the section titled "Collage" in Chapter 6.

Food-Related Experiences

Field Trips

bakery	flour mill
berry patch	food processing plant
bottling plant	garden
butcher shop	grain field or mill
cannery	greenhouse
cheese factory	grocery or local market
cold-storage plant	kitchen (restaurant or home of a
dairy farm	teacher or child)
dairy processing plant	natural food store
farms (animal, produce)	nut store
fields (corn, potato, peanut,	orchard (seasonal)
pumpkin)	picnic
fish hatchery or market	pizza parlor
fishing at a local lake or river	poultry or turkey ranch
(close supervision is mandatory)	restaurant (specialty, ethnic)

Resource People (use appropriate aids)

baker	fisher
beekeeper	grocer
butcher	milk carrier
chef	miller
cook at your center or local	parent to demonstrate prepa-
school	ration and use of products
farmer with produce to tell how	poultry rancher
food is prepared for market	others particularly interesting
and how he sells it (crate, truck-	to the children
load, pound)	

Children enjoy eating and learning etiquette, and they experience greater satisfaction when they have been a part of the preparation.

Songs

Many good songs concern food. Check your favorite songbooks.

HEALTH

The health of young children is not an isolated or unimportant factor; however, an in-depth discussion about the growth and development of young children is not appropriate here. Nevertheless, it is important to note that the integration of hereditary and environmental influences, attitudes and actions, and opportunities and deprivations will have a bearing on their health.

Strong bodies can be strengthened or weakened, as can weak bodies. The genetics of the child sets limits for her potential, but external forces (disease, pollution, poverty, and so on) influence the child's attainment.

In recent years forces have been pulling against each other; health, nutrition, and well-being have been stressed by some and resisted by others (reduction in physical-education emphasis and financial backing, increased availability of drugs, inaccurate and inappropriate media advertising, fewer educational and career opportunities for the poor, reduced food and social programs, increased environmental pollution, and others).

It is during the early developing years that children adopt models, establish patterns, and set goals. Adults who interact with these children have the responsibility and opportunity to influence them in happy, healthful, and productive ways by planning activities to increase and encourage physical development (see Gabbard & LeBlanc, 1986); being aware of and preventing harmful environmental effects (see Noyes, 1987); reducing disease through research, immunizations, and education (see Aronson, 1991); and increasing their awareness of harmful agents and activities (see Lasky & Eichelberger, 1985).

Always practice good health habits: proper purchase, preparation, storage, and disposal of food items; hand and body cleanliness; proper disposal of waste; avoidance of contagion or infection by using rubber gloves for certain procedures; knowledge and practice of good first-aid procedures for accidents and other emergencies; and others of general or specific nature. Some state laws mandate procedures for training or interaction with young children or those in groups.

Children with Chronic Illnesses

Children with chronic illnesses need not be restricted from group participation unless it is recommended by a physician, even though it is difficult for some children to stay healthy in a schooling setting or among peers. Not only may chronically ill children be absent more frequently than other children, they also may experience more injuries (Goldberg, 1994).

Dramatic play and other experiences that help ill children deal with their experiences helps them, and other classmates, understand and accept health problems. See References at the end of this chapter for resources on chronic illnesses.

Medicaid

According to Chavkin and Pizzo in the NAEYC Public Policy Report:

> Medicaid reimbursement may be available to fund early childhood programs to:
>
> inform parents about or help them locate and/or travel to sites of health and developmental assessment and services for Medicaid-eligible children;
>
> transport Medicaid-eligible children (with their parents or other attendants) to necessary medical care;
>
> provide some preventive health services, such as developmental assessments;
>
> provide remediation and treatment services to children with special needs; and
>
> provide medical day care pursuant to a plan established by a qualified health professional (e.g., a nurse) designed to treat or remediate a physical or mental illness or condition of children. (Chavkin & Pizzo, 1992, p. 39)

Conclusion

"[W]hen so many young children are going without immunizations and preventive health care . . . and so many families are looking for special child care—early childhood programs have a unique opportunity to help. Developing a partnership with Medicaid is one way to realize this opportunity" (Chavkin & Pizzo, 1992, p. 42).

Examples of Health Care

1. Our local medical facility (Utah Valley Regional Medical Center, 1996) has issued information regarding infection control policies and procedures for day care of employee children:
   "Purpose. Recommendations of the Centers for Disease Control, the American Academy of Pediatrics, and the Utah Department of Health for the prevention, control, and management of infections in day care will be implemented. Center Child Day Care Standards of the Utah State Dept. of Social Services will be met or exceeded to prevent the spread of disease." Also included in the publication is information related to medical and health requirements for day care;

Children are interested in their bodies and in ways to maintain good health.

medical care after admission; sanitation—diapering, communicable diseases; and Appendix A of the UVRMC manual, which discusses infection, mode of transmission, incubation period, period of communicability, management of an infected child or adult, and management of exposed children and adults.

2. The ten most common health problems in school are divided by Needleman and Needleman (1995) into three categories as:
   - Chronic conditions, such as allergies and asthma;
   - Mishaps, such as scrapes and cuts, bumps on the head, sand in the eyes, and splinters
   - Infections, such as conjunctivitis, head lice, chicken pox, strep throat, and lingering coughs.

3. Practical health-related exercises are outlined and discussed (Werner, Timms, & Almond, 1996):
   a. Children may have boundless energy and move constantly, but they also may be less than healthy.
   b. Coronary heart disease may have its origins in childhood (Lauer et al., 1975; Newman et al., 1986). Data show that only 2 percent of adults who were inactive as children become active as adults, according to a national fitness survey conducted in England (Activity and Health Research, 1992) and it is suspected that patterns are similar in the United States.
   c. The best guideline for young children is to offer them both a mixture of free play and guided exploration or discovery, such as music and movement and vigorous games—both types of play promote health.
   d. Activities must be fun for each child.
   e. Some children are absorbed in activities for long periods of time; others have relatively short attention spans.
   f. Healthy atmospheres include both indoor and outdoor play.

Proposed Policies

A proposed policy regarding comprehensive services for young children and families by the year 2001 includes the following (Lombardi, 1992):

1. policies and funding that respond to local needs
2. policies, funding, and professional preparation that ensure comprehensive services
3. collaboration as a way to achieve comprehensive services
4. efforts to provide continuous services from birth through age 8
5. continuous effort to promote full cost of quality (pp. 24–25)

In an effort to promote the welfare of young children, NAEYC has recommended revision of its ethics code to include, emphasize, and uphold laws protecting children from abuse and neglect ("Ethics Code Revision," 1992).

Recall from Chapter 1 that the national education strategy proposes goals for young children and families. Goal 1 reads:

Readiness for school by the year 2000: All children in America will start school ready to learn.

Part C reads:

Children will receive the nutrition and health care needed to arrive at school with healthy minds and bodies. (U.S. Department of Education, 1991. Also reported by Hostetler, 1991, pp. 2 and 57–58.)

According to the FYI report in *Young Children*, 48(3) (March 1993):

The State of America's Children presents current data revealing the decline in child and family well-being in 1992 and calls for "immediate investment so that millions of children are not left behind—unready for school and victims of needless illness, disability, and death."

This new annual report from the Children's Defense Fund cites that in most states, fewer than 60% of two-year-olds are fully immunized; one in five children—14.3 million—lived in poverty in 1992, the highest number since 1965; and half of all states spent less than $25 on child care and early childhood education per child under age 14. (p. 31)

Assistance to Parents

Some parents are very aware about and active in handling the health needs of their children. Others are unaware, confused, helpless, or uninterested. Teachers of young children can discuss health issues with the parents or provide information for them through the activities at school. For example, some children wear shoes that do not support the best growth of their feet, but they wear them because they are affordable, available, or just handed down. Frequently teachers pay attention to the footwear of children only when shoes seem to be a problem (the child isn't walking correctly; complains about pain in his feet, knees, or back; falls often; doesn't like climbing or running; can't keep up with others; removes his shoes; wears out his shoes unevenly; and so on). According to the American Academy of Pediatrics (1992), the healthiest footwear, developmentally speaking,

is flexible, light-weight, quadrangular, porous, and should fit properly. Shoes that are too short compress the toes and create deformity. Shoes that are too long cause children to be clumsy and to trip and fall. Sole friction should be equivalent to that of the bare foot. Slippery (leather) soles and soles that generate excessive friction (some rubber soles) should be avoided. Toddlers' shoes should extend above the ankle to prevent children from slipping while running.

And from Cane and Van Enoo (1992):

[A] young foot or ankle that is weak will eventually cause further problems. For example, a foot that is turned inward (excessive pronation) may cause the heel to go out, the arch to fall, the foot to flatten, and the ankle to turn in; these problems may cause the body to compensate, stressing or misaligning the knee, hip, and spine. Like a building with a faulty foundation, the child is at risk. (p. 42)

Although teachers want the best situation for the child, they should be sensitive to the abilities and feelings of the parents. Rather than seeming to "attack" parents who already feel guilty or neglectful, try to approach the parents in a positive, supportive, and helpful way. When necessary, have some suggestions for the parents to ponder and places where they can seek medical help or counseling.

Teachers should be constantly alert for ways to promote good health in themselves and in the children. One item, frequently avoided, includes information about and preparation for a visit to a medical person—dentist, doctor, clinic, hospital, or other health care. Advance information tends to put one's mind at ease. A doctor visited a preschool group and showed what he carried in his bag, how he used the instruments, and how he liked to help people—frequently reminding the children that he was unable to give any shots today. A 3-year-old was prepared for his tonsillectomy. When he went to the hospital for the surgery, he knew what was going to happen and kept asking, "Where are the Popsicles?" He seemed more calm than his parents.

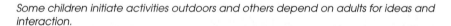

Some children initiate activities outdoors and others depend on adults for ideas and interaction.

Reflection

From the suggested health items for young children found in Figure 11.6, sequence the main categories and then sequence individual items within each group (that is, which main categories and which subitems should precede others?). Feel free to add other items. After making a tentative prioritization of categories and subtopics, select one subtopic and brainstorm important concepts and activities to present to young children.

Immunizations

Immunization is the most effective way to prevent many infectious diseases in children.

The American Academy of Pediatrics recommends that children be immunized according to a schedule they have established. Child care providers in centers or family day care homes can help reduce these risks. They can: (1) get training in health and safety;

Figure 11.6
Proposed Health Curriculum for Young Children

Priority	Major Topic	Subtopics
	Physical health	Senses
		General hygiene
		Dental hygiene
		Nutrition
		Exercise, relaxation, sleep
		Illness and prevention
		Substance-abuse prevention (drugs, alcohol, tobacco)
		First aid
		Abuse (physical, mental, sexual, other)
		Handicaps
		Environment (pollution, disasters)
		Other (identify)
	Mental health	Self-esteem
		Identifying and expressing one's feelings
		Identifying and accepting others' feelings
		Emotional neglect
		Abuse
		Disabilities or gifts
		Other (identify)
	Family living	Diversity within families
		Cultural diversity
		Socioeconomic differences
		Prenatal development
		Problems (death, divorce, illness, diverse parenting styles)
		Sibling rivalry
		Moving
		Other (identify)

Figure 11.7
Immunization Schedule

IMMUNIZE BY 2

Utah Department of Health
Immunization Program

It's Up To You

Recommended Immunization Schedule*

Age → Vaccine ↓	Birth	2 Months	4 Months	6 Months	12–15 Months	4–6 Years	11–12 Years
Hep B	X	X		X			X[1]
DTP/DTaP[2]		X	X	X	X	X	
Hib		X	X	X	X		
Polio[3]		X	X		X	X	
MMR					X	X	
Td							X
Chicken pox					X[4]		X[4]

*Your child's immunization schedule may vary depending upon your provider's judgment and the vaccine manufacturer's recommendations.

1. This series is recommended for adolescents who have not already received 3 doses of hepatitis B vaccine.
2. Your provider may offer DTaP as an alternative to DTP.
3. Two doses of IPV followed by two OPV is recommended, but all IPV or OPV are acceptable.
4. Chicken pox vaccine may be given to children at or after 12 months of age, if they have not had chicken pox. At 11 to 12 years of age, chicken pox vaccine is encouraged for children not previously vaccinated or who lack a reliable history of chicken pox.

(2) maintain current immunization records on all staff and children in their center or home; (3) identify health resources in the community that families can use to get immunizations; (4) encourage low-income families to explore eligibility for medical coverage under Medicaid; (5) require full immunizations for all staff and children in the center and home; (6) develop a written procedure to keep families informed when infectious disease occurs in the center or home. ("Immunizations Urged for Children in Out-of-Home Care," 1992)

See Figure 11.7 for the immunization schedule recommended by the Utah Department of health, which is similar to the one recommended by the American Academy of Pediatrics.

An essential resource for family day-care homes and centers is *Caring for Our Children: National Standards for Health and Safety in Out-of-Home Child Care,* published by the American Academy of Pediatrics and the American Public Health Association. To obtain this manual, contact the American Academy of Pediatrics, P.O. Box 927, 141 NW Point Boulevard, Elk Grove Village, IL 60009-0927.

Those who care for or teach children in groups have concern about HIV infection (AIDS) as well as common childhood diseases. Although new information may be coming frequently, it may be overshadowed by myth, rumors, fears, and speculation. For the latest facts, contact your local or state health department. Basically, "studies continue to show lack of transmission from HIV-infected individuals by nonsexual contact, even under conditions of close contact such as occurs among children and staff in group programs" "New Guidelines on HIV Infection (AIDS) Announced for Group Programs," 1989, p. 51); however, cleanliness and precautions are always in order.

According to the American Academy of Pediatrics Task Force on Pediatric AIDS (1988), the following guidelines are suggested for infection control in early-childhood programs relative to HIV infections:

1. HIV-infected children should be admitted to group programs if their health, neurological development, behavior, and immune status are appropriate.

Such decisions should be made on an individual basis by qualified people with expertise regarding HIV infection and AIDS, including the child's physician. This decision should take into account both the efficacy of program participation for the infected child and whether the child poses a potential threat to others.

2. Most infected children, particularly those too young to walk, pose no threat to others. HIV-infected children who persistently bite others or who have oozing skin lesions may theoretically transmit the virus, although such transmission has not been conclusively demonstrated.

Reports available at this time definitely indicate that biting *does not* transmit HIV infection from an infected biter to the person bitten unless the biter has a bloody mouth. The principal concern is whether blood from the infected person is transferred; few bites draw blood.

3. Screening children for the presence of the HIV antibody prior to program entry is not warranted or recommended.

4. Parents of children attending group programs do not have the right to know the HIV status of other children in the program. Caregivers and teachers need to know when a child has immunodeficiency, regardless of cause, so that precautions can be taken to protect the child from other infections. However, this does not require knowledge of HIV status.

5. Programs offering services specifically for children with HIV infections may provide appropriate alternative placements for individual children, but separate programs are not necessary for infection control and should not be used to segregate children.

6. Because it is not always known when children are infected with HIV or other infectious agents, precautions should be taken to reduce the risk of infection. Recommended practices include promptly cleaning soiled surfaces with disinfectant using disposable towels and tissues with proper disposal, and avoiding exposure of mucous membranes or any open skin lesion to blood or blood-contaminated body fluid (by using disposable gloves, for example).

Exercise

When one approaches a situation with enthusiasm and a good attitude, the positive feelings spread—but the opposite could just as well be true: A bad attitude, lack of enthusiasm, and a negative feeling can cause even the best ideas to fail! So it is with exercise; however, it does seem that children have boundless energy for activity.

You don't have to provide formal fitness training for enjoyment and benefit. Start out slowly and with skills the children can already do (most of them are more limber than adults, but they still must begin slowly). Remember that young children need to move often; when they have been sedentary for a period, introduce some fun movement activities. They can help initiate ideas.

Music, rhythm, and feeling add enjoyment. Just keep the activities within the abilities of the children. A group of 2- and 3-year-olds enjoyed a story about a parade. They even liked playing instruments, but when they were asked to play their instruments and march at the same time, their confusion increased and their desire decreased.

Obstacle courses take on a new twist when children are asked for suggestions and help in arranging the items. What could we do with this box? Who can do a different thing with the ball?

Children are in constant motion and don't often need encouragement to run, climb, jump, or combine motor skills. Records with and without instructions can be used over and over again.

Developmentally Appropriate Exercise for Children

Because young children have small bodies and limited muscular endurance, they easily and quickly tire—three to five minutes may be the limit of their endurance during lively play. Within minutes they are back at the activity.

Active play need not be limited to outdoors or a certain time period during the day. Refer to Chapter 7, Music and Movement Education, and Chapter 12, Transition Activities, where discussions and/or activities are suggested for both locomotor and nonlocomotor actions.

Preschool and child-care teachers are always expected to include lots of vigorous physical activity in their daily programs; however, there is seldom a physical-education or music/movement-education specialist on the staff; therefore, planners of physical activity often have little or no physical-education training for working with the young child.

A simple set of guidelines that both physical-education specialists and early-childhood teachers can use is provided by Werner, Timms, and Almond (1996):

1. Allow children to make individual decisions about when to join or terminate an activity.
2. Creative simple fitness activities that allow everyone to succeed.
3. Suggest actions—many young children are visual learners.

Without suggestion or example, some children omit physical exercise from their daily routines.

4. Keep directions simple. Use cue or key words in your verbal descriptions.

5. Change activities often.

6. Allow maximum practice opportunity—provide a piece of equipment for everyone.

7. Encourage more active play; show enthusiasm and play actively with the children yourself.

And I would like to add:

8. If necessary, limit the number of children participating at one time due to lack of equipment, space, endurance, interest, safety, or other limitations.

9. Use props (music, scarves, hats, and so on) that enhance the experience.

10. Review Chapter 7, Music and Movement Education.

Reflection

Keeping in mind the interests and skills of preschool children, make some guidelines for use in an exercise program for young children. Consider the following items:

1. The physical abilities and endurance of the children (the need of some to settle down and the need of others to liven up)
2. How exercises enlarge, stretch, or strain developing muscles and other parts of their bodies
3. Ways to encourage children and their personal satisfaction
4. Amount of time (daily/monthly, spontaneous/planned)
5. Warm-up and cool-off activities and times
6. How to build endurance
7. Sequence and routine
8. Special clothing or equipment
9. New or more complex activities or uses of equipment

APPLICATION OF PRINCIPLES

1. Make a list of foods typical of your area, such as fruit, vegetables, meat, and seafood. Tell how you could utilize each of these in your center.

2. Design a lesson plan based on nutrition. Use it in your center.

3. Provide materials and opportunities for your children to practice good sanitary procedures such as washing hands, cleaning nails, and covering clothes.

4. Make a chart of basic nutrients and their sources. Check the information against the food served in your center over the past week. What nutrients need to be included more often in foods you serve? How often are "harmful" ingredients (sugar, caffeine, chocolate, salt, and other additives) served? Should a specific attempt be made to reduce their use?

5. If possible, provide weekly opportunities in food preparation. Use the checklist in Figure 11.4.

6. Make a nutritious snack schedule for one month. Also make a quantity and price list. Compare the various menus for food value and cost.

7. Check each child's personal record to see if she has food allergies, dislikes, or cultural restrictions. How do you handle these limitations?

8. Using a week's menu from a child-care center or recalling your own food intake for one week, record the number of times the following foods were eaten:

Now, compare the food intake for one week with the Department of Agriculture Food Guide Pyramid (Figure 11.1) to see if the intake was in accordance with their recommendations.

Food Intake Chart					
	Mon.	Tues.	Wed.	Thurs.	Fri.
Fruit citrus other					
Vegetables green/yellow starchy other					
Dairy products milk cheese yogurt cottage cheese other					
Meat/alternatives meat fish poultry eggs other					
Grains bread nuts/seeds pasta rice other					

9. Make a weekly meal schedule in which you introduce a new food, outline hygiene and mealtime behavior, encourage sensory enjoyment of foods, and provide for child participation daily. Indicate child-oriented goals, preparation of the teacher, materials needed, and anticipated results.

10. Make a list of the most common fruits in your locality, specifying whether or not they are seasonal. Then list at least four ways each fruit could be served to increase its familiarity and versatility. (Remember to use different combinations.) How many of these fruits and methods could children assist in preparing and/or serving?

11. Make a list of favorite snacks of young children. Make a list of your favorite snacks. Evaluate both lists according to the nine principles at the beginning of this chapter. Make a substitute list of more nutritious foods for young children and yourself. Plan and serve these snacks for a two-week period.

12. Using the curriculum checklist in Figure 4.2, see how many ways food can be integrated into the curriculum.

13. Design and present a lesson on health care or personal grooming that would be appropriate for the children in your classroom.

14. Prepare a lesson on first aid or health. Present it to the parents.

15. What health conditions need to be improved in your area? How can you assist?

16. Check with local clinics or health departments as to immunization information and dates. Encourage parents to have their child's immunizations current.

17. Design and implement a day (or week) lesson plan related to health and/or safety for young children.

18. Provide a one-week exercise plan that includes daily locomotor activities to be used (a) indoors, (b) outdoors, and (c) spontaneously without props. If possible, implement your plan. Note the responses of the children. Would you need to revise your plans? If so, how?

19. How do you personally feel about health and exercise? Do you make them a part of your daily living? How could you use one or both to a better advantage?

For a miniplan on nutrition and health, see Appendix C.

REFERENCES

Activity and Health Research (1992). *Allied Dunbar National Fitness Survey.* London: Sports Council and Health Education Authority.

Alles-White, M. L., & P. Welch (1985). Factors affecting the formation of food preferences in preschool children. *Early Child Development and Care,* 21, 265–276.

American Academy of Pediatrics (1992). *Caring for our children. National health and safety standards: Guidelines for out-of-home child care programs.* Elk Grove Village, IL: Author.

American Academy of Pediatrics Task Force on Pediatric AIDS (1988, November). Pediatric guidelines for infection control of human immunodeficiency virus (Acquired Immunodeficiency Virus) in hospitals, medical offices, schools, and other settings. *Pediatrics,* 82(5), 801–807.

American Dietetic Association (1994). Position of the American Dietetic Association: Nutrition standards for child care programs. *Journal of American Dietetic Association,* 94, 323–328.

American Psychiatric Association (1981). *Diagnostic manual for mental disorders,* Vol. 4. Washington, DC: Author.

Aronson, S. (1991). *Health and safety.* New York: Harper-Collins.

Baumrind, D. (1973). The development of instrumental competence through socialization. In Pick, A. D. (ed.), *Minnesota Symposium on Child Psychology,* Vol. 7. Minneapolis, MN: University of Minnesota Press.

Birch, L. L. (1980). Effects of peer models' food choices and eating behaviors on preschoolers' food preferences. *Child Development,* 51, 489–496.

Birch, L. L., S. L. Johnson, & J. A. Fisher (1995). Research in review: Children's eating: The development of food-acceptance patterns. *Young Children,* 50(2), 71–78.

Birch, L. L., S. Zimmerman, & H. Hind (1980). The influence of social-effective contact on the formation of children's food preferences. *Appetite: Journal for Intake Research,* 3, 353–360.

Bomba, A. K., B. Oakley, & K. B. Knight (1996, September). Planning the menu of the child care center. *Young Children,* 51(6), 62–67.

Brown, M. (1986). *Stone soup.* New York: Macmillan Child Group.

Cane, E., & R. Van Enoo (1992, March). Teachers! Be on the lookout for tell-tale signs of foot problems: Simple clues for the perceptive teacher. *Young Children,* 47(3), 42.

Chavkin, D., & P. D. Pizzo (1992, March). Public policy report: Medicaid and child care: Good partnership potential. *Young Children,* 47(3), 39–42.

Cosgrove, M. S. (1991, March). Cooking in the classroom: The doorway to nutrition. *Young Children,* 46(3), 43–46.

Dietz, W. (1991). Factors associated with childhood obesity. *Nutrition,* 7, 290–291.

Endres, J. B., & R. E. Rockwell (1994). *Food, nutrition, and the young child,* 4th edition. New York: Merrill/Macmillan.

Ethics code revision: Recommended Changes in the NAEYC Code of Ethical Conduct (1992, March). *Young Children,* 47(3), 12.

FYI (for your information): A decline in child & family well-being. *Young Children* 48(3), p. 31.

Gabbard, C., & B. LeBlanc. (1986). *Health-related fitness and young children.* EDRS ED266879.

Glasser, A. (1964). Nursery school can influence foods acceptance. *Journal of Home Economics,* 56, 680–683.

Goldberg, E. (1994, January). Including children with chronic health conditions: Nebulizers in the classroom. *Young Children,* 49(2), 34–37.

Hostetler, L. (1991, November). Healthy environments: Our goal one for young children. *Young Children,* 47(1), 2457–58.

Immunizations urged for children in out-of-home care. (1992, Nov.). *Competence,* 9(3), 5.

Klefstad, J. (1995, September). Cooking in the kindergarten. *Young Children,* 50(6), 32–33.

Lasky, P. A., & K. M. Eichelberger (1985, January). Health-related views and self-care behaviors of young children. Special issue: The family and health care. *Family Relations Journal of Applied Family and Child Studies,* 34(10), 13–18.

Lauer, R. N., W. E. Connor, P. E. Leaverton, M. A. Reiter, & W. R. Clarke (1975). Coronary heart disease risk factors in school children: The Muscadine study. *Journal of Pediatrics,* 86(5), 697–706.

Lombardi, J. (1992, May). Viewpoint: Early childhood 2001—Advocating for comprehensive services. *Young Children,* 47(4), 24–25.

National Association for the Education of Young Children (NAEYC) (1989). *Child care and ill children and healthy child care practices: A resource guide.* Washington, DC: NAEYC.

Needleman, R., & G. Needleman (1995, November/December). Ten most common health problems in school. *Scholastic Early Childhood Today,* 10(3), 22–23.

New guidelines on HIV infection (AIDS) announced for group programs (1989, January). *Young Children,* 44(2), 51.

Newman, W. P., D. S. Friedman, A. W. Voors, P. D. Gard, S. R. Srinivasan, J. L. Cresanta, G. D. Williamson, L. W. Webber, & G. S. Berenson (1986). Relation of serum lipoproteins and systolic blood pressure to early atherosclerosis: The Bogalusa heart study. *New England Journal of Medicine,* 31(3), 138–144.

Noyes, D. (1987, September). Indoor pollutants: Environmental hazards to young children. *Young Children,* 42(6), 57–65.

Phillips, M. G. (1986, Spring). Home economics and Head Start: A partnership to strengthen nutrition services to preschool children. *Journal of Home Economics,* 78(1), 43–45.

Pipes, P. (1985). *Nutrition in infancy and childhood,* 3rd edition. St. Louis, MO: Mosby.

Powers, H., & J. Presley (1978). *Food power: Nutrition and your child's behavior.* New York: St. Martin's Press.

Sampson, H. A., L. Mendelson, & J. P. Rosen (1992). Fatal and near-fatal anaphylactic reaction to food in children and adolescents. *New England Journal of Medicine,* 37(6), 480–484.

Seefeldt, C. (1980). *A curriculum for the child care centers,* 2nd edition. Columbus, OH: Merrill/Macmillan.

Serious allergic reactions to foods in children. (1992, September). *Child Health Alert.*

Taylor, B. J. (1997). *Early childhood program management: People and procedures,* 163–190. Upper Saddle River, NJ: Prentice-Hall.

Thurston, E. W. (1979). *The parents' guide to better nutrition for tots to teens (and others).* New Canaan, CT: Keats.

U.S. Department of Agriculture (1992, April). *Nutrition guidance for the child nutrition programs.* Washington, DC 20250. Developed jointly by the U.S. Departments of Agriculture and Health and Human Services.

U.S. Department of Education (1991). *America 2000: An education strategy.* Washington, DC: Author.

U.S. Department of Health and Human Services (1994). *Head Start program performance standards.* 45-CFR 1304. Washington, DC: Author.

Utah Valley Regional Medical Center (1996). Infection control policies and procedures for day care. Provo, UT: Utah Valley Regional Medical Center.

Werner, P., S. Timms, & L. Almond. (1996, Sept). Health stops: practical ideas for health-related exercise in preschool and primary classrooms. *Young Children,* 51(6), 48–55.

Worthington, R. B. (1981). *Contemporary developments in nutrition.* St. Louis, MO: Mosby.

Resources on Chronic Illnesses

Educational planning for students with chronic health conditions. Educational Rights Specialist, 79 Elmore Street, Newton, MA 02159, C/O Ellie Goldberg. Send a self-addressed, stamped business envelope.

Plaut, T. (1988). *Children with asthma: A manual for parents.* Amherst, MA: Pedipress. (800) 344-7798.

Plaut, T. (1991). *One minute asthma.* (English 1991, or Spanish, 1992). Amherst, MA: Pedipress. (800) 344-7798.

Sander, N. (1989). *A parent's guide to asthma.* New York: Doubleday.

Sander, N. (1991). *So you have asthma, too.* Research Triangle Park, NC: Allen & Hansburys.

Savage, E. D. (1989). *Winning over asthma.* Washington, DC: Asthma & Allergy Foundation of America.

Zeiger, R. S., & A. Munoz-Furlong. (1992). *Off to school with food allergies: A guide for parents and teachers.* The Food Allergy Network, 4744 Holly Avenue, Fairfax, VA 22030. Two-booklet set: $8 plus $2.50 shipping and handling.

Transition Activities

CHAPTER 12

MAIN PRINCIPLES

1. Periods between activities or locations require careful planning, variety, and cooperation.

2. Good transition periods accomplish the following:

    a. provide good learning opportunities

    b. reduce random and disruptive behavior

    c. promote confidence, independence, and inner control

    d. meet individual and group needs

    e. increase participation

    f. add variety to the curriculum

Looking at a group of young children absorbed in a curriculum area, such as art or music, and then later looking at these same children absorbed in another curriculum area, perhaps now in language arts or science, one wonders how the teacher moves these children from one topic (or area) to another so the children will again find interest and motivation. Or does the change involve chaos, undesired behavior, noise, and frustration for both the teacher and the children?

When a teacher plans the daily schedule, are there provisions for the in-between periods (described by Berk [1976] as periods between activities, generally involved in reading, wandering, exploring, and waiting)? In studying several different kinds of nursery schools, Berk reported that transitions occupy from 20 to 35 percent of activity time in nursery school (depending on the school, the particular day, and the skill and planning contributed by the teacher). These periods consume a sizable amount of time, which can be either utilized or wasted. Those who make teaching look so easy and flow so smoothly attend to both transition and curriculum components.

It has been suggested that a number of factors contribute to difficulties around transition time, including boredom, the insistence on conformity, the absence of a future orientation in some children, the absence of clearly defined tasks, and a possible fear of failure (Hirsch, n.d.). Careful planning on the part of teachers at these times can reduce the negative behavior and attitudes that may occur.

Transition periods can make the day flow smoothly, or they can make the day seem choppy and out of control. Once the children get ahead of the teacher and the schedule, it is difficult for the teacher to regain control.

Times when schedules need attention are when children change activity or location. Activity changes include arrival of the children, opening time or free play, completion of an activity, moving between activities (sometimes from more desired to less desired ones, such as napping), waiting for an activity to begin (such as waiting for a ride, a visitor, or a group member), and preparing for departure. Change of location includes going outside or to another room, lunchtime, napping, field trips, and departure. Separation of the children from the parents or from the center may cause some children to feel anxious. A wise teacher will have several available techniques for working with children under these circumstances.

At times children may see transitions differently than do adults and will delay, resist, refuse, or ignore interruptions to pleasurable or interesting activities. Teachers should show respect for the children at these times by discussing with them the changes and expectations. Ordinarily the children will want to take responsibility when they know what is to be done, what is expected, or what comes next. Cleanup can be an enjoyable activity and a good learning experience for the children. They should be involved in it, and teachers can encourage their participation by giving them attention and honest approval. Situations where children just wait while the teacher cleans up the present activity and prepares the following one are inappropriate.

Well-planned transitions, those that are of interest and meet the needs of the children in a particular group, add much value to a classroom. Lest there be a misunderstanding, transitions are not to be interpreted as another period for academic performance. True, knowledge and opportunities are there, but transitions are used for a change of pace and place, even though learning occurs simultaneously. Consider the following as advantages.

Misbehavior Can Be Reduced or Avoided

Informed children (those who know what is expected of them and what to expect from the program, the schedule, and the teachers) become involved in undesirable behavior less frequently. With a little warning (first to those at the activities that re-

Things that are unusual, even if they are scary, get immediate attention of the children.

quire the most time or effort in cleaning up, or to the children who are dawdlers), the children can finish a present task and move easily to the next one.

Children Grow Individually

When teachers believe that children are competent, dependable, and trustworthy, the children act in these ways. Children can learn and practice independence ("I can do it myself"), gain confidence, and build inner control through good transition planning on the part of the teacher. Children like to help make decisions (when feasible), to feel some control over their actions and lives, and to be independent. These traits can be developed at school because of their knowledge of the program and the environment.

Development Occurs

Transitions can enhance areas of skill and personal development.

Physical

Activities can be provided to exercise large and small muscles through perceptual-motor and eye-hand coordination, balance, body movement, self-help, and other opportunities.

Cognitive

Children exercise memory and recall in cleanup, in refreshing previous concepts, in imaginative and creative thinking about old and new concepts, and in understanding their world.

Emotional

Children take pride in the appearance of their classroom and in developing good work habits.

Social

During transitions, children learn how to work cooperatively with others and to see each other's views. They learn how to build and strengthen relationships with peers and adults.

Learning Is Increased

Young children need firsthand, or concrete, experiences; therefore, transition activities that focus on sensory development are essential. Numerous opportunities to hear, smell, feel, see, and taste are especially good learning reinforcers for young children.

Rather than use transition times as stallers, the teacher can use these periods productively to disseminate new information, to review and reinforce old information, or to build personal relationships.

Language Can Be Practiced

Some teachers use a particular sound (bell, chords on piano, lights flickered, record, and so on) to warn children about the impending change of activity. When they do this, they do two things: (1) they forfeit an opportunity to practice language

Teachers can preassess current knowledge, introduce new concepts, or reinforce previous teaching during a transition period.

skills, and (2) they teach children to respond to external stimuli. The practice of using sounds could be used as a shaping tool until the children get the routine, but should then be replaced by verbal interaction and by the children taking more responsibility for their own behavior.

Teachers Can Be Better Prepared

Teachers use the physical environment in planning movement and participation activities so children will not be restricted by furniture or people. Teachers organize their teaching materials to be easily accessible, appropriate, and interesting. Teachers schedule activities and routines to meet the needs of individual children, small groups, and the whole group.

GOOD TRANSITION ACTIVITIES

A good transition activity will accomplish one or more of the following: enable the child to see the conclusion or completion of an activity; allow for child involvement and independence; set the mood for the next activity; reinforce ideas already learned; preassess the present knowledge of the child; serve as a valuable teaching time in all areas of development; help the child build good relationships with others; and add interest and variety to the daily schedule. Thus, the activity should:

1. Provide a variety of experiences. Using the same finger play or song day after day may discourage children from coming. Make it so exciting that the children will be there in order not to miss something!

2. Encourage self-control. When moving from one room or location to another, try putting something on the floor for the children to follow (yarn or paper objects such as footprints) or give them a particular way to go (for example, jumping like a frog) *until* they have established the routine. *Then* try saying that all those wearing shoes (or green, or stripes) can go to the next activity or place. Still later on, just tell them what is expected ("We're going to lunch now"), and let them take responsibility for getting there. It removes the external control and helps them build internal control, independence, and self-confidence—very important steps. To reiterate this point: At first give the children a specific idea of how to go and where they are expected to go; then move to verbalization and independence building. Teachers who must always tell children what to do and how to do it do not have confidence in the children or themselves.

3. Prepare the children for what is to follow (snack, story, going outside). A transition period may be used as specific preparation for an activity or as a quieting time for the children.

4. Meet the needs, interests, and developmental abilities of the children. Transition time should encourage participation, provide some learning, and be enjoyable and flexible. The teacher should watch the children for clues as to length, type of activity, and expectations.

5. Be started by the teacher when the first children arrive in the area. Other children will finish their activities and join the group. If a teacher waits until all the children are there before she begins, there is no incentive for the children to get there. "Why hurry so you can wait?"

Tips for Better Transitions

- Have the next activity or location prepared before terminating the present activity.

- Allow a realistic amount of time for the transition.

- Give sufficient warning about the impending change.

- Avoid having all children move at once. Forming lines and waiting for others create noise, crowded situations, competition, frustration, and aggression.

- Have a positive attitude and act in a calm, respectful way with a conviction in your voice that the children will follow the requests.

- Allow for requests of and suggestions by the children.

- Use planned and spontaneous transitions to preassess new concepts to be taught or to reinforce knowledge previously taught.

- Avoid transition periods that are too long, too short, too boring, or too demanding.

- Use the same careful planning and considerations as for other activities. Appropriate transitions help children move through the routine with ease.

- Plan some transitions to quiet the children (to relax, to settle down, to think and reason, to apply and reinforce concepts); plan others to stimulate participation, cooperation, or activity.

If a teacher of young children is asked what part of the day is the most troublesome or frustrating, the answer is generally "When we're changing from one activity to another!" This is especially true with an inexperienced teacher. A bit of organization and planning, however, can change a dreaded period to one of pleasure and reward.

Webster's Tenth New Collegiate Dictionary defines transition as "a passage from one state, stage, subject, or place to another." When one works with young children, transitions occur frequently, from the time they enter the door until they leave for home. It is not like a formal high school or college class, where students enter at a specified time, hear a lecture on a designated topic, and then leave at the sound of a bell. Young children can be interested in an activity for a long period of time—in fact, they sometimes need to be reminded that it will soon be time for another activity. In a developmentally appropriate program, individual children move more frequently than those in more traditional or academic programs.

In an effort to find ways to reduce random behavior during transition from one activity to another, teachers should review the plan for the day before the children arrive. A few extra minutes spent on transition activities will be well worth the effort. During the meeting, a song can be reviewed, any activities using props readied, and specifics discussed with other teachers if their assistance is needed. A few extra activities should be ready to use when needed. Preparation before the children arrive pays off while they are there.

How can children be encouraged to clean up their toys and materials before moving on to the next activity? Possibly by observing when they begin to lose interest and then stepping in to suggest that the blocks be put on the shelf or to assist in clearing up the art materials and putting things away; possibly by giving a few minutes' warning; possibly by having something of interest planned and started before the children begin random or running behavior. What happens at transition times really depends on the teacher. If she stops to clean up or get involved with a single child, or is not ready for the next activity, the children usually go right on past her. Then she has difficulty regaining her lead. In a developmentally appropriate program, children may replace their personal work materials but leave the area or activity ready for other children.

Several studies have focused on the amount of time teachers and children spend in transitions. Berk (1976) found that for children under the age of 6, transitions were the most prominent activity in all schools studied, ranging from 20 percent of the time in the community day-care center to 30 to 35 percent in all settings, including a Head Start program and a Montessori preschool. That is a lot of time when children may not know what is expected of them, and can increase aggression, class disruption, or deviant behavior. Reporting on the behavior of passive and aggressive children who were not provided with positive transitions, Wolfgang (1977) observed that the passive child (1) remains stationary, showing no response to commands, (2) withdraws to some quiet place, or (3) silently does what he is told. Meanwhile, the aggressive child responds by (1) destroying materials, (2) throwing objects, (3) becoming verbally aggressive, or (4) running and forcing the teacher to chase her.

In the daily activities, most teachers plan for curriculum areas, such as art, free play, and music, but neglect transition times—and then wonder why they are so difficult to manage. When teachers do not know what to expect, how can the children know? Teachers who write into their lesson plan the specific activities to be used at transition times find control of the children much easier. Teachers should also try to delay unnatural breaks in classroom activity, minimize interruption of activities, and, when possible, allow completion of an activity before introducing another.

Transition times are not merely time consumers; they can be very valuable teaching times. Much learning and feedback comes at times when the group is small and time is available for informal conversation. Transition can be a time of relationship building, relaxation, or emotional or physical release.

It is fun to listen to a tape and try to follow the directions.

Routines

Children who know the routines and expectations find it easier to make changes from activities or locations—even though some changes flow more smoothly than others. It is when children are unsure that problems occur. Some of the daily routines are arrival, washing and toileting, resting, eating, and departure. In a developmentally appropriate program, there are fewer routines as a whole group and more individual changes.

Arrival

In a regular, short-day program, many of the children arrive simultaneously. Sometimes this creates confusion and sometimes it gives each child an opportunity to obtain desired toys, join playmates in a small group, and initiate an activity.

In full-day or long-hour programs (day care, for example), children are coming and going throughout the day. Interruptions must be tolerated by both children and adults.

As children arrive for any length of program, there will be a certain amount of confusion and time expended before they settle into play or activities.

Washing and Toileting

Some centers have specific times when they encourage children to wash and use the toilet (before eating, resting, or outside times). Some children need to be reminded frequently to use the toilet and wash their hands; other children recognize and meet their own needs.

When children use the restroom for washing/toileting as a group, confusion may result. Children may need help in finishing their tasks and moving out to make room for other children. Some children may use the excuse of having to wash or use the toilet when they are expected to be in a group time (storytime, meals, or outside). If they need to be at a certain place for a specific reason or length of time, remind these children beforehand to take care of these necessities.

Resting

Children enrolled in short-day programs usually do not have an organized or specific time or place for resting. Usually they move between active and quiet periods, so resting, per se, is not suggested; however, tired children are encouraged to rest when and if they need to.

In long-day programs, children may be expected to rest on a cot or bed (for a short time each morning and each afternoon with an actual sleeping time for younger children). Some teachers have found that "resting" is more of a frustration for them and the children than providing other options—a quiet activity or listening to a story or music. In some states, an individual place to rest and a specific time (or length of time) is required. Centers must conform to this requirement.

Eating

Eating can be a social time, but it also provides a time for relaxation and nourishment. Short-day programs may provide only a snack; however, long-day programs usually provide a morning snack (or breakfast), lunch, and an afternoon snack, providing part of the total daily nutritional requirements for each child.

Eating experiences can help the child become familiar with different kinds of food, practice group living (manners), and learn about foods and customs of other people. (See Chapter 11.)

Departure

It is just as important to give children attention and time to wind down school activities as it is to get them involved when they arrive. Sometimes parents are in a hurry and expect their children to drop everything and leave. A wise teacher helps the children finish tasks and be partially ready to depart when parents or car-pool drivers arrive. For security reasons, the center should require and have on file the names and/or identification of the people who are authorized to pick up each child. An authorized person should daily sign the child into the center and sign him out when he leaves.

Parents and teachers need to have personal contact often, and it may be at the beginning or the end of the child's day. Leaving the center should be as relaxed and joyful as possible.

TEACHING SUGGESTIONS

Following are some suggestions that could be used as transition activities. Use only those that are appropriate for your group of children and add other ideas of your own.

Animal

Have an animal concealed until group time. Then bring it into the group or take the children to the animal, whichever is more appropriate. Discuss, touch, and enjoy the animal.

Ball Toss

As each child (for example, John) comes to the group, the teacher says, "John is ready." Toss or roll a soft ball to the child, who returns it. Repeat as each child arrives.

Body Cards

The teacher shows large individual cards on which have been drawn different positions (see Figure 12.1). The children use their bodies to represent the symbols.

Another way to use body cards is to have individual silhouette figures cut out of tagboard (see Figure 12.2). The teacher holds up an example, and the children form that position with their bodies.

Chalkboard

With the teacher drawing stick figures, the children supply a story. It is surprising how rapidly the story content changes. Some children who do not ordinarily express themselves become verbal in such a setting. Accept the children's ideas and let the story flow freely. If children are able, have them draw some of the story on the chalkboard.

Figure 12.1
Body cards with stick figures representing different positions that children can imitate.

Children's Original Stories

Without Props or Aids

One day a group of children was waiting for storytime before the teacher was ready. One child volunteered, "I'll tell you a story." The other children agreed; so Dell moved to the place usually occupied by the teacher and told his story. It was short and to the point: "Once there was a dog." Then he returned to his place in the group. Other children wanted a turn. Some of the stories were familiar ones; some were make-believe. The children thoroughly enjoyed participating. Children who wanted to tell a story were given the chance, but those who did not were not forced to do so.

With Props or Aids

Paste pictures into an old book (for example, a dress pattern book) with a stiff back and heavy pages. (Children or teachers may do this.) At storytime, show the pictures and let the children make up a story. This can be used over and over.

Provide the children with flannel board cutouts and let them make up a story, or let them use visuals that teachers have previously used. The stories may be traditional or original.

Figure 12.2
Body cards with silhouette figures that children can imitate.

Cognitive Concepts

Suppose you want to see how children respond to certain situations. "I want to buy some oranges. Where do I go to get them?" "Where can I get a new collar for my dog?" This gives the children an opportunity to think. Before you respond, "No, you can't buy it there," ask for further clarification. The child may be perfectly correct!

Teach about prepositions by using an object in relationship to another object. "Where is the spoon?" (*over, under, beside, on,* or *in* the box). Then give the child a chance to place the object and tell its relationship. A better activity would be for the child to use her body in relationship to an object; however, space may be a limitation.

Enforcing Themes

Example 1

When a theme concerns air, use a canister vacuum with the hose attached to blow rather than suck air. Place the opening directly up, put a Ping-Pong ball on the opening, and turn on the vacuum. The ball bounces up and down.

Example 2

For a theme on magnets, tell the story *Mickey's Magnet* (Branley & Vaughan, 1956). Demonstrate how Mickey kept spilling and picking up pins. Then divide children into groups and give them objects and magnets. Let them determine which objects are attracted by the magnet.

Exercises

Exercises such as "Head, Shoulders, Knees, and Toes" help reduce some of the tensions and physical needs of children. Many exercises can be used.

With children sitting on the floor, legs outstretched, have them touch the opposite knee with their fingers. Try it with an elbow, then the nose.

Have the children pretend they are rag dolls. Help them relax by first hanging their heads, then moving their arms limply, then their legs, and so on until they are on the floor.

Have the children walk around the room as they think animals would walk, using their own creative imaginations without patterning from teachers.

Use some of the movement activities suggested in Chapter 7.

When stimulating activity occurs just before a quiet period, it is important to provide an activity immediately after it to relax the children. Some of the finger plays on the following pages work nicely for this purpose.

Feel Box

Take a small cardboard box (about 16 by 8 by 8 inches or a size that can be easily handled by a child) and cut out one side. On each end make holes large enough for the child's hands. Have the child put his hands in the ends and hold the open side

The teacher begins when the first children gather for a transition and then modifies or expands the activity as more children join in.

away from himself so that he cannot see inside the box, but so that the other children can. The child closes his eyes while the teacher places an object through the open side into the box. The child feels the object and tries to guess what it is.

Films

Films should never take the place of actual experience, but they can be used infrequently as supplements to firsthand experiences. Carefully evaluate each film as to length, concepts taught (including vocabulary), interest for the children, and value to be gained from the film. Consider also *whether this is the best way to teach a particular topic.*

Finger Plays

Children enjoy doing as well as seeing. Finger plays should be short and of interest to the children; some help teach number concepts. Teachers should know the finger plays well before attempting to teach them to the children; make sure all teachers with the group do the finger plays the same way. Following are some favorites (some by authors unknown, some used by permission) along with some body actions for children.

One Little Body

Two little hands go clap, clap, clap!　　　　　(Do actions as mentioned.)
Two little feet go tap, tap, tap!
Two little hands go thump, thump, thump!
Two little feet go jump, jump, jump!
One little body turns around;
One little body sits quietly down.

Hands

On my head my hands I place,
On my shoulders, on my face.
On my waist, and by my side;
Quickly at my back they hide.
I can wave them way up high,
Like the little birdies fly.
I can clap them; one, two, three.
Now see how quiet they can be.

Little Hands

Open, shut them; open, shut them;
Give a little clap.
Open, shut them; open, shut them;
Lay them in your lap.
Creep them, creep them slowly upward
To the rosy cheek;
Open wide the shining eyes,
Through the fingers peek.
Open, shut them; open, shut them;
To the shoulders fly;
Let them like the birdies flutter,

Flutter to the sky.
Falling, falling slowly downward,
Nearly to the ground;
Quickly raise them, all the fingers
Twirling round and round.
Open, shut them; open, shut them;
Give a little clap.
Open, shut them; open, shut them;
Lay them in your lap.
Creep them; creep them; creep them
Right up to your chin;
Open wide your little mouth,
But do not let them in!

Ten Little Fingers

Ten little fingers, and they all belong to me.
I can make them do things, would you like to see?
I can shut them up tight, or open them wide.
I can put them together, or make them all hide.
I can make them jump high. I can make them jump low.
I can fold them quietly, and hold them just so!

Where Is Thumbkin?

Where is Thumbkin? Where is Thumbkin?	(Hide hands behind back.)
Here I am. Here I am.	(Show one thumb, then the other.)
How are you today, sir?	
Very well, I thank you.	
Run away. Run away.	(Return each hand to back.)
Repeat song using:	(Repeat actions showing appropriate finger, then return hands to back.)
"Pointer" (index finger);	
"Tall Man" (middle finger);	
"Ring Man" (ring finger);	
"Baby" (little finger):	
and "All the Men" (all fingers at once).	

Night and Morning

This little boy is going to bed;	(Place first finger of right hand on palm of left hand.)
Down on the pillow he lays his head;	(Thumb of left hand is pillow.)
Pulls the covers up round him tight,	(Fingers of left hand close.)
And this is the way he sleeps all night!	
Morning comes, he opens his eyes;	(Open and blink eyes.)
Back with a toss the cover flies;	(Fingers of left hand open quickly.)
Up he jumps, is dressed and away.	(Right index finger is up and hopping away.)
Ready for frolic and play all day.	

Bunny Song

Here is my bunny with ears so funny,	(Right fist forms bunny, and two fingers the ears. Left hand is closed to make a "hole.")
And here is his hole in the ground.	
When a noise he hears,	
He pricks up his ears	
And jumps in his hole with a bound.	

Quacking Ducks

Five little ducks went out to play,	(Hold up five fingers.)
Over the hills and far away.	(Fingers run away.)
When the mother duck said,	(Make quacking motion
"Quack, quack, quack."	with both hands.)
Four little ducks came waddling back.	(Four fingers return.)
Four little ducks went out to play.	(Four fingers run away.)
(Continue words and motions until . . .)	
No little ducks came waddling back.	
BUT, when the mother duck said,	(Make deliberate
"QUACK, QUACK, QUACK!"	quacking motion.)
Five little ducks came waddling back!	(All fingers return.)

Five Little Squirrels

Five little squirrels sitting on a tree.	(Hold up hand.)
The first one said, "What do I see?"	(Shield eyes with hand.)
The second one said, "A man with a gun."	(Take aim.)
The third one said, "Oh! Let's run!"	(Hands run away.)
The fourth one said, "Let's hide in the shade."	
The fifth one said, "I'm not afraid!"	(Thumbs under armpits.)
Then "BANG!" went the gun	(Clap hands loudly.)
And away they all run.	(Hands go behind back.)

The Beehive

Here is the beehive.	(Close fist, thumb inside.)
Where are the bees?	
Hidden away where nobody sees.	

Teachers who require children to be ready and to participate as a group find less support and enthusiasm than teachers who are prepared for the first children and modify the activities as more children join in.

Soon they'll come creeping out of the hive;
One, two, three, four, five.   (Bring out finger with each
                                                number.)

BZZZZZZZ, BZZZZZZZ.   (Fingers and hands fly
                                                around.)

Five Little Kittens

There were five little kittens.   (Hold left hand up; with right hand
One little kitten went to sleep.   fold the left-hand fingers into the
Two little kittens went to sleep.   palm, one by one, starting with the
Three little kittens went to sleep.   little finger.)
Four little kittens went to sleep.
Five little kittens went to sleep.
All the kittens were fast asleep.

My Little Kitten

My little kitten ran up a tree.   (Fingers run up arms.)
And sat on a limb to look at me.   (Hands are placed on opposite
                                                shoulders.)

I said, "Come, kitty," and down he ran,   (Fingers run down arms.)
And drank all the milk   (Hand is cupped, opposite
I poured in his pan.   hand drinks.)

Eensy, Weensy Spider

Eensy, weensy spider   (Opposite thumbs and index fingers
Climbed up the water spout.   climb up each other.)
Down came the rain   (Quickly lower hands and arms.)
And washed the spider out.
Out came the sun   (Make circle of arms around head.)
And dried up all the rain.
So eensy, weensy spider
Climbed up the spout again.   (Repeat thumbs and finger motion.)

Here Is a Ball

A little ball,   (Make ball with fingers.)
A bigger ball,   (Make ball with both hands.)
A great big ball I see.   (Make ball with both arms.)
Now let's count the balls we've made.
One, two, three!   (Repeat previous three circles.)

My Dolly

This is how my dolly walks,   (Walk around a circle stiff-
This is how she walks, you see.   legged and arms raised.)
This is how my dolly runs,   (Run stiff-legged.)
This is how she runs, you see.
This is how my dolly talks,   (Bend over, say, "Mama, Mama.")
This is how she talks, you see.

The Fruit Tree

Way up high in the apple tree,   (Extend arms up high.)
Two little apples smiled down on me.   (Put hands around eyes.)

I shook that tree as hard as I could,	(Pretend to shake tree.)
And down came the apples;	(Arms move to ground.)
M-m-m-m, were they good!	(Rub stomach.)

Repeat poem and motions using different kinds of fruit: pear, peach, banana, orange, cherry, and so on.

For last verse, use a lemon tree. Last action is pulling a sour face and saying, "U-u-u-uh! They were sour!"

Jack-in-the-Box

Jack-in-the-Box, all shut up tight,	(Close fist with thumb inside and cover
Not a breath of air or a bit of light.	with palm of other hand, or curl up
How tired he must be, all folded up.	body on floor with arms around head.)
Let's open the lid, and up he'll jump.	(Thumbs pop out of fist, or child jumps up, extending arms.)

Guessing Games

Say: "I am thinking of something that _____ (give a couple of clues). Can you guess what it is?" (Use animals or transportation vehicles; describe a child.) Children can also take a turn giving clues.

Guests

Often bringing a guest into the school is easier than taking children on a particular field trip. By bringing the guest to school, the children can enjoy the experience in a familiar setting. This is often helpful.

A doctor, father of one child in the center, came to the school with his black bag. Rexene backed off, saying, "But I don't want a shot today." She was assured by the teachers and the doctor that he had not come to give shots that day. This particular doctor was a bone specialist. After showing the children all the things he carried in his bag, he asked, "Have any of you ever known someone who had broken a bone?" Some did, and some did not. He went on to explain how he helped people when they had a broken bone. He applied a cast to a teacher's arm for demonstration—none of the children would be his patient! How real the experience was to the children! They expressed sympathy to the teacher, as if she really had a broken arm. After the cast was dry, the doctor removed it. Many of the children were concerned, thinking he would cut off the teacher's arm with the cast. He took care to explain away all their fears and questions. After the cast was removed, the children said how glad they were that the teacher's arm was better. The children examined the cast, tried it on, and explored it in every way. This was an excellent experience for them because the doctor could communicate with them on their level. One child commented, "My dog has a broken leg, but he doesn't have a cast on." Shortly after this classroom experience, the teacher's own young son broke his arm, and she had information to make the experience less frightening for him.

A carpenter also paid a visit to a group of preschool children. The visit had been prearranged and well planned. Through his conversation, he helped the children to understand his occupation better. He brought a small door that was nearly completed and let the children finish it by putting screws in predrilled holes. He

Children enjoy transition activities that are varied and stimulating.

explained the use of all his tools, and, on departing, gave each child a carpenter's pencil. How busy the woodworking bench was that day!

A musician invited as a guest should be asked to explain about the instrument briefly and then play tunes that are familiar to the children. The children can listen to some selections, but they also enjoy participating. If the children are not allowed to touch or use the instrument, they may be able to sing or dance with the music. Although a guest may be very talented and want to display his or her skills, young children are easily bored and may walk out on the guest. The experience should be kept simple, therefore, with the length of the presentation varied according to the interests of the children.

Mirror Image

The teacher shows a mirror, and the children see how it reflects their movements and expressions. The mirror is removed and the teacher or a child makes movements for the others to reflect.

Musical Experiences

Children enjoy expressing themselves—verbally or physically—through music. Free, spontaneous movement should be encouraged. Occasional honest praise helps to motivate the quiet child.

A number of records and tapes encourage children to participate. When selecting this material, see that they give ideas, but do not restrict freedom to interpret actions. See music catalogues for possible selections.

Use the piano from time to time, sometimes to accompany songs, sometimes to teach specific concepts (high and low, loud and soft, fast and slow); sometimes encourage child participation (marching, moving to various rhythms).

Some of the ideas under the section titled "Exercises" could be used with the addition of music. For other specific suggestions, see activities listed at the end of Chapter 7.

Number Experiences

With the aid of a flannel board, chalkboard, bulletin board, finger plays, games, songs, and other methods, provide some relaxed and enjoyable but meaningful experiences with numbers. Many preschool children can do rote counting but still do not understand number symbols. For example, when interrupted in counting, they must return to the beginning—they cannot continue where they left off.

For some specific ideas, see finger plays listed previously that include numbers, see Chapter 9, or try some of the following. (*Note:* It is generally easier for young children to count forward than backward.)

This Old Man

This old man, he played one,
He played knick-knack on his thumb;
With a knick-knack, paddy-whack, give my dog a bone,
This old man came rolling home.
This old man, he played two (shoe); three (knee); four (door); five (hive); six
(sticks); seven (up to heaven); eight (gate); nine (vine); ten (hen).

One Red Valentine

One red valentine, two red valentines,
Three red valentines, four;
I'll snip and cut out color and paste
And then make twenty more.

Over in the Meadow
(Southern Appalachian folk song)

Over in the meadow in the sand in the sun
Lived an old mother turtle and her little baby one.
"Swim," said the mother; "I swim," said the one,
And he swam and was happy in the sand in the sun.

Over in the hollow in a pool in the bogs
Lived an old mother froggie and her two polliwogs.
"Kick," said the mother; "We kick," said the wogs,
Then they kicked and kicked into little green frogs.

Over in the meadow in a nest in the tree
Lived an old mother birdie and her little babies three.
"Sing," said the mother; "We sing," said the three
And they sang and were happy in the nest in the tree.

This song has 10 verses. For another version, see *Over in the Meadow* by John Langstaff (New York: Brace and World, 1957).

One Elephant
(Chilean folk song)

One elephant went out to play,   (Children extend arms down,
All on a spider's web one day.   clasp own hands,
He had such enormous fun,   pretend to walk like an ele-
He called on another elephant to come.   phant.)

Continue counting as "elephants" (children) are added to group. "Two elephants went out to play . . . Three elephants . . . Four elephants," and so on.

Three Blue Pigeons

(American folk song)

Three blue pigeons, sitting on the wall,
Three blue pigeons, sitting on the wall.
One flew away. Whee-ee-ee-ee!
Two blue pigeons, sitting on the wall,
Two blue pigeons, sitting on the wall.
One flew away. Whee-ee-ee-ee!

Repeat, using one blue pigeon, then no blue pigeons.

Five Little Buns

(Traditional English song)

Five little buns in a baker's shop,
Nice and round with sugar on the top,
Along came a little boy (girl) with a penny to pay,
And bought a sugar bun and took it right away.

Repeat, using four, three, two, one, and no little buns.

Five Little Chickadees

(Old counting song)

Five little chickadees peeping at the door,
One flew away and then there were four.
Refrain:
Chickadee, chickadee, happy and gay,
Chickadee, chickadee, fly away.
Four little chickadees sitting on a tree.
(Refrain)
Three little chickadees looking at you.
(Refrain)
Two little chickadees sitting in the sun.
(Refrain)
One little chickadee left all alone,
He flew away and then there were none.
(Refrain)

Nursery Rhymes

Young children enjoy the plays on words, repetition, and nonsense that are incorporated in nursery rhymes. Pictures add to the enjoyment. Through repetition they learn the rhymes without formal training. Nursery rhymes should be selected by the same criteria used for books. Avoid those that are violent or encourage aggression.

Following are some nursery rhymes familiar to most young children:

Curly Locks	Little Boy Blue
Hickory, Dickory, Dock!	Little Miss Muffet
Jack Be Nimble	To Market, to Market

Mary Had a Little Lamb	Little Jack Horner
Old King Cole	Simple Simon
Peter, Peter, Pumpkin Eater	Lucy Locket
Rub-a-Dub-Dub	Mary, Mary, Quite Contrary
Twinkle, Twinkle, Little Star	Pease Porridge Hot
Deedle, Deedle, Dumpling	Rock-a-Bye, Baby
Humpty Dumpty	Seesaw, Margery Daw
Little Bo Peep	Wee Willie Winkie

Original Stories from Adults

Perhaps you have written a story, or would like to, and are interested in the reactions of the children. You do not want to use it as your main story, but you do want to try it. Use it as the children are assembling for a group time. (Maybe a parent, a friend, or someone else has written a story and would like response from a group of young children. Try it for them, if you think it would be appropriate.)

Writing for young children is challenging. You need to know their interests, their needs, and some of their growth characteristics. Your story should be short, simple, and realistic. Writing in poetry form is stimulating and exciting. (See Chapter 5.)

Pantomime

Read a favorite story to the children. Briefly talk about it with the children. Help them identify some key concepts or characteristics. Encourage them to act it out. Sometimes they are better at pantomiming than at reciting.

Paper Bag

Give each child a paper sack and tell her to go around the room, putting into her sack objects of a certain color or shape (or other description). Examine the contents with the group.

Have two sacks or boxes with identical contents. Have a child feel in his sack and name an object in it. The second sack is handed to another child, who is requested to find the same object. Sacks are passed around until all the children have had a turn.

Give each child a paper sack. Go into the play yard or on a walk and ask them to either pick up garbage or bring back some things for making a picture. At group time, examine the contents and then proceed with the appropriate activity (keeping the community clean or appreciating things of beauty in nature).

Show a paper bag. Ask the children how many ways the bag can be used. Brainstorm. Try some of the ideas.

Pictures

Select with care the pictures you use with young children. Avoid confusion and distraction.

A teacher can show an interesting picture and start talking about it—the children will generally join in—or a teacher can hold up a picture and stimulate verbal responses by asking questions such as, "What do you think these children are doing?" "Would you like to do what they are doing?" "What time of year is shown in the picture?"

Younger children may need a special invitation or help from a teacher to join a group.

A bulletin board with selected pictures can also be very effective for discussion.

Do not hesitate to get quality (perhaps famous) artwork from the local library or other available sources. Help the children appreciate aesthetic values.

Poetry

Listen to the conversation of children; it is truly poetic! The play on words, the fun sounds, and the humor are delightful. Too often adults think that poetry has no place in the lives of young children. How wrong they are! An excellent introduction to poetry when a child is young is a priceless experience that will add greatly to his future enjoyment of it.

Young children thoroughly enjoy the rhythmic quality of poetry (nursery rhymes included). They can often be heard reciting a line, phrase, or entire poem as they play. It encourages them to sharpen their hearing perception. They begin to discriminate between similar sounds, they enjoy the sense and nonsense of poetry, and they learn new things.

Poetry should be a part of the teacher's repertoire. When appropriate, he can recite a poem, expressing his enjoyment of the verse and also showing the children that he values it.

Select poetry as carefully as you do other language experiences. Use it in a similar way: for a transition, to support areas of curriculum, to create interest, and to verbalize with the children. You can dramatize it or use it spontaneously or as a planned activity, with or without visual aids. If the children seem interested, use more verses; if they become restless, only a first verse or the first and last verses may be sufficient.

The teacher's attitude toward poetry will be influential. A teacher who enjoys and appreciates it will select and share it enthusiastically and will use different types: poems related to children's everyday experiences, nonsense verses for fun, poems that bring melody and rhythm to the ear, poems with special meaning, and poems that stimulate and encourage verbal exploration. Through repetition, not through rigid memorization, children learn and enjoy poetry.

As you can tell, using poetry with young children is one of my great favorites. When I was required to use poetry as a student in a children's literature class, the experience started off on a reluctant note. The children responded so well, my timidity vanished, and now it is impossible to get along without using it often in the classroom. If you cannot find a poem on a specific topic, you might even try writing your own.

Among the many excellent sources of poetry for young children are favorite authors such as Dorothy Aldis, Dorothy Baruch, Polly Chase Boyden, Marchette Chute, Rachel Field, Rose Fyleman, Josette Frank, Kate Greenaway, A. A. Milne, Elizabeth Madox Roberts, Carl Sandburg, Robert Louis Stevenson, and James S. Tippett.

Preparation for a Field Trip

Tell the children about an excursion just before you go. Help them to understand why you are going and what you will see and do. Set up the guidelines and make necessary stops at the bathroom and water fountain before leaving the center.

After a field trip, use transition time to discuss what happened, to ask and answer questions, or to draw or write a story of the group's experience.

For additional information about field trips, see Chapter 10.

Puppets

Several kinds of puppets are available and add interest to activities. Sack, finger, hand, sock, tube, clothespin, and stock puppets can be easily made and used by either children or teachers. Making something for later use (perhaps at group time) adds an element of anticipation for the children.

Make sure the puppets are realistically represented and that correct concepts are taught. This should be a learning experience as well as a fun one.

Some shy children who do not respond to a person will respond to a puppet. Use this experience to encourage verbalization, or have the puppet give instructions for the children to follow: "Lester, please hold a picture while we sing." "Mindy, please put the cow on the flannel board." "All hop like bunnies."

Set the guidelines to puppet use before the children become loud or aggressive. Merely saying "These are friendly puppets who have come to help us today" may deter any problems.

Rhyming Games

Read a poem, show objects, or tell the children certain words. Ask them to think of words that rhyme. Some of their responses will be very interesting.

Rhythms

For suggestions, see music and movement activities at the end of Chapter 7.

Role Playing

Encourage a child or children to act out a story or activity. Let others guess what it is. Give a turn to all who want one.

Science

If you are interested in having all the children participate in a science experience, this is an excellent time. Sometimes have the whole group together, and sometimes use small groups for discussion and participation.

For suggested activities, see Chapter 8.

Songs

Most children enjoy singing simple songs. Songs that use the names of the individual children tend to have magical power. (See "Mary Wore Her Red Dress" in *American Folk Songs for Children* by Ruth Seeger [1948].)

A review of Chapter 7, including how to teach a song to young children, might be appropriate at this stage.

Stories with Action

Have you ever been on an action walk with children? This activity brings out an element of suspense that delights each child.

The children and teachers sit on the floor, using their hands to make the sound effects: clapping for walking; rubbing the hands together for going through tall grass; gently pounding on the chest for going over a bridge; fists pounding on the legs for running. Use your own imagination and comments from the children to carry you through an enjoyable experience.

Several versions of an animal "hunt" are available. Ramsey and Bayless (1980) take a bear hunt; others take a tiger hunt; still others take a cougar hunt. Here is an original example of how such an activity could be used.

Let's Go Camping

Everyone sits down. The teacher begins; the children repeat what the teacher says and does and participate throughout the entire activity.

"Let's go camping." (Children repeat.) "We'll need our sleeping bags, food, ___ _____ , _____ ." (Children repeat.) Pretend to gather and pack items. "We have walked a long way." (Children repeat.) "I'm getting hungry." (Children repeat.) Pretend to fix and eat meal. "I'm getting so sleepy!" (Children repeat.) Yawn, stretch, and pretend to prepare sleeping bag and self for bed. "Let's crawl into our sleeping bags." (Children repeat.) Wiggle as if getting in and going to sleep. "Somebody is snoring!" (Children repeat.) Snore and blow out air. "Somebody is snoring louder than anyone else!" (Children repeat.) Snore and blow out air. _____ (use child's name) isn't sleepy; so he goes for a walk in the woods. As he is walking (slap hands rhythmically on the legs), he goes over some cobble rocks (make click with tongue in mouth); then he goes over a bridge (pound fists on legs); then he goes over some dry dirt (rub hands together). And do you know what he sees when he gets there? He sees a fire in the forest, and the wind is blowing the fire (put arms up in the air and wave back and forth, saying "Whoo-oo-oo, whoo-oo-oo!").

When he sees the fire, he runs back over the dry dirt (action), over the bridge (action), and over the cobble rocks (action) to the camp. He wakes everyone up and tells of the fire. All get up and run to the fire, first over the cobble rocks (action), then the bridge (action), and last over the dry dirt (action). They see the fire with the wind blowing it (action) and decide to go back and get some water (go back through actions). They get some buckets and pour water into them (say "shh-hhh-hh-pt") and go back to the fire (with actions). They pour the water on the fire that the wind is blowing ("whoo-oo-oo," slow down), and the fire goes out.

Now we're very tired; so we go back to the camp across the dry dirt, bridge, and rocks (very slow actions), crawl into our sleeping bags, and all start to snore (action). And guess who snores the loudest of all?

If this activity seems too long for the children, delete parts of it. Usually they respond, "Oh, let's do it again!"

Storybooks

Select an appropriate book, other than one to be used at actual storytime. Show the pictures to the children and stimulate their conversation.

A child may select a book she would like you to read for storytime. Use it while the children are gathering, but use the book you had already prepared for the entire group.

Surprise Box

Occasionally a teacher or a child can bring a surprise or gather up familiar things from the room. The teacher or a child feels the object in a box and describes it. Others try to guess its identity.

Talking Time for Children

Many opportunities should be provided for the young child to express himself and his ideas as well as to listen to others. Following are some ideas that have been tried and found to be effective:

- Ask which children in the group are absent that day. This helps the children to become more aware of each child.
- Talk about the weather. Has there been a recent change? What kinds of wearing apparel are appropriate for today?
- If you know a child has done or is about to do something exciting, let her share it with the group.
- Casually, get feedback from the children on certain concepts so that you will know if more time and information are needed.
- Talk about things the children have been doing during the morning. How did the finger paint feel? Was it fun to climb on the jungle gym? See other ideas presented in Chapter 5.

Children are more willing to terminate one activity and move to another when they assume some responsibility for their actions.

Think Box

Designate a good-sized box as the "think box." Use it as often as the value dictates. The teacher brings the box to group time and encourages verbal expression from the children. "What do you think is in the box today?" As the children guess, the teacher may add clues. For example, one day the box may include gloves—baseball glove, ski glove, boxing glove, lady's dress glove, and child's winter glove. The teacher says to the children, "What does a glove look like?" "How many kinds of gloves do you know about?" As the children name some that are in the box, she takes them out. The teacher may give added clues: "It's a kind of glove you play a game with," or "You wear it in the winter."

Another use of the think box is to have parents and children, the day before you use the box, bring things (something soft, something your favorite color, something about an animal, or a picture of something in your house). The enthusiasm of parents and children is usually high. On the teaching day have the child place his object in the box, unseen by others. At the appropriate time the child shows and tells about his object. The setting is very informal so that even the shy child participates. To prevent boredom, select a few different children to bring objects each time the box is used.

Television

Make a television screen by cutting a hole in a large box. Let the children take turns being the actors. You may want to encourage the children to use props.

Another idea is to use a box that is large enough to cut a screen that is visible to the group. Make a continuous story on butcher paper. Roll the story on a dowel and attach the other end of the story to another dowel. As you tell the story, unroll the pictures from one dowel to the other, showing the pictures through the screen.

APPLICATION OF PRINCIPLES

1. For one week, note the different activities used for transitions. Which ones do the children respond to best?

2. Be particularly aware of the children's actions, voices, and involvement during transitions. How does the tempo in the room change? Are teachers more concerned with things (cleanup, getting the next activity ready) or people? Use examples.

3. Plan and use a new transition activity. Begin it as the first children assemble. How do things change as more children join the activity?

4. Learn and use four new finger plays in the next month.

5. Memorize and use four poems. Stimulate children to use rhyming words and to write their own poems.

6. Make and use a plan that will use transition periods as learning experiences for children and teachers.

REFERENCES

Baker, B. R. (1986, Summer). Transition time: Make it a time of learning for children." *Day Care and Early Education, 36–38.*

Berk, L. (1976, November). How well do classroom practices reflect teacher goals? *Young Children, 32,* 64–81.

Branley, F. M., & E. K. Vaughan (1956). *Mickey's magnet.* New York: Scholastic Book Services.

Hirsch, E. S. (n. d.). *Transition periods: Stumbling blocks of education.* New York: Early Childhood Education Council of New York City.

Langstaff, J. (1957). *Over in the meadow.* New York: Brace & World.

McAfee, O. D. (1985, September). Circle time: Getting past "Two Little Pumpkins." *Young Children, 40*(6), 24–28.

Ramsey, M. E., & K. M. Bayless (1980). *Kindergarten: Programs and practices.* St. Louis, MO: Mosby.

Seeger, R. (1948). *American folk songs for children,* 130–131. Garden City, NY: Doubleday.

Wolfgang, C. (1977). *Helping aggressive and passive preschoolers through play.* New York: Merrill/Macmillan.

EARLY-CHILDHOOD THEORISTS AND PRACTICES

"*Developmentally appropriate practices* result from the process of professionals making decisions about the well-being and education of children based on at least three important kinds of information or knowledge about: (1) *child development and learning,* (2) *the strengths, interests, and needs of each individual child in the group,* and (3) *the social and cultural contexts in which children live*" (Bredekamp & Copple, 1997, p. 8 & 9).

NAEYC has modified its former standards from "either/or" to "both/and" thinking: For example: Children (1) construct their own understanding of concepts *and* benefit from instruction by more competent peers and adults; (2) learn through integration of curriculum *and* in-depth study; (3) benefit from making choices *and* from having boundaries; and (4) develop their own self-identity *and* respect for differences of others. Additional examples are given in the NAEYC position statement (Bredekamp & Copple, 1997, p. 23)

For more details about each theorist, see Chapter 1.

HIGHLIGHTS ABOUT IMPORTANCE OF PLAY FROM EDUCATORS

(Listed Alphabetically)

John Dewey (1859–1952)

Dewey called for educational institutions to provide children with opportunities to learn from real objects and productive experiences similar to a home experience. He promoted constructing one's own ideas and learning in lieu of traditional methods that relied on memorizing symbols and digesting facts, seeing Froebel's "gifts" as contrived rather than real experiences.

Social negotiation and cooperation were emphasized in Dewey's philosophy. He encouraged children to invent tools, use constructive and make-believe play, and strive for practical and aesthetic successes.

Dewey believed that the major role of the teacher was (1) to provide a carefully prepared environment—carpentry, weaving, cooking, and local geography were essentials (Dewey, 1904/1964); (2) to ask questions and provide extensions that would broaden the child's understandings across several subject areas; and (3) to use peer pressure and self-rewards as a replacement for external adult discipline.

Dewey viewed learning as "a continuing reconstruction of experience" (1959, p. 27), and education as "a process of continual reorganizing, reconstructing, transforming" (1966, p. 50). Distinct from traditional education, in which teaching is conceived as a "pouring in" (1966, p. 38) and learning as "passive absorption" (1966, p. 38), Dewey saw education as being a social direction through "a joint activity" (1966, p. 39) within which people consciously refer to each other's use of materials, tools, ideas, capacities, and applications" (Rankin, 1997, p. 73).

Dewey placed value on teachers being responsive, observant, and learners as well as teachers: not to impose certain ideas or habits on the child, but, as a member of the community, to select influences that will affect the child and assist in her proper response to these influences (1959, p. 24).

Erik Erikson (1902–1994)

See information listed in Chapter 1.

Erikson identified the preschool years as a period when a sense of initiative, responsibility, and independence were developing. Time for change appears ripe for preschool children. (1950a). The theme for the 1950 White House Conference *Personality in the Making* represented Erikson's theory. Each of his eight steps to a healthy personality is a foundation for the next steps (Erikson, 1950a).

Erikson's work added the idea of play as mastery over situations through experimentation and planning to its role in mastering unconscious impulses and conflicts and in promoting conflict resolution and ego strength (1950b).

Friedrich Froebel (1792–1852)

Born in Germany, Froebel was an idealist. He felt that childhood represents a noble and malleable phase of human life, and that both humanity and nature reflect a unity with God. Froebel also emphasized the importance of the child's self-activity.

A Froebelian curriculum includes free play; directed singing and movement games; originated, promoted, and carefully sequenced "gifts" (specially designed materials he believed would help children develop knowledge of forms of life, beauty, and mathematics); and "occupations" (constructive play activities such as weaving, clay modeling, paper folding, and embroidery that focused children's attention and exercised fine motor skills) to guide and structure play. Froebel instructed teachers to observe and gently guide, but not to interfere with children's creative processes.

Believing that Froebel was an atheist, the German government banned kindergarten education in 1851; however, Froebel's ideas and materials were widely disseminated throughout the world. They were rigidly supported in the United States, especially by Susan Blow. Other liberal progressives (led by Patty Smith Hill and Elizabeth Peabody) believed that Froebel's principles had become severely distorted in the American kindergartens and sought major changes.

Lucy Sprague Mitchell (1878–1954); Caroline Pratt (1867–1968); Harriet Johnson (1867–1934)

Pratt, the designer of wooden unit blocks which are enthusiastically and frequently used in preschool and kindergarten classrooms today, and Mitchell opened the Play School in New York City in the 1920s. They adopted Dewey's emphasis on local geography (field trips), the school as an extended family, play with real objects, and language and storytelling using the children's own experiences. In the Play School, the role of the teacher was that of "guide and stage manager," teacher-researcher, observer and note taker, and parent-educator. Spontaneous play and interests from home were welcomed and carefully observed by the teacher in planning curriculum.

In the 1920s, Mitchell teamed up with Johnson to create a nursery school (believed by some to be the first genuine nursery school in the United States) under the Bureau of Educational Experiments (BEE) in New York, developing imaginative language and literacy curriculum. The BEE school later became the Bank Street College of Education, a respected institution in the field today.

Maria Montessori (1870–1952)

Maria Montessori was born in Italy; by profession she was a physician, psychiatrist, and educator. She gleaned many of her ideas from careful observation of infants from low-income or abandoned backgrounds and from caregivers in Rome (Montessori, 1936, 1964). Her methods, toys, and materials spread worldwide, and her influence is still felt in classrooms today.

Her philosophy was somewhat similar to that of her contemporaries Froebel and Dewey, but she added new elements about early-childhood development and education by developing self-correcting toys and materials. She believed that children should be clean (she worked mostly with "slum" children); to that end, she prescribed specific and sequential steps in personal care—handwashing, for example.

Montessori felt that children should select their own materials and assume responsibility for cleanup as well. She disapproved of rewards and punishment and believed that the child's self-dignity could best be developed by intrinsic motivation. In a nutshell, a good Montessori teacher operates on three principles: a carefully prepared environment, an attitude of humility, and respect for children's individuality (Montessori, 1936).

Jean Piaget (1896–1980)

Piaget's theories included the following: (1) Activity directed by the child is primary in his development (Van Hoorn et al., 1993, p. 237); (2) Through her own initiative and effort, the child modifies and builds upon already constructed mental patterns to try to make sense of new experiences (Cowan, 1978); and (3) Knowledge is based on what the individual child brings to each situation rather than on what he accumulates from the environment (Van Hoorn et al., 1993, p. 15).

Piaget's influence began in the 1950s, accelerated in the 1960s, and is very influential at present. An early contemporary of Lev Vygotsky, Piaget and his work became more widely known because of the suppression of Vygotsky's writings in Russia at the time. Both educators' theories have become influential in the educational theory and practice of the 1970s, 1980s, and 1990s. They both place emphasis on play in intellectual development and provide strong arguments for children's use of objects and in interaction with peers as the basis for early-childhood curriculum.

"Piaget assumed that the child's thought becomes more like that of the adult when children become developmentally ready to notice deficiencies in their immature, illogical reasoning and abandon it in favor of a logical approach to the world. Indeed, Piaget regarded the thought of the young child and that of more mature peers and adults not as collaborative and complementary but rather as in conflict" (Tudge & Winterhoff, 1993, p. 74)

Piaget's work is described as a cognitive-developmental theory: Children "construct" their own knowledge, facilitated by the teacher, through reflection on their experiences, their choices, and playing with peers. Learning and development are separate entities, but learning depends on development. (See Berk & Winsler, 1995, pp. 100–103).

Piaget was a strong supporter of play and hands-on experiences. He believed that children progress through universal and invariant sequences of development (maturation and transactions), with each stage marked by a characteristic way of organizing thoughts and activities; in other words, children actually think differently than adults. (See Chapter 1.) He encouraged learning centers with materials for art, block play, writing, drawing, dramatic play, and exploration with raw materials (dirt, sand, water, and so on) for both individual and group projects (DeVries & Kohlberg, 1987; Wasserman, 1990).

Lev Vygotsky (1896–1934)

Because of political suppression by the Russian government, Vygotsky's work was little known, even though he wrote copiously, was a contemporary of Piaget, and shared ideas in common with Piaget.

Vygotsky believed that play is a central feature of early-childhood curriculum. Make-believe (1) is the ultimate activity for nurturing capacities that are crucial for academics as well as later-life success (Berk & Winsler, 1995, p. 79); (2) helps children understand the meaning and function of culture, life plans, and volitional motives (Vygotsky, 1978, p. 2); and (3) is valuable for stretching children's development (zone of proximal development): children function above their normal level of ability when challenged by peers in their play; and (4) "make-believe is the ultimate activity for nurturing capacities that are crucial for academic as well as later-life success" (Berk & Winsler, 1995, p. 79).

According to Vygotsky, play has two critical features: "all representational play creates an imaginary situation that permits the child to grapple with unrealized desires, and it contains rules for behavior that children must follow to successfully act out the play scene" (Berk, 1994, p. 32). This theory is described as a sociocultural theory (Berk & Winsler, 1995, p. 100); learning and development combine in a complex interrelated fashion such that *instruction leads, or elicits, development.* Language is central; teachers ask real and important questions to determine what children know about the world. There are no single "right answers." The child is active; social environments collaborate to produce development (Berk & Winsler, 1995, p. 101). Vygotsky's main tenet is that "people are products of their social and cultural worlds and that to understand children, we must understand the social, cultural, and societal contexts in which they develop" (Berk & Winsler, 1995, p. 1).

Four distinct characteristics of Vygotsky-based curricular reform in his early childhood classrooms are (1) heavy emphasis on teacher-child and child-child relationships; (2) use of whole-language theory rather than meaningless drills; (3) relevant activities related to children's interests and competencies; and (4) suggested broadening of ZPD to expert partners, such as mixed-age grouping (Moll & Whitmore, 1993).

Scaffolding, a term not introduced by Vygotsky but used to describe his work, denotes important components of tutoring (Wood, 1989) and connotes and supports a sensitive cooperation promoting children to take over more responsibility for tasks as their skill increases (Berk & Winsler, 1995, p. 32).

Both Vygotsky and Piaget credited each other for help in their theories— Vygotsky about Piaget's work of self-directed speech in cognitive development ([1934] 1986) and Piaget about Vygotsky's interpretation of egocentric speech ([1962] 1979). "In sum, Piaget and Vygotsky both started with the same basic view of the child as a biological organism. Piaget focused on what it is within the organism that leads to cognitive change. Vygotsky explored how social experience might cause important revisions in the child's thinking to come about" (Berk & Winsler, 1995, p. 109). "Because of shared basic beliefs about development, the two theories are best viewed as complementary rather than in opposition to one another; as checks and balances" (Glassman, 1994, p. 186).

SELECTED REFERENCES

Berk, L. E. (1994, November). Vygotsky's theory: The importance of make-believe play. *Young Children*, 50(1), 30–39.

Berk, L. E., & A. Winsler (1995). *Scaffolding children's learning: Vygotsky and early childhood education. Research in Practice*, Vol. 7. Washington, DC: NAEYC.

Bredekamp, S., & C. Copple (eds.) (1997). *Developmentally appropriate practice in early childhood programs*, revised edition. Washington, DC: NAEYC.

Cowan, P. A. (1978). *Piaget with feeling; Cognitive, social, and emotional dimensions*. New York: Holt, Rinehart & Winston.

DeVries, R., & L. Kohlberg. (1987). *Programs of early childhood: A constructivist view*. New York: Longman.

Dewey, J. (1900). *The school and society*. Chicago: University of Chicago Press.

Dewey, J. (1959). *My pedagogic creed*. In Dworkin, M. S. (ed.), *Dewey on education*. New York: Teachers College Press.

Dewey, J. (1904/1964). The relation of theory to practice in education. In Archambault, R. (ed.), *John Dewey on education: Selected writings*, 313–338. New York: Random House.

Dewey, J. (1966). *Democracy and education*. New York: Free Press.

Erikson, E. H. (1950a). *A healthy personality for your child*. Midcentury White House Conference on Children and Youth, December 1950. Washington, DC: U. S. Government Printing Office.

Erikson, E. (1950b). *Childhood and society*. New York: Norton.

Erikson, E. H. (1977). *Toys and reasons*. New York: Norton.

Erikson, E. H. (1980). *Identity and the life cycle*. New York: Norton.

Froebel, F. (1975). *The education of man*. New York: Appleton.

Glassman, M. (1994). All things being equal: The two roads of Piaget and Vygotsky. *Developmental Review*, 14, 186–214.

Moll, L. C., & K. F. Whitmore (1993). Vygotsky in classroom practice: Moving from individual transmission to social transaction. In Forman, E. A., N. Minick, & C. A. Stone (eds.), *Contexts for learning*, 19–42. New York: Oxford University Press.

Montessori, M. (1912). *The Montessori method: Scientific pedagogy as applied to child education in "The Children's Houses,"* with additions and revisions. Trans. A. E. George, with introduction by H. W. Holes. New York: Stokes. (Original work published 1909).

Montessori, M. (1936). *The secret of childhood*. Bombay, India: Orient Longman.

Montessori, M. (1964). *The Montessori method*. New York: Schocken.

Rankin, B. (1997). Education as collaboration: Learning from and building on Dewey, Vygotsky, and Piaget. In Hendrick, J. (ed.), *First steps toward teaching the Reggio way*, 70–83. Upper Saddle River, NJ: Prentice-Hall.

Piaget, J. [1962] (1979). Comments on Vygotsky's critical remarks. *Archives of Psychology* 47: 237–49.

Tudge, J. R. H., & P. A. Winterhoff (1993). Vygotsky, Piaget, and Bandura: Perspectives on the relations between the social world and cognitive development. *Human Development*, 36, 61–81.

Van Hoorn, J., P. Nourot, B. Scales, & K. Alward. (1993). *Play at the center of the curriculum*. New York, Macmillan.

Vygotsky, L. S. [1934] (1986). *Thought and language*, trans. A. Kozulin. Cambridge, MA: MIT Press.

Vygotsky, L. S. (1967). Play and its role in the mental development of the child. In Bruner, J., A. Jolly, & K. Sylva (eds.), *Play: Its role in development and evolution*. New York: Basic.

Vygotsky, L. S. (1978). *Mind in society: The development of higher psychological processes*. Cambridge, MA: Harvard University Press.

Wasserman, S. (1990). Serious players in the primary classroom: Empowering children through active learning experiences. New York: Teachers College Press.

Wood, D. J. (1989). Social interaction as tutoring. In *Interaction in human development*, eds. M. H. Bornstein & J. S. Bruner, 59–80. Hillsdale, NJ: Erlbaum.

SUGGESTED CURRICULUM TOPICS

These topics are provided for teachers to use to give stimulation to the classroom while focusing on the interests and needs of their students. They can also be used successfully in webbing concepts of depth and breadth. (See Chapter 4, Curriculum Development.)

Animals

- Care of animals
- Names of young and adult animals
- Names of male and female animals
- Where and how animals live
- How animals help people
- Coverings (shell, fur, feathers)
- Products obtained from animals
- Good pets
- Wild animals
- Circus animals
- Protection (claws, camouflage, hibernation)
- Characteristics of animals

Birds

- Names of birds
- Sounds made by birds
- Where birds live
- How birds feed their young
- How birds help people (beauty, sound, eating insects)
- Kinds of nests
- Kinds of eggs birds lay (color, size)
- Characteristics of birds
- Habits of birds (nesting, migrations)

Categories

- Grouping (vehicles, food, animals, birds, clothing, furniture, persons, buildings, toys, plants, containers, appliances, things to write with, and building, garden, or household tools)

- Multiple classification (things that can be classed in more than one category)
- Ways to help discriminate between categories (senses, experiences)
- Why categories are useful and helpful

The Children

- Learning one's own name and worth
- Learning names of other children, teachers, nurse, others
- Where to hang clothing
- Self-confidence
- Good self-image
- Parts of the body
- Complying with requests
- Self-mastery and control

Clothing

- Names of garments
- Seasons for wearing different types of clothing
- Sequence for putting on clothing
- Types of fabrics (cotton, wool, leather, plastic)
- Clothing for different occasions (play, party, sleeping)
- Different types of fasteners on clothing (zippers, buttons, snaps)
- Uses of certain pieces of clothing (shoes, hats)
- Color or patterning in clothing (printed, woven)
- Learning to dress and undress dolls

Color

- Names of the primary and secondary colors
- How various colors are made
- Shades of the same color
- How various colors make you feel
- Uses of colors (for example, red for danger)
- Colors of specific objects (fruits, vehicles, animals)
- How colors are made and actually making some (berries, leaves)
- Tie-dyeing experience

Communication

- Physical and verbal communication
- Learning about different languages
- Different forms of communication (radio, television, newspaper, books, telephone)
- Proper names of people, places, and things so that we understand meanings
- How some animals help carry messages (dogs, pigeons)
- Learning to recognize objects from verbal descriptions only

- Telling something interesting about oneself or an activity
- Learning to follow simple directions

The Community

- Locations within the community
- Kinds of buildings, industries, parks, highways
- Recognizing community landmarks
- Different communities

Community Helpers

- Firefighter, police officer, letter carrier, doctor, nurse, dentist, baker, milk carrier, grocer, merchant, miner, farmer, fisher (places of work, activities, services)
- How community helpers work together
- Recognizing community helpers by uniforms or clothing

Comparatives

- Learning names and relationships by comparing two things (biggest/smallest, hottest/coldest, heaviest/lightest; bigger/smaller, fatter/skinnier, taller/shorter; too loud/too soft, too long/too short)
- Learning names and relationships by comparing more than two things (big, bigger, biggest; short, shorter, shortest; long, longer, longest)
- Learning that one object can be big when compared to some things and small when compared to others
- The concept of *middle*
- Ordinal (first, second, third) and cardinal (1, 2, 3) numbers
- Learning opposites through comparisons (soft, rough)

Days of the Week

- Names of the days of the week
- Why days have special names
- Sequence of the days
- Activities for certain days (for example, Saturday or Sunday)
- Learning about the calendar (days, weeks, months)

Environment

- Characteristics of the community (lakes, mountains)
- What pollution is and how to help prevent it
- Natural resources (coal, gas, oil)
- Conservation of natural resources (forests, water)
- Recycling (water, paper, metal)
- How to respect public property

Families

- Learning what a family is
- Learning the immediate family (mother, father, sister, brother, baby)
- Learning the extended family (aunts, uncles, cousins, grandparents)
- What families do together
- Different jobs and responsibilities of family members
- Friends and their names
- Learning about people (physical characteristics, abilities, likes, and so on)
- How to entertain guests
- How to get along with family members
- Good social techniques

Food (see the sections on food in Chapter 8 and Chapter 11)

- Names of various foods
- Tasting various foods
- Learning about taste (sweet, sour, salty, bitter)
- Preparing food in a variety of ways
- Plant parts used as food (roots, stalk, flower)
- Things that look alike but taste different (salt, sugar, baking soda)
- Food consumed by animals
- Preparing for and participating in lunch or snack
- Good diet (pyramid group)
- Where food products come from (animals, farms and gardens, factories)
- Ways of preparing food (raw, boiled, baked)
- Learning when food is unripe, ripe, and overripe
- Things *not* to be eaten (poisons, medicines)

Growing Things (see the sections on plants and nature in Chapter 8)

- Names of common flowers and plants
- How to care for plants
- Different things that plants grow from (bulb, seed, starts)
- Parts of the plant (root, stalk, vine, leaf, flower)
- Parts of plants that are edible (root—carrot, turnip; head—lettuce, cabbage; stalk—celery)
- Sizes and kinds of seeds
- Length of growing time (for example, rapid for grass and beans; more slowly for corn and squash)
- Fruits grown on trees
- Things needed for growth (sunlight, water, warmth)
- Food that grows above and below the ground
- Growing things that are not edible
- Storing fruit and vegetables

    ○ Why food is washed or cleaned before eating

    ○ Growing things for beauty (shrubs, trees, flowers) and consumption (fruit, vegetables)

Health and Cleanliness

    ○ How to clean various body parts (hair, nails, skin, teeth)

    ○ Reasons for keeping clean and healthy

    ○ How to keep healthy (exercise, rest, clothing)

    ○ Proper diet

    ○ Poisonous plants

    ○ Professional people who help us

Holidays

    ○ Names of holidays

    ○ Activities unique to holidays

    ○ Importance of holidays to children (birthdays, religious holidays, national, cultural, local, and other important days. (See also Chapter 10)

    ○ Which holidays come during which seasons

    ○ Family customs for various holidays

    ○ National, religious, cultural, and personal holidays of self and others

    ○ Preparing for and participating in child-centered holiday activities

Homes

    ○ Where each child lives

    ○ What a house looks like (inside and out)

    ○ Different types of homes in the community

    ○ Care of homes (inside and out)

    ○ Household equipment and appliances (brushes, mixers, and so on)

    ○ Repair and building tools

    ○ Homes in other countries or areas

    ○ Furnishing rooms

    ○ Building materials

    ○ Visiting a home or apartment

    ○ Performing tasks

Identification

    ○ Matching animals (mother and young)

    ○ Categorizing what is sold in a specific type of store

    ○ Selecting a type of store for a certain item

    ○ Things that belong together (fork and spoon, hat and coat, shoe and sock)

    ○ How to recognize something by one or more of the senses

    ○ How to group objects with similar characteristics (color, material, shape)

    ○ How to distinguish between objects

Machines

- Machines for the home or for industry: how they work and what their function is
- Learning to operate machines (mixer, eggbeater, gears)
- How machines make work easier

Materials

- Names of different building materials (brick, wood, fiber glass, cement, steel, cinder blocks)
- Names and uses of materials (metal, glass, plaster, paper, cardboard, cloth fabrics, leather, rubber, foil)
- Fabrics (waterproof, resilient, inexpensive)

Mathematics (see Chapter 9)

- How to count using familiar things (children, blocks, crackers, clapping)
- Counting similar and dissimilar objects
- Recognizing written symbols
- Learning about parts (fractions) of the whole (for example, a wheel is part of a wagon)
- Exploring with unit blocks (using different shapes and numbers to make other shapes)
- Making things equal
- Learning to tell different things by their number (phone, sport participant, house, time)
- Buying by weight, size, amount
- Mathematical terms (more, less, how many)

Music (see Chapter 7)

- Singing songs
- Playing and listening to records and tapes
- Names and uses of musical instruments
- Ways of making sounds
- Classes of instruments (wind, percussion, string)
- Different ways music makes us feel
- Learning to participate with music
- Discovering rhythm in everyday life (clocks, water dripping, walking)
- Observing different instruments being played
- Imitating music or movement in nature (trees, animals, water)

Objects

- Names of parts of an object (for example, a pencil has a point, lead, a shaft, and an eraser)
- Different materials used to make same or different objects
- Specific uses of different objects (spoon, screwdriver, belt)

○ Identifying objects through one or more of the senses

○ Naming several objects used for the same purpose (for example those that hold water or improve surroundings)

Opposites

○ Learning opposites (big/little, fat/skinny, loud/soft, hot/cold, long/short, fast/slow, wet/dry, smooth/rough, tall/short, dark/light)

○ Combining opposites (big, rough, and dark)

○ Discrimination (an object may be big compared to some things and small compared to others)

Pattern

○ Learning about different patterns (striped, flowered, polka-dot, plaid, plain, checked)

○ Learning whether the pattern is woven into fabric or printed

○ Creating one's own patterns using art materials

○ How patterns (shapes) are combined in environment

Piagetian Concepts

○ Conservation of volume or substance

○ Reversibility (water to ice to water)

○ Weight of objects (in hand or scale)

○ How objects can be grouped in a variety of ways (color, shape, size, material)

○ Discovering that learning is enhanced through the senses and movement (sensorimotor skills)

Plurals

○ Regular plurals (formed by adding *s* or *es*)

○ Irregular plurals (foot/feet, child/children, man/men, tooth/teeth, mouse/mice, sheep/sheep)

○ Terms used for more than one of an object (*many, few, group, some*)

○ When one object is called a "pair" (scissors, glasses, pants)

Prepositions

○ Names and relationship of various prepositions (*in, on, over, under, next to, in front of, in back of, inside, outside, between*)

○ How to carry out simple commands

○ Using one's body in space to learn prepositions (obstacle course)

The Preschool

○ Labels for materials and objects in the room

○ Storage place for toys

○ Places for certain activities

○ Learning about adults and children

○ Limits, responsibilities, and privileges

○ Learning routine

Safety

- ○ Times and places to be careful (roads, around water)
- ○ How to prevent accidents
- ○ Care of injuries
- ○ Professional people who help us
- ○ Safety at school and home
- ○ Reasons for limits under different circumstances
- ○ Using tools and materials

Science (see Chapter 8)

- ○ Magnets
- ○ Magnifying glasses
- ○ How to measure
- ○ Heat and how it changes various things
- ○ Light and prisms
- ○ Heavy and light objects
- ○ Liquids, solids, and gases
- ○ Physical science
- ○ Social science
- ○ Producing and preparing food
- ○ Working with levers
- ○ Biological science
- ○ Discovering things about community, nation, and universe
- ○ How to get along with others

Seasons

- ○ Naming the seasons and characteristics of each season
- ○ What people do during different seasons
- ○ What people wear during different seasons
- ○ How seasons affect families, animals, and plants
- ○ Identifying different seasons from pictures

Shapes

- ○ Names of shapes (square, circle, triangle, rectangle, oval, diamond, trapezoid)
- ○ Uses of different shapes
- ○ Looking for various shapes in the room
- ○ Discussing shapes in our daily lives
- ○ Why certain things are the shapes they are (for example, a wheel)
- ○ How various shapes are formed (two semicircles make a circle; two triangles, a trapezoid)
- ○ How similar objects (leaves, flowers) are different shapes
- ○ Making an original design using a variety of shapes (an art project or manipulative experience, for example)

- Characteristics of various shapes (a triangle has three corners; the lines in a square are the same length)

Sound (see Chapters 6 and 8)

- Listening for sounds in everyday life
- Distinguishing things by sound only
- Differences in sound (high or low, loud or soft)
- Different ways of making sounds
- Making sounds of animals
- Making sounds of transportation vehicles
- Making sounds that express different emotions
- Saying rhyming words

Temperature

- Terms used with heat (hot/warm, cold/cool, hot/cold)
- Temperature and the seasons
- Temperature and heat in cooking
- How a thermometer registers heat or cold

Time

- Learning about the present, past, and future (may be difficult to grasp)
- Sequence (before and after)
- Ways to tell time (clock, sun, sundial)
- Things to do in daylight and in the dark

Transportation

- Names of kinds of transportation (boat, airplane, bus, train, automobile)
- Ways transportation works
- What different vehicles carry and how it feels to ride in each
- Learning about vehicles
- Wheels and how they work
- Transportation in air (airplanes, balloons, helicopters); in water (boats, submarines, ferries); on land (cars, trucks, buses); and underground (subways)
- Animals used for transportation (horse, camel, elephant)
- Animals used for carrying (burro, llama)

SUGGESTED MINIPLANS FOR CURRICULUM CHAPTERS

Build upon the interests and suggestions of children. Avoid rigidity and teacher-directed learning. As a foundation for this information, refer to Chapter 4 for discussion and to review the planning steps as follows:

Step 1: Preassess present knowledge or abilities

Step 2: Identify concepts

Step 3: Overview the schedule and complete the plan

Step 4: Implement the plan in the classroom

Step 5: Evaluate the plan and the day

Step 6: Modify the plan for follow-up or expansion of the theme

From the following suggestions, enhance, select, or abandon any ideas for a personal plan that would better suit you and the children in your classroom. (Suggestions are given here to indicate the variety of ways to preassess, to expedite the use of examples, and to encourage the teacher to be innovative within the interests and skills of the children.) The individual teacher is expected to make a completed plan.

SUGGESTIONS RELATED TO LANGUAGE ARTS (CHAPTER 5)

Language arts include reading, listening, writing, and speaking. Young children are not readers, although they enjoy looking at books and hearing stories. Their writing skills are undeveloped, both in using writing implements and in composing their thoughts. For these reasons, a miniplan is proposed here that encourages children to do what they do best—speak! Young children need to speak fluently and confidently; therefore, this plan is centered on the child's self-image.

These miniplans will follow the previous format; however, they will be in less detail to reduce redundancy—the reader should refer to the previous plan for ideas, sequence, and support.

Step 1: Preassess Present Knowledge or Abilities

- Observe the children to determine the ranges of self-image. (Some verbal children are confident and others are insecure. Some nonverbal children are confident and others are insecure.) After making written or mental notes about the confidence and security of each child in your classroom, share your thoughts with other teachers for accuracy, then observe the children again in different activities to solidify or modify the individual assessment.

Step 2: Identify Concepts

○ Note that sometimes concepts are actual statements or ideas that could be made to children, sometimes they are ideas on which to build, sometimes they remind teachers of goals, sometimes they are forthright statements of fact, and sometimes they indicate a direction that can be used or modified at the time of teaching.

○ One of your goals in using *this* plan is to help each child feel good about himself. Avoid comparison between children, among cultures, and within personal preference. Each child is special and has individual worth. Aim for personal and group concepts by highlighting individual assets, by helping each child feel more confident than before the topic, and by helping the children acknowledge and appreciate the uniqueness of each child. All comments, actions, and encouragement must be honest and sincere, and teachers must realize that to develop a good self-image is an ongoing—never a one-time—procedure!

○ After carefully identifying how each child feels about herself, write some proposed individual and group concepts. For example, from observation and consultation, you may note that the children speak in varying degrees of loudness, interact within a select group, avoid certain types of activities, and are either passive or active depending on who is participating or the tone of the activity. For this exercise, assume that the following concepts are appropriate:

Because children use different pitches and kinds of responses, teachers should listen intently when a child is speaking. (Sarah yells for attention, Juan withdraws, Peter speaks too rapidly, Ana is bilingual and gets the languages mixed, and so on.)

Focus: By listening carefully and giving the child full attention, the child will be able to express himself more freely and feel that what is said is of worth.

Different activities encourage or discourage child participation. More active settings (blocks, riding toys, climbing, and so on) discourage younger, less developed, and insecure children from participating.

Focus: Invite reticent children to participate by limiting the size of the group and by staying close by for verbal and physical support, when needed. This will give the children an opportunity to participate without being overwhelmed by the noise and skills of more active children.

Initiate activities by using more quiet children as the nucleus (introducing a new toy, helping with visuals, leading an activity, and so on).

Focus: Avoid putting a child on the spot or insisting he be the center of attention when this is uncomfortable for the child.

Encourage children to talk about themselves and others in a positive and supportive way.

Focus: Help each child think and speak positively, comfortably, and happily about herself and others.

Step 3: Make an Overview, Select and Schedule Activities, and Complete the Plan

- Encourage a shy or reticent child to participate in a small group.
- Give honest verbal, facial, and physical support to each child.
- Provide activities that call the child's attention to constructive things about his body and abilities:

  Draw or trace an outline of the child's body and encourage the child to color or cut it out (include ponytails, boots, and so on).

  Provide materials and activities that are open-ended (child's choice rather than patterned).

  Provide puzzles of body parts, occupations, cultures, and so on.

  Help the children to learn about and use tools properly (woodworking, scissors, cooking utensils).

  Display the child's work at school and home.

  Encourage children to work in pairs, as buddies, or in teams.

  Give the child a respectable responsibility, such as preparing snack and tables, holding doors open, watering plants, caring for pets, putting away toys, getting needed items, and so on.

  Do a simple game such as "Do as I'm Doing," where the child sets the activity (but be ready with some suggestions).

- Talk about similar and different physical characteristics of the children—who has blue eyes, how many have blond hair, and so on. Do this in a way that attracts children to each other—never as a judgment of better or best.
- Consider the group carefully to determine which (if any) children are ready for a show-and-tell activity or if it will become too teacher-centered. A similar idea could be used with a friend or small group of children so the child does not feel intimidated.
- Well-placed pictures in the classroom will give children information about different activities, cultures, locations, and so on. Such pictures often encourage individual or group conversations.
- If possible, see the child in settings outside the classroom (home visits, shopping, at the park, and so on).
- Occasionally have a parent or family member visit the classroom and tell something special about the child. Or the teacher could have a conversation with a family member and casually mention something special about a child.
- Do activities where the names of the children are emphasized or play noncompetitive games where children are described and others try to guess who it is, and so on. Call the children by their names and encourage others to do so also.

Procedures

- Focus on some general group concepts or goals and highlight one or two children.
- Make children feel that they belong: on the entry door, place a small photograph of each child who belongs in that room, give each one a place for personal items, and identify it with a label, picture, or sticker.

○ Never compare the children to each other. Rather, help each child to see personal progress—running faster, doing harder activities, verbalizing rather than using physical attacks, getting taller, and so on.

○ Have quiet areas where children can sit, look at books, play in quiet activities, or visit with one another.

○ Place appropriate books, flannel boards and characters, and other visual aids where children will use them. Consider such things as developmental abilities of the children, present interests or ideas to be introduced, good cultural and role models, children interacting with other children, and so on.

○ When possible, assist the children in making rules that are important for specific situations and help them to understand the reasons of rule making. Where rules are necessary, help the children discuss the problems and how to resolve them.

Many of these suggestions could be used on any day with any topic; however, try to fit some, all, or substitutions into a session that would enhance the self-image of each and every child. Incidentally, you could be increasing the self-image of teachers and supporting staff as well!

Step 4: Implement the Plan

○ With a completed plan, the needed materials, support of teachers, and enthusiasm, you are ready to have a fun and important period with the children. Note their reactions, their comments, and their interactions. What new combinations of children did you see as a result of the activities or ideas? Which children were more or less verbal today? How will you plan to help the children further develop friendships and increase their understanding of themselves and others?

Step 5: Evaluate the Plan

○ Armed with your plan and your notes, pause for a thoughtful evaluation of what occurred during play and activity periods. Which of your ideas were most successful—and why? Where was the activity or interaction terminated abruptly because of lack of time or too many choices? When did you hear children referring to other children by name—were there increases over previous times?

Step 6: Modify the Plan for Follow-Up or Expansion of the Theme

○ Promotion of good self-image in children has just begun. Note which children are more popular and which are less popular within the group. Make mental or written notes as to how to help all children learn to interact more favorably with all children. Make a reminder (perhaps a chart) to help you relate with all children. Every single day all teachers should have private or small-group conversations with each child. It may help to focus on one or two children each week, but never overlook any child—whether it is focus week or not. Often feedback from parents will help build a stronger relationship with each child. If a child feels ignored or disliked, she may resort to negative behavior just to be noticed! Don't let this happen in your classroom!

○ In every session, deliberately plan something that will build good personal and group relationships. (For example, in books, stories, and visual aids, select those that are complimentary, are nonstereotypical, show variety [ethnicity, age, handicaps, abilities, and so on], encourage cooperation, and can be put into immediate use by the children.)

SUGGESTIONS RELATED TO A SENSORY EXPERIENCE (CHAPTER 6)

Step 1: Preassess Present Knowledge about Sound

○ Show objects that make specific sounds (bell ringing, water dripping, clock ticking, and so on). Have a child imitate a sound of one of the objects and ask the other children to select the proper object. With very young children, make sure the object is familiar and has a definite sound. Some children will describe sounds differently for the same object. Accept their ideas unless they are totally inappropriate.

○ Have objects behind a screen. Make the sound of each object separately and ask the children to identify the object. Use familiar objects and then introduce a new or slightly more difficult one.

○ Show pictures of objects and have the children imitate the sound identified with each object. In order to make this an effective experience, include some objects that are noiseless (a cotton ball dropped on the table, a Band-Aid being applied, a spider walking, and so on).

○ Prerecord familiar indoor and outdoor sounds on a tape recorder. As the tape is played, have the children imitate the sound (brushing teeth, answering phone, raking leaves, and so on). Then play a series of sounds and help the children make a sequential story using the sounds.

○ Ask the children to listen to sounds during a play period and then share their findings during a group time. Teachers may need to add visuals or clues to help the children remember over a period of time.

○ Using one item (perhaps a musical instrument), demonstrate and help the children identify characteristics of that item (fast, slow; high, low; sharp, sustained; loud, soft; and so on).

○ Talk about how sounds help people: warning (emergency vehicles), schedules (bells, timers, telephones), pleasure (sports whistles, music), and others.

○ Sing a song that has different sounds, such as "The Wheels on the Bus," "Old McDonald Had a Farm," or others. Accept the sounds the children offer. Even sing the song different ways. For example, the horn on the bus may go "beep, beep, beep" or "honk, honk, honk." It really doesn't have to have *one* specific sound.

Step 2: Identify Concepts

○ The teacher identifies some basic concepts and begins a tentative plan as to which concepts would interest or bore the children, where the concepts would be most appropriately placed, what would be a reasonable length of time, and other considerations.

Step 3: Make an Overview, Select and Schedule Activities, and Complete the Plan

- An inexhaustible list is made of activities and materials that would present clear and accurate concepts about hearing—based on the current developmental level of the children for whom the plan is intended. Some ideas are included in the plan, others are excluded entirely or held for future teaching; however, the entire list is retained for future use.

- Suppose the teacher narrows down the prospective ideas to talking with the children at group time; playing a sound game; using a story, a tape recorder, and a workable telephone; placing pictures of noisy and quiet items on the walls; and an art activity.

  Preassessment is completed and one or more of the ideas suggested in Step 1, or personally developed ideas, are selected.

- Prior to the teaching day, the teacher preassesses current knowledge of the children using one or more of the ideas suggested in Step 1 or personally developed ideas. (Items usually included on the plan are general findings of the preassessment, suggested concepts, an outline for the day's activities, evaluation suggestions, and follow-through for parents (see Daily Planning Outline [Figure 4.3]).

  For this example, consider the following:

General Findings

- Some children readily recognize and imitate sounds in the classroom and home.
- Some children need the object and sound to make a clear distinction.
- Several of the children offer no comments when listening to sounds in general; others boisterously make requested sounds and volunteer others.
- Focusing on sound would be of interest and value to the children at this time.

Concepts to Be Taught

These are broad enough for the needs of individual children, yet specific enough to have a focus.

Suppose the teacher selects one or more of the following:

- Sounds are all around us.
- Sounds have different meanings.
- Different sounds make us feel differently.
- Caring for our ears is important because they help us identify sounds.

Outline for the Day's Activities

- Assume that the session is for a half day and is divided into four periods: arrival, activity playtime, gathering time, and departure (closing). Activity playtime and gathering time may occur more than once during the day. For some suggestions, see Figure C.1.

Step 4: Implement the Plan

- The plan is carried out. Teachers take *quick* notes of things that went well, things that were troublesome, comments and activities of children, and other occurrences that reflect on the plan and individual children.

Figure C.1
Suggestions for a Miniplan Involving Sound

Curriculum Area	Activity Playtime (large block of time)	Gathering Time (smaller block of time)
Creative, Artistic, and Sensory Expression (Chapter 6)	Transportation vehicles near blocks, housekeeping area with household utensils, pictures placed at eye level, books and tapes in a reading area, prerecorded sound tape and player, self-selection of toys. At this or a selected time the teachers and children could go on a listening walk in their school, on the playground, or nearby. Climbing and riding toys, digging and hauling tools, running and playing activities are available. Some children continue the idea of listening for sounds.	Sound experiences (values of being in a group include: verbalizing and listening, broader understanding of topic, interaction with teacher and group, cooperation); pictures associated with sounds; tape for identifying and/or imitating household, community, transportation, and animal sounds; identifying sounds of items not visible (bell, clock, eggbeater or mixer, squeaky toy, musical instrument, and so on); informal discussion about care, importance, and use of ears using a large model ear; importance of sounds: danger or safety, pleasant and soothing, activity, reminders (whistles, bells, warnings), and so on; story and tape "The Listening Walk" by Paul Showers (or an original story and tape) are used; snack of foods that make sounds (crunching of apples or celery, munching of crackers, squeaking of raisins, and so on).

Step 5: Evaluate the Plan

○ In planning (and *before* the plan is implemented), the teacher records some areas of focus for evaluation, hoping or assuming there will be some comments, questions, or suggestions relating to the plan. These are the items for discussion but may include spontaneous ones as well.

○ After implementing the plan, teachers use the evaluation as a period of sharing notes and feelings in a discussion rather than as a checklist. Why were some things successful and others unsuccessful? Notations of additions, deletions, substitutions, and so on are made right on the plan for future reference.

Step 6: Modify the Plan for Follow-Up or Expansion of the Theme

○ The teachers discuss the comments and actions of the children, then note on the plan some ideas for future teaching on this same topic. What children understood the concepts? Which ones showed special interest in the topic? How could you increase the knowledge of the immature children *and* the mature children without boring some and frustrating others? Young children need many opportunities to learn about their world as an entity in itself and as a part of their global world. Return to Chapter 1 and review the discussion of the Reflection symbol.

○ The plan, notes, teaching aids, and so on are filed for future use. This gives the teacher incentive to try the topic again soon—either with the same children, with a different group, or as a stepping stone for review or for integrated or more complex information.

SUGGESTIONS RELATED TO MUSIC AND MOVEMENT (CHAPTER 7)

Although some teachers are very hesitant to teach about music (rhythm, musical instruments, sound, and so on), it seems that even more teachers feel that physical activity will come whether or not there are attempts to promote it. True, many children learn to run, jump, and climb without adult interference; however, because of the impact one feels related to one's body performance, the miniplan for this chapter will be on development for both large and small muscles.

Step 1: Preassess Present Abilities

○ Focusing on the motor skills of each child, the teacher can determine how the child feels about himself. Age must be a factor in assessing the small- and large-muscle development of each child. Younger and inexperienced children practice large-muscle skills (running, climbing, carrying, and so on). As the child feels more confidence in using large muscles through opportunities and experience, the control and use of small muscles takes on new importance; therefore, expect skills to be at different levels for different children, expect children to use their bodies differently, expect attitudes about their abilities to be different, and expect some children to avoid experiences that may indicate their immaturity.

○ In determining the small motor skills of the children, provide activities in which eye-hand coordination is important (cutting with *good* scissors, pegs and boards, puzzles, threading, pouring, and so on). Get a feeling for the individual child and for the group (some do this, most do that, none do that).

○ In determining the large motor skills of the children, provide activities in which arms and legs are used individually or together (climbing, pedaling, catching, running, and so on). Get a feeling for the individual child and for the group (some, most, one).

Step 2: Identify Concepts

○ Note which children seem deficient in small, large, or both motor skills. Note which children seem proficient in one or both motor skills.

○ Make this a fun experience—one that the children will enjoy and want to repeat by themselves or through assistance. Emphasis on this topic is not to make children perform better for us but to give them opportunities that increase their self-image, provide additional experiences, and stimulate interaction with peers and adults.

○ For *this* exercise, concepts will be related to teaching techniques and activities rather than direct statements about the learning of the children.

○ Activities emphasizing the use of small or large muscles may be inappropriate for some children in their present state of development.

○ Some activities and materials may be growth-promoting for some children and growth-stunting for others.

○ Many children practice small- and/or large-muscle development through ideas and opportunities that interest them—not necessarily only those that are teacher-oriented.

Step 3: Make an Overview, Select and Schedule Activities, and Complete the Plan

Overview the supporting activities for this plan; suggestions are given for curriculum areas or time periods.

Activity Playtime

Free Play

○ *Table toys* (usually small-muscle or eye-hand coordination): puzzles; pegs and boards; stringing objects; small building materials; frames or opportunities (housekeeping area) for lacing, tying, buttoning, zipping, dressing; pouring water or sensory materials (wheat, rice, flour); books and visual aids with flannel boards; and so on

○ *Floor toys* (usually large-muscle coordination): blocks, transportation vehicles, jungle gyms

○ *Art:* scissors (good quality), tearing, pasting, painting with brushes, block or stamp printing, collage, crayons, felt pens, finger painting, clothespins for hanging artwork

○ *Outdoors* (usually large-muscle activities): walking boards, boxes, obstacle course, wheel toys, climbing gyms, nets, ladders, woodworking tools, Frisbees, balls, parachute, gardening, games

Gathering Time

○ *Stories:* Engage children in physical activities, art activities, activities with pets, and planting (See Chapter 6 for related literature)

○ *Snack:* soft spreads (butter, peanut butter) with small knives and crackers/bread, pouring own beverage (sponges handy and no pressure), finger foods (vegetables, fruit), and so on. Children can help prepare and serve food.

○ *Music:* rhythm instruments, participation records, finger plays, songs

○ *Games:* "Head, Shoulders, Knees, and Toes," "If You're Happy and You Know It," "Hokey Pokey," "Do as I'm Doing," the sponge game. *Note:* Use games that encourage children to participate in their own ways and at their own speed—*avoid* games that teach competition between children or that reveal immaturity of the child ("Simon Says," musical chairs, and so on).

○ Completing the plan

From these options, a completed plan could be as follows:

Activity Playtime:

○ *Housekeeping area:* Dress-up clothes, dishes, food cartons, dolls, stuffed animals, and so on

- *Table toys:* Puzzles of children and activities; small plastic bricks, cash register and tokens, stringing large beads

- *Floor toys:* Large unit blocks with various types of vehicles; a portable climbing gym; perhaps hula hoops to define a space for a child

- *Quiet area:* Cozy reading corner with books, pillows, stuffed toys

- *Sponge game:* Each child is given a sponge approximately 4 by 6 inches. Color is no consideration. The leader (teacher or child) gives ideas and children perform them: "Put the sponge on your head." "Put the sponge on your foot," and so on. Sometimes the instructions include "See if you can walk with the sponge on your head without the sponge falling off," or "Get on your hands and knees, put the sponge on your back, and keep it from falling off."

- Tell a story about a child who learns to do more things because he is getting older, more experienced, or more confident (for example, Krauss, *The Growing Story*, published in 1947 by Harper's Children's Books; see Chapter 6, or write an original story appropriate for the children in this classroom).

Now complete the plan following your schedule and the needs of the children in the particular group. Provide for activity time, gathering time, outdoor activities, creative art, music, and so on.

Step 4: Implement the Plan

- Note carefully the way the children (individually and collectively) respond to activities, peers, adults, and materials. Make short notes throughout the day.

Step 5: Evaluate the Plan

- Using the notes from Step 4 and recalling individual children and activities, share ideas and feelings about the day with other staff members. What indications were there that the plan was successful or unsuccessful? Which children were involved and which children seemed to be discouraged? Give examples. Plan additional moderate stretching for each child, and each day include some type of physical- and self-image-promoting ideas.

Step 6: Modify the Plan for Follow-Up or Expansion of the Theme

- From experiencing the day with the children and through careful observation, what would you include or exclude the next time this topic is introduced? How important is it that children are encouraged at their present stage and find success for at least trying the activities? Plan additional moderate stretching activities for each child. Include some type of self-image-promoting ideas daily. Discuss how the staff can give *honest, sincere* praise to each child. Which would be more appropriate: (1) other days focused on large/small-muscle development, or (2) planning carefully for each child? A good self-image is important for children and adults. Begin now to promote healthy concepts in yourself, the children, other staff members, and other contacts.

Add music to activities and have a whole new experience.

SUGGESTIONS RELATED TO BIOLOGICAL AND PHYSICAL SCIENCE (CHAPTER 8)

For simplification, two broad categories of science have been identified: biological and physical. For books and other teaching materials, see both biological and physical references in Chapter 8.

Science can be one of the most exciting, interesting, challenging, and fun topics for young children. They are interested in everything—especially when they discover things for themselves.

Almost everything can fit into science in one or many ways, but as an example, we will use water, a very common, inexpensive, mesmerizing, and versatile medium. It is hoped the reader will be willing to provide simple water experiences for our youngest children and then to develop the topic in a variety of ways for older children. Today adults spend much time researching the properties and benefits of water, results of drought and pollution, and water's other characteristics and uses. It is vital to our survival.

Step 1: Preassess Present Knowledge

○ Tubs and water for bathing dolls, plastic animals, doll clothes, pouring and measuring, cleanup after art or other activities, painting metal or nonharmful surfaces with a brush and bucket of water, or other water activities more suited to your location, facilities, and staff

○ Adding water to other media: powdered paint, frozen juices, sensory table, recipes, and so on

○ Washing fruits and/or vegetables for snack or lunch

○ An experience related to cleanliness of the body (personal habits) and clothes (washing, frequent changes, proper fit, and so on)

○ Caring for classroom or family pets

○ Different weather conditions: heat, snow, rain, fog

○ Water play outdoors (hose, small wading pool, bathing suits, buckets)

○ Occupations that depend on water

○ Caring for plants and gardens

○ Different climates or physical locations (near bodies of water, deserts, cold regions)

○ And many more suggestions—some of them more appropriate for some locations, ages, or situations and others less appropriate until the children have more experience and background in the topic

○ The teacher should have some ideas about what to preassess and what will be presented to the children; otherwise, the preassessment could be long, frustrating, and meaningless. Remember that most children (young and old) thoroughly enjoy pouring and measuring water. Help them to move beyond this stage and still enjoy the simple properties of water.

Step 2: Identify Concepts

○ For a very young child or one who has had little experience with water except to drink it or splash in it during a bath or on a hot day: This child will thoroughly enjoy pouring, spilling on herself and the floor, and taking an occasional drink. She will be totally absorbed and it will be important for her to have a comfortable feeling about her actions—even though a puddle will occur. The child is learning about the properties of water and what she can do with it. Pouring will be inaccurate as eye-hand coordination begins. When the child tires of the activity, give her a sponge or towel and help her wipe up the excess water, all the time talking about the activity and the feelings it brought. Provide this type of experience frequently along with other pouring and water experiences: helping pour her own beverage, cleaning up, and using water in a variety of ways.

○ For the older preschool child who has had some water and pouring experiences: He will still want to pour and measure. He will recognize the use of water in other activities: mixing paint, playing at the sensory table, watering plants and animals, and so on. He is now ready for some expanding experiences. One day you may provide objects for the children to predetermine if the objects will sink or float (providing proper jargon). Another day, experiment with evaporation or the three different properties of water (liquid, solids, gases). Still another day, talk about occupations related to water because of community dependency on water. Your teaching and provision of activities and information will all be on the appropriate level of the children because you have preassessed well and have patiently led the children to this point of understanding.

Step 3: Overview the Schedule, Select Activities and Materials, and Complete the Plan

Few teachers have children of the same developmental and interest level in their preschool classrooms, so plan some basic or repeated experiences for the younger or less mature children and also consider the older and more mature children. Plan to challenge both younger and older children—but at their pace and interest level.

○ In science activities, plan to use many open-ended materials: those that can be continued for a period of time or can be terminated easily, according to the child's interests. Insisting that a child remain at an activity a certain length of time or to a certain point of completion could discourage him from coming to an activity at another time. Likewise, help the child develop enough interest that the activity offers something to him now and for the future.

○ Along with focused activities, set out some familiar activities so the child can move to areas of interest. Help the children to see how ideas fit together. Listen to the children. Pick up on their interests for future science experiences.

○ In spontaneous ways (singing, poetry, conversation, activities) show the children some of the marvels of our world. Reward the children for showing new interest, curiosity, or discovering something. That's what science is all about!

○ It certainly isn't necessary to set up a theme or period on science. You can teach it in many ways every day, but once in a while it is stimulating to focus on some scientific ideas.

Step 4: Implement the Plan

Throughout each day, teachers (adults) should be constantly aware of the many planned and spontaneous scientific happenings that are meaningful to the children and their understanding of their environment. Build on them by providing verbal support, physical proximity, and additional materials, and by encouraging the children to work together.

Step 5: Evaluate the Plan

- Reflect on how the children approached and used the situations that were provided for them. Could these experiences be enhanced and used again, or were they not on target for these children on this day?

- Which children participated in group activities? Which comments of the children led you to believe that they had either understood or misunderstood the concepts presented? Which activities need to be repeated on a simplified level and which ones were too familiar or too easy for the children? How can you tell if any learning occurred? Discuss the feelings (excited, frustrated, challenged, satisfied, indifferent, and so on) of the adults who interacted with the children. How can you encourage children and adults to be excited about science experiences? Which activities or children got out of control, what were the causes, and were these situations healthy or detrimental to the topic?

Step 6: Modify the Plan for Follow-Up or Expansion of the Theme

- Teachers should be constantly alert for comments or activities of the children that reflect on scientific concepts. Teachers can reinforce or clarify concepts by having a repertoire of poems, songs, activities, suggestions, and physical and verbal support ready for spontaneous interaction.

- Children can learn that there are many ways to solve problems—not just one stereotyped way. But to learn this, they must experience the environment on their own developmental level, according to their own personal time schedule, and in an accepting and loving environment. Children should not be afraid to explore and experiment within guidelines that protect them from harm, imposing on the rights of others, and becoming stagnant.

- Become a careful observer and listener. Note the many different ways water could be introduced into your classroom and the many benefits children would gain from such exposure. How can you tie water into snack/lunch? Into a gathering time? Into outdoor play? When would it be better for individual play rather than a group setting? What community activities require water for their success? How could you incorporate water into other curriculum areas, such as language arts, sensory experiences, social science, health, or mathematics?

SUGGESTIONS RELATED TO MATHEMATICS (CHAPTER 9)

The theme for this section is numbers and counting.

Step 1: Preassess Present Knowledge

Adults can determine the understanding and limitations of number symbols, number concepts, and number uses of young children as adults talk with or observe the play of these children.

Here are some quick and easy ways to determine number knowledge of young children.

○ Count aloud from 1 to 10 with the children (use no visual aids). See how many can count correctly.

○ Count objects aloud from 1 to 10 with the children.

○ Invite a couple of children to help set the table for snack or lunch. How many napkins, chairs, and so on will you need at each table? Does the teacher need to place the correct number of chairs and tell the children to put a napkin by each chair, or can the teacher tell the children a number of places to set?

○ As a table activity, a game, or a one-on-one activity, have a set of number cards. Showing the cards individually, ask the child to say the number of the symbol shown. Or hand the child a set of numbers 1 to 10 and ask that they be put in order. For the child who is having difficulty with these requests, end the experience here for now. For the child who can do this easily, see if she can put them in descending order. For the child who can do both of these things easily, mix some number symbols with some letters of the alphabet and ask the child to make a stack of numbers and one of letters.

○ Do some finger plays involving numbers. Remember that ascending counting is much easier for young children than descending counting.

○ Ask a child his age. Note whether he tells a number, shows a number of fingers, or uses both a number and finger gestures; do they correspond? (For example, does the child say "I'm two" but display four fingers?) (I had a verbal, intelligent 3-year-old boy in a group who insisted that he was "40" no matter how often or when you asked him.)

○ Use spinner games. If necessary, help the children relate the number spun on the spinner with the written number and how to move that many spaces.

○ For less experienced children, do spontaneous counting when appropriate. For more experienced children, help them use numbers in their play. ("There are four boys and one apple. How can we cut the apple so each boy can have an equal part of the apple?") ("How many firefighter hats do we need so everyone can have one?" or "How can we share four hats when there are six children?") Some children think that size has to do with quantity—for example, coin concepts are difficult, some children would rather have a penny or nickel than a dime because of size.

○ Listen carefully to the conversation of the children. They frequently use numbers. Do they use them correctly? Do the other children understand their meaning?

○ Be careful to help children build positive concepts about numbers. Drill, excessive repetition, boredom, pressure, or performance can be detrimental to young children.

○ In ways to improve communication, use stories, songs, and other opportunities to introduce verbal and written language and number concepts. (Examples: After reading *Ask Mr. Bear* by M. Flack [1991, Macmillan Children's Book Group], help the children count the number of animals or suggested gifts for the child's mother; set out a flannel board and number cutouts for manipulation and discussion; display pictures related to number—one dog, two cats, three birds; provide a set of hand puppets, then help the children count them and separate them into groups: family, animals, birds, and so on.)

Step 2: Identify Concepts

There will probably be great variation in the knowledge and use of numbers for young children. Many activities can be provided that will allow the child to explore and experiment at an individual pace. In this way older children are likely to assist younger or less experienced children, but may not be able to explain the reasoning behind number use. For very young children, ability to count or identify number symbols is of limited value.

- Children of similar (and different) ages have a different knowledge base regarding numbers and counting.
- Using numbers can simplify some tasks.
- A healthy attitude about numbers and mathematical concepts sets a good basis for later knowledge.

    Note: Identify concepts for a particular group of children based on their present knowledge and good later learning habits. The three suggestions given here are general.

Step 3: Make an Overview, Select and Schedule Activities, and Complete the Plan

- Think about the concepts to be emphasized. Carefully consider what activities or parts of the day would be most useful to present information or activities. Make the activities fit naturally into the flow of the schedule—a teacher may see a relationship between concepts and activities, but children might not. Watch for spontaneous opportunities to talk about numbers without unduly promoting them.
- Most of the activities should be open-ended: things that a child can do at her present stage of development but that are also slightly challenging. Less experienced children may try to use materials in unique or unrelated ways; more advanced children may go beyond your planning. Make quick but careful notations of the behavior and comments of different children so that follow-up planning will be valuable.
- More awareness will be generated on the topic while planning is in progress, so make some questions or identify focal points for discussion that will follow the implementation of the plan.

Step 4: Implement the Plan

- Throughout the period when the plan is used, make observations and notations for future building of number concepts, but do not let note taking distract you from interacting with the children. Use number concepts when possible, but do not overload the children by overemphasis on the topic.

Step 5: Evaluate the Plan

- This is where the questions or concerns identified in Step 3 will become of value. Were the concerns justified? What changes would make the topic and the plan more appropriate for another time or another group of children?

How were the time periods handled? Also raise new questions, ask for feelings and suggestions of staff members, and discuss behavior of individual children as well as the group as a whole.

Step 6: Modify the Plan for Follow-Up or Expansion of the Theme

- How can numbers, counting, and mathematical concepts be a part of daily routines without boring the children?
- How can staff members help children enjoy and use number concepts in their daily lives?
- How can number concepts be integrated naturally into other curriculum areas—art, science, language arts, and so on?
- Which children are still in the one-to-one correspondence stage? What are some interesting ideas to give them more experience?
- Which children could accurately count to 10 before this experience? Which children can now accurately count to 10? Which children can now accurately count beyond 10? How can number experiences be enriched for them?
- How can staff members help children develop a positive attitude toward number use? What are good ways to assist children to count accurately? What are some *spontaneous* ways to introduce numbers? What are some *planned* ways to introduce numbers?
- What is the attitude of staff members toward number concepts? Do they need assistance in changing from a negative to a positive attitude? If so, how can this be accomplished?

SUGGESTIONS RELATED TO SOCIAL STUDIES (CHAPTER 10)

There are many lesson plan topics that could easily and profitably be addressed in this chapter. Learning about oneself, one's family and surroundings, varied occupations, field trips, and other subtopics are but a few examples; however, a very timely topic is getting along with others who are similar to and different from us. This topic should be planned for and considered each and every day. Here is a suggested, tentative plan encouraging teachers and children to be more aware of their environment, the people in it, and different sets of circumstances.

Step 1: Preassess Present Knowledge

- In most groups of children receiving care and education outside the home, there are children and adults of diverse races, backgrounds, goals, and attitudes. Also, most young children are not yet prejudiced or competitive. Table C.1 shows a number of areas to preassess.
- As is very evident, there are many aspects of an anti-bias curriculum. It would be overwhelming and foolish to think one can teach all the necessary concepts *in one day* or *only once.*

Table C.1
Encouraging Harmony, Understanding, and Social Relationships in Young Children

FOCUS	CONSIDERATIONS
Race	Make notations about the ethnic background of each person in the classroom—not in an effort to categorize individuals, but to plan for diversity in teaching. Lack of ethnic diversity is not an excuse to avoid it. Children need to learn about ethnic and other differences in a warm, accepting atmosphere.
Culture	There are more aspects to culture than how a person dresses or what he eats. These can become more apparent through firsthand experiences.
Gender	It no longer is appropriate to classify people or occupations based on gender.
Age	Individuals of all ages should receive and give respect to others. Very young children have different needs than older children, just as young adults differ from elderly people.
Socioeconomic status	Many young children are unaware of or unconcerned with monetary conditions; however, many young children live in economically deprived situations. Differences can be understood and handled through teaching and learning experiences in the classroom.
Abilities or disabilities	There is much focus on and awareness of individuals with differing abilities and needs. When young children are made aware of these differences, they respond much more positively than when they are exposed to these differences at an older age.
Home situations	No two children experience the same situations at home. Some must deal with low self-esteem, disabilities, divorce and/or dual custody, death of a loved one, absence of one or both parents (war, separation), illness/disease (temporary or terminal), multigenerational living, adoptive or foster homes, poverty, security, hygiene, lack of medical and dental attention, immunizations, and other circumstances.
Personal characteristics	Low self-esteem, physical appearance, skills (physical, verbal, intellectual), social attitude, allergies.

Step 2: Identify Concepts

- This type of teaching needs to go on every day, in every activity, and with every person. It is more about teaching *attitudes* than a topic. The teacher needs to carefully consider the composition of the group (children and adults) and make some short-range and long-range plans—then teach with patience, love, and understanding.

- No specific concepts are given for this example because each group of children is so different. Teachers can observe situations and then discuss them and children in staff meetings in order to determine a positive approach for this group of children at this particular time.

Step 3: Make an Overview, Select and Schedule Activities, and Complete the Plan

- Have individual family members share some of their customs (beginning with food and dress, but going beyond as the children can assimilate the information).
- Have pictures, songs, visual aids, and so on available, and talk about how occupations can be performed by males and females.
- If someone in the group has a disability, talk about it. If not, visit someone who is disabled.
- Openly talk about diseases—communicable, terminal.
- See the breakdown in Step 1. Write new suggestions/ideas.
- Write new pertinent suggestions/ideas.

Step 4: Implement the Plan

Step 5: Evaluate the Plan

When evaluating each plan, note especially the daily focus on the progress of positive attitudes and/or suggestions for creating and promoting an anti-bias curriculum.

- Note the attitudes and activities of different children as they enlarge their group of friends, as they build tolerance and acceptance, and as they express themselves verbally.

Step 6: Modify the Plan for Follow-Up or Expansion of the Theme

- As it is a lifelong task to help promote love and understanding of other people, watch for children and adults who need extra support because of their diversity or because of their attitudes. (Check Chapter 10 for supplementary books on this topic.)

SUGGESTIONS RELATED TO NUTRITION AND HEALTH (CHAPTER 11)

The theme for this section is that good food helps build strong bodies.

Step 1: Preassess Present Knowledge

- Based on the concepts to be introduced or enhanced, devise a number of ways of finding out what the children already know—without resorting strictly to questioning, especially closed-ended questions. Watch and listen to the children during their play, provide props that will suggest the topic, and note what would be important for them to know about nutrition (do they appear to be well nourished, have infrequent illnesses, have habits of cleanliness, enjoy various foods, and so on?).
- List several ways to preassess the children.

Step 2: Identify Concepts

Based on your preassessment, how could a topic on nutrition benefit the children and/or their families? What simple, basic concepts are important for them at this time and stage of development? Introduce some familiarity but slightly stretch their thinking and behavior.

- Some foods are better for the body than are other foods.
- Children can help select, prepare, and serve healthy foods.
- Healthy food helps the body have more energy.
- It is important to have clean hands when handling food.
- Besides good food, other things help promote a strong body, such as good personal habits, checkups, rest and exercise, the environment, and other things. (This will be a casual mention so the children will realize that *not* just good food keeps them healthy. This could be a later topic.)
- For teachers and children: If young children learn about nutrition at a young age and discuss the knowledge often, they may be more conscious of eating good food and developing nutrition goals.
- As you identify concepts to emphasize, also think about some discussion questions for the evaluation after the plan has been implemented. (Which children commented about the topic? How could you tell if the children gained *correct* concepts? If you were to use this plan again, on which activities would you put more or less emphasis? How would you make a follow-up plan and how soon would you reintroduce the topic?)

Step 3: Make an Overview, Select and Schedule Activities, and Complete the Plan

- Begin with a general schedule overview. Fill in the curriculum and time periods with activities and materials appropriate for the theme. Add, delete, and substitute activities that would be most meaningful to these children. Eliminate activities that do not fit naturally or smoothly into the schedule. (Some diversions from the theme would be expected.)
- To give versatility to planning, rather than putting this topic into a time and activity frame, brainstorm how to best support the identified concepts. Consider the following: The first exposure to the topic should be an overview. Then make follow-up plans to discuss specific types of food—perhaps a plan on fruit, one on vegetables, one on grains, one on meat and meat products, one on dairy products, or any combination that meets the needs of the children in the group.
- Display and discuss the Food Group Pyramid by the U.S. Department of Agriculture. (Show an example.) Make individual puzzles out of the pyramid so that when the children put them together (or paste them on paper), they get the idea that the food in the bigger pieces should be eaten more frequently than those pictures in the smaller pieces.
- In your planning, be sure to include nutritional food and nonnutritional food, so the children have many opportunities to decide between food items. They need to make comparisons and evaluations (would it be healthier to eat potato chips or grapes—and why?). Should candy, for instance, never be

consumed? Some families have limited food, cultural preferences, or no knowledge about nutrition. How could this plan make a difference in family buying and eating?

- Have empty cartons, packages, and so on of actual food products available in the housekeeping area.

- Have pictures of the same food as fresh and processed (for example, a fresh apple, juice, and sauce, or grains in various forms).

- Talk about the taste of food without getting too far from today's goal. If appropriate, mention the four tastes (salty, sweet, sour, and bitter), but leave a discussion about the taste buds and specific personal preferences for follow-up topics.

- Sometime and somewhere during the day, provide a tasting time for the children. Whenever possible, let the children assist in preparing, serving, and cleaning up snack and/or lunch tables. (Would it be possible to make and bake bread, cook applesauce or spaghetti in the classroom, or have each child bring a piece of fruit or a vegetable to make a salad or stone soup [see Brown, M., *Stone Soup*, Macmillan Children's Book Group, 1986, Chapter 11, and other references related to food]?)

- Encourage the children to help prepare some nutritious snacks. Stress the importance of cleanliness of hands, surfaces, and utensils when preparing or eating food.

- Have a variety of pictures of food, both nutritious and junk. Provide a bulletin board divided into two parts. Talk with the children about which foods help bodies grow strong and which foods are not beneficial. Help them understand why the food is healthy or unhealthy. They may indicate that all their preferences (high sugar, fat, and/or salt content) are healthy just because they like them or eat them often. Watch your terminology carefully so you give the right information and ideas to the children. Bear in mind that adults most often select, serve, and influence the food choices of children.

- Plant a garden, but realize that it takes a long time to mature.

- Provide good books on food in the reading-browsing area. (See Chapter 11 for suggestions.)

- Informally or formally, indoors or outdoors, individually or in groups, sing songs, read poetry, and have informal discussions about good food.

- Suggested ideas show how the topic could be used during activity or free-selection play, in gathering times, informally around the classroom and playground, or formally with a group of children. The topic fits well with different curriculum areas—science, art, music, language arts, and so on. Consider carefully whether food items should be used in art projects. Some argue that with food shortages, malnutrition, health problems, and costs, food should not be wasted on art projects when others items could easily be substituted. Perhaps an occasional potato or fruit print or grain collage would invite children to an art activity. You decide. Refer to the section titled "Collage" in Chapter 6 for a discussion of this issue.

Using some, all, or none of the suggestions, write a plan that would be beneficial to the children you will teach.

Step 4: Implement the Plan

- Make short notes about various children, activities, and behavior to stimulate discussion at evaluation time.

Step 5: Evaluate the Plan

° Throughout the session, record quick notes about the high and low points of the session and follow up with a teacher discussion after the children depart. Begin your evaluation by asking for and making general comments about the concepts and actions of the children. Encourage and listen to comments of other adults in the classroom. Did they see and hear what you saw and heard? How beneficial was the day for the children? Were the concepts and activities appropriate or inappropriate for the children—and why?

Step 6: Modify the Plan for Follow-Up or Expansion of the Theme

° While the topic and participation are fresh in your mind, suggest some ways to build a follow-up lesson on this topic or ways to integrate it with other information when the children show interest and readiness.

° Return to Step 2 and review your evaluation thoughts. Were the ideas on- or off-target according to the results of the day?

° Teachers who feel they have taught a topic "once and for all" need to remember that not only do children learn through appropriate repetition, but they also learn by integrating a topic into other topics, activities, and interactions.

° Other contributors to a strong body include cleanliness (hand washing, teeth brushing, and so on); exercise; rest; immunizations; a nonpolluted environment (air, water, soil); proper clothing for an activity and the weather; health care and medical/dental checkups; and others.

° Topics related to health and safety include household products; unsafe play activities and toys (ropes, sharp objects); avoiding those who are ill; choosing good friends and activities; understanding making, and supporting rules; reporting hazardous things or unfriendly individuals; and others.

RECIPES

RECIPES FOR CREATIVE AND ARTISTIC EXPRESSION

Beads

½ c salt   ¼ c water (heated)
¼ c cornstarch   food coloring (optional)

Dissolve salt in heated water; stir in cornstarch and food coloring (optional). Knead until smooth. Pinch off small amounts, form into shapes, stick small dowels or pencils through them, and place on waxed paper. When beads are dry, slip off sticks and thread onto yarn.

Salt Ceramic

½ c cornstarch   1 c salt
½ c boiling water

Mix ingredients in top of double boiler. Cook, stirring constantly, 2 to 3 minutes, until so thick that mixture follows spoon in stirring. When consistency of bread dough, dump onto waxed paper to cool. Knead with hands several minutes. Store in airtight container.

Salt Beads

Use Salt Ceramic recipe, but add 1 tsp food coloring.
Roll into balls. Use toothpick or nail to make holes. Let dry and then string.

Earth Clay

Put desired amount of water in earthen jar. Gradually add clay powder, stirring until mixture reaches consistency of sticky bread dough. Let stand overnight. Knead powder into clay until desired consistency.

Cooked-Dough Clay (Recommended)

2 c flour
4 tsp cream of tartar
2 T oil
spice such as cinnamon or
  cloves for scent (optional)

1 c salt
2 c water
food coloring (optional)

Mix flour, salt, and cream of tartar in heavy aluminum pan. Add and mix water, oil, food coloring, and spice. Heat on stove 3 minutes or until mixture pulls away from pan. Remove from heat and knead immediately. Store in airtight container. Clay keeps for several months.

Flour-Salt Dough

1½ c flour
½ c water
food coloring (optional)

½ c salt
¼ c vegetable oil

Mix flour and salt. Slowly add water, oil, and food coloring (optional). Knead well. Store in refrigerator in closed container or plastic bag. Can be baked at 225° for 2 hours. Color or decorate, if desired.

Cornstarch Dough

2 c salt
1 c cornstarch

1⅓ c cold water, divided

Mix salt and ⅔ c water in pan and bring to a boil. In separate bowl, stir cornstarch and remaining water thoroughly. Combine mixtures and cook over low heat for several minutes. Turn onto lightly floured surface and knead well. Store, covered, in refrigerator.

Ooblick

2 c warm water   3 c cornstarch

Mix ingredients with hands in a bowl. It becomes solid when resting, but turns into a liquid when handled. The warmth of the hands produces the change.

Glarch

1 c liquid starch   1 c Elmer's glue

Pour liquid starch over glue and gently fold together with a spoon. Once glue solidifies, pour off extra starch. Glarch becomes harder and more rubbery as it is worked. Once it is quite solid, rinse under cold water to remove starch.

Basic Finger Paint

Food coloring or tempera paint can be used for coloring in this section, but food coloring really stains hands, clothes, tabletops, and so on.

Method 1

> 3 c soap *flakes*   water
>   (such as Ivory)

Put soap in a medium-sized bowl. Gradually add water. Beat with a rotary or electric beater to a soft, smooth consistency that holds a peak. Color, if desired.

Method 2

> 1 c laundry starch   1 c cold water
> 2 c hot water   1 c soap flakes
> glycerin

Moisten laundry starch with cold water. Add hot water and cook until thick. Remove from heat and add soap flakes and a few drops of glycerin.

Method 3

> 1 c flour   1 tsp salt
> 3 c cold water

Mix together in a double boiler flour, salt, and cold water. Cook until thick, beating with an eggbeater or electric mixer.

Cornstarch Finger Paint

> ½ c cornstarch   4 c boiling water

Dissolve cornstarch in just enough cold water to make a thick paste. Add to boiling water and stir. Let mixture come to boil again. Cooling causes paint to thicken slightly.

Salt and Flour Finger Paint

> 1 c flour   1½ c salt
> ¾ c water   food coloring

Stir flour and salt into water. Add food coloring. Paint will have grainy quality.

Liquid Starch Finger Paint

Pour liquid starch on damp surface.

Starch and Gelatin Finger Paint

½ c laundry starch   ¾ c cold water, divided
1 envelope unflavored gelatin   2 c hot water
½ c soap flakes

Combine laundry starch and ½ c cold water in saucepan. Soak gelatin in ¼ c cold water. Add hot water to starch mixture and cook, stirring constantly over medium heat, until mixture comes to a boil and is clear. Remove from heat and blend in softened gelatin. Add soap flakes and stir until mixture thickens and soap is thoroughly dissolved. Makes about 3 cups.

RECIPES FOR FOOD

Breads

Streamlined White Bread

1¼ c warm water   1 pkg active dry yeast
   (not hot—100° to 115°F)   2 T soft shortening
2 tsp salt   2 T sugar
3 c sifted flour, divided

In mixer bowl, dissolve yeast in warm water. Add shortening, salt, sugar, and half the flour. Beat 2 minutes at medium speed on mixer, or 300 vigorous strokes by hand. Scrape sides and bottom of bowl frequently. Add remaining flour and blend with spoon until smooth. Scrape batter from sides of bowl. Cover with cloth and let rise in warm place (85°F) until double, about 30 minutes. (If kitchen is cool, place dough on rack over bowl of hot water and cover with a towel.) Stir down batter by beating about 25 strokes. Spread batter evenly in greased loaf pan, 8½ by 4½ by 2¾ inches or 9 by 5 by 3 inches. Batter will be sticky. Smooth out top of loaf by flouring hand and patting into shape. Again let rise in warm place until batter reaches ¼ inch from top of 8½-inch pan or 1 inch from top of 9-inch pan, about 40 minutes. Heat oven to 375°F. Bake 45 to 50 minutes or until brown. To test loaf, tap the top crust; it should sound hollow. Remove immediately from pan. Place on cooling rack or across bread pans. Brush top with melted butter or shortening. Do not place in direct draft. Cool before cutting. A sawtooth knife is especially good for cutting. Slice with a sawing motion rather than pressing down, making slices slightly thicker than usual. Makes one loaf.

Individual Bun Recipe (ingredients for each child)

1 tsp soft margarine   1 tsp sugar
1 T flour   1 tsp fruit (currants)
1½ T milk-and-egg mixture
(2 eggs to 1 pt of milk whipped
together for group to share)

Blend margarine and sugar in small bowl or plastic carton. Add flour, fruit, and milk-and-egg mixture. Stir. Put in baking papers in muffin tin. Bake at 350°F until golden brown.

Breadsticks

1 pkg refrigerator biscuits	¼ c melted butter, divided
sesame seeds	

Shape biscuits into 6- to 8-inch-long sticks. Place half of the butter in 9-by-12-inch baking pan. Put sticks in butter. Pour rest of butter over sticks. Sprinkle sticks with seeds. Bake 10 minutes at 400°F.

Cheese Biscuits

½ c soft margarine	2 c flour
2 c grated cheese (mild cheddar)	2 c rice cereal (such as Rice Krispies)

Mix together margarine, flour, grated cheese, and rice cereal. Roll into small balls, then flatten. Place on greased cookie sheet. Bake 8 to 10 minutes at 375°F. Makes about 40 biscuits.

Apple Biscuits

1 c crushed Wheat Chex	½ c grated unpeeled apples
½ c apple juice	2 c biscuit mix
nutmeg and cinnamon	

Mix Wheat Chex and apples. Add apple juice. Combine biscuit mix and small amount of nutmeg and cinnamon. Stir into crumb mixture. Mix well. Spoon onto greased cookie sheet. Bake at 450°F for 10 minutes. Makes 16 to 18 servings.

Simple Pizza

½ English muffin	1 T tomato sauce
oregano	salami slices (optional)
cheese slices	

Spread English muffin with tomato sauce. Sprinkle lightly with oregano. Place one slice salami on sauce (optional). Top with slice of cheese. Place on baking sheet. Bake about 10 minutes at 425°F or until cheese is bubbly.

Indian Fry Bread

1 pkg yeast	1 c warm milk
¼ c oil	1 T sugar
3 c flour	1 tsp salt
oil for frying	

Dissolve yeast in warm milk. Add oil and sugar. Measure and combine flour and salt in mixing bowl; add other ingredients. Dough should be soft but not sticky; more flour may be needed. Divide into portions and let the children knead it for 5 minutes. Lightly oil inside of large bowl. Make ball of all dough and place in bowl. Turn dough over so oiled side is up. Cover with plastic or damp clean towel. Let rise until double in bulk (about 2 hours). Punch down. Pull off chunks about size of table-tennis ball; roll into a flat circle about ¼ inch thick. Heat ½ inch oil until hot. Fry to golden brown; turn over. Remove and drain on paper towels. Eat while warm. Serves 16 to 18 children.

Dairy

Butter

½ pt cream   salt
yellow food coloring

Put cream in a pint jar. *Cream should be at room temperature and should be several days old.* Shake it until it thickens, about 10 minutes. Add salt to taste. Drain. Pour cold water over it and keep pouring buttermilk off. Cream with a spoon until all buttermilk is drained off. Add yellow food coloring. (Butter can also be made by putting cream in small baby-food jars so more children can participate.)

Cottage Cheese

2 c whole milk (fresh or soured)   1 T vinegar
salt

Stir and cook milk over medium heat until bubbles begin to form on top. Remove from heat and stir in vinegar. Stir gently and watch for curds, which form quickly. Liquid is whey. Stir occasionally as mixture cools. Gather curds in strainer, gently pressing curds so that whey is removed. Add salt to taste.

Homemade Yogurt

½ gal fresh milk   ½ c powdered milk
1 pt plain commercial yogurt

Boil milk for 4 minutes. Insert thermometer and cool to 100° to 125°F. Add powdered milk and yogurt. Spoon into warm, clean jars. Put lids on. Put warm water (100° to 125°F) in deep pan; put jars in (water should cover at least one half of jar). Turn to low heat (about 125°F) for 2 to 4 hours. Remove when contents become firm. Refrigerate.

For additional batches, save one jar to use as next starter (can be used several times, then begin again with commercial yogurt).

At serving time, add fruit or 2 T frozen orange juice, or eat plain.

Cookies

Drop Cookies

Peanut Butter Cookies

1½ c sifted flour   1 tsp baking soda
½ c white sugar   1 c brown sugar
dash of salt   ½ c peanut butter
½ c butter or margarine, melted   1 egg

Sift flour and baking soda together once. Mix together dry ingredients. Add peanut butter, butter, and egg. Make balls the size of English walnuts, place on oiled cookie sheet 3 inches apart, and press down with fork. Bake at 375°F until light brown. Makes 3 dozen cookies, mild in flavor.

Oatmeal Cookies

1 c white sugar	½ tsp salt
1 c shortening	½ tsp baking soda
3 eggs	1 tsp cinnamon
2 c flour	1 c raisins (covered with
½ tsp allspice	water and simmered for
½ tsp ground cloves	5 min.)
6 T raisin liquid	2 c oatmeal
1 c nuts	

Cream white sugar and shortening; add eggs and beat. Sift dry ingredients and add to creamed mixture. Add raisin liquid alternately with oatmeal. Add raisins and nuts. Mix well. Bake at 375°F for 15 minutes. Makes about 5 dozen.

Snickerdoodles

1 c shortening	1½ c + 2 tsp sugar, divided
2 eggs	2½ c flour
2 tsp cream of tartar	2 tsp baking soda
½ tsp salt	1 tsp cinnamon

Cream shortening and 1½ c sugar. Add eggs and stir. Sift dry ingredients (except cinnamon) together and add. Mix well and roll in cinnamon mixed with remaining sugar. Bake at 350°F for 8 to 10 minutes. Makes about 2½ dozen.

No-Bake Oatmeal Cookies

3 c quick oats	3 T carob
2 c sugar	½ c milk
½ c peanut butter	¼ lb butter or margarine

Mix oats and carob together in bowl. In saucepan, mix and boil sugar, milk, peanut butter, and butter or margarine for 1 minute. Pour hot sugar mixture over oat mixture and mix well. Drop by spoon onto waxed paper.

Chinese No-Bake Cookies

¼ lb margarine (1 stick)	2 c sugar
½ c milk	½ tsp salt
2 T peanut butter	1 tsp vanilla
2 c oats	2 c Chinese noodles

Mix together margarine, sugar, milk, and salt in a heavy saucepan and bring to a rolling boil. Boil 1 minute. Add the rest of the ingredients. Mix and drop on waxed paper or oiled cookie sheet and chill.

Energy Cookies

1 c brown sugar	1½ c corn or peanut oil
4 c uncooked rolled oats	½ c maple syrup
3 c unbleached white flour	6 T milk
2 c dates (chopped and pitted)	

Beat sugar and oil. Add oats, syrup, flour, and milk. Stir in dates. Roll into small balls, then flatten on oiled cookie sheet. Bake 15 to 20 minutes at 350°F. Makes 5 dozen.

Rolled Cookies

Buttermilk Cookies

1 c shortening	2 c sugar
3 eggs, beaten	1 c buttermilk
6 c flour	1 tsp baking soda
¼ tsp nutmeg or other spice	

Cream the shortening; add the sugar gradually and blend thoroughly. Add beaten eggs and buttermilk. Add sifted dry ingredients, mixing well. Chill. Roll to a thickness of about ⅛ inch; spread with sugar and cut. Place on greased cookie sheet and bake at 375°F for 10 to 12 minutes.

Grandma Milne's Sugar Cookies

1 c shortening	2 c sugar
2 eggs	2 tsp baking soda in a little
5 to 6 c flour	hot water
2 heaping tsp cream of	1 c milk
tartar	
2 tsp vanilla	

Cream shortening and sugar; add eggs and soda. Sift flour and cream of tartar. Add dry ingredients to shortening mixture alternately with milk. Add vanilla. Bake at 350° to 375°F for 12 minutes.

Carolyn's Cookies

4 c flour	1 c sugar
4 tsp baking powder	½ tsp salt
1 c shortening	4 eggs, well beaten
⅓ c milk	1 tsp vanilla

Sift dry ingredients together. Cut in shortening as in pie dough. Add eggs, milk, and vanilla. Roll out and cut. Bake at 400°F until brown. Makes about 5 dozen.

Coloring for Sugar Cookies

1 egg yolk	1 tsp water
different food coloring	

Beat egg yolk with water. Divide into containers and add different food coloring to each. Brush onto cookies before baking. If not cooked too long, the color is good.

Gingerbread Figures

1 c molasses	1 c shortening
1 c sugar	1 egg
1 tsp vanilla	2 tsp baking soda dissolved in
5 c flour	½ c hot water
¼ tsp ground cloves	1 tsp cinnamon
1 tsp salt	½ tsp ginger

Simmer together molasses and shortening for 15 minutes. Cream together sugar, egg, and vanilla. Add baking soda dissolved in hot water; add to sugar-and-egg mixture. Add molasses mixture. Sift together flour, cloves, cinnamon, salt, and ginger. Add to molasses and sugar-and-egg mixtures and stir until flour is well mixed. Roll thin and cut with cookie cutter. Bake 10 minutes in 375°F oven. This dough does not stick to the pan. Children can cut and place the figures in the pan.

Grandma's Gingerbread Dough

5½ c flour	1 tsp baking soda
1 tsp salt	3 tsp cinnamon
2 tsp ginger	2 tsp ground cloves
1 tsp nutmeg	⅓ tsp cardamom
1 c shortening or margarine	1 c white or brown sugar
1 c molasses	1 egg

Sift together flour, soda, salt, and five spices. Cream shortening and sugar until fluffy; add egg and molasses. Beat at least 8 to 10 minutes. Add flour mixture a little at a time. Can be rolled into log shape and frozen for up to six months. Bake at 315° to 325°F for 15 to 20 minutes.

Fruity Finger Food

4 envelopes of unflavored gelatin
4 c fruit juice (such as apple, cranberry, lemon-lime, orange juice drink)

In medium saucepan, sprinkle unflavored gelatin over 1 c juice; let stand 1 minute. Stir over low heat until gelatin is completely dissolved, about 3 minutes. Stir in remaining 3 c juice. Pour into 9-inch-square, nonstick baking pan. Chill until firm, about 3 hours. To serve, cut into 2-inch squares or press cookie cutter shapes into pan. Remove carefully with thin, flexible metal spatula. Makes about 9 treats.

Index